MILESTONE DOCUMENTS
OF AMERICAN LEADERS

Exploring the Primary Sources
of Notable Americans

MILESTONE DOCUMENTS OF AMERICAN LEADERS

Exploring the Primary Sources
of Notable Americans

Volume 2
Du Bois – Jay

Paul Finkelman
Editor in Chief

James A. Percoco
Consulting Editor

Ｓ Schlager Group

Milestone Documents of American Leaders
Copyright © 2009 by Schlager Group Inc.

All rights reserved. No part of this book may be reproduced or utilized in any form or by any means, electronic or mechanical, including photocopying, recording, or by any information storage or retrieval systems, without permission in writing from the publisher. For information, contact:

Schlager Group Inc.
2501 Oak Lawn Avenue, Suite 440
Dallas, Texas 75219
USA

You can find Schlager Group on the World Wide Web at
http://www.schlagergroup.com
Text and cover design by Patricia Moritz

Printed in the United States of America
10 9 8 7 6 5 4 3 2 1

ISBN: 978-0-9797758-5-7

This book is printed on acid-free paper.

Contents

Volume 1: Abigail Adams to Frederick Douglass

VOLUME 2: W. E. B. DU BOIS TO JOHN JAY

MILESTONE DOCUMENTS OF AMERICAN LEADERS

Exploring the Primary Sources of Notable Americans

W. E. B. Du Bois (AP/Wide World Photos)

W. E. B. Du Bois   1868–1963

Educator, Journal Editor, and Civil Rights Activist

Featured Documents
- "Strivings of the Negro People" (1897)
- "The Parting of the Ways" (1904)
- "Agitation" (1910)
- "Returning Soldiers" (1919)
- "Marxism and the Negro Problem" (1933)

Overview

William Edward Burghardt Du Bois was born on February 23, 1868, in Great Barrington, Massachusetts, and raised by his mother. In spite of the poverty of his childhood, Du Bois excelled in school and achieved one of the most impressive educations of his generation. He received bachelor degrees from Fisk University and Harvard University, pursued graduate work at Harvard and Germany's University of Berlin, and earned his PhD in history from Harvard in 1895. He received a faculty appointment at Wilberforce University in 1894, worked for the University of Pennsylvania on a study of blacks in Philadelphia in 1896, and joined the faculty of Atlanta University in 1897. In 1910 he left Atlanta and took a paid position as the director of publishing and research for the newly founded National Association for the Advancement of Colored People (NAACP). He served in that position and also as the founding editor of the NAACP journal, the *Crisis*, subtitled *A Record of the Darker Races*, until 1934, when he resigned over a policy dispute.

Following his departure from the NAACP, Du Bois returned to Atlanta University and to academic scholarship for ten years. In 1943, at the age of seventy-six, he was forced to retire from the university, and he accepted a position back at the NAACP. By this time, Du Bois was clearly out of step with the civil rights organization; his increasingly leftist, pro-Soviet politics and his criticism both of U.S. foreign policy and of the NAACP director Walter White cost him his job in 1948. In the late 1940s and early 1950s Du Bois became involved in leftist organizations, continued condemning the United States and its foreign policy while praising the Soviet Union, and ran for public office as a nominee of the American Labor Party. These activities made him a target of the post–World War II "red scare" inspired by Senator Joseph McCarthy. Although he was acquitted of charges related to his involvement with radical antiwar organizations, his passport was suspended from 1951 to 1958. When he regained the right to travel abroad, he made a series of trips, including highly publicized visits to East Germany, the Soviet Union, and Communist China. Du Bois's continued pro-Communist political radicalism isolated him from the emerging civil rights movement. In 1961, disillusioned with the United States, Du

Bois formally joined the U.S. Communist Party before relocating to the newly independent nation of Ghana. In 1963 he became a citizen of his adopted country; on August 27, 1963, he died at the age of ninety-five.

Du Bois was the leading African American intellectual of his day. He first established his credentials with his scholarly publications on the Atlanta slave trade and on Philadelphia's black community. In 1897 he began to define his political and racial views, moving from academic work to political and social activism; his publication of "Strivings of the Negro People" in the *Atlantic Monthly* brought him national attention. Six years later, his classic work *The Souls of Black Folk* cemented his intellectual credentials. His involvement with the Niagara Movement beginning in 1905 and with the National Association for the Advancement of Colored People made him the most significant of Booker T. Washington's critics and the most prominent and most respected head of the early-twentieth-century campaign for civil rights. In his books and articles, especially those published in the *Crisis*, Du Bois developed ideas that were fundamental to his vision of race in America and to the long struggle against discrimination and for equality. While he found himself increasingly out of the mainstream civil rights movement following his departure from the NAACP in 1934, Du Bois remained one of the giants among twentieth-century American intellectuals.

Explanation and Analysis of Documents

Du Bois came of age during the nadir of race relations in the United States. The gains that African Americans had achieved during Reconstruction were undone as segregation became the standard across the country, southern states denied blacks the right to vote or participate in the political process, and the nation was swept by an epidemic of racial violence, especially in the form of lynching. Du Bois himself, despite his superior education and record of scholarship, could not obtain a faculty position in a "white" college or university. This was the reality that Du Bois confronted as he began his career as a professor and intellectual, and he chose to address the era's racial injustice with his pen. Five documents can trace the development and evolution of his political thought from the beginning of his

1868

■ **February 23**
W. E. B. Du Bois is born in Great Barrington, Massachusetts.

1895

■ **June**
Du Bois receives a PhD from Harvard University.

1897

■ **August**
Du Bois publishes an expanded version of his January speech to the American Negro Academy under the title "Strivings of the Negro People" in the *Atlantic Monthly*.

1897

■ **September**
Du Bois takes a teaching position at Atlanta University.

1903

■ **Spring**
Du Bois publishes *The Souls of Black Folk*.

1904

■ **April**
Du Bois criticizes Booker T. Washington's leadership in "The Parting of the Ways," published in *World Today*.

1905

■ **July 11–14**
Du Bois participates in the meeting of African American leaders in Niagara Falls, Ontario, that results in the organization of the Niagara Movement.

1909

■ **May 31**
Du Bois participates in the mixed-race meeting in New York City that leads to the creation of the National Association for the Advancement of Colored People the following year.

career in the late nineteenth century to his resignation from the NAACP in 1934. The first two, "Strivings of the Negro People" and "The Parting of the Ways," were published in mainstream intellectual journals; the final three, "Agitation," "Returning Soldiers," and "Marxism and the Negro Problem," appeared in the *Crisis*.

◆ **"Strivings of the Negro People"**

For the twenty-nine-year-old Du Bois, 1897 was a breakthrough year. His accomplishments thus far were impressive: He had earned his doctorate in history from Harvard University and had published his dissertation as *The Suppression of the African Slave-Trade to the United States of America, 1638–1870*, the first monograph in Harvard's series on history; he had completed two years as a professor at Wilberforce; and he had begun work on his groundbreaking study of the Negro in Philadelphia. Yet to this point he was relatively unknown. In January 1897, Du Bois delivered his first major public address at the inaugural meeting of the American Negro Academy. This speech, "The Conservation of Races," elevated the status of the young scholar among the African American intellectual elite. In August, Du Bois published a reworked version of the speech in the *Atlantic Monthly*, the nation's premier literary/intellectual magazine, which served to introduce him to the white intellectual elite.

"Strivings of the Negro People" contains the best statement of Du Bois's early efforts to define the complexity of race in America and its impact on the African American people. He opens the essay dramatically, immediately establishing the racial divide "between me and the other world" and defining the white world's essential assumption about African Americans through the ever-unspoken question "How does it feel to be a problem?" Drawing on concepts of race that he had picked up at the University of Berlin, Du Bois sets the African American within the context of all the world's races, adapting the concept of immutable races that differ one from the other primarily in terms of the talents and gifts they have brought forth. Du Bois's racial structure contains seven groups, with the Negro "a sort of seventh son, born with a veil, and gifted with second-sight in this American world,—a world which yields him no self-consciousness, but only lets him see himself through the revelation of the other world." The unique situation of African Americans is that they exist within the white world, not truly visible but veiled and denied consciousness by prejudice that allows them to see themselves only in the white world's terms. This situation creates a duality within the black psyche—one in which "one ever feels his two-ness,—an American, a Negro; two souls, two thoughts, two unreconciled strivings; two warring ideals in one dark body."

In defining the resolution or escape for the duality of the Negro soul, Du Bois rejects both assimilation within white American culture, which would destroy black identity, and the nationalistic embrace of pure African culture, which would deprive black people of the gifts of America. The middle ground is to embrace both sides of this divided consciousness, allowing one "to be both a Negro and an American without being cursed and spit upon by his fellows, without losing the opportunity of self-development." In taking this approach, Du Bois advocates neither amalgamation and denial of racial divisions nor racial separatism.

After establishing the nature of African American identity, Du Bois makes his case for equal rights. Noting the recent demise of the degradation of chattel slavery, he recounts the difficult road that blacks had traveled during their three decades of freedom. While acknowledging but not apologizing for missteps and errors, he emphasizes the political and social needs of his race—education of both hand and mind; political rights, including the ballot; and freedom, "the freedom of life and limb, the freedom to work and think." With this accomplished, Du Bois perceives an America where racial identity does not vanish but strengthens as blacks achieve full racial consciousness and, in so doing, share in American ideals and contribute their strength to the nation.

Du Bois uses the national platform that the *Atlantic Monthly* provided to define a new concept of race and the role of African Americans in the United States. He sees race as something to be embraced, not overcome; race denotes difference, not superiority or inferiority. The observable problems in the African American community—poverty, ignorance, crime—resulted from the stultifying effects of centuries of slavery, and blacks were now striving both to overcome the discrimination and prejudice that blocked their progress and to compete. Du Bois concludes that America would be enriched by the different but equally valuable contributions that each race brought to it.

◆ **"The Parting of the Ways"**

By 1904 Du Bois had concluded that the path chosen by Booker T. Washington to lead African Americans to their destiny was flawed and that, both for his own career and for the well-being of his people, he needed to advocate the pursuit of a different direction. Through the first few years of the twentieth century the young Du Bois and the well-established Washington had formed an alliance. The concepts Du Bois had presented in his *Atlantic Monthly* essay did not conflict with Washington's teachings. However, the deterioration of civil rights, the rise in racial violence, and the increasing political influence of Washington convinced Du Bois of the need to chart another path. He had voiced mild criticism in his review of Washington's autobiography *Up from Slavery*, and he included additional criticism in his chapter on Washington in *The Souls of Black Folk*. As the split became irrevocable, Du Bois addressed his position in his essay "The Parting of the Ways," published in April 1904 in *World Today*, a small journal of politics and culture.

Du Bois crafted this essay carefully; after all, he was challenging the authority of the most prominent African American, who had a great deal of respect among whites. Interestingly, Du Bois never mentions Booker T. Washington by name. However, he clearly separates himself from Washington and writes as though the reader knows, perhaps through the essay's title, that he is doing so. He

Time Line

1910

■ **August**
Du Bois resigns from Atlanta University and moves to New York to serve as member of the board of directors and director of publications and research for the NAACP.

■ **November**
In the first issue of the *Crisis*, which he established and edited, Du Bois publishes the editorial "Agitation."

1918

■ **July**
Du Bois writes a controversial essay in the *Crisis*, "Close Ranks," urging African Americans to put aside racial grievances and support the war effort.

1918–1919

■ **December 1918– February 1919**
Du Bois travels to France, where he attempts to influence the peace conference on colonialism, investigates the treatment of African American troops in France, and helps organize the Pan-African Congress held in Paris.

1919

■ **May**
Du Bois publishes "Returning Soldiers" in the *Crisis*.

1926

■ **August 14**
Du Bois arrives in the Soviet Union on a fact-finding trip. After spending almost two months there, he returns praising the Bolshevik Revolution and the Soviet Union.

1933

■ **May**
As part of a series of essays redefining his political views, Du Bois addresses the relevance of Marxism in "Marxism and the Negro Problem."

begins, in the first sentence, by listing the areas of contention that he has with Washington: "First, the scope of education; second, the necessity of the right of suffrage; third, the importance of civil rights; fourth, the conciliation of the South; fifth, the future of the race in this country." To establish his credentials, Du Bois then connects himself with previous black leaders, especially the revered Frederick Douglass and Alexander Crummell. His argument is that the unnamed Washington's emphasis on economic development, what Du Bois labels the "gospel of money," neglected higher education and equal rights. Du Bois contends that the Tuskegee president remained silent as African Americans lost their political rights, were subjected to Jim Crow laws, and faced the terror of lynching. While the accuracy of Du Bois's charges against Washington can be debated, they struck a chord among northern blacks who were already disenchanted with Washington's southern-directed leadership. They also applauded the hint of militancy in Du Bois's criticism, especially his concluding exhortation to African Americans to struggle unceasingly for black rights, and even if they fail, to "die trying."

◆ **"Agitation"**

In the years that followed the publication of "The Parting of the Ways," the rift between Du Bois and Washington deepened. In 1905 Du Bois joined with other more militant African Americans to establish the Niagara Movement and push their civil rights agenda. However, they lacked the financial resources to successfully challenge Washington's political power or to pursue their goals. In 1909 Du Bois joined with white liberals to create the National Negro Committee, which would found the National Association for the Advancement of Colored People in 1910. That year Du Bois became the only African American on the NAACP board and launched the organization's monthly magazine, the *Crisis*. Du Bois now had a position with a well-funded civil rights organization that shared his political views and was editing a journal that provided him with an outlet through which to expound on his views. In the first issue of the *Crisis*, Du Bois published the essay "Agitation," arguing for the active confrontation of racism and inequality.

"Agitation" was one of the shortest essays that Du Bois wrote but clearly communicated his point. As a political approach, agitation was central to the tactics of the *Crisis* and the NAACP. Du Bois remarks, "The function of this Association is to tell this nation the crying evil of race prejudice. It is a hard duty but a necessary one—a divine one." Agitation, he argues, is an essential means of forcing awareness of social evils into the public consciousness; it is particularly necessary to prevent the public from turning a blind eye to the social evils faced by African Americans. Du Bois thus justifies the use of agitation to combat racial injustice. It is significant that Du Bois chose the topic of agitation for one of his first editorials in the *Crisis*. While Booker T. Washington did speak out on issues like segregation, voting rights, and lynching and was not the accommodationist he often is accused of being, he did avoid direct confrontation with southern racists and southern leaders. Du Bois did not take his civil rights battles to the streets, but he was confrontational in his writing and in the positions he took, and he made sure that agitation defined the tone of the NAACP.

◆ "Returning Soldiers"

During the decade following its founding, the *Crisis*, under Du Bois's direction, became the most influential African American monthly magazine in the country. It sustained agitation for racial justice and also reported on political, economic, social, and intellectual affairs of interest to American blacks. During World War I, Du Bois wrote an editorial, "Close Ranks," urging blacks to set aside their grievances and join with their fellow Americans in support of the war. No essay that Du Bois wrote brought him as much criticism, especially from left-wing antiwar activists like A. Philip Randolph, who accused Du Bois of betraying the black race. When the war ended, Du Bois attempted to reassert his leadership and regain his reputation as a stalwart campaigner for racial justice. In May 1919 he penned "Returning Soldiers," a virtual call to arms instructing returning black veterans to bring home the struggle they had engaged in to make the world safe for democracy. This was one of Du Bois's most militant and threatening essays, and it clearly anticipated the lynchings and race riots that made 1919, with its "red summer," one of the most violent and oppressive years in the nation's history.

Du Bois begins his message to black soldiers by acknowledging their service and sacrifice and reminding them that while they fought gladly for humanity and against the threat of Germany, they also fought with much bitterness for "the dominant southern oligarchy entrenched in Washington" and for "the America that represents and gloats in lynching, disfranchisement, caste, brutality and devilish insult." The returning soldiers come home having been changed by the experience of war. They have become more aware of the injustice in America and less willing to be patient and accommodating in the face of this injustice. Instead, eyes opened by war, they stand tall and "look America squarely in the face and call a spade a spade."

Du Bois proceeds to list the sins America has regularly committed against its black citizens and to define the impact of these sins in harsh and graphic terms. The sins include lynching; disfranchisement; withholding access to education; robbing blacks of their land, their labor, and opportunity; and insulting blacks and depriving them of their dignity. Despite this reality, African Americans donned the nation's uniform and fought and died for their country, and, if called upon, they would do so again. But Du Bois insists that it is now time to "fight a sterner, longer, more unbending battle against the forces of hell in our own land." In his closing lines, Du Bois turns poet and pens verse of resistance: "We *return*. We *return from fighting*. We *return fighting*." He then concludes with a promise that "we will save" democracy in the United States of America, "or know the reason why." This essay was Du Bois at his most militant. While the decade that followed brought dra-

Karl Marx (AP/Wide World Photos)

matic changes, including the Great Migration of blacks out of the South, the Harlem Renaissance, the rise of the "New Negro," and the rise and fall of the black nationalist Marcus Garvey, it did not bring the promised democracy and justice for African Americans.

◆ "Marxism and the Negro Problem"

The 1920s was a decade of change for Du Bois. Following World War I, he became involved in a series of Pan-African Congresses that focused attention on the ties among the peoples of the African diaspora and on the struggle for the liberation of colonial peoples. In 1926 he made his first trip to the Soviet Union; he returned enamored of the Bolshevik Revolution and from then on grew more and more committed to Socialism. Also by the mid-1920s Du Bois was losing his clout within the NAACP, in part because of his political shift to the left but also because of a personal clash with the executive director, Walter White. Reflecting these changes, in the early 1930s Du Bois began to explore broader political themes, especially in his writings. Through 1933 and early 1934 he published a series of essays redefining his political views, addressing such topics as Pan-Africanism and segregation; in May 1933, he took a critical look at the relevance of Marxism for African Americans.

President of Ghana, Dr. Kwame Nkrumah, second from right, talks with the ninety-three-year-old scholar Dr. W. E. B. Du Bois shortly before opening the World Peace Conference in Accra, Ghana, June 21, 1962.
(AP/Wide World Photos)

Du Bois opens "Marxism and the Negro Problem" by extolling *Das Kapital* (translated as *Capital*) as one of the great books of Western civilization and its author, Karl Marx, as a genius. He then provides a brief summary of the fundamental elements of Marx's analysis of society, focusing on the relationship between capital and labor, on the surplus value created by labor, and on the inevitable social revolution that will be provoked by the capitalist's control of this surplus value and the exploitation of labor. With this as his background, Du Bois then assesses the relevance of Marxism to the economic realities faced during the Great Depression of the 1930s, especially with respect to American labor and African Americans. His general conclusion is that while Marx's analysis is astute as applied to the realities of the mid-nineteenth century, historical events and factors of the twentieth century, especially in the United States, impinged on some of Marx's assumptions and projections. One of these factors was the emergence of imperialist capitalism worldwide and the use of white proletariats to subjugate usually nonwhite colonial proletariats; a second factor was the division that racism imposed on the American proletariat.

Regarding labor and capital in the United States, Du Bois's adaptation of Marxist analysis is straightforward. The first African Americans were overwhelmingly laborers. White labor, however, not only refused to join with black labor but also actively participated in the racial suppression of African Americans. Consequently, both the broader labor movement and Socialism in the United States were rendered impotent. White labor was too frightened of black labor to unite with them; Socialism also failed to safeguard the privileged position of white labor. Communism, in turn, which alone promotes racial equality, could not attract white members because of that commitment to equality. In Du Bois's view, only in the "hearts of black laborers" are found the ideals of democracy and equality, which might someday lead to Marx's vision of a workers' utopia becoming a reality.

Impact and Legacy

In many ways, the 1933 essay "Marxism and the Negro Problem" marked the end of the intellectual trajectory that Du Bois began in 1897 with "Strivings of the Negro People." Du Bois was by then sixty-five, an age when most careers are drawing to a close. His departure from the NAACP the following year virtually ended his career in civil rights. However, this point marked the beginning of another thirty-year career for Du Bois as an academic, an intellectual, and, more and more, a political radical and internationalist. More than any other person, Du Bois brought race to the forefront of historical analysis of American society; he believed that understanding race was fundamental to understanding America. His concept of racial identity as something to be preserved rather than overcome, as expressed in his 1897 article, formed the basis for his concept of civil rights as something deserved by African Americans, not to be earned by them. While Du Bois did not see his decades of work on behalf of the black race bear the fruit he sought—and ironically left the United States just as the civil rights movement was achieving its first victories—his work was fundamental to the developing of concepts and the defining of objectives at the heart of the civil rights movement.

Key Sources

The major repository for Du Bois's papers is at the University of Massachusetts Amherst, in the W. E. B. Du Bois Papers, Department of Special Collections and University Archives. Many of the papers in this collection were microfilmed in 1980, and the seventy-nine-reel set is widely available in research libraries around the country. The most noted published collections of Du Bois's papers are two titles edited by his close friend the historian Herbert Aptheker: *The Correspondence of W. E. B. Du Bois*—Vol. 1: *Selections, 1877–1934* (1973); Vol. 2: *Selections, 1934–1944* (1976); and Vol. 3: *Selections, 1944–1963* (1978)—and *Against Racism: Unpublished Essays, Papers, Addresses, 1887–1961* (1988). Two other important published collections of Du Bois's work are *Writings: W. E. B. Du Bois* (1986) and David Levering Lewis, ed., *W. E. B. Du Bois: A Reader* (2005). The documentary *W. E. B. Du Bois: A Biography in Four Voices* (1996), directed by Louis Massiah and narrated by Toni Cade Bambara, Amiri Baraka, Wesley Brown, and Thulani Davis is available in DVD and VCR formats, and is the best film study of Du Bois.

Further Reading

■ Books

Blum, Edward J. *W. E. B. Du Bois: American Prophet.* Philadelphia: University of Pennsylvania Press, 2007.

Lewis, David Levering. *W. E. B. Du Bois.* Vol. 1: *Biography of a Race, 1868–1919.* New York: Henry Holt, 1993; Vol. 2: *The Fight*

"*One ever feels his two-ness,—an American, a Negro; two souls, two thoughts, two unreconciled strivings; two warring ideals in one dark body, whose dogged strength alone keeps it from being torn asunder. The history of the American Negro is the history of this strife,—this longing to attain self-conscious manhood, to merge his double self into a better and truer self.*"

("Strivings of the Negro People")

"*The plain result of this propaganda has been to help the cutting down of educational opportunity for Negro children, the legal disfranchisement of nearly 5,000,000 of Negroes and a state of public opinion which apologizes for lynching, listens complacently to any insult or detraction directed against an eighth of the population of the land, and silently allows a new slavery to rise and clutch the South and paralyze the moral sense of a great nation.*"

("The Parting of the Ways")

"*The way for black men to-day to make these rights the heritage of their children is to struggle for them unceasingly, and if they fail, die trying.*"

("The Parting of the Ways")

"*The function of this Association is to tell this nation the crying evil of race prejudice. It is a hard duty but a necessary one—a divine one.*"

("Agitation")

"*We stand again to look America squarely in the face and call a spade a spade. We sing: This country of ours, despite all its better souls have done and dreamed, is yet a shameful land.*"

("Returning Soldiers")

"*In the hearts of black laborers alone, therefore, lie those ideals of democracy in politics and industry which may in time make the workers of the world effective dictators of civilization.*"

("Marxism and the Negro Problem")

for Equality and the American Century, 1919–1963. New York: Henry Holt, 2000.

Marable, Manning. *W. E. B. Du Bois: Black Radical Democrat.* Boston: Twayne Publishers, 1986.

Meier, August. *Negro Thought in America, 1880–1915: Racial Ideologies in the Age of Booker T. Washington.* Ann Arbor: University of Michigan Press, 1963.

Moore, Jacqueline M. *Booker T. Washington, W. E. B. Du Bois, and the Struggle for Racial Uplift.* Wilmington, Del.: Scholarly Resources, 2003.

Rampersad, Arnold. *The Art and Imagination of W. E. B. Du Bois.* Cambridge, Mass.: Harvard University Press, 1976.

Rudwick, Elliott M. *W. E. B. Du Bois: Propagandist of the Negro Protest.* New York: Atheneum, 1969.

Wolters, Raymond. *Du Bois and His Rivals.* Columbia: University of Missouri Press, 2002.

■ **Web Sites**

"Du Bois Central." University of Massachusetts Amherst Web site. http://www.library.umass.edu/spcoll/collections/dubois/index.htm.

—Cary D. Wintz

Questions for Further Study

1. Early in his career, Du Bois advocated that African Americans strive to occupy a "middle ground" between white American culture and black African culture. What did Du Bois mean by this?

2. Summarize the fundamental difference between Du Bois's view of racial issues and that of Booker T. Washington. On what basis was Du Bois critical of Washington's views?

3. Describe the impact of World War I on Du Bois's views concerning race relations.

4. In your view, what was the appeal of Marxism and Communism to an African American intellectual such as Du Bois in the 1920s and beyond? How did the advent of the Great Depression contribute to that appeal?

5. Compare Du Bois's views on race relations with those of Charles Hamilton Houston, particularly Houston's views in "Educational Inequalities Must Go!" What common ground do the two writers occupy? Do you detect any differences in their points of view?

"STRIVINGS OF THE NEGRO PEOPLE" (1897)

Between me and the other world there is ever an unasked question: unasked by some through feelings of delicacy; by others through the difficulty of rightly framing it. All, nevertheless, flutter round it. They approach me in a half-hesitant sort of way, eye me curiously or compassionately, and then, instead of saying directly, How does it feel to be a problem? they say, I know an excellent colored man in my town; or, I fought at Mechanicsville; or, Do not these Southern outrages make your blood boil? At these I smile, or am interested, or reduce the boiling to a simmer, as the occasion may require. To the real question, How does it feel to be a problem? I answer seldom a word....

After the Egyptian and Indian, the Greek and Roman, the Teuton and Mongolian, the Negro is a sort of seventh son, born with a veil, and gifted with second-sight in this American world, a world which yields him no self-consciousness, but only lets him see himself through the revelation of the other world. It is a peculiar sensation, this double-consciousness, this sense of always looking at one's self through the eyes of others, of measuring one's soul by the tape of a world that looks on in amused contempt and pity. One ever feels his two-ness, an American, a Negro; two souls, two thoughts, two unreconciled strivings; two warring ideals in one dark body, whose dogged strength alone keeps it from being torn asunder. The history of the American Negro is the history of this strife, this longing to attain self-conscious manhood, to merge his double self into a better and truer self. In this merging he wishes neither of the older selves to be lost. He does not wish to Africanize America, for America has too much to teach the world and Africa; he does not wish to bleach his Negro blood in a flood of white Americanism, for he believes foolishly, perhaps, but fervently that Negro blood has yet a message for the world. He simply wishes to make it possible for a man to be both a Negro and an American without being cursed and spit upon by his fellows, without losing the opportunity of self-development.

This is the end of his striving: to be a co-worker in the kingdom of culture, to escape both death and isolation, and to husband and use his best powers. These powers, of body and of mind, have in the past been so wasted and dispersed as to lose all effectiveness, and to seem like absence of all power, like weakness. The double-aimed struggle of the black artisan, on the one hand to escape white contempt for a nation of mere hewers of wood and drawers of water, and on the other hand to plough and nail and dig for a poverty-stricken horde, could only result in making him a poor craftsman, for he had but half a heart in either cause. By the poverty and ignorance of his people the Negro lawyer or doctor was pushed toward quackery and demagogism, and by the criticism of the other world toward an elaborate preparation that overfitted him for his lowly tasks. The would-be black savant was confronted by the paradox that the knowledge his people needed was a twice-told tale to his white neighbors, while the knowledge which would teach the white world was Greek to his own flesh and blood. The innate love of harmony and beauty that set the ruder souls of his people a-dancing, a-singing, and a-laughing raised but confusion and doubt in the soul of the black artist; for the beauty revealed to him was the soul-beauty of a race which his larger audience despised, and he could not articulate the message of another people.

This waste of double aims, this seeking to satisfy two unreconciled ideals, has wrought sad havoc with the courage and faith and deeds of eight thousand thousand people, has sent them often wooing false gods and invoking false means of salvation, and has even at times seemed destined to make them ashamed of themselves. In the days of bondage they thought to see in one divine event the end of all doubt and disappointment; eighteenth-century Rousseauism never worshiped freedom with half the unquestioning faith that the American Negro did for two centuries. To him slavery was, indeed, the sum of all villainies, the cause of all sorrow, the root of all prejudice; emancipation was the key to a promised land of sweeter beauty than ever stretched before the eyes of wearied Israelites. In his songs and exhortations swelled one refrain, liberty; in his tears and curses the god he implored had freedom in his right hand. At last it came, suddenly, fearfully, like a dream. With one wild carnival of blood and passion came the message in his own plaintive cadences:

"Shout, O children!
Shout, you're free!
The Lord has bought your liberty!"

Years have passed away, ten, twenty, thirty. Thirty years of national life, thirty years of renewal and development, and yet the swarthy ghost of Banquo sits in its old place at the national feast....

The freedman has not yet found in freedom his promised land. Whatever of lesser good may have come in these years of change, the shadow of a deep disappointment rests upon the Negro people, a disappointment all the more bitter because the unattained ideal was unbounded save by the simple ignorance of a lowly folk.

A people thus handicapped ought not to be asked to race with the world, but rather allowed to give all its time and thought to its own social problems. But alas! while sociologists gleefully count his bastards and his prostitutes, the very soul of the toiling, sweating black man is darkened by the shadow of a vast despair. Men call the shadow prejudice, and learnedly explain it as the natural defense of culture against barbarism, learning against ignorance, purity against crime, the "higher" against the "lower" races.... But before that nameless prejudice that leaps beyond all this he stands helpless, dismayed, and well-nigh speechless; before that personal disrespect and mockery, the ridicule and systematic humiliation, the distortion of fact and wanton license of fancy, the cynical ignoring of the better and boisterous welcoming of the worse, the all-pervading desire to inculcate disdain for everything black, from Toussaint to the devil, before this there rises a sickening despair that would disarm and discourage any nation save that black host to whom "discouragement" is an unwritten word.

They still press on, they still nurse the dogged hope, not a hope of nauseating patronage, not a hope of reception into charmed social circles of stock-jobbers, pork-packers, and earl-hunters, but the hope of a higher synthesis of civilization and humanity, a true progress....

The ideals of physical freedom, of political power, of school training, as separate all-sufficient panaceas for social ills, became in the third decade dim and overcast. They were the vain dreams of credulous race childhood; not wrong, but incomplete and oversimple. The training of the schools we need to-day more than ever, the training of deft hands, quick eyes and ears, and the broader, deeper, higher culture of gifted minds. The power of the ballot we need in sheer self-defense, and as a guarantee of good faith. We may misuse it, but we can scarce do worse in this respect than our whilom masters. Freedom, too, the long-sought, we still seek, the freedom of life and limb, the freedom to work and think. Work, culture, and liberty, all these we need, not singly, but together; for to-day these ideals among the Negro people are gradually coalescing, and finding a higher mean-

Glossary

Banquo	a character in William Shakespeare's *Macbeth* whom Macbeth has murdered; Macbeth later sees a ghost of Banquo in an empty seat at a banquet
Israelites	the "chosen people" of the Hebrew Bible whose Exodus and quest for the "promised land" is chronicled in the first five books of the biblical Old Testament
Mechanicsville	the site of a major U.S. Civil War battle in Virginia in 1862
Rousseauism	the philosophy of Jean-Jacques Rousseau (1712–1778), who believed that humans in the state of nature were good but that they were corrupted by society
seventh son	a figure of legend, folklore, and mythology, as well as in the Bible; one who will reveal his power gradually; sometimes regarded as an "ugly duckling" that evolves into a swan
Teuton	an early Germanic tribe
twice-told tale	a phrase from William Shakespeare's *King John* ("Life is as tedious as a twice-told tale") and used by the American writer Nathaniel Hawthorne as the title of a short-story collection
Toussaint	Toussaint Louverture (ca. 1743–1803), a black slave who organized a slave insurrection in Haiti

ing in the unifying ideal of race, the ideal of fostering the traits and talents of the Negro, not in opposition to, but in conformity with, the greater ideals of the American republic, in order that someday, on American soil, two world races may give each to each those characteristics which both so sadly lack....

Merely a stern concrete test of the underlying principles of the great republic is the Negro problem, and the spiritual striving of the freedmen's sons is the travail of soul whose burden is almost beyond the measure of their strength, but who bear it in the name of an historic race, in the name of this the land of their fathers' fathers, and in the name of human opportunity.

"THE PARTING OF THE WAYS" (1904)

The points upon which American Negroes differ as to their course of action are the following: First, the scope of education; second, the necessity of the right of suffrage; third, the importance of civil rights; fourth, the conciliation of the South; fifth, the future of the race in this country.

The older opinion as built up under the leadership of our great dead, Payne, Crummell, Forten and Douglass, was that the broadest field of education should be opened to black children; that no free citizen of a republic could exist in peace and prosperity without the ballot; that self-respect and proper development of character can only take place under a system of equal civil rights; that every effort should be made to live in peace and harmony with all men, but that even for this great boon no people must willingly or passively surrender their essential rights of manhood; that in future the Negro is destined to become an American citizen with full political and civil rights, and that he must never rest contented until he has achieved this.

Since the death of the leaders of the past there have come mighty changes in the nation. The gospel of money has risen triumphant in church and state and university. The great question which Americans ask to-day is, "What is he worth?" or "What is it worth?" The ideals of human rights are obscured, and the nation has begun to swagger about the world in its useless battleships looking for helpless peoples whom it can force to buy its goods at high prices. This wave of materialism is temporary; it will pass and leave us all ashamed and surprised; but while it is here it strangely maddens and blinds us. Religious periodicals are found in the van yelling for war; peaceful ministers of Christ are leading lynchers; great universities are stuffing their pockets with greenbacks and kicking the little souls of students to make them "move faster" through the courses of study, the end of which is ever *"Etwas schaffen"* and seldom *"Etwas sein."* Yet there are signs of change. Souls long cramped and starved are stretching toward the light. Men are beginning to murmur against the lower tendencies and the sound of the Zeitgeist strikes sensitive ears with that harrowing discord which prefigures richer harmony to come.

Meantime an awakening race, seeing American civilization as it is, is strongly moved and naturally misled. They whisper: What is the greatness of the country? Is it not money? Well then, the one end of our education and striving should be moneymaking. The trimmings of life, smatterings of Latin and music and such stuff—let that wait till we are rich. Then as to voting, what is the good of it after all? Politics does not pay as well as the grocery business, and breeds trouble. Therefore get out of politics and let the ballot go. When we are rich we can dabble in politics along with the president of Yale. Then, again the thought arises: What is personal humiliation and the denial of ordinary civil rights compared with a chance to earn a living? Why quarrel with your bread and butter simply because of filthy Jim Crow cars? Earn a living; get rich, and all these things shall be added unto you. Moreover, conciliate your neighbors, because they are more powerful and wealthier, and the price you must pay to earn a living in America is that of humiliation and inferiority.

No one, of course, has voiced this argument quite so flatly and bluntly as I have indicated. It has been expressed rather by the emphasis given industrial and trade teaching, the decrying of suffrage as a manhood right or even necessity, the insistence on great advance among Negroes before there is any recognition of their aspirations, and a tendency to minimize the shortcomings of the South and to emphasize the mistakes and failures of black men. Now, in this there has been just that degree of truth and right which serves to make men forget its untruths. That the shiftless and poor need thrift and skill, that ignorance can not vote intelligently, that duties and rights go hand in hand, and that sympathy and understanding among neighbors is prerequisite to peace and concord, all this is true. Who has ever denied it, or ever will? But from all this does it follow that Negro colleges are not needed, that the right of suffrage is not essential for black men, that equality of civil rights is not the first of rights and that no self-respecting man can agree with the person who insists that he is a dog? Certainly not, all answer.

Yet the plain result of the attitude of mind of those who, in their advocacy of industrial schools, the unimportance of suffrage and civil rights and conciliation, have been significantly silent or evasive as to higher training and the great principle of free self-respecting manhood for black folk the plain result of this propaganda has been to help the cutting down of educational opportunity for Negro children, the legal disfranchisement of nearly 5,000,000 of Negroes and a state of public opinion which apologizes for lynching, listens complacently to any insult or detraction directed against an eighth of the population of the land, and silently allows a new slavery to rise and clutch the South and paralyze the moral sense of a great nation.

What do Negroes say to this? I speak advisedly when I say that the overwhelming majority of them declare that the tendencies to-day are wrong and that the propaganda that encouraged them was wrong. They say that industrial and trade teaching is needed among Negroes, sadly needed; but they unhesitatingly affirm that it is not needed as much as thorough common school training and the careful education of the gifted in higher institutions; that only in this way can a people rise by intelligence and social leadership to a plane of permanent efficiency and morality....

Moreover, notwithstanding speeches and the editorials of a subsidized Negro press, black men in this land know that when they lose the ballot they lose all. They are no fools. They know it is impossible for free workingmen without a ballot to compete with free workingmen who have the ballot; they know there is no set of people so good and true as to be worth trusting with the political destiny of their fellows, and they know that it is just as true to-day as it was a century and a quarter ago "Taxation without representation is tyranny."

Finally, the Negro knows perfectly what freedom and equality mean—opportunity to make the best of oneself, unhandicapped by wanton restraint and unreasoning prejudice. For this the most of us propose to strive. We will not, by word or deed, for a moment admit the right of any man to discriminate against us simply on account of race or color.... We refuse to kiss the hands that smite us, but rather insist on striving by all civilized methods to keep wide educational opportunity, to keep the right to vote, to insist on equal civil rights and to gain every right and privilege open to a free American citizen.

But, answer some, you can not accomplish this. America will never spell opportunity for black men; it spelled slavery for them in 1619 and it will spell the same thing in other letters in 1919. To this I answer simply: I do not believe it. I believe that black men will become free American citizens if they have the courage and persistence to demand the rights and treatment of men, and cease to toady and apologize and belittle themselves. The rights of humanity are worth fighting for. Those that deserve them in the long run get them. The way for black men to-day to make these rights the heritage of their children is to struggle for them unceasingly, and if they fail, die trying.

Glossary

etwas schaffen	German for "do something"
etwas sein	German for "be something"
greenbacks	dollars, money
Jim Crow cars	late-nineteenth-century and early-twentieth-century laws and customs that kept African Americans segregated and in a subservient position; "cars" refers to railroad cars
Payne, Crummell, Forten and Douglass	Daniel A. Payne (1811–1893), an author, educator, and clergyman associated with the African Methodist Episcopal Church; Alexander Crummell (1819–1898), an African American clergyman and missionary; James Forten (1766–1842), an African American businessman and abolitionist; Frederick Douglass (1818–1895), a prominent African American author and abolitionist
Zeitgeist	a German word literally meaning "spirit of the time"

"AGITATION" (1910)

Some good friends of the cause we represent fear agitation. They say: "Do not agitate—do not make a noise; *work*." They add, "Agitation is destructive or at best negative—what is wanted is positive constructive work."

Such honest critics mistake the function of agitation. A toothache is agitation. Is a toothache a good thing? No. Is it therefore useless? No. It is supremely useful, for it tells the body of decay, dyspepsia and death. Without it the body would suffer unknowingly. It would think: All is well, when lo! danger lurks.

The same is true of the Social Body. Agitation is a necessary evil to tell of the ills of the Suffering. Without it many a nation has been lulled to false security and preened itself with virtues it did not possess.

The function of this Association is to tell this nation the crying evil of race prejudice. It is a hard duty but a necessary one—a divine one. It is Pain; Pain is not good but Pain is necessary. Pain does not aggravate disease—Disease causes Pain. Agitation does not mean Aggravation—Aggravation calls for Agitation in order that Remedy may be found.

Glossary

dyspepsia	literally, indigestion; often used to suggest ill humor or disgruntlement

"Returning Soldiers" (1919)

We are returning from war! THE CRISIS and tens of thousands of black men were drafted into a great struggle. For bleeding France and what she means and has meant and will mean to us and humanity and against the threat of German race arrogance, we fought gladly and to the last drop of blood; for America and her highest ideals, we fought in far-off hope; for the dominant southern oligarchy entrenched in Washington, we fought in bitter resignation. For the America that represents and gloats in lynching, disfranchisement, caste, brutality and devilish insult—for this, in the hateful upturning and mixing of things, we were forced by vindictive fate to fight, also.

But today we return! We return from the slavery of uniform which the world's madness demanded us to don to the freedom of civil garb. We stand again to look America squarely in the face and call a spade a spade. We sing: This country of ours, despite all its better souls have done and dreamed, is yet a shameful land.

It *lynches*.

And lynching is barbarism of a degree of contemptible nastiness unparalleled in human history. Yet for fifty years we have lynched two Negroes a week, and we have kept this up right through the war.

It *disfranchises* its own citizens.

Disfranchisement is the deliberate theft and robbery of the only protection of poor against rich and black against white. The land that disfranchises its citizens and calls itself a democracy lies and knows it lies.

It encourages *ignorance*.

It has never really tried to educate the Negro. A dominant minority does not want Negroes educated. It wants servants, dogs, whores and monkeys. And when this land allows a reactionary group by its stolen political power to force as many black folk into these categories as it possibly can, it cries in contemptible hypocrisy: "They threaten us with degeneracy; they cannot be educated."

It *steals* from us.

It organized industry to cheat us. It cheats us out of our land; it cheats us out of our labor. It confiscates our savings. It reduces our wages. It raises our rent. It steals our profit. It taxes us without representation. It keeps us consistently and universally poor, and then feeds us on charity and derides our poverty.

It *insults* us.

It has organized a nation-wide and latterly a world-wide propaganda of deliberate and continuous insult and defamation of black blood wherever found. It decrees that it shall not be possible in travel nor residence, work nor play, education nor instruction for a black man to exist without tacit or open acknowledgment of his inferiority to the dirtiest white dog. And it looks upon any attempt to question or even discuss this dogma as arrogance, unwarranted assumption and treason.

This is the country to which we soldiers of Democracy return. This is the fatherland for which we fought! But it is our fatherland. It was right for us to fight. The faults of our country are our faults. Under similar circumstances, we would fight again. But by the God of Heaven, we are cowards and jackasses if now that that war is over, we do not marshal every ounce of our brain and brawn to fight a sterner, longer, more unbending battle against the forces of hell in our own land.

We *return*.
We *return from fighting*.
We *return fighting*.

Make way for Democracy! We saved it in France, and by the Great Jehovah, we will save it in the United States of America, or know the reason why.

Glossary

Jehovah	the name often given to God in Hebrew Scripture

"Marxism and the Negro Problem" (1933)

There are certain books in the world which every searcher for truth must know: the Bible, *Critique of Pure Reason*, *Origin of Species*, and Karl Marx's *Capital*....

The task which Karl Marx set himself was to study and interpret the organization of industry in the modern world....

The gist of that philosophy is that the value of products regularly exchanged in the open market depends upon the labor necessary to produce them; that capital consists of machines, materials and wages paid for labor; that out of the finished product, when materials have been paid for and the wear and tear and machinery replaced, and wages paid, there remains a surplus value. This surplus value arises from labor and is the difference between what is actually paid laborers for their wages and the market value of the commodities which the laborers produce. It represents, therefore, exploitation of the laborer, and this exploitation, inherent in the capitalistic system of production, is the cause of poverty, of industrial crises, and eventually of social revolution.

This social revolution, whether we regard it as voluntary revolt or the inevitable working of a vast cosmic law of social evolution, will be the last manifestation of the class struggle, and will come by inevitable change induced by the very nature of the conditions under which present production is carried on. It will come by the action of the great majority of men who compose the wage-earning proletariat, and it will result in common ownership of all capital, the disappearance of capitalistic exploitation, and the division of the products and services of industry according to human needs, and not according to the will of the owners of capital....

Perhaps nothing illustrates this better than recent actions in the United States: our re-examination of the whole concept of Property; our banking moratorium; the extraordinary new agriculture bill; the plans to attack unemployment, and similar measures. Labor rather than gambling is the sure foundation of value and whatever we call it—exploitation, theft or business acumen—there is something radically wrong with an industrial system that turns out simultaneously paupers and millionaires and sets a world starving because it has too much food.

What now has all this to do with the Negro problem? First of all, it is manifest that the mass of Negroes in the United States belong distinctly to the working proletariat.... Nevertheless, this black proletariat is not a part of the white proletariat....

And while Negro labor in America suffers because of the fundamental inequities of the whole capitalistic system, the lowest and most fatal degree of its suffering comes not from the capitalists but from fellow white laborers. It is white labor that deprives the Negro of his right to vote, denies him education, denies him affiliation with trade unions, expels him from decent houses and neighborhoods, and heaps upon him the public insults of open color discrimination.

It is no sufficient answer to say that capital encourages this oppression and uses it for its own ends.... But the bulk of American white labor is neither ignorant nor fanatical. It knows exactly what it is doing and it means to do it. William Green and Mathew Woll of the A. F. of L. have no excuse of illiteracy or religion to veil their deliberate intention to keep Negroes and Mexicans and other elements of common labor, in a lower proletariat as subservient to their interests as theirs are to the interests of capital.

This large development of a petty bourgeoisie within the American laboring class is a post-Marxian phenomenon and the result of the tremendous and world wide development of capitalism in the 20th Century....

Thus in America we have seen a wild and ruthless scramble of labor groups over each other in order to climb to wealth on the backs of black labor and foreign immigrants. The Irish climbed on the Negroes. The Germans scrambled over the Negroes and emulated the Irish. The Scandinavians fought forward next to the Germans and the Italians and "Bohunks" are crowding up, leaving Negroes still at the bottom chained to helplessness, first by slavery, then by disfranchisement and always by the Color Bar.

The second influence on white labor both in America and Europe has been the fact that the extension of the world market by imperial expanding industry has established a world-wide new proletariat of colored workers, toiling under the worst conditions of 19th century capitalism, herded as slaves and serfs and furnishing by the lowest paid wage in modern history a mass of raw material for industry. With this largess the capitalists have consolidated their economic power, nullified universal suffrage and bribed the white workers by high wages, visions of wealth and the opportunity to drive "niggers." Soldiers and sailors from the white workers are used to keep "darkies" in their "places" and white foremen and engineers have been established as irresponsible satraps in China and India, Africa and the West Indies, backed by the organized and centralized ownership of machines, raw materials, finished commodities and land monopoly over the whole world.

How now does the philosophy of Karl Marx apply today to colored labor? First of all colored labor has no common ground with white labor. No soviet of technocrats would do more than exploit colored labor in order to raise the status of whites. No revolt of a white proletariat could be started if its object was to make black workers their economic, political and social equals. It is for this reason that American socialism for fifty years has been dumb on the Negro problem, and the communists cannot even get a respectful hearing in America unless they begin by expelling Negroes....

Under these circumstances, what shall we say of the Marxian philosophy and of its relation to the American Negro? We can only say, as it seems to me, that the Marxian philosophy is a true diagnosis of the situation in Europe in the middle of the 19th Century.... But it must be modified in the United States of America and especially so far as the Negro group is concerned. The Negro is exploited to a degree that means poverty, crime, delinquency and indigence. And that exploitation comes not from a black capitalistic class but from the white capitalists and equally from the white proletariat...

Meantime, comes the Great Depression. It levels all in mighty catastrophe. The fantastic industrial structure of America is threatened with ruin. The trade unions of skilled labor are doubletongued and helpless. Unskilled and common white labor is too frightened at Negro competition to attempt united action. It only begs a dole. The reformist program of Socialism meets no response from the white proletariat because it offers no escape to wealth and no effective bar to black labor, and a mud-sill of black labor is essential to white labor's standard of living. The shrill cry of a few communists is not even listened to, because and solely because it seeks to break down barriers between black and white. There is not at present the slightest indication that a Marxian revolution based on a united class-conscious proletariat is anywhere on the American far horizon. Rather race antagonism and labor group rivalry is still undisturbed by world catastrophe. In the hearts of black laborers alone, therefore, lie those ideals of democracy in politics and industry which may in time make the workers of the world effective dictators of civilization.

Glossary

Bohunks	a slur used against people of east-central European descent
Critique of Pure Reason	a book by Immanuel Kant (1724–1804) published in 1781 and widely considered one of the most important works in the history of philosophy
Mathew Woll	Matthew Woll (1880–1956), vice president of the American Federation of Labor from 1919 to 1955
Origin of Species	*On the Origin of Species*, a book by Charles Darwin (1809–1882) published in 1859 and important in the early history of the science of evolutionary biology
petty bourgeoisie	Anglicized form of the French *petite bourgeoisie*, referring to a social class above the proletariat but below that of the bourgeoisie, or upper class; generally shopkeepers and small business owners
proletariat	the laboring class, usually used in reference to industrial workers
soviet	a governing council, usually in a Communist country
William Green	president of the American Federation of Labor from 1924 until his death (1873–1952)

Allen Dulles (Library of Congress)

ALLEN DULLES

1893–1969

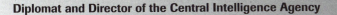

Diplomat and Director of the Central Intelligence Agency

Featured Documents
◆ "The Present Situation in Germany" (1945)
◆ Television Interview on the Soviets' Intentions (1956)
◆ Address on the Soviet Military Threat (1959)

Overview

Allen W. Dulles was born on April 7, 1893, in Watertown, New York, one of five children brought up in a family dedicated to public service. Dulles was related to two secretaries of state, John W. Foster and Robert Lansing. Allen's brother John Foster later became secretary of state in the administration of Dwight Eisenhower. Dulles earned B.A. and M.A. degrees from Princeton (in 1914 and 1916, respectively) and then entered the diplomatic service, attending peace negotiations at the end of World War I and serving in various posts in European capitals. When he returned to Washington, D.C., in 1922, he began attending law school at George Washington University; he graduated in 1926 and joined the law firm of Sullivan & Cromwell, where his brother John Foster Dulles was a managing partner.

Not a litigator, Dulles specialized in helping the firm's clients with their international business. His office was on Wall Street, and while living in New York City he joined the Council on Foreign Relations. He also continued to take government assignments, representing the U.S. government at the League of Nations armament conference in 1932–1933. During World War II, Dulles joined the Office of Strategic Services (OSS), the precursor of the Central Intelligence Agency (CIA). This new position marked his departure from conventional diplomacy, as he now began a career as a covert operative, penetrating the German Foreign Ministry and gathering information about the 1944 assassination attempt on the German leader Adolf Hitler. For the next eight years Dulles continued to work on intelligence matters, engaging in covert operations as well as in considerable assessment of the CIA as an organization. In 1953, President Eisenhower named Dulles director of the CIA.

Dulles became an activist, initiating operations to destabilize governments in Iran and Guatemala that were deemed threats to U.S. security. Similar efforts to drive Fidel Castro from power in Cuba, however, failed in the infamous Bay of Pigs invasion in 1961. Shortly thereafter Dulles resigned as director of the CIA. In retirement, Dulles wrote several books about spying and intelligence gathering and served on the Warren Commission, established by President Lyndon B. Johnson to investigate the assassination of President John F. Kennedy.

Dulles did not merely write for his colleagues and speak to fellow professionals—as he did in his *Foreign Affairs* articles and interviews. His appearances on television, his public speeches, and his books aimed at a general audience made him in the popular mind one of the country's master spies and a foremost authority on the cold war. In 1963 he published *The Craft of Intelligence*, considered one of the classics in the field. In 1968 he edited the volume *Great True Spy Stories*.

Dulles's most notable contributions, perhaps, were his understanding of developments in Germany—both before and after World War II—and his dedication to countering the Soviet threat, especially in the form of propaganda and efforts of the Soviet intelligence agencies to undermine the will of the Western governments to oppose Communist infiltrations of governments in Europe, Asia, and South and Central America. Dulles's speeches and interviews focused on mobilizing the efforts of government and other public leaders as well as the population at large to oppose the spread of Communism and the power of the Soviet Union.

Explanation and Analysis of Documents

In both private meetings (such as the off-the-record briefing on the situation in Germany at the Council on Foreign Relations) and in public speeches and television appearances, Allen Dulles remained remarkably consistent: He perceived the Soviet Union as a major threat to world peace—specifically to the stable relations that ought to have prevailed between the United States and its former enemies, especially Germany. The right way to rebuild international relations after World War II, Dulles argued, was to forge close bonds with the Germans. He acknowledged the need to punish those Germans whose actions led to or perpetuated the war, but he also believed that Germany could not be reformed without the cooperation of its citizens, who had to be turned into good allies with a stake in world peace. Thus, the Soviet Union was a threat not only because it challenged and attempted to subvert U.S. supremacy in international relations but also because the Russians sought to rule through coercion, not cooperation. They wanted to dominate Eastern Europe, turning countries into Soviet satellites rather than reaching compromises and means of accommodation with neighboring nations. To Dulles, Europe could prosper only if Germany were restored to robust health as a sovereign power.

Dulles saw Soviet Communism as a more or less monolithic system that was slow to change and unlikely to devel-

Time Line

1893	■ **April 7** Allen W. Dulles is born in Watertown, New York.
1914	■ Dulles earns a B.A. degree from Princeton.
1916	■ Dulles earns an M.A. degree from Princeton; he then joins the diplomatic service, working in Vienna, Berne, Berlin, Constantinople, and Geneva until 1925.
1926	■ Dulles earns a law degree from George Washington University and joins the law firm of Sullivan & Cromwell, to advise clients on international affairs.
1942	■ Dulles joins the Office of Strategic Services.
1944	■ Dulles engages in covert actions that penetrate the German Foreign Ministry.
1945	■ **December** Dulles delivers remarks concerning the postwar situation in Germany at an off-the-record meeting of the Council on Foreign Relations.
1948	■ Dulles issues highly critical reports of U.S. intelligence activities and calls for a reorganization of intelligence agencies.
1953	■ Dulles is appointed director of the Central Intelligence Agency; he shortly supervises operations that assist in overthrowing the governments of Iran and Guatemala.

op the sort of democratic institutions he deemed essential in the free world. He distrusted leaders like the Soviet premier Nikita Khrushchev, who talked of reform while keeping rigid control over the political apparatus and people.

♦ "The Present Situation in Germany"

Dulles's remarks at the Council on Foreign Relations occurred in the uncertain period right after the end of World War II. Germany was an occupied country, with authority divided among the Soviet Union and its allies, the United States, France, and Great Britain. Tensions were high in Berlin, situated in East Germany, where Soviet power prevailed. The beginnings of the cold war, in which the United States and the Soviet Union would compete as superpowers seeking to extend their international influence, centered on Berlin, a flashpoint that could conceivably set off another world war. At issue was the way in which Europe would recover and the roles the United States and the Soviet Union would play in that recovery. For the Soviets, gaining control of Berlin was crucial, since it would serve as a focal point in their effort to dominate Eastern Europe by holding a large part of Germany, the country that had decimated the Soviet Union and had started two world wars. The Soviets were determined never to put their own land at such risk again. But the United States interpreted Soviet aggressiveness in Eastern Europe not merely as a defensive strategy but as part of Communism's quest for world domination. The United States prided itself on defending what it called the "free world." Like the Soviet Union, the United States had its spies and intelligence-gathering agencies—the CIA in particular, which Allen Dulles was shaping to comport with U.S. desires to block or contain Soviet influence everywhere.

In early December 1945, Dulles was preparing to retire from government service after having spent the war in the OSS in close contact with the German resistance to Hitler and then as an observer of the early stages of German postwar reconstruction. In this context, he delivered remarks as part of an off-the-record meeting of the Council on Foreign Relations. Dulles begins by describing the current situation: Germany was still suffering the ravages of defeat, with a barely functioning economy. Security seemed a lesser problem. No underground group existed that could challenge the occupying authorities. Finding competent people to reconstruct the country was proving difficult, however, since many anti-Nazis qualified to work had been out of the country and were out of touch with the current conditions. As a result, at least some former Nazi Party members had to be employed.

Dulles provides examples of the complexities of evaluating Nazi Party membership. Some had joined merely to obtain or retain their employment; others might have served the Nazi government in some capacity but were not party members and did not believe in Nazi ideology. Yet certain regulations restricted such people from employment in postwar Germany. Nazi control had spread through so many institutions—such as banking—that it proved difficult to find anyone who had not collaborated with the regime in some way, no matter how minor or even unintentional. Many Germans had been deprived of basic rights, Dulles admits, but with seventy thousand arrests, it became impossible to devote much time to individual cases. The first priority was to ensure the occupation of Germany, Dulles notes, expressing his reluctance to criticize the American occupation.

Dividing Germany into four zones—as per agreements between America and its allies—had proved unworkable, in Dulles's opinion, especially since neither the United States nor the Soviet Union was willing to cede power to the other. Even worse, U.S. occupation authorities worried over American reactions to any efforts to rebuild Germany, which might be characterized as restoring the country's power to make war. And the Soviet Union's intentions were unclear: Did it mean to rebuild its part of Germany or allow it to remain in ruins? In Dulles's view, the Soviets were not making much progress in transforming East Germany using Communist methods.

Dulles takes a dim view of Soviet behavior, noting how Soviet troops had pillaged the country and were behaving like "thugs." The Soviets had reneged on their promises at the meeting in Yalta, Ukraine, to respect the rights of Germans and other defeated nations. Consequently, Dulles believes that much bitterness could result from the Soviet occupation of East Germany. To Dulles, the problems in Germany seem nearly insurmountable because of the scant trust between the occupying Americans and the German populace still angry over the war's outcome. Women had had no influential roles in Nazi Germany, and it was difficult to see how they could be enlisted to ameliorate the country's plight. Similarly, serious doubts had been raised about involving the churches in political reform. And yet Dulles could not see how Europe could prosper if Germany did not become a productive state.

Dulles holds out some hope that perhaps local government could be revived in Germany and the elements behind the attempt on Hitler's life in 1944 could be relied upon to lead reconstruction efforts. But as long as the Soviet Union occupied part of Germany, Dulles could see no way to reestablish a central government. Thus, at the time of these remarks, Dulles was well on his way to formulating a policy that would result in a separate West Germany, in which the United States would be free to reconstitute a German democracy without the interference of the Soviet Union.

◆ **Television Interview on the Soviets' Intentions**

Dulles appeared on American television at a crucial moment in the Soviet Union's history. Nikita Khrushchev had emerged as a powerful leader after a power struggle following the death of Joseph Stalin in 1953. Although Khrushchev had served as one of Stalin's loyal lieutenants, he recognized the need for reform, especially to dispel the climate of paranoia and panic that Stalin's purges had provoked. At a Communist Party congress in 1956, Khrushchev delivered an unusually frank speech, revealing Stalin's persecution and murder of party members. The ramifications of Khrushchev's attack on Stalin were incal-

Time Line	
1956	■ **June 14** In a television interview conducted by Representative Harold C. Ostertag of New York, Dulles discusses his belief in the Soviet intention to spread Communism.
1959	■ **December 4** Dulles gives a speech to the National Association of Manufacturers on the threat posed by the Soviet Union.
1961	■ Dulles plays a key role in planning the Bay of Pigs invasion of Cuba; he later resigns as director of the Central Intelligence Agency.
1963	■ Dulles is appointed to the Warren Commission to investigate the assassination of President John F. Kennedy.
1969	■ **January 9** Dulles dies in Washington, D.C.

culable, as it led to the disaffection of many loyal Communists who could no longer support Stalinism and coincided with efforts in Eastern Europe to relax the grip of Soviet-backed regimes that were restricting free speech and basic human rights. It was natural, then, that Dulles—charged with monitoring and curbing Soviet efforts to subvert democratic movements and spread Communism abroad—should be questioned about Khrushchev's motives and the impact his anti-Stalin policies would have on the CIA and other American governmental institutions.

In this interview, conducted on June 14, 1956, by Representative Harold C. Ostertag of New York, a deeply skeptical Dulles warns against taking Khrushchev's words at face value. He expresses the belief that the Soviet premier was attacking Stalin as a ploy, in the hope of convincing the Soviet people that the new regime was renouncing tyranny. But Soviet intentions had not changed; that is, world dominance remained the Communist program. Dulles shows far less concern for Stalin's crimes, simply acknowledging the leader's murderous behavior.

Asked about the Soviet public's response to Khrushchev's revelations about Stalin, Dulles states that there was much confusion because Stalin had been built

The bipartisan presidential commission (with Dulles at far left) named to investigate the assassination of President John F. Kennedy meets for the first time Dec. 5, 1963, at the National Archives Building in Washington, D.C. (AP/Wide World Photos)

up for so long as the country's savior-hero. Radically changing public opinion in Russia would be difficult, Dulles points out, given that the current leaders were part of the apparatus that Stalin himself had instituted. But perhaps they could at least alleviate some of the public anxiety that Stalin's brutal methods had stimulated. The Soviet government would function better, Dulles suggests, if the tension Stalin had introduced into the system dissipated.

On the topic of Soviet intentions in Berlin, Dulles reiterates his disbelief that the Russians would leave Germany or allow the United States to dominate it. He alludes to the Berlin blockade (June 24, 1948, to May 11, 1949), when the Russians attempted to close off access to the western sectors of the city. In response, the United States and its allies successfully organized an airlift that supplied the beleaguered city. Considered the first crisis of the cold war, the airlift had shown Western determination and ingenuity, revealing capability far greater than the Soviets had supposed in their drive to get the United States and its allies out of Germany. Although the Soviets could prevent the unification of Germany, they also realized, Dulles points out, that the Americans could not be forced out of the country.

Dulles's worries about the recovery of West Germany had disappeared; in the next few years its thriving economy was to have no counterpart in East Germany, where the Soviets were still trying to develop an alternative to the Western model. West Germany, Dulles points out, was a

great example of what a free people could do. Asked about China's plans for attacking Formosa (Taiwan), Dulles hesitates to make a prediction. He observes the potentially hostile situation, given the Chinese threat to invade the island that had become the home of the National Revolutionary Army, which had fled the mainland when the Communists took power. Similarly, Dulles could not say what would happen in South Korea, although he notes that the failure to unify the country during the Korean War perhaps meant that the North Koreans and their allies (the Chinese) would not make another effort to invade the South.

On the subject of nuclear arms, Dulles refuses to be specific, except to state his doubt that the Russians had an overall lead in the development of intercontinental missiles. It was not his expertise or his responsibility, however, to make such comparisons. Dulles seeks to dispel any notions that U.S. intelligence, the military, and other government organizations were in disarray. He notes his belief that these institutions were coordinating their efforts and would avoid another Pearl Harbor, when the United States had succumbed to a surprise Japanese attack, which initiated American engagement in World War II.

◆ Address on the Soviet Military Threat

Dulles begins his speech on December 4, 1959, to the National Association of Manufacturers noting that he had likewise addressed them in 1947 on the threat the Soviet

Union posed to the rule of law in a free society. Not much had changed since then, he emphasizes. Premier Khrushchev had just made a much-publicized trip to the United States, bragging that his form of government would eventually overcome America. Dulles reminds his audience that although earlier Soviet leaders had predicted the demise of capitalism, the success of the Marshall Plan for rebuilding Europe after the war and U.S. prosperity had made the next generation of Soviet leaders shift their argument to claims that they would surpass their rivals in industrial output.

Dulles expresses doubt that the Soviet economy could surpass the U.S. system. He observes that instead, with the resources of an economy half the size of America's, the Soviet government was using its wealth to bolster national power instead of its people's welfare. During this period the Soviet Union produced inferior goods for domestic consumption, whereas U.S. businesses had concentrated on improving products for consumers. The scene of competition between the superpowers had shifted from Europe to other parts of the world. The Soviet Union had failed to wreck U.S. efforts to improve Western Europe's economy, and so now Khrushchev and his cohort were focusing on the rest of the world, hoping to persuade the so-called uncommitted, or "nonaligned," nations to support the Soviet cause. American business, Dulles implies, needed to deal with the Soviet effort to improve relations with other countries through the use of foreign aid and trade.

Although the Soviet leader spoke of "coexistence," in fact, they were as hostile and aggressive as ever. Dulles reminds the manufacturers that the Soviet Union had tried to undermine governments in Greece, Turkey, and Korea and just recently had again threatened the United States with its nuclear arsenal. His warning occurred at a time when at least some American businessmen would have preferred to increase trade and cooperation with the Soviet Union, presuming, perhaps, that peace could be preserved through such exchanges. Dulles was reminding his audience that the underlying principles of Soviet policy had not changed, even if the wording sounded pacific. And to Dulles, the proof that basic Soviet behavior had not changed was the way the "hard core" Communist leaders of Eastern Europe remained in control.

American businessmen had little to fear from economic competition with the Soviet Union, Dulles assures his listeners in the second part of his speech. But the Soviet factor would nevertheless have a significant impact on how American business competed in the rest of the world. Thus, Dulles is describing a political climate far subtler than that of the early days of the cold war. He concedes that a direct U.S.-Soviet confrontation leading to a hot war seemed less likely but suggests that the spread of Communism by other means was more likely than ever. Quoting a "wise European," Dulles argues that the nuclear stalemate (whereby neither the United States nor the Soviet Union could destroy the other without inflicting severe, perhaps irrevocable, damage to itself) benefited the Soviet Union's long-term goals. In this sense, peace, rather than war, was likely to work to Khrushchev's advantage.

With each side bearing such awesome power to destroy the world, certain approaches would be more important than ever, Dulles insists in the third part of his speech. First of all, the United States and its allies would have to remain vigilant, to ensure that the Soviet Union would never suppose that it could win a war. So long as the Soviets feared massive retaliation, the United States and its allies would be able to compete with the Soviet Union's drive to increase its influence as a world power.

Second, every effort would have to be made to contain regional conflicts, the small wars that had potential to draw in the superpowers and become big wars. Third, the United States would have to display willingness to combat Soviet aggressiveness. Unless the United States proved willing to use its weapons, the Soviet Union might miscalculate and operate under the impression that the Western powers were not strong enough to risk war. War could thus result from a misunderstanding—from the Soviet belief that America might not be strong enough to stand up to Soviet military threats. Dulles states that although he did not think the present situation invited such misunderstanding, he wanted the nation to ensure that this would remain the case "tomorrow." In other words, the United States would have to be proactively anti-Communist so that the Soviet Union would never mistake the desire for peace for an unwillingness to go to war.

Dulles expresses a primary concern for complacency. The Soviets were increasing their military capabilities, such that the United States could not afford to remain content with its current preparedness for war. This kind of thinking—often viewed as contributing to the establishment of the national security state—was in part the product of Dulles's belief that tensions between the United States and the Soviet Union were inevitable so long as the Communist system worked to spread its ideas abroad. Without some kind of agreement on disarmament, he concludes, the Soviet Union would quite likely reach parity with the United States at least in military and industrial terms.

As Dulles reminds the businessmen he was addressing, rather than taking profits, the Soviets were plowing their proceeds back into the military-industrial complex, outspending U.S. investment in the same areas. Dulles then brings his audience to the heart of his message: While American industrialists were concentrating on the domestic market, manufacturing products that did not add to national strength, the Soviets were doing the opposite, producing far fewer items for individual, domestic consumption so as to concentrate the country's vast resources on machinery and military equipment. In effect, Dulles worries that American know-how was operating in a vacuum and, even worse, dragging down the nation's ability to compete with an antagonistic superpower. He forthrightly remarks, "For a contestant engaged in a vital economic race with a lean and well-muscled opponent, we persist in carrying a prodigious burden of fat on our backs."

Pursuing his point that Soviet objectives had not changed, Dulles notes in the fifth part of his address

"Germany today is a problem of extraordinary complexity. For two and one-half years the country has been a political and economic void in which discipline was well-maintained. There is no dangerous underground operating there now although some newspapers in the United States played up such a story. The German leaders, of course, could not admit defeat and today the attitude of the people is not so much a feeling of shame and guilt as one of having been let down by their leaders."

("The Present Situation in Germany")

"The Russians are acting little better than thugs. They have wiped out all the liquid assets. No food cards are issued to Germans, who are forced to travel on foot into the Russian zone, often more dead than alive. An iron curtain has descended over the fate of these people and very likely conditions are truly terrible."

("The Present Situation in Germany")

"I think the Kremlin is now dominated by a bunch of tyrants, but I think they feel it will be useful for the future, if they can persuade the people of the Soviet Union that they are doing away with tyranny."

(Television Interview on the Soviets' Intentions)

"West Germany is the showcase of the free world. Here's the free world working, and you contrast the marvelous economic, industrial and overall situation of West Germany and West Berlin with the East—That is the greatest contrast of the slave type of life and the free type of life."

(Television Interview on the Soviets' Intentions)

"A decade ago Moscow was speaking to us in threatening terms because we were giving aid overseas to meet the danger of economic breakdown and communist takeover in large parts of Europe. Now they propose to compete with us on a worldwide basis in the field of overseas aid and trade, hoping to win over the uncommitted nations of the world."

(Address on the Soviet Military Threat)

Khrushchev's recent speeches, especially one given in 1956 at a reception for Western ambassadors at the Polish embassy in Moscow, in which the Soviet premier proclaimed, "We will bury you!" This was to be accomplished by the Soviet role in rapidly industrializing the developing world. The Soviet Union would brandish the success and prestige of its space program in promising to modernize the newly independent nations just emerging from colonial rule. Even though the U.S. government understood that Khrushchev could not ultimately satisfy the expectations engendered by foreign aid, his regime effectively established areas of influence, preempting U.S. efforts in the regions in question. Economic aid coupled with the shrewd use of media, like the radio, and Communist parties' adept employment of "cover" groups (youth, professional, and veterans organizations), allowed the Soviets to spread Communist propaganda while professing to work for peaceful coexistence. Communists thus sought both converts and world domination, Dulles concludes in the seventh part of his speech.

Summing up his years of observing the Soviet Union, Dulles reports seeing a few signs that it might be lessening its grip on Eastern Europe, but he ends his speech by broadly cautioning his audience that Americans had to pursue a vigorous, multifaceted approach. A nuclear stalemate would not be sufficient to protect U.S. security, since the Soviet Union would be likely to press its ideology on others through political, economic, social, and secretive forms of manipulation.

Impact and Legacy

Allan Dulles played a key role in forming what came to be called the national security state. He took a fledgling organization, the OSS, developed to gather intelligence on enemies of the United States during World War II, and transformed it into a proactive CIA, concerned not merely with gathering intelligence but further with shaping the course of world affairs. The new agency would allow America to know what friends, rivals, and enemies were doing as well as what they were planning. Under Dulles's direction, if other nations acted in ways that were inimical to U.S. interests, the CIA believed that it should initiate actions that would defend the nation. This meant that certain gov-

Questions for Further Study

1. In his report on the situation in Germany in 1945, Dulles refers to an "iron curtain" that "has descended" across Central Europe. This statement calls to mind the famous words of Winston Churchill, describing the division of Europe between the non-Communist and Communist zones: "From Stettin in the Baltic to Trieste in the Adriatic, an 'iron curtain' has descended across the Continent." Churchill made that statement in 1946, and, in fact, the phrase "iron curtain" has a long history. Research the ways in which that term has been used and discuss the changing meanings of the phrase. Do you think it is an effective metaphor for the situations it has been used to describe? Why or why not?

2. Compare the 1956 Dulles television interview with present-day news and interview shows. How would the interview process today be different—perhaps more engaging or entertaining to viewers who are used to a great deal more sensory stimulation than their counterparts half a century ago? What things have not changed? Do you think Ostertag does a good job of asking questions and that Dulles answers them successfully?

3. Discuss the economic issues raised by Dulles in his 1959 address to manufacturers—particularly, the distinctions between capital-based and consumer-based economies. Explain the difference in emphasis between the Soviet and American economies, and critique the conclusions that Dulles draws. Do you agree with him that, in emphasizing consumer goods over capital production, the U.S. economy was soft and flabby compared with that of the Soviets? Likewise, evaluate the Soviets' economic principles as discussed by Dulles. For example, as he noted, Communists dismissed the Marshall Plan as "merely a means of unloading excess commodities and capital." How valid is their position on this and other issues mentioned in the speech?

4. Compare and contrast Dulles's ideas and forms of expressions with those of his brother, John Foster Dulles, secretary of state under the Dwight Eisenhower administration. In what ways are their viewpoints similar, particularly with regard to the spread of Communism and its threat to the United States? In what ways are they different?

ernments (those of Iran and Guatemala, for example) should be overthrown and others combated with disinformation and other forms of subversion that would neutralize threats against the United States.

That the CIA established its power and influence covertly meant that congressional oversight of this government agency and its budget was problematic. The CIA argued that it could not be effective if its plans, procedures, and accounting were publicly acknowledged in the kinds of hearings routinely held by congressional committees. Consequently, the CIA under Dulles and his successors became the subject of much speculation, especially as to its methods and adherence to democratic principles.

Unquestionably, Dulles brought to government an expertise in world affairs and a capacity for behind-the-scenes maneuvering that often benefited U.S. interests. At the same time, his role in establishing the CIA as a covert organization raises questions about the extent to which a government body can act in secret and remain democratic, especially since some of Dulles's failures—notably the Bay of Pigs invasion—actually hurt U.S. relations with other countries and compromised the nation's standing in Central and South America. Critics of Dulles and the CIA have asked whether the United States even has the right to engage in regime change, thus overthrowing the concept of state sovereignty. On the one hand, the CIA gave American diplomacy and statecraft a new tool in dealing with a dangerous world; on the other hand, some of the CIA's actions seem to have subverted international law and, in the long term, to have worked against U.S. interests.

Key Sources

The Allen W. Dulles Papers (primarily 1918–1969) are located at the Seeley G. Mudd Manuscript Library of Princeton University. This comprehensive collection includes professional correspondence, reports, lectures, and administrative papers based on what the CIA collected from Dulles's home office in 1969. The agency continues to hold the originals of these papers and redacted the copies sent to Princeton in 2007. *The Craft of Intelligence* (1963) is often cited as one of the classic discussions of intelligence work. In this book Dulles explains the work of the CIA and of other intelligence agencies (such as that of the Soviets) and their involvement in coups and other political activities and shows keen insight into the strengths and weaknesses of spying and other covert actions. *Germany's Underground* (1947) is Dulles's classic account of German resistance to the Nazis during World War II.

Further Reading

■ Books

Grose, Peter. *Gentleman Spy: The Life of Allen Dulles*. Amherst: University of Massachusetts Press, 1996.

Mosley, Leonard. *Dulles: A Biography of Eleanor, Allen, and John Foster Dulles and Their Family Network*. New York: Dial Press, 1978.

Srodes, James. *Allen Dulles: Master of Spies*. Washington, D.C.: Regnery, 1999.

■ Web Sites

"Allen W. Dulles Papers: Digital Files Series, 1939–1977: Finding Aid." Princeton University "Mudd Manuscript Library" Web site. http://diglib.princeton.edu/ead/eadGetDoc.xq?id=/ead/mudd/public policy/MC019.09.EAD.xml.

—Carl Rollyson

"The Present Situation in Germany" (1945)

Germany today is a problem of extraordinary complexity. For two and one-half years the country has been a political and economic void in which discipline was well-maintained. There is no dangerous underground operating there now although some newspapers in the United States played up such a story. The German leaders, of course, could not admit defeat and today the attitude of the people is not so much a feeling of shame and guilt as one of having been let down by their leaders.

Economically and industrially, Germany has scraped the bottom of the barrel, and there are few shops with anything to sell. As soon as you attempt to get Germany to tick and to make arrangements for a government, the lack of men becomes apparent at once. Most men of the caliber required suffer a political taint. When we discover someone whose ability and politics are alike acceptable, we usually find as we did in one case that the man has been living abroad for the past ten years and is hopelessly out of touch with the local situation. We have already found out that you can't run railroads without taking in some Party members....

We tried hard to find financial advisers, but most of the bankers who had been in Germany in the Twenties and Thirties had by this time been liquidated. I found a banker in the prisoner's cage who had been arrested on an automatic charge because in the early part of the war he had been appointed custodian for the property of an alien, a post he later resigned. I am told that during the period of his responsibility he discharged his trust with scrupulous honesty. I had to bring his case before the Joint Chiefs of Staff in Washington before I was permitted to use him. Then there was Doctor Sauerbruch, one of the leading surgeons in Berlin. Him, also, I found in a cage. It took a cable to London from Washington to get his case straightened out and get him released for useful service, and this had no sooner been done when a few days later the British rearrested him because he came under some other category.

In our zone we arrested 70,000 people. There was no such thing as a habeas corpus and there was no forum to which one could apply for a hearing, although later on we did set up a tribunal of sorts. I do not blame our people too much for this state of affairs. After all, we could not examine each case individually in the early days when the chief task was to occupy Germany in the most effective manner.

The present political set-up in Germany is based on the agreements reached at Tehran, Yalta, and Potsdam....We have chopped up Baden, Württemburg, and Hesse into artificial zones. In the case of Saxony, the Russian zone cuts off the American and British zones from their counterparts there. It is difficult to see how the Allies could have done otherwise inasmuch as the Russians would not consent to British and American domination of Germany and the Americans and British likewise refused to consider letting Russia get an advantage. Even so, very little progress is being made toward the centralization of the various services....

In the zone under Russian control the application of Soviet doctrines is thus far confined largely to paper. The Russians are finding it a little difficult to mix collectivist doctrines, including the nationalization of banks, a new system of land tenure, and the creation of a small farmer class, with the set-up as it existed under the Nazis and more broadly under a capitalist economy.

We, ourselves, have excellent men on the job.... Yet I am inclined to think that the problems inherent in the situation are almost too much for us. Our people in Germany are unduly fearful of criticism in the United States. For example, the road between Frankfurt and Wiesbaden is so full of holes that it is almost impossible to drive over it, and one cannot cross the Main between those two places because all the bridges are down. But no repairs are made since the Army feels certain it would be criticized for "restoring the German war potential."

Industry in Germany is at its lowest ebb except for some coal mining in the Ruhr. The minute one considers what industries should be allowed to function and how best to prime the pump in order to set them going, some very real and serious difficulties appear.

So far as the treatment of industry in various zones is concerned, the Russian policy is particularly hard to fathom. It is hard to say whether the Russians really intend to tear down the zone for the purpose of building up Russia, but there is some evidence pointing that way. The Russians have torn up all the double tracks, they are keeping all able-bodied German prisoners, and they have taken East a great many industrialists, bankers, scientists, and the like.

Russian standing in their zone is low. Russian troops are living off the land, and have looted far more than anyone else. They have gone about Berlin looting workers' houses in very much the same way they did in Hungary. This seems to indicate that in both localities the Communist party is not very strong.... It is difficult to say what is going on, but in general the Russians are acting little better than thugs. They have wiped out all the liquid assets. No food cards are issued to Germans, who are forced to travel on foot into the Russian zone, often more dead than alive. An iron curtain has descended over the fate of these people and very likely conditions are truly terrible. The promises at Yalta to the contrary, probably 8 to 10 million people are being enslaved. Unquestionably Germany should be punished. In this instance, however, I think there will remain a legacy of bitterness which will not bode well for the future.

I have already said that the problem of Germany very nearly defies a successful solution. The question is: What can we do? The first step is to get together in dealing with what is at bottom a common prob-lem. Next, we must find people we can use. We might use the churches which did not knuckle under to Hitler, although it is questionable in the minds of some people whether churches should get into poli-tics. We might also consider the survivors of the affair of July 20 [the 1944 assassination attempt on Hitler] and see what material the trade unions can furnish. Finally, we can screen the prisoners of war.

The women will not be much help to us, although in theory they could be. A saying now current in Ger-many is that today most of the able-bodied men are women. Hitler had an enormous hold over them and Eva Braun's existence appeared to be unknown to most of them. They are extremely bitter. Altogether the problem deserves very careful study.

I think it may well become necessary for us to change the form of our occupation. Thus far there has been very little disturbance or misbehavior on the part of our troops. I think we ought to use small, highly mechanized units and put our reliance on planes. These forces I would quarter outside of the cities, lest their presence create a talking point for

Glossary

collectivist	referring to any political system (but especially totalitarian ones such as Nazism and Communism) that emphasizes the collective or group over the individual
double track	a dual system of railroad tracks, such that trains can travel in opposite directions, as contrasted with a single track, on which trains traveling in opposite directions must share the track and be scheduled accordingly
Eva Braun	the mistress of Adolf Hitler
food cards	ration cards
habeas corpus	Latin for "we demand the body"; the legal right of an accused person not to be held or detained without the opportunity of being formally charged for specific crimes
land tenure	individual land ownership
liquid assets	items of value that can be easily exchanged—cash, precious metals, or precious gems
Party members	former members of the Nazi party
prime the pump	government stimulation of an economy through spending, lowered taxes or interest rates, or other means
quarter	give temporary living accommodations to
tear down the zone for the purpose of building up Russia	a reference to the fact that during and after World War II, the Soviet dictator Joseph Stalin arranged to have whole factories and even towns moved from the Soviets' western frontiers to the interior of the nation
Tehran, Yalta, and Potsdam	three major conferences of the Allied leadership in World War II

German propaganda against the occupation.... Germany ought to be put to work for the benefit of Europe and particularly for the benefit of those countries plundered by the Nazis....

Until the Russians get out—and there is no indication that they intend to—there can be no central administration. Hence I think it will be necessary to attempt to build up local government, not in the sense of trying to divide Germany but to provide some means of administration.

Dulles, Allen

TELEVISION INTERVIEW ON THE SOVIETS' INTENTIONS (1956)

HCO: It is my privilege to have as my guest today the Director of our Central Intelligence Agency, Mr. Allen W. Dulles. It is Mr. Dulles' job to coordinate our worldwide intelligence activities, so that those who are responsible, shall be aware at all times of any threat to our country's security and safety....

Allen, I suppose the most absorbing development in modern history is the current drive in Russia to destroy Stalin's prestige. What is the meaning of that campaign?

AWD: They are trying to persuade the peoples of the Soviet bloc that they are doing away with tyranny. Now I don't believe they are. I think the Kremlin is now dominated by a bunch of tyrants, but I think they feel it will be useful for the future, if they can persuade the people of the Soviet Union that they are doing away with tyranny....

HCO: Is there any reason to think the Communists have changed their goals along with their leadership?

AWD: No, I don't believe they have. They think the softer line may get them further than the hard, rigid line of Stalin.

HCO: What effect is this sudden switch from hot to cold, so far as Stalin is concerned, having on the minds of the Russian people?

AWD: Well, Harold, I think they're pretty badly befuddled. Here for twenty-twenty-five years, they've built Stalin up to be their great hero. He brought their country from being a third or fourth rate country to being the second greatest country in the world....He led them to victory in a World War, and they made him a great hero. All of the history books are full of the Stalin legend. All of a sudden now they tell the people this fellow was no good. Not only that, but he was a murderer, he was inept in his leadership and everything of that kind, even in his military leadership. Well I don't believe you can do that to a people.

HCO: Granted that the people are befuddled, are the Kremlin leaders downgrading Stalin in order to upgrade themselves?

AWD:...I don't think they're really going to upgrade themselves, because you can't turn around, after you've been a man's friend and profited by all the honors that he's given you, and that's happened to the present leaders of the Kremlin—it was Stalin that made them—you can't turn around and destroy your benefactor and really think it's going to make you stand higher in the minds of the people. But I think that they feel that they've got to get rid of this very hard line. The people were beginning to be very uneasy....

HCO: What is going to happen to Berlin and the situation with respect to unification of Germany?

AWD: Obviously the Communists would like to get us out of Berlin. They're working to try to do that. But having failed in their great effort, at the time of the blockade, I don't think they feel they can move in on us now....

HCO: What did appear to be the purpose was that they were trying to foist on the world, the free world and the United States, the fact they had transferred jurisdiction to the East German Democratic Republic, that phony government that's now in charge of East Germany.

AWD: Well, they're trying to build up something that will be a counterpoise to West Germany. West Germany is the showcase of the free world. Here's the free world working, and you contrast the marvelous economic, industrial and overall situation of West Germany and West Berlin with the East—That is the greatest contrast of the slave type of life and the free type of life. And they don't like that.

HCO: Let's turn to another part of the world. Are the Red Chinese preparing to attack Formosa?

AWD: That's a tough one....The Chinese Communists are building up their strength in that part of the world opposite Formosa. They're building airfields, they're bringing in more troops, and they are in a military position where they might try to attack some outposts. Whether they will do it or not—that's another question.

HCO: Well, how about South Korea?

AWD: South Korea at the moment—the Chinese Communists are taking their troops out of North Korea to quite a large extent. And I would doubt whether, having failed in a particular area, as clearly as they have, they would start something new there right away. But still, they have the force; on the other side of the Yalu, the troops will be there. And if it was in the interests of their policy to do so, they could start something.

HCO: Allen, we hear an awful lot, and we read in the press arguments over whether Russia is ahead of us in the development of atomic energy and the development of the intercontinental ballistic missile. Are the Russians ahead of us in these developments?

AWD: Harold, in my job, I give intelligence and information on where the Russians stand: that is my job, and I'm not really in the job of making comparisons. I'm not an expert on the American position. But maybe departing from that sort of basic philosophy that I have in my work, I can say this, that overall, in the atomic field, I feel quite sure they aren't ahead of us. They are putting a great deal of stress now on building up nuclear power in the electrical field. And they have a very dramatic program, announced recently in their sixth five-year plan. Overall, though, they're certainly not ahead of us....

HCO: Well, how about the intercontinental ballistic missile? Would you say they are ahead of us or behind us?

AWD: I don't want to make a comparison there. It's very difficult to do it. They have made quite a lot of progress in that field. But I have no evidence that they're ahead of us.

HCO: Speaking of intelligence, many of us are aware that our military—the Army, the Navy and the Air Force, all have their intelligence; we have our FBI and Secret Service—are the intelligence services of our government, Allen, effectively coordinated as a team, or are we going off in all directions?

AWD: I think now we have a very good team, Harold. I'm very glad that these services are there, that they are effective, because the military people are the most adept at getting and analyzing military information and we work very closely together. We meet together every week and we coordinate our work and there is very good cooperation among the intelligence services. We don't want another Pearl Harbor, you know.

Glossary

intercontinental ballistic missile	the opposite of a guided missile, in that its course cannot be altered once it is fired; distinguished from shorter-range missiles in its capacity to travel more than 3,500 miles
Kremlin	technically, a medieval fortress in Moscow, around which government buildings grew, leading to the use of the term as a reference to the Russian or Soviet government as a whole
opposite Formosa	across the Taiwan Strait, a body of water that separates mainland China from Taiwan (formerly, Formosa)
sixth five-year plan	initiated by Stalin, one of several attempts to rapidly develop Soviet industry through centralized planning, coordination, and implementation; the sixth plan ran from 1956 to 1960
Stalin	Joseph Stalin (1879–1953), absolute dictator of the Soviet Union
Yalu	the river that forms the boundary between China and North Korea

ADDRESS ON THE SOVIET MILITARY THREAT (1959)

Twelve years ago, on December 3, 1947, I had the honor of addressing the 52nd Annual Congress of American Industry, held by your Association. My subject on that occasion, as now, was, the Soviet Challenge. I then stated that this was a challenge to the United States "to prove that the system of free men under law can survive."

This is still a challenge. Only a few weeks ago Khrushchev amiably advised us, as he left the United States, that Communism would in time take us over.

In 1947 the Soviets were basing their hopes—not so much on the economic and industrial might of their own system, as on their forecast of the imminent collapse of our free enterprise society.

Then it was Stalin, Molotov and Vishinsky who warned us and told the world that our Marshall Plan was merely a means of unloading excess commodities and capital to avoid an impending American crisis.

These old Soviet leaders have gone and so have gone many of their arguments. Their successors have largely abandoned the thesis of an early demise of capitalism due to its own defects. Now they boast that over the years, say by 1970, they will surpass us in total industrial output.

This is a boast which is not likely to be realized unless we "rest on our oars." What is of more immediate concern to us is the fact that the Soviets are using their growing industrial strength, which is still less than one-half of our own, largely to promote their national power aims rather than to give a fuller life to their own people. We are doing just the opposite.

A decade ago Moscow was speaking to us in threatening terms because we were giving aid overseas to meet the danger of economic breakdown and communist takeover in large parts of Europe. Now they propose to compete with us on a worldwide basis in the field of overseas aid and trade, hoping to win over the uncommitted nations of the world.

Then, though they had no atomic bombs, the Soviets were using the threat of their great conventional forces to help undermine Greece and Turkey and then later to menace the Free World in Berlin and Korea.

Now, while they preach coexistence and economic and industrial competition with the West, they also, on occasions, this week in fact, rattle the threat of ballistic missiles and give their support to the "hard core" Communists in their uneasy European satellites.

As representatives of this 64th Congress of American Industry, you have a legitimate interest in what your most aggressive foreign competitor, the Sino-Soviet Bloc, is doing and planning. Today this is not because this competitor is seriously threatening your domestic or even your foreign markets. It is rather because the pattern of this competitor's conduct and the impact of the Bloc's growing industrial power may have an important influence on the future direction of American industry and of our economy.

A wise European remarked to me the other day that in his opinion, the danger of war had receded, but that the dangers from international communism in other fields had increased.

In saying this he had two major thoughts in mind:

First, that the military situation would become a nuclear stalemate, the United States with its allies and the Sino-Soviet Bloc each having a sufficient supply of nuclear weapons and the means of delivery to inflict unacceptable damage on the other.

Second that, under these conditions, the competition might shift, at least for a time, from the military to the political and economic sectors with the Free World and free enterprise competing for the uncommitted world against all forms of penetration by international communism....

It does not require recourse in secret data to reach the following conclusion: That over the immediate future both the United States and the Soviet Union will be continuing to equip themselves with nuclear weapons and with the means of delivery...adequate to constitute a grave deterrent to war by either side. The impact of this mutual growing capability is already having its effect on the international scene.

However, for the deterrent to be effective, other conditions must be met; among them are the following:

(1) The United States and its allies of the Free World must continue to maintain a military defensive and retaliatory power such that no increase in Sino-Soviet military power could lead the latter to believe that they had gained clear superiority over us.

(2) Regional strife among powers having no nuclear capabilities must be quarantined or

limited. History has shown us small wars breed great wars and chain reactions with unforeseen consequences may result from them.

(3) There must be no doubt in the minds either of the leaders in Moscow or Peiping that the initiation by them of a war of aggression would be met with adequate force. Hence we must make the strength of our military position, and our readiness to use it in defense against communist aggression, so clear that there can be no misunderstanding on the part of the Soviet....

I doubt whether the leaders of international communism misunderstand or miscalculate our posture today. They must *not* do so tomorrow. The prevention of misunderstanding is a continuing task. We must not slip into an attitude of complacency which might lead the Communists to have doubts about our intentions. They must not be allowed to feel that the threat of nuclear blackmail could be used to push us out of any position that is vital to our security, on the mistaken theory that it is not worth the risk of a nuclear conflict.

Today the Soviets with a Gross National Product and an industrial capacity less than one-half of ours are nevertheless allocating to the national power sector of their economy, including military hardware and industrial plant for war purposes, an effort roughly equivalent to ours.

If they continue their industrial growth rate, at some eight to nine per cent per annum as is likely, the Soviets will be able, if they choose, substantially to increase their military effort.

Certainly until a system of controlled disarmament is devised, we cannot safely relax in the field of our military strength as the primary deterrent to the danger of communist aggression....

The commanding role of investment in Soviet economic growth is dramatically illustrated by their Seven Year Plan, which runs through 1965. Capital investment in industry for the year 1959, the initial year of the plan, will be approximately equal, measured in dollars, to industrial investment in the United States.

Furthermore, the Soviets' absolute volume of investment in such productive areas as the iron, steel and nonferrous industries, as well as in machinery manufacturing, will be substantially greater than that of the United States.

These massive investment expenditures are being fed into an industrial system whose output in 1958 was only about 40 per cent of the United States. Under such high pressure fueling, the Soviet industrial plant can hardly fail to grow considerably faster than that of the United States.

Turning to the consumers field, the picture is entirely different. While they have been slightly increasing the production of consumer goods over the past few years, their consuming public fares badly in comparison with our own. In 1958, Soviet citizens had available for purchase about one-third of the total goods and services available to Americans. For example, the Soviets were then producing on an average one automobile for every 50 we produced....

Certainly it is true that a major thrust of our economy is directed into the production of the consumer type of goods and services, which add little to the sinews of our national strength. On the other hand, the major thrust of Soviet economic development, and its high technological skills and resources, are directed toward specialized industrial, military and national power goals.

For a contestant engaged in a vital economic race with a lean and well-muscled opponent, we persist in carrying a prodigious burden of fat on our backs.

Soviet postwar economic expansion, as well as its advances in the military field, have also permitted the Kremlin to adopt an aggressive program in the less developed countries of the Free World. In these newly emergent and fragile nations, the Soviet leaders have been advancing their cause by a combination of economic penetration, political warfare, and subversion.

The basic strategy of international communism, with its primary emphasis on measures short of war, has remained remarkably unchanged since the death of Stalin. So too have its objectives.

These were never more bluntly stated than in Khrushchev's recent speeches.

Obviously referring to the phrase attributed to him, "We will bury you," he explained last summer that when he said that communism would be the graveyard of capitalism, he did not mean that communists would take shovels and start digging; "History," he said, "would take care of capitalists." They too, he suggested, would become museum pieces, and added that, "If there were a God and he could act, he would take a good broom and sweep you out."

Let us have a look at the brooms Khrushchev proposes to use.

First economic penetration of the uncommitted world.

Quick industrialization is the goal of the new and emerging countries, as well as of many of the older countries which have been backward industrially. It is no answer to such aspirations to suggest that the type of industrialization they want is premature, unwise or over-costly....

The example of the Soviet Union attracts them. Here they see a nation which, in the course of 30 years since their revolutionary growing pains ended about 1928, has achieved second place in the world industrially.

The newly emerging States want results.... They understand full well that the Soviets first got a rocket to the moon and some of them are deluded by the belief that the Kremlin can also give them a painless industrial transformation. Soviet propaganda tells them this is so and that communism will deliver the goods. It is a potent argument....

The Soviets, abetted by the Chinese Communists and their European Satellites, can easily maintain their present level of aid and trade and in the coming decade they may well divert larger absolute amounts to woo the uncommitted areas of the world. As the Soviet and Chinese Communist industrial production advances, the threat of the spread of communism through trade and aid into uncommitted areas of the world will be proportionately increased.

Another broom which international communism proposes to use against the Free World is political warfare.

Here they have an aggressive campaign based on a series of very positive programs with political, economic and cultural objectives. It involves the radio and other means of mass communication, as well as the written and spoken word; subtle political intrigue based on the control and manipulation of communist parties and communist fronts on a worldwide basis.

It includes the use of various "cover" organizations which pretend to represent youth, labor, professional groups and veterans. They become the agencies for spreading communist doctrine throughout the Free World. In their subversive arsenal, they also have organizations which use the slogans of "peace," friendship and coexistence.

This challenge is being pressed forward under the growing threat of Soviet industrial, scientific and technical advances and under the cover of the Kremlin's posture of coexistence. It is a challenge which is the more dangerous because it is cleverly and clandestinely conducted, and even the Communist role is concealed as far as possible.

To meet this threat we must understand it. To penetrate the subtleties of the Soviet political, economic, and psychological drive is harder to do than to understand the military threat. Weapons of war are visible, tangible, and comprehensible. The impact of an idea, of a subversive political movement, of a disguised economic policy is more subtle....

The communists have no reason to be confident that they have an adequate answer to our military retaliatory power. They do feel, however, that they still have the ability to close off their own frontiers, their air space and their rigidly controlled society to ideas from abroad. They have their Iron Curtains not only on their frontiers but within the country. They even try to draw down this Curtain within the minds of their own people.

Recently we see some evidence here and there of a slight raising of their curtain. There is somewhat less jamming and a wider play of American news items in the Soviet press. If this were to continue and develop it would be one of the most encouraging signs in our relations with the USSR. It would be an act, a deed on their part, as contrasted with mere pronouncements about coexistence.

A third broom the Soviets have been subtly using against us is the penetration and subversion of governments which do not "cooperate" with Moscow or Peiping. A classical example here was Czechoslovakia, more than ten years ago.... Popular front governments are still being planned by Moscow for several countries which today have close relations with us....

It is Moscow's desire to move very secretly in this field and not to allow its hand to be shown as directly supporting local Communist parties either in this Hemisphere or elsewhere....

In these comments, I have tried to give some idea of the nature and dimensions of the Soviet challenge in the military, political, and economic fields.

My conclusion is that even if a nuclear stalemate should tend to lessen the immediate danger of war, we would still be faced with a serious challenge....

Certainly we have not answered the challenge if we limit ourselves merely to meeting the Kremlin's military threat.

These facts should bring us to a sober appraisal of the best means of marshalling our very great assets and capabilities—in concert with our like-minded friends and allies. Today the Free World has a wide margin of industrial superiority over the Communist world. Are we applying this superiority in the proper way to the proper ends?

This we must do within the framework of freedom—not regimentation as practiced in the Soviet Union. It must be done with due regard for the legitimate aspirations of our people for a fuller life—not by asking them to accept the drab existence imposed

Document Text

on the Soviet people. However,…the fateful competition with communism has a first claim on our energies and our interests and calls for subordination of our private interests to the paramount public interest.

You, yourselves, with your wide interests and responsibilities could do much to help make this society of ours become more responsive to the challenge of the day.

Glossary

capital investment	investment in factories and other items that are not ends in themselves but means of producing further income
Czechoslovakia, more than ten years ago	though Czechoslovakia made an attempt at free elections in 1946, in 1948 the Communists seized power in that country
European Satellites	six nations in eastern Europe—Poland, East Germany, Czechoslovakia, Hungary, Romania, and Bulgaria—that were under the control of the Soviet Union during the years of the cold war
Gross National Product	the overall annual productivity, in estimated dollar value, for a given country
industrial plant	factories, machines, and all other means of production
jamming	electromagnetic interference with radio signals, a practice often used by police states such as the Soviet Union to prevent citizens from hearing information other than government propaganda
Marshall Plan	officially known as the European Recovery Program, a massive U.S. effort to rebuild Europe after World War II
Molotov and Vishinsky	Vyacheslav Molotov and Andrey Vyshinsky, two leading figures in the regime of the Soviet dictator Joseph Stalin
nonferrous	unrelated to iron or steel
Peiping	another name for Beijing; variant of "Peking"
Popular front governments	governments that comprised a variety of parties, mostly on the Left—including Communists, who in most cases exercised all real control
Seven Year Plan	a mistaken reference to the seventh five-year plan, an attempt at rapid modernization under government control in the Soviet Union that lasted from 1961 to 1965
the Sino-Soviet Bloc	dating from the Communist takeover of China in 1949, the acting in concert of Soviet and Chinese Communists, a somewhat uneasy relationship
the uncommitted world	a term, like "third world," for those nations that were not firmly in the American or Soviet spheres of influence

John Foster Dulles (AP/Wide World Photos)

JOHN FOSTER DULLES   1888–1959

U.S. Senator and Secretary of State

Featured Documents

◆ Radio and Television Address on Communism in Guatemala (1954)
◆ Address to the United Nations on the Suez Crisis (1956)
◆ Address on U.S. Policy toward Communist China (1957)
◆ News Conference on U.S. Relations with Latin American Nations (1958)

Overview

Born in Washington, D.C., on February 25, 1888, John Foster Dulles came from a family of clerics and politicians. His father was a Presbyterian minister, and his maternal grandfather served as secretary of state under Benjamin Harrison. Dulles went to Princeton University, followed by George Washington University Law School. With the help of his grandfather, he gained employment at the Sullivan & Cromwell law firm, where he quickly rose through the ranks, eventually becoming sole managing partner of the firm. Dulles always had political aims, however, and gained experience dealing with politicians under his grandfather's tutelage. He advised Thomas Dewey throughout his election campaign in 1948 and was active in drafting the Charter of the United Nations. He also served as U.S. delegate to the United Nations for three years. He thought his chance to become a major political player had arrived in 1949 when Governor Dewey appointed him as a New York senator after a resignation left the position vacant, but he lost the seat in the following election. He then decided to confine his political activity to appointed positions. When Dwight Eisenhower became president in 1953, he appointed Dulles secretary of state. During his time in that position, Dulles revolutionized American foreign policy and set in motion policy trends that continue to this day. He died shortly after retiring from office, on May 24, 1959.

Dulles was born into privilege, and his ideas, speeches, and writings demonstrate as much. In his youth he attended parties with his grandfather and became acquainted with some of the most powerful men in Washington, including William Howard Taft, Grover Cleveland, and Woodrow Wilson. He did not actually graduate from George Washington Law School, instead opting to take the bar without a degree. When New York law firms did not take him seriously, he turned to his grandfather to secure a position. Despite the low pay he received as a clerk at Sullivan & Cromwell, he lived very well, since his grandfather allowed him access to his inheritance. At the firm he dealt with the international business elite and adopted the belief that American business interests were one and the same with its policy interests. His experience with the moneyed elite influenced his decisions throughout his life as well as his view of world affairs.

Religion also played a major role in shaping Dulles's consciousness. Multiple generations of his family had been clergymen, and he had also planned to enter the clergy until he attended university. Although he dedicated himself to the study of law rather than religion, his commitment to the teachings of the church did not waver. As an adult, he was an elder of the Presbyterian Church and on the board of directors of Union Theological Seminary. Dulles did not see his position as a civil servant as divorced from his religious devotion; on the contrary, he relied upon his religious beliefs to guide his policy decisions.

Dulles formatively altered American foreign policy. While two of the major ideas governing American foreign policy during the cold war, "containment" and "the domino theory," had already been established when he came into office, Dulles changed the way that these ideas were used in practice. He also introduced new concepts to America's cold war policy. He had a strong conviction that Communism was the greatest danger to the free world, both strategically and morally. He advocated "liberation" in place of containment, for example. The concept most associated with Dulles, however, is "brinkmanship." With brinkmanship, Dulles advocated bringing the country to the brink of war without ultimately engaging in armed conflict. During his tenure in office, however, Dulles rarely used brinkmanship, instead employing covert action or establishing treaties with other countries.

Explanation and Analysis of Documents

Dulles was one of the first secretaries of state of the cold war era. Steadfast in his beliefs and an experienced orator, Dulles adeptly explained the Eisenhower administration's foreign policy decisions in public forums. Particularly when controversial matters needed to be addressed, Dulles, rather than Eisenhower, publicly spoke about them. In the conformist 1950s, when critiques of U.S. cold war policy were considered tantamount to embracing Communism, Dulles's unflinching commitment to destroying the global Communist threat was widely embraced and almost never challenged. Dulles's complete conviction of the righteousness of the anti-Communist cause as well as the significance of his role in the battle against Communism contributed to the strength of his public orations. He never faltered or reconsidered his position in interviews, and his responses, like his speeches, tended to have a pros-

1888

- **February 25**
  John Foster Dulles is born
  in Washington, D.C.

1949

- **July 7**
  Dulles is appointed
  senator from New York
  after the position is
  vacated.

1951

- **September 8**
  The United States and the
  Allied powers sign a peace
  treaty with Japan drafted
  by Dulles.

1953

- **January 26**
  Dulles becomes secretary
  of state under President
  Dwight Eisenhower.

- **August 19**
  The Iranian prime minister
  Mohammad Mossadeq is
  overthrown in a coup
  planned by Dulles and his
  brother Allen, director of
  the Central Intelligence
  Agency.

1954

- **June 27**
  The Guatemalan president
  Jacobo Arbenz Guzmán
  resigns in response to
  tactics employed by Dulles
  to force his abdication.

- **June 30**
  Dulles delivers an address
  on radio and television
  about Communism in
  Guatemala.

- **September 8**
  The Southeast Asia Treaty
  Organization, largely
  Dulles's brainchild, is
  created.

1956

- **November 1**
  Dulles delivers a speech
  and presents the U.S.
  resolution concerning the
  Suez crisis to the UN
  General Assembly.

1957

- **June 28**
  Dulles delivers an address
  on U.S. policy toward
  Communist China.

elytizing quality. Influenced by his experience as a church leader, Dulles presented matters in terms of good and evil or black and white; based on his reasoning, gray areas did not exist. Four documents—his radio and television address on Communism in Guatemala, his speech to the United Nations on the Suez crisis, his address on U.S. policy toward Communist China, and his news conference on U.S. Relations with Latin American nations—exemplify his unbending belief in the righteousness of his own actions and his ability to present his actions, as well as the policies of the Eisenhower administration, in an altruistic manner.

◆ **Radio and Television Address on Communism in Guatemala**

In 1954 the United States became embroiled in a conflict with Jacobo Arbenz Guzmán, the reformist president of Guatemala. Dulles stood at the forefront of this conflict—and, as some argued, was its major instigator. Dulles had two major concerns with the changes occurring in Guatemala under Arbenz. Publicly, Dulles complained that Arbenz was a stooge of international Communism and that, as per the domino theory, his rule opened the door to Communist infiltration throughout the Western Hemisphere. Privately, Dulles was also concerned about the financial effects of Arbenz's agrarian reform on the United Fruit Company, for which Dulles and his brother, Allen, both sat on the board of directors. Dulles attempted to cajole Arbenz into resigning, first individually and then with the aid of the Organization of American States. When that failed, John Dulles and Allen Dulles, director of the Central Intelligence Agency, recruited, trained, and funded Guatemalans (primarily military men disenchanted with Arbenz's policies), who then overthrew the Arbenz regime in June 1954. In this statement, which Dulles issued shortly after the coup, he explains the geostrategic reasons for U.S. interest in Guatemala while downplaying economic concerns. Here, as elsewhere, he does not divulge his role in the coup, instead claiming, "The situation is being cured by the Guatemalans themselves."

Dulles begins his address by painting a picture of events in Guatemala as he wanted the American public to see them. He omits information that did not conform to his narrative and at times presents speculation as fact. Throughout the first portion, Dulles emphasizes the connection between the Arbenz regime and international Communism. Little of the address discusses events and politics in Guatemala as such. He instead speaks in broad terms, presenting the Guatemalan situation in the context of "Soviet despotism" and casting the situation as a conflict between the "inter-American system" and "the Kremlin." Careful not to blame Guatemala or specific Guatemalans for the situation that had unfolded, Dulles explains that over the previous ten years international Communists infiltrated all aspects of Guatemalan politics and society, so that they eventually pulled the strings of both the congress and the president. He points out that although Guatemala was a small country, it was of great significance.

Dulles then focuses on the support for a new Guatemalan regime shared by the other countries in the

Organization of American States. He brings up the March 1954 meeting in the Venezuelan capital, in which a declaration condemning incursions of international Communism into the Western Hemisphere was adopted, with Guatemala as the only dissenting state. In Dulles's version of events, the Declaration of Caracas caused the international Communists controlling Guatemala to begin a massive offensive, ordering arms from abroad, increasing efforts to take over neighboring countries, and ruthlessly suppressing internal political dissent. Events had actually unfolded somewhat differently in early 1954. Dulles attended the meeting of the Organization of American States determined to see the passage of a declaration condemning the Arbenz regime. He easily obtained the support of Latin America's various authoritarian leaders, many of whom were cut from the same cloth as Carlos Castillo Armas, a Guatemalan opponent of Arbenz, and courted U.S. support. Those who did not initially support the resolution were coerced into doing so. Mexico and Argentina, two of the most powerful Latin American nations, abstained from voting. Arbenz, recognizing the gravity of the situation, returned to his country, believing that he faced imminent attack from a militarily superior enemy, and began to search for an arms supplier. After pursuing a number of unsuccessful avenues, he received a shipment of arms from Czechoslovakia on May 15, 1954. It was on the basis of this transaction that Dulles believed the alliance between Arbenz and the Soviet Union to be clearly established.

In the final section, Dulles addresses U.S. economic interests in Guatemala for the only time during the speech, in describing recent events in Guatemala and assuring both Americans and Guatemalans that the recent coup would have positive ramifications for all. Dulles mentions the tumultuous relationship between Guatemala and the United Fruit Company in response to what he characterizes as unjust Communist claims that the United States was merely motivated by imperialist concerns. He states that although the dispute between the fruit company and the Guatemalan government was regrettable, it was "relatively unimportant." Dulles continues by informing the public that Arbenz had resigned under pressure from "patriots" "led by Col. Castillo Armas." According to Dulles, Guatemala was thus newly free from the despotic representatives of international Communism and the Guatemalan people could now determine their own fate. He concludes with two major points. First, he warns of the continued need to vigilantly guard against Communism; the danger of Communist infiltration still remained. In addition, he assures the Guatemalan people that the U.S. government would continue to support their country.

Both the American public and Dulles's government colleagues seem to have reacted positively to his address. Few in the government knew the extent of Dulles's role in the coup, and nearly no one in the private sector had knowledge about events on the ground in Guatemala at the time of Armas's coup. In 1954, as throughout his career, Dulles was received as a virulent "cold warrior" who took necessary measures to protect his country. His description of the

Time Line

| 1958 | ■ **May 20** Dulles speaks at a news conference on U.S. relations with Latin American nations. |
| 1959 | ■ **April 15** Dulles resigns as secretary of state owing to illness. ■ **May 24** Dulles dies in Washington, D.C. |

threat posed by Guatemala was based on the domino theory, which American politicians and civilians living in 1954 knew well. His presentation of the events that unfolded in Guatemala would have sounded familiar; the public had no reason to challenge his version.

For many years following the Armas coup, "Operation Success," as it was dubbed by the Central Intelligence Agency, was regarded as a model for U.S. response to the perceived threat of Communism throughout the globe. It was not until the failed attempt to train, arm, and fund Cuban expatriates to invade Cuba and overthrow Fidel Castro's regime in 1961 that American policy makers discovered that the model masterminded by Dulles would not always succeed. Nonetheless, covert operations modeled on Operation Success continued into the 1980s, often bringing the desired results.

◆ **Address to the United Nations on the Suez Crisis**

In 1956 a crisis arose in the Middle East. Many factors contributed to the crisis, including the ongoing border conflict between Egypt and Israel, British desires to maintain control of shipping in the region, and American and Soviet attempts to demonstrate regional dominance. The Egyptian president Gamal Abdel Nasser stood at the center of the conflict. Owing to ongoing warfare with Israel, Nasser began seeking to purchase arms. In 1955, after the United States had avoided his requests for months, Nasser finally accepted a shipment of arms from Czechoslovakia, a nation in the Communist bloc, which infuriated Secretary of State Dulles. Nasser likewise appealed to the United States and the British for funding to build the dam that he believed would increase Egypt's prosperity. Despite the initially lukewarm response from the United States, the U.S. and British governments eventually agreed to contribute to the project on the condition that the remaining funds come in the form of a loan from the World Bank. In July 1956, however, Dulles reneged on the offer. In response, Nasser nationalized the Suez Canal, claiming he now needed the canal's revenue to support the dam project. Israel, whose shipments were already forbidden by Nasser from passing through the canal, increased its arms purchases from France and entered into an alliance with the British and

A plane drops leaflets on Guatemalans listening to Col. Carlos Castillo Armas's speech, following his successful revolt against the ousted government of the leftist President Jacobo Arbenz Guzmán. (AP/Wide World Photos)

French. Meanwhile, Dulles and the British agreed to hold an international conference in London to deal with the situation. But the conference failed to accomplish concrete changes, and Britain and France began plotting with Israel to regain control of the canal. On October 29, Israel attacked Egypt, and Britain and France sent troops to seize the canal under the guise of peacemaking. When Nasser refused to hand the canal over to the European powers, the British and French began bombing Egypt. President Eisenhower sent Dulles to the United Nations to deal with the problem. The resolution introduced to the Security Council by the United States was vetoed, but the council decided that the matter should go before the General Assembly. Dulles delivered this speech, which included the new U.S. resolution, to the General Assembly on November 1, 1956.

Dulles opens the speech by lamenting the disagreement between the United States and Israel, France, and Great Britain, the latter two of which had been long-standing allies. He notes that because the disagreement was so uncommon, the United States had reevaluated its position—but, despite reconsideration, its stance on the Suez

Canal crisis remained unchanged. He observes that the current meeting marked the first time that the United Nations was summoned in accord with the "Uniting for Peace" resolution, which calls for the General Assembly to convene if the Security Council cannot resolve a matter of international security.

For much of the speech, Dulles describes the events leading up to the crisis, although he avoids mentioning the role of U.S. diplomacy in aggravating Nasser. He depicts Britain and France as the aggressors, pointing out that while they claimed that their action derived from a desire to secure the canal, they had also admitted their intent to gain control of it. In several instances, he hints that Britain and France had acted out of self-interest rather than from a desire to reestablish peace. In turn, rather than absolving Egypt of blame for the current hostilities, he criticizes that country for violating armistice agreements, ignoring the UN mandate to allow the passage of goods to Israel through the canal, accepting Soviet arms, and violating the treaty that gave control of the Suez Canal to the Universal Suez Canal Company. Dulles also spends much time outlining the decisions made at the London conference, lamenting how Great Britain and France brought the matter to the Security Council but later resorted to the use of force. If the United Nations accepted injustice and faltered on its commitment to renouncing the use of force, Dulles argues, it would become a powerless organization, and the world would face imminent doom.

Dulles continues by suggesting what the United Nations needed to do in response to the Suez crisis. At this point he presents the U.S. resolution, proposing six changes aimed at ending the conflict in Egypt. The resolution calls, first, for a cease-fire; second, for any country subject to the aforementioned armistice agreements to return their forces to territory within the stipulated national boundaries; third, for members of the United Nations to avoid importing any new arms to the region; fourth, for steps to be taken to reopen the Suez Canal following the cease-fire; fifth, for the UN secretary-general to study the progress made as a result of the resolution and report it to the Security Council and the General Assembly; and sixth, for the United Nations to stay in emergency session until the conditions of the resolution are met. After reading the U.S. resolution, Dulles admits that it was incomplete and certainly would not solve all of the problems in the region. But, he contends, something had to be done to end the ongoing conflict.

In closing, Dulles tries to impress upon his audience the importance of passing the resolution. He states that if the United Nations were not to take action immediately, the conflict in and around Egypt would most likely broaden. In addition, Dulles fears that if the United Nations were not to take action it would be viewed as weak, and other countries would begin using force without fear of reprisal. He even states that while he once thought that World War II represented the worst of war, he now believes that the future holds worse misfortune.

Dulles's speech evidently impressed the General Assembly; the following day, it voted to adopt the U.S. resolution, and France, Great Britain, and Israel immediately began withdrawing forces from the region. Dulles and Eisenhower had also hoped that the stance against Great Britain and France would distance the United States from the former imperial superpowers and help it win the support of nonaligned nations, but the resolution and speech seemed to have little effect on international views of the United States. To Dulles's chagrin, the Soviet Union actually made concrete gains in the region as a result of the crisis. In addition to cementing regional trade and arms sales, the USSR threatened on November 5 to take military action against Great Britain and France if they did not pull out of the region. Both were already in the process of withdrawing their troops as stipulated by the U.S. resolution, but the Soviets spun the situation in the media so that many people worldwide believed that the crisis was resolved by the Soviet Union, not the United States or United Nations.

◆ Address on U.S. Policy toward Communist China

Dulles did not mince words when discussing the Communist nation of China. In this address, delivered in June 1957, he immediately casts the People's Republic of China as an aggressive, violent, expansionist global threat that despises the United States for interfering with its moves toward global domination. He sums up the U.S. refusal to recognize China by stating that it is in the best interest of the United States to support "free" nations and contrary to U.S. interests to support Communist regimes. Therefore, he states, the United States is opposed to allowing China entrance into the United Nations and refuses to trade or converse with China.

Dulles continues by explaining that American dealings with the Soviet Union after its revolution in 1917 set a precedent for current policy toward Communist China. He notes that for sixteen years following the Russian Revolution, the United States recognized the government in exile of Alexander Kerensky (the non-Communist leader of the Russian revolution who was later deposed by the Bolsheviks) as the legitimate government of Russia, recognizing the USSR in 1933 only as part of its effort to curb Japanese imperialism in Asia. Furthermore, he argues, the United States had no indication in 1933 that the Soviet Union would act aggressively, imperialistically, or in a manner that would threaten American interests; at that time, the USSR had not acted aggressively for over ten years and had not mistreated American citizens. In the context of world politics, then, U.S. recognition of Communist Russia was appropriate. In contrast, Dulles states, recognition of Communist China in 1957 would be contrary to American interests. He states that unlike the USSR in 1933, China in 1957 had an immediate history of aggression and did not show an inclination toward changing policy. Furthermore, he accuses China of abusing American citizens and of violating international agreements. If the United States were to recognize China, Dulles claims, mainland Chinese, Taiwanese, and the Chinese diaspora who hoped to see the Communist regime overthrown would be disappointed. U.S. recognition would furthermore encourage China's admission into the United Nations, which Dulles deems inappropriate given China's history of aggression.

In the remaining portion of the address, Dulles rebuts the major arguments made in favor of diplomatic recognition of China. In response to the argument that the Communists in China had held power for a duration deserving of recognition, Dulles contends that diplomatic recognition remained a privilege that the regime did not deserve. He claims that the United States did not withhold recognition spitefully but instead because it recognized regimes that both demonstrated the ability to govern and represented the will of their people. Responding to a second major argument, that recognition of Communist China was inevitable, Dulles contends that it was not inevitable and that the global community had the power to determine its own destiny. He reinforces this claim by stating that Communist governments were not nearly as strong as many observers believed and therefore would not enjoy the longevity of democracies. Finally, he argues against the proposition that in recognizing China the United States might bring about the downfall of the Soviet Union because the two Communist powers might turn on each other. He compares such a tactic to working with one of the Axis powers during World War II in the hope that they might eventually turn against one another.

In concluding, Dulles reiterates the reasons for U.S. denial of diplomatic recognition to China. He again levies the charges that Communist China was aggressive, ignored international law, and was generally "uncivilized." He assures his audience that international Communism is a temporary fixture in world politics and that in refusing to recognize Communist China the United States sought to hasten its fall rather than prolong it. Dulles's views on the necessity of denying the People's Republic of China diplomatic recognition and admission to the United Nations governed American decisions relating to the country for a decade and a half. A major shift did not occur until President Richard Nixon visited China in 1972 and decided to extend recognition; as Dulles had feared, it was subsequently admitted to the United Nations.

◆ **News Conference on U.S. Relations with Latin American Nations**

The precedent set by Dulles in dealing with Arbenz in Guatemala did not escape the attention of people throughout Latin America. In the late 1950s the United States maintained its policy of steadfastly supporting authoritarian rulers if they protected American business interests and opposed Communism, as in Venezuela. There, however, in January 1958, a military junta with popular support overthrew the ruling dictator, Marcos Pérez Jiménez. The U.S. reaction to the coup only further angered Venezuelans: First, the United States provided refuge for both Pérez Jiménez and his national security police chief, one of the most hated men in Venezuela. Then Harold "Duke" Haight, the president of the largest American oil company in Venezuela, made widely publicized remarks disparaging the junta's decision to increase taxes on foreign oil companies. Finally, the Eisenhower administration began discussing a curbing of Venezuelan oil imports, which Venezuelans interpreted as an economic attack on the new regime.

During this tumultuous period the Eisenhower administration decided to send Vice President Richard Nixon on a tour of Latin America, in an effort to both strengthen ties to hemispheric allies and improve the image of the United States in Latin America. When Nixon and his wife arrived in Venezuela on May 13, 1958, they were greeted at the airport by throngs of angry protesters who yelled at and spit on them. As they drove through the capital city of Caracas, they were attacked by an angry mob, had the windows of their vehicle smashed, and eventually had to run through the street with the aid of Secret Service officers and take refuge in the residence of the American ambassador. They fled the country a few days later. Americans were shocked to hear of the events. In this context, Dulles held a news conference on May 20. His aims were to quiet concerns over the Caracas incident and to clarify foreign policy in the Western Hemisphere for the American public.

He begins by denying that any deep-seated anti-American sentiment existed in Venezuela. He insists that the actions against Nixon that began on May 13 did not represent the sentiments of Venezuelans in general. Instead, he attributes the protests during Nixon's visit to a limited group of people acting out and claims that expatriates had returned from abroad in the aftermath of Pérez Jiménez's abdication and unfairly blamed the United States for Venezuela's problems. He also argues that the recent regime change had created an unstable environment owing to a shortage of law enforcement in the streets, which had allowed the mob activity to take place. Dulles insists that the State Department had not miscalculated in sending Nixon to Caracas, stating that America should not hide from any potentially explosive situation, since doing so would only encourage mob activity and international Communism. He concludes that the State Department's only miscalculation was in believing that Venezuela would adequately protect the U.S. vice president.

Dulles proceeds to address the critique that the United States immorally dealt with dictatorships in Latin America. He contends that the foreign policy of the United States could not be conducted if diplomats always had to distinguish "good government" from "bad government." Doing so, he argues, would require an inappropriate degree of involvement in the domestic politics of other countries. Instead, he states, the United States would deal with whatever governments were in power, unless there exist what he obliquely refers to as "reasons" not to, such as in Communist China. Dulles concludes the conference with a discussion of the significance of relations with Latin America to U.S. foreign policy more generally. He considers relations with Latin America to be equally important to those with other regions and extols the virtues of the Organization of American States. He repeatedly states that perhaps the misconception that Latin America held an inferior position in foreign policy considerations existed because most meetings related to Latin American policy were conducted in Washington, not requiring him to travel, and therefore received little attention in the press. Finally, he argues that when one includes private trade and investment in considerations of foreign relations, Latin America is clearly quite important to the United States.

Impact and Legacy

Dulles was a controversial figure in his own day and remains so in the present. While the public applauded many of his policy decisions, he was sometimes chastised for his single-mindedness. President Eisenhower strongly critiqued Dulles's decisions during the Suez crisis, for example, and his obituaries were not uniformly positive. In general, however, politicians and the public condoned his policy decisions. His policy of "brinkmanship," in particular, was embraced by the American public. Americans feared the possibilities of the nuclear age in the 1950s, and most believed that the United States represented the best hope for humanity. Their sense of national pride and religious beliefs gave them much in common with Dulles.

"*Guatemala is a small country. But its power, standing alone, is not a measure of the threat. The master plan of international communism is to gain a solid political base in this hemisphere, a base that can be used to extend Communist penetration to the other peoples of the other American Governments.*"

(Radio and Television Address on Communism in Guatemala)

"*I have said and deeply believe that peace is a coin which has two sides— one of which is the avoidance of the use of force and the other is the creation of conditions of justice—and in the long run you cannot expect one without the other.*"

(Address to the United Nations on the Suez Crisis)

"*If we seemed to waver and to compromise with communism in China, that would in turn weaken free Asia resistance to the Chinese Communist regime and assist international communism to score a great success in its program to encircle us.*"

(Address on U.S. Policy toward Communist China)

"*There is often an optical illusion which results from the fact that police states, suppressing differences, give an external appearance of hard permanency, whereas the democracies, with their opposition parties and often speaking through different and discordant voices, seem the unstable, pliable members of the world society.*"

(Address on U.S. Policy toward Communist China)

"*You can talk about dictators and nondictators, but it isn't quite as easy to classify on that basis. There are quasi-dictators and almost-dictators and 'dictators of the proletariat' and all sorts of things in gradations.*"

(News Conference on U.S. Relations with Latin American Nations)

The public later learned much more about the covert operations that Dulles had ignited, largely contributing to an increasingly negative view of him. As the consequences of those actions have been borne out, particularly in Central America during the 1980s and in the Middle East more recently, critiques and negative views of him have increased. Yet people also remember Dulles and his legacy fondly. Steadfast in his belief in American superiority and unbending in negotiations, Dulles represents for some the type of diplomacy that made the United States a superpower.

The language and tone of Dulles's speeches reflect his privileged background. At times, particularly in dealing with reporters, he came across as condescending. Indeed, Dulles came from a position of social, economic, and educational privilege. He believed that he was better suited than anyone else to run the foreign affairs of the United States, and his speeches reflect this belief. He also firmly believed that his policies were in the best interest of the people of the United States. Even when he clearly misrepresented circumstances or his own actions, he did not believe that he was doing so in a sinister manner or for selfish reasons. He truly envisioned himself as a warrior against evil. Dulles's speeches offer a lens through which to view not only some of the most significant foreign policy decisions of the twentieth century but also the mentality that allowed for the persistence of the cold war.

Key Sources

The John Foster Dulles Papers, held at Princeton University, are available to view at the Princeton University Library's Department of Rare Books and Special Collections. Some of Dulles's correspondence is held in the Dulles Family Collection at the Tarlton Law Library at the University of Texas. Many of Dulles's speeches also appear in Arthur M. Schlesinger, Jr., ed., *The Dynamics of World Power: A Documentary History of United States Foreign Policy, 1945–1973*. In *War, Peace, and Change* (1939), Dulles discusses the potential problems of nationalism as well as the necessity of international organizations for maintaining

Questions for Further Study

1. What role did Dulles's early religious education and continuing spiritual commitment play in shaping his thinking? What strengths did he most likely gain from this element in his background, and in what ways might it have limited his vision?

2. Dulles's 1954 television address regarding Guatemala as well as his 1958 news conference on U.S. relations with Latin America bristle with dire warnings of Communist infiltration of the New World. Compare this with the actual record of events that followed, including Communist takeovers in Cuba and Nicaragua and the attempt to establish Communist regimes in Grenada, El Salvador, and other countries. How accurate was Dulles's assessment? Despite these warnings, how did Communists manage to make the progress that they did in Latin America and the Caribbean during the latter half of the twentieth century?

3. Was Dulles correct in the assessment of Communist China that he offers in his 1957 address? In particular, was he right in saying that while U.S. recognition of the Soviet Union had been necessary, America should withhold such recognition from the Communist Chinese? Did he accurately assess the unity of aims between Moscow and Beijing? And was he correct in his analysis of China as an expansionist power? Finally, how might Dulles have regarded the subsequent opening of relations with China under President Richard Nixon in 1972 and the emergence of China as an economic powerhouse in the early twenty-first century?

4. If Dulles were alive today, he would see that Communism, the principal force opposing American interests in the world of his time, has lost most of its influence—only to be overtaken by a potentially even more formidable threat in the form of Muslim extremism. Meanwhile, the Communist system lingers on in Cuba and North Korea and in a modified form in China, while a number of former Soviet republics—including the Russian Federation itself—show signs of returning to Communist practices. Pretend that you are Dulles glimpsing the world of the early twenty-first century, and discuss your reactions. In what ways are things very different from what you envisioned at the height of the cold war? And in what ways is the world situation much as you imagined it in the 1950s?

global peace. In *War or Peace* (1950), he criticizes the policy of containment pursued by the administration of President Harry S. Truman and advocates a far more aggressive policy toward destroying global Communism.

Further Reading

■ Books

Hoopes, Townsend. *The Devil and John Foster Dulles*. Boston: Little, Brown, 1973.

Kinzer, Stephen. *Overthrow: America's Century of Regime Change from Hawaii to Iraq*. New York: Times Books, 2007.

Pruessen, Ronald W. *John Foster Dulles: The Road to Power*. New York: Free Press, 1982.

Toulouse, Mark G. *The Transformation of John Foster Dulles: From Prophet of Realism to Priest of Nationalism*. Macon, Ga.: Mercer University Press, 1985.

—G. Mehera Gerardo

RADIO AND TELEVISION ADDRESS ON COMMUNISM IN GUATEMALA (1954)

Tonight I should like to talk with you about Guatemala. It is the scene of dramatic events. They expose the evil purpose of the Kremlin to destroy the inter-American system, and they test the ability of the American States to maintain the peaceful integrity of this hemisphere. For several years international communism has been probing here and there for nesting places in the Americas. It finally chose Guatemala as a spot which it could turn into an official base from which to breed subversion which would extend to other American Republics. This intrusion of Soviet despotism was, of course, a direct challenge to our Monroe Doctrine, the first and most fundamental of our foreign policies....

In Guatemala, international communism had an initial success. It began 10 years ago, when a revolution occurred in Guatemala. The revolution was not without justification. But the Communists seized on it, not as an opportunity for real reform, but as a chance to gain political power.

Communist agitators devoted themselves to infiltrating the public and private organizations of Guatemala. They sent recruits to Russia and other Communist countries for revolutionary training and indoctrination in such institutions as the Lenin School at Moscow. Operating in the guise of "reformers," they organized the workers and peasants under Communist leadership. Having gained control of what they call "mass organizations," they moved on to take over the official press and radio of the Guatemalan Government. They dominated the social security organization and ran the agrarian reform program. Through the technique of the "popular front" they dictated to the Congress and the President.

The judiciary made one valiant attempt to protect its integrity and independence. But the Communists, using their control of the legislative body, caused the Supreme Court to be dissolved when it refused to give approval to a Communist-contrived law. Arbenz, who until this week was President of Guatemala, was openly manipulated by the leaders of communism.

Guatemala is a small country. But its power, standing alone, is not a measure of the threat. The master plan of international communism is to gain a solid political base in this hemisphere, a base that can be used to extend Communist penetration to the other peoples of the other American Governments. It was not the power of the Arbenz government that concerned us but the power behind it.

If world communism captures any American State, however small, a new and perilous front is established which will increase the danger to the entire free world and require even greater sacrifices from the American people.

This situation in Guatemala had become so dangerous that the American States could not ignore it. At Caracas last March the American States held their Tenth Inter-American Conference. They then adopted a momentous statement. They declared that "the domination or control of the political institutions of any American State by the international Communist movement...would constitute a threat to the sovereignty and political independence of the American States, endangering the peace of America."

There was only one American State that voted against this declaration. That State was Guatemala.

This Caracas declaration precipitated a dramatic chain of events. From their European base the Communist leaders moved rapidly to build up the military power of their agents in Guatemala. In May a large shipment of arms moved from behind the Iron Curtain into Guatemala. The shipment was thought to be secreted by false manifests and false clearances. Its ostensible destination was changed three times while en route.

At the same time, the agents of international communism in Guatemala intensified efforts to penetrate and subvert the neighboring Central American States. They attempted political assassinations and political strikes. They used consular agents for political warfare.

Many Guatemalan people protested against their being used by Communist dictatorship to serve the Communists' lust for power. The response was mass arrests, the suppression of constitutional guaranties, the killing of opposition leaders, and other brutal tactics normally employed by communism to secure the consolidation of its power....

Throughout the period I have outlined, the Guatemalan Government and Communist agents throughout the world have persistently attempted to obscure the real issue—that of Communist imperialism—by claiming that the United States is only interested in protecting American business. We regret that there have been disputes between the Guatemalan Government and the United Fruit Company. We have urged repeatedly that these disputes be submitted for settlement to an international tribunal or to international arbitration. That is the way to dispose of problems of this sort. But this issue is relatively unimportant. All who know the temper of the U.S. people and Government must realize that our overriding concern is that which, with others, we recorded at Caracas, namely the endangering by international communism of the peace and security of this hemisphere

The people of Guatemala have not been heard from. Despite the armaments piled up by the Arbenz government, it was unable to enlist the spiritual cooperation of the people.

Led by Col. Castillo Armas, patriots arose in Guatemala to challenge the Communist leadership—and to change it. Thus, the situation is being cured by the Guatemalans themselves.

Last Sunday, President Arbenz of Guatemala resigned and seeks asylum. Others are following his example.

Tonight, just as I speak, Col. Castillo Armas is in conference in El Salvador with Colonel Monzon, the head of the Council which has taken over the power in Guatemala City. It was this power that the just wrath of the Guatemalan people wrested from President Arbenz, who then took flight.

Now the future of Guatemala lies at the disposal of the Guatemalan people themselves. It lies also at the disposal of leaders loyal to Guatemala who have not treasonably become the agents of an alien despotism which sought to use Guatemala for its own evil ends....

Above all, we can be grateful that there were loyal citizens of Guatemala who, in the face of terrorism and violence and against what seemed insuperable odds, had the courage and the will to eliminate the traitorous tools of foreign despots.

The need for vigilance is not past. Communism is still a menace everywhere. But the people of the United States and of the other American Republics can feel tonight that at least one grave danger has been averted. Also an example is set which promises increased security for the future. The ambitious and unscrupulous will be less prone to feel that communism is the wave of their future.

In conclusion, let me assure the people of Guatemala. As peace and freedom are restored to that sister Republic, the Government of the United States will continue to support the just aspirations of the Guatemalan people. A prosperous and progres-

Glossary

false manifests and false clearances	falsified shipping documents and records
from behind the Iron Curtain	from somewhere in the Communist world, in this case Czechoslovakia
Kremlin	technically, a medieval fortress in Moscow, around which government buildings grew, leading to the use of the term as a reference to the Russian or Soviet government as a whole
Lenin School at Moscow	the International Lenin School, which operated from 1926 to 1938 as an institution for the indoctrination of some three thousand foreign youth
Monroe Doctrine	a doctrine formulated in 1823 by John Quincy Adams as secretary of state to President James Monroe, prohibiting outside interference in the Western Hemisphere
popular front	coalitions of mostly leftist parties by which Communists sought to gain control of non-Communist countries
United Fruit Company	a U.S.-based corporation (1899–1970) that exercised enormous influence over nations in and around the Caribbean during the first half of the twentieth century
used consular agents for political warfare	planted propagandists and agitators, disguised as diplomatic personnel, in other countries

sive Guatemala is vital to a healthy hemisphere. The United States pledges itself not merely to political opposition to communism but to help to alleviate conditions in Guatemala and elsewhere which might afford communism an opportunity to spread its tentacles throughout the hemisphere. Thus we shall seek in positive ways to make our Americas an example which will inspire men everywhere.

ADDRESS TO THE UNITED NATIONS ON THE SUEZ CRISIS (1956)

I doubt that any delegate ever spoke from this forum with as heavy a heart as I have brought here tonight. We speak on a matter of vital importance, where the United States finds itself unable to agree with three nations with whom it has ties, deep friendship, admiration and respect, and two of whom constitute our oldest, most trusted and reliable allies....

What are the facts that bring us here?

There is, first of all, the fact that there occurred beginning last Monday a deep penetration of Egypt by Israeli forces. Then, quickly following up upon this action, there came action by France and the United Kingdom in subjecting Egypt first to a 12-hour ultimatum and then to armed attack, which is now going on from the air with the declared purpose of gaining temporary control of the Suez Canal, presumably to make it more secure.

Then there is the third fact that the matter, having been brought to the Security Council, was sought to be dealt with by a resolution which was vetoed by the United Kingdom and by France, which cast the only dissenting votes against the resolution. Thereupon, under the provisions of the Uniting for Peace resolution, the matter came here under a call from the Secretary General, instituted by a vote of seven members of the Security Council, requiring that this Assembly convene in emergency session within 24 hours....

We are not blind, Mr. President, to the fact that what has happened in the last two or three days comes out of a murky background. But we have come to the conclusion that these provocations, serious as they are, cannot justify the resort to armed force which has occurred within the last two and three days, and which is going on tonight....

But, Mr. President, if we were to agree that the existence of injustices in the world, which this organization so far has been unable to cure, means that the principle of renunciation of force is no longer respected, and that there still exists the right wherever a nation feels itself subject to injustice to resort to force to try to correct that injustice, then, Mr. President, we would have, I fear, torn this Charter into shreds and the world would again be a world of anarchy. And all the great hopes that are placed in this organization and in our Charter would have vanished and we would be as we were, when World War II

began, with only another tragic failure in place of what we hoped would be—and still can hope will be—a barrier against the recurrence of a world war which, as our Preamble says, has "twice in our lifetime...brought untold sorrow to mankind...."

It is animated by such considerations, Mr. President, that the United States has introduced a resolution which I should like to read to you:...

"Noting the disregard on many occasions by parties to the Israel-Arab Armistice Agreements of 1948 of the terms of such agreements, and that the armed forces of Israel have penetrated deeply into Egyptian territory in violation of the General Armistice Agreement between Egypt and Israel; Noting that armed forces of France and the United Kingdom are conducting military operations against Egyptian territory;

Noting that traffic through the Suez Canal is now interrupted to the serious prejudice of many nations;

Expressing its grave concern over these developments:

1. Urges as a matter of priority that all parties now involved in hostilities in the area agree to an immediate cease-fire and as part thereof halt the movement of military forces and arms into the area;

2. Urges the parties to the Armistice Agreements promptly to withdraw all forces behind the Armistice lines, to desist from raids across the Armistice lines into neighboring territory, and to observe scrupulously the provisions of the Armistice Agreements;

3. Recommends that all members refrain from introducing military goods in the area of hostilities and in general refrain from any acts which would delay or prevent the implementation of this resolution;

4. Urges that upon the cease-fire being effective steps be taken to reopen the Suez Canal and restore secure freedom of navigation;

5. Requests the Secretary General to observe and promptly report on the compliance with this resolution, to the Security Council and to the General Assembly, for such further action as they may deem appropriate in accordance with the Charter;

6. Decides to remain in emergency session pending compliance with this resolution."

That, Mr. President, is the proposal of the United States Delegation....

I have said and deeply believe that peace is a coin which has two sides—one of which is the avoidance of the use of force and the other is the creation of conditions of justice—and in the long run you cannot expect one without the other.

I do not by the form of this resolution want to seem in any way to believe that this situation can be adequately taken care of merely by the steps that are in this resolution. There needs to be something better than the uneasy armistices which have existed now for these eight years between Israel and the Arab neighbors; there needs to be a greater sense of confidence and security in the free and equal operation of the Canal than has existed since three months ago when President Nasser seized the Suez Canal Company. These things I regard of the utmost importance....

I fear that if we do not act and act promptly, and if we do not act with sufficient unanimity of opinion so that our recommendations carry a real influence, there is great danger that what is started and what has been called a police action may develop into something which is far more grave. Even if that does not happen, the apparent impotence of this organization to deal with this situation may set a precedent which will lead other nations to attempt to take into their own hands the remedying of what they believe to be their injustices. If that happens, the future is dark indeed.

We thought when we wrote the Charter in San Francisco in 1945 that we had seen perhaps the worst in war, that our task was to prevent a recurrence of what had been, and indeed what then had been was tragic enough. But now we know that what can be will be infinitely more tragic than what we saw in World War II.

Glossary

police action	military action undertaken without a formal declaration of war
prejudice	denial of legal rights
Secretary General	legislative head of the United Nations General Assembly, chosen through a process of election by that body
Security Council	the UN Security Council, consisting of five permanent members (Russia, China, France, Britain, and the United States), all of which have veto power, and ten elected members
two of whom	Britain and France but not Israel (the third nation mentioned) because that nation was only eight years old at the time
Uniting for Peace resolution	United Nations General Assembly Resolution 377, adopted November 3, 1950, and providing that when the Security Council fails to act on an issue, owing to disagreement between two or more of its members, that issue would be placed before the General Assembly

ADDRESS ON U.S. POLICY TOWARD COMMUNIST CHINA (1957)

On the China mainland 600 million people are ruled by the Chinese Communist Party. That party came to power by violence and, so far, has lived by violence.

It retains power not by will of the Chinese people but by massive, forcible repression. It fought the United Nations in Korea; it supported the Communist war in Indochina; it took Tibet by force. It fomented the Communist Huk rebellion in the Philippines and the Communists' insurrection in Malaya. It does not disguise its expansionist ambitions. It is bitterly hateful of the United States, which it considers a principal obstacle in the way of its path of conquest....

As regards China, we have abstained from any act to encourage the Communist regime—morally, politically, or materially. Thus:

We have not extended diplomatic recognition to the Chinese Communist regime;

We have opposed its seating in the United Nations;

We have not traded with Communist China or sanctioned cultural interchanges with it.

These have been, and are, our policies. Like all our policies, they are under periodic review....

United States diplomatic recognition of Communist China would have the following consequences:

(1) The many mainland Chinese, who by Mao Tse-tung's own recent admission seek to change the nature of their government, would be immensely discouraged.

(2) The millions of overseas Chinese would feel that they had no Free China to which to look....This would be a tragedy for them; and it would imperil friendly governments already menaced by Chinese Communist subversion.

(3) The Republic of China, now on Taiwan, would feel betrayed by its friend. That Government was our ally in the Second World War and for long bore alone the main burden of the Far Eastern war. It had many tempting opportunities to compromise with the Japanese on terms which would have been gravely detrimental to the United States. It never did so....

(4) The free Asian governments of the Pacific and Southeast Asia would be gravely perplexed. They are not only close to the vast Chinese land mass, but geographically and, to some extent, politically, they are separated as among themselves. The unifying and fortifying influence is, above all, the spirit and resolution of the United States. If we seemed to waver and to compromise with communism in China, that would in turn weaken free Asia resistance to the Chinese Communist regime and assist international communism to score a great success in its program to encircle us.

United States recognition of Communist China would make it probable that the Communist regime would obtain the seat of China in the United Nations. That would not be in the interest either of the United States or of the United Nations.

The United Nations is not a reformatory for bad governments. It is supposedly an association of those who are already "peace-loving" and who are "able and willing to carry out" the charter obligations. The basic obligation is not to use force, except in defense against armed attack.

The Chinese Communist regime has a record of successive armed aggressions, including war against the United Nations itself, a war not yet politically settled but discontinued by an armistice. The regime asserts not only its right but its purpose to use force if need be to bring Taiwan under its rule....

These are the considerations which argue for a continuance of our present policies. What are the arguments on the other side?

There are some who say that we should accord diplomatic recognition to the Communist regime because it has now been in power so long that it has won the right to that.

That is not sound international law. Diplomatic recognition is always a privilege, never a right.

Of course, the United States knows that the Chinese Communist regime exists....

But diplomatic recognition gives the recognized regime valuable rights and privileges, and, in the world of today, recognition by the United States gives the recipient much added prestige and influence at home and abroad.

Of course, diplomatic recognition is not to be withheld capriciously. In this matter, as others, the United States seeks to act in accordance with principles which contribute to a world society of order under law....

Another argument beginning to be heard is that diplomatic recognition is inevitable, so why not now?

First, let me say emphatically that the United States need never succumb to the argument of "inevitability." We, with our friends, can fashion our own destiny. We do not accept the mastery of Communist forces.

And let me go on to say: Communist-type despotisms are not so immutable as they sometimes appear. Time and circumstances work also upon them.

There is often an optical illusion which results from the fact that police states, suppressing differences, give an external appearance of hard permanency, whereas the democracies, with their opposition parties and often speaking through different and discordant voices, seem the unstable, pliable members of the world society.

The reality is that a governmental system which tolerates diversity has a long life expectancy, whereas a system which seeks to impose conformity is always in danger. That results from the basic nature of human beings. Of all the arguments advanced for recognition of the Communist regime in China, the least cogent is the argument of "inevitability."

There are some who suggest that, if we assist the Chinese Communists to wax strong, then they will eventually break with Soviet Russia and that that is our best hope for the future....

Perhaps, if the ambitions of the Chinese Communists are inflated by successes, they might eventually clash with Soviet Russia. Perhaps, too, if the Axis Powers had won the Second World War, they would have fallen out among themselves. But no one suggested that we should tolerate and even assist an Axis victory because in the end they would quarrel over the booty—of which we would be part....

The capacity to change is an indispensable capacity. Equally indispensable is the capacity to hold fast that which is good. Given those qualities, we can hopefully look forward to the day when those in Asia who are yet free can confidently remain free and when the people of China and the people of America can resume their long history of cooperative friendship.

Glossary

diplomatic recognition	formal, established interactions between nations based on their mutual agreement that each has the legal right to exist in its present form
Huk	the Hukbalahap, the military wing of the Philippine Communist Party, which waged war against its nation's pro-Western government from 1946 to 1954
Indochina	the area of Southeast Asia under French control from the nineteenth century until the middle of the twentieth, when Communist revolutions established the nations of Vietnam, Cambodia, and Laos
insurrection in Malaya	the difficult transition (1946–1966) from British colonialism to independence experienced by the Southeast Asian nation now known as Malaysia, a period that included the uprising to which Dulles alludes
Mao Tse-tung	Mao Zedong (1893–1976), Chinese Communist leader from the establishment of the People's Republic in 1949 to his death

News Conference on U.S. Relations with Latin American Nations (1958)

In the first place I would not say that there is any general or preponderant anti-American sentiment among the people of Venezuela. You cannot judge a people on the basis of sporadic, organized outbursts of rowdyism. I am confident that what happened there is not a reflection of the general views of the Venezuelan people.

Now there have been developments which have made it easier for those who want to organize these demonstrations to do so. One of them has been the shift in the oil situation. That is an economic cause. The oil, instead of being in short supply, as it was during the Suez crisis, has come into oversupply, and that has required some voluntary restrictions on oil imports into the United States, including those from Venezuela. As an economic factor, that has come into the situation.

Then there is a political factor in that, after the overthrow of the 10-year rule of Jimenez, a good many refugees came back to Venezuela and tended to blame their situation on the United States. Furthermore, there was a sort of vacuum of power, which always encourages rowdyist elements to come to the forefront. We know ourselves that, when there is not an adequate police force, as when there is a disaster or something which eliminates the ordinary forces of law and order, rowdyism takes command. I do not think it is sound to judge the basic sentiments of the Venezuelan nation and the Venezuelan people on the basis of what took place when Mr. Nixon was there....

I believe myself, in the light of what we knew before Vice President Nixon went there, it was a quite correct judgment on his part to go. I think, if we had all known what was going to happen there and had been able to foresee the events, probably he would not have gone. But, you know, if you don't go to places because of threats, you will be locked up at home. I have never gone to any country in the world, hardly, but what I have had threats and there have been demonstrations of one sort or another. It is so with the Vice President, who has also visited a great many countries. If you allow yourself to be deterred by threats of that kind, the result is that the Communists will imprison you at home....

We try to conduct our relations with all the governments of the world on the basis of dealing with the government which is, in fact, in power, unless we have reasons, as we have in Communist China, for not recognizing it.

On the basis of noninterference with the internal affairs of countries and in the case of South America—Latin America—we tried to deal with those governments on the basis of our appraisal as to whether they were a good government or a bad government, whether they were a dictatorial or not a dictatorial government, we would find ourselves, I am afraid, deeply enmeshed in their internal affairs.

As you know, one of the cardinal doctrines for this hemisphere, which is affirmed and reaffirmed on every occasion by the American Republics, is the doctrine of noninterference in the internal affairs of other countries. Their economic and political interdependence with the United States is such that to a peculiar degree—a greater degree than probably any other area in the world—if we attempted to adjust our relations according to our appraisal of their government, we would become involved in their internal affairs.

I would like to point out there is no clearcut distinction. You can talk about dictators and nondictators, but it isn't quite as easy to classify on that basis. There are quasi-dictators and almost-dictators and "dictators of the proletariat" and all sorts of things in gradations. If you begin to grade and say, if it is a certain type of government, you give 100 percent support, and, if it is not quite as good by our standards, you give 90 percent, and, if it is less good, you give 70 percent support, that would get us involved in an intolerable situation.

It is obvious the American Government and the American nation and the American people like to see governments which rest upon the consent of the governed and where the governed are educated people able to carry the responsibilities of self-government. Wherever that exists, there almost automatically results a closer and more intimate friendly relationship than where that doesn't exist. But any formula whereby we try to apply a sort of slide rule to their governments would be, in fact, an interference in their internal affairs....

I would like to say this: that relations with Latin America have never been in any subordinated category....

I suppose we devote as much time and thought to the problems of the Americas as we do to the problems of any other region in the world. I say it is less conspicuous because it is done quietly here in Washington and does not entail arrival statements and departure statements and all the business that goes with these trips. But there has never been a downgrading.

Now there is another point that I want to make, which is the fact that our relations with the American Republics are more on a basis of private activity and relatively less on a basis of governmental activity than with certain other areas of the world. There is a tremendous private trade.

Now when the Soviets talk about "aid," they include trade. If we included trade, the figures would be massive. There is more private trade between the United States and Latin America than between any of the other—more than Canada and more than any other country in the world, if you lump the Latin American countries together.

There is a big flow of private American capital that goes to these countries, and there are very large loans by the Export-Import Bank. So that the activities in relation to Latin America are not all reflected by activities that take place here in the Department of State. It is a very good thing that that is the case. It is abnormal, under our form of society, to have to deal with other countries through … special grant-aid, Government-sponsored projects, and so forth. It is a healthy thing, and good for both of us, that so much can be done in this other way. But when you are thinking about what is done, the level of interest and concern, don't write off the tremendous volume of private trade, the tremendous volume of private capital, and the loaning facilities of the Export-Import Bank. If you take all those things into account, you will see that the interest and concern of the United States with Latin America is very great indeed.

Glossary

capital	funds for investment
dictators of the proletariat	a sarcastic reference to "dictatorship of the proletariat," the Marxian concept of rule by workers, or the proletariat, that would follow Communist revolution
Export-Import Bank	the Export-Import Bank of the United States, established in 1934 as a credit agency to facilitate international trade
one of the cardinal doctrines for this hemisphere… noninterference	a reference to the Monroe Doctrine, formulated in 1823 by John Quincy Adams as secretary of state to President James Monroe, which prohibits outside interference in the Western Hemisphere
shift in the oil situation	a proposal by the Dwight Eisenhower administration to limit U.S. oil imports from Venezuela—a key element in that nation's economy at that time

President Charles de Gaulle of France (left), Premier Harold Macmillan of Great Britain (center), and President Dwight D. Eisenhower are shown at the end of a failed summit conference on disarmament between Western nations and leaders of the Soviet Union. (AP/Wide World Photos)

DWIGHT D. EISENHOWER   1890–1969

Thirty-fourth President of the United States

Featured Documents
- ◆ First Inaugural Address (1953)
- ◆ "Cross of Iron" Speech (1953)
- ◆ Atoms for Peace Speech (1953)
- ◆ Special Message to Congress on the Eisenhower Doctrine (1957)
- ◆ Second Inaugural Address (1957)
- ◆ Farewell Address (1961)

Overview

Dwight David Eisenhower was born in Denison, Texas, in 1890 and grew up in Abilene, Kansas. Throughout his life he exemplified the plainspoken midwestern values that marked his childhood. He graduated from the U.S. Military Academy at West Point and went on to a distinguished career in the military. During World War II he led the invasion of Normandy, France, in 1944 and was the supreme commander of Allied forces in Western Europe. He later became the first military commander of the North Atlantic Treaty Organization (NATO). Eisenhower was not affiliated with either major American political party, but a draft effort led him to enter the Republican presidential nomination campaign, and he won the 1952 election. Eisenhower thus became the first elected Republican chief executive since 1928 and the first president born in Texas, and he was the only career military officer elected president in the twentieth century. He was reelected by a large margin in 1956. Indeed, during his two terms, Eisenhower emerged as one of the most popular presidents of the century, in accord with his campaign slogan "I like Ike." He presided over the maturation of the cold war and a period of domestic prosperity that was marked by rising consumer culture and the beginnings of the modern civil rights movement. Eisenhower died in Washington, D.C., on March 28, 1969.

Eisenhower's popularity transcended party politics, and he helped solidify the emerging bipartisan consensus on foreign policy that would mark U.S. politics for the remainder of the cold war. He ended the Korean War, and his tenure also marked the end of the era of political suspicion and fear fostered by Senator Joseph McCarthy in his crusade to root out Communists in the U.S. government. Eisenhower developed a new mode of national security, dubbed the "New Look," using covert operations to achieve foreign policy goals, with notable interventions in Iran (1953) and Guatemala (1954). He increased the nation's reliance on nuclear weapons as a deterrent against the Soviet Union, including through the development of the hydrogen bomb, but concurrently launched the Atoms for Peace initiative, which led to the creation of the International Atomic Energy Agency. Eisenhower adroitly managed the 1956 Suez crisis (following Egypt's decision to nationalize the Suez Canal) and then issued the Eisenhower Doctrine to counter Soviet influence in the Middle East in 1957, pledging U.S. economic and military assistance to nations facing Soviet aggression. He also further strengthened U.S.-European security ties. He continued military aid to France in Indochina and then was instrumental in the creation of non-Communist South Vietnam. Despite his security initiatives, the president was credited with reducing tensions with the Soviet Union. Eisenhower also oversaw the beginnings of the space race and dramatically bolstered funding for the National Aeronautics and Space Administration.

The Eisenhower presidency was a period of expansive domestic economic growth. Personal incomes almost doubled during his eight years in office, and both inflation and unemployment remained low. Home ownership increased dramatically, and consumers enjoyed a range of new products. Eisenhower pursued moderate domestic and economic programs but also endeavored to maintain a balanced budget (with his administration achieving surpluses in three of the budget years). Although he was criticized by conservatives within his party, Eisenhower expanded Social Security and low-income housing, and his administration established the Department of Health, Education, and Welfare. The nation's modern interstate system was initiated during his tenure and was later named the "Eisenhower Interstate System" in his honor. Eisenhower had a mixed civil rights record, acting progressively on occasion. In 1957 he deployed the U.S. Army to integrate the high school in Little Rock, Arkansas, following the 1954 landmark civil rights case *Brown v. Board of Education*. Further, he introduced the 1957 and 1960 Civil Rights Acts.

Eisenhower reshaped U.S. politics by moderating Republicans and moving the party to the center. This laid the foundation for the modern Grand Old Party. Eisenhower's popularity helped Republicans recapture both houses of Congress in 1954, but his appeal was mainly personal and failed to dramatically help the party in future elections, including his 1956 landslide victory, when Republicans were unable to regain control of Congress. Although he cultivated a reputation as a chief executive who delegated power and responsibility, Eisenhower was intimately involved in decision making and policy development. He

1890

- **October 14**
Dwight David Eisenhower is born in Dennison, Texas.

1915

- Eisenhower graduates from West Point and is commissioned in the U.S. Army.

1935–1939

- Eisenhower serves as an aide to General Douglas MacArthur in the Philippines.

1943

- **December 24**
Eisenhower is appointed Supreme Allied Commander of the Western European Allies during World War II.

1944

- Eisenhower commands the planning and invasion of France.

1945

- **May 7**
Eisenhower accepts the surrender of Germany.

1950–1952

- Eisenhower serves as the first supreme commander of the North Atlantic Treaty Organization.

1952

- **November 4**
Eisenhower is elected president of the United States.

1953

- **January 20**
Eisenhower delivers his first inaugural address.

- **April 16**
Eisenhower delivers his "cross of iron" speech, also known as the "chance for peace" speech.

- **July 27**
A ceasefire agreement ends the Korean War.

- **December 8**
Eisenhower gives his Atoms for Peace speech before the United Nations.

maintained his personal popularity throughout his presidency, with approval ratings above 70 percent.

Explanation and Analysis of Documents

Eisenhower was president of the United States during a golden age of relative peace and prosperity that followed World War II and the opening years of the cold war. He was not a great orator, as he lacked the eloquence of Franklin D. Roosevelt or the intensity of Harry S. Truman. His speaking style during his prepared speeches was often described as plain, quiet, and blunt. This suited him well during an age when the availability and popularity of television expanded greatly. His oratory style and appearance conveyed a confident, grandfatherly image that resonated well with Americans. At a time of uncertainty about the growing power of the Soviet Union, Eisenhower was able to reassure Americans, and the public responded with a high degree of trust in the president. Eisenhower was not comfortable speaking extemporaneously. During press conferences, his answers were often confused and rambling. He was the first president to have an official speechwriter, Emmet J. Hughes, although many had previously used speechwriters in an unofficial manner. Eisenhower's style and his approach toward public speaking are demonstrated in six documents, all prepared speeches: his first inaugural address; the "cross of iron" speech, in which he expresses a desire for peace with the Soviet Union; his Atoms for Peace address to the United Nations, in which he advocates the peaceful use of nuclear energy; his promulgation of the Eisenhower Doctrine, in which he offers expanded U.S. aid to countries confronted by Soviet interventionism; his second inaugural address, entitled "The Price of Peace"; and his final official address, in which he warns of the dangers posed by the growing military-industrial complex within the United States.

◆ First Inaugural Address

Eisenhower was a moderate Republican and not overtly partisan, but he was well aware of his historic place as the nation's first Republican president in twenty years. Consequently, in his inaugural address he attempted to balance calls for bipartisanship with a message of change. Eisenhower begins his address of January 20, 1953, with a prayer in which he calls for Americans to be treated equally "regardless of station, race or calling." He also urges cooperation among those in the United States who "hold to differing political faiths." Eisenhower was able to effectively maintain a bipartisan consensus on foreign policy for most of his presidency. After the Democrats regained control of Congress following the 1954 midterm elections, Eisenhower reached out to congressional Democrats. He developed a working, though often tense, relationship with Lyndon Johnson, the Democratic Senate leader, and took a variety of steps to increase cooperation between the White House and Capitol Hill. For instance, the president directed agency heads to consult with Democratic committee chairmen in Congress before launching new programs or initiatives. Throughout the remainder of his presidency, Eisenhower frequently appealed for bipartisanship on major foreign policy and domestic issues.

Eisenhower devotes most of the rest of his first address as the new president to emphasizing the need for U.S. leadership in the worldwide struggle between freedom and oppression. He emphasizes the commonality of the United States and its major allies, including the British and French, and links the ongoing conflicts in Korea, Malaysia, and Indochina as all part of the larger conflict against Communist oppression. Eisenhower speaks of the trials and sacrifices that the United States endured in the past three decades, including the Great Depression, World War II, and the growing cold war. He notes that the United States did not seek to be a world leader, but that role had been thrust upon the nation.

Eisenhower pledges that his administration will be guided by nine principles. He asserts that the best way to achieve peace is through diplomatic strength and a willingness to reduce arms through negotiation and international treaty. He categorically rejects appeasement, however, and declares that "in the final choice a soldier's pack is not so heavy a burden as a prisoner's chains." Still, he notes that the United States would "never use our strength to try to impress upon another people our own cherished political and economic institutions"—a pledge that would later be broken through the use of covert operations and support for pro-American elements in countries such as Iran and Guatemala. Eisenhower affirms U.S. support for the United Nations and stresses the importance of strengthening the world body so that it could be more effective and better able to deal with international crises. He further pledges support for free and open trade and calls for the fulfillment of the charter of the United Nations through the creation of regional organizations. During his first term, he endeavored to strengthen NATO and was instrumental in the expansion of the alliance in 1955 to include West Germany. His administration would attempt to follow up on the success of NATO through the creation of regional collective defense organizations, including the Southeast Asia Treaty Organization in 1954 and the Central Treaty Organization, also known as the Baghdad Pact, in 1955. Both organizations were modeled after NATO and designed to contain Soviet expansion. The Southeast Asia Treaty Organization's members were Australia, France, New Zealand, Pakistan, the Philippines, Thailand, the United Kingdom, the United States, South Korea, and South Vietnam, while the Central Treaty Organization included Iran, Iraq, Turkey, Pakistan, and the United Kingdom.

In his first inaugural, Eisenhower goes on to seek to address charges that U.S. foreign policy was too focused on Europe and the ongoing conflict in Korea. Toward the end of his address, he states that "we hold all continents and peoples in equal regard and honor." He also rejects the notion that any one people or race might be inferior to another. This reflects Eisenhower's general opposition to colonialism. Throughout his presidency Eisenhower reiter-

ated support for independence movements, but his rhetoric did not always coincide with U.S. policy. For instance, the United States continued to support colonial powers such as Britain and France. The president did pressure France to relinquish control of Indochina, which led to the establishment of North and South Vietnam. He also opposed the Anglo-French-Israeli occupation of the Suez Canal in 1956 and forced the invading party to withdraw.

Eisenhower concludes his address by reminding Americans that "each citizen plays an indispensable role" in the global struggle against oppression and tyranny. He emphasizes the need for the United States to be a model for the rest of the world. In one of the closing lines, the new president states, "Whatever America hopes to bring to pass in the world must first come to pass in the heart of America." Many African Americans hoped that this sentiment was an indication of Eisenhower's support for civil rights.

◆ "Cross of Iron" Speech

Just months after he entered office, Eisenhower expanded on many of his foreign policy principles in a speech before the American Society of Newspaper Editors. Given on April 16, 1953, the speech came just over a month after

Time Line

1954

■ **March 1**
The United States detonates the first war-ready hydrogen bomb.

1956

■ **November 6**
Eisenhower is reelected president of the United States.

1957

■ **January 5**
In a special address to Congress the president promulgates the Eisenhower Doctrine.

■ **January 21**
Eisenhower delivers his second inaugural address, entitled "The Price of Peace."

1961

■ **January 17**
Eisenhower delivers his farewell address, also known as the "military industrial complex" speech.

1969

■ **March 28**
Eisenhower dies in Washington, D.C.

President Dwight D. Eisenhower and the country's new first lady, Mamie, wave to spectators from an open car as they leave the capitol at the start of the inauguration parade, January 20, 1953. (AP/Wide World Photos)

the death of the Soviet dictator Joseph Stalin. The address is alternatively known as either the "cross of iron" speech or the "chance for peace" speech. It was primarily written by Eisenhower's longtime aide Charles Douglas "C. D." Jackson. Eisenhower hoped to take advantage of new leadership in the Soviet Union to reduce U.S.-Soviet tensions. While he was a staunch proponent of a strong national defense, the former general also hoped to reduce military spending in order to increase funding for domestic programs.

Eisenhower begins the address by contrasting the paths of the United States and the Soviet Union. He asserts that in the post–World War II era, the United States and the Soviet Union, former wartime allies, were taking different approaches, with one promoting freedom, the other tyranny. In the first part of the speech Eisenhower addresses the differences between the two superpowers, highlighting what he describes as "clear precepts" that govern U.S. foreign policy, including multilateralism, the right of both political and economic self-determination, and the belief that security should be based on "just relations," not on the development of weapons or a powerful military. He contends that, on the other hand, for the Soviet Union "security was to be found, not in mutual trust and mutual aid but in force: huge armies, subversion, rule of neighbor nations." The president argues that the Soviets were actually undermining their own security through the post–World War II arms race with the West, which unified former wartime enemies such as France and Germany against the Soviet Union. He further notes that by diverting a growing amount of resources to the military, the Kremlin was reducing Soviet economic growth and the standard of living of its people.

Eisenhower points out that the arms race has hurt the people of the West as well. He declares, "We pay for a single destroyer with new homes that could have housed more than 8,000 people," and he cites other examples of how mil-

itary spending takes resources away from the economy and society. In a stern tone, he declares that the contemporary arms race has left "humanity hanging from a cross of iron" (giving the address the name by which it would be known).

Seeking to ameliorate the social, economic, and political costs of the cold war, Eisenhower proposes five broad areas in which the United States and the Soviet Union could reduce global tensions. First, he calls for limitations on the sizes of national militaries under an internationally agreed-upon standard. Second, he proposes restrictions on the proportion of a country's gross domestic product that could be devoted to the military. Third, he suggests that nuclear energy be used only for peaceful purposes and that there be an eventual ban on atomic weapons. Fourth, he proposes a prohibition on other forms of weapons of mass destruction. Fifth, the president calls for the United Nations to monitor compliance with his proposals and to develop an inspections system.

Eisenhower concludes his speech by challenging the Soviet Union with a series of questions. He asks if the Soviets could be ready to end military aid to North Korea and to work with the United States to create a lasting peace on the Korean peninsula. He questions whether the new Soviet leaders would allow the countries of Eastern Europe the freedom to choose their own political and economic systems. He also reiterates his call for the United Nations to monitor disarmament. Eisenhower closes by declaring that the United States did not have ulterior motivations but that his proposals came "from our calm conviction that the hunger for peace is in the hearts of all peoples—those of Russia and of China no less than of our own country."

The Soviets did not act on Eisenhower's peace proposals. Instead, Stalin's death ushered in a period of internal strife, as various leaders struggled to consolidate power and rule the Soviet Union. It was not until September 1953 that Nikita Khrushchev emerged as the leader within the Kremlin. Khrushchev, in fact, initiated a series of political reforms centered on a de-Stalinization plan intended to remove the worst excesses of the former regime. However, he continued to face resistance, including an aborted coup attempt in 1957. It was not until 1958 that Khrushchev was able to fully consolidate power. Throughout this period, his attention was focused on internal Soviet politics, and he was either unable or unwilling to pursue Eisenhower's arms control proposals.

◆ Atoms for Peace Speech

Eisenhower expanded his call for the peaceful use of nuclear energy in an address before the United Nations on December 8, 1953. The early drafts of this speech were also done by Charles Douglas Jackson. With continuing uncertainty about the leadership of the Soviet Union, Eisenhower hoped to use the United Nations to develop a global consensus on the use of nuclear power for peaceful energy production. He also sought to end the growing arms race between the United States and the Soviet Union, to fulfill one of the principles of his foreign policy and so that he could redirect resources toward domestic programs.

Finally, Eisenhower hoped to use the world body to develop tools to prevent nuclear proliferation.

Eisenhower's address came after the UN General Assembly adopted Resolution 715 on November 28, 1953. The resolution reiterated that the United Nations had a responsibility and interest in arms control and urged member states to work with the UN Disarmament Commission to facilitate global disarmament. The address also followed a five-day summit between Eisenhower, the British prime minister Winston Churchill, and the French prime minister Joseph Laniel that began on December 4, 1953. At that meeting, Churchill reported that British emissaries had approached the new Soviet government in an effort to gauge the possibility of détente. The British diplomats had been rebuffed, but the three Western leaders agreed that they should continue overtures to the Soviets and follow through on an earlier proposal by Eisenhower for four-party arms control talks that would include the United States, France, Great Britain, and the Soviet Union.

In the Atoms for Peace speech, Eisenhower begins by addressing the dangers posed by the growing nuclear arsenals. The president notes that the current atomic weaponry of the United States "exceeds by many times the total equivalent of the total of all bombs and all shells that came from every plane and every gun in every theatre of war in all the years of the Second World War." He also points out that a growing number of countries, including the Soviet Union, either had or were acquiring nuclear weapons technology. The president acknowledges that the United States had closely collaborated with Canada and the United Kingdom in the development of atomic weapons.

Eisenhower strongly affirms that the United States would use nuclear weapons to retaliate against any atomic attack on its soil, pledging that the nation would "inflict terrible losses upon an aggressor." The president then makes a transition, however, into a series of proposals to reduce the threat of nuclear armageddon. He assures the Soviet Union that the United States was seeking peace, not conflict, and a way to reduce nuclear stockpiles.

The president then invokes UN Resolution 715 and notes that the document calls for the creation of a "subcommittee consisting of representatives of the Powers principally involved" to develop a report for the world body on how to proceed with disarmament. In response to the resolution, then, Eisenhower proposes that the nations currently producing nuclear materials provide a proportion of that material to a new body, an international atomic energy agency, which would operate under the auspices of the United Nations. Eisenhower envisions that the agency would be "responsible for the impounding, storage and protection of the contributed fissionable and other materials." The atomic energy agency would also be directed to "apply atomic energy to the needs of agriculture, medicine and other peaceful activities." Furthermore, the agency would be tasked with providing "abundant electrical energy in the power-starved areas of the world." He notes that the United States would be "proud" to be involved in the endeavor. To demonstrate his seriousness, Eisenhower declares his

readiness to submit a multifaceted plan to the U.S. Congress that would encourage the peaceful use of nuclear energy throughout the world, reduce the nation's atomic weapons arsenal, and launch a new round of disarmament discussions with the Soviet Union, thus demonstrating that "the great Powers of the earth, both of the East and of the West, are interested in human aspirations first rather than in building up the armaments of war."

Although his proposals for détente with the Soviet Union did not come to fruition, the creation of the International Atomic Energy Agency, as Eisenhower named it, was unanimously approved by the United Nations in October 1956, and the agency began operations the following year. It was indeed charged with promoting the peaceful use of nuclear power and discouraging the proliferation of atomic weapons. The agency would emerge as one of the most important institutions of the United Nations and would play a major role in subsequent world affairs, including the negotiations surrounding the 1968 Nuclear Non-Proliferation Treaty and both the 1991 and 2003 wars in the Persian Gulf.

◆ **Special Message to Congress on the Eisenhower Doctrine**

By 1957 Eisenhower's hopes for détente were gone, and his administration had adopted an increasingly hard line against the Soviet Union. The year before, the Soviets invaded Hungary to overthrow a reformist government, and American policy makers believed that the Kremlin would use military force to expand its sphere of influence. After the 1956 Suez crisis, the Soviets attempted to increase their presence in the Middle East, specifically in Egypt. In response, Eisenhower proposed a series of measures that he articulated in a speech to Congress on January 5, 1957, measures collectively known as the Eisenhower Doctrine.

The president used the model of the 1947 Truman Doctrine, which promised military and economic assistance to countries that confronted Communist aggression. While the Truman Doctrine was initially applied to Greece and Turkey, the Eisenhower Doctrine would cover the Middle East. Eisenhower understood the strategic and economic importance of the region and wanted to safeguard its oil supplies. He also believed that with support from the United States, countries in the region could become democratic.

In his message to Congress, Eisenhower declares the world to be at a critical period, as an increasingly aggressive Soviet Union was seeking to bring countries under its sway. Eisenhower proclaims, "The Middle East has abruptly reached a new and critical stage in its long and important history." He states that the United States "supports without reservation the full sovereignty and independence of each and every nation of the Middle East." This statement was somewhat disingenuous in light of U.S. actions in Iran, but Eisenhower and many of his advisers perceived that American covert actions in Iran and other areas had been taken to prevent Soviet takeover. In the speech, the president acknowledges that the death of Stalin could have ushered in a new era in East-West relations but that the invasion of Hungary dashed any hopes for détente.

While the United Nations was the preferred avenue through which to settle international disputes, Eisenhower notes that the Soviet Union had vetoed attempts to compel the withdrawal of foreign forces from Hungary. Consequently, the president argues that the world could not depend on the United Nations to protect small countries from aggression.

Transitioning briefly to domestic concerns, Eisenhower notes that the White House and Congress had often reached across party divides to forge bipartisan foreign policy and protect the "national integrity of other free nations." He also points out that the United States shared defense agreements with forty-two nations and that these arrangements reinforced the collective defense mission of the United Nations.

Eisenhower proposes that the United States initiate programs of economic and military cooperation with nations of the Middle East. He informs Congress that he would ask for $200 million annually to support countries in the region. He also asks for Congress's assent to allow the president to use military force to protect nations facing "overt armed aggression from any nation controlled by International Communism." Eisenhower ties the new doctrine to previous actions by the United States and links the policy to a worldwide struggle between democracy and tyranny that began prior to World War II. He proclaims that the United States had already undertaken significant sacrifices to protect nations around the globe and that "these sacrifices, by which great areas of the world have been preserved to freedom, must not be thrown away."

The Eisenhower Doctrine was first invoked in 1958 when the president deployed fourteen thousand troops to Lebanon in response to a request by that country's president. The troops were able to end an ongoing civil war and stabilize the country; U.S. forces were withdrawn after three months. This was the only occasion during his presidency when Eisenhower ordered the deployment of a significant U.S. military force.

◆ Second Inaugural Address

Eisenhower was elected by a landslide in the 1956 election. He won 57.4 percent of the popular vote to Adlai Stevenson's 42 percent and 457 electoral votes to Stevenson's 73. His second inaugural address, entitled "The Price of Peace," was one of the most eloquent speeches that he gave while president. It was also one of the best inaugural addresses in U.S. history. Eisenhower spoke in broad generalities and discussed the contemporary state of world affairs in a much grander fashion than in many of his previous speeches.

The address was delivered on January 21, 1957, in the aftermath of the Soviet invasion of Hungary and the subsequent promulgation of the Eisenhower Doctrine. Therein, the reelected president calls on Americans to bear the economic, social, and military costs necessary to contain Communism and to promote freedom throughout the globe.

Eisenhower describes the abundance and prosperity that marked the United States and contrasts the nation's freedoms and high standard of living with the poverty and oppression afflicting so many around the world. Eisenhower notes that "new forces and new nations stir and strive across the earth" and that many of the world's people were entering new struggles to gain "freedom from grinding poverty." He declares that the United States, seeking to counter the forces of oppression, has one overriding "firm and fixed purpose—the building of a peace with justice in a world where moral law prevails."

The rest of the speech focuses on what the president describes as "the price of this peace." He argues that the United States would need not only to build and maintain a strong national defense but also to reach out and help other nations counter the growing threats on the international stage. This was especially important for the newly independent states emerging from the shadows of colonialism, as these countries were particularly vulnerable to the influence of outside forces. Eisenhower calls for Americans to use their scientific and technical skills to help reinforce democracy and free-market economies in developing nations. He contends that by lifting people out of poverty and ensuring their political freedom, the United States could prevent the threat of totalitarianism. However, this was a task that the country should not undertake in isolation; it should instead work through its allies and the United Nations to develop comprehensive approaches to global problems. Many historians have contended that the former general was warning against imperial overstretch, the tendency of powerful states to overextend military and economic resources in efforts to gain global primacy or even outright hegemony. Eisenhower assures other nations that the United States did not seek to exert undue power or control over their affairs. He affirms that the United States respected the independence of other countries and that "we no more seek to buy their sovereignty than we would sell our own."

During the 1956 election campaign, the president and many of his advisers became increasingly concerned that the prosperity of the United States would weaken the commitment of Americans to the cold war struggle and return the nation to the isolationism of the 1920s. Consequently, in his second inaugural address, Eisenhower warns of the dangers of isolationism. He points out that the nation's prosperity is based on economic interdependence and that the United States could not shut itself off from the rest of the world and maintain its standard of living. He also firmly declares that no nation could be a "fortress"; rather, efforts to build a "shelter" against the outside world were likely to result in a "prison."

Far more dramatic than his first inaugural speech, Eisenhower's 1957 address was designed for an international audience. Toward the end of the speech, the president reaches out to the Soviet Union and declares that the United States did not "dread" but instead welcomed the educational and industrial advances of the Soviet Union. Eisenhower asserts that he and the American people looked forward to the day when the two countries might "freely meet in friendship." He concludes by reaffirming the commitment of the United States to help overcome the divides separating the world and reduce the tensions of the contemporary superpower conflict.

Over the next three years Eisenhower worked to develop a nuclear test ban treaty with the Soviet Union. In July 1959 Vice President Richard Nixon went to the Soviet Union as part of a goodwill exhibition. In September, Khrushchev became the first Soviet leader to visit the United States after Eisenhower invited him to attend a summit at Camp David and to tour parts of the United States. However, the downing of an American U-2 spy plane over the Soviet Union in 1960 revived tensions and precluded the finalization of any comprehensive arms control agreement.

◆ **Farewell Address**

After the 1960 presidential election, Eisenhower's chief aides strongly encouraged him to deliver a farewell address. Eisenhower spoke to the nation on January 17, 1961, four days before John F. Kennedy was inaugurated. The speechwriter Malcolm Moos drafted the initial address, which was modified both by Eisenhower and by other staffers and advisers. In the speech the outgoing president bids farewell to the nation and wishes his successor well. He also states his belief that during his tenure relations between the executive and legislative branches had generally been cordial and productive and that the two branches had cooperated on the nation's vital interests. He speaks of the need for a strong military to deter aggression against the United States and to maintain peace.

The bulk of the address is concerned with the growing military-industrial complex in the United States. Eisenhower notes that the dangers the country faced in the world required a permanent defense industry, which, when combined with the direct spending on the military, absorbed more money each year than "the net income of all United States corporations." During his second term, defense spending accounted for about 53 percent of total government expenditures (some $49 billion per year) and about 10 percent of the nation's gross domestic product. This occurred despite the president's efforts to reduce overall government spending. However, Eisenhower's efforts and the growing economy did reduce the government's share of the gross domestic product from 24.5 percent to 20.05 percent. In the farewell address, Eisenhower accepts the need for the defense sector but reminds Americans that military planning, procurement, and research now touched the lives of almost every citizen. He notes that the present combination of an expansive military and an equally significant arms industry was "new in the American experience."

Eisenhower goes on to warn Americans that while the industrial defense sector was necessary, the nation needed to be vigilant to ensure that that sector did not acquire undue influence or undermine democracy. The former war hero's most famous line in the speech is his caution that "we must guard against the acquisition of unwarranted influence, whether sought or unsought, by the military

industrial complex." He cautions Americans to be ever vigilant to ensure that the military and the armaments sector fulfill their roles in safeguarding the nation without undermining the very ideals and principles they were supposed to protect. Eisenhower also advises the nation to be careful lest the best and brightest scholars be absorbed into the military-industrial complex. He notes the possibility that a "scientific technological elite" could emerge that would unduly influence public policy and divert government resources into projects and ventures that were not necessarily in the best interests of the nation.

Eisenhower concludes by declaring that it is the duty of the nation's leaders to strike the appropriate balance in dealing with the military-industrial complex. He also renews his call for détente and expresses his disappointment that significant arms control measures had not been achieved during his administration. Eisenhower's warning about the dangers of the military-industrial complex has resonated through the years with many Americans. Eisenhower's status as a former general and leader during World War II gave him a high degree of credibility on security matters, and he correctly foresaw the potential dangers of the growing relationship between the military and defense firms.

Impact and Legacy

Eisenhower remained immensely popular after he left office. Although he was not a great orator, his grandfatherly style and appearance reassured Americans, who remembered his presidency as a period of peace and prosperity between the Korean War and the Vietnam War. On several occasions, most notably in his second inaugural address and in the military-industrial speech, Eisenhower was eloquent and convincing, and the public regarded him with a high degree of trust. Consequently, as president, he was able to maintain a consensus on foreign and security policy in Congress and among the American public. While his arms-control efforts were not successful, Eisenhower and his administration were able to preserve the status quo in the cold war struggle and avoid major armed conflict with the Soviet Union or its proxies.

Eisenhower's calm, reassuring tone matched the general mood of the 1950s as an era of wealth and progress for most Americans. However, such prosperity was not universal. Groups such as African Americans remained excluded from the mainstream of U.S. political, social, and economic life. In addition, Eisenhower's oft-stated support for national sovereignty did not match the reality of his administration's actions in areas such as Iran and Guatemala.

Having learned firsthand of the horrors of war during his service in the military, Eisenhower sincerely sought to reduce superpower tensions and end the arms race between the United States and the Soviet Union. He also saw détente as a means to lessening U.S. defense spending and diminishing the dangers of the military-industrial complex. His opposition to imperialism was real, and his actions during the 1956 Suez crisis were a testament to his

"*Freedom is pitted against slavery; lightness against the dark.*"
(First Inaugural Address)

"*This is not a way of life at all, in any true sense. Under the cloud of threatening war, it is humanity hanging from a cross of iron.*"
("Cross of Iron" Speech)

"*Today, the United States stockpile of atomic weapons, which, of course, increases daily, exceeds by many times the total equivalent of the total of all bombs and all shells that came from every plane and every gun in every theatre of war in all the years of the Second World War.*"
(Atoms for Peace Speech)

"*Russia's rulers have long sought to dominate the Middle East. That was true of the Czars and it is true of the Bolsheviks.*"
(Special Message to Congress on the Eisenhower Doctrine)

"*From the deserts of North Africa to the islands of the South Pacific one third of all mankind has entered upon an historic struggle for a new freedom; freedom from grinding poverty.*"
(Second Inaugural Address)

"*We must use our skills and knowledge and, at times, our substance, to help others rise from misery, however far the scene of suffering may be from our shores. For wherever in the world a people knows desperate want, there must appear at least the spark of hope, the hope of progress—or there will surely rise at last the flames of conflict.*"
(Second Inaugural Address)

"*In the councils of government, we must guard against the acquisition of unwarranted influence, whether sought or unsought, by the military industrial complex.*"
(Farewell Address)

support for political self-determination. Ultimately, Eisenhower's public speeches and addresses reflected his idealism and desire for peace, while his policies often echoed his military background and his experiences during World War II. Initially many scholars assessed Eisenhower as an average president who often delegated matters to his chief advisers and cabinet officers. However, his status has improved over time as new evidence of his effectiveness and active role in decision making has emerged. Eisenhower is now generally rated as one of the top ten presidents of American history.

Key Sources

Johns Hopkins University Press has published a collection of Eisenhower's public and private papers from World War II through his presidency, including letters and his diary, titled *The Papers of Dwight David Eisenhower*. There is also an electronic version of the publication provided by the Eisenhower Memorial Commission (http://www.eisenhowermemorial.org/presidential-papers/index.htm). The National Archives has a collection of all of Eisenhower's official documents from his presidency. The archives and the Eisenhower Presidential Library have a digitization program through which original documents can be viewed online (http://www.eisenhower.archives.gov/dl/digital_docu

ments.html). A selection of Eisenhower's letters and correspondence with his wife are contained in *Letters to Mamie* (1978). Johns Hopkins University Press also published a collection of his prewar papers, *Eisenhower: The Prewar Diaries and Selected Papers, 1905–1941* (1998).

Further Reading

■ Articles

De Santis, Vincent P. "Eisenhower Revisionism."*Review of Politics* 38, no. 2 (April 1976): 190–207.

Greenstein, Fred I. "Eisenhower as an Activist President: A Look at New Evidence." *Political Science Quarterly* 94, no. 4 (Winter 1979–1980): 575–599.

Hart, John. "Eisenhower and the Swelling of the Presidency." *Polity* 24, no. 4 (Summer 1992): 673–691.

Immerman, Richard H. "Eisenhower and Dulles: Who Made the Decisions?" *Political Psychology* 1, no. 2 (Autumn 1979): 21–38.

■ Books

Ambrose, Stephen. *Eisenhower*. 2 vols. New York: Simon and Schuster, 1983–1984.

Questions for Further Study

1. Eisenhower was often ridiculed by intellectuals, many of whom regarded him as a bumbler and a do-nothing, yet much historical scholarship in later years has shown him to be a shrewd leader who, while fully involved in the issues of his day, presented the nation with a relaxed, calming image. Discuss Eisenhower's leadership style, goals, and values as expressed in his speeches. In what ways can he be justly credited for America's successes in the 1950s, and what failures can be attributed to him?

2. Compare Eisenhower's foreign policy, in the Eisenhower Doctrine and other speeches, to that of other presidents. Consider, for instance, how he expanded the Truman Doctrine, and address the issue of how consistent his ideas were with the principles set forth in the Monroe Doctrine.

3. What kind of world might have been created if the proposals in Eisenhower's Atoms for Peace speech had been put into action? Examine this question not only from the standpoint of the potential positive results he describes but also that of the pitfalls that such a proposal might have met in the international arena. Be sure to address the most notable concrete effect of that speech and his ideas on disarmament generally, the International Atomic Energy Agency.

4. It is interesting that Eisenhower, a military man and a conservative, coined the term *military-industrial complex* in his farewell address. Discuss what he meant by this expression and why he considered it so dangerous. How did other political figures in later years take up this issue, and what impact have such critics (beginning with Eisenhower) had on slowing the expansion of the military-industrial complex?

Brands, H. W. *Cold Warriors: Eisenhower's Generation and American Foreign Policy*. New York: Columbia University Press, 1988.

Dockrill, Saki. *Eisenhower's New-Look National Security Policy, 1953–61*. New York: St. Martin's Press, 1996.

Hewlett, Richard G., and Jack M. Holl. *Atoms for Peace and War, 1953–1961: Eisenhower and the Atomic Energy Commission*. Berkeley: University of California Press, 1989.

Korda, Michael. *Ike: An American Hero*. New York: Harper, 2007.

Lee, R. Alton. *Dwight D. Eisenhower, Soldier and Statesman*. Chicago: Nelson-Hall, 1981.

Perret, Geoffrey. *Eisenhower*. New York: Random House, 1999.

Rabe, Stephen G. *Eisenhower and Latin America: The Foreign Policy of Anticommunism*. Chapel Hill: University of North Carolina Press, 1988.

■ **Web Sites**

"Dwight David Eisenhower (1890–1969)." Miller Center of Public Affairs "American President: An Online Reference Resource" Web site. http://millercenter.org/academic/americanpresident/eisenhower.

—Tom Lansford

FIRST INAUGURAL ADDRESS (1953)

Give us, we pray, the power to discern clearly right from wrong, and allow all our words and actions to be governed thereby, and by the laws of this land. Especially we pray that our concern shall be for all the people regardless of station, race or calling.

May cooperation be permitted and be the mutual aim of those who, under the concepts of our Constitution, hold to differing political faiths; so that all may work for the good of our beloved country and Thy glory. Amen....

Freedom is pitted against slavery; lightness against the dark.

The faith we hold belongs not to us alone but to the free of all the world. This common bond binds the grower of rice in Burma and the planter of wheat in Iowa, the shepherd in southern Italy and the mountaineer in the Andes. It confers a common dignity upon the French soldier who dies in Indo-China, the British soldier killed in Malaya, the American life given in Korea.

We know, beyond this, that we are linked to all free peoples not merely by a noble idea but by a simple need. No free people can for long cling to any privilege or enjoy any safety in economic solitude. For all our own material might, even we need markets in the world for the surpluses of our farms and our factories. Equally, we need for these same farms and factories vital materials and products of distant lands. This basic law of interdependence, so manifest in the commerce of peace, applies with thousand-fold intensity in the event of war....

In pleading our just cause before the bar of history and in pressing our labor for world peace, we shall be guided by certain fixed principles. These principles are:

1. Abhorring war as a chosen way to balk the purposes of those who threaten us, we hold it to be the first task of statesmanship to develop the strength that will deter the forces of aggression and promote the conditions of peace. For, as it must be the supreme purpose of all free men, so it must be the dedication of their leaders, to save humanity from preying upon itself.

   In the light of this principle, we stand ready to engage with any and all others in joint effort to remove the causes of mutual fear and distrust among nations, so as to make possible drastic reduction of armaments. The sole requisites for undertaking such effort are that—in their purpose—they be aimed logically and honestly toward secure peace for all; and that—in their result—they provide methods by which every participating nation will prove good faith in carrying out its pledge.

2. Realizing that common sense and common decency alike dictate the futility of appeasement, we shall never try to placate an aggressor by the false and wicked bargain of trading honor for security. Americans, indeed, all free men, remember that in the final choice a soldier's pack is not so heavy a burden as a prisoner's chains.

3. Knowing that only a United States that is strong and immensely productive can help defend freedom in our world, we view our Nation's strength and security as a trust upon which rests the hope of free men everywhere. It is the firm duty of each of our free citizens and of every free citizen everywhere to place the cause of his country before the comfort, the convenience of himself.

4. Honoring the identity and the special heritage of each nation in the world, we shall never use our strength to try to impress upon another people our own cherished political and economic institutions.

5. Assessing realistically the needs and capacities of proven friends of freedom, we shall strive to help them to achieve their own security and well-being. Likewise, we shall count upon them to assume, within the limits of their resources, their full and just burdens in the common defense of freedom.

6. Recognizing economic health as an indispensable basis of military strength and the free world's peace, we shall strive to foster everywhere, and to practice ourselves, policies that encourage productivity and profitable trade.

For the impoverishment of any single people in the world means danger to the well-being of all other peoples.

7. Appreciating that economic need, military security and political wisdom combine to suggest regional groupings of free peoples, we hope, within the framework of the United Nations, to help strengthen such special bonds the world over. The nature of these ties must vary with the different problems of different areas.

   In the Western Hemisphere, we enthusiastically join with all our neighbors in the work of perfecting a community of fraternal trust and common purpose.

   In Europe, we ask that enlightened and inspired leaders of the Western nations strive with renewed vigor to make the unity of their peoples a reality. Only as free Europe unitedly marshals its strength can it effectively safeguard, even with our help, its spiritual and cultural heritage.

8. Conceiving the defense of freedom, like freedom itself, to be one and indivisible, we hold all continents and peoples in equal regard and honor. We reject any insinuation that one race or another, one people or another, is in any sense inferior or expendable.

9. Respecting the United Nations as the living sign of all people's hope for peace, we shall strive to make it not merely an eloquent symbol but an effective force. And in our quest for an honorable peace, we shall neither compromise, nor tire, nor ever cease....

We must be willing, individually and as a Nation, to accept whatever sacrifices may be required of us. A people that values its privileges above its principles soon loses both.

These basic precepts are not lofty abstractions, far removed from matters of daily living. They are laws of spiritual strength that generate and define our material strength. Patriotism means equipped forces and a prepared citizenry. Moral stamina means more energy and more productivity, on the farm and in the factory. Love of liberty means the guarding of every resource that makes freedom possible—from the sanctity of our families and the wealth of our soil to the genius of our scientists.

And so each citizen plays an indispensable role. The productivity of our heads, our hands and our hearts is the source of all the strength we can command, for both the enrichment of our lives and the winning of the peace.

No person, no home, no community can be beyond the reach of this call. We are summoned to act in wisdom and in conscience, to work with industry, to teach with persuasion, to preach with conviction, to weigh our every deed with care and with compassion. For this truth must be clear before us: whatever America hopes to bring to pass in the world must first come to pass in the heart of America.

Glossary

appeasement	a policy of giving in to the demands of aggressive powers in the hope that this will cause them to stop their aggression
impress	force
Malaya	a Southeast Asian nation, now known as Malaysia, that went through a difficult transition from British colonialism to full independence in the years 1946–1966

"CROSS OF IRON" SPEECH (1953)

The way chosen by the United States was plainly marked by a few clear precepts, which govern its conduct in world affairs.

First: No people on earth can be held, as a people, to be an enemy, for all humanity shares the common hunger for peace and fellowship and justice.

Second: No nation's security and well-being can be lastingly achieved in isolation but only in effective cooperation with fellow nations.

Third: Any nation's right to a form of government and an economic system of its own choosing is inalienable.

Fourth: Any nation's attempt to dictate to other nations their form of government is indefensible.

And fifth: A nation's hope of lasting peace cannot be firmly based upon any race in armaments but rather upon just relations and honest understanding with all other nations....

The Soviet government held a vastly different vision of the future.

In the world of its design, security was to be found, not in mutual trust and mutual aid but in force: huge armies, subversion, rule of neighbor nations. The goal was power superiority at all cost. Security was to be sought by denying it to all others.

The result has been tragic for the world and, for the Soviet Union, it has also been ironic....

Every gun that is made, every warship launched, every rocket fired signifies, in the final sense, a theft from those who hunger and are not fed, those who are cold and are not clothed. This world in arms is not spending money alone.

It is spending the sweat of its laborers, the genius of its scientists, the hopes of its children.

The cost of one modern heavy bomber is this: a modern brick school in more than 30 cities.

It is two electric power plants, each serving a town of 60,000 population.

It is two fine, fully equipped hospitals. It is some 50 miles of concrete highway.

We pay for a single fighter plane with a half million bushels of wheat.

We pay for a single destroyer with new homes that could have housed more than 8,000 people.

This, I repeat, is the best way of life to be found on the road the world has been taking.

This is not a way of life at all, in any true sense. Under the cloud of threatening war, it is humanity hanging from a cross of iron....

As progress in all these areas strengthens world trust, we could proceed concurrently with the next great work—the reduction of the burden of armaments now weighing upon the world. To this end we would welcome and enter into the most solemn agreements. These could properly include:

1. The limitation, by absolute numbers or by an agreed international ratio, of the sizes of the military and security forces of all nations.

2. A commitment by all nations to set an agreed limit upon that proportion of total production of certain strategic materials to be devoted to military purposes.

3. International control of atomic energy to promote its use for peaceful purposes only and to insure the prohibition of atomic weapons.

4. A limitation or prohibition of other categories of weapons of great destructiveness.

5. The enforcement of all these agreed limitations and prohibitions by adequate safeguards, including a practical system of inspection under the United Nations....

This idea of a just and peaceful world is not new or strange to us. It inspired the people of the United States to initiate the European Recovery Program in 1947. That program was prepared to treat, with like and equal concern, the needs of Eastern and Western Europe.

We are prepared to reaffirm, with the most concrete evidence, our readiness to help build a world in which all peoples can be productive and prosperous....

The monuments to this new kind of war would be these: roads and schools, hospitals and homes, food and health.

We are ready, in short, to dedicate our strength to serving the needs, rather than the fears, of the world.

We are ready, by these and all such actions, to make of the United Nations an institution that can effectively guard the peace and security of all peoples.

I know of nothing I can add to make plainer the sincere purpose of the United States.

I know of no course, other than that marked by these and similar actions, that can be called the highway of peace.

I know of only one question upon which progress waits. It is this:

What is the Soviet Union ready to do?

Whatever the answer be, let it be plainly spoken....

The test of truth is simple. There can be no persuasion but by deeds.

Is the new leadership of the Soviet Union prepared to use its decisive influence in the Communist world, including control of the flow of arms, to bring not merely an expedient truce in Korea but genuine peace in Asia?

Is it prepared to allow other nations, including those of Eastern Europe, the free choice of their own forms of government?

Is it prepared to act in concert with others upon serious disarmament proposals to be made firmly effective by stringent U.N. control and inspection?

If not, where then is the concrete evidence of the Soviet Union's concern for peace?

The test is clear.

There is, before all peoples, a precious chance to turn the black tide of events. If we failed to strive to seize this chance, the judgment of future ages would be harsh and just.

If we strive but fail and the world remains armed against itself, it at least need be divided no longer in its clear knowledge of who has condemned humankind to this fate.

The purpose of the United States, in stating these proposals, is simple and clear.

These proposals spring, without ulterior purpose or political passion, from our calm conviction that the hunger for peace is in the hearts of all peoples—those of Russia and of China no less than of our own country.

They conform to our firm faith that God created men to enjoy, not destroy, the fruits of the earth and of their own toil.

Glossary

European Recovery Program	official name for the Marshall Plan, a U.S. effort to rebuild Europe after World War II
race in armaments	competition to produce weapons and build armies

ATOMS FOR PEACE SPEECH (1953)

Today, the United States stockpile of atomic weapons, which, of course, increases daily, exceeds by many times the total equivalent of the total of all bombs and all shells that came from every plane and every gun in every theatre of war in all the years of the Second World War. A single air group whether afloat or land based, can now deliver to any reachable target a destructive cargo exceeding in power all the bombs that fell on Britain in all the Second World War.

But the dread secret and the fearful engines of atomic might are not ours alone.

In the first place, the secret is possessed by our friends and allies, the United Kingdom and Canada, whose scientific genius made a tremendous contribution to our original discoveries and the designs of atomic bombs.

The secret is also known by the Soviet Union. The Soviet Union has informed us that, over recent years, it has devoted extensive resources to atomic weapons. During this period the Soviet Union has exploded a series of atomic devices, including at least one involving thermo-nuclear reactions....

Should such an atomic attack be launched against the United States, our reactions would be swift and resolute. But for me to say that the defense capabilities of the United States are such that they could inflict terrible losses upon an aggressor, for me to say that the retaliation capabilities of the United States are so great that such an aggressor's land would be laid waste, all this, while fact, is not the true expression of the purpose and the hopes of the United States.

To pause there would be to confirm the hopeless finality of a belief that two atomic colossi are doomed malevolently to eye each other indefinitely across a trembling world. To stop there would be to accept helplessly the probability of civilization destroyed, the annihilation of the irreplaceable heritage of mankind handed down to us from generation to generation, and the condemnation of mankind to begin all over again the age-old struggle upward from savagery towards decency, and right, and justice. Surely no sane member of the human race could discover victory in such desolation. Could anyone wish his name to be coupled by history with such human degradation and destruction? Occasional pages of history do record the faces of the "great destroyers," but the whole book of history reveals mankind's never-ending quest for peace and mankind's God-given capacity to build....

We never have, and never will, propose or suggest that the Soviet Union surrender what rightly belongs to it. We will never say that the peoples of the USSR are an enemy with whom we have no desire ever to deal or mingle in friendly and fruitful relationship....

There is at least one new avenue of peace which has not been well explored—an avenue now laid out by the General Assembly of the United Nations.

In its resolution of 28 November 1953 (resolution 715 (VIII)) this General Assembly suggested: "that the Disarmament Commission study the desirability of establishing a sub-committee consisting of representatives of the Powers principally involved, which should seek in private an acceptable solution and report...on such a solution to the General Assembly and to the Security Council not later than 1 September 1954."...

I therefore make the following proposal.

The governments principally involved, to the extent permitted by elementary prudence, should begin now and continue to make joint contributions from their stockpiles of normal uranium and fissionable materials to an international atomic energy agency. We would expect that such an agency would be set up under the aegis of the United Nations. The ratios of contributions, the procedures and other details would properly be within the scope of the "private conversations" I referred to earlier....

The atomic energy agency could be made responsible for the impounding, storage and protection of the contributed fissionable and other materials. The ingenuity of our scientists will provide special safe conditions under which such a bank of fissionable material can be made essentially immune to surprise seizure.

The more important responsibility of this atomic energy agency would be to devise methods whereby this fissionable material would be allocated to serve the peaceful pursuits of mankind. Experts would be mobilized to apply atomic energy to the needs of agriculture, medicine and other peaceful activities. A special purpose would be to provide abundant electrical energy in the power-starved areas of the world....

The United States would be more than willing— it would be proud to take up with others "principally involved" the development of plans whereby such peaceful use of atomic energy would be expedited....

I would be prepared to submit to the Congress of the United States, and with every expectation of approval, any such plan that would, first, encourage world-wide investigation into the most effective peacetime uses of fissionable material, and with the certainty that the investigators had all the material needed for the conducting of all experiments that were appropriate; second, begin to diminish the potential destructive power of the world's atomic stockpiles; third, allow all peoples of all nations to see that, in this enlightened age, the great Powers of the earth, both of the East and of the West, are interested in human aspirations first rather than in building up the armaments of war; fourth, open up a new channel for peaceful discussion and initiative, at least a new approach to the many difficult problems that must be solved in both private and public conversations if the world is to shake off the inertia imposed by fear and is to make positive progress towards peace.

Glossary

aegis	protection
colossi	giants
elementary prudence	simple common sense
Security Council	the United Nations body responsible for maintaining international security
thermo-nuclear reactions	fusion, or the joining of atomic nuclei, which produces an even more powerful weapon (the so-called hydrogen bomb) than fission, or splitting

SPECIAL ADDRESS TO CONGRESS ON THE EISENHOWER DOCTRINE (1957)

The Middle East has abruptly reached a new and critical stage in its long and important history. In past decades many of the countries in that area were not fully self-governing.... Our country supports without reservation the full sovereignty and independence of each and every nation of the Middle East....

Russia's rulers have long sought to dominate the Middle East. That was true of the Czars and it is true of the Bolsheviks....

The reason for Russia's interest in the Middle East is solely that of power politics. Considering her announced purpose of Communizing the world, it is easy to understand her hope of dominating the Middle East....

Stalin's death brought hope that this pattern would change. And we read the pledge of the Warsaw Treaty of 1955 that the Soviet Union would follow in satellite countries "the principles of mutual respect for their independence and sovereignty and noninterference in domestic affairs." But we have just seen the subjugation of Hungary by naked armed force. In the aftermath of this Hungarian tragedy, world respect for and belief in Soviet promises have sunk to a new low. International Communism needs and seeks a recognizable success....

Our thoughts naturally turn to the United Nations as a protector of small nations.... The United Nations was able to bring about a cease-fire and withdrawal of hostile forces from Egypt because it was dealing with governments and peoples who had a decent respect for the opinions of mankind as reflected in the United Nations General Assembly. But in the case of Hungary, the situation was different. The Soviet Union vetoed action by the Security Council to require the withdrawal of Soviet armed forces from Hungary. And it has shown callous indifference to the recommendations, even the censure, of the General Assembly. The United Nations can always be helpful, but it cannot be a wholly dependable protector of freedom when the ambitions of the Soviet Union are involved....

It is nothing new for the President and the Congress to join to recognize that the national integrity of other free nations is directly related to our own security.

We have joined to create and support the security system of the United Nations. We have reinforced the collective security system of the United Nations by a series of collective defense arrangements. Today we have security treaties with 42 other nations which recognize that our peace and security are intertwined. We have joined to take decisive action in relation to Greece and Turkey and in relation to Taiwan....

The action which I propose would have the following features.

It would, first of all, authorize the United States to cooperate with and assist any nation or group of nations in the general area of the Middle East in the development of economic strength dedicated to the maintenance of national independence.

It would, in the second place, authorize the Executive to undertake in the same region programs of military assistance and cooperation with any nation or group of nations which desires such aid.

It would, in the third place, authorize such assistance and cooperation to include the employment of the armed forces of the United States to secure and protect the territorial integrity and political independence of such nations, requesting such aid, against overt armed aggression from any nation controlled by International Communism....

The present proposal would, in the fourth place, authorize the President to employ, for economic and defensive military purposes, sums available under the Mutual Security Act of 1954, as amended, without regard to existing limitations.

The legislation now requested should not include the authorization or appropriation of funds because I believe that, under the conditions I suggest, presently appropriated funds will be adequate for the balance of the present fiscal year ending June 30. I shall, however, seek in subsequent legislation the authorization of $200,000,000 to be available during each of the fiscal years 1958 and 1959 for discretionary use in the area, in addition to the other mutual security programs for the area hereafter provided for by the Congress....

The proposed legislation is primarily designed to deal with the possibility of Communist aggression, direct and indirect....

Experience shows that indirect aggression rarely if ever succeeds where there is reasonable security against direct aggression; where the government disposes of loyal security forces, and where economic conditions are such as not to make Communism seem an attractive alternative....

It is my hope and belief that if our purpose be proclaimed, as proposed by the requested legislation, that very fact will serve to halt any contemplated aggression. We shall have heartened the patriots who are dedicated to the independence of their nations. They will not feel that they stand alone, under the menace of great power....

And as I have indicated, it will also be necessary for us to contribute economically to strengthen those countries, or groups of countries, which have governments manifestly dedicated to the preservation of independence and resistance to subversion. Such measures will provide the greatest insurance against Communist inroads. Words alone are not enough....

In the situation now existing, the greatest risk, as is often the case, is that ambitious despots may miscalculate. If power-hungry Communists should either falsely or correctly estimate that the Middle East is inadequately defended, they might be tempted to use open measures of armed attack. If so, that would start a chain of circumstances which would almost surely involve the United States in military action. I am convinced that the best insurance against this dangerous contingency is to make clear now our readiness to cooperate fully and freely with our friends of the Middle East in ways consonant with the purposes and principles of the United Nations. I intend promptly to send a special mission to the Middle East to explain the cooperation we are prepared to give....

Indeed, the sacrifices of the American people in the cause of freedom have, even since the close of World War II, been measured in many billions of dollars and in thousands of the precious lives of our youth. These sacrifices, by which great areas of the world have been preserved to freedom, must not be thrown away.

In those momentous periods of the past, the President and the Congress have united, without partisanship, to serve the vital interests of the United States and of the free world.

Glossary

appropriation	the act of setting aside public funds for a specific purpose
Bolsheviks	technically the term for the Social Democratic (Communist) Party faction that seized control of Russia in 1917; used here to refer to Soviet Communists in general
Mutual Security Act of 1954	an act of Congress providing for U.S. developmental assistance to countries deemed strategically important
national integrity	genuine independence, as opposed to being a puppet state under the control of a superpower
Security Council	the United Nations body responsible for maintaining international security, which consists of five permanent members (Russia, China, France, Britain, and the United States) and ten elected members
subjugation of Hungary by naked armed force	a reference to the violent repression by Soviet forces of a popular uprising against Communist rule in Hungary in 1956
Warsaw Treaty of 1955	a military, social, and political pact between the Soviet Union and most Communist nations of Eastern Europe

SECOND INAUGURAL ADDRESS (1957)

We live in a land of plenty, but rarely has this earth known such peril as today.

In our nation work and wealth abound. Our population grows. Commerce crowds our rivers and rails, our skies, harbors, and highways. Our soil is fertile, our agriculture productive. The air rings with the song of our industry—rolling mills and blast furnaces, dynamos, dams, and assembly lines—the chorus of America the bountiful.

This is our home—yet this is not the whole of our world. For our world is where our full destiny lies—with men, of all people, and all nations, who are or would be free. And for them—and so for us—this is no time of ease or of rest.

In too much of the earth there is want, discord, danger. New forces and new nations stir and strive across the earth, with power to bring, by their fate, great good or great evil to the free world's future. From the deserts of North Africa to the islands of the South Pacific one third of all mankind has entered upon an historic struggle for a new freedom; freedom from grinding poverty. Across all continents, nearly a billion people seek, sometimes almost in desperation, for the skills and knowledge and assistance by which they may satisfy from their own resources, the material wants common to all mankind.

No nation, however old or great, escapes this tempest of change and turmoil. Some, impoverished by the recent World War, seek to restore their means of livelihood. In the heart of Europe, Germany still stands tragically divided. So is the whole continent divided. And so, too, is all the world.

The divisive force is International Communism and the power that it controls.

The designs of that power, dark in purpose, are clear in practice. It strives to seal forever the fate of those it has enslaved. It strives to break the ties that unite the free. And it strives to capture—to exploit for its own greater power—all forces of change in the world, especially the needs of the hungry and the hopes of the oppressed.

Yet the world of International Communism has itself been shaken by a fierce and mighty force: the readiness of men who love freedom to pledge their lives to that love. Through the night of their bondage, the unconquerable will of heroes has struck with the swift, sharp thrust of lightning. Budapest is no longer merely the name of a city; henceforth it is a new and shining symbol of man's yearning to be free.

Thus across all the globe there harshly blow the winds of change. And, we—though fortunate be our lot—know that we can never turn our backs to them.

We look upon this shaken earth, and we declare our firm and fixed purpose—the building of a peace with justice in a world where moral law prevails.

The building of such a peace is a bold and solemn purpose. To proclaim it is easy. To serve it will be hard. And to attain it, we must be aware of its full meaning—and ready to pay its full price.

We know clearly what we seek, and why.

We seek peace, knowing that peace is the climate of freedom. And now, as in no other age, we seek it because we have been warned, by the power of modern weapons, that peace may be the only climate possible for human life itself....

We are called to meet the price of this peace.

To counter the threat of those who seek to rule by force, we must pay the costs of our own needed military strength, and help to build the security of others.

We must use our skills and knowledge and, at times, our substance, to help others rise from misery, however far the scene of suffering may be from our shores. For wherever in the world a people knows desperate want, there must appear at least the spark of hope, the hope of progress—or there will surely rise at last the flames of conflict.

We recognize and accept our own deep involvement in the destiny of men everywhere. We are accordingly pledged to honor, and to strive to fortify, the authority of the United Nations. For in that body rests the best hope of our age for the assertion of that law by which all nations may live in dignity....

For one truth must rule all we think and all we do. No people can live to itself alone. The unity of all who dwell in freedom is their only sure defense. The economic need of all nations—in mutual dependence—makes isolation an impossibility; not even America's prosperity could long survive if other nations did not also prosper. No nation can longer be a fortress, lone and strong and safe. And any people, seeking such shelter for themselves, can now build only their own prison.

Our pledge to these principles is constant, because we believe in their rightness.

We do not fear this world of change. America is no stranger to much of its spirit. Everywhere we see the seeds of the same growth that America itself has known. The American experiment has, for generations, fired the passion and the courage of millions elsewhere seeking freedom, equality, and opportunity. And the American story of material progress has helped excite the longing of all needy peoples for some satisfaction of their human wants. These hopes that we have helped to inspire, we can help to fulfill.

In this confidence, we speak plainly to all peoples.

We cherish our friendship with all nations that are or would be free. We respect, no less, their independence. And when, in time of want or peril, they ask our help, they may honorably receive it; for we no more seek to buy their sovereignty than we would sell our own. Sovereignty is never bartered among freemen.

We honor the aspirations of those nations which, now captive, long for freedom. We seek neither their military alliance nor any artificial imitation of our society. And they can know the warmth of the welcome that awaits them when, as must be, they join again the ranks of freedom.

We honor, no less in this divided world than in a less tormented time, the people of Russia. We do not dread, rather do we welcome, their progress in education and industry. We wish them success in their demands for more intellectual freedom, greater security before their own laws, fuller enjoyment of the rewards of their own toil. For as such things come to pass, the more certain will be the coming of that day when our peoples may freely meet in friendship.

So we voice our hope and our belief that we can help to heal this divided world. Thus may the nations cease to live in trembling before the menace of force. Thus may the weight of fear and the weight of arms be taken from the burdened shoulders of mankind.

Glossary

blast furnaces	furnaces used for producing iron and other ores
Budapest	capital of Hungary, where much of the resistance fighting took place during the 1956 revolt against Soviet rule
dynamos	electrical generators
meet	pay
our substance	our possessions
rolling mills	factories for shaping metals

FAREWELL ADDRESS (1961)

In this final relationship, the Congress and the Administration have, on most vital issues, cooperated well, to serve the national good rather than mere partisanship, and so have assured that the business of the Nation should go forward. So, my official relationship with the Congress ends in a feeling, on my part, of gratitude that we have been able to do so much together....

A vital element in keeping the peace is our military establishment. Our arms must be mighty, ready for instant action, so that no potential aggressor may be tempted to risk his own destruction....

Until the latest of our world conflicts, the United States had no armaments industry. American makers of plowshares could, with time and as required, make swords as well. But now we can no longer risk emergency improvisation of national defense; we have been compelled to create a permanent armaments industry of vast proportions. Added to this, three and a half million men and women are directly engaged in the defense establishment. We annually spend on military security more than the net income of all United States corporations.

This conjunction of an immense military establishment and a large arms industry is new in the American experience. The total influence—economic, political, even spiritual—is felt in every city, every State house, every office of the Federal government. We recognize the imperative need for this development. Yet we must not fail to comprehend its grave implications. Our toil, resources and livelihood are all involved; so is the very structure of our society.

In the councils of government, we must guard against the acquisition of unwarranted influence, whether sought or unsought, by the military industrial complex. The potential for the disastrous rise of misplaced power exists and will persist.

We must never let the weight of this combination endanger our liberties or democratic processes. We should take nothing for granted. Only an alert and knowledgeable citizenry can compel the proper meshing of the huge industrial and military machinery of defense with our peaceful methods and goals, so that security and liberty may prosper together....

The prospect of domination of the nation's scholars by Federal employment, project allocations, and the power of money is ever present and is gravely to be regarded. Yet, in holding scientific research and discovery in respect, as we should, we must also be alert to the equal and opposite danger that public policy could itself become the captive of a scientific technological elite.

It is the task of statesmanship to mold, to balance, and to integrate these and other forces, new and old, within the principles of our democratic system—ever aiming toward the supreme goals of our free society.

Another factor in maintaining balance involves the element of time. As we peer into society's future, we—you and I, and our government—must avoid the impulse to live only for today, plundering, for our own ease and convenience, the precious resources of tomorrow. We cannot mortgage the material assets of our grandchildren without risking the loss also of their political and spiritual heritage. We want democracy to survive for all generations to come, not to become the insolvent phantom of tomorrow....

Disarmament, with mutual honor and confidence, is a continuing imperative. Together we must learn how to compose differences, not with arms, but with intellect and decent purpose. Because this need is so sharp and apparent I confess that I lay down my official responsibilities in this field with a definite sense of disappointment. As one who has witnessed the horror and the lingering sadness of war—as one who knows that another war could utterly destroy this civilization which has been so slowly and painfully built over thousands of years—I wish I could say tonight that a lasting peace is in sight.

Glossary

allocations	portions of money set aside for specific purposes
plowshares ... swords	terminology derived from several Bible verses contrasting peaceful and military purposes

Stephen J. Field (Library of Congress)

STEPHEN J. FIELD

1816–1899

Supreme Court Justice

Featured Documents
- *Cummings v. Missouri* (1867)
- *Munn v. Illinois* (1876)
- *Ho Ah Kow v. Nunan* (1879)
- "The Centenary of the Supreme Court of the United States" (1890)

Overview

Stephen Johnson Field was born into a prominent family in Haddam, Connecticut, on November 4, 1816. He graduated at the top of his class from Williams College in 1837 and studied law in the office of his brother David Dudley Field. The California gold rush enticed Field to travel to California in 1849; instead of mining, however, he turned to law and politics. The following year, Field was elected as a Democrat to the California assembly, where he served one term and was pivotal in codifying civil and criminal procedures. Field soon became one of the most prominent attorneys in California. In 1857 Field was elected to the California Supreme Court and became chief justice there in 1859. Because he was both colorful and dogmatic, Field made numerous enemies as well as friends. In 1863 Congress increased the size of the U.S. Supreme Court with the addition of a tenth seat in an attempt to garner further support in California for the Civil War. Although he was a Democrat, Field was a strong supporter of the Union cause. President Abraham Lincoln's nomination of Field to the U.S. Supreme Court was promptly confirmed by the Senate. Field continued his interest in politics, making unsuccessful bids for the Democratic presidential nomination in 1880 and 1884. Field would serve on the Supreme Court until December 1897, long enough to set a new record for service. He died in Washington, D.C., on April 9, 1899, less than eighteen months after leaving the court.

On the Supreme Court, Field became the most influential justice of the Gilded Age. His constitutional philosophy was derived from precepts of natural law (holding that there were certain eternal principles inherent in the universe and that laws must embody these principles to be regarded as legitimate) and his aversion to special privileges and class legislation, akin to Andrew Jackson's. Field championed a broad reading of the Fourteenth Amendment, adopted in 1868, to safeguard inalienable rights that did not expressly appear in the Constitution. A central principle of Field's constitutionalism was an attachment to individual liberty, a concept he defined largely but not exclusively in terms of economic freedom. Like most of his contemporaries on the bench, Field demonstrated little interest in equality as a constitutional norm. For example, he consistently refused to use the Fourteenth Amendment to shield blacks from discrimination by the states. Rather than defer to legislative judgments, Field believed that courts should actively safeguard individual rights, especially property and contractual rights.

An important dimension of Field's individualistic belief was deep hostility to government policies aimed at redistribution. He especially disliked property confiscation, and he played a leading role in persuading the Supreme Court to construe narrowly the power of Congress to confiscate Confederate-owned property after the Civil War. Field similarly sought to circumscribe state regulation of railroad and utility charges, fearing that the exercise of such power might constitute a kind of confiscation of property through the imposition of rates that were too low to support commerce. Field's disdain for redistributive programs was also evident in his frequent votes to invoke the contract clause to block efforts by local governments to repudiate their bonded debt. The most dramatic sign of Field's anti-redistributive principles was his joining the majority in *Pollock v. Farmers' Loan and Trust Co.* (1895) to invalidate the 1894 income tax as an unconstitutional direct tax. The basic issue in this case was the legitimacy of using federal taxing authority to alter the market-determined distribution of wealth. Such a levy was odious to Field, who saw it as a form of class legislation. Still, it would be a mistake to caricature Field as a one-sided defender of business interests. He voted to uphold numerous health and safety regulations that were within the scope of traditional state police power. Field was also skeptical of government-conferred monopoly privilege and was sympathetic to the claims of employees injured in industrial accidents. He was concerned to safeguard what he saw as the natural rights of individuals to follow ordinary avocations. Field contributed significantly to the interpretation of the Fourteenth Amendment, although the Supreme Court never protected property rights and entrepreneurial freedom to the extent he desired. Field had an irascible personality and a tendency to hold grudges that made him a vexing colleague of his fellow justices. By the mid-1890s he had become increasingly feeble and wrote few opinions. He died in 1899 at the age of eighty-four.

Explanation and Analysis of Documents

Field joined the U.S. Supreme Court in 1863 when American society was experiencing sweeping changes.

1816

■ **November 4**
Stephen J. Field is born in
Haddam, Connecticut.

1837

■ Field graduates as
valedictorian from Williams
College.

1841

■ Field is admitted to the
New York bar and begins
a seven-year partnership
with his older brother,
David Dudley Field.

1850

■ Field is elected to the
California Assembly and
serves one term.

1857

■ Field is elected to the
Supreme Court of
California.

1859

■ Field is selected to be
chief justice of the
California Supreme Court.

1863

■ **May 20**
Field takes the oath as the
tenth justice on the U.S.
Supreme Court.

1867

■ **January 14**
Field delivers the Court's
opinion in *Cummings v.
Missouri.*

1877

■ **March 1**
The case of *Munn v. Illinois*
is decided, with Field
delivering a dissenting
opinion.

1879

■ Field delivers a circuit
court opinion in *Ho Ah
Kow v. Nunan.*

1890

■ Field delivers an address
on the centenary of the
Supreme Court of the
United States.

Early in his tenure, issues arising from the Civil War and Reconstruction dominated the Court's docket. The emergence of a new industrial order and large-scale corporate enterprises were also raising novel constitutional questions. The justices grappled with increased regulation of the economy in a constitutional system committed to private property and limited government. A central question was the extent to which the Fourteenth Amendment (1868) altered the federal-state balance and protected economic freedom from state regulation. The Fourteenth Amendment conferred citizenship upon all persons born in the United States and declared that no state could abridge "the privileges or immunities" of citizens, deprive any person of "life, liberty, or property, without due process of law," or deny any person "the equal protection of the laws."

Field was a champion of individual liberty, which in his mind included entrepreneurial freedom. Anxious to safeguard liberty by confining the reach of government, he insisted that the due process clause of the Fourteenth Amendment protected substantive rights. Substantive due process meant that there were certain individual rights, such as the right to acquire property or enter contracts, which government could not arbitrarily abridge. Thus, the due process norm limited legislative power. The due process clause provides both procedural and substantive protection of individual rights. The procedural component of due process requires fair procedures before an individual can be deprived of life, liberty, or property. The substantive component imposes an absolute limit on governmental action regardless of the procedure followed. Field envisioned an active role for the federal judiciary in upholding rights from state abridgement. Although his ideas were often advanced in dissenting opinions, his thinking came to dominate the Court in the late nineteenth century. Four documents demonstrate Field's mode of judicial analysis and his view of the role of the Supreme Court: his opinion for the Court in *Cummings v. Missouri*, his dissenting opinion in *Munn v. Illinois*, his circuit court opinion in *Ho Ah Kow v. Nunan*, and his address on the centenary of the Supreme Court.

◆ ***Cummings v. Missouri***

Following the Civil War, many states passed laws requiring any person in public office or in certain professions to take a loyalty oath to the Union. These laws were intended to prevent those who had supported or sympathized with the Confederacy from gaining a position of influence or power. It was feared that southern sympathizers in government might undermine the Union victory on the battlefield. The Missouri state constitution included such an oath provision. John A. Cummings was a Catholic priest in Missouri who refused to take the loyalty oath and continued to preach. Fined $500, he appealed to the Missouri Supreme Court, which upheld the requirement. On appeal to the U.S. Supreme Court, David Dudley Field, the brother of Justice Field, argued on behalf of Cummings. Writing for a five to four majority, Justice Field ruled that the oath provisions were ex post facto laws that punish a person for acts that had not been criminal at the time they were committed and constituted bills of attainder, or legislation that inflicts punishment on a person without a judicial trial.

The Bill of Rights was originally understood to apply only to the federal government, and so *Cummings* turned to the specific constitutional restrictions on state power. Article I, Section 10 of the U.S. Constitution bars states from passing any laws that are either ex post facto or bills of attainder. Since both provisions pertained to punishments, the first question was whether the loyalty oath provisions in Missouri's constitution amounted to penalties. The state of Missouri argued that in order to punish a person, he or she must be deprived of life, liberty, or property and that the loyalty oaths were merely a qualification for holding office or pursuing lawful avocations. Rejecting this contention, Field insists in this opinion that the laws were designed to punish persons who refused to take the oath and were not designed to establish fitness for the designated posts: "The oath could not ... have been required as a means of ascertaining whether parties were qualified or not for their respective callings or the trusts with which they were charged." Invoking the Declaration of Independence, he maintains that the pursuit of happiness encompasses "all avocations, all honors, all positions" and "deprivation or suspension of any of these rights for past conduct" is a penalty.

Once the Court had decided that the loyalty oaths constituted punishment for those who refused to take the oath, it held that the laws were, in fact, both bills of attainder and ex post facto laws. Field writes that the clauses in question "subvert the presumptions of innocence" and alter the fundamental rules of evidence. The laws are aimed at past rather than future actions. They assume guilt and forced parties to prove their innocence by the only means available, an expurgatory oath—an oath that swore that a person had never been a Confederate supporter or sympathizer. Field maintains that the laws are also bills of attainder because they do not afford an individual the right to a trial for removal of the disability. He concludes that if states were allowed to circumvent the provision of the federal Constitution directed at protecting the liberty of all citizens, there would be no guarantee anywhere in the Constitution that could not likewise be evaded. The immediate impact of the *Cummings* decision was to undercut efforts to keep former Confederates from regaining political and professional ascendancy. Field's opinion remains good law. It was invoked by the Supreme Court in subsequent cases dealing with loyalty oaths in the twentieth century. The decision continues to be cited by federal courts and discussed by scholars in the twenty-first century.

◆ Munn v. Illinois

By the 1870s railroads were increasingly dominating American economic life. Merchants and farmers were often dependent on rail services to ship their goods to distant markets. There were chronic complaints about excessive and discriminatory freight charges. Resentment over alleged rate discrimination was at the root of the clamor for governmental regulation. Although some of the charges

Time Line

1897

■ **December 1**
Field retires from the Supreme Court with the longest record of service to that point.

1899

■ **April 9**
Field dies in Washington, D.C., at the age of eighty-four.

directed at railroads were exaggerated, the railroads did exercise virtually unchecked authority to fix charges and determine the level of service they supplied. In addition to these economic concerns, many observers feared that railroads also enjoyed undue political clout in legislative bodies. Finally, railroads were the most visible symbol of the emerging industrial order and the national market for goods. As such, they were often treated as scapegoats for larger economic frustrations felt by segments of the public.

Growing sentiment against the railroads found expression in the so-called Granger laws passed in a number of midwestern states. These laws established powerful commissions that were authorized to set maximum rates for railroads and related businesses. Arguing that these rate regulations would retard the construction of new lines, the railroad companies engineered repeal or modification of some Granger laws. They also challenged the constitutionality of rate regulations by states in a group of cases that raised key questions about state authority to control charges for use of private property. A crucial line of inquiry was whether the rate-regulation laws constituted the confiscation of property without due process of law, in violation of the Fourteenth Amendment.

In a cluster of decisions known as the Granger Cases, the Supreme Court rejected the constitutional attack on the authority of states to set rates. At issue in the most important case, *Munn v. Illinois* (1877), was an Illinois law regulating the charges for storing grain in elevators. Chief Justice Morrison R. Waite declares in the majority opinion that "when private property is devoted to a public use, it is subject to public regulation." Waite agrees that owners of property "clothed with a public interest" were entitled to reasonable compensation, but he insists that the determination of such compensation was a legislative and not a judicial task. "For protection against abuses by the legislature," Waite observes, "the people must resort to the polls, not the courts." Adopting a narrow view of the protection given private property under the Fourteenth Amendment's due process clause, he thus seemingly shut the door on judicial review of state-imposed rates.

Field vigorously disagreed, articulating the view that the due process clause of the Fourteenth Amendment protected economic liberty from state regulation. In his dissent he first maintains that property ownership went beyond title and possession and included the right to use and derive income

Periodical illustration showing a Chinese person asking a missionary why he may go to heaven but not to the United States, to which the missionary replies, "There is no labor vote in heaven." (Library of Congress)

from the property. Field then insists that the due process clause "has a much more extended operation" than courts had previously recognized. The due process norm, he continues, "has been supposed to secure to every individual the essential conditions for the pursuit of happiness" and should therefore not be construed "in any narrow or restricted sense." He next broadly defines liberty as more than freedom from physical restraint. To Field, liberty encompassed the right of a person to "pursue such callings and avocations as may be most suitable to develop his capacities." In a key portion of his dissent Field states that property should receive the same "liberal" protection as liberty.

Turning to the question of state rate regulation, Field observes:

> If the legislature of a State, under the pretense of providing for the public good, or for any other reason, can determine, against the consent of the owner, the uses to which private property shall be devoted, or the prices which the owner shall receive for its uses, it can deprive him of the property as completely as by a special act for its confiscation or destruction.

Field concludes by insisting that constitutional protection of property was meaningless unless it extended to use and income as well as title and possession. Although Field did not prevail in *Munn*, his dissent paved the way for heightened judicial scrutiny of railroad rate regulations in

the late nineteenth century. Equally important, his expansive definition of liberty and property would prove influential as courts grappled with the scope of the due process guarantee. Field did much to advance the view that due process guaranteed substantive rights.

◆ Ho Ah Kow v. Nunan

Until 1891 the Supreme Court justices were required to serve as judges for their respective circuit courts twice a year. In 1879, while presiding on the circuit court in California, Field heard the case of *Ho Ah Kow v. Nunan*. The large-scale immigration of Chinese laborers into the United States had fueled virulent anti-Chinese sentiment on the West Coast. There was persistent pressure to halt further Chinese immigration and to restrict Chinese immigrants already in the United States. In 1870 the California legislature passed an ordinance requiring boardinghouses to provide at least five hundred cubic feet of air per person. Any person occupying a room that did not meet these specifications could be punished by a fine of $50 or imprisonment. This law was aimed at the ever-expanding Chinese immigrant population in the state. The Chinese largely frustrated the law by accepting jail terms rather than paying the fines. To give the statute more teeth, San Francisco's Board of Supervisors then passed a city ordinance directing jailers to cut the hair of every male prisoner to a uniform length of one inch. It was well known that hair braided into a queue had spiritual meaning for Chinese men. Hence, the ordinance would either intimidate them into paying the fine rather than accepting imprisonment and having their hair cut or punish them further if they were imprisoned. In 1878 Ho Ah Kow was convicted of violating the statute. Defaulting on his fine, he was imprisoned, and the sheriff cut his queue. Ho Ah Kow sued the sheriff under a federal civil rights statute. When the case came to him, Field struck down the city ordinance, finding a host of objections.

The state of California argued that the ordinance was a mere sanitary regulation put in place to help identify prisoners as well as to prevent disease. In his opinion, Field dismisses this argument, pointing out that if the ordinance had been enacted for sanitary reasons, it would have applied to both men and women rather than simply to men. Field states that it would also have been implemented for parties awaiting trial as well as for those convicted. He insists that the clipping of the hair was done neither for sanitary reasons nor for identification purposes. Instead, it was done to add to the severity of the punishment for Chinese prisoners. Significantly, Field refuses to accept the supposed health rationale at face value. Instead, he looks beyond the language of the statute and makes an independent determination that the alleged justification was merely a pretext. It followed that the city council had no authority to enact an ordinance that added to punishments set by state law.

Field's primary reason for overturning the queue ordinance was that it amounted to class legislation in violation of the equal protection clause of the Fourteenth Amendment. He reasons in his opinion that the ordinance, though phrased in general terms, put a special burden on Chinese prisoners. It was common knowledge, Field states, that the ordinance effectively singled out Chinese males. At this point in time, the Bill of Rights was generally regarded as inapplicable to the states, yet Field strikingly argues that the city ordinance amounted to a cruel and unusual punishment as forbidden in the U.S. Constitution.

An underlying issue in *Ho Ah Kow* was the extent of state authority. Field writes that a state could exclude aliens who were diseased, convicts, paupers, or others likely to become a burden. Beyond such restrictions, steps to prevent further Chinese immigration were the responsibility of the federal government. Field attempts to minimize any negative impact that this case would have for his political ambitions in the eyes of the majority anti-Chinese element in California by observing that he had always regarded the mass immigration of the Chinese into California as a serious evil. However, Field argues that spiteful legislation would do little to alleviate this problem. Notwithstanding his defense of the rights of Chinese immigrants in *Ho Ah Kow*, Field's record in handling numerous Chinese immigrant cases was not consistent. As he notes in the document, Field believed that the remedy for continued Chinese immigration must be found at the federal level. In 1882 Congress passed the Chinese Exclusion Act to severely limit such immigration. Speaking for the Supreme Court, Field upheld the power of Congress to exclude foreigners. Still, he gained a reputation as a defender of the Chinese against discrimination. As a result, despite his disclaimer, Field became politically unpopular in California.

◆ "The Centenary of the Supreme Court of the United States"

In February 1790 the Supreme Court met in New York City, the temporary capital of the new Republic, for its first term, as required by the Judiciary Act of 1789. As there were no cases pending, the Court held an organizational meeting. It appointed officers, framed rules, and provided for the formation of a bar. One hundred years later, in 1890, the New York State Bar Association sponsored a celebration of this event. Chief Justice Melville W. Fuller asked Justice Field to deliver an address on behalf of the Court. These remarks provide a revealing look into Field's philosophy of law as it had developed toward the end of his career.

Several themes dominate this address. Throughout his comments Field emphasizes the limitations on legislative power and the importance of judicial review to invalidate laws inconsistent with the Constitution. He highlights the importance of the Civil War Amendments to the Constitution, noting that they greatly enlarged federal jurisdiction but did not fundamentally alter the dual nature of the system of government. Under the doctrine of dual federalism, the federal and state governments exercised separate and independent powers, and neither could encroach on the authority of the other. Field felt that many areas of laws were reserved to the states but that the Civil War Amendment increased federal authority to safeguard individual rights. Field was greatly concerned about the impact on

American society of industrialization and the emergence of large-scale corporate enterprise. He was as uneasy with corporate power as he was with legislation that restrained the rights of property owners. In this speech he defends judicial activism as a means of safeguarding traditional values and defusing social tensions. Underscoring a major and recurring issue in his thinking, Field asserts that the right to pursue ordinary vocations and enjoy the fruits of one's labor is an essential element of freedom. Field points out the changing nature and increasing size of the Supreme Court's docket. Indeed, he stresses that many cases arose from causes that had not existed earlier in the nineteenth century. He expresses concern about delays in the administration of justice and calls for steps to relieve the Court's crowded docket. Finally, Field echoes the views of the framers by emphasizing that property rights and personal rights are interdependent and both are deserving of judicial solicitude. He famously observes that "protection to property and persons cannot be separated."

Impact and Legacy

Field was one of the most important justices to sit on the Supreme Court. Although at first he was often in the minority, Field's opinions had a profound impact on the way in which courts viewed the guarantees of the Fourteenth Amendment and defined liberty. The opinion in *Cummings v. Missouri*, for example, exemplifies Field's commitment to individual liberty in a decisive manner. *Cummings*, coupled with his circuit court opinion in *Ho Ah Kow v. Nunan*, underscores Field's determination to defy public opinion in order to vindicate the rights of the aggrieved individuals and groups.

In analyzing Field's language in these documents, it is important to recognize both short-term and long-term impacts. Field's views, which assigned a high value to the rights of property owners, private economic ordering, and limited government, gained ascendency on the Supreme Court in the 1890s and continued to dominate that body until 1937. Field, then, was a prophet of a jurisprudence that emphasized entrepreneurial liberty as the cornerstone of constitutional law. As the documents make clear, Field's interpretation of the Constitution was grounded in his conception of liberty. As his 1890 address on the centenary of the Supreme Court makes clear, he was concerned about the growth of large-scale corporate enterprise, but he insisted throughout his career that the best way to protect liberty was to restrain governmental power. After 1937, with the political and constitutional triumph of the New Deal, the Supreme Court abandoned property-conscious constitutionalism and greatly enlarged the scope of permissible government regulation of economic activity. Hence, Field's dogged defense of economic individualism was relegated to the history books.

Other aspects of Fields legacy, however, were destined to have a lasting influence. As shown in his 1890 centenary address, Field was a vigorous proponent of a strong federal

"

"The Constitution deals with substance, not shadows."

(*Cummings v. Missouri*)

"If the legislature of a State, under pretense of providing for the public good, can determine, against the consent of the owner, the uses to which private property shall be devoted, or the prices which the owner shall receive for its uses, it can deprive him of the property as completely as by a special act for its confiscation or destruction."

(*Munn v. Illinois*)

"All that is beneficial in property arises from its use, and the fruits of that use; and whatever deprives a person of them deprives him of all that is desirable or valuable in the title and possession."

(*Munn v. Illinois*)

"Besides, we cannot shut our eyes to matters of public notoriety and general cognizance. When we take our seats on the bench we are not struck with blindness, and forbidden to know as judges what we see as men."

(*Ho Ah Kow v. Nunan*)

"As population and wealth increase—as the inequalities in the conditions of men become more and more marked and disturbing—as the enormous aggregation of wealth possessed by some corporations excites uneasiness lest their power should become dominating in the legislation of the country, and thus encroach upon the rights or crush out the business of individuals of small means—as population in some quarters presses upon the means of subsistence, and angry menaces against order find vent in loud denunciations—it becomes more and more the imperative duty of the court to enforce with a firm hand every guarantee of the constitution."

("The Centenary of the Supreme Court of the United States")

"It should never be forgotten that protection to property and persons cannot be separated. Where property is insecure the rights of persons are unsafe."

("The Centenary of the Supreme Court of the United States")

"

judiciary. He certainly helped to pave the way for more aggressive exercise of judicial power in the twentieth century. Moreover, Field became the prototype of an activist judge. He frequently used dissenting and concurring opinions to advance his constitutional doctrines. His dissent in *Munn v. Illinois* is a good example of how a dissenting opinion could eventually sway the Court and persuade fellow justices to purse a path first marked by Field. Finally, Field's insistence upon a broad reading of the guarantees of the Fourteenth Amendment and his view that the due process clause protected economic rights has been transformed by the Supreme Court to provide a basis for upholding a variety of personal rights. A study of Field's language thus affords insights into how a key Supreme Court justice reacted to the social and economic challenges of the late nineteenth century and how he promoted the expansive interpretation of the Fourteenth Amendment that eventually gained currency.

Key Sources

Several archives contain letters and documents pertaining to Stephen J. Field. Among the most helpful are the Matthew Deady Collection, Oregon Historical Society, and the Stephen J. Field Collection, Bancroft Library, University of California at Berkeley. Field's *Personal Reminiscences of Early Days in California* (1877), written with George C. Gorham, was reprinted in 1968.

Further Reading

■ Articles

McCurdy, Charles W. "Justice Field and the Jurisprudence of Government-Business Relations: Some Parameters of Laissez-Faire Constitutionalism, 1863–1897." *Journal of American History* 61 (1975): 970–1005.

■ Books

Ely, James W., Jr. *The Chief Justiceship of Melville W. Fuller, 1888–1910.* Columbia: University of South Carolina Press, 1995.

Fiss, Owen M. *History of the Supreme Court of the United States,* Vol. 8: *Troubled Beginnings of the Modern State, 1888–1910.* New York: Macmillan, 1993.

Kens, Paul. *Justice Stephen Field: Shaping Liberty from the Gold Rush to the Gilded Age.* Lawrence: University Press of Kansas, 1997.

Swisher, Carl Brent. *Stephen J. Field, Craftsman of the Law.* 1930. Reprint. Chicago: University of Chicago Press, 1969.

Urofsky, Melvin I., ed. *The Supreme Court Justices: A Biographical Dictionary.* New York: Garland Publishers, 1994.

White, G. Edward. *The American Judicial Tradition: Profiles of Leading American Judges.* 3rd ed. New York: Oxford University Press, 2007.

—James Ely

Questions for Further Study

1. During the more than three decades that Stephen Field served on the Supreme Court, American government, politics, and society underwent profound and sweeping changes. Which of these changes is reflected in the documents, and how did Field respond to them?

2. In *Cummings v. Missouri*, Field voted to strike down a Missouri law requiring a loyalty oath. On what constitutional basis did Field regard such a requirement as unlawful?

3. How did Field apply his concept of economic liberty in *Munn v. Illinois*? How did this view of economic liberty affect the economic expansion of the nation during the post–Civil War period?

4. In *Ho Ah Kow v. Nunan*, Field argued that while a particular law on its face might seem to apply to everyone, in practice it could affect only a racial, ethnic, or other group, making it unconstitutional. How did he apply this view to Chinese immigrants in this case?

5. Summarize Field's views on the relationship, specifically the power balance, between the federal and state governments.

6. Compare John Marshall Harlan's dissent in the Civil Rights Cases with Field's views on civil rights as expressed in *Ho Ah Kow v. Nunan* and in "The Centenary of the Supreme Court of the United States."

CUMMINGS V. MISSOURI (1867)

The oath could not, therefore, have been required as a means of ascertaining whether parties were qualified or not for their respective callings or the trusts with which they were charged. It was required in order to reach the person, not the calling. It was exacted, not from any notion that the several acts designated indicated unfitness for the callings, but because it was thought that the several acts deserved punishment, and that for many of them there was no way to inflict punishment except by depriving the parties, who had committed them, of some of the rights and privileges of the citizen.

The disabilities created by the constitution of Missouri must be regarded as penalties—they constitute punishment. We do not agree with the counsel of Missouri that "to punish one is to deprive him of life, liberty, or property, and that to take from him anything less than these is no punishment at all." The learned counsel does not use these terms—life, liberty, and property—as comprehending every right known to the law. He does not include under liberty freedom from outrage on the feelings as well as restraints on the person. He does not include under property those estates which one may acquire in professions, though they are often the source of the highest emoluments and honors. The deprivation of any rights, civil or political, previously enjoyed, may be punishment, the circumstances attending and the causes of the deprivation determining this fact. Disqualification from office may be punishment, as in cases of conviction upon impeachment. Disqualification from the pursuits of a lawful avocation, or from positions of trust, or from the privilege of appearing in the courts, or acting as an executor, administrator, or guardian, may also, and often has been, imposed as punishment....

The theory upon which our political institutions rest is, that all men have certain inalienable rights—that among these are life, liberty, and the pursuit of happiness; and that in the pursuit of happiness all avocations, all honors, all positions, are alike open to everyone, and that in the protection of these rights all are equal before the law. Any deprivation or suspension of any of these rights for past conduct is punishment, and can be in no otherwise defined....

The counsel for Missouri closed his argument in this case by presenting a striking picture of the struggle for ascendency in that State during the recent Rebellion between the friends and the enemies of the Union, and of the fierce passions which that struggle aroused. It was in the midst of the struggle that the present constitution was framed, although it was not adopted by the people until the war had closed. It would have been strange, therefore, had it not exhibited in its provisions some traces of the excitement amidst which the convention held its deliberations....

"No State shall pass any bill of attainder, *ex post facto* law, or law impairing the obligation of contracts."

A bill of attainder is a legislative act which inflicts punishment without a judicial trial.

If the punishment be less than death, the act is termed a bill of pains and penalties. Within the meaning of the Constitution, bills of attainder include bills of pains and penalties. In these cases the legislative body, in addition to its legitimate functions, exercises the powers and office of judge; it assumes, in the language of the text-books, judicial magistracy; it pronounces upon the guilt of the party, without any of the forms or safeguards of trial; it determines the sufficiency of the proofs produced, whether conformable to the rules of evidence or otherwise; and it fixes the degree of punishment with its own nations of the enormity of the offence....

If the clauses of the second article of the constitution of Missouri, to which we have referred, had in terms declared that Mr. Cummings was guilty, or should be held guilty, of having been in armed hostility to the United States, or of having entered that State to avoid being enrolled or drafted into the military service of the United States, and, therefore, should be deprived of the right to preach as a priest of the Catholic Church, or to teach in any institution of learning, there could be no question that the clauses would constitute a bill of attainder within the meaning of the Federal Constitution. If these clauses, instead of mentioning his name, had declared that all priests and clergymen within the State of Missouri were guilty of these acts, or should be held guilty of them, and hence be subjected to the like deprivation, the clauses would be equally open to objection. And, further, if these clauses had declared that all such priests and clergymen should be so held guilty, and be thus deprived, provided they did not, by a day designated, do certain specified acts, they would be no less within the inhibition of the Federal Constitution.

In all these cases there would be the legislative enactment creating the deprivation without any of the ordinary forms and guards provided for the security of the citizen in the administration of justice by the established tribunals.

The results which would follow from clauses of the character mentioned do follow from the clauses actually adopted. The difference between the last case supposed and the case actually presented is one of form only, and not of substance. The existing clauses presume the guilt of the priests and clergymen, and adjudge the deprivation of their right to preach or teach unless the presumption be first removed by their expurgatory oath—in other words, they assume the guilt and adjudge the punishment conditionally. The clauses supposed differ only in that they declare the guilt instead of assuming it. The deprivation is effected with equal certainty in the one case as it would be in the other, but not with equal directness. The purpose of the lawmaker in the case supposed would be openly avowed; in the case existing it is only disguised. The legal result must be the same, for what cannot be done directly cannot be done indirectly. The Constitution deals with substance, not shadows. Its inhibition was levelled at the thing, not the name. It intended that the rights of the citizen should be secure against deprivation for past conduct by legislative enactment, under any form, however disguised. If the inhibition can be evaded by the form of the enactment, its insertion in the fundamental law was a vain and futile proceeding.

We proceed to consider the second clause of what Mr. Chief Justice Marshall terms a bill of rights for the people of each State—the clause which inhibits the passage of an *ex post facto* law.

By *ex post facto* law is meant one which imposes a punishment for an act which was not punishable at the time it was committed; or imposes additional punishment to that then prescribed; or changes the rules of evidence by which less or different testimony is sufficient convict than was then required....

The clauses in the Missouri constitution, which are the subject of consideration, do not, in terms, define any crimes, or declare that any punishment shall be inflicted, but they produce the same result upon the parties, against whom they are directed, as though the crimes were defined and the punishment was declared. They assume that there are persons in Missouri who are guilty of some of the acts designated. They would have no meaning in the constitution were not such the fact. They aimed at past acts, and not future acts. They were intended especially to operate upon parties who, in some form or manner, by action or words, directly or indirectly, had aided or countenanced the Rebellion, or sympathized with parties engaged in the Rebellion, or had endeavored to escape the proper responsibilities and duties of a citizen in time of war; and they were intended to operate by depriving such persons of the right to hold certain offices and trusts, and to pursue their ordi-

Glossary

bill of attainder	a legislative act that declares a person or group of persons guilty of a crime without benefit of a trial
countenanced	tolerated
emoluments	earnings and benefits from employment
estates	generally property, especially land; here, a figure of speech suggesting accumulation of wealth
***ex post facto* law**	retroactive law that imposes a punishment for acts not illegal at the time they were committed
expurgatory	serving to cleanse or purify something that is offensive
judicial magistracy	the concept of judges and courts acting as magistrates, thus improperly assuming the powers of the executive branch of government
Mr. Chief Justice Marshall	John Marshall (1755–1835), chief justice of the United States from 1801 until his death

nary and regular avocations. This deprivation is punishment; nor is it any less so because a way is opened for escape from it by the expurgatory oath. The framers of the constitution of Missouri knew at the time that whole classes of individuals would be unable to take the oath prescribed. To them there is no escape provided; to them the deprivation was intended to be, and is, absolute and perpetual. To make the enjoyment of a right dependent upon an impossible condition is equivalent to an absolute denial of the right under any condition, and such denial, enforced for a past act, is nothing less than punishment imposed for that act. It is a misapplication of terms to call it anything else....

And this is not all. The clauses in question subvert the presumptions of innocence, and alter the rules of evidence, which heretofore, under the universally recognized principles of the common law, have been supposed to be fundamental and unchangeable. They assume that the parties are guilty; they call upon the parties to establish their innocence; and they declare that such innocence can be shown only in one way—by an inquisition, in the form of an expurgatory oath, into the consciences of the parties....

The provision of the Federal Constitution, intended to secure the liberty of the citizen, cannot be evaded by the form in which the power of the State is exerted. If this were not so, if that which cannot be accomplished by means looking directly to the end, can be accomplished by indirect means, the inhibition may be evaded at pleasure. No kind of oppression can be named, against which the framers of the Constitution intended to guard, which may not be effected.

Munn v. Illinois (1876)

Field dissent

The doctrine of the State court, that no one is deprived of his property, within the meaning of the constitutional inhibition, so long as he retains its title and possession, and the doctrine of this court, that, whenever one's property is used in such a manner as to affect the community at large, it becomes by that fact clothed with a public interest, and ceases to be *juris private* only, appear to me to destroy, for all useful purposes, the efficacy of the constitutional guaranty. All that is beneficial in property arises from its use, and the fruits of that use; and whatever deprives a person of them deprives him of all that is desirable or valuable in the title and possession. If the constitutional guaranty extends no further than to prevent a deprivation of title and possession, and allows a deprivation of use, and the fruits of that use, it does not merit the encomiums it has received. Unless I have misread the history of the provision now incorporated into all our State constitutions, and by the Fifth and Fourteenth Amendments into our Federal Constitution, and have misunderstood the interpretation it has received, it is not thus limited in its scope, and thus impotent for good. It has a much more extended operation than either court, State or Federal, has given to it. The provision, it is to be observed, places property under the same protection as life and liberty. Except by due process of law, no State can deprive any person of either. The provision has been supposed to secure to every individual the essential conditions for the pursuit of happiness; and for that reason has not been heretofore, and should never be, construed in any narrow or restricted sense.

No State "shall deprive any person of life, liberty, or property without due process of law," says the Fourteenth Amendment to the Constitution. By the term "life," as here used, something more is meant than mere animal existence. The inhibition against its deprivation extends to all those limbs and faculties by which life is enjoyed. The provision equally prohibits the mutilation of the body by the amputation of an arm or leg, or the putting out of an eye, or the destruction of any other organ of the body through which the soul communicates with the outer world. The deprivation not only of life, but whatever God has given to everyone with life, for its growth and enjoyment, is prohibited by the provision in question, if its efficacy be not frittered away by judicial decision.

By the term "liberty," as used in the provision, something more is meant than mere freedom from physical restraint or the bounds of a prison. It means freedom to go where one may choose, and to act in such manner, not inconsistent with the equal rights of others, as his judgment may dictate for the promotion of his happiness; that is, to pursue such callings and avocations as may be most suitable to develop his capacities, and give to them their highest enjoyment.

The same liberal construction which is required for the protection of life and liberty, in all particulars in which life and liberty are of any value, should be applied to the protection of private property. If the legislature of a State, under pretense of providing for the public good, or for any other reason, can determine, against the consent of the owner, the uses to which private property shall be devoted, or the prices which the owner shall receive for its uses, it can deprive him of the property as completely as by a special act for its confiscation or destruction. If, for instance, the owner is prohibited from using his building for the purposes for which it was designed,

Glossary

construction	interpretation
construed	interpreted
encomiums	praises
juris private	private use

it is of little consequence that he is permitted to retain the title and possession; or, if he is compelled to take as compensation for its use less than the expenses to which he is subjected by its ownership, he is, for all practical purposes, deprived of the property, as effectually as if the legislature had ordered his forcible dispossession. If it be admitted that the legislature has any control over the compensation, the extent of that compensation becomes a mere matter of legislative discretion. The amount fixed will operate as a partial destruction of the value of the property, if it fall below the amount which the owner would obtain by contract, and practically, as a complete destruction, if it be less than the cost of retaining its possession. There is, indeed, no protection of any value under the constitutional provision, which does not extend to the use and income of the property, as well as to its title and possession.

HO AH KOW V. NUNAN (1879)

The validity of this ordinance is denied by the plaintiff on two grounds: 1. That it exceeds the authority of the board of supervisors, the body in which the legislative power of the city and county is vested; and 2. That it is special legislation imposing a degrading and cruel punishment upon a class of persons who are entitled, alike with all other persons within the jurisdiction of the United States, to the equal protection of the laws. We are of opinion that both these positions are well taken....

The cutting off the hair of every male person within an inch of his scalp, on his arrival at the jail, was not intended and cannot be maintained as a measure of discipline or as a sanitary regulation. The act by itself has no tendency to promote discipline, and can only be a measure of health in exceptional cases. Had the ordinance contemplated a mere sanitary regulation it would have been limited to such cases and made applicable to females as well as to males, and to persons awaiting trial as well as to persons under conviction. The close cutting of the hair which is practiced upon inmates of the state penitentiary, like dressing them in striped clothing, is partly to distinguish them from others, and thus prevent their escape and facilitate their recapture. They are measures of precaution, as well as parts of a general system of treatment prescribed by the directors of the penitentiary under the authority of the state, for parties convicted of and imprisoned for felonies. Nothing of the kind is prescribed or would be tolerated with respect to persons confined in a county jail for simple misdemeanors, most of which are not of a very grave character. For the discipline or detention of the plaintiff in this case, who had the option of paying a fine of ten dollars, or of being imprisoned for five days, no such clipping of the hair was required. It was done to add to the severity of his punishment....

The claim, however, put forth that the measure was prescribed as one of health is notoriously a mere pretense. A treatment to which disgrace is attached, and which is not adopted as a means of security against the escape of the prisoner, but merely to aggravate the severity of his confinement, can only be regarded as a punishment additional to that fixed by the sentence. If adopted in consequence of the sentence it is punishment in addition to that imposed by the court; if adopted without regard to the sentence it is wanton cruelty.

In the present case, the plaintiff was not convicted of any breach of a municipal regulation, nor of violating any provision of the consolidation act. The punishment which the supervisors undertook to add to the fine imposed by the court was without semblance of authority. The legislature had not conferred upon them the right to change or add to the punishments which it deemed sufficient for offenses; nor had it bestowed upon them the right to impose in any case a punishment of the character inflicted in this case. They could no more direct that the queue of the plaintiff should be cut off than that the punishments mentioned should be inflicted. Nor could they order the hair of any one, Mongolian or other person, to be clipped within an inch of his scalp. That measure was beyond their power....

The second objection to the ordinance in question is equally conclusive. It is special legislation on the part of the supervisors against a class of persons who, under the constitution and laws of the United States, are entitled to the equal protection of the laws. The ordinance was intended only for the Chinese in San Francisco. This was avowed by the supervisors on its passage, and was so understood by everyone. The ordinance is known in the community as the "Queue Ordinance," being so designated from its purpose to reach the queues of the Chinese, and it is not enforced against any other persons. The reason advanced for its adoption, and now urged for its continuance, is, that only the dread of the loss of his queue will induce a Chinaman to pay his fine. That is to say, in order to enforce the payment of a fine imposed upon him, it is necessary that torture should be superadded to imprisonment. Then, it is said, the Chinaman will not accept the alternative, which the law allows, of working out his fine by his imprisonment, and the state or county will be saved the expense of keeping him during the imprisonment. Probably the bastinado, or the knout, or the thumbscrew, or the rack, would accomplish the same end; and no doubt the Chinaman would prefer either of these modes of torture to that which entails upon him disgrace among his countrymen and carries with it the constant dread of misfortune and suffering after death. It is not creditable to the humanity and civilization of our people, much less to their Christianity, that an ordinance of this character was possible.

The class character of this legislation is none the less manifest because of the general terms in which it is expressed. The statements of supervisors in debate on the passage of the ordinance cannot, it is true, be resorted to for the purpose of explaining the meaning of the terms used; but they can be resorted to for the purpose of ascertaining the general object of the legislation proposed, and the mischiefs sought to be remedied. Besides, we cannot shut our eyes to matters of public notoriety and general cognizance. When we take our seats on the bench we are not struck with blindness, and forbidden to know as judges what we see as men; and where an ordinance, though general in its terms, only operates upon a special race, sect or class, it being universally understood that it is to be enforced only against that race, sect or class, we may justly conclude that it was the intention of the body adopting it that it should only have such operation, and treat it accordingly. We may take notice of the limitation given to the general terms of an ordinance by its practical construction as a fact in its history, as we do in some cases that a law has practically become obsolete. If this were not so, the most important provisions of the constitution, intended for the security of personal rights, would, by the general terms of an enactment, often be evaded and practically annulled. The complaint in this case shows that the ordinance acts with special severity upon Chinese prisoners, inflicting upon them suffering altogether disproportionate to what would be endured by other prisoners if enforced against them. Upon the Chinese prisoners its enforcement operates as "a cruel and unusual punishment."

Many illustrations might be given where ordinances, general in their terms, would operate only upon a special class, or upon a class, with exceptional severity, and thus incur the odium and be subject to the legal objection of intended hostile legislation against them. We have, for instance, in our community a large number of Jews. They are a highly intellectual race, and are generally obedient to the laws of the country. But, as is well known, they have peculiar opinions with respect to the use of certain articles of food, which they cannot be forced to disregard without extreme pain and suffering. They look, for example, upon the eating of pork with loathing. It is an offense against their religion, and is associated in their minds with uncleanness and impurity. Now, if they should in some quarter of the city overcrowd their dwellings and thus become amenable, like the Chinese, to the act concerning lodging-houses and sleeping apartments, an ordinance of the supervisors requiring that all prisoners confined in the county

jail should be fed on pork would be seen by everyone to be leveled at them; and, notwithstanding its general terms, would be regarded as a special law in its purpose and operation. During various periods of English history, legislation, general in its character, has often been enacted with the avowed purpose of imposing special burdens and restrictions upon Catholics; but that legislation has since been regarded as not less odious and obnoxious to animadversion than if the persons at whom it was aimed had been particularly designated.

But in our country hostile and discriminating legislation by a state against persons of any class, sect, creed or nation, in whatever form it may be expressed, is forbidden by the fourteenth amendment of the constitution. That amendment in its first section declares who are citizens of the United States, and then enacts that no state shall make or enforce any law which shall abridge their privileges and immunities. It further declares that no state shall deprive any person (dropping the distinctive term citizen) of life, liberty or property, without due process of law, nor deny to any person the equal protection of the laws. This inhibition upon the state applies to all the instrumentalities and agencies employed in the administration of its government, to its executive, legislative and judicial departments, and to the subordinate legislative bodies of counties and cities. And the equality of protection thus assured to everyone whilst within the United States, from whatever country he may have come, or of whatever race or color he may be, implies not only that the courts of the country shall be open to him on the same terms as to all others for the security of his person or property, the prevention or redress of wrongs and the enforcement of contracts; but that no charges or burdens shall be laid upon him which are not equally borne by others, and that in the administration of criminal justice he shall suffer for his offenses no greater or different punishment....

We are aware of the general feeling—amounting to positive hostility—prevailing in California against the Chinese, which would prevent their further immigration hither and expel from the state those already here. Their dissimilarity in physical characteristics, in language, manners and religion would seem, from past experience, to prevent the possibility of their assimilation with our people. And thoughtful persons, looking at the millions which crowd the opposite shores of the Pacific, and the possibility at no distant day of their pouring over in vast hordes among us, giving rise to fierce antagonisms of race, hope that some way may be devised to prevent their further immigration. We feel the force and importance of these considerations; but the remedy for the apprehended evil is to be sought from the general government, where, except in certain cases, all power over the subject lies. To that government belong exclusively the treaty-making power and the power to regulate commerce with foreign nations, which includes intercourse as well as traffic, and, with the exceptions presently mentioned, the power to prescribe the conditions of immigration or importation of persons.… For restrictions necessary or desirable in these matters, the appeal must be made to the general government; and it is not believed that the appeal will ultimately be disregarded. Be that as it may, nothing can be accomplished in that direction by hostile and spiteful legislation on the part of the state, or of its municipal bodies, like the ordinance in question—legislation which is unworthy of a brave and manly people. Against such legislation it will always be the duty of the judiciary to declare and enforce the paramount law of the nation.

Glossary

animadversion	harsh criticism
bastinado	a beating, particularly on the soles of the feet
cognizance	knowledge
consolidation act	a statute that made the boundaries of the city and the county of San Francisco, California, the same; similar acts were passed in other city and counties, including Denver, Colorado, and Philadelphia, Pennsylvania
knout	a whip with multiple thongs

"THE CENTENARY OF THE SUPREME COURT OF THE UNITED STATES" (1890)

The legislation required by the exigencies of the civil war, and following it, and the constitutional amendments which were designed to give farther security to personal rights, have brought before the court questions of the greatest interest and importance, calling for the most earnest and laborious consideration. Indeed, the cases which have come before this court, springing from causes which did not exist during the first quarter of the century, exceed, in the magnitude of the property interests involved, and in the importance of the public questions presented, all cases brought within the same period before any court of Christendom.

Whilst the constitutional amendments have not changed the structure of our dual form of government, but are additions to the previous amendments, and are to be considered in connection with them and the original constitution as one instrument, they have removed from existence an institution which was felt by wise statesmen to be inconsistent with the great declarations of right upon which our government is founded; and they have vastly enlarged the subjects of Federal jurisdiction. The amendment declaring that neither slavery nor involuntary servitude, except as a punishment for crime, shall exist in the United States or any place subject to their jurisdiction, not only has done away with the slavery of the black man, as it then existed, but interdicts forever the slavery of any man, and not only slavery, but involuntary servitude—that is, serfage, vassalage, villeinage, peonage, and all other forms of compulsory service for the mere benefit or pleasure of others. As has often been said, it was intended to make every one born in this country a free man and to give him a right to pursue the ordinary vocations of life without other restraint than such as affects all others, and to enjoy equally with them the fruits of his labor. The right to labor as he may think proper without injury to others is an element of that freedom which is his birthright.

The amendment, declaring that no State shall make or enforce any law which shall abridge the privileges or immunities of citizens of the United States, nor deprive any person of life, liberty or property without due process of law, nor deny to any person within its jurisdiction the equal protection of the laws, has proclaimed that equality before the law shall forever be the governing rule of all the States of the Union which every person however humble may invoke for his protection. In enforcing these provisions, or considering the laws adopted for their enforcement, or laws which are supposed to be in conflict with them, difficult and far-reaching questions are presented at every term for decision.

Up to the middle of the present century the calendar of the court did not average 140 cases a term, and never amounted at any one term to 300 cases; the calendar of the present term exceeds 1,500. In view of the condition of the court,—its crowded docket,—the multitude of questions constantly brought before it of the greatest and most extended influence—surely it has a right to call upon the country to give it assistance and relief. Something must be done in that direction and should be done speedily to prevent the delays to suitors now existing. To delay justice is as pernicious as to deny it....

To retain the respect and confidence conceded in the past, the court, whilst cautiously abstaining from assuming powers granted by the constitution to other departments of the government, must unhesitatingly and to the best of its ability enforce, as heretofore, not only all the limitations of the constitution upon the Federal and State governments, but also all the guarantees it contains of the private rights of the citizen, both of person and of property. As population and wealth increase—as the inequalities in the conditions of men become more and more marked and disturbing—as the enormous aggregation of wealth possessed by some corporations excites uneasiness lest their power should become dominating in the legislation of the country, and thus encroach upon the rights or crush out the business of individuals of small means—as population in some quarters presses upon the means of subsistence, and angry menaces against order find vent in loud denunciations—it becomes more and more the imperative duty of the court to enforce with a firm hand every guarantee of the constitution. Every decision weakening their restraining power is a blow to the peace of society and to its progress and improvement. It should never be forgotten that protection to property and persons cannot be separated. Where property is insecure the rights of persons are unsafe. Protection to the one goes with protection to the other; and there can be neither prosperity nor progress where either is uncertain.

That the Justices of the Supreme Court must possess the ability and learning required by the duties of their office, and a character for purity and integrity beyond reproach, need not be said. But it is not sufficient for the performance of his judicial duty that a judge should act honestly in all that he does. He must be ready to act in all cases presented for his judicial determination with absolute fearlessness. Timidity, hesitation and cowardice in any public officer excite and deserve only contempt, but infinitely more in a judge than in any other, because he is appointed to discharge a public trust of the most sacred character....

If he is influenced by apprehensions that his character will be attacked, or his motives impugned, or that his judgment will be attributed to the influence of particular classes, cliques or associations, rather than to his own convictions of the law, he will fail lamentably in his high office.

Glossary

exigencies	emergencies; urgent situations
institution which was felt by wise statesmen...	slavery
interdicts	forbids
peonage	the condition of paying off a debt through forced labor
pernicious	harmful, deadly
serfage	the condition of being a serf
vassalage	a position of subjection or subordination
villeinage	a tenant bound to the land and subject to the land's owner

Felix Frankfurter (Library of Congress)

FELIX FRANKFURTER 1882–1965

Supreme Court Justice

Featured Documents
- ◆ *Minersville School District v. Gobitis* (1940)
- ◆ *Colegrove v. Green* (1946)
- ◆ *Cooper v. Aaron* (1958)
- ◆ *Gomillion v. Lightfoot* (1960)

Overview

Before Felix Frankfurter came to the U.S. Supreme Court, he had had a long and accomplished career as a liberal political activist and academic. Most onlookers assumed that he would continue to function in both roles on the Court but that his liberalism, rather than his academic nature, would predominate. In fact, it was his academic side that did. Frankfurter's penchant for pedantry combined with his philosophy of deference to legislative and administrative decision making, and the result muted both others' expectations and his own judicial accomplishments. His philosophy of judging, which emphasized process over results, was designed to be a value-neutral method of reaching a decision. This *process jurisprudence*, as it has come to be known, has been championed by some as an admirable form of judicial restraint. To others, Frankfurter's brand of judging more closely resembled abdication of responsibility.

Perhaps ironically, given Frankfurter's avowedly impersonal approach to his job on the Court, more than one Frankfurter observer has associated the justice's uncommonly reverential attitude toward the institutions of American government and their codified roles with his biography. Born in Vienna, Austria, in 1882, Frankfurter immigrated to the United States with his family when he was twelve years old. Like many other European immigrants, the Frankfurters settled on the Lower East Side of Manhattan. Within five years, however, the Frankfurters had moved uptown to the more affluent Yorkville section of New York City. Felix discovered his own route to upward mobility to be in education, entering City College in 1901 and going from there to Harvard Law School, where he graduated first in his class in 1906. At Harvard, Frankfurter was introduced to the case method, an innovative, ostensibly scientific method of studying law.

But Harvard also introduced Frankfurter to the kind of idealism about the law espoused by Louis D. Brandeis, the "people's attorney," who would later become both a Supreme Court justice and one of Frankfurter's closest friends. Frankfurter followed Brandeis's example by choosing a career in public service, beginning with a position in the office of Henry L. Stimson, the U.S. Attorney for New York. Frankfurter had a gift for friendship, and his alliance with Stimson stood him in good stead as he followed the latter to Washington to serve in the administrations of

Presidents Theodore Roosevelt and William Howard Taft. Stimson left Washington after the election of Woodrow Wilson, and Frankfurter followed shortly thereafter when he was invited to join the Harvard Law School faculty. Frankfurter had, of course, logged a sterling academic record while at Harvard, but it was a talk he had delivered in 1912 at the twenty-fifth anniversary of the *Harvard Law Review* that seems to have clinched the job. That speech, which emphasized the limited role of courts in interpreting economic regulation, stressed the necessity of permitting legislatures to experiment in order to meet the shifting necessities of a changing world. "The Constitution," Frankfurter intoned prophetically, "was not intended to limit this field of experimentation" (Urofsky, p. 7).

Frankfurter taught at Harvard, focusing on the new field of administrative law, from 1914 until he joined the Supreme Court in 1939, but his commitment to public service and to economic progressivism frequently took him far from Cambridge, Massachusetts. Together with the editors Walter Lippmann and Walter Weyl, he was instrumental in founding the influential political and cultural magazine *New Republic*. Although he had never been an observant Jew, at the urging of Brandeis, Frankfurter helped spearhead the new American Zionist movement. After lobbying in support of Brandeis's ultimately successful Supreme Court nomination, Frankfurter took over his friend's role defending progressive labor legislation for the National Consumers' League.

During World War I, Frankfurter served as secretary and counsel to the Mediation Commission on Labor Problems, established to settle defense industry strikes, and chaired the War Labor Policies Board. These experiences familiarized him with labor politics, and he came to sympathize with those he viewed as underdogs, such as the radical labor leader Thomas Mooney. After the war, Frankfurter helped found the controversial American Civil Liberties Union. And in 1927 he took up the even more controversial cause of the immigrant anarchists Nicola Sacco and Bartolomeo Vanzetti, whom many believed had been framed for murder. The article he published in the prestigious *Atlantic Monthly* focused on the judicial overreaching that marred the Sacco and Vanzetti trial, and it cemented Frankfurter's reputation in some quarters as a radical.

In 1932 Frankfurter turned down a seat on the Massachusetts Supreme Judicial Court and took up the cause of

Time Line

1882
- **November 15**
  Felix Frankfurter is born in Vienna, Austria.

1902
- Frankfurter graduates from City College of New York with high honors.

1906
- Frankfurter graduates first in his class from Harvard Law School.
- Frankfurter becomes an assistant to the U.S. Attorney for New York Henry L. Stimson.

1911
- Frankfurter becomes a law officer in the Bureau of Insular Affairs, handling legal matters concerning America's overseas territories.

1914
- Frankfurter joins the faculty of Harvard Law School, where he teaches criminal and administrative law.
- Frankfurter helps start the *New Republic* by writing articles and performing editorial duties.
- Frankfurter takes up a role as Louis Brandeis's assistant in the fledgling American Zionist movement.

1917
- **January 19**
  Frankfurter begins working as counsel for the National Consumers' League, arguing on behalf of state regulation of minimum wages and maximum work hours.
- **April**
  Frankfurter takes a leave of absence from Harvard to serve as assistant to Secretary of War Newton D. Baker.
- **September**
  Frankfurter is appointed counsel to President Woodrow Wilson's Mediation Commission.

Franklin Delano Roosevelt. When Roosevelt moved into the White House in 1933, Frankfurter became one of the president's staunchest "Brain Trust" lieutenants, supporting New Deal legislation and supplying bright young Harvard Law graduates—who came to be known as Frankfurter's "Happy Hot Dogs"—to staff the administration. Roosevelt rewarded him first with an offer to become solicitor general (which Frankfurter declined), and then, in 1939, with a nomination to replace Benjamin Cardozo on the Supreme Court. Owing to Frankfurter's activism on behalf of liberal causes and his continuing alliance with Roosevelt, observers expected him to continue along a progressive track once on the Court. A few years earlier, the previously conservative Court had experienced a profound reorientation in response to Roosevelt's ultimately unsuccessful plan to pack it with supporters, and during Frankfurter's tenure this leftward shift intensified. But Frankfurter, who many believed would assume intellectual leadership of the Court, was obliged to take a back seat as his onetime friend, Hugo Black, acted as midwife to the birth of new individual rights. Frankfurter, ideologically opposed to abstract principles and political outcomes, reconciled with his archrival only toward the end of their mutual Court tenures, by which time Black had drifted closer to Frankfurter's judicial conservatism. Frankfurter retired from the Court in 1962 after suffering a debilitating stroke. He died two and a half years later, at the age of eighty-two.

Explanation and Analysis of Documents

Felix Frankfurter remains something of enigma. An activist in early life, after his appointment to the Supreme Court, he came to stand for a restraint that seemed at odds with his past. The opinions he wrote while he was on the Court also often seem to contradict themselves. In one of the earliest, *Minersville School District v. Gobitis*, Frankfurter's opinion for the majority nullified the First Amendment right to free exercise of religion by upholding the school district's right to expel students whose faith prohibited them from saluting the flag. In contrast, in one of his last opinions, *Gomillion v. Lightfoot*, he was willing to sidestep his own carefully formulated prohibition against adjudicating apportionment disputes so that he could strike down a state law that discriminated against black voters. One plausible explanation of his opinion for the Court in *Gomillion* is that by authoring it, Frankfurter was able to support a political issue he personally favored while at the same time formulating a rationale that preserved the holding of *Colegrove v. Green*, the embodiment of his philosophy of judicial restraint. Perhaps nothing he wrote on the Court better exhibits Frankfurter's need to have the last word than his concurring opinion in the landmark desegregation case *Cooper v. Aaron*. Unlike most concurrences, it takes issue not with the majority's logic but with its tone. In the end, perhaps, it can be said that Frankfurter's vaulting intellect betrayed him, making him the enemy of his colleagues rather than making him their leader.

◆ Minersville School District v. Gobitis

Gobitis was the first of two flag-salute cases that came before the Court in the late 1930s and early 1940s. The issue involved in both, whether a regulation mandating schoolchildren to salute the flag of the United States violated the free exercise clause of the First Amendment, was not entirely new, as it had already been the subject of major litigation in seven states by the time the Court agreed to hear *Gobitis*. Mandatory flag pledges had always been associated with a rise in patriotic feelings during times of war. The first such laws had been passed during the Spanish-American War, and many more states adopted flag-salute requirements during World War I. *Gobitis*, which the Court handed down even as the English were fleeing the Nazis by evacuating Dunkirk, had been heard and decided just as America was beginning to feel the heat generated by a second major war that was about to become a global one.

Gobitis revolved around Lillian and William Gobitis, who were twelve and ten years old when they were expelled from public school in Minersville, Pennsylvania, for refusing to salute the flag. The Gobitis children belonged to a family who had recently joined the Jehovah's Witnesses, a faith group that in 1935 had adopted a doctrine stating that flag saluting was idolatry. Jehovah's Witnesses were encouraged to stand up for their right to religious freedom by refusing to pledge their allegiance to the flag, an act some other Americans equated with demonstrating Nazi sympathies. Such notions were common in Minersville, which in the 1940s was 90 percent Roman Catholic. The Gobitis children were taunted by their schoolmates, the Gobitis family endured a boycott of their store, and eventually the Commonwealth of Pennsylvania decreed that Lillian and William could be ousted from the public school system without appeal.

The Minersville School District lost two lower court proceedings before the case came before the Supreme Court, where Justice Frankfurter, a naturalized American citizen who took the nation's ideals and its symbols very seriously, was assigned to write the opinion for the eight-member Court majority. For Frankfurter, the Court clearly had no right to override the judgment and prerogatives of local authorities:

> To stigmatize legislative judgment in providing for this universal gesture of respect for the symbol of our national life in the setting of the common school as a lawless inroad on that freedom of conscience which the Constitution protects, would amount to no less than the pronouncement of pedagogical and psychological dogma in a field where courts possess no marked and certainly no controlling competence.

In a file devoted to the flag-salute cases, Frankfurter left a handwritten note that conveys similar—if more personal—sentiments: "No duty of judges is more important nor more difficult to discharge than that of guarding against reading their personal and debatable opinions into the Case" (Urofsky, p. 52). To guard against what he saw as fatal

Time Line	
1918	**■ March** Frankfurter is sent abroad to explore European reactions to Wilson's "fourteen points" peace proposal. **■ May** President Wilson names Frankfurter chairman of the War Labor Policies Board.
1919	**■ Spring** Frankfurter serves as Zionist delegate to the Paris Peace Conference that formally ends World War I.
1920	**■** Frankfurter helps found the American Civil Liberties Union.
1927	**■ March** Frankfurter's article attacking irregularities in the murder trial of anarchist immigrants Nicola Sacco and Bartolomeo Vanzetti appears in the *Atlantic*.
1939	**■ January 30** Frankfurter joins the U.S. Supreme Court as an associate justice.
1940	**■ June 3** The Court hands down its decision in *Minersville School District v. Gobitis*, with Frankfurter writing the majority opinion.
1946	**■ June 10** The Court hands down its opinion in *Colegrove v. Green*, for which Frankfurter wrote the plurality opinion.
1958	**■ September 12** The Court hands down its opinion in *Cooper v. Aaron*, for which Frankfurter wrote a concurring opinion.

Time Line

1960

■ **November 14**
The Court hands down its opinion in *Gomillion v. Lightfoot*, with Frankfurter writing the opinion of a unanimous Court.

1962

■ **August 28**
Frankfurter retires from the Court after suffering a debilitating stroke.

1965

■ **February 22**
Frankfurter dies in Washington, D.C., from congestive heart failure.

subjectivity, Frankfurter goes to the opposite extreme in *Gobitis*, asking, first, whether the goal of the legislation mandating the flag salute was legitimate and, second, whether the means of enforcing this law was reasonable. Because these questions form a simple arithmetic, the answer seemed almost a foregone conclusion: The "felt necessities" of a nation threatened with war outweigh any First Amendment claims to freedom of religious observance.

In making this two-step analysis, Frankfurter was following the same formula the Court had employed for decades when evaluating the constitutionality of economic regulations. At the dawn of a new legal era, with its increasing emphasis on individual rights, the standards for finding laws that affected the freedoms of individuals constitutional would be considerably tightened, requiring that the state's interest in the law be compelling and its methods of enforcement the least restrictive available. But before this change could take place, the Court had to accept the notion that the Fourteenth Amendment—which defines citizenship and grants equal protection under the law to all U.S. citizens—had incorporated the entitlements memorialized in the Bill of Rights, making them applicable at the state level. Frankfurter does not do so in *Gobitis*, instead adhering to the notion the Court had enunciated three years earlier in *Palko v. Connecticut* (1937), that only those protections "of the very essence of a scheme of ordered liberty" could be made to apply to state laws. Frankfurter never did accept the incorporation doctrine, applying portions of the Bill of Rights to the states. Even as the Court moved beyond the formulation responsible for *Gobitis*, Frankfurter declined to move with it.

Public reaction to *Gobitis* was swift. At the same time that most members of the media criticized the opinion, they were reporting the attacks on Jehovah's Witnesses that inevitably followed. Largely as a result of this violence, *Gobitis* proved to be one of the shortest-lived of Supreme Court precedents. Two years later, in *Jones v. Opelika* (1942), a case concerning the refusal of some Jehovah's Witnesses to pay a license fee allowing them to distribute religious pamphlets, three other justices joined Harlan Stone, who had been the lone dissenter in *Gobitis*, in dissenting from the majority's decision against the Jehovah's Witnesses. These three also appended a note in their joint dissenting opinion indicating that they thought the majority's opinion was in line with *Gobitis*, which they now felt had been wrongly decided. The following year, in *West Virginia Board of Education v. Barnette* (1943), the Court revisited the issue of Jehovah's Witnesses and the flag salute. The Court's decision overturned *Gobitis*.

◆ *Colegrove v. Green*

At the time *Colegrove v. Green* was decided, the Court was operating with only seven members. Chief Justice Harlan F. Stone had died unexpectedly just after oral arguments had been heard in the case, and Justice Robert Jackson was presiding over the Nazi trials in Nuremberg, Germany. This fact, combined with a plurality vote among the remaining members, made *Colegrove*'s status as precedent less than secure. The decision also prominently featured the ideological rift between Frankfurter and Hugo Black over the incorporation doctrine and judicial activism.

Kenneth W. Colegrove, a professor at Northwestern University, sued the governor of Illinois, Dwight H. Green, over the state's 1901 apportionment law. Professor Colegrove alleged that, owing to its obsolescence, the law violated the Fourteenth Amendment ban against abridgement of the right to vote, violated the Article I guarantees concerning apportionment of congressmen, and violated the Article IV guarantee that every state shall have a republican form of government. Professor Colegrove was also banking on a spate of recent successful voting-rights cases based on equal protection arguments. What distinguished *Colegrove* from these preceding decisions, however, is that they had involved African American voters, the very individuals the Fourteenth Amendment was designed to protect. Speaking for the four-member majority, Frankfurter declares that the case before the Court involves a political question, one the judiciary is not qualified to decide. At best, the Court can declare the Illinois electoral system invalid, but doing so would simply leave the state without districts. If the state chose not to redraw district lines, the election of representatives would of necessity take place on a statewide basis, an eventuality Congress had deemed undesirable and inequitable a century earlier when it had mandated districting. By meddling in state districting, Frankfurter says, the Court would be meddling in the state's political processes and therefore overreaching the Court's constitutionally granted powers.

The "political question" doctrine Frankfurter refers to originated with the Dorr Rebellion in 1842, when armed residents of Rhode Island protested a state law granting only landowners the right to vote. When the Supreme Court was asked to decide the legitimacy of the state government in *Luther v. Borden* (1849), the justices ducked the issue by declaring it a "political question" they had no authority to decide. Over the ensuing decades, the Court frequently invoked the doctrine in order to avoid dealing

Seven of nine black students walk onto the campus of Central High School in Little Rock, Arkansas, with a National Guard officer as an escort on October 15, 1957. (AP/Wide World Photos)

with certain types of issues. Frankfurter, an ardent advocate of judicial restraint, sought to do the same. The problem with his analysis, however, is that a legislature elected by malapportioned districts would almost certainly not change those districts unless forced to do so. Nonetheless, two other justices agreed with Frankfurter's logic. A fourth, Wiley B. Rutledge, wrote a concurrence indicating that while he thought the Court could address reapportionment issues, he was voting with Frankfurter to uphold the lower court's dismissal of Colegrove's case because the situation in Illinois could not be rectified before the next election. The shortness of the time remaining made it doubtful whether action could, or would, be taken in time to secure for petitioners the effective relief they sought.

The majority in *Colegrove* was thus the slimmest possible. Nonetheless, for the next sixteen years, the Court declined to reenter the reapportionment "political thicket." When it finally did so, in *Baker v. Carr* (1962), it robbed *Colegrove* of all power. Although *Baker* did not explicitly overturn *Colegrove*, simply by granting jurisdiction in

Baker—the case that helped establish the principle of "one person, one vote"—the Court breached the bulwark Frankfurter had erected against judicial activism, thereby opening the way to a new era of Court-mandated societal reforms.

◆ ***Cooper v. Aaron***

In 1954, with *Brown v. Board of Education*, the Supreme Court handed down one of its most historically significant opinions. The burden of *Brown* was to overturn *Plessy v. Ferguson* (1896) and thereby end more than a half-century of "separate but equal" legal racial segregation. The Court did so by taking up the issue of school desegregation, but mandating this change proved difficult. The next year, in *Brown v. Board of Education II* (1955), the Court ordered states to desegregate their public schools "with all deliberate speed," putting the onus of enforcement on lower federal courts. Predictably, many southern states dragged their feet—in no small part because President Dwight Eisenhower's well-known personal dislike of the *Brown* decision provided no moral support for moving forward and perhaps even encouraged delay on the part of noncompliant states. The standstill ended in 1958 with *Cooper v. Aaron*.

The state of Arkansas responded to *Brown II* by formulating a plan that would proceed glacially toward integration, beginning with a mere handful of African American students being admitted to only one school, Central High School in Little Rock, in the fall of 1957. The Little Rock chapter of the National Association for the Advancement of Colored People decided to sue in federal court in order to expedite the desegregation process, choosing as litigants a number of children whose applications to all-white schools had been rejected. John Aaron was only the first of these named plaintiffs, just as William G. Cooper, president of the Little Rock School District, was only one of the named defendants. The school district won at trial, and this judgment was upheld by the Eighth District Court of Appeals, which held that the school district's plan was prompt and reasonable.

In the interim between the hearing and its appeal, voters had adopted a state constitutional amendment opposing school integration, while another suit, intended to stop implementation of the limited integration plan, wended its way to the Eighth Circuit. The Arkansas governor, Orval Faubus, then appeared on television to announce that, owing to threats of violence, he was ordering the state national guard to prevent integration at Central High. The next day, Judge Ronald Davis of the federal district court ordered the school to integrate on schedule and also requested that the U.S. Department of Justice intervene to enjoin Governor Faubus from executing his order. On September 23, 1957, nine black students, the "Little Rock Nine," entered Central High School under the protection of the city police department. Their attendance lasted only a few hours, however, because of the large crowds demonstrating outside the school. President Eisenhower could not ignore Faubus's challenge to federal power, and two days later he sent members of the 101st Airborne Division to escort the Little Rock Nine to Central High. Federalized national guardsmen replaced the army troops and remained in place for the remainder of the school year.

Although Judge Davis's ruling had been upheld in federal appellate court, yet another lawsuit sought to delay desegregation because of continued threats of violence. As that case was working its way through the courts, in August 1958 the Supreme Court met in special session for only the third time in its history to hear arguments for and against delaying the Arkansas school desegregation plan. The case presented two primary questions: Would a postponement violate the constitutional rights of the black students? Were the state governor and legislature bound by decisions of the U.S. Supreme Court? The justices agreed quickly and unanimously that the equal protection clause of the Fourteenth Amendment demanded that the Arkansas desegregation plan go forward as planned. They further agreed that the supremacy clause of Article VI bound state governments to Supreme Court decisions. At Justice Frankfurter's suggestion, for the first time in the

Court's history and as an indication of its solidarity, every justice signed the Court's opinion. The other justices were therefore astonished on September 29, when the Court convened to announce its decision, to hear Frankfurter say that he had written a separate concurring opinion memorializing his disagreement with some of the language in the Court's opinion, which had been written by Justice William Brennan.

Frankfurter's concurrence differs little from the Court's opinion: No state can interfere with the authority of the federal government as outlined in the Constitution. Without adherence to law, anarchy reigns—just as it did during the Civil War. And law cannot yield to force, for the constitutional rights of a minority are at stake, rights that must be upheld lest the rest of American society succumb to a breakdown in the order imposed by law. But then Frankfurter closes with a bow to what he sees as the different sensibilities of white southerners. *Brown II*, he implies, recognized differing needs among different communities—and recognized that it would take cooperation from local authorities to make desegregation work. The eloquent words of Abraham Lincoln's first inaugural address failed to avert war, but the compassion implicit in "the better angels of our nature" helped overcome seemingly insurmountable differences.

Frankfurter claimed that his decision to concur separately grew out of a long-standing and special relationship with southern lawyers, on whose respect for the law he felt desegregation ultimately depended. In the midst of oral argument in *Cooper*, he had asked Chief Justice Earl Warren to make a similar bow to the school district's lawyer. Warren refused. Frankfurter believed that Warren lacked a proper sense of the delicacy of the situation and, in essence, made an end run around the chief justice and the rest of the Court. Warren, not surprisingly, felt betrayed. Justices William Brennan and Hugo Black drafted a separate concurrence to distance themselves from Frankfurter but were dissuaded from publishing it. Whatever Frankfurter's motives, his attempt at a grace note did little good. *Cooper* initially stiffened resistance to desegregation. It would take another six years of struggle on the part of civil rights activists before the Civil Rights Act of 1964 forced the South to desegregate.

◆ *Gomillion v. Lightfoot*

Charles G. Gomillion was one of a number of black citizens of Tuskegee, Alabama, who sued Phil M. Lightfoot, Tuskegee's mayor, as well as other city and county officials over a gerrymandering scheme that changed city boundaries into a "strangely irregular twenty-eight-sided figure" that deprived all but four or five of Tuskegee's registered African American voters of their franchise in municipal elections while not depriving a single white citizen of his or her right to vote. Lawyers for Tuskegee and Macon County repeatedly cited in their briefs and oral arguments the holding of *Colegrove v. Green*, the 1946 redistricting case in which Justice Frankfurter claimed that questions of legislative apportionment were beyond the reach of the judici-

"Conscientious scruples have not, in the course of the long struggle for religious toleration, relieved the individual from obedience to a general law not aimed at the promotion or restriction of religious beliefs."

(*Minersville School District v. Gobitis*)

"This is one of those demands on judicial power, which cannot be met by verbal fencing about 'jurisdiction.' It must be resolved by considerations on the basis of which this Court, from time to time, has refused to intervene in controversies. It has refused to do so because due regard for the effective working of our Government revealed this issue to be of a peculiarly political nature and therefore not meet for judicial determination."

(*Colegrove v. Green*)

"To sustain this action would cut very deep into the very being of Congress. Courts ought not to enter this political thicket. The remedy for unfairness in districting is to secure State legislatures that will apportion properly…. The Constitution has many commands that are not enforceable by courts…. The Constitution has left the performance of many duties in our governmental scheme to depend…, ultimately, on the vigilance of the people in exercising their political rights."

(*Colegrove v. Green*)

"On the few tragic occasions in the history of the Nation, North and South, when law was forcibly resisted or systematically evaded, it has signalled the breakdown of constitutional processes of government on which ultimately rest the liberties of all. Violent resistance to law cannot be made a legal reason for its suspension without loosening the fabric of our society."

(*Cooper v. Aaron*)

"A statute which is alleged to have worked unconstitutional deprivations of petitioners' rights is not immune to attack simply because the mechanism employed… is a redefinition of municipal boundaries…. While in form this is merely an act redefining metes and bounds… the inescapable human effect… is to despoil colored citizens, and only colored citizens, of their… voting rights. That was not Colegrove v. Green."

(*Gomillion v. Lightfoot*)

ary. It was poetic justice that Frankfurter was now obliged to write the opinion of the unanimous *Gomillion* Court.

Frankfurter needed to defend both his earlier opinion and his core value of judicial restraint. He does so by declaring that the Tuskegee law, unlike that addressed in *Colegrove*, was intended to injure only black voters and was therefore a violation of the Fifteenth Amendment, which prohibits states from denying anyone the right to vote on account of race, color, or previous condition of servitude. As such, the case concerned not a political question but a violation of the Constitution. Furthermore, Frankfurter says, while *Colegrove* concerned legislative inaction over a lengthy period, the law currently before the Court was of recent vintage and plainly reflected legislative intent to deprive black citizens of Tuskegee of their right to vote. State power—even when employed in a "political" redefinition of municipal boundaries—could not be used in violation of a right conferred by the Constitution.

Frankfurter's analysis contains an inherent contradiction: What is to prevent white citizens suffering disenfranchisement from seeking similar relief? While the intent of the Fifteenth Amendment might have been to ensure African American suffrage, the words of the amendment make it applicable to all "citizens of the United States." In a concurring opinion, Justice Charles Whittaker argues that the equal protection clause of the Fourteenth Amendment offers a clearer basis for disallowing the type of racially discriminatory apportionment under consideration in *Gomillion*. Whittaker would soon be proved right: Just days after the *Gomillion* decision was handed down, the Court indicated its intention to hear another reapportionment case, *Baker v. Carr* (1962). Frankfurter urged his fellow justices not to take on *Baker*, which he considered to involve a political question; granting jurisdiction would necessitate overruling *Colegrove*. Justice William Brennan's opinion for the Court in *Baker* did not explicitly overturn *Colegrove*. Brennan noted, however, that four of the seven justices in *Colegrove* had expressed their belief that the Court did have jurisdiction but that one of the four, fearing a remedy could not be found before the next election for the malapportionment alleged in the case, had voted with Frankfurter not to consider an appeal in *Colegrove*. It was a fine point without much resonance for anyone other than Frankfurter: *Baker* would mark the inauguration of the reapportionment revolution and the end of Frankfurter's Supreme Court career.

Questions for Further Study

1. It has been said that Frankfurter's reputation rests largely on his work before his appointment to the Supreme Court. Compare and contrast these two phases of his professional life, and address the reasons why he is today considered one of the most controversial judges of his time.

2. It is perhaps ironic that as members of the Jehovah's Witness sect, the Gobitis children refused to salute the U.S. flag: in less than two years, armed forces under that flag would go to war against Hitler's Germany, where Jehovah's Witnesses were a target for extermination. Nevertheless, to salute the flag would have been against their religious beliefs. Using *Minersville School District v. Gobitis* as a point of reference, discuss the issue of religious freedom when it comes into conflict with federal or state law. Consider other examples, such as military service for Quakers and other pacifist sects or drug laws as they pertain to Native American peyote ceremonies.

3. Evaluate Frankfurter's controversial opinion in *Colegrove v. Green*. Although he has been judged harshly for this ruling, there is certainly a strong argument for his stance that the federal government had no right to intervene in a state's electoral redistricting process. Do you agree with his claim that the issue in *Colegrove* was a "political question" not to be decided in a court of law? What about his statement that "the Constitution has many commands that are not enforceable by courts"? In fact, the courts themselves, strictly speaking, do not enforce anything; that is the job of the executive branch. What did Frankfurter mean by this statement, and was he correct?

4. Why did Frankfurter, after insisting that all justices sign the opinion in *Cooper v. Aaron*, then submit a separate concurring opinion? What point was he trying to make?

5. Examine the contrasting opinions of Frankfurter and his much younger colleague, William Brennan, in *Colegrove*, *Gomillion v. Lightfoot*, and *Baker v. Carr*.

Impact and Legacy

It has to be said that Felix Frankfurter's accomplishments before joining the Court outweigh his accomplishments while on the high bench. Once the erstwhile progressive activist donned the jurist's robe, he reverted to the professorial role he had filled even during the whirlwind days of the New Deal, when he wielded enormous—if unofficial—power. But once exposed to the public's watchful eye, the former power broker suddenly lost his ability or his willingness to wield his power. Justice Frankfurter's watchwords were *discretion* and *deference*. He never wanted the Court to overstep its bounds, to tread on ground occupied by the other branches of government. It seemed that the former teacher of administrative law wanted—above all else—to sit on the Court as a sort of super administrator, one who viewed his primary job to be instructing his colleagues on the finer points of the law while restraining them from making any judgments or gestures that could be construed as political.

Frankfurter has been called the most controversial justice of his day—perhaps because he did not meet the expectations of those who believed that his powerful intellect and commitment to liberal causes would inevitably result in his becoming the Court's leader, if not its chief justice. Instead, time seems to have passed Frankfurter by, leaving as his major judicial legacy a case, *Colegrove v. Green*, that was a kind of seawall against the tide of social change that eventually overwhelmed it. His most lasting achievement may, in fact, have been his two-plus decades at Harvard Law School, where he influenced so many of the young minds that went on to shape the nation's future.

Key Sources

Frankfurter left a lengthy paper trail. Most of his papers, dating from his time at Harvard and his tenure on the Court, reside in the manuscript collections at Harvard Law School. Papers concerning his many years devoted to political reform have been deposited in the Manuscript Division of the Library of Congress. Those concerning his work with the Zionist organization can be found in the Central Zionist Archives in Jerusalem, Israel. Frankfurter kept up a lively correspondence with many prominent individuals, so selected letters can be found in such places as the Learned Hand Papers at the Harvard Law School Library, and the Louis D. Brandeis Papers at the University of Louisville Law School Library. Published collections of Frankfurter's works include Archibald MacLeish and E. F. Prichard, eds., *Law and Politics: Occasional Papers of Felix Frankfurter, 1913–1938* (1939); Philip B. Kurland, ed., *Felix Frankfurter on the Supreme Court: Extrajudicial Essays on the Court and the Constitution* (1970); Philip Elman, ed., *Of Law and Men: Papers and Addresses of Felix Frankfurter, 1939–1956* (1956); and Joseph P. Lash, ed., *From the Diaries of Felix Frankfurter* (1975).

Further Reading

■ Articles

Danzig, Richard. "Justice Frankfurter's Opinions in the Flag Salute Cases: Blending Logic and Psychologic in Constitutional Decisionmaking," *Stanford Law Review* 36 (1984): 675–723.

■ Books

Baker, Leonard. *Brandeis and Frankfurter: A Dual Biography*. New York: Harper and Row, 1984.

Coleman, William T., Jr. "Mr. Justice Frankfurter: Civil Libertarian as Lawyer and as Justice." In *Six Justices on Civil Rights*, ed. Donald J. Rotunda. New York: Oceana, 1983.

Freyer, Tony Allan. *Little Rock on Trial: Cooper v. Aaron and School Desegregation*. Lawrence: University Press of Kansas, 2007.

Murphy, Bruce Allen. *The Brandeis/Frankfurter Connection: The Secret Political Activities of Two Supreme Court Justices*. New York: Oxford University Press, 1982.

Parrish, Michael E. *Felix Frankfurter and His Times: The Reform Years*. Glencoe, Ill.: Free Press, 1982.

Simon, James F. *The Antagonists: Hugo Black, Felix Frankfurter and Civil Liberties in Modern America*. New York: Simon and Schuster, 1989.

Urofsky, Melvin I. *Felix Frankfurter: Judicial Restraint and Individual Liberties*. Boston: Twayne, 1991.

—Lisa Paddock

MINERSVILLE SCHOOL DISTRICT V. GOBITIS (1940)

We must decide whether the requirement of participation in such a ceremony, exacted from a child who refuses upon sincere religious grounds, infringes without due process of law the liberty guaranteed by the Fourteenth Amendment.

Centuries of strife over the erection of particular dogmas as exclusive or all-comprehending faiths led to the inclusion of a guarantee for religious freedom in the Bill of Rights. The First Amendment, and the Fourteenth through its absorption of the First, sought to guard against repetition of those bitter religious struggles by prohibiting the establishment of a state religion and by securing to every sect the free exercise of its faith. So pervasive is the acceptance of this precious right that its scope is brought into question, as here, only when the conscience of individuals collides with the felt necessities of society.

Certainly the affirmative pursuit of one's convictions about the ultimate mystery of the universe and man's relation to it is placed beyond the reach of law. Government may not interfere with organized or individual expression of belief or disbelief. Propagation of belief—or even of disbelief in the supernatural—is protected, whether in church or chapel, mosque or synagogue, tabernacle or meetinghouse. Likewise the Constitution assures generous immunity to the individual from imposition of penalties for offending, in the course of his own religious activities, the religious views of others, be they a minority or those who are dominant in government....

But the manifold character of man's relations may bring his conception of religious duty into conflict with the secular interests of his fellow-men. When does the constitutional guarantee compel exemption from doing what society thinks necessary for the promotion of some great common end, or from a penalty for conduct which appears dangerous to the general good? To state the problem is to recall the truth that no single principle can answer all of life's complexities. The right to freedom of religious belief, however dissident and however obnoxious to the cherished beliefs of others—even of a majority—is itself the denial of an absolute. But to affirm that the freedom to follow conscience has itself no limits in the life of a society would deny that very plurality of principles which, as a matter of history, underlies protection of religious toleration....

Our present task then, as so often the case with courts, is to reconcile two rights in order to prevent either from destroying the other. But, because in safeguarding conscience we are dealing with interests so subtle and so dear, every possible leeway should be given to the claims of religious faith.

In the judicial enforcement of religious freedom we are concerned with a historic concept....The religious liberty which the Constitution protects has never excluded legislation of general scope not directed against doctrinal loyalties of particular sects. Judicial nullification of legislation cannot be justified by attributing to the framers of the Bill of Rights views for which there is no historic warrant. Conscientious scruples have not, in the course of the long struggle for religious toleration, relieved the individual from obedience to a general law not aimed at the promotion or restriction of religious beliefs. The mere possession of religious convictions which contradict the relevant concerns of a political society does not relieve the citizen from the discharge of political responsibilities. The necessity for this adjustment has again and again been recognized. In a number of situations the exertion of political authority has been sustained, while basic considerations of religious freedom have been left inviolate.... In all these cases the general laws in question, upheld in their application to those who refused obedience from religious conviction, were manifestations of specific powers of government deemed by the legislature essential to secure and maintain that orderly, tranquil, and free society without which religious toleration itself is unattainable. Nor does the freedom of speech assured by Due Process move in a more absolute circle of immunity than that enjoyed by religious freedom. Even if it were assumed that freedom of speech goes beyond the historic concept of full opportunity to utter and to disseminate views, however heretical or offensive to dominant opinion, and includes freedom from conveying what may be deemed an implied but rejected affirmation, the question remains whether school children, like the Gobitis children, must be excused from conduct required of all the other children in the promotion of national cohesion. We are dealing with an interest inferior to none in the hierarchy of legal values. National unity is the basis of national security....Situations like the present are phases of the profoundest problem confronting a democracy—the problem which Lincoln cast in memorable dilemma: "Must a government of necessity be too strong for the liberties of its people, or too weak to maintain its own existence?" No mere textual reading or logical talisman can solve the dilemma. And when the issue demands judicial determination, it is not the personal notion of judges of what wise adjustment requires which must prevail....

The case before us is not concerned with an exertion of legislative power for the promotion of some specific need or interest of secular society—the protection of the family, the promotion of health, the common defense, the raising of public revenues to defray the cost of government. But all these specific activities of government presuppose the existence of an organized political society. The ultimate foundation of a free society is the binding tie of cohesive sentiment. Such a sentiment is fostered by all those agencies of the mind and spirit which may serve to gather up the traditions of a people, transmit them from generation to generation, and thereby create that continuity of a treasured common life which constitutes a civilization. "We live by symbols." The flag is the symbol of our national unity, transcending all internal differences, however large, within the framework of the Constitution. This Court has had occasion to say that "...the flag is the symbol of the nation's power,—the emblem of freedom in its truest, best sense....It signifies government resting on the consent of the governed; liberty regulated by law; the protection of the weak against the strong; security against the exercise of arbitrary power; and absolute safety for free institutions against foreign aggression."...

The case before us must be viewed as though the legislature of Pennsylvania had itself formally directed the flag-salute for the children of Minersville; had made no exemption for children whose parents were possessed of conscientious scruples like those of the Gobitis family; and had indicated its belief in the desirable ends to be secured by having its public school children share a common experience at those periods of development when their minds are supposedly receptive to its assimilation, by an exercise appropriate in time and place and setting, and one designed to evoke in them appreciation of the nation's hopes and dreams, its sufferings and sacrifices. The precise issue, then, for us to decide is whether the legislatures of the various states and the authorities in a thousand counties and school districts of this country are barred from determining the appropriateness of various means to evoke that uni-

fying sentiment without which there can ultimately be no liberties, civil or religious. To stigmatize legislative judgment in providing for this universal gesture of respect for the symbol of our national life in the setting of the common school as a lawless inroad on that freedom of conscience which the Constitution protects, would amount to no less than the pronouncement of pedagogical and psychological dogma in a field where courts possess no marked and certainly no controlling competence. The influences which help toward a common feeling for the common country are manifold. Some may seem harsh and others no doubt are foolish. Surely, however, the end is legitimate. And the effective means for its attainment are still so uncertain and so unauthenticated by science as to preclude us from putting the widely prevalent belief in flag-saluting beyond the pale of legislative power. It mocks reason and denies our whole history to find in the allowance of a requirement to salute our flag on fitting occasions the seeds of sanction for obeisance to a leader.

The wisdom of training children in patriotic impulses by those compulsions which necessarily pervade so much of the educational process is not for our independent judgment. Even were we convinced of the folly of such a measure, such belief would be no proof of its unconstitutionality. For ourselves, we might be tempted to say that the deepest patriotism is best engendered by giving unfettered scope to the most crochety beliefs. Perhaps it is best, even from the standpoint of those interests which ordinances like the one under review seek to promote, to give to the least popular sect leave from conformities like those here in issue. But the court-room is not the arena for debating issues of educational policy. It is not our province to choose among competing considerations in the subtle process of securing effective loyalty to the traditional ideals of democracy, while respecting at the same time individual idiosyncrasies among a people so diversified in racial origins and religious allegiances. So to hold would in effect make us the school board for the country. That authority has not been given to this Court, nor should we assume it.

We are dealing here with the formative period in the development of citizenship. Great diversity of psychological and ethical opinion exists among us concerning the best way to train children for their place in society. Because of these differences and because of reluctance to permit a single, iron-cast system of education to be imposed upon a nation compounded of so many strains, we have held that, even though public education is one of our most cherished democratic institutions, the Bill of Rights bars a state from compelling all children to attend the public schools.... But it is a very different thing for this Court to exercise censorship over the conviction of legislatures that a particular program or exercise will best promote in the minds of children who attend the common schools an attachment to the institutions of their country.

What the school authorities are really asserting is the right to awaken in the child's mind considerations as to the significance of the flag contrary to those implanted by the parent. In such an attempt the state is normally at a disadvantage in competing with the parent's authority, so long—and this is the vital aspect of religious toleration—as parents are unmolested in their right to counteract by their own persuasiveness the wisdom and rightness of those loyalties which the state's educational system is seeking to promote. Except where the transgression of constitutional liberty is too plain for argument, personal freedom is best maintained—so long as the

remedial channels of the democratic process remain open and unobstructed—when it is ingrained in a people's habits and not enforced against popular policy by the coercion of adjudicated law. That the flag salute is an allowable portion of a school program for those who do not invoke conscientious scruples is surely not debatable. But for us to insist that, though the ceremony may be required, exceptional immunity must be given to dissidents, is to maintain that there is no basis for a legislative judgment that such an exemption might introduce elements of difficulty into the school discipline, might cast doubts in the minds of the other children which would themselves weaken the effect of the exercise.

The preciousness of the family relation, the authority and independence which give dignity to parenthood, indeed the enjoyment of all freedom, presuppose the kind of ordered society which is summarized by our flag. A society which is dedicated to the preservation of these ultimate values of civiliza-

Glossary

binding tie of cohesive sentiment	shared beliefs that serve to unite a society
compounded of so many strains	made up of so many elements and influences
due process of law	the right of an individual accused of a crime to be formally charged and tried
Fourteenth Amendment... through its absorption of the First	reference to the fact that whereas the First Amendment guarantees free speech under federal law, the Fourteenth extends that guarantee to individuals under state law
immunity	freedom from prosecution
leave from conformities	exemption from abiding by rules
nor does the freedom of speech... a more absolute circle of immunity	freedom of speech is not more important or valid than freedom of religion
occasions the seeds of sanction for obeisance to a leader	opens up the possibility of dictatorship
plurality of principles	variety of competing ideas
so to hold	to take such a position
talisman	magic charm

tion may in self-protection utilize the educational process for inculcating those almost unconscious feelings which bind men together in a comprehending loyalty, whatever may be their lesser differences and difficulties. That is to say, the process may be utilized so long as men's right to believe as they please, to win others to their way of belief, and their right to assemble in their chosen places of worship for the devotional ceremonies of their faith, are all fully respected.

Judicial review, itself a limitation on popular government, is a fundamental part of our constitutional scheme. But to the legislature no less than to courts is committed the guardianship of deeply-cherished liberties.…Where all the effective means of inducing political changes are left free from interference, education in the abandonment of foolish legislation is itself a training in liberty. To fight out the wise use of legislative authority in the forum of public opinion and before legislative assemblies rather than to transfer such a contest to the judicial arena, serves to vindicate the self-confidence of a free people.

COLEGROVE V. GREEN (1946)

We are of opinion that the petitioners ask of this Court what is beyond its competence to grant. This is one of those demands on judicial power which cannot be met by verbal fencing about "jurisdiction." It must be resolved by considerations on the basis of which this Court, from time to time, has refused to intervene in controversies. It has refused to do so because due regard for the effective working of our Government revealed this issue to be of a peculiarly political nature and therefore not meet for judicial determination.

This is not an action to recover for damage because of the discriminatory exclusion of a plaintiff from rights enjoyed by other citizens. The basis for the suit is not a private wrong, but a wrong suffered by Illinois as a polity.... In effect this is an appeal to the federal courts to reconstruct the electoral process of Illinois in order that it may be adequately represented in the councils of the Nation. Because the Illinois legislature has failed to revise its Congressional Representative districts in order to reflect great changes, during more than a generation, in the distribution of its population, we are asked to do this, as it were, for Illinois. Of course no court can affirmatively remap the Illinois districts so as to bring them more in conformity with the standards of fairness for a representative system. At best we could only declare the existing electoral system invalid. The result would be to leave Illinois undistricted and to bring into operation, if the Illinois legislature chose not to act, the choice of members for the House of Representatives on a state-wide ticket. The last stage may be worse than the first. The upshot of judicial action may defeat the vital political principle which led Congress, more than a hundred years ago, to require districting.... Assuming acquiescence on the part of the authorities of Illinois in the selection of its Representatives by a mode that defies the direction of Congress for selection by districts, the House of Representatives may not acquiesce. In the exercise of its power to judge the qualifications of its own members, the House may reject a delegation of Representatives-at-large.... Nothing is clearer than that this controversy concerns matters that bring courts into immediate and active relations with party contests. From the determination of such issues this Court has traditionally held aloof. It is hostile to a democratic system to involve the judiciary in the politics of the people. And it is not less pernicious if such judicial intervention in an essentially political contest be dressed up in the abstract phrases of the law.

The petitioners urge with great zeal that the conditions of which they complain are grave evils and offend public morality. The Constitution of the United States gives ample power to provide against these evils. But due regard for the Constitution as a viable system precludes judicial correction. Authority for dealing with such problems resides elsewhere. Article I, section 4 of the Constitution provides that "The Times, Places and Manner of holding Elections for... Representative, shall be prescribed in each State by the Legislature thereof; but the Congress may at any time by Law make or alter such Regulations,..." The short of it is that the Constitution has conferred upon Congress exclusive authority to secure fair representation by the States in the popular House and left to that House determination whether States have fulfilled their responsibility. If Congress failed in exercising its powers, whereby standards of fairness are offended, the remedy ultimately lies with the people. Whether Congress faithfully discharges its duty or not, the subject has been committed to the exclusive control of Congress. An aspect of government from which the judiciary, in view of what is involved, has been excluded by the clear intention of the Constitution cannot be entered by the federal courts because Congress may have been in default in exacting from States obedience to its mandate.

The one stark fact that emerges from a study of the history of Congressional apportionment is its embroilment in politics, in the sense of party contests and party interests. The Constitution enjoins upon Congress the duty of apportioning Representatives "among the several States... according to their respective Numbers,..." Article I, 2. Yet, Congress has at times been heedless of this command and not apportioned according to the requirements of the Census. It never occurred to anyone that this Court could issue mandamus to compel Congress to perform its mandatory duty to apportion.... Until 1842 there was the greatest diversity among the States in the manner of choosing Representatives because Congress had made no requirement for districting. Congress then provided for the election of Represen-

Frankfurter, Felix

tatives by districts. Strangely enough the power to do so was seriously questioned; it was still doubted by a Committee of Congress as late as 1901....Throughout our history, whatever may have been the controlling Apportionment Act, the most glaring disparities have prevailed as to the contours and the population of districts....

To sustain this action would cut very deep into the very being of Congress. Courts ought not to enter this political thicket. The remedy for unfairness in districting is to secure State legislatures that will apportion properly, or to invoke the ample powers of Congress. The Constitution has many commands that are not enforceable by courts because they clearly fall outside the conditions and purposes that circumscribe judicial action....The Constitution has left the performance of many duties in our governmental scheme to depend on the fidelity of the executive and legislative action and, ultimately, on the vigilance of the people in exercising their political rights.

Glossary

apportionment	the act of dividing a state or other entity into legislative districts
cannot be met by verbal fencing	cannot be settled simply by arguing
due regard for the Constitution ... precludes judicial correction	if one takes the Constitution seriously, then it is not possible to use the courts to change it
mandamus	a court order requiring another court to perform a particular action
meet	appropriate
the popular House	the House of Representatives
until 1842	a reference to the Dorr Rebellion, in which a group led by Thomas Dorr of Rhode Island agitated for expansion of voting rights in that state to include all white men, not just property owners

COOPER V. AARON (1958)

Frankfurter concurrence

While unreservedly participating with my brethren in our joint opinion, I deem it appropriate also to deal individually with the great issue here at stake.

By working together, by sharing in a common effort, men of different minds and tempers, even if they do not reach agreement, acquire understanding and thereby tolerance of their differences. This process was under way in Little Rock. The detailed plan formulated by the Little Rock School Board, in the light of local circumstances, had been approved by the United States District Court in Arkansas as satisfying the requirements of this Court's decree in *Brown v. Board of Education.* The Little Rock School Board had embarked on an educational effort "to obtain public acceptance" of its plan. Thus the process of the community's accommodation to new demands of law upon it, the development of habits of acceptance of the right of colored children to the equal protection of the laws guaranteed by the Constitution, had peacefully and promisingly begun. The condition in Little Rock before this process was forcibly impeded by those in control of the government of Arkansas....

All this was disrupted by the introduction of the state militia and by other obstructive measures taken by the State. The illegality of these interferences with the constitutional right of Negro children qualified to enter the Central High School is unaffected by whatever action or non-action the Federal Government had seen fit to take. Nor is it neutralized by the undoubted good faith of the Little Rock School Board in endeavoring to discharge its constitutional duty.

The use of force to further obedience to law is in any event a last resort and one not congenial to the spirit of our Nation. But the tragic aspect of this disruptive tactic was that the power of the State was used not to sustain law but as an instrument for thwarting law. The State of Arkansas is thus responsible for disabling one of its subordinate agencies, the Little Rock School Board, from peacefully carrying out the Board's and the State's constitutional duty. Accordingly, while Arkansas is not a formal party in these proceedings and a decree cannot go against the State, it is legally and morally before the Court.

We are now asked to hold that the illegal, forcible interference by the State of Arkansas with the continuance of what the Constitution commands, and the consequences in disorder that it entrained, should be recognized as justification for undoing what the School Board had formulated, what the District Court in 1955 had directed to be carried out, and what was in process of obedience. No explanation that may be offered in support of such a request can obscure the inescapable meaning that law should bow to force. To yield to such a claim would be to enthrone official lawlessness, and lawlessness if not checked is the precursor of anarchy. On the few tragic occasions in the history of the Nation, North and South, when law was forcibly resisted or systematically evaded, it has signalled the breakdown of constitutional processes of government on which ultimately rest the liberties of all. Violent resistance to law cannot be made a legal reason for its suspension without loosening the fabric of our society. What could this mean but to acknowledge that disorder under the aegis of a State has moral superiority over the law of the Constitution? For those in authority thus to defy the law of the land is profoundly subversive not only of our constitutional system but of the presuppositions of a democratic society. The State "must ... yield to an authority that is paramount to the State."...

The duty to abstain from resistance to "the supreme Law of the Land," U.S. Const., Art. VI 2, as declared by the organ of our Government for ascertaining it, does not require immediate approval of it nor does it deny the right of dissent. Criticism need not be stilled. Active obstruction or defiance is barred. Our kind of society cannot endure if the controlling authority of the Law as derived from the Constitution is not to be the tribunal specially charged with the duty of ascertaining and declaring what is "the supreme Law of the Land."...Particularly is this so where the declaration of what "the supreme Law" commands on an underlying moral issue is not the dubious pronouncement of a gravely divided Court but is the unanimous conclusion of a long-matured deliberative process. The Constitution is not the formulation of the merely personal views of the members of this Court, nor can its authority be reduced to the claim that state officials are its controlling interpreters. Local customs, however hardened by time, are not decreed in heaven. Habits and feelings they engender may be counteracted and moderated. Experience attests that such local habits and feelings will yield, gradually though this be, to law and education. And educational influences are exerted not only by explicit teaching. They vigorously flow from the fruitful exercise of the responsibility of those charged with political official power and from the almost unconsciously transforming actualities of living under law.

The process of ending unconstitutional exclusion of pupils from the common school system—"common" meaning shared alike—solely because of color is no doubt not an easy, overnight task in a few States where a drastic alteration in the ways of communities is involved. Deep emotions have, no doubt, been stirred. They will not be calmed by letting violence loose—violence and defiance employed and encouraged by those upon whom the duty of law observance should have the strongest claim—nor by submitting to it under whatever guise employed. Only the constructive use of time will achieve what an advanced civilization demands and the Constitution confirms.

For carrying out the decision that color alone cannot bar a child from a public school, this Court has recognized the diversity of circumstances in local school situations. But is it a reasonable hope that the necessary endeavors for such adjustment will be furthered, that racial frictions will be ameliorated, by a reversal of the process and interrupting effective measures toward the necessary goal? The progress that has been made in respecting the constitutional rights of the Negro children, according to the graduated plan sanctioned by the two lower courts, would have to be retraced, perhaps with even greater difficul-

ty because of deference to forcible resistance. It would have to be retraced against the seemingly vindicated feeling of those who actively sought to block that progress. Is there not the strongest reason for concluding that to accede to the Board's request, on the basis of the circumstances that gave rise to it, for a suspension of the Board's non-segregation plan, would be but the beginning of a series of delays calculated to nullify this Court's adamant decisions in the Brown case that the Constitution precludes compulsory segregation based on color in state-supported schools?

That the responsibility of those who exercise power in a democratic government is not to reflect inflamed public feeling but to help form its understanding, is especially true when they are confronted with a problem like a racially discriminating public school system. This is the lesson to be drawn from the heartening experience in ending enforced racial segregation in the public schools in cities with Negro populations of large proportions. Compliance with decisions of this Court, as the constitutional organ of the supreme Law of the Land, has often, throughout our history, depended on active support by state and local authorities. It presupposes such support. To withhold it, and indeed to use political power to try to paralyze the supreme Law, precludes the maintenance of our federal system as we have known and cherished it for one hundred and seventy years.

Lincoln's appeal to "the better angels of our nature" failed to avert a fratricidal war. But the compassionate wisdom of Lincoln's First and Second Inaugurals bequeathed to the Union, cemented with blood, a moral heritage which, when drawn upon in times of stress and strife, is sure to find specific ways and means to surmount difficulties that may appear to be insurmountable.

Glossary

constitutional organ	functional entity, such as a court, whose authority comes from the Constitution
the organ of our Government	the Constitution

GOMILLION V. LIGHTFOOT (1960)

At this stage of the litigation we are not concerned with the truth of the allegations, that is, the ability of petitioners to sustain their allegations by proof. The sole question is whether the allegations entitle them to make good on their claim that they are being denied rights under the United States Constitution. The complaint, charging that Act 140 is a device to disenfranchise Negro citizens, alleges the following facts: Prior to Act 140 the City of Tuskegee was square in shape; the Act transformed it into a strangely irregular twenty-eight-sided figure as indicated in the diagram appended to this opinion. The essential inevitable effect of this redefinition of Tuskegee's boundaries is to remove from the city all save only four or five of its 400 Negro voters while not removing a single white voter or resident. The result of the Act is to deprive the Negro petitioners discriminatorily of the benefits of residence in Tuskegee, including, inter alia, the right to vote in municipal elections.

These allegations, if proven, would abundantly establish that Act 140 was not an ordinary geographic redistricting measure even within familiar abuses of gerrymandering. If these allegations upon a trial remained uncontradicted or unqualified, the conclusion would be irresistible, tantamount for all practical purposes to a mathematical demonstration, that the legislation is solely concerned with segregating white and colored voters by fencing Negro citizens out of town so as to deprive them of their pre-existing municipal vote.

It is difficult to appreciate what stands in the way of adjudging a statute having this inevitable effect invalid in light of the principles by which this Court must judge, and uniformly has judged, statutes that, howsoever speciously defined, obviously discriminate against colored citizens. "The [Fifteenth] Amendment nullifies sophisticated as well as simpleminded modes of discrimination."…

The complaint amply alleges a claim of racial discrimination. Against this claim the respondents have never suggested, either in their brief or in oral argument, any countervailing municipal function which Act 140 is designed to serve. The respondents invoke generalities expressing the State's unrestricted power—unlimited, that is, by the United States Constitution—to establish, destroy, or reorganize by contraction or expansion its political subdivisions, to wit, cities, counties, and other local units. We freely recognize the breadth and importance of this aspect of the State's political power. To exalt this power into an absolute is to misconceive the reach and rule of this Court's decisions in the leading case of *Hunter v. Pittsburgh*, and related cases relied upon by respondents.…

In short, the cases that have come before this Court regarding legislation by States dealing with their political subdivisions fall into two classes: (1) those in which it is claimed that the State, by virtue of the prohibition against impairment of the obligation of contract (Art. I, 10) and of the Due Process Clause of the Fourteenth Amendment, is without power to extinguish, or alter the boundaries of, an existing municipality; and (2) in which it is claimed that the State has no power to change the identity of a municipality whereby citizens of a pre-existing municipality suffer serious economic disadvantage.

Neither of these claims is supported by such a specific limitation upon State power as confines the States under the Fifteenth Amendment. As to the first category, it is obvious that the creation of municipalities—clearly a political act—does not come within the conception of a contract under the Dartmouth College case. As to the second, if one principle clearly emerges from the numerous decisions of this Court dealing with taxation it is that the Due Process Clause affords no immunity against mere inequalities in tax burdens, nor does it afford protection against their increase as an indirect consequence of a State's exercise of its political powers.

Particularly in dealing with claims under broad provisions of the Constitution, which derive content by an interpretive process of inclusion and exclusion, it is imperative that generalizations, based on and qualified by the concrete situations that gave rise to them, must not be applied out of context in disregard of variant controlling facts. Thus, a correct reading of the seemingly unconfined dicta of Hunter and kindred cases is not that the State has plenary power to manipulate in every conceivable way, for every conceivable purpose, the affairs of its municipal corporations, but rather that the State's authority is unrestrained by the particular prohibitions of the Constitution considered in those cases.

The Hunter opinion itself intimates that a state legislature may not be omnipotent even as to the disposition of some types of property owned by municipal corporations. Further, other cases in this Court have refused to allow a State to abolish a municipality, or alter its boundaries, or merge it with another city, without preserving to the creditors of the old city some effective recourse for the collection of debts owed them....

This line of authority conclusively shows that the Court has never acknowledged that the States have power to do as they will with municipal corporations regardless of consequences. Legislative control of municipalities, no less than other state power, lies within the scope of relevant limitations imposed by the United States Constitution. The observation in *Graham v. Folsom* becomes relevant: "The power of the State to alter or destroy its corporations is not greater than the power of the State to repeal its legislation."...

If all this is so in regard to the constitutional protection of contracts, it should be equally true that, to paraphrase, such power, extensive though it is, is met and overcome by the Fifteenth Amendment to the Constitution of the United States, which forbids a State from passing any law which deprives a citizen of his vote because of his race. The opposite conclusion, urged upon us by respondents, would sanction the achievement by a State of any impairment of voting rights whatever so long as it was cloaked in the garb of the realignment of political subdivisions....

The respondents find another barrier to the trial of this case in *Colegrove v. Green*. In that case the Court passed on an Illinois law governing the arrangement of congressional districts within that State. The complaint rested upon the disparity of population between the different districts which rendered the

Glossary

Act 140	the Tuskegee redistricting ordinance
Due Process Clause	a guarantee, under the Fifth and Fourteenth Amendments, of the individual's right to be formally charged for a crime and granted a fair trial
gerrymandering	political redistricting intended to benefit certain groups at the expense of others
Graham v. Folsom	a 1906 Supreme Court decision concerning "the power of the state to alter or destroy its municipal corporations"
Hunter v. Pittsburgh	a 1907 Supreme Court case involving redistricting
in disregard of variant controlling facts	without taking into account other significant factors
inter alia	among other things
invalid	without legal justification or right
metes and bounds	a legal description for a piece of real estate, involving markers and directional headings to clearly identify the boundaries of the parcel
Mr. Justice Holmes	Oliver Wendell Holmes, Jr. (1841–1935)
municipal corporations	city or town governments
Nixon v. Herndon	a 1927 case in which the Supreme Court struck down a Texas law that prevented blacks from voting in the Democratic primaries
plenary	planning
respondents	parties against whom a case is brought by the petitioners
sanction	grant approval to
viz.	abbreviation for the Latin *videlicet*, meaning "for example"

effectiveness of each individual's vote in some districts far less than in others. This disparity came to pass solely through shifts in population between 1901, when Illinois organized its congressional districts, and 1946, when the complaint was lodged. During this entire period elections were held under the districting scheme devised in 1901. The Court affirmed the dismissal of the complaint on the ground that it presented a subject not meet for adjudication. The decisive facts in this case, which at this stage must be taken as proved, are wholly different from the considerations found controlling in Colegrove.

That case involved a complaint of discriminatory apportionment of congressional districts. The appellants in Colegrove complained only of a dilution of the strength of their votes as a result of legislative inaction over a course of many years. The petitioners here complain that affirmative legislative action deprives them of their votes and the consequent advantages that the ballot affords. When a legislature thus singles out a readily isolated segment of a racial minority for special discriminatory treatment, it violates the Fifteenth Amendment. In no case involving unequal weight in voting distribution that has come before the Court did the decision sanction a differentiation on racial lines whereby approval was given to unequivocal withdrawal of the vote solely from colored citizens. Apart from all else, these considerations lift this controversy out of the so-called "political" arena and into the conventional sphere of constitutional litigation.

In sum, as Mr. Justice Holmes remarked, when dealing with a related situation, in *Nixon v. Herndon*, "Of course the petition concerns political action," but "The objection that the subject matter of the suit is political is little more than a play upon words." A statute which is alleged to have worked unconstitutional deprivations of petitioners' rights is not immune to attack simply because the mechanism employed by the legislature is a redefinition of municipal boundaries. According to the allegations here made, the Alabama Legislature has not merely redrawn the Tuskegee city limits with incidental inconvenience to the petitioners; it is more accurate to say that it has deprived the petitioners of the municipal franchise and consequent rights and to that end it has incidentally changed the city's boundaries. While in form this is merely an act redefining metes and bounds, if the allegations are established, the inescapable human effect of this essay in geometry and geography is to despoil colored citizens, and only colored citizens, of their theretofore enjoyed voting rights. That was not *Colegrove v. Green*.

When a State exercises power wholly within the domain of state interest, it is insulated from federal judicial review. But such insulation is not carried over when state power is used as an instrument for circumventing a federally protected right. This principle has had many applications. It has long been recognized in cases which have prohibited a State from exploiting a power acknowledged to be absolute in an isolated context to justify the imposition of an "unconstitutional condition." What the Court has said in those cases is equally applicable here, viz., that "Acts generally lawful may become unlawful when done to accomplish an unlawful end,... and a constitutional power cannot be used by way of condition to attain an unconstitutional result."

BENJAMIN FRANKLIN

1706   Pennsylvania   1790

Benjamin Franklin   (AP/Wide World Photos)

BENJAMIN FRANKLIN 1706–1790

Scientist, Diplomat, and Founding Father

Overview

To the student of history, it may seem as though almost everything Benjamin Franklin wrote was a milestone in some way. For instance, in the sciences, he conducted groundbreaking research in electricity, identified and charted the Gulf Stream, proved that lead was poisonous and was sickening those who worked with it, and even worked out new ship rigging that took better advantage of the wind. In his writings on society and politics, it is hard to find a work without at least a nugget of insight into how people govern their personal and public affairs and how they might better govern themselves. By the 1750s he was well aware that he was famous and admired, and he took his status seriously, believing that it put him under obligations to sacrifice his leisure time for the sake of public service. When he wrote for publication, he did so knowing that what he wrote would be read in part because it was written by the widely admired Ben Franklin. He also knew that much of the world would judge Americans on the basis of what he himself said and achieved. To the learned people of the world, to the political leaders of the world, and to the ordinary people of the world, he represented the surprises of America and of Americans and was a living example that Americans could equal and even exceed Europeans in learning, in genius, and in achievement.

Franklin was one of the greatest communicators America has ever seen. He claimed to have mastered writing through independent effort of his own as a child; he had only about two years of formal schooling. In his autobiography he often mentions reading and writing as essential to an individual person's success in American society. In his descriptions of his countrymen, he creates an image of them as self-made successes who as early settlers, through their own hard work and risk taking, built a strong society in which even those born into poverty could have a chance to become prosperous. He indeed seems to have believed it his duty to participate in social causes, as he helped found a fire department, a lending library, and other institutions. He was looked to for leadership by those around him, and he dutifully, though sometimes reluctantly, accepted posts that he had not sought, such as postmaster and delegate to Pennsylvania's legislature.

Franklin's personal life was not as exemplary as his public one. He left his wife alone for years at a time while he was in Europe representing Pennsylvania and America. Sometimes even the siblings he loved most would not hear from him for as long as three years. He made friends easily but sometimes shed them seemingly without a sense of loss. These and other faults he recognized, often mentioning them to make fun of himself or to remind others that he was just a man. Although he confessed to thinking himself better than he admitted in print, his writings were composed with a degree of humility that seems odd for so great a man. But Franklin had one of the world's sharpest minds, and through his humility he was able to put his ideas forward without his fame intruding.

Explanation and Analysis of Documents

Franklin had many facets to his life, of which writing was only one. For most of his lifetime he was physically strong and fit. On sea voyages he would swim in the ocean, circumnavigating the ship on which he was sailing and taking the opportunity to observe sharks and other mysteries of the sea. He was an outdoorsman who had a vigorous life on city streets and in the countryside. But his writings outlived him, and it is through them that he is now best known. He valued clarity in his writing, which has resulted in some misunderstandings about his artistry. Some critics have foolishly insisted that he lacked a poetic sensibility or that he sacrificed art for plainness. The following texts prove both charges to be incorrect. Instances of sharp, powerful metaphorical imagery may be found even in his essays of persuasion, and they are abundant in his writings about the friction between America and Great Britain as well as in those about his hopes for a unified America with a republican government emerging from the Revolutionary War. In Franklin's vision for America, every person would be a sovereign, most answerable to himself or herself for success and failure, for whom happiness would be a life well lived.

1706

■ **January 17**
Benjamin Franklin is born in Boston, Massachusetts.

1718

■ Franklin becomes an apprentice in his brother James's printing business.

1729

■ Franklin buys the *Pennsylvania Gazette*.

1731

■ **November**
Franklin establishes a subscription library in Philadelphia.

1732

■ **December**
Franklin publishes his first almanac under the pseudonym Richard Saunders, known as *Poor Richard's Almanack*.

1737

■ Franklin is named postmaster of Philadelphia, a post he holds until 1753.

1743

■ **May 14**
Franklin distributes "A Proposal for Promoting Useful Knowledge among the British Plantations in America," which results in the founding of the American Philosophical Society in 1744.

1751

■ Franklin begins a fourteen-year stint as a member of the Pennsylvania Assembly.

■ **May 9**
"Exporting of Felons to the Colonies," which appears in the *Pennsylvania Gazette*, signals a shift in Franklin's attitude toward Great Britain and its treatment of Americans.

1753

■ Franklin becomes North America's deputy postmaster general, serving until 1774.

◆ **"A Proposal for Promoting Useful Knowledge among the British Plantations in America"**

During 1743 Franklin distributed this document among people of learning and of wealth as part of his effort to create a society that would promote learning in natural philosophy, what would now be called the sciences. He seems to have hoped that such a society would do for America what the Royal Academy did for Britain. Even at this early date, Franklin was thinking that the American colonies would need to help themselves rather than rely on the mother country and the Royal Academy to include them in the benefits enjoyed by British subjects elsewhere. This document became the foundation document for the American Philosophical Society in 1744.

Worthy of note is the opening paragraph, in which Franklin mentions "a long tract of continent, from Nova Scotia to Georgia" to be included in his proposed society. Throughout his life, he tried to include Canadians in social and political developments in America but was chronically disappointed by his failure to persuade Canadians to participate in American affairs. He believes, he says, that America has developed enough economically to afford to have people work on the sciences. His use of the word *leisure* does not accord with how it is usually used nowadays. To Franklin, leisure time was time to be spent usefully, not in rest or play. When he mentions *leisure*, he means time spent studying, writing, painting, conducting experiments, and making useful inventions.

When he suggests that the society include at least one expert in various sciences, he does so in the hope of spurring cross-fertilization, with each science learning from the other sciences to produce comprehensive advances in learning. He worries that the discoveries and inventions of too many Americans are being lost for lack of communication. Ever pragmatic in his thought, Franklin hopes that his proposed society will result in the spread of ideas and inventions throughout the colonies, not only preserving those ideas and inventions but also generating better ways of living that would continue America's growth into a society with a robust economy. As is common in Franklin's writing, he thinks of the colonies as one collective community rather than several, and his proposed society is a way to help Americans think of themselves as having a unified destiny.

◆ **"Exporting of Felons to the Colonies"**

For much of his life, Franklin was a Loyalist—that is, he was faithful to the colonies' mother country, Great Britain—and he often urged those who were angry at Great Britain to restrain their emotions and to work within that nation's governing system. By 1751 Franklin's mind was shifting toward rebellion. He was not only a powerful thinker but also a versatile one who would shift his views when he believed facts required him to do so. "Exporting of Felons to the Colonies," written in the form of a letter to the *Pennsylvania Gazette*, is a satire that reveals how unhappy Franklin had become with Great Britain's policies in the American colonies. The letter shows the influence of Jonathan Swift, who was the greatest satirist in the English language in the

1700s and, like Franklin, was very critical of Great Britain's policies toward its subjects. In this letter Franklin pretends to thank Great Britain for sending its most vile criminals to live in the American colonies while actually elaborating on an analogy that displays his anger toward the British policy of exporting criminals to America, where they prey on Americans. Franklin signs this satire "Americanus" to imply that he speaks for all Americans in protesting a policy that is detrimental and even hateful to Americans.

Franklin cites as inspiration for his satire an article in the *Pennsylvania Gazette* in which the British Parliament cites its reason for voiding a law forbidding the transportation of criminals from Britain to the American colonies, as "such Laws are against the Publick Utility, as they tend to prevent the IMPROVEMENT *and* WELL PEOPLING *of the Colonies.*" Franklin suggests that Americans should show their gratitude by capturing rattlesnakes and sending them to England, especially to government officials, to improve Britain the same way Britain improves America by sending human rattlesnakes. Franklin notes that Great Britain would get the better of the deal because America receives criminals who rape and give venereal disease to daughters, stab wives, corrupt and kill sons, and slit the throats of husbands as well as commit burglaries, shoplifting, and robbery, whereas all rattlesnakes do is bite and kill only an occasional child. On the other hand, the rattlesnakes would be educational, because they could help British gentry better "learn to creep, and to insinuate, and to slaver, and to wriggle into Place (and perhaps to poison such as stand in their Way)."

◆ **"The Way to Wealth"**

In 1757 Franklin voyaged to England, where he would remain until 1762. He wished to promote his vision of Americans as equals of the English in a nation that spanned the Atlantic, including Great Britain and its colonies as one, united people. He also hoped to persuade Parliament to end the proprietorship of the Penn family in Pennsylvania. He believed that the power granted to the Penn family hindered the economic growth of Pennsylvania and infringed on the civil rights of most Pennsylvanians. By this time, he was world famous and admired as one of the great thinkers of his time, and he hoped that his personal prestige would help him in his efforts. While on his voyage to England, he revisited his writings for his *Poor Richard's Almanack* series. He gathered together some of his sayings, both original and borrowed, and seems to have chosen to have fun with them and with his personal fame.

He begins by making sly jokes about himself in his persona as Richard Saunders—his pen name for his almanacs. For instance, he notes how he is being quoted by people and admits the pleasure he takes in it, even though, as was well known, many of his pithy sayings are borrowed from writings of the past and from folklore. Franklin's ability to gently poke fun at himself was part of his charm, and he was well practiced in it; it accounts for part of the fun of reading "The Way to Wealth." Also part of the fun is the character of Father Abraham, who recites and explains the sayings of Poor Richard. Although he is supposed to be a revered

Time Line

1757

■ **July 7**
During a voyage to England, Franklin pulls together many of his maxims from editions of *Poor Richard's Almanac* and organizes them into a lecture by a fictional old man. The result is "The Way to Wealth," published as the preface to the 1758 edition of *Poor Richard Improved.*

1771

■ **July–August**
Franklin begins writing his autobiography, which remains unfinished at his death in 1790.

1773

■ **September 11**
In "Rules by Which a Great Empire May Be Reduced to a Small One," presented in the *Public Advertiser,* Franklin lays out grievances that will be fundamental to provoking the American Revolution.

1775

■ **May**
Franklin is elected to the Second Continental Congress.

1776

■ **June**
Franklin joins a committee for writing the Declaration of Independence.

1777

■ **February 18**
Purported date for the writing of "The Sale of the Hessians," a letter fabricated by Franklin as being from a German count and first published on an unknown date, one of the most widely read documents during the Revolutionary War.

1778

■ **February 6**
Franklin signs the Treaty of Alliance with France.

1781

■ **June**
Franklin, John Adams, Thomas Jefferson, and John Jay begin negotiations with Great Britain to end the Revolutionary War.

1783

■ **September 3**
Franklin and the other negotiators sign the Treaty of Paris, ending official hostilities between Great Britain and America.

1787

■ **May–September**
Franklin serves as a delegate to the Constitutional Convention.

■ **September 17**
On the closing day of the Constitutional Convention, a speech of Franklin's detailing his opinions of the document is read to the convention by another delegate because Franklin is sick.

1789

■ **November 9**
Franklin signs his "Address to the Public" on behalf of Pennsylvania's abolition society, urging that African Americans be educated and be given opportunity for employment as free people.

1790

■ **April 17**
Franklin dies in Philadelphia.

older gentleman, he delivers his wisdom more as a harangue than as sensible advice, and his audience ignores his message, benefiting not at all from what Richard Saunders thinks is an admirable recitation of his favorite sayings.

The harangue opens with a typical Franklin premise: that sloth and idleness shorten life and are at the source of poverty. Implicit in this view are Franklin's beliefs that liberty creates opportunities for becoming wealthy and that the freedom to pursue wealth is essential to happiness. His view of a happy life was not that wealth made a person happy or that being free of care made a person happy; rather, he took the classical view, dating as far back as the writings of Aristotle and being a view he had in common with many of the future leaders of the American Revolution,

that happiness consisted of a complete life well lived and that the ability to pursue wealth, rather than wealth itself, could be an important part of developing a happy life. In this line of thought, he tended to focus on the individual person's wealth rather than the community's wealth, but he believed that anyone who was wealthy should devote his or her leisure time to advancing the lot of others. In "The Way to Wealth," he is careful to state that a person should be charitable. When Father Abraham mentions the many ways money is wasted, he sets charity apart because charitable works are of significant personal as well as social benefit.

Much may be made of the seeming severity of Father Abraham's strictures, but Franklin writes tongue in cheek throughout. For instance, regarding the comments about money wasted in convivial company on food and drink, Franklin himself loved rich foods. Further, he found life-long pleasure in seeking out cheerful company in taverns and may rarely have thought his money spent on ale to have been wasted. On the other hand, he was a remarkably self-controlled man who rarely ate or drank to excess and avoided situations in which he might overindulge in his favorite pleasures. One of the key elements of "The Way to Wealth" may be the implied conclusion, underneath all the warnings and clever sayings, that moderation in pleasure and seriousness both may lead to a life of comfort.

Some of Franklin's literary artistry may be seen in how he structures Father Abraham's harangue. Franklin was not just a great thinker, he was also a great writer who wrote with power in his letters and with bitingly sharp phrases when addressing wrongdoing. He said that he regarded clarity as the most important quality of his writing, but his pursuit of clarity did not lead to dry, lifeless lectures. He seems to have always had an audience in mind, and he wrote to attract the interest of that audience. In the case of "The Way to Wealth," the audience was an American one, from Nova Scotia to Georgia. His readers probably looked forward to reading the Poor Richard books for pleasant diversion as well as sound advice.

To express his ideas in a way that attracts attention in "The Way to Wealth," he uses a metaphor that aptly conveys his thesis and binds together all of Father Abraham's somewhat wandering thoughts. When the people around Father Abraham bemoan their high taxes and ask him for advice on how to bear the financial burden, he transfers the responsibility for the difficulties of his audience from the government to his listeners themselves. The metaphor, then, is that idleness, pride, and foolishness are taxes: "We are taxed twice as much by our Idleness, three times as much by our Pride, and four times as much by our Folly; and from these Taxes the Commissioners cannot ease or deliver us by allowing an Abatement." Freedom to act does not mean freedom from responsibility; money lost through the taxation even of one-tenth of a person's wealth is not equal to the taxation incurred through a lack of personal responsibility. Once that precept is understood, it is no wonder that those in Father Abraham's audience ignore his advice and continue to waste money. After all, they had begun by blaming government taxation for their woes and were perhaps little interested in blaming themselves.

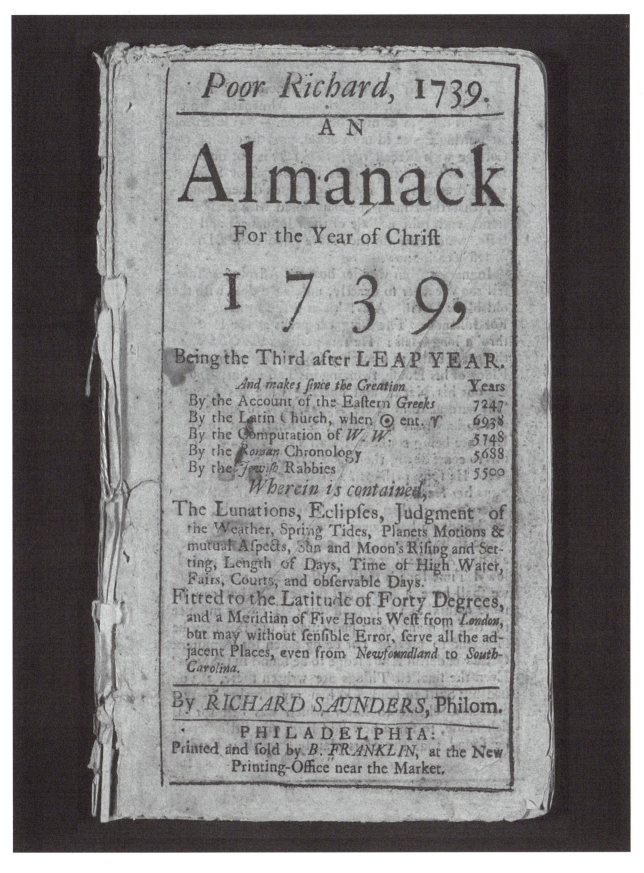

The cover page of **Poor Richard: An Almanac** *(1739) by "Richard Saunders" (one of Franklin's pseudonyms)*
(AP/Wide World Photos)

◆ "Rules by Which a Great Empire May Be Reduced to a Small One"

This satire's itemization of American grievances toward Great Britain is among the best such elaborations written prior to the Declaration of Independence. A comparison of the two documents suggests that the United States owed much to Franklin's identifying and explaining why the American colonies were effectively being driven out of the British Empire. Rarely did the author achieve a more powerful phrasing of exactly what angered Americans. The logical consequence of all that Franklin enumerates is revolution. When he wrote this document, presented in the *Public Advertiser* in September 1773, his hopes for a great empire in which Americans were equal to the English still lingered in him, but as a pragmatic man he had come to see himself and other Americans as a people separate from the English.

The satire imagines that there were a set of instructions given to the Earl of Hillsborough (Wills Hill, first Marquess of Downshire), Great Britain's minister in charge of affairs with the American colonies, at the moment he took office. The voice of "Rules by Which a Great Empire May Be Reduced to a Small One" is distinctly Franklin's, written in a robust, direct manner that he may have intended to represent the way liberated Americans should speak. In its bitterness and anger, it echoes "Exporting of Felons to the Colonies." In its detailed accounts of injustices, every American could see expressed with clarity what he or she had in common with other Americans in their desire for liberty and fairness.

Franklin itemizes the Americans' grievances, assigning them Roman numerals from one to twenty. The result is a nuanced work that defies quick reading. The first point is simple enough: To diminish an empire, begin by alienating the outer fringes of the empire. The second point strikes at the heart of Franklin's disappointments with Great Britain. He had long harbored a vision of the British Empire as greater than it was; in this vision the colonies of Great Britain would become integral, equal parts of the empire, with a parliament elected by English subjects equally from former colonies that had become as much a part of the homeland as England itself. He saw in Great Britain's behavior a failure of foresight that was leading to catastrophe, as the colonists were made to feel like aliens rather than fellow countrymen. In the third and fourth points, Franklin notes reasons why colonists are deserving of the respect of the motherland, having built a society themselves, at their own expense and risk, even while showing love and friendship toward Great Britain.

In the fifth through twentieth points, Franklin notes the conduct of Great Britain's government that has pushed Americans into reluctantly believing that their best interests would be served by being a people independent of Great Britain. He notes the broad perception that the justice system imposed by the British government is unfair, with foreign judges, many incompetent or criminals themselves, running the trials of Americans; he notes the misrule and corruption of governors imposed on colonies; he notes the injustice of taxes imposed by a parliament in which the colonies are not represented; he notes that the American people had given much willingly to the defense of the realm.

That the ideas that would be embodied in the Bill of Rights were being promulgated prior to America's Declaration of Independence is well demonstrated in the tenth point, in which Franklin writes that while Americans thought they should be protected by the English constitution, they were being denied such rights as habeas corpus and freedom to choose one's own religion. The phrase "that they are at present under a power something like that spoken of in the scriptures, which can not only kill their bodies, but damn their souls to all eternity, by compelling them, if it pleases, to worship the Devil" draws deeply from American anger and typifies the power of the satire as a whole. The eleventh through fourteenth points expand on the ways in which tax collection has been made odious and the mother country has actively thwarted justice in the colonies. The foolish conduct of Great Britain's government has made Americans an oppressed people.

◆ "The Sale of the Hessians"

This short work, a letter fabricated by Franklin as being from a German count, was one of the most widely read and influential of Franklin's Revolutionary writings. Its compactness and the stark inhumanity assigned to the leaders of the Hessians make "The Sale of the Hessians" a literary hammer blow. It piles on statistics of deaths and of payments for the dead in a ghastly businesslike manner, with sheer greed as its unifying theme. Franklin makes any gallantry among the Hessians seem like utter folly, because their bravery in battle only results in their dying for a cause not their own, with each death resulting in the enrichment of their overlords. For Franklin's readers, "The Sale of the Hessians" was a sharp, direct depiction of the evil that opposed the American Revolution.

◆ Speech at the Conclusion of the Constitutional Convention

Franklin was very ill during the Constitutional Convention of 1787 but attended anyway; he and George Washington were the two indispensable members of the convention. Both were almost universally known in America and were held in almost universally high esteem by Americans. Franklin's closing speech for the convention was read for him because he was too weak to do so himself. As he notes, the convention did not go the way he had wanted: "I do not entirely approve of this Constitution at present." He did not like the idea of the Senate, as he had favored the federal government's consisting of a single legislative body like the House of Representatives. He had not wanted there to be a powerful office of president; rather, he had favored multiple executives being responsible to the legislature, with each executive running only a portion of the executive government. He had wanted the presidency to be unpaid, with other government offices entitling the public servants only to enough compensation to cover their lost incomes; the payments would not be so high that people would be attracted to the positions because of the money rather than because of the duty of public service.

On the other hand, Franklin praises the work of the delegates to the convention and expresses surprise at how well they have crafted the Constitution, notwithstanding his objections. In urging that those who object to parts of the Constitution should nonetheless vote for the whole, he is self-consciously using his public persona to influence events. In this speech he is the thoughtful, modest family elder—a popular image of him among Americans. Where others might not have been able to do so, he could urge a convention composed of strong-minded and opinionated people to forsake their differences and for the common good give the new nation a functional government.

◆ "An Address to the Public"

From time to time Franklin had owned slaves, but in midlife he decided that slavery was a social evil. At the time he composed "An Address to the Public," Franklin was seriously ill. He was in constant torment and took laudanum (tincture of opium) to ease his pain. Most of the time, he could not hold even a pen, and he dictated his writings to others, which was probably the case for "An Address to the Public." Obviously handicapped by disease, Franklin might well have rested without anyone thinking badly of him for doing so, but he knew that he was one of the most famous people in the world and that his word on any subject was given great weight by readers and listeners. Thus, in one of his final efforts at improving society, he aided the Pennsylvania Society for Promoting the Abolition of Slavery in its efforts to raise funds for the rescue and education of slaves.

◆ *Autobiography*

Franklin's *Autobiography* is not only a landmark of American literature but also a significant statement on what distinguishes Americans from other people. By the summer of 1771, Franklin was already world famous and known to nearly every American, as he was aware, so he began his memoirs as a way to elaborate on how he became successful. The autobiography is at first addressed to his son William, but this changes to a broader address to the general public, perhaps because during the Revolutionary War, William, as a royal governor, remained a Loyalist.

As published in the modern era, the *Autobiography* is presented in four parts, not by design but because Franklin worked on it at four separate times of his life. The first part was written when he was sixty-five years old; he wrote to explain how he, one of seventeen children from a poor family, had become rich, popular, and even famous. Thus, the first part of the *Autobiography* provides an example of how someone could do what Franklin had done with his life. It is a classic American rags-to-riches story in which a modest but plucky young man masters a trade, builds wealth in part by overmastering his desires for idle pleasures and luxuries, and wins friends through his kindness and honesty. Franklin did not work again on his memoirs until he was in France in 1784. His point of view shifts somewhat because his imagined audience has changed; he no longer pretends to be explaining his life to his son, instead communicating to a broader readership. By the time he undertook the writing of the latter parts, Franklin was crippled, his body emaciated from the effects of laudanum; thus, they were most likely dictated in part. He left off his life story before recounting his elder years, the years during which he was a Revolutionary who helped shape world-altering events.

Remarkably, Franklin's *Autobiography*, written as it was in chunks during periods of his life that were significantly different from one another, is unified in its themes, even if its tone becomes somewhat more serious in the final passages. It is a portrait of what an American can be: a self-creating being who views life as limitless in its possibilities, who through forthrightness, hard work, and good sense can become his or her own sovereign. The *Autobiography* is also a book of persuasion, as it urges its readers to imitate its main character. This aspect of the book calls for caution on the part of the reader, because the character described in the book is not exactly the real-life Franklin but instead a version of Franklin. For instance, the main character supposedly abstains from drink, to the amusement of those around him, but the Franklin of flesh and blood enjoyed spirits, especially, late in life, wine. There are actually multiple Franklins in the text. The protagonist is Franklin the modest, self-disciplined American rising in prosperity. Another is Franklin the narrator, making jokes at his own expense, disarming with his plain language, and using his great powers of persuasion to convince his audience of his vision of what America is and ought to be.

Impact and Legacy

Lengthy tomes could be devoted entirely to Franklin's effect on people, society, science, and history. When he chose to be, he was a beguiling writer skilled in persuading people, even without appearing as though he were doing anything but entertaining. The way he wrote, how he behaved in public, and even what he wore were aspects of Franklin that many Americans imitated. His wearing Quaker-style clothing and a fur cap, while representing the United States in France, not only endeared him to the French, who saw him as representing what they admired most about Americans, but indeed served to show that Americans, simply by being themselves, could mix with even European high society and be accepted as sovereign beings. Although Franklin seems to have preferred to persuade subtly, in the matter of American independence he often wrote with savage intensity. His "Rules by Which a Great Empire May Be Reduced to a Small One" anticipates the Declaration of Independence in its drumbeat of grievances against the British government. Such writings stirred his fellow colonists and gave their resentments focus and direction. In the minds of many Americans and people around the world, once Franklin turned his pen toward independence, he became the author not only of the Revolution but furthermore of the Republic that emerged from it.

Although Franklin's political achievements draw attention away from his many other achievements, his legacy extends into aspects of life throughout the world. His vision

"There are many in every province in circumstances that set them at ease, and afford leisure to cultivate the finer arts and improve the common stock of knowledge."

("A Proposal for Promoting Useful Knowledge among the British Plantations in America")

"What is a little Housebreaking, Shoplifting, or Highway Robbing; what is a Son now and then corrupted and hang'd, a Daughter debauch'd and pox'd, a Wife stabbed, a Husband's Throat cut, or a Child's Brains beat out with an Axe, compared with this 'IMPROVEMENT and WELL PEOPLING of the Colonies!'"

("Exporting of Felons to the Colonies")

"We are taxed twice as much by our Idleness, three times as much by our Pride, and four times as much by our Folly."

("The Way to Wealth")

"They will probably complain to your parliaments,... Let the Parliaments flout their claims, reject their petitions, refuse even to suffer the reading of them, and treat the petitioners with the utmost contempt."

("Rules by Which a Great Empire May Be Reduced to a Small One")

"Thus I consent, Sir, to this Constitution, because I expect no better, and because I am not sure that it is not the best."

(Speech at the Conclusion of the Constitutional Convention)

"Slavery is such an atrocious debasement of human nature, that its very extirpation, if not performed with solicitous care, may sometimes open a source of serious evils."

("An Address to the Public")

"These [subscription] libraries have improved the general conversation of the Americans, made the common tradesmen and farmers as intelligent as most gentlemen from other countries, and perhaps have contributed in some degree to the stand so generally made throughout the colonies in defence of their privileges."

(Autobiography)

of an ideal society not only influenced the writing of the Constitution but also affected the lives of everyday people. His notions that public service was every person's duty and that even in quotidian matters people could better their lives and the lives of others have found receptive readers from his own era to the present. In his day many people regarded Franklin as the greatest natural philosopher (scientist) of the age. Franklin tried to make all of his scientific research useful in some way. For instance, his curiosity about electricity led him to make numerous discoveries that unified the concepts of electricity and lightning, and he took pains to put what he learned to use by inventing the lightning rod. He viewed science as a social obligation, and inventions of his, such as the lightning rod and the Franklin stove, were simply given to the world. His discovery and charting of the Gulf Stream reshaped navigation at sea. His studies of the movements of wind and water were applied to generating power. He affected the fields of astronomy, physics, chemistry, mechanical engineering, hydrology, and medicine as well as government and society. In almost every aspect of his public life Franklin reshaped the future.

Key Sources

Franklin's writings are available as *The Writings of Benjamin Franklin* (1905–1907), edited by Albert Henry Smyth. Publication of the scholarly *Papers of Benjamin Franklin*, edited by Leonard W. Labaree et al., began in 1959; several volumes were still in progress as of 2008. The papers are available online (http://franklinpapers.org/franklin/). There are numerous editions of Franklin's *Autobiography* and selected writings. Three of the best are *The Autobiography and Other Writings*, edited by Peter Shaw (1982); *The Autobiography and Other Writings*, edited by Kenneth Silverman (1986); and *The Autobiography and Other Writings*, edited by L. Jesse Lemisch, with an afterword by Carla Mulford (2001).

Further Reading

■ Books

Anderson, Douglas. *The Radical Enlightenments of Benjamin Franklin*. Baltimore: Johns Hopkins University Press, 1997.

Brands, H. W. *The First American: The Life and Times of Benjamin Franklin*. New York: Doubleday, 2000.

Dray, Philip. *Stealing God's Thunder: Benjamin Franklin's Lightning Rod and the Invention of America*. New York: Random House, 2005.

Isaacson, Walter. *Benjamin Franklin: An American Life*. New York: Simon & Schuster, 2003.

Morgan, Edmund S. *Benjamin Franklin*. New Haven, Conn.: Yale University Press, 2002.

Questions for Further Study

1. Among the most talented writers in the America of his time, Franklin had an ability to influence his readers and listeners regardless of his tone. In some works, most notably his speech at the Constitutional Convention, that tone was deadly serious, but he also knew how to employ cutting sarcasm in other writings, such as "The Sale of the Hessians." Compare and contrast the more earnest and sincere Franklin with the satirical Franklin. Is either approach more effective? Why? How does he adapt his approach to the occasion or question at hand?

2. One of Franklin's influences as a writer was Jonathan Swift, the English satirist and social commentator best known for *Gulliver's Travels*. Swift had a great talent for using absurdity to point out what he considered absurdity; similarly, Franklin takes on a deliberately ludicrous tone when discussing the ineptitude and cruelty of the British. Try writing your own version of a humorous social critique in the style of Franklin and Swift, using an issue in the national or local news. Then discuss the process. Was it easier or more difficult than you initially expected? What were some of the challenges?

3. Consider one of Franklin's more obviously serious writings, such as his "Proposal for Promoting Useful Knowledge" or his address to the public on slavery. What are his principal points and how well does he argue for them?

4. Examine the writing in Franklin's *Autobiography*. Is he a good storyteller? How does he describe himself—for instance, does he poke fun at himself? How does the Ben Franklin of the *Autobiography* differ from the "real" Ben Franklin, if at all?

Schiff, Stacy. *A Great Improvisation: Franklin, France, and the Birth of America*. New York: Henry Holt, 2005.

Wood, Gordon S. *The Americanization of Benjamin Franklin*. New York: Penguin, 2004.

—Kirk H. Beetz

"A Proposal for Promoting Useful Knowledge among the British Plantations in America" (1743)

Philadelphia, May 14, 1743.

The English are possessed of a long tract of continent, from Nova Scotia to Georgia, extending north and south through different climates, having different soils, producing different plants, mines, and minerals, and capable of different improvements, manufactures, &c.

The first drudgery of settling new colonies, which confines the attention of people to mere necessaries, is now pretty well over; and there are many in every province in circumstances that set them at ease, and afford leisure to cultivate the finer arts and improve the common stock of knowledge. To such of these who are men of speculation, many hints must from time to time arise, many observations occur, which if well examined, pursued, and improved, might produce discoveries to the advantage of some or all of the British plantations, or to the benefit of mankind in general.

But as from the extent of the country such persons are widely separated, and seldom can see and converse or be acquainted with each other, so that many useful particulars remain uncommunicated, die with the discoverers, and are lost to mankind; it is, to remedy this inconvenience for the future, proposed,

That one society be formed of virtuosi or ingenious men, residing in the several colonies, to be called The American Philosophical Society, who are to maintain a constant correspondence.

That Philadelphia, being the city nearest the centre of the continent colonies, communicating with all of them northward and southward by post, and with all the islands by sea, and having the advantage of a good growing library, be the centre of the Society.

That at Philadelphia there be always at least seven members, viz. a physician, a botanist, a mathematician, a chemist, a mechanician, a geographer, and a general natural philosopher, besides a president, treasurer, and secretary.

That these members meet once a month, or oftener, at their own expense, to communicate to each other their observations and experiments, to receive,

Glossary

&c	etc.
all philosophical experiments	those pursuits that at present have no practical application but might in the future
arts	professions and specialties
assaying of ores	determining the values of metals that have been mined
making such as are useful, but particular...more general	making more widely available those methods and plants presently available only on certain plantations
natural philosopher	scientist
province	area
raising and conveying of water	pumping water from a source and moving it, for instance, through pipes
situation	location
virtuosi	highly accomplished individuals
viz.	abbreviation for the Latin *videlicet*, meaning "for example"

read, and consider such letters, communications, or queries as shall be sent from distant members; to direct the dispersing of copies of such communications as are valuable, to other distant members, in order to procure their sentiments thereupon.

That the subjects of the correspondence be: all new-discovered plants, herbs, trees, roots, their virtues, uses, &c.; methods of propagating them, and making such as are useful, but particular to some plantations, more general; improvements of vegetable juices, as ciders, wines, &c.; new methods of curing or preventing diseases; all new-discovered fossils in different countries, as mines, minerals, and quarries; new and useful improvements in any branch of mathematics; new discoveries in chemistry, such as improvements in distillation, brewing, and assaying of ores; new mechanical inventions for saving labour, as mills and carriages, and for raising and conveying of water, draining of meadows, &c.; all new arts, trades, and manufactures, that may be proposed or thought of; surveys, maps, and charts of particular parts of the sea-coasts or inland countries; course and junction of rivers and great roads, situation of lakes and mountains, nature of the soil and productions; new methods of improving the breed of useful animals; introducing other sorts from foreign countries; new improvements in planting, gardening, and clearing land; and all philosophical experiments that let light into the nature of things, tend to increase the power of man over matter, and multiply the conveniences or pleasures of life.

"EXPORTING OF FELONS TO THE COLONIES" (1751)

Franklin, Benjamin

To THE PRINTERS OF THE [Pennsylvania] *GAZETTE*

By a Passage in one of your late Papers, I understand that the Government at home will not suffer our mistaken Assemblies to make any Law for preventing or discouraging the Importation of Convicts from Great Britain, for this kind Reason, "That such Laws are against the Publick Utility, as they tend to prevent the IMPROVEMENT *and* WELL PEOPLING *of the Colonies.*"

Glossary

all Commerce implies Returns	all economic exchanges require that each side gets something
Clime	climate
debauch'd and pox'd	raped and infected with sexually transmitted diseases
Felons-convict	prisoners who have been sentenced for felonies, or serious crimes
in the Light of	in the guise of, or under the pretense of being
Is not Example more prevalent than Precept?	suggestion that experiences in real life are more useful than mere ideas
Newgates	prisons, from the name of a famous prison in London
Our Mother	England, the "mother country"
Publick Utility	usefulness to the public
Risque	risk
sanguinary	bloody or bloodthirsty
St. James's Park	an area of London near the center of the British government
such as are adequate to the Favour	responses that are worthy of the good grace shown by the British Crown
suffer	allow
they may possibly change their Natures, if they were to change the Climate	they (rattlesnakes) might behave differently in a different location
Thou shalt bruise his head	a quote from Genesis 3:15, in which God condemns the snake in the Garden of Eden
Transportation	removal or deportation, particularly of prisoners
when the Conveniencies far exceed…	when the benefits outweigh the costs

Such a tender parental Concern in our Mother Country for the Welfare of her Children, calls aloud for the highest Returns of Gratitude and Duty. This every one must be sensible of: But 'tis said, that in our present Circumstances it is absolutely impossible for us to make such as are adequate to the Favour. I own it; but nevertheless let us do our Endeavour. Tis something to show a grateful Disposition.

In some of the uninhabited Parts of these Provinces, there are Numbers of these venomous Reptiles we call RATTLE-SNAKES; Felons-convict from the Beginning of the World: These, whenever we meet with them, we put to Death, by Virtue of an old Law, *Thou shall bruise his Head*. But as this is a sanguinary Law, and may seem too cruel; and as however mischievous those Creatures are with us, they may possibly change their Natures, if they were to change the Climate; I would humbly propose, that this general Sentence of Death be changed for Transportation.

In the Spring of the Year, when they first creep out of their Holes, they are feeble, heavy, slow, and easily taken; and if a small Bounty were allow'd per Head, some Thousands might be collected annually, and transported to Britain. There I would propose to have them carefully distributed in St. James's Park, in the Spring-Gardens and other Places of Pleasure about London; in the Gardens of all the Nobility and Gentry throughout the Nation; but particularly in the Gardens of the Prime Ministers, the Lords of Trade and Members of Parliament; for to them we are most particularly obliged.

There is no human Scheme so perfect, but some Inconveniencies may be objected to it: Yet when the Conveniencies far exceed, the Scheme is judg'd rational, and fit to be executed. Thus Inconveniencies have been objected to that good and wise Act of Parliament, by virtue of which all the Newgates and Dungeons in Britain are emptied into the Colonies.

It has been said, that these Thieves and Villains introduced among us, spoil the Morals of Youth in the Neighbourhoods that entertain them, and perpetrate many horrid Crimes: But let not private Interests obstruct publick Utility. Our Mother knows what is best for us. What is a little Housebreaking, Shoplifting, or Highway Robbing; what is a Son now and then corrupted and hang'd, a Daughter debauch'd and pox'd, a Wife stabbed, a Husband's Throat cut, or a Child's Brains beat out with an Axe, compared with this "IMPROVEMENT and WELL PEOPLING of the Colonies!"

Thus it may perhaps be objected to my Scheme, that the Rattle-Snake is a mischievous Creature, and that his changing his Nature with the Clime is a mere Supposition, not yet confirm'd by sufficient Facts. What then? Is not Example more prevalent than Precept? And may not the honest rough British Gentry, by a Familiarity with these Reptiles, learn to creep, and to insinuate, and to slaver, and to wriggle into Place (and perhaps to poison such as stand in their Way) Qualities of no small Advantage to Courtiers! In comparison of which "IMPROVE-MENT and PUBLIC UTILITY," what is a Child now and then killed by their venomous Bite,… or even a favourite Lap Dog?

I would only add, that this exporting of Felons to the Colonies, may be consider'd as a Trade, as well as in the Light of a Favour, Now all Commerce implies Returns: Justice requires them: There can be no Trade without them. And Rattle-Snakes seem the most suitable Returns for the Human Serpents sent us by our Mother Country. In this, however, as in every other Branch of Trade, she will have the Advantage of us. She will reap equal Benefits without equal Risque of the Inconveniencies and Dangers. For the Rattle-Snake gives Warning before he attempts his Mischief; which the Convict does not. I am Yours, &c.

AMERICANUS.

"The Way to Wealth" (1758)

"Friends," says he [Father Abraham], "and Neighbours, the Taxes are indeed very heavy, and if those laid on by the Government were the only Ones we had to pay, we might more easily discharge them; but we have many others, and much more grievous to some of us. We are taxed twice as much by our Idleness, three times as much by our Pride, and four times as much by our Folly; and from these Taxes the Commissioners cannot ease or deliver us by allowing an Abatement. However let us hearken to good Advice, and something may be done for us; God helps them that help themselves, as Poor Richard says, in his Almanack of 1733.

"It would be thought a hard Government that should tax its People one-tenth Part of their Time, to be employed in its Service. But Idleness taxes many of us much more, if we reckon all that is spent in absolute Sloth, or doing of nothing, with that which is spent in idle Employments or Amusements, that amount to nothing. Sloth, by bringing on Diseases, absolutely shortens Life. Sloth, like Rust, consumes faster than Labour wears; while the used Key is always bright, as Poor Richard says. But dost thou love Life, then do not squander Time, for that's the stuff Life is made of, as Poor Richard says. How much more than is necessary do we spend in sleep, forgetting that The sleeping Fox catches no Poultry, and that There will be sleeping enough in the Grave, as Poor Richard says.

Glossary

Calling	a job one was born to do
doing to the Purpose	working with a definite aim in mind
Drive thy Business, let not that drive thee	stay in control of your job and your concerns, so that they do not control you
Handle your Tools without Mittens	do not be afraid to get your hands dirty or to be fully engaged in your work
He that hath a Trade hath an Estate	if one is capable of doing something to earn money, one has a fortune already
he that lives upon Hope will die fasting	if a person simply hopes for something, without working for it, he will never achieve it
Industry need not wish	someone who is willing to work hard does not have to merely wish for rewards but is capable of achieving them
Nor will the Bailiff or the Constable enter…	an industrious man will not be in trouble with the law, particularly for unpaid debts or taxes
Office	job
then Help Hands, for I have no Lands	even if I have no property by which to earn an income, I can earn an income with my labor
the used Key is always bright	when a key is used frequently, it remains smooth and polished; similarly, work makes people better
weak-handed	lacking capability
well followed	well done, or ably carried out

"Time be of all Things the most precious, wasting Time must be, as Poor Richard says, the greatest Prodigality; since, as he elsewhere tells us, Lost Time is never found again; and what we call Time enough, always proves little enough: Let us then up and be doing, and doing to the Purpose; so by Diligence shall we do more with less Perplexity. Sloth makes all Things difficult, but Industry all easy, as Poor Richard says; and He that riseth late must trot all Day, and shall scarce overtake his Business at Night; while Laziness travels so slowly, that Poverty soon overtakes him, as we read in Poor Richard, who adds, Drive thy Business, let not that drive thee; and Early to Bed, and early to rise, makes a Man healthy, wealthy, and wise.

"So what signifies wishing and hoping for better Times. We may make these Times better, if we bestir ourselves. Industry need not wish, as Poor Richard says, and he that lives upon Hope will die fasting. There are no Gains without Pains; then Help Hands, for I have no Lands, or if I have, they are smartly taxed. And, as Poor Richard likewise observes, He that hath a Trade hath an Estate; and he that hath a Calling, hath an Office of Profit and Honour; but then the Trade must be worked at, and the Calling well followed, or neither the Estate nor the Office will enable us to pay our Taxes. If we are industrious, we shall never starve; for, as Poor Richard says, At the working Man's House Hunger looks in, but dares not enter. Nor will the Bailiff or the Constable enter, for Industry pays Debts, while Despair encreaseth them, says Poor Richard. What though you have found no Treasure, nor has any rich Relation left you a Legacy, Diligence is the Mother of Good-luck as Poor Richard says and God gives all Things to Industry. Then plough deep, while Sluggards sleep, and you shall have Corn to sell and to keep, says Poor Dick. Work while it is called To-day, for you know not how much you may be hindered To-morrow, which makes Poor Richard say, One to-day is worth two To-morrows, and farther, Have you somewhat to do To-morrow, do it To-day. If you were a Servant, would you not be ashamed that a good Master should catch you idle? Are you then your own Master, be ashamed to catch yourself idle, as Poor Dick says. When there is so much to be done for yourself, your Family, your Country, and your gracious King, be up by Peep of Day; Let not the Sun look down and say, Inglorious here he lies. Handle your Tools without Mittens; remember that The Cat in Gloves catches no Mice, as Poor Richard says. 'Tis true there is much to be done, and perhaps you are weak-handed, but stick to it steadily; and you will see great Effects, for Constant Dropping wears away Stones, and by Diligence and Patience the Mouse ate in two the Cable; and Little Strokes fell great Oaks, as Poor Richard says in his Almanack, the Year I cannot just now remember."

"Rules by Which a Great Empire May Be Reduced to a Small One" (1773)

I address myself to all ministers who have the management of extensive dominions, which from their very greatness are become troublesome to govern, because the multiplicity of their affairs leaves no time for fiddling.

I. In the first place, gentlemen, you are to consider, that a great empire, like a great cake, is most easily diminished at the edges. Turn your attention, therefore, first to your remotest provinces; that, as you get rid of them, the next may follow in order.

II. That the possibility of this separation may always exist, take special care the provinces are never incorporated with the mother country; that they do not enjoy the same common rights, the same privileges in commerce; and that they are governed by severer laws, all of your enacting, without allowing them any share in the choice of the legislators. By carefully making and preserving such distinctions, you will (to keep to my simile of the cake) act like a wise gingerbread baker, who, to facilitate a division, cuts his dough half through in those places where, when baked, he would have it broken to pieces....

IV. However peaceably your colonies have submitted to your government, shewn their affection to your interests, and patiently borne their grievances; you are to suppose them always inclined to revolt, and treat them accordingly. Quarter troops among them, who by their insolence may provoke the rising of mobs, and by their bullets and bayonets suppress them. By this means, like the husband who uses his wife ill from suspicion, you may in time convert your suspicions into realities.

V. Remote provinces must have Governors and Judges, to represent the Royal Person, and execute everywhere the delegated parts of his office and authority. You ministers know, that much of the strength of government depends on the opinion of the people; and much of that opinion on the choice of rulers placed immediately over them. If you send them wise and good men for governors, who study the interest of the colonists, and advance their prosperity, they will think their King wise and good, and that he wishes the welfare of his subjects. If you send them learned and upright men for Judges, they will think him a lover of justice. This may attach your provinces more to his government. You are therefore to be careful whom you recommend for those offices. If you

can find prodigals, who have ruined their fortunes, broken gamesters or stockjobbers, these may do well as governors; for they will probably be rapacious, and provoke the people by their extortions....

VIII. If, when you are engaged in war, your colonies should vie in liberal aids of men and money against the common enemy, upon your simple requisition, and give far beyond their abilities, reflect that a penny taken from them by your power is more honourable to you, than a pound presented by their benevolence; despise therefore their voluntary grants, and resolve to harass them with novel taxes. They will probably complain to your parliaments, that they are taxed by a body in which they have no representative, and that this is contrary to common right. They will petition for redress. Let the Parliaments flout their claims, reject their petitions, refuse even to suffer the reading of them, and treat the petitioners with the utmost contempt. Nothing can have a better effect in producing the alienation proposed; for though many can forgive injuries, none ever forgave contempt....

X. Possibly, indeed, some of them might still comfort themselves, and say, "Though we have no property, we have yet something left that is valuable; we have constitutional liberty, both of person and of conscience. This King, these Lords, and these Commons, who it seems are too remote from us to know us, and feel for us, cannot take from us our Habeas Corpus right, or our right of trial by a jury of our neighbours; they cannot deprive us of the exercise of our religion, alter our ecclesiastical constitution, and compel us to be Papists, if they please, or Mahometans." To annihilate this comfort...And, lest the people should think you cannot possibly go any farther, pass another solemn declaratory act, "that King, Lords, Commons had, hath, and of right ought to have, full power and authority to make statutes of sufficient force and validity to bind the unrepresented provinces IN ALL CASES WHATSOEVER." This will include spiritual with temporal, and, taken together, must operate wonderfully to your purpose; by convincing them, that they are at present under a power something like that spoken of in the scriptures, which can not only kill their bodies, but damn their souls to all eternity, by compelling them, if it pleases, to worship the Devil....

XV. Convert the brave, honest officers of your navy into pimping tide-waiters and colony officers of the customs. Let those, who in time of war fought gallantly in defence of the commerce of their countrymen, in peace be taught to prey upon it. Let them learn to be corrupted by great and real smugglers; but (to shew their diligence) scour with armed boats every bay, harbour, river, creek, cove, or nook throughout the coast of your colonies; stop and detain every coaster, every wood-boat, every fisherman, tumble their cargoes and even their ballast inside out and upside down; and, if a penn'orth of pins is found unentered, let the whole be seized and confiscated....

XIX. Send armies into their country under pretence of protecting the inhabitants; but, instead of garrisoning the forts on their frontiers with those troops, to prevent incursions, demolish those forts, and order the troops into the heart of the country, that the savages may be encouraged to attack the frontiers, and that the troops may be protected by the inhabitants. This will seem to proceed from your ill will or your ignorance, and contribute farther to produce and strengthen an opinion among them, that you are no longer fit to govern them.

Glossary

common right	natural rights, or good behavior according to common sense
customs	taxes on imports
despise therefore their voluntary grants	look down on the things they give you freely
ecclesiastical constitution	religious practices
gamesters or stockjobbers	gamblers or corrupt stockbrokers
garrisoning	placing troops in a permanent or semipermanent location
Habeas Corpus	Latin for "you shall have the body"; the right of the accused to be formally charged of a crime, rather than be imprisoned without trial
if a penn'orth of pins is found unentered	if a penny's worth of pins (or any other insignificant item) has not been accounted for
Mahometans	Muslims
nothing can have a better effect in producing the alienation proposed	nothing can do more to turn them against you
Papists	Catholics
a penny taken from them … a pound presented by their benevolence	it is better to force them to give up a small amount than to receive a larger amount freely given
pimping tide-waiters	dishonest sailors who simply wait for the easiest opportunities to go out to sea
the Royal Person	the king or queen
savages	a reference to Native Americans
shewn	shown
vie in liberal aids	compete to give as much as possible

"The Sale of the Hessians" (1777)

From the Count De Schaumbergh to the Baron Hohen-Dorf, Commanding the Hessian Troops in America.

Rome, February 18, 1777.

Monsieur Le Baron:

On my return from Naples, I received at Rome your letter of the 27th December of last year. I have learned with unspeakable pleasure the courage our troops exhibited at Trenton, and you cannot imagine my joy on being told that of the 1,950 Hessians engaged in the fight, but 345 escaped. There were just 1,605 men killed, and I cannot sufficiently commend your prudence in sending an exact list of the dead to my minister in London. This precaution was the more necessary, as the report sent to the English ministry does not give but 1,455 dead. This would make 483,450 florins instead of 643,500 which I am entitled to demand under our convention. You will comprehend the prejudice which such an error would work in my finances, and I do not doubt you will take the necessary pains to prove that Lord North's list is false and yours correct.

Glossary

convention	agreement
Count De Schaumbergh ... Baron Hohen-Dorf	fictional characters of Franklin's devising
Don't economize them	don't spare their lives
Dr. Crumerus	fictional character of Franklin's invention
farthing	a very small amount of money
florin	a unit of currency used in southern Germany at the time
guinea	a gold coin in the British currency of the time, equivalent to one pound and one shilling
Hessians	soldiers from the German state of Hesse hired to fight on the British side in the American Revolution
Lord North	prime minister of Great Britain from 1770 to 1782
Major Maundorff	fictional character created by Franklin
recall the life of	bring back from the dead
the 300 Lacedaemonians ...	reference to the Battle of Thermopylae in 480 BC, where King Leonidas of Sparta (also called Lacedaemon) led three hundred soldiers in a fight to the death against a vastly larger Persian invading force
they pay me as killed for all who die from disease	Franklin's fictional count receives just as much money for a man who dies of disease as for one who dies in battle
massacre of Trenton	reference to the Battle of Trenton (New Jersey), on December 26, 1776, where some nine hundred (out of a force of fourteen hundred) Hessians were captured by the Americans

The court of London objects that there were a hundred wounded who ought not to be included in the list, nor paid for as dead; but I trust you will not overlook my instructions to you on quitting Cassel, and that you will not have tried by human succor to recall the life of the unfortunates whose days could not be lengthened but by the loss of a leg or an arm. That would be making them a pernicious present, and I am sure they would rather die than live in a condition no longer fit for my service. I do not mean by this that you should assassinate them; we should be humane, my dear Baron, but you may insinuate to the surgeons with entire propriety that a crippled man is a reproach to their profession, and that there is no wiser course than to let every one of them die when he ceases to be fit to fight.

I am about to send to you some new recruits. Don't economize them. Remember glory before all things. Glory is true wealth. There is nothing degrades the soldier like the love of money. He must care only for honour and reputation, but this reputation must be acquired in the midst of dangers. A battle gained without costing the conqueror any blood is an inglorious success, while the conquered cover themselves with glory by perishing with their arms in their hands. Do you remember that of the 300 Lacedaemonians who defended the defile of Thermopylae, not one returned? How happy should I be could I say the same of my brave Hessians!

It is true that their king, Leonidas, perished with them: but things have changed, and it is no longer the custom for princes of the empire to go and fight in America for a cause with which they have no concern.

And besides, to whom should they pay the thirty guineas per man if I did not stay in Europe to receive them? Then, it is necessary also that I be ready to send recruits to replace the men you lose. For this purpose I must return to Hesse. It is true, grown men are becoming scarce there, but I will send you boys. Besides, the scarcer the commodity the higher the price. I am assured that the women and little girls have begun to till our lands, and they get on not badly. You did right to send back to Europe that Dr. Crumerus who was so successful in curing dysentery. Don't bother with a man who is subject to looseness of the bowels. That disease makes bad soldiers. One coward will do more mischief in an engagement than ten brave men will do good. Better that they burst in their barracks than fly in a battle, and tarnish the glory of our arms. Besides, you know that they pay me as killed for all who die from disease, and I don't get a farthing for runaways. My trip to Italy, which has cost me enormously, makes it desirable that there should be a great mortality among them. You will therefore promise promotion to all who expose themselves; you will exhort them to seek glory in the midst of dangers; you will say to Major Maundorff that I am not at all content with his saving the 345 men who escaped the massacre of Trenton. Through the whole campaign he has not had ten men killed in consequence of his orders. Finally, let it be your principal object to prolong the war and avoid a decisive engagement on either side, for I have made arrangements for a grand Italian opera, and I do not wish to be obliged to give it up. Meantime I pray God, my dear Baron de Hohendorf, to have you in his holy and gracious keeping.

SPEECH AT THE CONCLUSION OF THE CONSTITUTIONAL CONVENTION (1787)

Mr. President,

I confess, that I do not entirely approve of this Constitution at present; but, Sir, I am not sure I shall never approve it; for, having lived long, I have experienced many instances of being obliged, by better information or fuller consideration, to change my opinions even on important subjects, which I once thought right, but found to be otherwise. It is therefore that, the older I grow, the more apt I am to doubt my own judgment of others. Most men, indeed, as well as most sects in religion, think themselves in possession of all truth, and that wherever others differ from them, it is so far error. Steele, a Protestant, in a dedication, tells the Pope, that the only difference between our two churches in their opinions of the certainty of their doctrine, is, the Romish Church is infallible, and the Church of England is never in the wrong. But, though many private Persons think almost as highly of their own infallibility as of that of their Sect, few express it so naturally as a certain French Lady, who, in a little dispute with her sister, said, "But I meet with nobody but myself that is always in the right."…

In these sentiments, Sir, I agree to this Constitution, with all its faults, if they are such; because I think a general Government necessary for us, and there is no form of government but what may be a blessing to the people, if well administered; and I believe, farther, that this is likely to be well administered for a course of years, and can only end in despotism, as other forms have done before it, when the people shall become so corrupted as to need despotic government, being incapable of any other. I doubt, too, whether any other Convention we can obtain, may be able to make a better constitution; for, when you assemble a number of men, to have the advantage of their joint wisdom, you inevitably assemble with those men all their prejudices, their passions, their errors of opinion, their local interests, and their selfish views. From such an assembly can a perfect production be expected? It therefore astonishes me, Sir, to find this system approaching so near to perfec-

Glossary

abroad	outside this group
Babel	a reference to the biblical Tower of Babel, as described in Genesis 11
Convention	agreement
doubt a little of his own infallibility	realize that he might be wrong
a general Government	a central or federal government, as opposed to a loose alliance of states
the opinions I have had of its errors I sacrifice to the common good	I will give up my disagreements so as to advance the larger cause
Partisans	fierce supporters
put his name to this Instrument	sign this document
the Romish Church	the Catholic Church
Steele	Irish writer and politician Richard Steele (1672–1729)

tion as it does; and I think it will astonish our enemies, who are waiting with confidence to hear, that our councils are confounded like those of the builders of Babel, and that our States are on the point of separation, only to meet hereafter for the purpose of cutting one another's throats. Thus I consent, Sir, to this Constitution, because I expect no better, and because I am not sure that it is not the best. The opinions I have had of its errors I sacrifice to the public good. I have never whispered a syllable of them abroad. Within these walls they were born, and here they shall die. If every one of us, in returning to our Constituents, were to report the objections he has had to it, and endeavour to gain Partisans in support of them, we might prevent its being generally received, and thereby lose all the salutary effects and great advantages resulting naturally in our favour among foreign nations, as well as among ourselves, from our real or apparent unanimity. Much of the strength and efficiency of any government, in procuring and securing happiness to the people, depends on opinion, on the general opinion of the goodness of that government, as well as of the wisdom and integrity of its governors. I hope, therefore, for our own sakes, as a part of the people, and for the sake of our posterity, that we shall act heartily and unanimously in recommending this Constitution, wherever our Influence may extend, and turn our future thoughts and endeavours to the means of having it well administered.

On the whole, Sir, I cannot help expressing a wish, that every member of the Convention who may still have objections to it, would with me on this occasion doubt a little of his own infallibility, and, to make manifest our unanimity, put his name to this Instrument.

"AN ADDRESS TO THE PUBLIC" (1789)

It is with peculiar satisfaction we assure the friends of humanity, that, in prosecuting the design of our association, our endeavours have proved successful, far beyond our most sanguine expectations.

Encouraged by this success, and by the daily progress of that luminous and benign spirit of liberty, which is diffusing itself throughout the world, and humbly hoping for the continuance of the divine blessing on our labours, we have ventured to make an important addition to our original plan, and do therefore earnestly solicit the support and assistance of all who can feel the tender emotions of sympathy and compassion, or relish the exalted pleasure of beneficence.

Slavery is such an atrocious debasement of human nature, that its very extirpation, if not performed with solicitous care, may sometimes open a source of serious evils.

The unhappy man, who has long been treated as a brute animal, too frequently sinks beneath the common standard of the human species. The galling chains, that bind his body, do also fetter his intellectual faculties, and impair the social affections of his heart. Accustomed to move like a mere machine, by the will of a master, reflection is suspended; he has not the power of choice; and reason and conscience have but little influence over his conduct, because he is chiefly governed by the passion of fear. He is poor and friendless; perhaps worn out by extreme labour, age, and disease.

Under such circumstances, freedom may often prove a misfortune to himself, and prejudicial to society.

Attention to emancipated black people, it is therefore to be hoped, will become a branch of our national policy; but, as far as we contribute to promote this emancipation, so far that attention is evidently a serious duty incumbent on us, and which we mean to discharge to the best of our judgment and abilities.

To instruct, to advise, to qualify those, who have been restored to freedom, for the exercise and enjoyment of civil liberty, to promote in them habits of industry, to furnish them with employments suited to their age, sex, talents, and other circumstances, and to procure their children an education calculated for their future situation in life; these are the great outlines of the annexed plan, which we have adopted, and which we conceive will essentially promote the public good, and the happiness of these our hitherto too much neglected fellow-creatures.

A plan so extensive cannot be carried into execution without considerable pecuniary resources, beyond the present ordinary funds of the Society. We hope much from the generosity of enlightened and benevolent freemen, and will gratefully receive any donations or subscriptions for this purpose, which may be made to our treasurer, James Starr, or to James Pemberton, chairman of our committee of correspondence.

Signed, by order of the Society,

B. FRANKLIN, President.

Philadelphia, 9th of November, 1789.

Glossary

annexed	attached
galling	agonizing
peculiar	particular
reflection is suspended	he (the slave) is prevented from having an ability to think
sanguine	enthusiastic
sometimes	eventually
The unhappy man	the slave

Autobiography (1771–1790)

A friendly correspondence as neighbours and old acquaintances had continued between me and Mrs. Read's family, who all had a regard for me from the time of my first lodging in their house. I was often invited there and consulted in their affairs, wherein I sometimes was of service. I piti'd poor Miss Read's unfortunate situation, who was generally dejected, seldom chearful, and avoided company. I considered my giddiness and inconstancy when in London as in a great degree the cause of her unhappiness, tho' the mother was good enough to think the fault more her own than mine, as she had prevented our marrying before I went thither, and persuaded the other match in my absence. Our mutual affection was revived, but there were now great objections to our union. The match was indeed looked upon as invalid, a preceding wife being said to be living in England; but this could not easily be prov'd, because of the distance; and, tho' there was a report of his death, it was not certain. Then, tho' it should be true, he had left many debts, which his successor might be call'd upon to pay. We ventured, however, over all these dif-

Glossary

apprehended	expected
correspondence	interaction
disquisitions	formal or scholarly discussions
erratum	error
the general conversation of the Americans	the public intellectual life
his death	that of the other young man interested in Miss Read
I set on foot	I began
the Junto	a discussion group established by Franklin in Philadelphia in 1727
Mr. Grace	Robert Grace, a friend of Franklin's
Mrs. Read	the mother of Franklin's future wife, Deborah Read
my giddiness and inconstancy	my unreliability
scrivener	professional secretary or copyist
state	statement, sometimes used with "of" to mean "statement on"
subscription library	a lending library supported by regular monthly dues, or subscriptions
throve	past tense of "thrive"; succeeded
thus clubbing our books to a common library	donating our books to a regular lending library
with establish'd correspondence	with regular clients

ficulties, and I took her to wife, September 1, 1730. None of the inconveniences happened that we had apprehended; she proved a good and faithful help-mate, assisted me much by attending the shop; we throve together, and have ever mutually endeavour'd to make each other happy. Thus I corrected that great erratum as well as I could. About this time, our club meeting, not at a tavern, but in a little room of Mr. Grace's, set apart for that purpose, a proposition was made by me, that, since our books were often referr'd to in our disquisitions upon the queries, it might be convenient to us to have them altogether where we met, that upon occasion they might be consulted; and by thus clubbing our books to a common library, we should, while we lik'd to keep them together, have each of us the advantage of using the books of all the other members, which would be nearly as beneficial as if each owned the whole. It was lik'd and agreed to, and we fill'd one end of the room with such books as we could best spare. The number was not so great as we expected; and tho' they had been of great use, yet some inconveniences occurring for want of due care of them, the collection, after about a year, was separated, and each took his books home again. And now I set on foot my first project of a public nature, that for a subscription library. I drew up the proposals, got them put into form by our great scrivener, Brockden, and, by the help of my friends in the Junto, procured fifty subscribers of forty shillings each to begin with, and ten shillings a year for fifty years, the term our company was to continue. We afterwards obtain'd a charter, the company being increased to one hundred: this was the mother of all the North American subscription libraries, now so numerous. It is become a great thing itself, and continually increasing. These libraries have improved the general conversation of the Americans, made the common tradesmen and farmers as intelligent as most gentlemen from other countries, and perhaps have contributed in some degree to the stand so generally made throughout the colonies in defence of their privileges....

In 1733 I sent one of my journeymen to Charleston, South Carolina, where a printer was wanting. I furnish'd him with a press and letters, on an agreement of partnership, by which I was to receive one-third of the profits of the business, paying one-third of the expense. He was a man of learning, and honest but ignorant in matters of account; and, tho' he sometimes made me remittances, I could get no account from him, nor any satisfactory state of our partnership while he lived. On his decease, the business was continued by his widow, who, being born and bred in Holland, where, as I have been inform'd, the knowledge of accounts makes a part of female education, she not only sent me as clear a state as she could find of the transactions past, but continued to account with the greatest regularity and exactness every quarter afterwards, and managed the business with such success, that she not only brought up reputably a family of children, but, at the expiration of the term, was able to purchase of me the printing-house, and establish her son in it. I mention this affair chiefly for the sake of recommending that branch of education for our young females, as likely to be of more use to them and their children, in case of widowhood, than either music or dancing, by preserving them from losses by imposition of crafty men, and enabling them to continue, perhaps, a profitable mercantile house, with establish'd correspondence, till a son is grown up fit to undertake and go on with it, to the lasting advantage and enriching of the family.

Margaret Fuller (Library of Congress)

MARGARET FULLER   1810–1850

Editor, Journalist, and Woman's Rights Activist

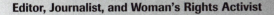

Featured Documents
- "A Short Essay on Critics" (1840)
- *Summer on the Lakes, in 1843* (1844)
- *Woman in the Nineteenth Century* (1845)

Overview

Sarah Margaret Fuller was born in Cambridgeport (now part of Cambridge), Massachusetts, in 1810. Her childhood was dominated by her father, Timothy Fuller, who gave her a rigorous education in literature and philosophy at home. Influenced by such German Romantic writers as Johann Goethe, she embraced the belief that God was found in both man and nature and that each individual was responsible for his or her own moral advancement. After the death of her father in 1835 she began teaching, first in Providence, Rhode Island, and then at an experimental Boston school conducted by Bronson Alcott, an important figure in the Transcendentalist movement. Fuller became a close friend and creative ally of other Transcendentalists, most notably Ralph Waldo Emerson. Her brilliance and energy won her many admirers in Boston's intellectual circles, though others found her arrogant and domineering. Her eloquence as a speaker led her to conduct a series of so-called Conversations held around the Boston area. These were actually courses in philosophy and aesthetics, primarily for women, that attracted a devoted following.

In 1840 Fuller became editor of the *Dial*, a small but highly influential magazine featuring contributions by Emerson, Alcott, Henry David Thoreau, and other Transcendentalist writers. Besides editing the writings of others, she contributed numerous critical essays and literary reviews over the publication's four-year life span. As a critic, she championed free expression in American writing and advocated greater equality between the sexes. Fuller's combination of scholarship, idealism, and mystical insight brought her detractors as well as devotees. Her refusal to take a deferential "feminine" tone as a writer infuriated her male peers. Her fellow critic Edgar Allan Poe reputedly claimed that humanity could be broken down into men, women, and Margaret Fuller.

Fuller's travels among the frontier communities of the American Midwest resulted in her first book, *Summer on the Lakes, in 1843*. Restless for new challenges, she accepted the editor Horace Greeley's offer to join the staff of the *New-York Tribune* in 1844. Arguably the first female investigative journalist in American history, she delved into such topics as slavery, urban poverty, and prison reform. While she was at the *Tribune*, she published her controversial work *Woman in the Nineteenth Century* in 1845, followed by *Papers on Literature and Art* in 1846. That same year

she sailed to Europe for a long-delayed Continental tour, during which she met Thomas Carlyle, George Sand, and other leading writers and thinkers. While visiting Italy in 1847, Fuller met and fell in love with the Marchese Giovanni Angelo d'Ossoli. Fuller shared Ossoli's commitment to Italian revolutionary nationalism and helped direct a hospital for war victims during the siege of Rome in 1848. The couple had a son in September 1848 and married in the spring of 1850. In May of that year Fuller, with her husband and child, set sail for America. They were killed in a shipwreck during a storm off Fire Island, New York, in July. Fuller's body was never recovered.

Explanation and Analysis of Documents

Fuller gained wide notice during the 1840s as one of the American Transcendentalist movement's leading voices. Her work shared ideas in common with those of Emerson, Alcott, Thoreau, and other writers, yet reflected distinctive concerns that were Fuller's own. Through her published work, she sought to influence public opinion beyond the intellectual confines of her native New England. Fuller advocated freedom of expression tempered by high critical standards as a literary reviewer. As a journalist and travel writer, she sought to apply her reformist ideals to factual reportage. Her desire to advance women's rights in American society led her to take on the conventions of her time as an essayist and author. Fuller's works "A Short Essay on Critics," *A Summer on the Lakes, in 1843*, and *Woman in the Nineteenth Century* demonstrate her wide scope as a writer and her forward-thinking views about artistic, philosophical, and social questions.

◆ "A Short Essay on Critics"
Margaret Fuller's role as the first editor of the *Dial* grew out of her participation in the Transcendental Club, an informal discussion group of Boston-area intellectuals. Her formidable knowledge—particularly of classical and modern European literature—more than qualified her for membership. Along with her friends Ralph Waldo Emerson and Bronson Alcott, Fuller believed that the ideas of the Transcendentalists should be discussed in an American periodical. The *Dial* was announced in May 1840 with the intention of accomplishing this goal. Among its chief aims was to improve the standards of American criticism and to

1810

■ **May 23**
Sarah Margaret Fuller is
born in Cambridgeport,
Massachusetts.

1836

■ **December**
Fuller begins teaching
foreign language courses
at the Temple School in
Boston.

1839

■ **November 6**
Fuller begins a series of
Conversations at the
Peabody House in Boston.

1840

■ **July**
The first issue of the *Dial*
is published, edited by
Fuller and containing her
"Short Essay on Critics."

1843

■ **July**
Fuller publishes her essay
"The Great Lawsuit: Man
vs. Men, Woman vs.
Women" in the *Dial*.

1844

■ **June**
Fuller publishes *Summer
on the Lakes, in 1843*.

■ **December**
Fuller joins the staff of the
New-York Tribune.

1845

■ **February**
Fuller publishes *Woman in
the Nineteenth Century*.

1846

■ **August 1**
Fuller sails for Europe.

1849

■ **June**
Fuller reports on the siege
of Rome for the *Tribune*.

1850

■ **July 19**
Fuller dies in a shipwreck
off Fire Island, New York.

expose readers to new modes of writing. In defining this mission as editor, Fuller had to reconcile the widely differing aesthetic ideas of the *Dial*'s contributors, which ranged from the mystical pronouncements of Alcott to the more conventional commentaries of Theodore Parker and George Ripley. In the first issue of the *Dial*, published in July 1840, Fuller sketched out critical standards that were clear in principle yet expansive enough to encompass a wide range of artistic visions. In the process she helped establish herself (rivaled only by Edgar Allan Poe) as the most significant American literary critic of her time.

Fuller begins her essay by stating her desire to "investigate the laws of criticism as a science," a difficult task considering the warring conceptions of what criticism should be. She acknowledges that some critics write as a form of pure personal expression while others are hacks writing only for money. Despite this difference, she hopes to forge "laws" of criticism that members of the "republic of letters" can agree upon. She compares the representatives of various literary factions to members of the Amphictyonic council, an association of regional councils in classical Greece charged with protecting temples and sacred sites. Rather than advocating her own critical standards directly, she hopes to set them forth by implication by describing the most common types of critics.

In the second and third paragraphs Fuller begins to introduce terms derived from the German idealist school of writers and philosophers, whom she refers to as "our German benefactors." In particular, she draws upon the ideas of Goethe and Thomas Carlyle in developing a comprehensive approach to criticism. Those who take the most impressionistic (or subjective) approach are criticized by Fuller as often irresponsible and lacking in scholarly method. Critics of the "subjective class" write out of emotion and base their opinions on nothing more than their likes and dislikes. Fuller's comments can be taken as a veiled criticism of certain Transcendentalist writers, including some who contributed to the *Dial*. Alcott and the poet Jones Very were prone to base their authority as critics upon inner revelations, or messages from God. Even Emerson preferred to advocate poetically rather than debate artistic points from logical standards. Fuller's comments here can be seen as a gentle warning against falling into subjective excess.

Moving on, Fuller considers the "apprehensive" critics, who seek to understand a creative work by fully entering into its creator's ideas and methods. Echoing Goethe's thoughts on the subject, she mostly approves of this sympathetic approach to a writer's inner world, though she wonders if critics are serving as witnesses rather than acting as true critics. While respecting the apprehensive critics' function, Fuller shows greater appreciation for "comprehensive" critics, those who can judge the ability of the artist to succeed on his own terms. Beyond this ability, such critics are able to apply "analogies of the universe" to measure an artist's work against "an absolute, invariable principle." Such a principle should sustain a critic's efforts, but it should not be constricted by narrow rules or formulas. Fuller does not spell out how principles can be distinguished from rules and formulas, but her ambiguity may be intentional. Like most of the Transcendentalist circle, Fuller avoided hard distinctions even when trying to craft aesthetic guidelines.

Having established these categories, Fuller focuses on more immediate issues involving the working critic in the sixth through eighth paragraphs. She pays honor to critics by acknowledging their poetic and philosophical qualities. Writing with the blend of the mystical and the practical that was a hallmark of the New England Transcendentalists, she praises the critic as someone who can translate an artist's "divine" creations into objective, accessible terms. In a sense, the critic is able to reveal things to the public that artists do not understand themselves. This function is not as exalted as that of the artists, but it does require rigor and seriousness. Unconsciously or not, Fuller is marking out her own path as a critic here. She describes her gifts quite accurately when she states that a critic of poetry "must want nothing of what constitutes the poet, except the power of creating forms and speaking in music." While her peers sometimes found her prose style lacking in finesse, few doubted her sensitivity or sound judgment as a critic.

The essay's eighth paragraph alludes to standards of criticism modeled on philosophic inquiry and based upon rigid moral principles. Such eighteenth-century English writers as Samuel Johnson and Edmund Burke applied an absolute, classically based standard of beauty and harmony to the arts. In Fuller's time, established Boston literary figures, such as George Ticknor and Edward Everett, upheld this classical tradition and were appalled at the broader outlook championed by the German idealists and American Transcendentalists. Fuller attempts to walk a line between the two extremes by rejecting the "hard cemented masonry of method" favored by conservative critics while reaffirming the need for objective "inquiry" and for seeking standards beyond the individual artist.

Fuller continues to try to find a middle path. She insists upon the right to classify a work of art by considering the qualities it lacks as well as those it possesses. A portion or aspect of the work should be measured against its overall intention. Balancing this is the recognition that a critic should not pretend to be an "infallible adviser" talking down to readers. This sort of arrogance has undermined the stature of critics and the journals that publish them, she feels. For all the skepticism these journals have aroused, they have not outlived their usefulness. Fuller may be thinking of the *North American Review* and similar conservative publications when she mentions "vehicle[s] for the transmission of knowledge" that still have a role to play in American culture.

Rather than defending the conservative old order, Fuller is more interested in noting the influence of democracy upon the new critical standards of her country. America, she insists, longs for honest expression and is tired of the "judicious man" who calculates his words. As if anticipating the emergence of Walt Whitman some fifteen years in the future, she sees the value in the "crude, rash, ill-arranged" artistic voice that speaks truthfully even as it challenges the notions of good taste. This earnest tone is needed in criticism. Writing with rising intensity, Fuller condemns the "uniformity of tone" that makes a journal's contents safe and predictable. Invoking the ever-new qualities of nature (a favorite theme among Transcendentalist writers), she urges "freshness of thought" in critical writing in order to stimulate similar qualities in the general reader.

Fuller stresses that equality is needed in the world of ideas as well as in the social and political spheres. She looks forward to meeting the critic as an equal instead of deferring to an authority figure. To make this meeting of equals possible, the critic must be honest and forthright, inspiring the reader to think and not simply assimilate information. Ultimately, the critic should become strong and firm enough to be the friend, rather than the instructor, of the reader. By engaging in sympathetic dialogue with an inspired audience, the critic might well resemble Fuller in her role as the leader of her Conversations.

◆ Summer on the Lakes, in 1843

In the spring of 1843 Fuller accepted an offer from her friends James Freeman Clarke and Sarah Clarke to accompany them on a trip through the Great Lakes region. After visiting Niagara Falls and traveling across Lake Michigan to Chicago, Fuller and Sarah Clarke embarked on an extended journey across the Illinois prairie. Although the roads were poor and the accommodations rough, Fuller found inspiration in the open expanses of the countryside. She was also impressed by the efforts of American and European pioneers to begin new lives in scattered settlements. As she traveled, Fuller spoke to people she encountered, kept a journal, and wrote letters to friends back home. Upon her return to Cambridge she gathered further information about North America's western region at the Harvard College Library, becoming the first woman reader allowed into its stacks. The result of her efforts was *Summer on the Lakes, in 1843*, published in 1844.

In the extract from the book included here, Fuller begins by presenting a glimpse of a thriving frontier society populated by settlers who are isolated by distance but united in common purpose. As she looks more closely, she sees the differing experiences of the sexes in these communities. The men have chosen to immigrate to the West, but the women have been forced to adapt to western conditions as best they can. Referring especially to female settlers from urban American and British backgrounds, Fuller describes how ill prepared they are to enjoy the outdoor pleasures of the region. Mothers and daughters are left to maintain households without any help. These observations of Fuller's push back against the stereotype of the rugged pioneer woman that was quickly becoming part of American folklore.

Perhaps because of her own highly cultured background Fuller shows particular insight into the conditions of educated middle- and upper-class women on the frontier. She notes that their education has made them "ornaments of society," rather than individuals able to cope with life on

Horace Greeley, editor of the New-York Tribune *(Library of Congress)*

the prairie. Their upbringing has, in fact, hindered their ability to perceive the natural beauty around them. Fuller mentions their inability to "ride, to drive, to row, alone," making a call for feminine self-sufficiency she would intensify in later writings.

Fuller looks to the daughters of such women for any hope of a better future. But she fears that the outlook of their mothers will limit their ability to fully embrace rural life. She blames "the fatal spirit of imitation, of reference to European standards" as the source of this inhibiting influence. This desire to break with Old World standards and establish uniquely American cultural forms is found throughout the writings of Fuller, Emerson, Thoreau, and other Transcendentalist thinkers. In Fuller's case, the issue takes on an acutely personal dimension as she laments the stunting of youthful spirit by mothers overly concerned with "delicacy." The "language of nature" is ignored in favor of "education" that stultifies.

In conceiving of something better Fuller imagines frontier schools that could awaken students to life around them instead of merely teaching them to imitate the ways of the urban East. In drawing a contrast to the rough but wholesome culture of the American West, she cites "some English Lady Augusta"—referring to Augusta Bruce, an intimate friend and attendant to Britain's Queen Victoria—as a model of female refinement. Such Old World elegance

could pale in comparison with the "new, original, enchanting" kind arising on the frontier. Fuller envisions a new sort of woman emerging out of the West, one both skilled in the domestic arts and capable of embracing the natural world around her. Such a woman would not suffer from the lack of petty big-city pleasures.

Summer on the Lakes, in 1843 met with a mixed critical reception. Some reviewers complained of its lack of structure and its passages of stiff, overly mannered prose. But the *Christian Examiner* spoke for Fuller's admirers when it praised the book as "a work of varied interest, rich in fine observation, profound reflection and striking anecdote" (qtd. in Myerson, p. 3).

◆ *Woman in the Nineteenth Century*

Fuller first outlined her ideas about gender equality in her article "The Great Lawsuit: Man vs. Men, Woman vs. Women," published in the *Dial* in July 1843. This analysis of the unequal status of women in American society attracted a good deal of notice and earned the praise of the editor Horace Greeley, who urged Fuller to expand it into a book. After accepting Greeley's offer to join the staff of his *New-York Tribune*, Fuller completed the book that would be published as *Woman in the Nineteenth Century* by the firm of Greeley and McElrath in February 1845.

She begins by linking the cause of feminine equality to the struggle against slavery. She notes the inability of a widow to receive a full inheritance after the death of a spouse, making her less than an adult under the law. Turning the issue of money around, she describes the way in which irresponsible and abusive husbands can live off the incomes of their wives with impunity. She particularly condemns the ability of fathers to take custody of children from their mothers, no matter how ill suited to parenthood such fathers might be. This state of affairs is evidence, she says, that men hold "a tone of feeling toward women as toward slaves," able to impose their will without legal restraint.

Fuller emphasizes that men do not feel that women are capable of self-sufficiency and full citizenship. Men believe that women are not able to use "the gift of reason" fully and therefore must be kept under men's guidance. Fuller's own experiences as a critic and journalist had brought her into contact with such opinions. When she refers to male comments and offhand jokes about women, she is probably recalling the belittling reception that she encountered as an assertive, intellectually gifted woman. Because of her experiences, Fuller agrees with "many reformers" that women need to represent their own interests in order to gain greater equality, rather than relying upon men to act for them.

She then attacks the belief that women are meant to remain within the "inner circle" of the home for their own protection. No matter what such an allegedly protective circle consists of—whether she is the favorite of a king or a lowly washerwoman—a woman's lot has all too often been one of drudgery or slavery. The stress of public life pales beside the physical hardships that women constantly endure. Fuller points to the examples of stage actresses and female Quaker preachers to refute the idea that women cannot achieve prominence in the world without losing their femininity. If women moved more freely in the larger world, they would be no more attracted to trivial social diversions than men are.

There is a fundamental inequality of power between the sexes, Fuller says. Men cannot be trusted to "do justice to the interests of woman" because they cannot rise above the belief that "woman was made *for man*." Fuller makes distinctions between types of men in their opinions of women—the worst offender, she says, is "the man of the world" who writes its laws and manages its practical affairs. Despite all this, Fuller affirms her hope. She declares that a new world of harmony would begin if the barriers blocking women's progress were removed. She writes with mystically tinged language of the "divine energy" that would be unleashed once equality was achieved. To reach this goal, men must acknowledge that women's freedom is a birthright and not a concession granted by superior beings to inferior ones. Fuller makes a direct comparison between the subjugation of woman and the enslavement of African Americans, and in both cases, she declares, women and slaves are accountable only to God, not to man.

Fuller recognizes that women have exercised a measure of power even during their oppression. However, by acting in an indirect and manipulative fashion, they have harmed themselves in the process. Far better is the sort of wholesome, honest influence that comes when men and women stand together as equals. This equality is simply a fulfillment of America's basic principles. Fuller stresses once again that women must look to one another rather than to men to obtain this equality. The only assistance Fuller asks for is the removal of "arbitrary barriers" blocking women's advancement.

In her writing Fuller displays an understanding of American race and class distinctions. Using an incident recounted in Edward Fitzgerald's travels among Native Americans, she describes how issues of status affect the relations of men and women. She declares that if women carry themselves with dignity and self-confidence, they will naturally win the respect of men—much as Ceres, the Roman goddess of agriculture, commanded reverence for her life-sustaining power.

Fuller expects that the achievement of equality between the sexes will be a gradual process. But if it comes all at once, she hazards no doubt that women's innate sense of balance will ensure that a radical overturn of society would not result. Still, there is no retreating from the idea of free vocational choice—she declares that women can be anything, even sea captains. She alludes to such examples of female heroism as Agostina Domenech (known as the Maid of Saragossa, who fought in the Spanish War of Independence in 1808), the Suliote women who died fighting the Ottoman Turks in 1803, and Countess Emelia Plater (a Polish nationalist who led troops against the Russians in 1830–1831). If women are not allowed to make their own decisions and fulfill their potential, they become stunted and unhappy. To support this view, Fuller refers to the writings of the French socialist philosopher François-Marie-

Charles Fourier, who declared in *The Theory of the Four Movements* (1808) that "the extension of women's privileges is the general principle for all social progress" (qtd. in LeGates, p. 163).

While acknowledging that most women will not choose to work outside the home, Fuller makes clear that the exceptional woman who wants to do so deserves to be encouraged. With rising force, she stresses that her call for equal opportunity for men and women will correct an unnatural imbalance. The fact that women have often had "an excessive devotion" to men has given the latter a godlike status, preventing an honest relationship between the sexes. By stating that women should live first for the sake of God, Fuller challenges the conventional Victorian-era belief that men's role as head of the household is divinely mandated. In Fuller's view, a woman is debasing herself (and by implication being impious) by exalting a man beyond his humanity. If she desires to give and receive love, she can do so only by being a strong and fulfilled human being. She cannot look to man for her salvation.

Woman in the Nineteenth Century stirred considerable controversy. As with Fuller's previous book, it was faulted by some for lack of organization and an overly verbose style. Many critics (mostly male) objected to her questioning traditional gender roles. A smaller number praised the book as a needed attack upon outmoded ideas. In hindsight the book can be seen as the most important feminist work in the English language since Mary Wollstonecraft's *Vindication of the Rights of Woman* (1792).

Impact and Legacy

It was often said by Fuller's friends and colleagues that her writing lacked the brilliance of her conversation. Fuller acknowledged that writing was a difficult process for her—"my voice excites me, my pen never," she said (qtd. in Richardson, p. 238). Even so, the ideas contained in her written works have been recognized as some of the most influential of her generation. In many ways Fuller anticipated the work of feminist cultural critics in the twentieth century. She likewise displayed a wide-ranging commitment to democracy and human rights that was significantly ahead of her time. More than this, she became a role model as a boldly independent woman who pushed against social restrictions and risked her safety as a European war correspondent.

These documents show Fuller's complexity as a social critic and artist. A love for the classical world is reflected in her allusions to ancient Greek myth and culture, and her desire for less tradition-bound modes of expression color her critical writings. She both embodied the genteel literary standards of her era and anticipated the rise of naturalism in American letters at the end of the nineteenth century. Her ideas about literature and social reform sought to reconcile the need for individual fulfillment with higher standards for humanity as a whole. While her works of advocacy, such as *Woman in the Nineteenth Century*, can be taken as mani-

"*Critics are poets cut down, says some one—by way of jeer; but, in truth, they are men with the poetical temperament to apprehend, with the philosophical tendency to investigate. The maker is divine; the critic sees this divine, but brings it down to humanity by the analytic process.*"

("A Short Essay on Critics")

"*The richer the work, the more severe should be its critic; the larger its scope, the more comprehensive must be his power of scrutiny.*"

("A Short Essay on Critics")

"*Everywhere the fatal spirit of imitation, of reference to European standards, penetrates, and threatens to blight whatever of original growth might adorn the soil.*"

(*Summer on the Lakes, in 1843*)

"*Methods copied from the education of some English Lady Augusta, are as ill suited to the daughter of an Illinois farmer, as satin shoes to climb the Indian mounds. An elegance she would diffuse around her, if her mind were opened to appreciate elegance; it might be of a kind new, original, enchanting, as different from that of the city belle as that of the prairie torch-flower from the shopworn article that touches the cheek of that lady within her bonnet.*"

(*Summer on the Lakes, in 1843*)

"*A house is no home unless it contains food and fire for the mind as well as for the body.*"

(*Woman in the Nineteenth Century*)

"*We would have every arbitrary barrier thrown down. We would have every path laid open to woman as freely as to man.*"

(*Woman in the Nineteenth Century*)

"*But if you ask me what offices they may fill, I reply—any. I do not care what case you put; let them be sea-captains, if you will.*"

(*Woman in the Nineteenth Century*)

festos for equality and justice, they are also very personal expressions filled with passion as well as thoughtful commentary. Fuller's best work displays a courage and prescience that makes her relevant for new generations of readers.

Key Sources

The largest collection of Margaret Fuller's papers is found at the Houghton Library of Harvard University. The Boston Public Library and the Massachusetts Historical Society also possess important documents. Most of Fuller's major writings are in print. *The Portable Margaret Fuller*, edited by Mary Kelley (1994), provides a good sampling of her works. The American Transcendentalism Web site (http://www.vcu.edu/engweb/transcendentalism/index.html) offers Fuller texts, biographical information, and critical analysis.

Further Reading

■ Books

Blanchard, Paula. *Margaret Fuller: From Transcendentalism to Revolution*. New York: Delacorte, 1978.

Chevigny, Belle Gale. *The Woman and the Myth: Margaret Fuller's Life and Writings*. Rev. ed. Boston: Northeastern University Press, 1994.

Higginson, Thomas Wentworth. *Margaret Fuller Ossoli*. 1884. Reprint. New York: Haskell House, 1968.

LeGates, Marlene. *In Their Time: A History of Feminism in Western Society*. New York: Routledge, 2001.

Miller, Perry. *Margaret Fuller: American Romantic*. Garden City, N.Y.: Doubleday, 1963.

Myerson, Joel. *Margaret Fuller: Essays on American Life and Letters*. New Haven, Conn.: College and University Press, 1978.

Richardson, Robert D. *Emerson: The Mind on Fire*. Berkeley: University of California Press, 1995.

Von Mehren, Joan. *Minerva and the Muse: A Life of Margaret Fuller*. Amherst: University of Massachusetts Press, 1995.

Wade, Mason. *Margaret Fuller: Whetstone of Genius*. New York: Viking Press, 1940.

—Barry Alfonso

Questions for Further Study

1. Susan B. Anthony presents a picture of the position of women in "The Status of Woman, Past, Present, and Future." Compare her portrait with Fuller's in *Woman in the Nineteenth Century*, remembering that Fuller wrote about a half century before Anthony.

2. Similarly, Anthony took up the issue of the rights of women in "Is It a Crime for a Citizen of the United States to Vote?" How does her perspective in this document differ from that of Fuller?

3. When Fuller wrote "A Short Essay on Critics" in 1840, the United States was still a relatively new, untamed nation trying to find its way in the cultural sphere without a long tradition behind it. How does Fuller's analysis of literary criticism reflect this newness and untamed quality?

4. Do you see any contradiction or inconsistency in Fuller's views about western frontier women, expressed in *Summer on the Lakes, in 1843*, and the fact that she herself enjoyed a privileged, comfortable life as a highly educated woman in an eastern city?

5. Fuller has been regarded as a woman ahead of her time. What views did she express that are widely taken more or less for granted in the twenty-first century? How would she have received the views expressed by Alice Paul in her documents?

"A Short Essay on Critics" (1840)

An essay on Criticism were a serious matter; for, though this age be emphatically critical, the writer would still find it necessary to investigate the laws of criticism as a science, to settle its conditions as an art. Essays, entitled critical, are epistles addressed to the public, through which the mind of the recluse relieves itself of its impressions. Of these the only law is, "Speak the best word that is in thee." Or they are regular articles got up to order by the literary hack writer, for the literary mart, and the only law is to make them plausible. There is not yet deliberate recognition of a standard of criticism, though we hope the always strengthening league of the republic of letters must ere long settle laws on which its Amphictyonic council may act. Meanwhile let us not venture to write on criticism, but, by classifying the critics, imply our hopes and thereby our thoughts.

First, there are the subjective class, (to make use of a convenient term, introduced by our German benefactors.) These are persons to whom writing is no sacred, no reverend employment. They are not driven to consider, not forced upon investigation by the fact, that they are deliberately giving their thoughts an independent existence, and that it may live to others when dead to them. They know no agonies of conscientious research, no timidities of self-respect....They love, they like, or they hate; the book is detestable, immoral, absurd, or admirable, noble, of a most approved scope;—these statements they make with authority, as those who bear the evangel of pure taste and accurate judgment, and need be tried before no human synod. To them it seems that their present position commands the universe....

The value of such comments is merely reflex. They characterize the critic. They give an idea of certain influences on a certain act of men in a certain time or place. Their absolute, essential value is nothing. The long review, the eloquent article by the man of the nineteenth century are of no value by themselves considered, but only as samples of their kind. The writers were content to tell what they felt, to praise or to denounce without needing to convince us or themselves. They sought not the divine truths of philosophy, and she proffers them not if unsought.

Then there are the apprehensive. These can go out of themselves and enter fully into a foreign existence. They breathe its life; they live in its law; they tell what it meant, and why it so expressed its meaning. They reproduce the work of which they speak, and make it better known to us in so far as two statements are better than one. There are beautiful specimens in this kind. They are pleasing to us as bearing witness of the genial sympathies of nature....These, if not true critics, come nearer the standard than the subjective class, and the value of their work is ideal as well as historical.

Then there are the comprehensive, who must also be apprehensive. They enter into the nature of another being and judge his work by its own law. But having done so, having ascertained his design and the degree of his success in fulfilling it, thus measuring his judgment, his energy, and skill, they do also know how to put that aim in its place, and how to estimate its relations. And this the critic can only do who perceives the analogies of the universe, and how they are regulated by an absolute, invariable principle. He can see how far that work expresses this principle, as well as how far it is excellent in its details. Sustained by a principle, such as can be girt within no rule, no formula, he can walk around the work, he can stand above it, he can uplift it, and try its weight. Finally, he is worthy to judge it.

Critics are poets cut down, says some one—by way of jeer; but, in truth, they are men with the poetical temperament to apprehend, with the philosophical tendency to investigate. The maker is divine; the critic sees this divine, but brings it down to humanity by the analytic process. The critic is the historian who records the order of creation. In vain for the maker, who knows without learning it, but not in vain for the mind of his race.

The critic is beneath the maker, but is his needed friend. What tongue could speak but to an intelligent ear, and every noble work demands its critic. The richer the work, the more severe should be its critic; the larger its scope, the more comprehensive must be his power of scrutiny. The critic is not a base caviller, but the younger brother of genius. Next to invention is the power of interpreting invention; next to beauty the power of appreciating beauty....

The critic, then, should be not merely a poet, not merely a philosopher, not merely an observer, but tempered of all three. If he criticize the poem, he must want nothing of what constitutes the poet, except the power of creating forms and speaking in music. He must have as good an eye and as fine a sense; but if he had as fine an organ for expression also, he would make the poem instead of judging it. He must be inspired by the philosopher's spirit of inquiry and need of generalization, but he must not be constrained by the hard cemented masonry of method to which philosophers are prone. And he must have the organic acuteness of the observer, with a love of ideal perfection, which forbids him to be content with mere beauty of details in the work or the comment upon the work.

There are persons who maintain, that there is no legitimate criticism, except the reproductive; that we have only to say what the work is or is to us, never what it is not. But the moment we look for a principle, we feel the need of a criterion, of a standard; and then we say what the work is *not*, as well as what it *is*; and this is as healthy though not as grateful and gracious an operation of the mind as the other. We do not seek to degrade but to classify an object by stating what it is not. We detach the part from the whole, lest it stand between us and the whole. When we have ascertained in what degree it manifests the whole, we may safely restore it to its place, and love or admire it there ever after.

The use of criticism, in periodical writing is to sift, not to stamp a work. Yet should they not be "sieves and drainers for the use of luxurious readers," but for the use of earnest inquirers, giving voice and being to their objections, as well as stimulus to their sympathies. But the critic must not be an infallible adviser to his reader. He must not tell him what books are not worth reading, or what must be thought of them when read, but what he read in them. Wo[e] to that coterie where some critic sits despotic, intrenched behind the infallible "We."...

From these causes and causes like these, the journals have lost much of their influence. There is a languid feeling about them, an inclination to suspect the justice of their verdicts, the value of their criticisms. But their golden age cannot be quite past. They afford too convenient a vehicle for the transmission of knowledge; they are too natural a feature of our time to have done all their work yet....

But their country cannot long be so governed. It misses the pure, the full tone of truth; it perceives that the voice is modulated to coax, to persuade, and it turns from the judicious man of the world, calculating the effect to be produced by each of his smooth sentences, to some earnest voice which is uttering thoughts, crude, rash, ill-arranged it may be, but true to one human breast, and uttered in full faith, that the God of Truth will guide them aright....

Here, it seems to me, has been the greatest mistake in the conduct of these journals. A smooth monotony has been attained, an uniformity of tone, so that from the title of a journal you can infer the tenor of all its chapters. But nature is ever various, ever new, and so should be her daughters, art and literature. We do not want merely a polite response to what we thought before, but by the freshness of thought in other minds to have new thought awakened in our own. We do not want stores of information only, but to be roused to digest these into knowledge. Able and experienced men write for us, and we would know what they think, as they think it not for us but for themselves. We would live with them, rather than be taught by them how to live; we would catch the contagion of their mental activity, rather than have them direct us how to regulate our own. In books, in reviews, in the senate, in the pulpit, we wish to meet thinking men, not schoolmasters or pleaders. We wish that they should do full justice to their own view, but also that they should be frank with us, and, if now our superiors, treat us as if we might some time rise to be their equals. It is this true manliness, this firmness in his own position, and this power of appreciating the position of others, that alone can make the critic our companion and friend.

Glossary

caviller	one who quibbles or raises petty objections
coterie	a clique
epistles	letters
evangel	gospel
girt	bound

SUMMER ON THE LAKES, IN 1843 (1844)

A pleasant society is formed of the families who live along the banks of this stream upon farms. They are from various parts of the world, and have much to communicate to one another. Many have cultivated minds and refined manners, all a varied experience, while they have in common the interests of a new country and a new life. They must traverse some space to get at one another, but the journey is through scenes that make it a separate pleasure. They must bear inconveniences to stay in one another's houses; but these, to the well-disposed, are only a source of amusement and adventure.

The great drawback upon the lives of these settlers, at present, is the unfitness of the women for their new lot. It has generally been the choice of the men, and the women follow, as women will, doing their best for affection's sake, but too often in heart-sickness and weariness. Beside it frequently not being a choice or conviction of their own minds that it is best to be here, their part is the hardest, and they are least fitted for it. The men can find assistance in field labor, and recreation with the gun and fishing-rod. Their bodily strength is greater, and enables them to bear and enjoy both these forms of life.

The women can rarely find any aid in domestic labor. All its various and careful tasks must often be performed, sick or well, by the mother and daughters, to whom a city education has imparted neither the strength nor skill now demanded.

The wives of the poorer settlers, having more hard work to do than before, very frequently become slatterns; but the ladies, accustomed to a refined neatness, feel that they cannot degrade themselves by its absence, and struggle under every disadvantage to keep up the necessary routine of small arrangements.

With all these disadvantages for work, their resources for pleasure are fewer. When they can leave the housework, they have not learnt to ride, to drive, to row, alone. Their culture has too generally been that given to women to make them "the ornaments of society." They can dance, but not draw; talk French, but know nothing of the language of flowers; neither in childhood were allowed to cultivate them, lest they should tan their complexions. Accustomed to the pavement of Broadway, they dare not tread the wild-wood paths for fear of rattlesnakes!

Seeing much of this joylessness, and inaptitude, both of body and mind, for a lot which would be full of blessings for those prepared for it, we could not but look with deep interest on the little girls, and hope they would grow up with the strength of body, dexterity, simple tastes, and resources that would fit them to enjoy and refine the western farmer's life.

But they have a great deal to war with in the habits of thought acquired by their mothers from their own early life. Everywhere the fatal spirit of imitation, of reference to European standards, penetrates, and threatens to blight whatever of original growth might adorn the soil.

If the little girls grow up strong, resolute, able to exert their faculties, their mothers mourn over their want of fashionable delicacy. Are they gay, enterprising, ready to fly about in the various ways that teach them so much, these ladies lament that "they cannot go to school, where they might learn to be quiet." They lament the want of "education" for their daughters, as if the thousand needs which call out their young energies, and the language of nature around, yielded no education.

Their grand ambition for their children is to send them to school in some eastern city, the measure most likely to make them useless and unhappy at home. I earnestly hope that, ere long, the existence of good schools near themselves, planned by persons of sufficient thought to meet the wants of the place and time, instead of copying New York or Boston, will correct this mania. Instruction the children want

Glossary

Broadway	major street in New York City's Manhattan
slatterns	untidy, dirty women

to enable them to profit by the great natural advantages of their position; but methods copied from the education of some English Lady Augusta, are as ill suited to the daughter of an Illinois farmer, as satin shoes to climb the Indian mounds. An elegance she would diffuse around her, if her mind were opened to appreciate elegance; it might be of a kind new, original, enchanting, as different from that of the city belle as that of the prairie torch-flower from the shopworn article that touches the cheek of that lady within her bonnet.

To a girl really skilled to make home beautiful and comfortable, with bodily strength to enjoy plenty of exercise, the woods, the streams, a few studies, music, and the sincere and familiar intercourse, far more easily to be met here than elsewhere, would afford happiness enough. Her eyes would not grow dim, nor her cheeks sunken, in the absence of parties, morning visits, and milliner's shops.

WOMAN IN THE NINETEENTH CENTURY (1845)

It may well be an Anti-Slavery party that pleads for Woman, if we consider merely that she does not hold property on equal terms with men; so that, if a husband dies without making a will, the wife, instead of taking at once his place as head of the family, inherits only a part of his fortune, often brought him by herself, as if she were a child, or ward only, not an equal partner.

We will not speak of the innumerable instances in which profligate and idle men live upon the earnings of industrious wives; or if the wives leave them, and take with them the children, to perform the double duty of mother and father, follow from place to place, and threaten to rob them of the children, if deprived of the rights of a husband, as they call them, planting themselves in their poor lodgings, frightening them into paying tribute by taking from them the children, running into debt at the expense of these otherwise so overtasked helots....I have seen the husband who had stained himself by a long course of low vice, till his wife was wearied from her heroic forgiveness, by finding that his treachery made it useless, and that if she would provide bread for herself and her children, she must be separate from his ill fame—I have known this man come to install himself in the chamber of a woman who loathed him, and say she should never take food without his company. I have known these men steal their children, whom they knew they had no means to maintain, take them into dissolute company, expose them to bodily danger, to frighten the poor woman, to whom, it seems, the fact that she alone had borne the pangs of their birth, and nourished their infancy, does not give an equal right to them....

But to return to the historical progress of this matter. Knowing that there exists in the minds of men a tone of feeling toward women as toward slaves, such as is expressed in the common phrase, "Tell that to women and children;" that the infinite soul can only work through them in already ascertained limits; that the gift of reason, Man's highest prerogative, is allotted to them in much lower degree; that they must be kept from mischief and melancholy by being constantly engaged in active labor, which is to be furnished and directed by those better able to think, &c., &c.,—we need not multiply instances, for who can review the experience of last week without recalling words which imply, whether in jest or earnest, these views, or views like these,—knowing this, can we wonder that many reformers think that measures are not likely to be taken in behalf of women, unless their wishes could be publicly represented by women?

That can never be necessary, cry the other side. All men are privately influenced by women; each has his wife, sister, or female friends, and is too much biased by these relations to fail of representing their interests; and, if this is not enough, let them propose and enforce their wishes with the pen. The beauty of home would be destroyed, the delicacy of the sex be violated, the dignity of halls of legislation degraded, by an attempt to introduce them there. Such duties are inconsistent with those of a mother; and then we have ludicrous pictures of ladies in hysterics at the polls, and senate-chambers filled with cradles.

But if, in reply, we admit as truth that Woman seems destined by nature rather for the inner circle, we must add that the arrangements of civilized life have not been, as yet, such as to secure it to her. Her circle, if the duller, is not the quieter. If kept from "excitement," she is not from drudgery. Not only the Indian squaw carries the burdens of the camp, but the favorites of Louis XIV accompany him in his journeys, and the washerwoman stands at her tub, and carries home her work at all seasons, and in all states of health. Those who think the physical circumstances of Woman would make a part in the affairs of national government unsuitable, are by no means those who think it impossible for the negresses to endure field work, even during pregnancy, or for the sempstresses to go through their killing labors....

As to the possibility of her filling with grace and dignity any such position, we should think those who had seen the great actresses, and heard the Quaker preachers of modern times, would not doubt that woman can express publicly the fulness of thought and creation, without losing any of the peculiar beauty of her sex....

As to her home, she is not likely to leave it more than she now does for balls, theatres, meetings for promoting missions, revival meetings, and others to which she flies, in hope of an animation for her existence commensurate with what she sees enjoyed by men. Governors of ladies' fairs are no less engrossed by such a charge, than the governor of a state by his;

presidents of Washingtonian societies no less away from home than presidents of conventions. If men look straitly to it, they will find that, unless their lives are domestic, those of the women will not be. A house is no home unless it contain food and fire for the mind as well as for the body....

As to men's representing women fairly at present, while we hear from men who owe to their wives not only all that is comfortable or graceful, but all that is wise, in the arrangement of their lives, the frequent remark, "You cannot reason with a woman," when from those of delicacy, nobleness, and poetic culture, falls the contemptuous phrase "women and children," and that in no light sally of the hour, but in works intended to give a permanent statement of the best experiences, when not one man, in the million, shall I say? no, not in the hundred million, can rise above the belief that woman was made *for man*, when such traits as these are daily forced upon the attention, can we feel that man will always do justice to the interests of woman? Can we think that he takes a sufficiently discerning and religious view of her office and destiny, *ever* to do her justice, except when prompted by sentiment, accidentally or transiently, that is, for the sentiment will vary according relations in which he is placed? The lover, the poet, the artist, are likely to view her nobly. The father and the philosopher have some chance of liberality; the man of the world, the legislator for expediency, none.

Under these circumstances, without attaching importance, in themselves, to the changes demanded by the champions of woman, we hail them as signs of the times. We would have every arbitrary barrier thrown down. We would have every path laid open to woman as freely as to man. Were this done, and a slight temporary fermentation allowed to subside, we should see crystallizations more pure and of more various beauty. We believe the divine energy would pervade nature to a degree unknown in the history of former ages, and that no discordant collision, but a ravishing harmony of the spheres, would ensue.

Yet, then and only then will mankind be ripe for this, when inward and outward freedom for woman as much as for man shall be acknowledged as a right, not yielded as a concession. As the friend of the negro assumes that one man cannot by right hold another in bondage, so should the friend of Woman assume that Man cannot by right lay even well-meant restrictions on Woman. If the negro be a soul, if the woman be a soul, appareled in flesh, to one Master only are they accountable. There is but one law for souls, and, if there is to be an interpreter of it, he must come not as man, or son of man, but as son of God....

I have aimed to show that no age was left entirely without a witness of the equality of the sexes in function, duty and hope.

Also that, when there was unwillingness or ignorance, which prevented this being acted upon, women had not the less power for their want of light and noble freedom. But it was power which hurt alike them and those against whom they made use of the arms of the servile; cunning, blandishment, and unreasonable emotion.

That now the time has come when a clearer vision and better action are possible. When man and woman may regard one another as brother and sister, the pillars of one porch, the priests of one worship.

I have believed and intimated that this hope would receive an ampler fruition, than ever before, in our own land.

And it will do so if this land carry out the principles from which sprang our national life.

I believe that, at present, women are the best helpers of one another.

Let them think; let them act; till they know what they need.

We only ask of men to remove arbitrary barriers. Some would like to do more. But I believe it needs that woman show herself in her native dignity, to teach them how to aid her; their minds are so encumbered by tradition.

When Lord Edward Fitzgerald travelled with the Indians, his manly heart obliged him at once to take the packs from the squaws and carry them. But we do not read that the red men followed his example, though they are ready enough to carry the pack of the white woman, because she seems to them a superior being.

Let woman appear in the mild majesty of Ceres, and rudest churls will be willing to learn from her.

You ask, what use will she make of liberty, when she has so long been sustained and restrained?

I answer; in the first place, this will not be suddenly given. I read yesterday a debate of this year on the subject of enlarging women's rights over property. It was a leaf from the class-book that is preparing for the needed instruction. The men learned visibly as they spoke. The champions of woman saw the fallacy of arguments on the opposite side, and were startled by their own convictions. With their wives at home, and the readers of the paper, it was the same. And so the stream flows on; thought urging action, and action leading to the evolution of still better thought.

But, were this freedom to come suddenly, I have no fear of the consequences. Individuals might commit excesses, but there is not only in the sex a reverence for decorums and limits inherited and enhanced from generation to generation, which many years of other life could not efface, but a native love, in Woman as Woman, of proportion, of "the simple art of not too much," a Greek moderation, which would create immediately a restraining party, the natural legislators and instructors of the rest, and would gradually establish such rules as are needed to guard, without impeding, life.

The Graces would lead the choral dance, and teach the rest to regulate their steps to the measure of beauty.

But if you ask me what offices they may fill, I reply—any. I do not care what case you put; let them be sea-captains, if you will. I do not doubt there are women well fitted for such an office, and, if so, I should be as glad to see them in it, as to welcome the maid of Saragossa, or the maid of Missolonghi, or the Suliote heroine, or Emily Plater.

I think women need, especially at this juncture, a much greater range of occupation than they have, to rouse their latent powers. A party of travellers lately visited a lonely hut on a mountain. There they found an old woman, who told them she and her husband had lived there forty years. "Why," they said, "did you choose so barren a spot?" She "did not know; *it was the man's notion.*"

And, during forty years, she had been content to act, without knowing why, upon "the man's notion." I would not have it so.

In families that I know, some little girls like to saw wood, others to use carpenters' tools. Where these tastes are indulged, cheerfulness and good-humor are promoted. Where they are forbidden, because "such things are not proper for girls," they grow sullen and mischievous.

Fourier had observed these wants of women, as no one can fail to do who watches the desires of little girls, or knows the ennui that haunts grown women, except where they make to themselves a serene little world by art of some kind. He, therefore, in proposing a great variety of employments, in manufactures or the care of plants and animals, allows for one third of women as likely to have a taste for masculine pursuits, one third of men for feminine.

Who does not observe the immediate glow and serenity that is diffused over the life of women, before restless or fretful, by engaging in gardening, building, or the lowest department of art? Here is something that is not routine, something that draws forth life towards the infinite.

I have no doubt, however, that a large proportion of women would give themselves to the same employments as now, because there are circumstances that must lead them. Mothers will delight to make the nest soft and warm. Nature would take care of that; no need to clip the wings of any bird that wants to soar and sing, or finds in itself the strength of pinion for a migratory flight unusual to its kind. The difference would be that *all* need

Glossary

churls	peasants, crude people without refinement or culture
dissolute	characterized by a lack of moral restraint, debauched
ennui	boredom
expediency	the quality of being practical, useful, or fit for the purpose
Graces	in Greek and Roman mythology, the personifications of joy, beauty, charm, happiness, and festivity
helots	in ancient Greece, serfs
Lord Edward Fitzgerald	Irish aristocrat (1763–1798) who traveled throughout Canada and what was then the territories west of the United States
Louis XIV	king of France (1638–1715)
profligate	wasteful, extravagant
Quaker	a member of a religious sect, more formally called the Religious Society of Friends, known for recognizing relative equality in women

not be constrained to employments for which *some* are unfit.

I have urged upon the sex self-subsistence in its two forms of self-reliance and self-impulse, because I believe them to be the needed means of the present juncture.

I have urged on woman independence of man, not that I do not think the sexes mutually needed by one another, but because in Woman this fact has led to an excessive devotion, which has cooled love, degraded marriage, and prevented either sex from being what it should be to itself or the other.

I wish woman to live, *first* for God's sake. Then she will not make an imperfect man her god, and thus sink to idolatry. Then she will not take what is not fit for her from a sense of weakness and poverty. Then, if she finds what she needs in Man embodied, she will know how to love, and be worthy of being loved.

William Lloyd Garrison (Library of Congress)

WILLIAM LLOYD GARRISON   1805–1879

Newspaper Editor and Abolitionist

Featured Documents
- "To the Public" (1831)
- "The Triumph of Mobocracy in Boston" (1835)
- "Declaration of Sentiments Adopted by the Peace Convention" (1838)
- "Address to the Friends of Freedom and Emancipation in the United States" (1844)
- Speech Relating to the Execution of John Brown (1859)
- Valedictory Editorial (1865)

Overview

William Lloyd Garrison was born in Newburyport, Massachusetts, on December 10, 1805. From his teens he worked in the newspaper-publishing business. Then, in 1831, he published the first issue of his Boston newspaper, the *Liberator*, which until the end of 1865 served as his personal vehicle for broadcasting his many controversial opinions, most notably that slavery must be immediately abolished and that people of all skin colors must be treated as equals. In 1833 he played a major role in the establishment of the American Anti-Slavery Society, which for the first time united black and white reformers of both genders in support of programs of mass agitation to promote immediate abolition and racial equality.

In the late 1830s Garrison adopted still more radical beliefs by embracing female equality and Christian pacifism, denying the literal truth of Scripture, rejecting the authority of religious denominations, and demanding the boycotting of governments and elections. By 1842, when he denounced the U.S. Constitution as a pro-slavery document and demanded that the free North secede from the slave South, he had become a divisive force within the abolitionist movement and a controversial figure in the nation's developing political crisis over slavery.

Throughout the 1840s and 1850s Garrison and his small circle continued to espouse a wide-ranging reform agenda through speeches and in the pages of the *Liberator*. In 1859, however, John Brown's insurrectionary raid on the federal armory at Harpers Ferry, Virginia, led Garrison to jettison his pacifism. When the Civil War began in 1861, he quickly became one of its most fervent supporters, demanding that all slaves be freed by force of arms. In 1865, after the ratification of the Thirteenth Amendment, abolishing slavery, Garrison closed the *Liberator* and ended his career. He died on May 24, 1879.

Garrison was perhaps the antebellum era's most innovative editorial agitator. In an era of rapidly expanding print and telegraphic communication, his ceaseless desire to promote himself as the nation's moral censor and his unerring capacity for challenging conventional values made it all but impossible for Americans to deny the moral problem of slavery. He accomplished his goals because of his exceptional talent as a polemicist and his inexhaustible love of ideological conflict. His temperament aligned him closely to the romantic impulses that inspired New England Transcendentalists and utopian reformers who, like him, were deeply suspicious of established institutions and who celebrated intuitive illuminations of God's "truth." In short, he addressed public opinion in idioms it instinctively understood.

Explanation and Analysis of Documents

Garrison's self-described roles were those of agitator, moral censor, prophet, and "universal reformer." His gifts were his extraordinary skills as an editorial polemicist and his resolve to follow the implications of his religious illuminations wherever they might lead him. In an age of rapidly multiplying editorial voices, Garrison proved to be a master of making himself (as he put it) "heard!" Six documents chart the course of Garrison's ideological evolution as an abolitionist from the start of his career to its end and give a flavor of his polemical approach as well: his 1831 introductory editorial in the *Liberator*, his description of his 1835 confrontation with a Boston antiabolitionist mob, his 1838 statement of belief in religious perfectionism, his 1844 justifications for condemning the U.S. Constitution, his 1859 abandonment of pacifist principles and defense of John Brown, and his valedictory editorial when terminating publication of the *Liberator* in 1865.

"To the Public"

By 1831 the young Garrison was evolving into an immediate abolitionist. He was also unemployed and without immediate prospects, having completed a brief but much-publicized sojourn in Baltimore's jail after being convicted for libeling a slave trader. While he was in Baltimore, Garrison had also boarded in the houses of several of the city's free black people, who had given him shocking first accounts of slavery's cruelties and the oppressiveness of racial prejudice. For these reasons the imperative that slavery must be abolished immediately and unconditionally stimulated Garrison's deep desires for success and recognition. It likewise spoke powerfully to his deeply felt obliga-

Time Line

1805

- **December 10**
  Garrison is born in
  Newburyport,
  Massachusetts.

1831

- **January 1**
  Garrison publishes the first
  issue of the *Liberator* with
  an opening statement
  entitled "To the Public."

1832

- **January 6**
  Garrison leads in founding
  the New England Anti-
  Slavery Society.

1833

- **December 4**
  Garrison leads in founding
  the American Anti-Slavery
  Society.

1835

- **November 7**
  Garrison publishes "The
  Triumph of Mobocracy in
  Boston" in the *Liberator*.

1838

- **September 18–20**
  The Peace Convention,
  designed to start a new
  movement to outlaw all
  forms of warfare, capital
  punishment, and state
  coercion, takes place in
  Boston.

- **September 28**
  Garrison publishes the
  "Declaration of Sentiments
  Adopted by the Peace
  Convention" in the
  Liberator, which he had
  issued at the Peace
  Convention held in Boston
  earlier that month.

1842

- Garrison promulgates the
  doctrine of northern
  secession from the Union.

1844

- **May 20**
  Garrison delivers "Address
  to the Friends of Freedom
  and Emancipation in the
  United States" to the
  executive committee of the
  American Anti-Slavery
  Society and publishes the
  address in the *Liberator* on
  May 31.

tion to expose the racial oppression about which his black associates had told him.

This editorial, from the inaugural issue of the *Liberator* on January 1, 1831, contains the most widely quoted words Garrison was ever to write. They constitute, above all, a compelling justification for his self-appointed role as an uncompromising moral censor and for his use of condemnatory rhetoric to forward the abolitionist cause. His promise that "I WILL BE HEARD" is almost invariably quoted in American history textbooks because it conveys so vividly his irrepressible zeal as well as the spirit of the immediate abolitionist movement.

Throughout the editorial Garrison presents himself as a solitary prophet whose mission it is to shock a morally slumbering nation into action. He emphasizes that public opinion in the North about slavery is even more blighted by prejudice and apathy than it is in the South and that overcoming such enormous obstacles requires the courage of spiritually inspired truth tellers precisely like him. His words are forceful: "I am aware, that many object to the severity of my language; but is there not cause for severity? I *will be* as harsh as truth, and as uncompromising as truth. On this subject, I do not wish to think, or speak, or write, with moderation." Invoking the values of the Declaration of Independence, he conflates the immediate freeing of all slaves with the highest callings of patriotism and explicitly rejects all appeals to gradualism—that is, the belief that slavery could gradually be ended. When rejecting moderation he also warns of slavery's corrosive impact on the sanctity of families. Appeals on behalf of the enslaved to the spirit of the American Revolution and to Christian values of family became two of the most powerful themes of those who called for immediate abolition.

♦ **"The Triumph of Mobocracy in Boston"**

By 1835 immediate abolitionists had coalesced into a tightly organized movement that was spreading its message throughout the nation by mobilizing speakers, founding newspapers, circulating handbills and petitions to the government, organizing rallies, and harshly criticizing all who supported slavery. Most controversially, abolitionists turned their meetings into what opponents criticized as dangerous assemblies that included women and African Americans in their deliberations. In the minds of the abolitionists' opponents, immediate abolition became synonymous with race mixing, fanaticism, and the overturning of the established social order. Abolitionists fell under siege from mobs that broke up their meetings, burned their publications, wrecked their printing presses, and terrorized free black communities. In 1832 a racially integrated school was attacked by a mob in Dover, Delaware, and a few years later a Quaker schoolteacher in Connecticut, Prudence Crandall, abandoned her attempt to maintain a school for black girls. Race riots provoked by white mobs took place in black neighborhoods in Pittsburgh, New York, Cincinnati, Boston, and Hartford, Connecticut. In Alton, Illinois, the Reverend Elijah Lovejoy was murdered by a mob as he guarded the printing press he used to print an antislavery newspaper. The U.S. postal service maintained a policy of not delivering antislavery materials to the South. In the midst of this turmoil, Garrison himself became a subject of enormous controversy as the movement's most notorious leader.

Fear of British subversion of American liberties added further to antiabolitionists' anxieties when Garrison hosted the controversial English abolitionist George Thompson in Boston in November 1835. Thompson, as a member of the British Parliament, was widely known in England for his lecture tours and legislation designed to end the slave trade. News that the Boston Female Anti-Slavery Society was convening to welcome him sent antiabolitionists into the streets. They intended to break up the women's meeting, capture Thompson and Garrison, and coat them with tar and feathers. While Thompson avoided trouble, Garrison did not. He confronted the mob as it broke into the meeting hall and was forced to find refuge in the Boston city jail.

In his description of the event, Garrison conveys his judgment on the moral character of his antagonists, likening them to a "troop of ravenous wolves." To him, the hypocrisy and venality of the mob were transparent. Their racial bigotry, disrespect for women, and contempt for civil liberties gave the lie to their self-proclaimed superiority as "respectable" and "influential" defenders of the social order. Instead, their disruptive actions confirmed that the corrupting influences of southern slavery were now reaching far into the free states, destroying northerners' rights of assembly and expression. The besieged abolitionist women, by contrast, embodied righteous purity, personal heroism, and civic responsibility. Unlike their supposedly upstanding opponents, it was actually they who represented patriotic values.

Garrison's warning that slavery in the South posed imminent dangers to freedom in the North proved persuasive to many who were otherwise unsympathetic to his cause. As he put it, "What will be the effect of this riot? Will it cause one abolitionist to swerve from the faith?…It will excite sympathy for the persecuted, and indignation against the persecutors; it will multiply sterling converts to our doctrines." Reacting negatively to the wave of antiabolitionist violence of the mid-1830s, an increasing number of northerners decided that the slave South did, indeed, represent a threat to their personal liberties and that an aggressive "Slave Power" must never be permitted to define the nation's course. In this respect, despite their continuing unpopularity, Garrison and his co-workers were forcing their fellow Americans to oppose slavery.

This document also reveals Garrison's admiration of the besieged female abolitionists and his desire to portray himself as their fearless protector. From the very first, Garrison clearly understood the extraordinary potential that reform-minded women represented for his cause. And, indeed, women quickly did come to dominate the movement's rank and file. Moreover, his eagerness to speak at the otherwise all-female meeting and act as these women's solitary male defender during the 1835 riot clearly prefigured his advocacy of women's rights two years later.

Time Line	
1854	■ **July 4** Garrison publicly burns a copy of the U.S. Constitution.
1859–1861	■ John Brown's raid on the federal arsenal at Harpers Ferry and the onset of Civil War lead Garrison to renounce his pacifist principles.
1859	■ **December 2** Garrison delivers his speech relating to the execution of John Brown and publishes the speech in the *Liberator* on December 16.
1861–1865	■ Garrison demands slave emancipation through military conquest of the South.
1865	■ **December 29** Garrison publishes the final issue of the *Liberator* with his valedictory editorial.
1879	■ **May 24** Garrison dies in New York City.

◆ **"Declaration of Sentiments Adopted by the Peace Convention"**

By 1838 the violence had subsided, leaving the abolitionists disturbed by its implications. In Garrison's view, the repression revealed a God-defying United States in which governments ruled by illegitimate force and people exploited one another through coercive relationships. In addition to southern slavery, Garrison now turned his opposition against what he took to be a variety of "godless" practices—the authority of religious denominations, the literal truth of Scripture, the legitimacy of government, and the subordination of women to men. By developing these novel doctrines, Garrison embraced a highly romantic expression of Protestantism known as *religious perfectionism* and an expanded sense of his role as a "universal reformer."

When moving in these directions, Garrison was heavily influenced by such charismatic religious utopians as John Humphrey Noyes, the controversial founder of the Oneida utopian community in New York State and the originator of the phrase *free love*. Perfectionism expressed a romantic aspiration to reject the sinful coercion of secular society by bringing the pacifying rule of Heaven directly to the earth. As perfectionists saw it, people must free themselves from enslaving institutions and live instead as Jesus had directed—in love and peace, freed from coercive relationships, and enjoying unqualified equality.

Equally influential in shaping Garrison's new beliefs were two spiritually questing sisters, Angelina and Sarah Grimké, who caused great controversy beginning in 1837 by challenging their fellow immediatists to endorse equal rights for women. To them, and to an increasing number of abolitionists of both genders, the oppression of women and southern slave owning appeared to be two closely interconnected forms of exploitation. They believed that moral consistency dictated that abolitionists must accord women complete equality within their movement—full voting rights, access to leadership positions, and freedom to speak as equals before the public. Each of these demands contradicted the prevailing beliefs that women resided in a sphere separate from men that protected their moral purity from the corruptions of the secular world.

Garrison's "Declaration of Sentiments Adopted by the Peace Convention" was put forward at the Peace Convention held in Boston from September 18 through 20, 1838. The document, which Garrison drafted and signed, conveys perfectionism's exalted desire to transcend man-made restrictions and to perfect the world through Christian love. "We cannot acknowledge allegiance to any human government," he declares. "Our country is the world, our countrymen are all mankind." In this declaration, Garrison envisions the government of God as sweeping aside not only armies and wars but also every agency that divides God's creations from one another. When prophesying a world "which has…no national partitions, no geographical boundaries…no distinction of rank, or division of caste, or inequality of sex," Garrison succinctly captures how he understood himself as a "universal reformer" and why he was suddenly becoming such a divisive influence within the abolitionist movement.

Many of Garrison's abolitionist colleagues rejected his new doctrines as offensive heresies and as distractions that crippled the cause of the slave. From 1838 onward, his ever more numerous opponents attempted to purge him and his followers, a process that concluded in failure when, in 1840, these critics instead seceded from the American Anti-Slavery Society to form their own new organizations. From that date onward, Garrison presided over a single diminished faction of an irreparably divided movement.

◆ "Address to the Friends of Freedom and Emancipation in the United States"

Garrison's "Address to the Friends of Freedom and Emancipation in the United States," which he published in May 1844 in the *Liberator*, summarizes the arguments supporting his most controversial political doctrine, that the free North must secede from the slave South and that abolitionists were morally compelled to withhold their allegiance from the Constitution of the United States. By 1844, in Garrison's view, the federal Union had clearly

proved an irredeemably tainted arrangement that guaranteed the continuing oppression of the enslaved. Therefore, he enjoins all abolitionists, "secede…from the government. Submit to its exactions, but pay it no allegiance, give it no voluntary aid. Fill no offices under it. Send no Senators or Representatives to the national or State Legislature."

On one level, Garrison's demand that there be "NO UNION WITH SLAVEHOLDERS" represented a logical culmination of the perfectionist views he had been exploring since the 1830s. In addition to denying the authority of churches and clergy, the idea that true Christians must now also withhold their allegiance to the state while submitting peacefully to its minimal requirements constituted his fullest vision of "universal reform." Sanctified people could actually conduct their lives according to the governance of God, Garrison contends, and liberate themselves from the coercive political demands of the unsanctified majority.

By propounding these doctrines Garrison established himself as an originator of civil disobedience doctrines advocated later by the Russian writer and pacifist Leo Tolstoy, the American Transcendentalist author Henry David Thoreau, the German Lutheran theologian Dietrich Bonhoeffer, and the American civil rights leader Martin Luther King, Jr. At the same time, as the document eloquently confirms, "NO UNION WITH SLAVEHOLDERS" was rooted in Garrison's bitter response to the hostility that he and his associates continued to experience. But most important was Garrison's heartfelt conviction that "three million" enslaved persons continue to be "crushed under the American Union!" Only by personally withdrawing from that Union and struggling peacefully to overthrow it would abolitionists sustain hope of abolishing slavery. Garrison's fundamental concern remained what it had always been—the liberation of the enslaved.

Obviously, Garrison's contention that the slaves would be emancipated only if the South were allowed to go its own way was logically dubious. At the same time, northern disunionism inspired rebuttals that developed enormous influence as the sectional conflict went forward. Dissenting responses from influential legal theorists such as Salmon P. Chase, that the Constitution was actually a document that barred slavery's westward expansion, were ultimately adopted by Abraham Lincoln's Republican Party.

◆ Speech Relating to the Execution of John Brown

On December 2, 1859, on the day that the abolitionist John Brown was hanged, Garrison delivered a speech in Boston, lamenting his death. This document conveys the collapse of Garrison's pacifist/perfectionist convictions and his sudden embrace of slave rebellion. After delivering these new opinions, he could no longer maintain his posture as a reforming perfectionist and found it increasingly easy to mix in the politics of the Civil War. The catalyst for Garrison's change of mind was John Brown's abortive raid on the federal arsenal in Harpers Ferry, West Virginia, in late 1859, after which he was tried and executed as a traitor. In the longer view, Garrison, like many other abolitionists, had increasingly flirted with violence ever since 1850, when, at slaveholders' insistence, Congress had passed a

THE BURNING OF THE UNITED STATES ARSENAL AT HARPER'S FERRY, 10 P.M. APRIL 18, 1861.—[SKETCHED BY D. H. STROTHER.]

The burning of the U.S. arsenal at Harpers Ferry, West Virginia (Library of Congress)

harsh new Fugitive Slave Law requiring U.S. citizens, including all northerners, to assist in the recapture of black escapees. Throughout the decade, black and white abolitionists united to protect fugitives from federal marshals, sometimes through mob action and occasionally by taking up arms. Meantime, violent conflicts in Kansas over slavery's possible extension into that territory added significantly to the atmosphere of confrontation.

As Garrison's speech makes clear, he, like many other abolitionists, saw himself as reenacting the struggles of 1776, when the "revolutionary fathers" embraced violence to face down compounding tyranny. As Garrison explains, Brown acted boldly as a latter-day George Washington or John Hancock when "striking a blow for freedom" by shedding slaveholders' blood. He was, Garrison insists, anything but a traitor, insurrectionist, and murderer. "If you believe in the right of assisting men to fight for freedom who are of your own color—(God knows nothing of color or complexion….)—then you must cover, not only with a mantle of charity, but with the admiration of your hearts, the effort of John Brown," he avers. How could Garrison have fallen so quickly from his perfectionist pacifism? As the document makes plain, he found Brown's violence appealing, and hence he resorted to tortured rationalizations. Brown, he argues, initially intended "nothing offensive, nothing aggressive," seeking only to supply weapons to slaves for

use in their own self-defense. When next Brown's "humanity overpowered his judgment" and he began firing on his enemies, admirable motives justified his course. By this time Garrison continues to maintain that he still was a nonresistant even while announcing that he is "prepared to say, 'Success to every slave insurrection in the South, and in every slave country.'"

When characterizing Brown as a hero, Garrison echoed many other militant abolitionists, black and white alike. Yet while most Republicans agreed with Abraham Lincoln that Brown was insane and his conduct unconscionable, Garrison's descent from perfectionism left him increasingly willing to support this new Republican Party. Although he continued to advocate northern disunion during the 1861 secession crisis, once Union troops mustered, Garrison embraced war. Henceforth he would act as the Republicans' harsh but loyal critic and never again as a "universal reformer."

◆ **Valedictory Editorial**

Following the ratification of the Thirteenth Amendment, which formally abolished slavery, Garrison declared his thirty-five-year mission completed, the abolitionist movement redundant, and the further publication of the *Liberator* unnecessary. His decision to retire came as the struggle to secure the rights of the just-emancipated slaves was only beginning. In this respect, it measures well exact-

"*I will be as harsh as truth, and as uncompromising as justice. On this subject, I do not wish to think, or speak, or write, with moderation.... I am in earnest—I will not equivocate—I will not excuse—I will not retreat a single inch—AND I WILL BE HEARD.*"

("To the Public")

"*Was it not a sublime spectacle to behold four or five thousand genteel ruffians courageously assembling together, to achieve so hazardous and glorious an exploit as the putting to flight one man and thirty defenseless females?*"

("The Triumph of Mobocracy in Boston")

"*Our motto is, 'NO UNION WITH SLAVEHOLDERS!'... Secede, then, from the government. Submit to its exactions, but pay it no allegiance, and give it no voluntary aid.*"

("Address to the Friends of Freedom and Emancipation in the United States")

"*Our country is the world, our countrymen are all mankind. We love the land of our nativity, only as we love all other lands. The interests, rights, liberties of American citizens are no more dear to us, than are those of the whole human race.*"

("Declaration of Sentiments Adopted by the Peace Convention")

"*As a peace man—an 'ultra' peace man—I am prepared to say, 'Success to every slave insurrection at the South, and in every slave country.'*"

("Speech Relating to the Execution of John Brown")

"*The object for which the Liberator was commenced—the extermination of chattel slavery—having been gloriously consummated, it seems to me specially appropriate to let its existence cover the historic period of the great struggle, leaving what remains to be done to complete the work of emancipation to other instrumentalities.*"

("Valedictory Editorial")

ly how conservative Garrison had become since abandoning his religious perfectionism during the Civil War.

Many of his oldest associates, most prominently Wendell Phillips, Frederick Douglass, and Elizabeth Cady Stanton, condemned his decision as an irresponsible abandonment of the struggle for racial equality at its most critical juncture and repulsed Garrison's attempt to disband the American Anti-Slavery Society. For the next five years, until 1870, this organization continued to battle for complete equality for African Americans. It played a vital role in the ratification of the Fourteenth Amendment (providing a broad definition of U.S. citizenship meant to secure the rights of former slaves) and the Fifteenth Amendment (banning race-based voting qualifications). Despite the promises he offered in this parting editorial to continue advocating for the rights of freed people, Garrison meantime remained largely uninvolved.

The document demonstrates how much more deeply preoccupied Garrison was with vindicating his own career by ending it in triumph than with continuing the struggle for equality. "Never had a journal to look such opposition in the face—never was one so constantly belied and caricatured," he claimed. And, still, he goes on, "no journal has been conducted with such fairness and impartiality;...none has so readily and exhaustively published, without note or comment, what its enemies have said to its disparagement, and the vilification of its editor." Garrison congratulates himself that "the object for which the *Liberator* was commenced—the extermination of chattel slavery—[has] been gloriously consummated." While he professes an ongoing commitment to the emancipated slaves, he reveals his self-satisfied naïveté when asserting that since the freed people were now being supported by "millions instead of hundreds for allies," an organized abolitionist movement was no longer needed. As the epic political battles to secure black equality played out during Reconstruction, Garrison remained secure in his belief that "his" abolitionist movement had already succeeded.

Impact and Legacy

Garrison's influence resonated far beyond his small circle of supporters. Southern slaveholders always regarded him as embodying all that was malignant about "Yankee" culture. The vast majority in the North also regarded him as a dangerous extremist and at times subjected him and other abolitionists to mob action. Yet his utopian approach provoked abolitionists who disagreed with him to develop alternate approaches to the problem of slavery that were more acceptable to the public at large. By the 1840s such dissidents had, for example, founded the Liberty Party, which attempted to further abolition through third-party politics. After Garrison proposed in 1842 that the North secede from the allegedly pro-slavery Union, debates multiplied over the federal government's powers respecting slavery and directly influenced Abraham Lincoln and the Republican Party.

Questions for Further Study

1. Whereas Garrison's fervent opposition to slavery seems only right to a modern American, some of the positions he expresses in the 1838 Peace Convention declaration remain out of the ordinary. Do you agree with his aims and with statements such as "the interests ... of American citizens are no more dear to us, than those of the whole human race"? What problems or pitfalls might arise from acting on the principles he outlines in the document?

2. Discuss Garrison's *religious perfectionism* and his stated desire to be a "universal reformer." Are these principles that can be applied in practice? What does his adoption of these ideas say about Garrison as an individual? How do you think he saw himself and his relationship to fellow humans (not just slaves)?

3. Trace the development of Garrison's views on the use of violence to obtain social justice. How did he go from being a pacifist to taking up the cause of the Union army?

4. Was Garrison right to close down the *Liberator* in 1865? Many critics within the abolitionist cause considered this an irresponsible move, but there is much to be said for the opposing viewpoint. With slavery abolished, he might justifiably have considered his work to be finished and could be regarded as acting with honesty and humility, rather than remaining active and perpetuating a career as a professional protester. What do you think?

5. Discuss Garrison's influence on the civil rights movement and on 1960s student radicalism.

Within the circle of reformers who supported him from the 1840s onward, Garrison was equally influential. The formal organization that advocated his views, the American Anti-Slavery Society, and its weekly newspaper, the *Anti-Slavery Standard*, were located in New York City. Boston, however, where Garrison published the *Liberator*, always remained the center of his movement. Here, beginning in the late 1830s, debates he provoked when insisting on equal rights for women nurtured the origins of the nation's first feminist movement, led initially by the abolitionists Lucretia Mott, Abby Kelley Foster, Angelina and Sarah Grimké, and Maria Weston Chapman. Throughout the antebellum decades, Boston "Garrisonianism" likewise provided crucial points of departure for the careers of important African American activists such as Charles Lennox Remond, William Nell, Nathaniel Paul, and Frederick Douglass. And, finally, Boston's Garrisonians played major roles during the 1840s and 1850s in transforming that city into a bastion of opposition to slavery and white supremacy. They led in efforts to protect fugitive slaves, agitated successfully for public school integration, opened the city to the cosmopolitan influence of British abolitionism, and during the Civil War pressed for the enlistment of black soldiers.

Garrison's greatest impact was his success in making slavery a pressing moral problem that white Americans could not choose to ignore. His exceptional polemical gifts, his egalitarian religious vision, and his personal fearlessness combined to ensure this result. Many of these same qualities also allowed him to inspire the nation's first feminists and to establish traditions of nonviolent resistance. At the same time, Garrison's strident language and extreme positions were deeply unsettling to southern slaveholders, who came in time to believe, incorrectly, that he spoke for a majority of northerners. In this respect, Garrison exercised a disproportionate influence in the political crisis that led to southern secession. In the longer view, during the Civil Rights era Garrison and the movement he so powerfully symbolized came to be regarded as powerful role models for the activism of that day.

Key Sources

The William Lloyd Garrison Papers at the Boston Public Library, the Smith College Library, and many smaller collections are comprehensively reprinted in Walter Merrill and Louis Ruchames, eds., *The Letters of William Lloyd Garrison, 1822–1879*, 6 vols. (1970–1979). Garrison's newspaper, the *Liberator*, is available on microfilm in many libraries.

Further Reading

■ Books

Mayer, Henry. *All on Fire: William Lloyd Garrison and the Abolition of Slavery*. New York: St. Martin's Press, 1998.

Stewart, James Brewer. *William Lloyd Garrison and the Challenge of Emancipation*. Arlington Heights, Ill.: Harlan Davidson, 1992.

———. *Holy Warriors: The Abolitionists and American Slavery*, rev. ed. New York: Hill and Wang, 1996.

—James Stewart

"To the Public" (1831)

During my recent tour for the purpose of exciting the minds of the people by a series of discourses on the subject of slavery, every place that I visited gave fresh evidence of the fact, that a greater revolution in public sentiment was to be effected in the free states—*and particularly in New-England*—than at the South. I found contempt more bitter, opposition more active, detraction more relentless, prejudice more stubborn, and apathy more frozen, than among slave owners themselves. Of course, there were individual exceptions to the contrary. This state of things afflicted, but did not dishearten me. I determined, at every hazard, to lift up the standard of emancipation in the eyes of the nation, *within sight of Bunker Hill and on the birth place of liberty*. That standard is now unfurled; and long may it float, unhurt by the applications of time or the missiles of a desperate foe—yes, till every chain be broken, and every bondsman set free! Let southern oppressors tremble—let all the enemies of the persecuted blacks tremble....

Assenting to the "self-evident truth" maintained in the American Declaration of Independence, "that all men are created equal, and endowed by their Creator with certain inalienable rights—among which are life, liberty and the pursuit of happiness," I shall strenuously then contend for the immediate enfranchisement of our slave population. In Park-street Church, on the Fourth of July, 1829, in an address on slavery, I unreflectingly assented to the popular but pernicious doctrine of gradual abolition. I seize this opportunity to make a full and unequivocal recantation, and thus publicly to ask pardon of my God, of my country, and of my brethren the poor slaves, for having stated a sentiment so full of timidity, injustice and absurdity....

I am aware, that many object to the severity of my language; but is there not cause for severity? I *will* be as harsh as truth, and as uncompromising as truth. On this subject, I do not wish to think, or speak, or write, with moderation. No! no! Tell a man whose house is on fire, to give a moderate alarm; tell him to moderately rescue his wife from the hands of the ravisher; tell the mother to gradually extricate her babe from the fire into which it has fallen;—but urge me not to use moderation in a cause like the present. I am in earnest—I will not equivocate—I will not excuse—I will not retreat a single inch—AND I WILL BE HEARD. The apathy of the people is enough to make every statue leap from its pedestal, and to hasten the resurrection of the dead.

It is pretended, that I am retarding the cause of emancipation by the coarseness of my invective, and the precipitancy of my measures. The *charge is not true*. On this question my influence—humble as it is—is felt at this moment to a considerable extent, and shall be felt in coming years—not perniciously, but beneficially—not as a curse, but as a blessing; and posterity will bear testimony that I was right. I desire to thank God, that he enables me to disregard "the fear of man which bringeth a snare," and to speak his truth in its simplicity and power. And here I close with this fresh dedication:

Oppression! I have seen thee, face to face,
And met thy cruel eye and cloudy brow;
But thy soul-withering glance I fear not now—
For dread to prouder feelings doth give place
Of deep abhorrence! Scorning the disgrace
Of slavish knees that at thy footstool bow,

Glossary

Afric's	Africa's
at every hazard	at all costs
equivocate	attempt to consider all sides of a question and thus not take a strong stand
ravisher	rapist
within sight of Bunker Hill	a place that saw one of the key battles of the Revolutionary War, a reference that notes the irony that so many years later millions of Americans were still not free

I also kneel—but with far other vow
Do hail thee and thy hord of hirelings base:—
I swear, while life-blood warms my throbbing veins,
Still to oppose and thwart, with heart and hand,
Thy brutalising sway—till Afric's chains
Are burst, and Freedom rules the rescued land,—
Trampling Oppression and his iron rod:
Such is the vow I take—SO HELP ME GOD!

"THE TRIUMPH OF MOBOCRACY IN BOSTON" (1835)

I shall give, as far as I am capable, an exact and faithful account of the ruthless disturbances which took place in Boston on Wednesday afternoon, Oct. 21st, and by which this city was suddenly transformed into an infuriated pandemonium. It is the most disgraceful event that has ever marred the character of Bostonians, whether reference be made to the time of its occurrence, or to the cause which was assailed, or to those who stood obnoxious to violent treatment. The recent pro-slavery meeting in Faneuil Hall supported the *theory* of despotism, and the tumultuous assembly of Wednesday carried it into *practice*—trampling all law and order, the constitution and personal liberty, public decorum and private decency, common humanity and Christian courtesy, into the dust. The light of day did not cause a blush, nor the certainty of exposure restrain from indecent and barbarous behavior, nor profession or station deter "respectable, wealthy and influential citizens" from enacting the part of ruffians and anarchists. All distinctions (excepting that of *color*, to the honor of the BLACK MAN be it recorded) were blended, for the purpose of gagging the advocates of freedom, and infusing new strength into the arm of the remorseless scourger of *Woman* at the South. The merchant and the aristocrat—the wealthy and the learned—the "respectable" and the "influential"—the professor and the profane—all were huddled together in thick and formidable array, with every variety of feeling, but with one prevalent design, namely, to insult, annoy and disperse the Female Anti-Slavery meeting, (brave, gentlemanly, chivalric men!) and to tar-and-feather, or put to death, GEORGE THOMPSON or myself! Was it not a sublime spectacle to behold four or five thousand genteel ruffians courageously assembling together, to achieve so hazardous and glorious an exploit as the putting to flight one man and thirty defenseless females…?

On ascending into the hall, I found about fifteen or twenty ladies assembled, sitting with cheerful countenances, and a crowd of noisy intruders (mostly young men) gazing upon them, through whom I urged my way with considerable difficulty. "That's Garrison," was the exclamation of some of these creatures as I quietly took my seat. Perceiving that they had no intention of retiring, I went to them and calmly said—"Gentlemen perhaps you are not aware that this is a meeting of the Boston *Female* Anti-Slavery Society, called and intended exclusively for *ladies*, and those only who have been invited to address them. Understanding this fact, you will not be so rude or indecorous as to thrust your presence upon this meeting. If, *gentlemen*," I pleasantly continued, "any of you are apprise me of the fact, give me your names, and I will introduce you to the rest of your sex, and you can take seats among them accordingly." I then sat down, and, for a moment, their conduct was more orderly. However, the stair-way and upper door of the hall were soon densely filled with a brazen-faced crew, whose behavior grew more and more indecent and outrageous. Perceiving that it would be impracticable for me, or any other person, to address the ladies; and believing, as I was the only male abolitionist in the hall, that my presence would serve as a pretext for the mob to annoy the meeting, I held a short colloquy with the excellent President of the Society, telling her that I would withdraw, unless she particularly desired me to stay. It was her earnest wish that I would retire, as well for my own safety as for the peace of the meeting. She assured me that the Society would resolutely but calmly proceed to the transaction of its business, and leave the issue with God.…

In the mean time, the crowd in the street had augmented from a hundred to thousands. The cry was for "Thompson! Thompson!"—but the Mayor had now arrived, and, addressing the rioters, he assured them that Mr. Thompson was not in the city, and besought them to disperse. As well might he have attempted to propitiate a troop of ravenous wolves. None went away—but the tumult continued to increase. It was apparent, therefore, that the hostility of the throng was not concentrated upon Mr. Thompson, but that it was as deadly against the Society and the Anti-Slavery cause.—This fact is worthy of special note—for it incontestably proves that the object of the "respectable and influential" rioters was to put down the cause of emancipation, and that Mr. Thompson furnished merely a pretext for five thousand "gentlemen" to mob thirty Christian women!…

What will be the effect of this riot? Will it cause one abolitionist to swerve from the faith? Will it prevent either men or women from assembling together, to devise ways and means for the destruction of the slave system? Will it stop the freedom of discussion?

Will it put down the *Liberator*? Will, it check the growth of the anti-slavery cause? Will it slacken my efforts? No! It will have a contrary effect. It will humble the pride of this city; it will rouse up and concentrate all that is left of the free spirit of our fathers; it will excite sympathy for the persecuted, and indignation against the persecutors; it will multiply sterling converts to our doctrines; it will increase the circulation of anti-slavery writings; it will substitute a thousand agitators in the place of one, and make the discussion of slavery paramount to all other topics; it will make the triumph of truth over error, and of liberty over oppression, and of law over jacobinism, and of republicanism over aristocracy, more signal and glorious; it will enable the most blind to see that the existence of Southern slavery is incompatible with the exercise of the rights and privileges of Northern freemen; and it will nerve my arm to strike heavier blows than ever upon the head of the monster OPPRESSION.

Faneuil Hall	a Boston meeting place, nicknamed "the Cradle of Liberty," where Samuel Adams and other Founders made important speeches during the American Revolution
George Thompson	prominent British politician and abolitionist (1804–1878)
jacobinism	the belief system of a radical group who brought about the Reign of Terror during the French Revolution; more generally, intolerance
nerve my arm	give me the strength and courage
the professor and the profane	a play on the expression *the sacred and the profane* (that is, the spiritual and the worldly) used here to mean "the educated and the uneducated"
signal	unusual

"Declaration of Sentiments Adopted by the Peace Convention" (1838)

We cannot acknowledge allegiance to any human government; neither can we oppose any such government, by a resort to physical force. We recognize but one KING and LAWGIVER, one JUDGE and RULER of mankind. We are bound by the laws of a kingdom which is not of this world; the subjects of which are forbidden to fight; in which MERCY and TRUTH are met together and RIGHTEOUSNESS and PEACE have kissed each other; which has no state lines, no national partitions, no geographical boundaries; in which there is no distinction of rank, or division of caste, or inequality of sex; the officers of which are PEACE, its exactors RIGHTEOUSNESS, its walls SALVATION, and its gates PRAISE; and which is destined to break in pieces and consume all other kingdoms.

Our country is the world, our countrymen are all mankind. We love the land of our nativity, only as we love all other lands. The interests, rights, liberties of American citizens are no more dear to us, than are those of the whole human race. Hence, we can allow no appeal to patriotism, to revenge any national insult or injury. The PRINCE OF PEACE, under whose stainless banner we rally, came not to destroy, but to save, even the worst of enemies. He has left us an example, that we should follow his steps. GOD COMMENDETH HIS LOVE TOWARD US, IN THAT WHILE WE WERE YET SINNERS, CHRIST DIED FOR US.

We conceive, that if a nation has no right to defend itself against foreign enemies, or to punish its invaders, no individual possesses that right in his own case. The unit cannot be of greater importance than the aggregate. If one man may take life, to obtain or defend his rights, the same license must necessarily be granted to communities, states, and nations. If *he* may use a dagger or a pistol, *they* may employ cannon, bomb-shells, land and naval forces. The means of self-preservation must be in proportion to the magnitude of interests at stake, and the number of lives exposed to destruction. But if a rapacious and bloodthirsty soldiery, thronging these shores from abroad, with intent to commit rapine and destroy life, may not be resisted by the people or magistracy, then ought no resistance to be offered to domestic troublers of the public peace, or of private security. No obligation can rest upon Americans to .regard foreigners as more sacred in their persons than themselves, or to give them a monopoly of wrong-doing with impunity....

We register our testimony, not only against all wars, whether offensive or defensive, but all preparations for war; against every naval ship, every arsenal, every fortification; against the militia system and a standing army; against all military chieftains and soldiers; against all monuments commemorative of victory over a foreign foe, all trophies won in battle; all celebrations in honor of military or naval exploits; against all appropriations for the defence of a nation by force and arms, on the part of any legislative body; against every edict of government, requiring of its subjects military service. Hence, we deem it unlawful to bear arms, or to hold a military office.

As every human government is upheld by physical strength, and its laws are enforced virtually at the point of the bayonet, we cannot hold any office which imposes upon its incumbent the obligation to compel men to do right, on pain of imprisonment or death. We therefore voluntarily exclude ourselves from every legislative and judicial body, and repudiate all human politics, worldly honors, and stations of authority. If *we* cannot occupy a seat in the legislature or on the bench, neither can we elect *others* to act as our substitutes in any such capacity.

Glossary

magistracy	courts
rapine	plunder or seizure of property

"ADDRESS TO THE FRIENDS OF FREEDOM AND EMANCIPATION IN THE UNITED STATES" (1844)

At the Tenth Anniversary of the American Anti-Slavery Society, held in the city of New-York, May 7th, 1844,—after grave deliberation, and a long and earnest discussion,—it was decided by a vote of nearly three to one of the members present, that fidelity to the cause of human freedom, hatred of oppression, sympathy for those who are held in chains and slavery in this republic, and allegiance to God; require that the existing national compact should be instantly dissolved; that secession from the government is a religious and political duty; that the motto inscribed on the banner of Freedom should be, NO UNION WITH SLAVEHOLDERS; that it is impracticable for tyrants and the enemies of tyranny to coalesce and legislate together for the preservation of human rights, or the promotion of the interests of Liberty; and that revolutionary ground should be occupied by all those who abhor the thought of doing evil that good may come, and who do not mean to compromise the principles of Justice and Humanity....

It matters not what is the theory of the government, if the practice of the government be unjust and tyrannical. We rise in rebellion against a despotism incomparably more dreadful than that which induced the colonists to take up arms against the mother country; not on account of a three-penny tax on tea, but because fetters of living iron are fastened on the limbs of millions of our countrymen, and our most sacred rights are trampled in the dust. As citizens of the State we appeal to the State in vain for protection and redress. As citizens of the United States, we are treated as outlaws in one half of the country, and the national government consents to our destruction. We are denied the right of locomotion, freedom of speech, the right of petition, the liberty of the press, the right peaceably to assemble together to protest against oppression and plead for liberty—at least in thirteen States of the Union. If we venture, as avowed and unflinching abolitionists, to travel South of Mason and Dixon's line, we do so at the peril of our lives. If we would escape torture and death, on visiting any of the slave States, we must stifle our conscientious convictions, bear no testimony against cruelty and tyranny, suppress the struggling emotion of humanity, divest ourselves of all letters and papers of an anti-slavery character, and do homage to the slaveholding power—or run the risk of a cruel martyrdom! These are appalling and undeniable facts.

Three millions of the American people are crushed under the American Union! They are held as slaves—trafficked as merchandize—registered as goods and chattels! The government gives them no protection—the government is their enemy—the government keeps them in chains! There they lie bleeding—we are prostrate by their side—in their sorrows and sufferings we participate—their stripes are inflicted on our bodies, their shackles are fastened on our limbs, their cause is ours! The Union which grinds them to the dust rests upon us, and

Glossary

existing national compact	the Constitution
Mason and Dixon's line	part of the borders between Pennsylvania, Maryland, Delaware, and West Virginia (then part of Virginia), surveyed by Charles Mason and Jeremiah Dixon in the 1760s, which became the boundary between free and slave states
nail your banners to the mast!	fly your flags!
revolutionary ground should be occupied by	the moral high ground belongs to

with them we will struggle to overthrow it! The Constitution, which subjects them to hopeless bondage, is one that we cannot swear to support! Our motto is, "NO UNION WITH SLAVEHOLDERS!"… Freemen! are you ready for the conflict? Come what may, will you sever the chain that binds you to a slaveholding government, and declare your independence? Up, then, with the banner of revolution!… Secede, then, from the government. Submit to its exactions, but pay it no allegiance, and give it no voluntary aid. Fill no offices under it. Send no Senators or Representatives to the national or State Legislature, for what you cannot conscientiously perform yourself, you cannot ask another to perform as your agent. Circulate a declaration of DISUNION FROM SLAVE HOLDERS, throughout the country. Hold mass meetings—assemble in conventions—nail your banners to the mast!

Speech Relating to the Execution of John Brown (1859)

The man who brands him [John Brown] as a traitor is a calumniator.… The man who says that his object was to promote murder, or insurrection, or rebellion, is, in the language of the apostle, "a liar, and the truth is not in him."…John Brown meant to effect, if possible, a peaceful exodus from Virginia, and had not his large humanity overpowered his judgment in regard to his prisoners, he would in all probability have succeeded, and not a drop of blood would have been shed. But it is asked, "Did he not have stored up a large supply of Sharp's rifles and spears? What did they mean?" Nothing offensive, nothing aggressive. Only this:—he designed getting as many slaves as he could to join him, and then putting into their hands those instruments for self-defense.…

Was John Brown justified in his attempt? Yes, if Washington was in his; if Warren and Hancock were in theirs. If men are justified in striking a blow for freedom, when the question is one of a three penny tax on tea, then, I say, they are a thousand times more justified, when it is to save fathers, mothers, wives and children from the slave coffle and the auction block, and to restore to them their God given rights. Was John Brown justified in interfering in behalf of the slave population of Virginia, to secure their freedom and independence? Yes, if LaFayette was justified in interfering to help our revolutionary fathers. If Kosciusko, if Pulaski, if Steuben, if De Kalb, if all who joined them from abroad were justified in that act, then John Brown was incomparably more so. If you believe in the right of assisting men to fight for freedom who are of your own color— (God knows nothing of color or complexion—human rights know nothing of these distinctions)—then you must cover, not only with a mantle of charity, but with the admiration of your hearts, the effort of John Brown at Harper's Ferry.…

I am a non-resistant, a believer in the inviolability of human life, under all circumstances; I, therefore, in the name of God, disarm John Brown, and every slave at the South. But I do not stop there; if I did, I should be a monster. I also disarm, in the name of God, every slaveholder and tyrant in the world. For wherever that principle is adopted, all fetters must instantly melt, and there can be no oppressed, and no oppressor, in the nature of things.…I am a non-resistant and I not only desire, hut have labored unremittingly to effect, the peaceful abolition of slavery, by an appeal to the reason and conscience of the slaveholder; yet, as a peace man—an 'ultra' peace

Glossary

Bunker Hill, and Lexington, and Concord	important battles of the Revolutionary War
calumniator	someone who knowingly and viciously lies
coffle	a group of captives bound together
his large humanity	his goodheartedness
LaFayette… Kosciusko…Pulaski …Steuben…De Kalb	foreign nationals who helped the Americans' cause in the Revolutionary War—Gilbert du Motier, marquis de Lafayette (1757–1834), French military officer and general in the Continental army; Polish national Thaddeus Kosciusko (1746–1817), who became an American citizen and general in the Continental army; Casimir Pulaski (1746–1779), Polish nobleman and general in the Continental army; Friedrich von Steuben (1730–1794), Prussian army officer and inspector general of the Continental army; Johann de Kalb (1721–1780), German soldier and general in the Continental army
Sharp's rifles	Sharps rifles, a popular brand of firearm designed by Christian Sharps

man—I am prepared to say, 'Success to every slave insurrection at the South, and in every slave country."… I do not see how I compromise or stain my peace profession in making that declaration. Whenever there is a contest between the oppressed and the oppressor,—the weapons being equal between the parties,—God knows my heart must be with the oppressed, and always against the oppressor. Therefore, whenever commenced, I cannot but wish success to all slave insurrections.…It is an indication of progress, and a positive moral growth, it is one way to get up to the sublime platform of non resistance, and it is God's method of dealing retribution upon the head of the tyrant. Rather than see men wear their chains in a cowardly and servile spirit, I would, as an advocate of peace, much rather see them breaking the end of tyrant with their chains. Give me, as a non resistant, Bunker Hill, and Lexington, and Concord, rather than the cowardice and servility of a Southern slave plantation.

VALEDICTORY EDITORIAL (1865)

I began the publication of the *Liberator* without a subscriber, and I end it—it gives me unalloyed satisfaction to say—without a farthing as the pecuniary result of the patronage extended to it during thirty-five years of unremitted labors.

From the immense change wrought in the national feeling and sentiment on the subject of slavery, the *Liberator* derived no advantage at any time in regard to its circulation. The original "disturber of the peace," nothing was left undone at the beginning, and up to the hour of the late rebellion, by Southern slaveholding villainy on the one hand, and Northern pro-slavery malice on the other, to represent it as too vile a sheet to be countenanced by any claiming to be Christian or patriotic; and it always required rare moral courage or singular personal independence to be among its patrons. Never had a journal to look such opposition in the face—never was one so constantly belied and caricatured. If it had advocated all the crimes forbidden by the moral law of God and the statutes of the State, instead of vindicating the sacred claims of oppressed and bleeding humanity, it could not have been more vehemently denounced or more indignantly repudiated. To this day—such is the force of prejudice—there are multitudes who cannot be induced to read a single number of it, even on the score of curiosity, though their views on the slavery question are now precisely those which it has uniformly advocated....Yet no journal has been conducted with such fairness and impartiality; none has granted such freedom in its columns to its opponents; none has so scrupulously and uniformly presented all sides of every question discussed in its pages; none has so readily and exhaustively published, without note or comment, what its enemies have said to its disparagement, and the vilification of its editor; none has vindicated primitive Christianity, in its spirit and purpose—"the higher law," in its supremacy over nations and governments as well as individual conscience—the Golden Rule; in its binding obligation upon all classes—the Declaration of Independence, with its self-evident truths—the rights of human nature, without distinction of race, complexion or sex—more earnestly or more uncompromisingly; none has exerted a higher moral or more broadly reformatory influence upon those who have given it a careful perusal; and none has gone beyond it in asserting the Fatherhood of God and the brotherhood of man. All this may be claimed for it without egotism or presumption....

In this connection, I must be permitted to express my surprise that I am gravely informed, in various quarters, that this is no time to retire from public labor; that though the chains of the captive have been

Glossary

impeach	question
instrumentalities	organizations
late rebel States	former states of the Confederacy
the late rebellion	the Civil War
on the score of	because of
sheet	newspaper
without a farthing as the pecuniary result of the patronage extended	without the slightest amount of financial benefit
yokes	restraints designed for keeping captives together in a group

broken, he is yet to be vindicated in regard to the full possession of equal civil and political rights; that the freedmen in every part of the South are subjected to many insults and outrages; that the old slaveholding spirit is showing itself in every available form; that there is imminent danger that, in the hurry of reconstruction and readmission to the Union, the late rebel States will be left free to work any amount of mischief; that there is manifestly a severe struggle yet to come with the Southern "powers of darkness," which will require the utmost vigilance and the most determined efforts on the part of the friends of impartial liberty—&c., &c., &c. Surely, it is not meant by all this that I am therefore bound to continue the publication of the *Liberator*; for that is a matter for me to determine, and no one else. As I commenced its publication with out asking leave of any one, so I claim to be competent to decide when it may fitly close its career.

Again—it cannot be meant, by this presentation of the existing state of things at the South, either to impeach my intelligence, or to impute to me a lack of interest in behalf of that race, for the liberation and elevation of which I have labored so many years! If, when they had no friends, and no hope of earthly redemption, I did not hesitate to make their cause my own, is it to be supposed that, with their yokes broken, and their friends and advocates multiplied indefinitely, I can be any the less disposed to stand by them to the last—to insist on the full Measure of justice and equity being meted out to them—to retain in my breast a lively and permanent interest in all that relates to their present condition and future welfare?…

The object for which the *Liberator* was commenced—the extermination of chattel slavery—having been gloriously consummated, it seems to me specially appropriate to let its existence cover the historic period of the great struggle, leaving what remains to be done to complete the work of emancipation to other instrumentalities (of which I hope to avail myself), under new auspices, with more abundant means, and with millions instead of hundreds for allies.…

BOSTON, DECEMBER 29, 1865.

Elbridge Gerry (Library of Congress)

ELBRIDGE GERRY 1744–1814

Governor, U.S. Congressman, and Fifth Vice President of the United States

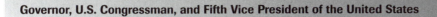

Featured Documents
- ◆ Letter to the Massachusetts Legislature on the U.S. Constitution (1787)
- ◆ First Reply to "A Landholder" (1788)
- ◆ Second Reply to "A Landholder" (1788)
- ◆ Letter to the Electors of Middlesex (1788)
- ◆ Speech on Paying Revolutionary War Debts (1790)

Overview

Elbridge Gerry was a prominent American Revolutionary and politician. In answer to oppressive British policies of colonial government, including special taxes on publications such as newspapers and the infamous tax on tea, he organized passive resistance, such as boycotts of certain British goods. When Great Britain blockaded and even occupied Boston (1775–1776), because the city was considered to be in a state of rebellion, he organized the smuggling of goods into Massachusetts through his hometown of Marblehead. During the privation brought on by the Revolutionary War, he helped provide those most affected with relief supplies.

Gerry was famous for being among the original signers of the Declaration of Independence, as a representative from Massachusetts. He also signed the Articles of Confederation, and he advocated the organization of the American states into a confederacy that would give the individual states wide discretion in the running of local affairs. He believed the U.S. Constitution to be too restrictive of what states could do, which is one reason why he refused to sign the document when he was a delegate to the Constitutional Convention in Philadelphia in 1787. This refusal meant that he was frequently condemned in print as being selfish or otherwise ill-intentioned. His greatest worry about the Constitution was that it gave the new central government too much power and failed to safeguard the civil rights of Americans. He had wanted a bill of rights included in the original Constitution and had spoken to the convention about his desire for explicit protections of civil liberties.

Of greatest concern for Gerry was freedom of the press. It was perhaps because he held high the principle of a press free from government regulation that he wrote as forthrightly as he did, insisting on his rights as a free citizen to speak his mind in public. In his writings he was often sarcastic, a trait that put off some readers, but he nonetheless presented his ideas with a refreshing forthrightness that allowed people to know exactly where he stood on social and political issues, and he was fearless in his expression of even very unpopular points of view. From the perspective of the twenty-first century, there seems no mistaking his views, yet in his own day his very forthrightness made some people suspicious of his motives, apparently in the belief

that there had to be opinions he was hiding behind his open facade. Gerry was a significant influence on the Bill of Rights, produced as the first ten amendments to the Constitution. During the period when the states were ratifying the Constitution, he argued vigorously for the states to require as a condition of ratification that a bill of rights be created by the First Congress. His hand can be seen not only in the federal protections of free press and free speech but also in the rights of citizens to bear arms in order to form state militias. He feared that the Senate and the presidency were too powerful and could fall into the hands of tyrants, and he therefore wanted states to be able to protect the rights of their citizens by having militias over which they had control and which could be used to resist an oppressive national army.

Although Gerry had a long career in politics, his writings of the era from the end of the Revolutionary War through the First Congress were his most influential. Throughout his political career, he believed that people were best served by local governments and feared that any federal government could possibly draw all power over people's lives to itself. Thus he advocated states being as independent of the federal government as possible in order to act as shields for their people against federal intrusions into their daily lives. It was his hope that the Bill of Rights would restrict the federal government enough to allow states to be independent in most matters while relying on federal law to protect citizens' freedom of speech, such that individuals could be independent participants in the local governments of towns, cities, and counties.

Explanation and Analysis of Documents

Gerry's views were taken seriously by his contemporaries, and his writings were carefully read by people involved in the politics of the day. Although he seems to have viewed himself primarily as a state politician rather than as a national one, his ideas were influential throughout the United States. His objections were taken into consideration not only in his home state of Massachusetts but throughout America as well, and his contentions were often the subjects of public replies by opponents of his views; thus, he was an important contributor to national

1744

- **July 17**
Elbridge Gerry is born in Marblehead, Massachusetts.

1762

- Gerry graduates from Harvard College.

1772

- **May**
Gerry is elected to the General Court of Massachusetts, the state legislature and venue for judicial appeals.

1776

- **February**
Gerry is made a Massachusetts representative to the Continental Congress, where he remains until 1780.

- **July**
Gerry signs the Declaration of Independence.

1783

- Gerry returns to what is now the Confederation Congress, serving until 1785.

1787

- **May–September**
Gerry is a delegate to the Constitutional Convention, where he refuses to sign the Constitution because it does not have a bill of rights.

- **October 18**
At the request of the Massachusetts legislature, Gerry explains his objections to the U.S. Constitution in the form of a letter.

1788

- **January 3**
In a first reply, Gerry answers accusations by an anonymous Connecticut landholder that he opposes the Constitution because he would lose money if the document were ratified.

debates on significant issues. His concerns about the creation of a bill of rights were echoed by other politicians, and they quite likely spurred some states to assert that their ratification of the U.S. Constitution was dependent on the First Congress's taking up the issues of civil rights protection under the new stronger central government.

The most influential of Gerry's documents were created during the period when the United States transitioned from the Articles of Confederation to the Constitution and in the early years of the new government. He was the northern states' most prominent opponent of the Constitution, and his letter to the Massachusetts legislature as well as his two replies to the Connecticut landholder explain his objections: the lack of a bill of rights and insufficient checks on the power of the presidency, Congress, and the judiciary. He found much of the political discourse of the era to be offensively crude, which may have accounted for the witty yet merciless response that he extended to his critics in his second reply to the landholder. In the House of Representatives, he frequently spoke out about how the new government was being organized, and he brought a moralizing tone to his speeches that evinced his determination that the federal government do right by individual citizens; such was the case in his speech urging that the plan to pay government debts as proposed by Alexander Hamilton include payment to those who had aided their individual states during the Revolutionary War and whose states could not pay them.

◆ **Letter to the Massachusetts Legislature on the U.S. Constitution**

Those who considered whether Massachusetts should ratify the U.S. Constitution were as wary as any others about what sort of government would emerge from the document. In general, the delegates knew what they did not want: the lack of direction that had emerged from the Articles of Confederation. Thus, in their consideration of the Constitution, which seemed to offer a more unified nation, they wanted to hear from Gerry, an outspoken opponent of the document who was also one of the most respected statesmen from Massachusetts. In response to a request to declare his objections to the Constitution, Gerry wrote an open letter to the legislature, dated October 18, 1787, providing a summary of concerns that were not only his own but also those of many who feared that the lack of a bill of rights would make the new Constitution an outline for tyranny.

Gerry had been publicly expressing his opinions at least since 1765, when he advocated passive resistance to the British government, and he had developed an approach to presenting his views that was comprehensive but direct. That he should begin his objections to the Constitution with the phrase "To this system I give my dissent" was typical of his writing. When he complains "that there is no adequate provision for a representation of the people—that they have no security for the right of election," he refers to senators being chosen by legislatures rather than by direct vote by the public. He had also made widely known his opinion that federal officers, especially in the House of Representatives, should face reelection every year. The obvious objection to this was that annual elections would be too unwieldy—that federal representatives would not have time to settle into their duties and get work done—but this is, in fact, what Gerry wanted; he wanted representatives to be made constantly uncomfortable so as to be inhibited from making laws that would increase their chances of holding their political positions semipermanently. He wanted the American people to have frequent opportunities to throw out politicians who failed to work for the public good.

An interesting aspect of this document is Gerry's noting that he had objected to the Constitutional Convention's choice to set aside the Articles of Confederation in favor of writing an entirely new document but had "acquiesced" in the decision of his colleagues. Another person might have walked out of the convention in protest, but Gerry was an advocate of constant engagement in the political process. He believed that if a democracy is to fully represent its citizens, those who lose in disputes over courses of action must not only acquiesce but also continue to participate, whether to further the collective effort or to yet seek to persuade people to their points of view.

The bulk of Gerry's argument in his letter to the Massachusetts legislature is devoted to his suspicion of big government, which is why he mentions the word *nation* as summarizing his apprehensions. He had wanted a government in which the individual states would handle almost all social policy but would be federated for the purposes of foreign policy and the waging of war. In being that of a nation, Gerry fears that the new government will be a central government that will dominate the states, being able to tell individual states what they can do. Rather than several states telling the federal government what it may do, the new government would supersede all state boundaries, making uniform laws that all states must follow. These circumstances, Gerry thought, could allow a small number of political leaders to form a tyranny under which states could not protect the rights of their people.

◆ First Reply to "A Landholder"

In general, Gerry did not reply to his critics. He had been making dangerous statements against the government in power ever since his early twenties, when he urged passive resistance to the laws imposed on the colonies by Great Britain; he had then been a target for hanging, thus making later attacks on him in the press seem unimportant by comparison. "A Landholder" was the name signed by someone who wrote several angry attacks on people who opposed the ratification of the Constitution; some historians believe that the person was a delegate to the Constitutional Convention—perhaps Oliver Ellsworth, who had been a delegate to the convention from Connecticut and would later be the nation's chief justice. The Connecticut landholder attacked Gerry for his failure to sign the Constitution at the end of the Constitutional Convention, implying that Gerry was not only unpatriotic but also a criminal who was motivated by greed. This is why Gerry states, in his reply published in the *Massachusetts Centinel*,

Time Line

1788

- **April 30**
  Hoping to encourage not only Massachusetts but also other states to demand a bill of rights, Gerry explains in a second reply to the landholder what worries him about a constitution that lacks explicit protections of civil rights.

1789

- **January**
  Gerry writes an open letter to the voters of the new congressional district of Middlesex asking that his name be withdrawn from candidacy for election to the U.S. House of Representatives.

- **March 4**
  Gerry begins four years of service in the U.S. House of Representatives.

1790

- **February 18**
  In the House, Gerry speaks in favor of the federal government's honoring debts incurred by the states during the Revolutionary War.

1797

- Gerry serves as an ambassador to France in an aborted attempt to negotiate peace that would become known as the XYZ Affair, returning to the United States in October 1798.

1800

- Gerry joins the Democratic-Republican Party.

1810

- **June 10**
  Gerry takes office as the elected governor of Massachusetts.

1812

- Gerry helps create the practice of gerrymandering by signing a bill to redraw his state's congressional districts in favor of his party.

Time Line

1813

■ **March 4**
Gerry is inaugurated vice
president of the United
States under James
Madison.

1814

■ **November 23**
Gerry dies in Washington,
D.C.

that he "could have no motives for preserving an office" because he had none he wished to preserve, addressing the landholder's suggestion that Gerry was fearful of losing income because he would lose status if the Constitution were ratified. The Connecticut landholder further suggested that Gerry held old currency issued under the Articles of Confederation that would become valueless under the proposed new government; Gerry makes clear that while he favored the new government's covering its old debts just as debts were covered under the Articles of Confederation, he himself held no such currency. In this document, Gerry presents himself as a moderate asking commonsense questions about how the new government would operate.

◆ **Second Reply to "A Landholder"**

The Connecticut landholder continued to attack Gerry in print. In so doing, he gave Gerry an opportunity to expand on his unpopular views while seeming to defend himself and his friends from the anonymous attacks. The Connecticut landholder seems to have known a great deal about what happened behind closed doors during the convention's deliberations, but in his second reply to the landholder, Gerry explodes that notion by noting several instances in which the landholder misstated what actually happened at the convention. The Connecticut landholder was perhaps simply a liar, or he may have been a poorly informed outsider.

Gerry's second reply, published in the *American Herald*, features an interesting style: He takes a sarcastic tone in which he belittles the Connecticut landholder with facetious praise. The tone is established at the outset, with Gerry noting that the landholder has "a modesty and delicacy peculiar to himself." The implication is that Gerry is choosing to take the high road in his statements, in contrast to the harsh, unpleasant language of the landholder. Being humorous, the phrase is likely to invite further reading by promising a clever, witty account of the author's views. The landholder suggests that Gerry was in disagreement with Luther Martin, another delegate to the Constitutional Convention—one of his seeming misstatements concerning the convention. In his reply to this charge Gerry fulfills the promise of his opening remarks by continuing to use sharp, witty locutions, when he says, "The Landholder has asserted, that Mr. Gerry 'uniformly opposed Mr. Martin's principles,' but this is a circumstance wholly unknown to Mr.

Gerry, until he was informed of it by the Connecticut Landholder." This particular phrasing deftly implies that the Connecticut landholder does not know what he is talking about, a theme found throughout the document, as Gerry repeatedly indicates that the Connecticut landholder is poorly informed about the issues he discusses. Gerry's referring to himself in the third person, as the Connecticut landholder would, heightens the arch tone of the document. What survives of the correspondence between Gerry and Luther Martin indicates that Gerry's account of their relationship is accurate. Martin had shared many of Gerry's misgivings about the proposed constitution. He had been a delegate representing Maryland at the Constitutional Convention, and he had likewise refused to sign the Constitution at the convention's end. He shared with Gerry a foreboding that the new federal courts would become oppressive, even dictatorial, and he advocated jury trials for cases taken before the Supreme Court as a means of tempering the power of Supreme Court justices.

In replying to the Connecticut landholder's charges, Gerry brings up the issues of public debt, libel, and patriotism. Although Gerry himself stood to gain little or nothing from the proposed new government's assuming of public debts, he was greatly concerned about people owed money for their services during the Revolutionary War; the issue of such debts was repeatedly the subject of debates in state legislatures. That Gerry should be concerned about debts owed by the federal government was a natural outgrowth of his concerns about the public welfare. During the 1760s and 1770s he had been much involved in trying to ease the suffering of common people through relief efforts. It is logical that he would wish to further aid the soldiers and civilians he had helped feed by having them repaid for their services and loans to the Revolutionary cause.

Libel was a hot topic in Gerry's era. After the Revolutionary War, Americans were frequently testing the limits of freedom of speech. Gerry was an advocate of the protection of freedom of speech by the Constitution. He was worried that the new government would suppress people's natural right to speak their minds, and he seems to have had good reason for his concerns. Later, the administration of John Adams would try to stifle disrespectful remarks about the president and the president's administration. Although Gerry calls the Connecticut landholder's attacks on him "libellous," he notably does not suggest that such remarks be suppressed, choosing ridicule as the best method of responding to the falsehoods that he says the landholder has uttered.

It is possible that accusations of being unpatriotic stung Gerry, because he suggests that the Connecticut landholder was in some way deficient of patriotism in the weakest part of his second reply. He suggests that the landholder's claim that Luther Martin was involved in an unethical scheme may indicate that the landholder is himself an unethical person who knows of no other way to advance a cause in politics than by being dishonest. Earlier in his document, Gerry criticizes the landholder for pretending to be able to read Martin's mind, but in his passage on patriotism he seems to be pretending to be able to read the Connecticut landholder's mind.

ARTICLES

OF

CONFEDERATION AND PERPETUAL UNION,

BETWEEN THE STATES OF

NEW-HAMPSHIRE,
MASSACHUSETTS-BAY,
RHODE-ISLAND,
CONNECTICUT,
NEW-YORK,
NEW-JERSEY,
PENNSYLVANIA,

The Counties of NEW-CASTLE KENT and SUSSEX on Delaware,
MARYLAND,
VIRGINIA,
NORTH-CAROLINA,
SOUTH-CAROLINA, AND
GEORGIA.

ART. I. THE name of this Confederacy shall be "THE UNITED STATES OF AMERICA."

ART. II. The said States hereby severally enter into a firm league of friendship with each other, for their common defence, the security of their liberties, and their mutual and general welfare, binding themselves to assist each other against all force offered to or attacks made upon them or any of them, on account of religion, sovereignty, trade, or any other pretence whatever.

ART. III. Each State reserves to itself the sole and exclusive regulation and government of its internal police in all matters that shall not interfere with the articles of this Confederation.

ART. IV. No State, without the consent of the United States in Congress Assembled, shall send any Embassy to or receive any embassy from, or enter into any conference, agreement, alliance or treaty with any King, Prince or State; nor shall any person holding any office of profit or trust under the United States or any them, accept of any present, emolument, office or title of any kind whatever from any King, Prince or foreign State; nor shall the United States Assembled, or any of them, grant any title of nobility.

ART. V. No two or more States shall enter into any treaty, confederation or alliance whatever between them without the consent of the United States in Congress Assembled, specifying accurately the purposes for which the same is to be entered into, and how long it shall continue.

ART. VI. No State shall lay any imposts or duties which may interfere with any stipulations in treaties hereafter entered into by the United States Assembled with any King, Prince or State.

A copy of the Articles of Confederation and Perpetual Union, the first constitution of the United States (AP/Wide World Photos)

The Constitutional Convention meets in Philadelphia in 1787 (AP/Wide World Photos)

◆ **Letter to the Electors of Middlesex**

In his open letter to the electors of Middlesex, Gerry addresses himself to the voters in a new congressional district in Massachusetts. In the letter, he professes that he does not wish to be elected to the House of Representatives, yet he clarifies his political views in such a way that he seems to be trying to appear uninterested in being a congressman while giving reasons why he should be chosen to represent Middlesex in Congress. In Gerry's day many people thought it proper for a politician to pretend to be indifferent to being elected to office while actually running for the office. As part of this approach, after winning an election, the politician might claim to have been drafted against his will by the admiring public and therefore to have a public mandate to pursue the policies he favored. On the other hand, Gerry had wished to take a break from politics and spend time working on his farm. Thus, he may truly have meant that he did not want people to vote for him.

There was a difference of opinion among many Americans in Gerry's day, as there is in the present day, over how an elected representative should make decisions. One opinion was that elected representatives should always set aside their personal views and vote on legislation the way the majority of their constituents wanted them to vote. With his remark "conceiving myself to be in a land of liberty, where the privilege of deliberating and voting with freedom would be firmly supported," Gerry seems to fall in line with the opposing opinion that an elected representative owed it to his constituents to vote according to his own best judgment. That Gerry should frame this notion in terms of freedom of thinking for oneself and voting accordingly was typical of his opinions, tying the freedoms of thought, of speech, and of voting together to form the foundation for his political views.

In most of this document, Gerry portrays himself as a wounded man afflicted unjustly by charges that he unpatriotically opposed the Constitution. He insists that fundamental to the new government must be the ability to speak one's political views in public, however unpopular they may be. Further, he insists that his political opponents have misled the public about his views on the Constitution. He had, he says, worked to create a balance of powers in the Constitution in order to protect the civil rights of citizens. His principles were such that, with the majority having spoken, he would abide by their decision and work within the rules of the Constitution. He makes it clear that regardless of people's opinions about his views, he intends to stick to them and would pursue a course that would result in amendments to the Constitution that would protect the civil rights of Americans.

◆ **Speech on Paying Revolutionary War Debts**

It may seem obvious that, in moral terms, the United States was obliged to repay people who contributed money and supplies to the American cause during the Revolutionary War as well as to pay the outstanding salaries of soldiers who served in the war, but such was not obvious to everyone during the early years of the new government under

"It was painful to me, on a subject of such national importance, to differ from the respectable members who signed the constitution: But conceiving as I did, that the liberties of America were not secured by the system, it was my duty to oppose it."

(Letter to the Massachusetts Legislature on the U.S. Constitution)

"It must be admitted, that a free people are the proper guardians of their rights and liberties—that the greatest men may err—and that their errors are sometimes of the greatest magnitude."

(Letter to the Massachusetts Legislature on the U.S. Constitution)

"His [Gerry's] objections are chiefly contained in his letter to the Legislature;…that his only motive for dissenting from the Constitution, was a firm persuasion that it would endanger the liberties of America; …that a representative of a free state, he was bound in honour to vote according to his idea of her true interest, and that he should do the same in similar circumstances."

(First Reply to "A Landholder")

"'Some of the powers of the federal legislature are ambiguous, and others (meaning the unlimited power of Congress, to keep up a standing army, in time of peace, and their entire controul of the militia) are indefinite and dangerous.'"

(Second Reply to "A Landholder")

"When the question on the constitution was put in the federal convention, conceiving myself to be in a land of liberty, where the privilege of deliberating and voting with freedom would be firmly supported, I voted against the constitution, because in my opinion, it was in many respects defective."

(Letter to the Electors of Middlesex)

"Amendments every citizen has a right to urge without exciting a spirit of persecution, which is unnecessary in a good cause, and never gains proselytes in a bad one."

(Letter to the Electors of Middlesex)

the U.S. Constitution. Many people believed that all debts incurred during the war and during the period of government under the Articles of Confederation were debts owed not by the new government but by old, defunct governments, such that the United States therefore owed no debts dating to before the Constitution was ratified. Others believed that the individual states were responsible for compensating soldiers levied by the states.

In late 1789 Secretary of Treasury Alexander Hamilton proposed to Congress that the United States pay even unpaid soldiers who had served in military units created by individual states rather than in the Continental army, as well as others who had supported the American effort by contributing their wealth to state defenses and troops. This was a measure that Gerry had long advocated; it ranked almost as high as the passage of a bill of rights on his personal agenda during his service in Congress. He viewed the measure as a moral issue, whereas opponents tended to view it strictly in monetary terms. Gerry offered a response to Hamilton's proposal in a speech to the House of Representatives in February of the following year. He was in a good position to know how the troops levied by individual states were regarded, having served in the Continental Congress: Those men "will not acknowledge any difference [in their rights], from their being enlisted by a State instead of Continental authority; yet that is the only distinction, for they were adopted by Congress, formed into one army,

fought the same battles, and shared in every hardship." Gerry makes the issue a patriotic one, noting the service and suffering of the people whom the measure proposed to pay.

An argument against Gerry's view was that the United States could not afford to make all of the designated payments. In his speech Gerry acknowledges that the nation's finances are "deranged," but he insists that the present uncertainty should not stop the nation from acknowledging debts that could be paid once the nation's finances were organized. He argues that the new federal government is better equipped than the states to gather the revenues necessary for meeting the debts and that America will prove rich enough to be able to pay them. To his mind, the people who served in state military units were one with the Continental army and therefore were rightly the responsibility of the new United States.

Impact and Legacy

In the later part of his life and for a few decades thereafter, Gerry was frequently criticized for having opposed the U.S. Constitution, a document to which most Americans became devoted. This criticism developed out of a failure on the part of historians to fully study Gerry's ideas and behavior. It certainly seems strange to some people that an outspoken opponent of the Constitution would

Questions for Further Study

1. Summarize the specific reasons Elbridge Gerry gave for not supporting ratification of the U.S. Constitution. Why did Gerry eventually come to support the Constitution, even though his objections were not initially answered?

2. In debates over ratification of the U.S. Constitution, many politicians and members of the public focused on the power relationship between the states and the federal government. On what basis did people such as Gerry believe that the Constitution granted too much power to the federal government?

3. Elbridge Gerry was a strong proponent of freedom of speech and of the press. How did this point of view influence his opinions as to the proper role of a legislator in voting on issues before a legislature?

4. In the twenty-first century, it is taken for granted that troops sent into a war against a foreign nation are under the authority of the federal government and are paid accordingly. During the Revolutionary War period, however, this was not necessarily the case; some troops were mustered by and were to be paid by the individual states. What impact did this difference have on post–Revolutionary War debates about the financial obligations of the new federal government?

5. Contrast Gerry's views with regard to ratification of the Constitution with those of Roger Sherman, particularly the views Sherman expressed in "Letters of a Countryman" (November 22, 1787). Similarly, how did Alexander Hamilton weigh in on this issue in Federalist 84?

consent to being elected to the House of Representatives in the First Congress, but Gerry's actions were actually consistent with his often-expressed views. He believed that for any system of democratic government to succeed and survive, people would have to confine their conflicts to reasoned argument, rather than resorting to the military battlefield. He likewise thought that those who lost the arguments would have to agree to work within the system in seeking to persuade people to change their minds. While serving in Congress, he did what he could to help modify the government and the Constitution to answer the objections he had raised when arguing against the founding document both at the convention and during ratification. When the Bill of Rights was passed, he believed that many of his objections had been answered, and he became a supporter of the amended U.S. Constitution.

In the modern era, Gerry seldom comes up in discussions of history or politics except as a creator of gerrymandering—the practice of linking disparate parts of a state to maximize the number of members of the House of Representatives from a particular party. Yet, he helped shape the U.S. Constitution in that, from the moment the Constitutional Convention decided to replace the Articles of Confederation altogether, he helped keep the concept of a bill of rights in the minds of the delegates and the public, and he helped ensure that such matters as freedom of the press and state militias were prominent parts of the Bill of Rights. During the nineteenth century, he was considered one of the most important framers of the Constitution and frequently appeared in discussions of the document's origins and intents. With the passage of time, other Founding Fathers who were more prolific in their writings or who had more successful careers in national politics came to dominate accounts of the Constitution's development, and Gerry eventually became more of a footnote in histories. Even so, the U.S. Constitution and the federal government based on it would have been different without Gerry's persistent advocacy for the protection of individual freedoms.

Key Sources

The Gerry Family Papers are held in the archives of Hartwick College, in Oneonta, New York, with a list of contents viewable online (http://info.hartwick.edu/library/archives/gerry/moreinfo.html). Some of Gerry's writings are found in Paul Leicester Ford, ed., *Essays on the Constitution of the United States, Published during Its Discussion by the People, 1787–1788* (1892). Among Gerry's writings, some of the most revealing of his political views are found in *A Study in Dissent: The Warren-Gerry Correspondence, 1776–1792* (1968), edited by C. Harvey Gardiner. *Elbridge Gerry's Letterbook: Paris, 1797–1798* (1966), edited by Russell W. Knight, tells of Gerry's activities while he served as an ambassador to France.

Further Reading

■ Articles

Kramer, Eugene F. "Some New Light on the XYZ Affair: Elbridge Gerry's Reasons for Opposing War with France." *New England Quarterly* 29, no. 4 (1956): 509–513.

■ Books

Austin, James T. *The Life of Elbridge Gerry*. 2 vols. Boston: Wells and Lilly, 1828–1829.

Billias, George A. *Elbridge Gerry, Founding Father and Republican Statesman*. New York: McGraw-Hill, 1976.

—Kirk H. Beetz

Letter to the Massachusetts Legislature on the U.S. Constitution (1787)

GENTLEMEN,

I have the honour to inclose, pursuant to my commission, the constitution proposed by the Federal Convention.

To this system I gave my dissent, and shall submit my objections to the honourable Legislature.

It was painful to me, on a subject of such national importance, to differ from the respectable members who signed the constitution: But conceiving as I did, that the liberties of America were not secured by the system, it was my duty to oppose it.—

My principal objections to the plan are that there is no adequate provision for a representation of the people—that they have no security for the right of election—that some of the powers of the Legislature are ambiguous and others are indefinite and dangerous—that the Executive is blended with and will have an undue influence over the Legislature—that the judicial department will be oppressive—that treaties of the highest importance may be formed by the President with the advice of two thirds of a *quorum* of the Senate—and that the system is without the security of a bill of rights. These are objections which are not local but apply equally to all the States.

As the convention was called for

the *sole* and *express* purpose of revising the Articles of Confederation, and reporting to Congress and the several Legislatures such alterations and provisions as shall render the Federal Constitution adequate to the exigencies of government and the preservation of the union,

I did not conceive that these powers extended to the formation of the plan proposed, but the Convention being of a different *opinion*, I acquiesced in *it*, being fully convinced that to preserve the union, an efficient government was indispensably necessary; and that it would be difficult to make proper amendments to the articles of Confederation.

The Constitution proposed has few, if any *federal* features, but is rather a system of *national* government: Nevertheless, in many respects I think it has great merit, and by proper amendments may be adapted to the "exigencies of government and the preservation of liberty."

The question on this plan involves others of the highest importance—1st. whether there shall be a dissolution of the *federal* government; 2dly, Whether the several State Governments shall be so altered, as in effect to be dissolved; and 3dly. Whether in lieu of the *federal* and state governments, the national constitution now proposed shall be instituted without amendments: Never perhaps were a people called on to decide a question of greater magnitude—Should the citizens of America adopt the plan as it now stands, their liberties may be lost: Or should they reject it altogether, Anarchy may ensue. It is evident therefore, that the subject should be well understood, lest they should refuse to *support* the government, after having *hastily* accepted it.

If those who are in favor of the Constitution, as well as those who are against it, should preserve moderation, their discussions may afford much information and finally direct to an happy issue.

It may be urged by some that an *implicit* confidence should be placed in the Convention: But, however respectable the members may be who signed the Constitution, it must be admitted, that a free people are the proper guardians of their rights and liberties—that the greatest men may err—and that their errors are sometimes of the greatest magnitude.

Glossary

***federal* features, but is rather a system of *national* government**	a distinction between a government that represents a federation of independent states and one that imposes a central government on the states
quorum	the minimum number of people required for a body to vote or take action

Others may suppose, that the Constitution may be safely adopted, because therein provision is made to *amend* it: But cannot *this object* be better attained before a ratification, than after it? And should a *free* people adopt a form of Government, under the conviction that it wants amendment?

And some may conceive, that if the plan is not accepted by the people, they will not unite in another: But surely whilst they have the power to amend, they are not under the necessity of rejecting it.

I have been detained here longer than I expected, but shall leave this place in a day or two for Massachusetts, and on my arrival shall submit the reasons (if required by the Legislature) on which my objections are grounded.

I shall only add, that as the welfare of the union requires a better Constitution than the Confederation, I shall think it my duty as a citizen of Massachusetts, to support that which shall be finally adopted, sincerely hoping it will secure the liberty and happiness of America.

I have the honour to be, Gentlemen, with the highest respect for the honourable Legislature and yourselves, your most obedient, and very humble servant.

E. Gerry

First Reply to "A Landholder" (1788)

You are desired to inform the publick from good authority, that Mr. GERRY, by giving his dissent to the proposed Constitution, could have no motives for preserving an office, for he holds none under the United States, or any of them; that he has not, as has been asserted, exchanged Continental for State Securities, and if he had, it would have been for his interest to have supported the new system, because thereby the states are restrained from impairing the obligation of contracts, and by a transfer of such securities, they may be recovered in the new federal court; that he never heard, in the Convention, a motion made, much less did make any, "for the redemption of the old continental money;" but that he proposed the public debt should be made neither better nor worse by the new system, but stand precisely on the same ground by the Articles of Confederation; that had there been such a motion, he was not interested in it, as he did not then, neither does he now, own the value of ten pounds in continental money; that he neither was called on for his reasons for not signing, but stated them fully in the progress of the business. His objections are chiefly contained in his letter to the Legislature; that he believes his colleagues men of too much honour to assert what is not truth; that his reasons in the Convention "were totally different from those which he published," that his only motive for dissenting from the Constitution, was a firm persuasion that it would endanger the liberties of America; that if the people are of a different opinion, they have a right to adopt; but he was not authorized to an act, which appeared to him was a surrender of their liberties; that a representative of a free state, he was bound in honour to vote according to his idea of her true interest, and that he should do the same in similar circumstances.

Cambridge, January 3, 1788.

Glossary

Continental	a reference to the paper money, designed by Benjamin Franklin, used during the Revolutionary War era

SECOND REPLY TO "A LANDHOLDER" (1788)

As the Connecticut Landholder's publications are dispersed throughout the state, it will be useful for the sake of truth to publish the following.

To the Public.

An elegant writer, under the signature of "A Landholder," having in a series of publications, with a modesty and delicacy peculiar to himself, undertaken to instruct members of legislatures, executives, and conventions, in their duty respecting the new constitution, is, in stating facts, unfortunate, in being repeatedly detected in errors; but his perseverance therein does honor "to his magnanimity," and reminds me of Dr. Sangerado (in Gil Blas) who being advised to alter his practice, as it was founded on false principles and destructive to his patients, firmly determined to pursue it, because he had written a book in support of it. Had our learned author, the modern Sangerado, confined himself to facts and to reasoning on the constitution, he might have continued to write without interruption from its opposers, until by instructing others, he had obtained that instruction which he seems to need, or a temporary relief from the ineviable malady, the cacoethes scribendi; but his frequent misrepresentations having exposed him to suspicions that as a disciple of Mandeville he was an advocate for vice, or that to correct his curiosity some humourist has palmed on him a spurious history of the proceedings of the federal convention, and exhibited his credulity as a, subject of ridicule, it is proper to set him right in facts, which, in almost every instance he has mistated.

In a late address to the honorable Luther Martin, Esquire, the Landholder has asserted, that Mr. Gerry "uniformly opposed Mr. Martin's principles," but this is a circumstance wholly unknown to Mr. Gerry, until he was informed of it by the Connecticut Landholder; indeed Mr. Gerry from the first acquaintance with Mr. Martin, has "uniformly had a friendship for him."

This writer has also asserted, "that the day Mr. Martin took his seat in convention, without requesting information, or to be let into the reasons of the adoption of what he might not approve, he opened against them in a speech which held during two days." But the facts are, that Mr. Martin had been a considerable time in convention before he spoke; that when he entered into the debates he appeared not to need "information," as he was fully possessed of the subject; and that his speech, if published, would do him great honor.

Another assertion of this famous writer is, that Mr. Gerry in "a sarcastical reply, admired the strength of Mr. Martin's lungs, and his profound knowledge in the first principles of government;" that "this reply" "left him a prey to the most humiliating reflections; but these did not teach him to bound his future speeches by the lines of moderation; for the very next day he exhibited, without a blush, another specimen of eternal volubility." This is so remote from the truth, that no such reply was made by Mr. Gerry to Mr. Martin, or to any member of the convention; on the contrary, Mr. Martin, on the first day he spoke, about the time of adjournment, signified to the convention that the heat of the season, and his indisposition prevented his proceeding, and the house adjourned without further debate, or a reply to Mr. Martin from any member whatever.

Again, the Landholder has asserted that Mr. Martin voted "an appeal should lay to the supreme judiciary of the United States for the correction of all errors both in law and fact," and "agreed to the clause that declares nine states to be sufficient to put the government in motion:" and in a note says, "Mr. Gerry agreed with Mr. Martin on these questions." Whether there is any truth in the assertions as they relate to Mr. Martin, he can best determine; but as they respect Mr. Gerry, they reverse the facts; for he not only voted against the first proposition (which is not stated by the Landholder, with the accuracy requisite for a writer on government) but contended for jury trials in civil cases, and declared his opinion, that a federal judiciary with the powers above mentioned, would be as oppressive and dangerous, as the establishment of a star-chamber, and as to the clause that "declares nine states to be sufficient to put the government in motion," Mr. Gerry was so much opposed to it, as to vote against it in the first instance, and afterwards to move for a reconsideration of it.

The Landholder having in a former publication asserted "that Mr. Gerry introduced a motion, respecting the redemption of old continental money" and the public having been informed by a paragraph in the Massachusetts Centinel, No. 32, of vol. 8, as well as by the honorable Mr. Martin, that neither Mr. Gerry, or any other member, had introduced such a proposition, the Landholder now says that "out of 126 days, Mr. Martin attended only 66," and then enquires "whether it is to be presumed that Mr. Martin could have been minutely informed, of all that happened in convention, and committees of convention, during the sixty days of absence?" and "Why is it that we do not see Mr. McHenry's verification of his assertion, who was of the committee for considering a provision for the debts of the union?" But if these enquiries were intended for subterfuges, unfortunately for the Landholder, they will not avail him: for, had Mr. Martin not been present at the debates on this subject, the fact is, that Mr. Gerry was not on a committee with Mr. McHenry, or with any other person, for considering a provision for the debts of the union, or any provision that related to the subject of old continental money; neither did he make any proposition, in convention, committee, or on any occasion, to any member of convention or other person, respecting the redemption of such money; and the assertions of the Landholder to the contrary, are altogether destitute of the shadow of truth.

The Landholder addressing Mr. Martin, further says, "Your reply to my second charge against Mr. Gerry, may be soon dismissed: compare his letter to the legislature of his state, with your defence, and you will find, that you have put into his mouth, objections different from anything it contains, so that if your representation be true, his must be false." The objections referred to, are those mentioned by Mr. Martin, as being made by Mr. Gerry, against the supreme power of Congress over the militia. Mr. Gerry, in his letter to the legislature, states as an objection, "That some of the powers of the federal legislature are ambiguous, and others (meaning the unlimited power of Congress, to keep up a standing army, in time of peace, and their entire controul of the militia) are indefinite and dangerous." Against both these did Mr. Gerry warmly contend, and why his representations must be false, if Mr. Martin's are true, which particularized what Mr. Gerry's stated generally, can only be discovered by such a profound reasoner, as the Connecticut Landholder.

The vanity of this writer, in supposing that his charges would be the subject of constitutional investigation, can only be equalled by his impertinence, in interfering with the politics of other states, or by his ignorance, in supposing a state convention could take cognizance of such matters as he calls charges, and that Mr. Gerry required a formal defence, or the assistance of his colleagues, to defeat the unprovoked and libellous attacks of the Landholder, or any other unprincipled revile.

The landholder says: "That Mr. Martin thought the deputy attorney-general of the United States, for the state of Maryland, destined for a different character, and that inspired him with the hope that he might derive from a desperate opposition, what he saw no prospect of gaining by a contrary conduct; but the landholder ventures to predict, that though Mr. Martin was to double his efforts he would fail in his object." By this we may form some estimate of the patriotism of the landholder, for, whilst he so readily resolves Mr. Martin's conduct into a manoeuvre for office, he gives too much reason to suppose, that he himself has no idea of any other motive in conducting politicks. But how can the landholder ascertain, that "Mr. Martin thought" the office mentioned "destined for a different character?" Was the landholder present at the destination? If so, it was natural for him, knowing there was a combination against Mr. Martin (however remote this gentleman was from discovering it) to suppose his accidental opposition to the complotters, proceeded from a discovery of the plot. Surely the landholder must have some reason for his conjecture respecting the motives of Mr. Martin's conduct, or to be subject to the charge of publishing calumny, knowing it to be such. If then, this great statesman was in a secret, which has been long impenetrable, he is now entitled to the honor of giving the public the most important information they have received, concerning the origin of the new constitution, and having candidly informed them who is not, he ought to inform who is to fill that office, and all others of the new federal government. It may then, in some measure be ascertained, what individuals have supported the constitution on principles of patriotism, and who under this guise have been only squabbling for office. Perhaps we shall find that the landholder is to have the contract for supplying the standing army under the new government, and that many others, who have recurred to abuse on this occasion, have some such happy prospects; indeed the landholder puts it beyond a doubt, if we can believe him, that it was determined in the privy council of this federal convention, that however Mr. Martin might advocate the new constitution, he should not have the office mentioned; for if this was not the case, how can the landholder so roundly assert that Mr. Martin could have no prospect by a contrary conduct of gaining the office, and so remarkably sanguine is the landholder, that the members of the privy council would be senators of the new Congress, in which case the elections would undoubtedly be made according to the conventional list of nominations, as that he ventures to predict, though Mr. Martin was to double his efforts, he would fail in his object. Thus whilst this blazing star of federalism is taking great pains to hold up Mr. Gerry and Mr. Mason [Jonathan Mason], as having held private meetings "to aggrandize old Massachusetts and the antient dominion" he has confessed enough to shew that his private meetings were solely to aggrandize himself.

Glossary

cacoethes scribendi	Latin for "an irresistible urge to write"
calumny	defamation, a false accusation
Gil Blas	a French novel, *L'Histoire de Gil Blas de Santillane*, written by Alain-René Lesage in the early eighteenth century
Luther Martin	one of the delegates to the Constitutional Convention who refused to sign the new Constitution (1748–1826)
magnanimity	generosity of spirit
Mandeville	Bernard de Mandeville (1670–1733), Dutch physician who moved to England, where he translated Continental literature into English and wrote satires
McHenry	James McHenry (1753–1816), delegate to the Constitutional Convention from Maryland
revile	here, an obsolete usage to refer to language that is abusive or contemptuous
sanguine	hopeful
shew	obsolete spelling of *show*
star-chamber	a legal body that issues arbitrary rulings in secret proceedings
subterfuges	misrepresentations, stratagems designed to deceive

Letter to the Electors of Middlesex (1788)

Friends and Fellow Citizens:

It appearing from your suffrages that I am one of your candidates for a federal representative, give me leave for this evidence of your confidence, to express my warmest acknowledgments, but at the same time to request that such of you as may again be disposed to honour me with your votes, will turn your attention to some other candidate; for although I have been long honoured with the confidence of my countrymen, and am conscious that a regard to their political happiness has been the sole motive of my conduct, yet circumstanced as I am, an election would by no means be agreeable.

Since however my name is again, without any effort or inclination of my own, brought into public view, I embrace this opportunity to explain that conduct, for which I have been treated with so much invective and abuse.

When the question on the constitution was put in the federal convention, conceiving myself to be in a land of liberty, where the privilege of deliberating and voting with freedom would be firmly supported, I voted against the constitution, because in my opinion, it was in many respects defective.

Had my opinion been founded in error, it would have been only an error of judgment. But five states having ratified the constitution, in the fullest expectation of amendments, and two having rejected it, no one can, I think, deny that my opinion has been confirmed by a majority of the union. An attempt has been made by means of invective, to impair or destroy the privilege mentioned; a privilege, which no good citizen will ever permit to die in his hands, and which the good sense of the community will protect as one of the pillars of a free state.

Some have endeavoured to represent me as an enemy to the constitution; than which nothing is more remote from truth. Since the commencement of the revolution, I have been ever solicitous for an efficient federal government, conceiving that without it we must be a divided and unhappy people. A government too democratical, I have deprecated; but wished for one that should possess power sufficient for the welfare of the union, and at the same time be so balanced as to secure the governed from the rapacity and domination of lawless and insolent ambition. To an unconditional ratification I was therefore opposed, because thereby every necessary amendment would be precarious. But as the system is adopted, I am clearly of opinion that every citizen of the ratifying states is in duty bound to support it, and that an opposition to a due administration of it would not only be unjustifiable, but highly criminal.

Amendments every citizen has a right to urge without exciting a spirit of persecution, which is unnecessary in a good cause, and never gains proselytes in a bad one. Every friend of a vigorous government must, as I conceive, be desirous of such amendments as will remove the just apprehensions of the people, and secure their confidence and affection. To defeat amendments of this description, must be in effect to defeat the constitution itself. When the question on amendments shall have received a constitutional decision, I shall cheerfully acquiesce, and in any event, shall be happy to promote the interests of the respectable county of Middlesex, of this commonwealth, and of the United States.

The part, which I have had to act, and the uncandid treatment, which I have received in this matter will, I trust, justify me in being thus explicit, for I am conscious that every part of my political conduct has had for its object, the public welfare.

Glossary

democratical	placing too much power in the hands of the people
deprecated	expressed disapproval
proselytes	adherents, supporters
suffrages	votes

SPEECH ON PAYING REVOLUTIONARY WAR DEBTS (1790)

It has been said, that Congress have no power to assume the State debts. This leads us to an inquiry into the power of Congress, and by referring to the constitution, we find that Congress are authorized to lay and collect taxes, &c. to pay the debts, and provide for the common defence and general welfare of the United States. If Congress have the power to pay debts, they have an implied right to examine what those debts are, and if they have been contracted fur the common defence there is no doubt but they are the debts of the United States; but supposing Congress unauthorized by the powers cited, they are, by the general clause, giving to Congress powers to make all laws necessary and proper for carrying into execution all the powers of the Constitution, or of any department or officer under it, fully authorized to judge of and determine the debts of the United States.

In order, then, to determine whether the debts of the States are the debts of the United States, let us consider who are the holders of the State certificates. Some of the State creditors were officers and soldiers of the late army. The first army of the United States was raised, armed, and cloathed by the States. The officers and soldiers thereof have as strong a claim on your justice for the money due them, as those who were established at the close of the war. They will not acknowledge any difference, from their being enlisted by a State instead of Continental authority; yet that is the only distinction, for they were adopted by Congress, formed into one army, fought the same battles, and shared in every hardship. Another part of the State creditors consists of men who furnished supplies for the Union during the late war. Most of them are of this class, and can any one, who recollects this circumstance, possibly imagine a difference between them and what are called Continental creditors? Part of the State debts were Continental debts, assumed by the States on the earnest recommendations of Congress. And other parts were occasioned by the States having undertaken, for their particular defence, expeditions against the common enemy, or having paid interest to their citizens on the Continental debt.

Gentlemen who reflect on the nature of the State Governments must be satisfied that it is impossible they should have incurred such immense debts on account of their civil lists and local institutions. On the contrary, it must be admitted, that every State has, by taxes and duties collected more than was sufficient to defray its own expenses; the surplus has been invariably applied to the discharge of the interest, or extinguishment of the principal debt incurred during the late war for general defence. Hence it must appear, that the debts now due by any State to its creditors are less than the aggregate of her demands against the Union. If, therefore, we assume the whole of their debts, we shall find they have still large demands against the Union.

Let us suppose, as stated by the gentleman from Maryland, that some of the State creditors will subscribe to the loan, and that others will not; where is the force of the objection? Let the State receive of the General Government interest for the unsubscribed part, and pay it to the non-subscribing creditors; but there is little doubt that every creditor will subscribe.

It was said the measure would raise the importance of the Union, and tend to depress the States. If it had that tendency I should oppose it; because I conceive that the Constitutional balance between the Union and States ought to be preserved, I view the constitutions of the United States and individual States as forming a great political machine, in which the small wheels are as essential as the large; and if the former are deranged, the system must be destroyed. I humbly conceive a contrary policy will have this effect; for, suppose the United States should refuse to assume the State debts, there is no doubt but Congress can make provision for the punctual payment of the holders of Continental certificates; but it is questionable whether the States can, each of them, make provision for their respective creditors; in case of their inability it will produce a clamor against them. The State creditors will have a high opinion of the honesty, integrity, and abilities of the General Government, while they will entertain a contrary opinion with respect to the State Government. Every such creditor will exert himself to support the former, and join in the clamor against the latter; they would allege that the State Governments were expensive and unjust; and it appears to me that the enemies of the State Governments would thus have a favorable opportunity, which their art and address would improve, to abolish the State constitutions. Should the National Government be disposed to depress the State Governments, I ask whether the States would not be better able to resist if they were clear of, than if encumbered with a debt? It is a common maxim, out of debt out of danger; but here gentlemen seem to reverse it, in debt out of danger. I cannot, therefore, agree with them.

I presume it is the wish of every gentleman to preserve the peace and harmony of the Union, and I submit to them, whether this effect is most likely to result from assuming or rejecting the State debts. If you reject the measure, you establish two contending parties, the Continental creditors, and State creditors. The latter will oppose every measure of the General Government, which they suppose is intended, in prejudice of themselves, to promote the interest of the former. It will sow discord among the citizens of the Union, tending to defeat the operation of both Federal and State Governments. From this I infer that a regard to the interest of the Continental creditors ought to induce us to agree to the assumption of the State debts; for the States, in making provision for their own creditors will be induced to extend their excise, as the only means of raising revenue, to all those articles which the General Government contemplates; hence will arise such clashing and interference as will involve both revenues in confusion, and defeat the collection. There is also danger that it might extend to injure the collection of impost; whereas a uniformity in the excise system would make it more productive, and tend to increase the impost also.

Some apprehension has been expressed that the State debts may not have been fairly liquidated. I should think, from a knowledge of the economy of the States, that they were more strictly liquidated than the Federal debt. The creditors in Massachusetts have had their accounts adjusted on as strict principles as could be adopted; and I suppose the other States have acted in the same manner.

It was also said, that we were unacquainted with the ability of the Union, and therefore it is improper to pledge the public faith for the payment of a debt which possibly may exceed that ability. I do not now, nor did I ever despair of the ability of the United States to pay their debts. Our finances, to be sure, are deranged; but we are taking measures to extricate ourselves from the evils resulting from such a situation. We are not to be deterred from ascertaining the amount of what we owe, because we have not at present revenue to pay the whole interest. Under our present circumstances it appears, from the Secretary's Report, that we are capable of paying two-thirds of the interest. With increasing resources, and a gradual diminution of the capital, we, may soon have it in our power to discharge the remainder. If we can now pay one half, or two-thirds, let us undertake it, and no more; because I would never subject this Government to a failure in its engagements; when our abilities increase, we can undertake what we are at this moment unable to perform. The Secretary goes on the principle of supporting the public contracts; he admits of no preference among the Continental creditors; and I shall be opposed to the giving any advantage to the injury of the State creditors. It will not be reasonable that a State should give up her resources for paying the interest on her debt, until her creditors are put on an equal footing with the Continental creditors; she requires this in justice, and asks nothing further.

Glossary

gentleman from Maryland	Congressman Michael J. Stone (1747–1812)
impost	a tax

Ruth Bader Ginsburg (AP/Wide World Photos)

RUTH BADER GINSBURG 1933–

Supreme Court Justice

Ginsburg, Ruth Bader

Featured Documents
- ◆ *United States v. Virginia* (1996)
- ◆ *Friends of the Earth, Inc. et al. v. Laidlaw Environmental Services, Inc.* (2000)
- ◆ *Stenberg, Attorney General of Nebraska, et al. v. Carhart* (2000)
- ◆ *Eldred v. Ashcroft* (2003)

Overview

Ruth Bader was born on March 15, 1933, in Brooklyn, New York. She graduated from Cornell University in 1954 and that year married Martin Ginsburg, a classmate. She enrolled at Harvard Law School, but after her husband found employment with a New York City law firm, she transferred to Columbia University, where she graduated tied for first in her class in 1959. That year she accepted a two-year clerkship for U.S. District Court Judge Edmund L. Palmieri in New York. After working on the Columbia Law School Project on International Procedure from 1961 to 1963, Ginsburg accepted a post as a law professor at Rutgers University, where she taught until 1972. She also served as volunteer counsel to the New Jersey chapter of the American Civil Liberties Union (ACLU). At the ACLU, Ginsburg litigated sex discrimination cases and cofounded the Women's Rights Project. Ironically, during her time at Rutgers she became pregnant with her son, James, and because she was not tenured, she concealed her pregnancy with oversized clothes. In 1972 Ginsburg accepted a position at Columbia University, the law school's first woman with the rank of full professor.

In 1980 President Jimmy Carter nominated Ginsburg as a justice on the U.S. Court of Appeals for the District of Columbia. Then, in 1993, President Bill Clinton nominated her to replace Justice Byron White on the U.S. Supreme Court. Ginsburg's reputation as a moderate on the U.S. Court of Appeals was helpful to her confirmation. In her years on the Supreme Court, her written decisions in numerous key cases made her a leading voice in the judicial branch for sex equality, thus expanding the rights of the American public, including both women and men.

Explanation and Analysis of Documents

Ruth Bader Ginsburg arrived at the Harvard Law School as a student without any sort of agenda. But her early commitment to women's rights and equality was perhaps forged when the dean of the law school asked her and her eight female classmates why they were taking up seats at the school that rightly should be occupied by men. If that were not enough, she was unable to win a clerkship for a U.S. Supreme Court justice because of her gender, and she did not receive a job offer from the New York City firm where she clerked during the summer before her final year in law school. Then, after she took a teaching position at the Rutgers University Law School, she discovered that she was being paid less than male colleagues with the same rank.

These circumstances motivated Ginsburg's preoccupation with civil rights generally and the rights of women in particular. During her academic years, when she also served as counsel for the ACLU, she took on a number of sex discrimination cases with a view to seeing gender equality afforded the same protections as racial equality under the equal protection clause of the Fourteenth Amendment to the Constitution. In such cases as *Frontiero v. Richardson* (1973), she argued that gender discrimination should be reviewed by the courts under the same strict scrutiny standard (the most stringent standard of judicial review used by U.S. courts) as race discrimination. In *Weinberger v. Wiesenfeld* (1975), she successfully argued that a provision of the Social Security Act denying widower fathers benefits provided to widow mothers discriminated against working women, since their Social Security taxes accrued fewer family benefits than those paid on behalf of working men. She also argued that the act denied men an opportunity equal to that of women to care for their children. In *Turner v. Department of Employment Security* (1975), she persuaded the Court to strike down a Utah law that made pregnant women ineligible for unemployment benefits. As a result of these and other cases, Ginsburg and the Women's Rights Project laid the groundwork for the passage of the Pregnancy Discrimination Act of 1978.

This passion for sexual equality continued during Ginsburg's tenure on the Supreme Court. For example, in *United States v. Virginia*, she supported equal rights (and opportunities) for women in higher education. On the issue of abortion rights, Ginsburg was critical of the Court's decision in the landmark 1973 case *Roe v. Wade*, arguing that the decision contributed to the divisiveness about abortion in the ensuing decades, yet she protected abortion rights in such cases as *Stenberg, Attorney General of Nebraska, et al. v. Carhart*. In other issues, she supported the rights of citizens to bring suit against companies that violated environmental protection laws. She showed her willingness to take the jurisprudence of other nations into account in her ruling on a case dealing with copyright law.

Time Line

1933

■ **March 15**
Ruth Bader is born in
Brooklyn, New York.

1954

■ Ginsburg graduates from
Cornell University.

1959

■ Ginsburg graduates from
Columbia Law School.

■ Ginsburg begins work as a
law clerk for U.S. District
Judge Edmund L. Palmieri,
a position she holds until
1961.

1963

■ Ginsburg joins the law
faculty at Rutgers
University and assists as
volunteer counsel to the
American Civil Liberties
Union in New Jersey.

1972

■ Ginsburg joins the law
faculty at Columbia, the
first woman with the rank
of full law professor at the
law school; founds and
serves as counsel for the
Women's Rights Project at
the American Civil Liberty
Union's New Jersey
affiliate; serves as general
counsel through 1980.

1974

■ Ginsburg joins the
American Civil Liberty
Union's national board of
directors and serves until
1980.

1978

■ **October 31**
Congress passes the
Pregnancy Discrimination
Act.

1980

■ **June 30**
Ginsburg is sworn in as a
U.S. Court of Appeals
judge for the District of
Columbia.

1993

■ **August 10**
Ginsburg is sworn in as
U.S. Supreme Court
justice.

◆ ***United States v. Virginia***

In this highly publicized 1996 case, Ginsburg, writing the majority opinion, had the opportunity to apply her knowledge and passion for gender equality to the postsecondary education context. This case involved a Fourteenth Amendment equal protection challenge by the United States to the Commonwealth of Virginia and the Virginia Military Institute (VMI), a public all-male military college. It was prompted by a complaint filed with the attorney general by a female high-school student seeking admission to VMI. After the district court ruled for VMI, the U.S. Court of Appeals for the Fourth Circuit reversed the decision and ordered the state of Virginia to remedy the constitutional violation. Although the district court then found the remedy to be constitutional, the case was appealed to the U.S. Supreme Court.

VMI is the only single-sex public institution of higher education in Virginia. Established in 1839, the school has the mission to create "citizen soldiers" and, as Ginsburg describes it, "to instill physical and mental discipline in its cadets and impart to them a strong moral code." Graduates of the school, Ginsburg writes, "leave VMI with heightened comprehension of their capacity to deal with duress and stress, and a large sense of accomplishment for completing the hazardous course." VMI argued that this type of education, based on the English public school model and once common to military instruction, which Ginsburg describes as "comparable in intensity to Marine Corps boot camp," was not suitable to a coeducational environment in general and specifically to female cadets.

Ginsburg notes, though, that the attributes needed to succeed in such an environment are not limited to males: "Neither the goal of producing citizen-soldiers nor VMI's implementing methodology is inherently unsuitable to women. And the school's impressive record in producing leaders has made admission desirable to some women." Nonetheless, Ginsburg goes on, "Virginia has elected to preserve exclusively for men the advantages and opportunities a VMI education affords." She notes that at the district court level, experts testified that "if VMI admitted women, 'the VMI ROTC experience would become a better training program from the perspective of the armed forces, because it would provide training in dealing with a mixed-gender army.'"

VMI argued that a single-sex, all-male public college (the only one in Virginia) provided diversity to an otherwise coeducational Virginia system and served an important governmental interest. Nevertheless, the state of Virginia proposed a parallel program for women that Ginsburg asserts was akin to the all-black colleges proposed by segregated southern universities in the 1940s and early 1950s in response to equal protection challenges. Virginia proposed the creation of the Virginia Women's Institute for Leadership, to be located at Mary Baldwin College, a private liberal arts school for women. The district court, treating VMI deferentially, found that Virginia's proposal satisfied the Constitution's equal protection requirement. The Fourth Circuit affirmed, applying the test of whether VMI and Virginia Women's Institute for Leadership students would receive "substantively comparable" benefits. The U.S. Supreme Court, disagreeing with the Fourth Circuit, held that the appropriate standard when a sex-based classification is used is, as Ginsburg states, "an exceedingly persuasive justification."

Ginsburg emphasizes that substantively speaking, the parallel program did not compare with that of VMI. She notes that the program's curriculum was limited in comparison with VMI's, adding that "while VMI offers degrees in liberal arts, the sciences, and engineering, Mary Baldwin, at the time of trial, offered only bachelor of arts degrees." Further, Ginsburg points out that "Mary Baldwin's own endowment is about $19 million; VMI's is $131 million." In addition, Ginsburg notes that "the average combined SAT score of entrants at Mary Baldwin is about 100 points lower than the score for VMI freshmen." She quotes the dean of Mary Baldwin College, who testified that Mary Baldwin's faculty held "significantly fewer Ph.D.'s than the faculty at VMI," and that the faculty "receives significantly lower salaries."

Ginsburg argues that the proposal that female applicants to Virginia Women's Institute for Leadership would have a "substantively comparable" experience and degree was not supported by the numbers or by history. Virginia argued that VMI's all-male student body was an important source of diversity, for it gave the state's students an alternative type of institution to attend. Ginsburg, however, emphasizes that recent history undermines this argument. It was the standard until relatively recently to segregate women from male university students and that after decades of slow change, Virginia's most prestigious institution of higher education, the University of Virginia, introduced coeducation and in 1972 began to admit women on an equal basis with men.

Referring to precedent, Ginsburg cites *Reed v. Reed*, a 1971 case in which the Court struck down an Idaho law that said that males must be preferred to females where several equally entitled persons are claiming to administer a decedent's estate. She writes: "In 1971, for the first time in our Nation's history, this Court ruled in favor of a woman who complained that her State had denied her the equal protection of its laws." After *Reed*, she says, "the Court has repeatedly recognized that neither federal nor state government acts compatibly with the equal protection principle when a law or official policy denies to women, simply because they are women, full citizenship stature—equal opportunity to aspire, achieve, participate in and contribute to society based on their individual talents and capacities."

Ginsburg notes that the heightened level of scrutiny used for Court review of gender classifications did not equate for all purposes with "classifications based on race or national origin." The Court, in decisions after the *Reed* case, "has carefully inspected official action that closes a door or denies opportunity to women (or to men)." She notes too that the inherent differences between men and women "remain cause for celebration, but not for denigration of the members of either sex or for artificial constraints on an individual's opportunity." Exhibiting a

Time Line

1996

■ **June 26**
Ginsburg delivers the Supreme Court's majority decision in *United States v. Virginia*.

2000

■ **January 12**
Ginsburg delivers the Supreme Court's majority decision in *Friends of the Earth, Inc. et al. v. Laidlaw Environmental Services, Inc.*

■ **June 28**
Ginsburg delivers a concurrence in *Stenberg, Attorney General of Nebraska, et al. v. Carhart*.

2003

■ **January 15**
Ginsburg delivers the Supreme Court's majority decision in *Eldred v. Ashcroft*.

nuanced approach, she concludes that the Court can use gender-based classifications to compensate women for economic inequities but not "to create or perpetuate the legal, social, and economic inferiority of women."

Ginsburg agrees with Virginia that "single-sex education affords pedagogical benefits to at least some students" and notes that those benefits are not contested in this case. She argues, though, that legal precedent requires that Virginia's reasons for using a gender-based classification not be accepted automatically but must be shown to be a "tenable justification" that describes "actual state purposes, not rationalizations for actions in fact differently grounded." She argues that on this important element of the law, Virginia's rationale for the benefits of single-sex education was not tenable and thus was discriminatory in violation of the equal protection clause.

Ginsburg emphasizes that VMI "offers an educational opportunity no other Virginia institution provides, and the school's 'prestige'—associated with its success in developing 'citizen-soldiers'—is unequaled." But, she writes, "Virginia has closed this facility to its daughters and, instead, has devised for them a 'parallel program,'" that fails to approach the standards set by VMI. Thus, she concludes, "Women seeking and fit for a VMI-quality education cannot be offered anything less, under the State's obligation to afford them genuinely equal protection."

◆ Friends of the Earth, Inc. et al. v. Laidlaw Environmental Services, Inc.

In this case, Ginsburg, again writing for the majority, interpreted a statutory provision in the Clean Water Act regarding standing to sue. A person has "standing" if that

Three of the first group of female cadets at the Virginia Military Institute (AP/Wide World Photos)

person is an injured party or otherwise has the right to claim injuries or enforce duties; people without standing have no right to sue. The Court here broadened standing for suing under environmental protection laws such as the Clean Water Act to include citizen groups. The Court held that citizens may have standing to sue for enforcement if they are "injured in fact" (versus actual harm), even if that injury consists of "concerns" about the polluter's activities; this harm can be redressed through a civil penalty such as a fine. Ginsburg's holding created a broad standard allowing more private citizens to seek enforcement of environmental laws when the government has not done so.

Friends of the Earth was a citizen suit filed by various environmental groups on behalf of private citizens who lived near North Carolina's North Tyger River. Laidlaw Environmental Services, Inc., dumped into this river industrial pollutants such as mercury in excess of its permitted allowance. The citizens refrained from using the river (such as swimming in it) because of their concern about the harmful effects of the pollutants. Normally, to win a lawsuit, a plaintiff has to show actual harm or damages; what makes this case important is that the plaintiffs were not required to do so. They feared the potential harmful effects of pollution but did not show any actual harm to themselves.

Ginsburg stated that the Court majority "see nothing 'improbable' about the proposition that a company's continuous and pervasive illegal discharges of pollutants into a river would cause nearby residents to curtail their recreational use of that waterway and would subject them to other economic and aesthetic harms." Such a proposition, which the district court agreed with, is "entirely reasonable" and enough for injury "in fact." Ginsburg's statement here is important because it greatly broadened the type of parties who may sue against an environmental polluter. It established that it is not necessary for a plaintiff to clear the often very high hurdle of showing that the defendant's pollution has caused specific harm. Such a burden of proof often requires scientific tests that are likely to be beyond the financial resources of private citizens.

The appellant-plaintiffs in this case argued that they would use the river if not for the pollutants discharged by

Laidlaw. Ginsburg argues that this conditional refraining from use of the river was not only reasonable but also was sufficient to show injury in fact. She argues that by allowing civil penalties through suits brought by citizen groups, the Court was affecting Congress's legislative intent to create a deterrent to polluters' future bad acts. She states, "Congress has found that civil penalties in Clean Water Act cases do more than promote immediate compliance by limiting the defendant's economic incentive to delay its attainment of permit limits; they also deter future violations. This congressional determination warrants judicial attention and respect."

◆ Stenberg, Attorney General of Nebraska, et al. v. Carhart

In this case, the Court revisited abortion, an issue important to Ginsburg's concern with gender equality. The case addressed the right of states to ban a particular type of abortion procedure called a "partial-birth" abortion. This phrase is widely used in the media to refer to a procedure that medical practitioners call an "intact dilation and extraction." It refers to a late-term abortion performed on a living fetus. As such, the matter is highly controversial, with opponents of partial-birth abortion seeing it as akin to infanticide. This appeal challenged a Nebraska law that outlawed partial-birth abortions. Justice Stephen Breyer, writing for the five-to-four majority, struck down the Nebraska law. The core of his argument was that the law criminalized partial-birth abortions in violation of the due process clause of the Fourteenth Amendment to the Constitution. Citing such precedent-setting cases as *Roe v. Wade* (1973) and *Planned Parenthood v. Casey* (1993), the Court majority maintained that Nebraska law placed an "undue burden" on a woman's right to an abortion.

Ginsburg voted with the majority, but in addition, she wrote a concurrence with the majority's decision because she wanted "only to stress that amidst all the emotional uproar caused by an abortion case, we should not lose sight of the character of Nebraska's 'partial birth abortion' law." She states that "as the Court observes, this law does not save any fetus from destruction, for it targets only 'a *method* of performing abortion.' Nor does the statute seek to protect the lives or health of pregnant women." She asserts that the important issue in this case is not that this form of abortion is any more gruesome than other forms of abortion but rather that with such bans, states seek to *limit* a woman's choice. She adds that "the most common method of performing previability second trimester abortions is no less distressing or susceptible to gruesome description." Ginsburg was careful to use the important term "previability" when describing the fetus in partial-birth abortions. Referring to *Planned Parenthood v. Casey*, she states that "a state regulation that 'has the purpose or effect of placing a substantial obstacle in the path of a woman seeking an abortion of a nonviable fetus' violates the Constitution." Noting the importance of choice, and in particular deference to the judgment of medical professionals, she states that "such an obstacle exists if the State stops a woman from choosing the procedure her doctor 'reasonably believes will best protect the woman in [the] exercise of [her] constitutional liberty.'" Ginsburg's careful jurisprudence is apparent here as she takes care to emphasize a particular aspect of the majority opinion in order to ensure that it does not get lost in the broader holding.

◆ Eldred v. Ashcroft

In this case, the U.S. Supreme Court, with Ginsburg writing for the majority, reviewed a challenge to the constitutionality of the 1998 Sonny Bono Copyright Term Extension Act (CTEA). Displaying her ability to rule on a range of complex legal issues, Ginsburg's opinion upheld CTEA, which extended copyright terms by twenty years from those established by the Copyright Act of 1976. CTEA applied to new as well as to existing copyrights. The legal issue in this case addressed the retroactive effect of CTEA. The plaintiffs, composed of groups such as Internet companies and publishers, argued that CTEA violated the U.S. Constitution's copyright clause (which protected copyrighted works for only a limited time period so that those works could be used to foster progress in science and the arts) and First Amendment guarantees of freedom of speech. The U.S. District Court of Columbia and the U.S. Court of Appeals for the District of Columbia both upheld the constitutionality of CTEA.

Ginsburg, in upholding the decisions of the lower courts, argues that CTEA did not exceed constitutional limits. She refers to various prior copyright acts from 1790 through 1976 that also provided retroactive extensions of copyright. In reviewing the copyright clause, Ginsburg argues that the language of the clause, as well as its intent, was not to describe a particular length of time for copyrights but rather only to set time limits generally. In addition, Ginsburg states that eighteenth-century copyright acts did not foresee the much longer life expectancy of today. In Ginsburg's view, CTEA is a "rational exercise of the legislative authority conferred by the Copyright Clause. On this point, we defer substantially to Congress…. The CTEA reflects judgments of a kind Congress typically makes, judgments the Court cannot dismiss as outside the Legislature's domain."

Ginsburg notes that an important reason for Congress's passage of CTEA was a 1993 European Union law that established a baseline copyright term of life plus seventy years but also denied this longer term to works produced in any non–European Union country whose laws did also provide the same extended term. Ginsburg states that "by extending the baseline United States copyright term,…Congress sought to ensure that American authors would receive the same copyright protection in Europe as their European counterparts." She states that by "retaining the general structure of the 1976 Act, the CTEA enlarges the terms of all existing and future copyrights by 20 years. For works created by identified natural persons, the term now lasts from creation until 70 years after the author's." She argues that this standard harmonizes the baseline U.S. copyright term with that adopted by the European Union. Therefore, Gins-

burg states that Congress contemplated that CTEA would provide incentive for American and other authors to publish works in the United States and take into account demographic, economic, and technological changes. CTEA, Ginsburg also argues, does not violate the First Amendment. She notes that the copyright clause was passed at roughly the same time as the First Amendment and that copyright law accommodates First Amendment interests. She states that U.S. copyright law makes only expression, not ideas, "eligible for copyright protection" and that it "strikes a definitional balance between the First Amendment and the Copyright Act by permitting free communication of facts while still protecting an author's expression."

Impact and Legacy

Ginsburg's advocacy on behalf of sex equality represents the common role that civil rights activists have played in American law. Advocating on behalf of those on the margins of American society, advocates such as Ginsburg extend basic rights to the mainstream of American society. The chief impact of her tenure on the Court of Appeals and on the Supreme Court was to extend the due process and equal protection clauses of the Fourteenth Amendment to matters of gender equality; prior to Ginsburg's efforts, there had been little effort to extend these kinds of constitutional protections to women.

Ginsburg's concern with the civil rights of women extended to other groups. She generally was regarded as a liberal judge on a wide range of social and criminal issues. She was also noteworthy for the deference she showed to the legal systems and laws of other nations, arguing that U.S. law, where possible, should harmonize with international law. She believed that the laws of other nations—on such issues as the war against terrorism, the treatment of enemy combatants, or the use of torture in interrogating terrorism suspects—contributed to evolving standards of what is morally, ethically, and legally right and that the United States can and should be at least in part guided by these standards.

Key Sources

In 1998 Ginsburg donated two collections of her papers, comprising more than sixteen thousand items, to the manuscript division of the Library of Congress. These papers include correspondence, speeches, documents related to major cases during her tenures as a Court of Appeals and Supreme Court justice, and papers related to her work for the ACLU (http://memory.loc.gov/ammem/awhhtml/awmss5/judg_attys.html). Additionally, Ginsburg is the author of numerous articles and tributes to other prominent figures in the legal community as well as of forewords to books about legal matters. An example is "Affirmative Action as an International Human Rights Dialogue," published in *The Brookings Review* (2000).

"The Court has repeatedly recognized that neither federal nor state government acts compatibly with the equal protection principle when a law or official policy denies to women, simply because they are women, full citizenship stature—equal opportunity to aspire, achieve, participate in and contribute to society based on their individual talents and capacities."

(*United States v. Virginia*)

"We see nothing 'improbable' about the proposition that a company's continuous and pervasive illegal discharges of pollutants into a river would cause nearby residents to curtail their recreational use of that waterway and would subject them to other economic and aesthetic harms. The proposition is entirely reasonable, the District Court found it was true in this case, and that is enough for injury in fact."

(*Friends of the Earth, Inc. et al. v. Laidlaw Environmental Services, Inc.*)

"A would-be polluter may or may not be dissuaded by the existence of a remedy on the books, but a defendant once hit in its pocketbook will surely think twice before polluting again."

(*Friends of the Earth, Inc. et al. v. Laidlaw Environmental Services, Inc.*)

"A state regulation that 'has the purpose or effect of placing a substantial obstacle in the path of a woman seeking an abortion of a nonviable fetus' violates the Constitution."

(*Stenberg, Attorney General of Nebraska, et al. v. Carhart*)

"Text, history, and precedent, we conclude, confirm that the Copyright Clause empowers Congress to prescribe 'limited Times' for copyright protection and to secure the same level and duration of protection for all copyright holders, present and future."

(*Eldred v. Ashcroft*)

"By extending the baseline United States copyright term to life plus 70 years, Congress sought to ensure that American authors would receive the same copyright protection in Europe as their European counterparts."

(*Eldred v. Ashcroft*)

Further Reading

■ Articles

Merritt, Deborah Jones, and David M. Lieberman. "Ruth Bader Ginsburg's Jurisprudence of Opportunity and Equality." *Columbia Law Review* 104, no. 1 (2004): 39–48.

■ Books

Baldwin, Louis. *Women of Strength: Biographies of 106 Who Have Excelled in Traditionally Male Fields, a.d. 61 to the Present*. Jefferson, N.C.: McFarland, 1996.

Campbell, Amy Leigh. *Raising the Bar: Ruth Bader Ginsburg and the ACLU Women's Rights Project*. Princeton, N.J.: Xlibris Corporation, 2003.

Perry, Barbara A. *"The Supremes": Essays on the Current Justices of the Supreme Court of the United States*. New York: P. Lang, 1999.

Tushman, Clare, ed. *Supreme Court Decisions and Women's Rights: Milestones to Equality*. Washington, D.C.: CQ Press, 2001.

Urofsky, Melvin I. *Biographical Encyclopedia of the Supreme Court: The Lives and Legal Philosophies of the Justices*. Washington, D.C.: CQ Press, 2006.

■ Web Sites

"Tribute: The Legacy of Ruth Bader Ginsburg and WRP Staff," American Civil Liberties Union Web site. http://www.aclu.org/womensrights/gen/24412pub20060307.html.

—Michael Chang and Michael J. O'Neal

Questions for Further Study

1. Why, according to Ginsburg, was Virginia's program at Mary Baldwin College, intended to parallel the program at the Virginia Military Institute, inadequate in providing equal opportunities for women?

2. In 1997, when women were first admitted to VMI, the dropout rate among male cadets after the first week was 5 percent, but the dropout rate among female cadets was about 3 percent (one of thirty female students). Do you believe that these figures justify Ginsburg's argument in *United States v. Virginia*? Why or why not?

3. The legal concept of "standing," or the right to bring a lawsuit, is critical in court cases. How did Ginsburg alter the concept of standing as it applied to environmental issues in *Friends of the Earth, Inc. et al. v. Laidlaw Environmental Services, Inc.*? Why was this alteration significant?

4. *Eldred v. Ashcroft* extended the length of copyright protection for literary and artistic works. Why, according to Ginsburg, does doing so not infringe the First Amendment freedom of speech rights of others who want to use the works?

5. Contrast Ginsburg's views regarding abortion with those expressed by William Rehnquist in his dissent in *Roe v. Wade*.

UNITED STATES V. VIRGINIA (1996)

Founded in 1839, VMI is today the sole single-sex school among Virginia's 15 public institutions of higher learning. VMI's distinctive mission is to produce "citizen-soldiers," men prepared for leadership in civilian life and in military service. VMI pursues this mission through pervasive training of a kind not available anywhere else in Virginia. Assigning prime place to character development, VMI uses an "adversative method" modeled on English public schools and once characteristic of military instruction. VMI constantly endeavors to instill physical and mental discipline in its cadets and impart to them a strong moral code. The school's graduates leave VMI with heightened comprehension of their capacity to deal with duress and stress, and a large sense of accomplishment for completing the hazardous course....

Neither the goal of producing citizen-soldiers nor VMI's implementing methodology is inherently unsuitable to women. And the school's impressive record in producing leaders has made admission desirable to some women. Nevertheless, Virginia has elected to preserve exclusively for men the advantages and opportunities a VMI education affords....

VMI produces its "citizen-soldiers" through "an adversative, or doubting, model of education" which features "[p]hysical rigor, mental stress, absolute equality of treatment, absence of privacy, minute regulation of behavior, and indoctrination in desirable values." As one Commandant of Cadets described it, the adversative method "dissects the young student," and makes him aware of his "limits and capabilities," so that he knows "how far he can go with his anger,...how much he can take under stress,...exactly what he can do when he is physically exhausted."

VMI cadets live in spartan barracks where surveillance is constant and privacy nonexistent; they wear uniforms, eat together in the mess hall, and regularly participate in drills. Entering students are incessantly exposed to the rat line, "an extreme form of the adversative model," comparable in intensity to Marine Corps boot camp. Tormenting and punishing, the rat line bonds new cadets to their fellow sufferers and, when they have completed the 7-month experience, to their former tormentors....

In the two years preceding the lawsuit, the District Court noted, VMI had received inquiries from 347 women, but had responded to none of them. "[S]ome women, at least," the court said, "would want to attend the school if they had the opportunity." The court further recognized that, with recruitment, VMI could "achieve at least 10% female enrollment"—a sufficient 'critical mass' to provide the female cadets with a positive educational experience." And it was also established that "some women are capable of all of the individual activities required of VMI cadets." In addition, experts agreed that if VMI admitted women, "the VMI ROTC experience would become a better training program from the perspective of the armed forces, because it would provide training in dealing with a mixed-gender army."

The District Court ruled in favor of VMI, however, and rejected the equal protection challenge pressed by the United States....The District Court reasoned that education in "a single-gender environment, be it male or female," yields substantial benefits. VMI's school for men brought diversity to an otherwise coeducational Virginia system, and that diversity was "enhanced by VMI's unique method of instruction." If single-gender education for males ranks as an important governmental objective, it becomes obvious, the District Court concluded, that the only means of achieving the objective "is to exclude women from the all-male institution-VMI."...

The Court of Appeals for the Fourth Circuit disagreed and vacated the District Court's judgment. The appellate court held: "The Commonwealth of Virginia has not...advanced any state policy by which it can justify its determination, under an announced policy of diversity, to afford VMI's unique type of program to men and not to women."...

The parties agreed that "some women can meet the physical standards now imposed on men," and the court was satisfied that "neither the goal of producing citizen soldiers nor VMI's implementing methodology is inherently unsuitable to women." The Court of Appeals, however, accepted the District Court's finding that "at least these three aspects of VMI's program—physical training, the absence of privacy, and the adversative approach—would be materially affected by coeducation." Remanding the case, the appeals court assigned to Virginia, in the first instance, responsibility for selecting a remedial course. The court suggested these options for the State: Admit women to VMI; establish parallel institutions or programs; or abandon state support, leaving VMI free to pursue its policies as a private institution....

In response to the Fourth Circuit's ruling, Virginia proposed a parallel program for women: Virginia Women's Institute for Leadership (VWIL). The 4-year, state-sponsored undergraduate program would be located at Mary Baldwin College, a private liberal arts school for women, and would be open, initially, to about 25 to 30 students. Although VWIL would share VMI's mission-to produce "citizen-soldiers"—the VWIL program would differ, as does Mary Baldwin College, from VMI in academic offerings, methods of education, and financial resources.

The average combined SAT score of entrants at Mary Baldwin is about 100 points lower than the score for VMI freshmen. Mary Baldwin's faculty holds "significantly fewer Ph.D.'s than the faculty at VMI," and receives significantly lower salaries, While VMI offers degrees in liberal arts, the sciences, and engineering, Mary Baldwin, at the time of trial, offered only bachelor of arts degrees. A VWIL student seeking to earn an engineering degree could gain one, without public support, by attending Washington University in St. Louis, Missouri, for two years, paying the required private tuition....

Virginia represented that it will provide equal financial support for in-state VWIL students and VMI cadets, and the VMI Foundation agreed to supply a $5.4625 million endowment for the VWIL program. Mary Baldwin's own endowment is about $19 million; VMI's is $131 million. Mary Baldwin will add $35 million to its endowment based on future commitments; VMI will add $220 million. The VMI Alumni Association has developed a network of employers interested in hiring VMI graduates. The Association has agreed to open its network to VWIL graduates, but those graduates will not have the advantage afforded by a VMI degree....

The court recognized that, as it analyzed the case, means merged into end, and the merger risked "bypass[ing] any equal protection scrutiny." The court therefore added another inquiry, a decisive test it called "substantive comparability." The key question, the court said, was whether men at VMI and women at VWIL would obtain "substantively comparable benefits at their institution or through other means offered by the [S]tate." Although the appeals court recognized that the VWIL degree "lacks the historical benefit and prestige" of a VMI degree, it nevertheless found the educational opportunities at the two schools "sufficiently comparable."...

The Fourth Circuit denied rehearing en banc.... Judge Motz agreed with Judge Phillips that Virginia

had not shown an "'exceedingly persuasive justification'" for the disparate opportunities the State supported....

We note, once again, the core instruction of this Court's pathmarking decisions in *J. E. B. v. Alabama ex rel. T. B.*, and *Mississippi Univ. for Women*: Parties who seek to defend gender-based government action must demonstrate an "exceedingly persuasive justification" for that action....

In 1971, for the first time in our Nation's history, this Court ruled in favor of a woman who complained that her State had denied her the equal protection of its laws. Since *Reed*, the Court has repeatedly recognized that neither federal nor state government acts compatibly with the equal protection principle when a law or official policy denies to women, simply because they are women, full citizenship stature—equal opportunity to aspire, achieve, participate in and contribute to society based on their individual talents and capacities.

Without equating gender classifications, for all purposes, to classifications based on race or national origin, the Court, in post-*Reed* decisions, has carefully inspected official action that closes a door or denies opportunity to women (or to men). To summarize the Court's current directions for cases of official classification based on gender: Focusing on the differential treatment or denial of opportunity for which relief is sought, the reviewing court must determine whether the proffered justification is "exceedingly persuasive." The burden of justification is demanding and it rests entirely on the State. The State must show "at least that the [challenged] classification serves 'important governmental objectives and that the discriminatory means employed' are 'substantially related to the achievement of those objectives.'" The justification must be genuine, not hypothesized or invented post hoc in response to litigation. And it must not rely on overbroad generalizations about the different talents, capacities, or preferences of males and females.

The heightened review standard our precedent establishes does not make sex a proscribed classification. Supposed "inherent differences" are no longer accepted as a ground for race or national origin classifications. Physical differences between men and women, however, are enduring: "[T]he two sexes are not fungible; a community made up exclusively of one [sex] is different from a community composed of both."

"Inherent differences" between men and women, we have come to appreciate, remain cause for celebration, but not for denigration of the members of either sex or for artificial constraints on an individual's opportunity. Sex classifications may be used to compensate women "for particular economic disabilities [they have] suffered," to "promot[e] equal employment opportunity," to advance full development of the talent and capacities of our Nation's people. But such classifications may not be used, as they once were, to create or perpetuate the legal, social, and economic inferiority of women.

Measuring the record in this case against the review standard just described, we conclude that Virginia has shown no "exceedingly persuasive justification" for excluding all women from the citizen-soldier training afforded by VMI....

Single-sex education affords pedagogical benefits to at least some students, Virginia emphasizes, and that reality is uncontested in this litigation. Similarly, it is not disputed that diversity among public educational institutions can serve the public good. But Virginia has not shown that VMI was established, or has been maintained, with a view to diversifying, by its categorical exclusion of women, educational opportunities within the State. In cases of this genre, our precedent instructs that "benign" justifications proffered in defense of categorical exclusions will not be accepted automatically; a tenable justification must describe actual state purposes, not rationalizations for actions in fact differently grounded....

Ultimately, in 1970, "the most prestigious institution of higher education in Virginia," the University of Virginia, introduced coeducation and, in 1972, began to admit women on an equal basis with men. A three-judge Federal District Court confirmed: "Virginia may not now deny to women, on the basis of sex, educational opportunities at the Charlottesville campus that are not afforded in other institutions operated by the [S]tate."...

VMI, too, offers an educational opportunity no other Virginia institution provides, and the school's "prestige"—associated with its success in developing "citizen-soldiers"—is unequaled. Virginia has closed this facility to its daughters and, instead, has devised for them a "parallel program," with a faculty less impressively credentialed and less well paid, more limited course offerings, fewer opportunities for military training and for scientific specialization. VMI, beyond question, "possesses to a far greater degree" than the VWIL program "those qualities which are incapable of objective measurement but which make for greatness in a...school," including "position and influence of the alumni, standing in the community, traditions and prestige." Women seeking and fit for a VMI-quality education cannot be offered anything less, under the State's obligation to afford them genuinely equal protection.

Glossary

en banc	literally, "on the bench"; refers to a case heard with the judges sitting together
endowment	the reserve of money and investments used to help fund an institution such as a college or university
fungible	alike; interchangeable
proscribed	prohibited
remanding	sending back to a lower court for further consideration
spartan	barren, primitive

FRIENDS OF THE EARTH, INC. ET AL. V. LAIDLAW ENVIRONMENTAL SERVICES, INC. (2000)

This case presents an important question concerning the operation of the citizen-suit provisions of the Clean Water Act. Congress authorized the federal district courts to entertain Clean Water Act suits initiated by "a person or persons having an interest which is or may be adversely affected." To impel future compliance with the Act, a district court may prescribe injunctive relief in such a suit; additionally or alternatively, the court may impose civil penalties payable to the United States Treasury. In the Clean Water Act citizen suit now before us, the District Court determined that injunctive relief was inappropriate because the defendant, after the institution of the litigation, achieved substantial compliance with the terms of its discharge permit. The court did, however, assess a civil penalty of $405,800. The "total deterrent effect" of the penalty would be adequate to forestall future violations, the court reasoned, taking into account that the defendant "will be required to reimburse plaintiffs for a significant amount of legal fees and has, itself, incurred significant legal expenses."

The Court of Appeals vacated the District Court's order. The case became moot, the appellate court declared, once the defendant fully complied with the terms of its permit and the plaintiff failed to appeal the denial of equitable relief....

We reverse the judgment of the Court of Appeals. The appellate court erred in concluding that a citizen suitor's claim for civil penalties must be dismissed as moot when the defendant, albeit after commencement of the litigation, has come into compliance....A defendant's voluntary cessation of allegedly unlawful conduct ordinarily does not suffice to moot a case. The Court of Appeals also misperceived the remedial potential of civil penalties. Such penalties may serve, as an alternative to an injunction, to deter future violations and thereby redress the injuries that prompted a citizen suitor to commence litigation....

The Constitution's case-or-controversy limitation on federal judicial authority, Art. III, §2, underpins both our standing and our mootness jurisprudence, but the two inquiries differ in respects critical to the proper resolution of this case, so we address them separately. Because the Court of Appeals was persuaded that the case had become moot and so held,

it simply assumed without deciding that FOE had initial standing. But because we hold that the Court of Appeals erred in declaring the case moot, we have an obligation to assure ourselves that FOE had Article III standing at the outset of the litigation....

Our decision in *Lujan v. National Wildlife Federation* is not to the contrary. In that case an environmental organization assailed the Bureau of Land Management's "land withdrawal review program," a program covering millions of acres, alleging that the program illegally opened up public lands to mining activities. The defendants moved for summary judgment, challenging the plaintiff organization's standing to initiate the action under the Administrative Procedure Act. We held that the plaintiff could not survive the summary judgment motion merely by offering "averments which state only that one of [the organization's] members uses unspecified portions of an immense tract of territory, on some portions of which mining activity has occurred or probably will occur by virtue of the governmental action."

In contrast, the affidavits and testimony presented by FOE in this case assert that Laidlaw's discharges, and the affiant members' reasonable concerns about the effects of those discharges, directly affected those affiants' recreational, aesthetic, and economic interests. These submissions present dispositively more than the mere "general averments" and "conclusory allegations" found inadequate in *National Wildlife Federation*. Nor can the affiants' conditional statements—that they would use the nearby North Tyger River for recreation if Laidlaw were not discharging pollutants into it—be equated with the speculative "'some day' intentions" to visit endangered species halfway around the world that we held insufficient to show injury in fact in *Defenders of Wildlife*.

Los Angeles v. Lyons, relied on by the dissent, does not weigh against standing in this case. In *Lyons*, we held that a plaintiff lacked standing to seek an injunction against the enforcement of a police chokehold policy because he could not credibly allege that he faced a realistic threat from the policy. In the footnote from *Lyons* cited by the dissent, we noted that "[t]he reasonableness of Lyons' fear is dependent upon the likelihood of a recurrence of the allegedly unlawful conduct," and that his "subjective apprehensions" that such a recurrence would even *take place* were not enough to support standing. Here, in contrast, it is undisputed that Laidlaw's unlawful conduct—discharging pollutants in excess of permit limits—was occurring at the time the complaint was filed. Under *Lyons*, then, the only "subjective" issue here is "[t]he reasonableness of [the] fear" that led the affiants to respond to that concededly ongoing conduct by refraining from use of the North Tyger River and surrounding areas. Unlike the dissent, we see nothing "improbable" about the proposition that a company's continuous and pervasive illegal discharges of pollutants into a river would cause nearby residents to curtail their recreational use of that waterway and would subject them to other economic and aesthetic harms. The proposition is entirely reasonable, the District Court found it was true in this case, and that is enough for injury in fact.

Laidlaw argues next that even if FOE had standing to seek injunctive relief, it lacked standing to seek civil penalties. Here the asserted defect is not injury but redressability. Civil penalties offer no redress to private plaintiffs, Laidlaw argues, because they are paid to the government, and therefore a citizen plaintiff can never have standing to seek them.

Laidlaw is right to insist that a plaintiff must demonstrate standing separately for each form of relief sought. But it is wrong to maintain that citizen plaintiffs facing ongoing violations never have standing to seek civil penalties.

We have recognized on numerous occasions that "all civil penalties have some deterrent effect." More specifically, Congress has found that civil penalties in Clean Water Act cases do more than promote immediate compliance by limiting the defendant's economic incentive to delay its attainment of permit limits; they also deter future violations. This congressional determination warrants judicial attention and respect. "The legislative history of the Act reveals that Congress wanted the district court to consider the need for retribution and deterrence, in addition to restitution, when it imposed civil penalties....[The district court may] seek to deter future violations by basing the penalty on its economic impact." It can scarcely be doubted that, for a plaintiff who is injured or faces the threat of future injury due to illegal conduct ongoing at the time of suit, a sanction that effectively abates that conduct and prevents its recurrence provides a form of redress. Civil penalties can fit that description. To the extent that they encourage defendants to discontinue current violations and deter them from committing future ones, they afford redress to citizen plaintiffs who are injured or threatened with injury as a consequence of ongoing unlawful conduct.

The dissent argues that it is the *availability* rather than the *imposition* of civil penalties that deters any particular polluter from continuing to pollute. This argument misses the mark in two ways. First, it overlooks the interdependence of the availability and the imposition; a threat has no deterrent value unless it is credible that it will be carried out. Second, it is

Glossary

affiant	a person whose has made an affidavit, or sworn statement
averments	statements
case-or-controversy limitation on federal judicial authority	requirement that the courts hear actual cases and not be called on to settle controversial issues
dispositively	having the quality of bringing about the disposition, or settlement, of a case.
equitable relief	a legal remedy ordered by a court, including an injunction, a restraining order, adherence to the terms of a contract, or other requirement; generally provided only when monetary damages are inappropriate
injunctive relief	a court-ordered prohibition of an act that has been requested by another party
moot	of no legal significance because the matter has been settled or previously decided
vacated	set aside

reasonable for Congress to conclude that an actual award of civil penalties does in fact bring with it a significant quantum of deterrence over and above what is achieved by the mere prospect of such penalties. A would-be polluter may or may not be dissuaded by the existence of a remedy on the books, but a defendant once hit in its pocketbook will surely think twice before polluting again.

STENBERG, ATTORNEY GENERAL OF NEBRASKA, ET AL. V. CARHART (2000)

Ginsburg concurrence

I write separately only to stress that amidst all the emotional uproar caused by an abortion case, we should not lose sight of the character of Nebraska's "partial birth abortion" law. As the Court observes, this law does not save any fetus from destruction, for it targets only "a *method* of performing abortion." Nor does the statute seek to protect the lives or health of pregnant women. Moreover, as Justice Stevens points out, the most common method of performing previability second trimester abortions is no less distressing or susceptible to gruesome description. Seventh Circuit Chief Judge Posner correspondingly observed, regarding similar bans in Wisconsin and Illinois, that the law prohibits the D & X procedure "not because the procedure kills the fetus, not because it risks worse complications for the woman than alternative procedures would do, not because it is a crueler or more painful or more disgusting method of terminating a pregnancy." Rather, Chief Judge Posner commented, the law prohibits the procedure because the State legislators seek to chip away at the private choice shielded by *Roe v. Wade*, even as modified by *Casey*.

A state regulation that "has the purpose or effect of placing a substantial obstacle in the path of a woman seeking an abortion of a nonviable fetus" violates the Constitution. Such an obstacle exists if the State stops a woman from choosing the procedure her doctor "reasonably believes will best protect the woman in [the] exercise of [her] constitutional liberty." Again as stated by Chief Judge Posner, "if a statute burdens constitutional rights and all that can be said on its behalf is that it is the vehicle that legislators have chosen for expressing their hostility to those rights, the burden is undue."

Glossary

D & X procedure	dilation and extraction, a method of performing abortion, generally between the twentieth and twenty-fourth weeks after conception, consisting of expansion of the cervix and removal of the fetus in sections; also a method used to remove a deceased fetus from the uterus of the mother
Previability	with respect to a fetus, the state of not yet being able to sustain life outside the womb
Seventh Circuit Chief Judge Posner	Richard Posner (1939–), a judge of the Seventh Circuit Court of Appeals (Chicago) from 1991 and chief judge from 1993 to 2000

ELDRED V. ASHCROFT (2003)

This case concerns the authority the Constitution assigns to Congress to prescribe the duration of copyrights. The Copyright and Patent Clause of the Constitution … provides as to copyrights: "Congress shall have Power…[t]o promote the Progress of Science…by securing [to Authors] for limited Times… the exclusive Right to their…Writings."…

The measure at issue here, the CTEA, installed the fourth major duration extension of federal copyrights. Retaining the general structure of the 1976 Act, the CTEA enlarges the terms of all existing and future copyrights by 20 years. For works created by identified natural persons, the term now lasts from creation until 70 years after the author's death. This standard harmonizes the baseline United States copyright term with the term adopted by the European Union in 1993.…

We address first the determination of the courts below that Congress has authority under the Copyright Clause to extend the terms of existing copyrights. Text, history, and precedent, we conclude, confirm that the Copyright Clause empowers Congress to prescribe "limited Times" for copyright protection and to secure the same level and duration of protection for all copyright holders, present and future.

The CTEA's baseline term of life plus 70 years, petitioners concede, qualifies as a "limited Tim[e]" as applied to future copyrights. Petitioners contend, however, that existing copyrights extended to endure for that same term are not "limited." Petitioners' argument essentially reads into the text of the Copyright Clause the command that a time prescription, once set, becomes forever "fixed" or "inalterable." The word "limited," however, does not convey a meaning so constricted. At the time of the Framing, that word meant what it means today: "confine[d] within certain bounds," "restrain[ed]," or "circumscribe[d]."… Thus understood, a time span appropriately "limited" as applied to future copyrights does not automatically cease to be "limited" when applied to existing copyrights. And as we observe, there is no cause to suspect that a purpose to evade the "limited Times" prescription prompted Congress to adopt the CTEA.

To comprehend the scope of Congress' power under the Copyright Clause, "a page of history is worth a volume of logic."…History reveals an unbroken congressional practice of granting to authors of works with existing copyrights the benefit of term extensions so that all under copyright protection will be governed evenhandedly under the same regime. As earlier recounted, the First Congress accorded the protections of the Nation's first federal copyright statute to existing and future works alike. Since then, Congress has regularly applied duration extensions to both existing and future copyrights.…

Further, although prior to the instant case this Court did not have occasion to decide whether extending the duration of existing copyrights complies with the "limited Times" prescription, the Court has found no constitutional barrier to the legislative expansion of existing patents. *McClurg v. Kingsland* is the pathsetting precedent. The patentee in that case was unprotected under the law in force when the patent issued because he had allowed his employer briefly to practice the invention before he obtained the patent. Only upon enactment, two years later, of an exemption for such allowances did the patent become valid, retroactive to the time it issued. *McClurg* upheld retroactive application of the new law. The Court explained that the legal regime governing a particular patent "depend[s] on the law as it stood at the emanation of the patent, together with such changes as have been since made; for though they may be retrospective in their operation, that is not a sound objection to their validity." Neither is it a sound objection to the validity of a copyright term extension, enacted pursuant to the same constitutional grant of authority, that the enlarged term covers existing copyrights.…

Satisfied that the CTEA complies with the "limited Times" prescription, we turn now to whether it is a rational exercise of the legislative authority conferred by the Copyright Clause. On that point, we defer substantially to Congress. ("[I]t is Congress that has been assigned the task of defining the scope of the limited monopoly that should be granted to authors … in order to give the public appropriate access to their work product.").

The CTEA reflects judgments of a kind Congress typically makes, judgments we cannot dismiss as outside the Legislature's domain. As respondent describes, a key factor in the CTEA's passage was a 1993 European Union (EU) directive instructing EU members to establish a copyright term of life plus 70 years.... Consistent with the Berne Convention, the EU directed its members to deny this longer term to the works of any non-EU country whose laws did not secure the same extended term. By extending the baseline United States copyright term to life plus 70 years, Congress sought to ensure that American authors would receive the same copyright protection in Europe as their European counterparts. The CTEA may also provide greater incentive for American and other authors to create and disseminate their work in the United States....

In addition to international concerns, Congress passed the CTEA in light of demographic, economic, and technological changes, and rationally credited projections that longer terms would encourage copyright holders to invest in the restoration and public distribution of their works....

In sum, we find that the CTEA is a rational enactment; we are not at liberty to second-guess congressional determinations and policy judgments of this order, however debatable or arguably unwise they may be. Accordingly, we cannot conclude that the CTEA—which continues the unbroken congressional practice of treating future and existing copyrights in parity for term extension purposes—is an impermissible exercise of Congress' power under the Copyright Clause....

Petitioners separately argue that the CTEA is a content-neutral regulation of speech that fails heightened judicial review under the First Amendment. We reject petitioners' plea for imposition of uncommonly strict scrutiny on a copyright scheme that incorporates its own speech-protective purposes and safeguards. The Copyright Clause and First Amendment were adopted close in time. This proximity indicates that, in the Framers' view, copyright's limited monopolies are compatible with free speech principles. Indeed, copyright's purpose is to *promote* the creation and publication of free expression. As *Harper & Row* observed: "[T]he Framers intended copyright itself to be the engine of free expression. By establishing a marketable right to the use of one's expression, copyright supplies the economic incentive to create and disseminate ideas."

In addition to spurring the creation and publication of new expression, copyright law contains built-in First Amendment accommodations. First, it distinguishes between ideas and expression and makes only the latter eligible for copyright protection. Specifically, 17 U.S.C. §102(b) provides: "In no case does copyright protection for an original work of authorship extend to any idea, procedure, process, system, method of operation, concept, principle, or discovery, regardless of the form in which it is described, explained, illustrated, or embodied in such work." As we said in *Harper & Row*, this "idea/expression dichotomy strike[s] a definitional balance between the First Amendment and the Copyright Act by permitting free communication of facts while still protecting an author's expression." Due to this dis-

Glossary

Berne Convention	an international agreement about copyrights, signed in Berne, Switzerland, in 1886
dichotomy	distinction
European Union	the economic and political union of twenty-seven European countries
Framing	the formation of the United States under the Constitution.
heightened judicial review under the First Amendment	more stringent evaluation by the Court because the matter involves a fundamental right under First Amendment freedom of speech
instant case	the present case; the case on which the Court is ruling
natural persons	actual human beings, as opposed to "fictitious persons" such as corporations.
"a page of history is worth a volume of logic"	quotation from Supreme Court justice Oliver Wendell Holmes, Jr., in *New York Trust Co. v. Eisner* (1921)
strict scrutiny	the Court's most stringent manner of reviewing a law, applied when fundamental rights are at issue

tinction, every idea, theory, and fact in a copyrighted work becomes instantly available for public exploitation at the moment of publication.

Second, the "fair use" defense allows the public to use not only facts and ideas contained in a copyrighted work, but also expression itself in certain circumstances. Codified at 17 U.S.C. §107 the defense provides: "[T]he fair use of a copyrighted work, including such use by reproduction in copies…, for purposes such as criticism, comment, news reporting, teaching (including multiple copies for classroom use), scholarship, or research, is not an infringement of copyright." The fair use defense affords considerable "latitude for scholarship and comment."

The CTEA itself supplements these traditional First Amendment safeguards. First, it allows libraries, archives, and similar institutions to "reproduce" and "distribute, display, or perform in facsimile or digital form" copies of certain published works "during the last 20 years of any term of copyright… for purposes of preservation, scholarship, or research" if the work is not already being exploited commercially and further copies are unavailable at a reasonable price. Second, Title II of the CTEA, known as the Fairness in Music Licensing Act of 1998, exempts small businesses, restaurants, and like entities from having to pay performance royalties on music played from licensed radio, television, and similar facilities.…

The CTEA…does not oblige anyone to reproduce another's speech against the carrier's will. Instead, it protects authors' original expression from unrestricted exploitation.

Emma Goldman (Library of Congress)

EMMA GOLDMAN   1869–1940

Anarchist and Journalist

Featured Documents
◆ "Anarchism: What It Really Stands For" (1917)
◆ "The Psychology of Political Violence" (1917)
◆ "Marriage and Love" (1917)
◆ Speech against Conscription and War (1917)

Overview

Emma Goldman was born June 27, 1869, in Kovno, Lithuania, which was then part of the Russian Empire. The Goldman family moved to St. Petersburg, where Emma's father experienced a series of business failures. Goldman often quarreled with her father, who failed to support his daughter's educational endeavors. In 1885 Goldman and her older sister Helena left Russia for the United States and settled with other family members in Rochester, New York, where Goldman began factory work as a seamstress. In February 1887 she married her fellow worker Jacob Kersner, but the marriage dissolved after a year, with Goldman moving to New York City in 1889.

Upon her arrival in the more cosmopolitan environment of New York City, Goldman met the anarchist Alexander Berkman, with whom she began a political and romantic relationship. Berkman introduced Goldman to another anarchist, Johann Most, an advocate for what anarchists called the propaganda of the deed, concluding that their direct action would motivate the masses to revolution. Most encouraged Goldman's involvement in the anarchist movement, although she would later split with her mentor. In 1892 Pennsylvania authorities violently suppressed a labor uprising in the steel plants of Andrew Carnegie in Homestead, Pennsylvania. Following the violent suppression of the steel strike, Berkman was imprisoned for his attempted assassination of the plant manager, Henry Clay Frick. Although no evidence was established linking Goldman to the act, she later acknowledged her involvement. Goldman was imprisoned for allegedly urging unemployed workers to revolt during the national financial crisis referred to as the Panic of 1893. After serving a ten-month sentence, she continued her political agitation, supporting herself by working as a midwife and nurse following study at the Vienna General Hospital in 1895 and 1896.

On September 6, 1901, President William McKinley was assassinated by the anarchist Leon Czolgosz. Goldman was arrested for her alleged association with the assassin but freed for lack of evidence. In 1906 Berkman was released from prison, and the couple began publication of the anarchist journal *Mother Earth*. In the pages of *Mother Earth* and in her public speeches over the next decade, Goldman addressed issues of anarchism, women's rights, patriotism, and labor organization. It was in *Mother Earth*

that she first published the essays "Anarchism: What It Really Stands For," "The Psychology of Political Violence," and "Marriage and Love."

In 1917 Berkman and Goldman were arrested for their opposition to conscription and American participation in World War I. Charged under the newly enacted Espionage Act, Goldman and Berkman were sentenced to two years in prison. Released during the zenith of America's "red scare"—a period of anti-Communism that followed World War I, in reaction to the Russian Revolution—Berkman and Goldman were deported to Russia.

Although she initially supported the Bolshevik seizure of power in Russia in 1917, Goldman expressed disillusionment with the centralized state evolving there. In 1921 she left Russia, living briefly in Germany before settling in London. Although many on the political left censured Goldman for her opposition to the Soviet state, the anarchist defended her views and assailed coercive states of both the political left and right in her autobiography, *Living My Life* (1931). Suffering from a stroke, Goldman died in Toronto on May 14, 1940.

Explanation and Analysis of Documents

From 1893 to 1917 Emma Goldman delivered numerous and controversial lectures regarding anarchism, women's rights, patriotism, and labor conditions. In addition to her efforts on the lecture circuit, in 1906 Goldman established the anarchist journal *Mother Earth*, which she edited in New York City's bohemian center of Greenwich Village. In 1910 several of Goldman's *Mother Earth* pieces were collected in the anthology *Anarchism and Other Essays*.

The piece "Anarchism: What It Really Stands For" is an excellent example of Goldman's writing regarding the philosophical roots of anarchism. While Goldman stresses the creative force of anarchism, many opponents of anarchy were appalled by its association with the violent "propaganda of the deed." Goldman was accused of participating in the attack on Henry Clay Frick as well as the assassination of President McKinley. In "The Psychology of Political Violence," Goldman enunciates her complex views on the means by which anarchists must challenge the economic exploitation and violence of capitalism. Goldman also focused upon the possibilities of anarchism to provide liberation for women—a topic

Time Line

1869

■ **June 27**
Emma Goldman is born in Kovno, Lithuania (then part of the Russian Empire).

1885

■ **December 29**
Goldman and her older sister Helena arrive in the United States.

1893

■ **August 21**
Goldman's speech to unemployed workers in New York City leads to her incarceration in Blackwell's Island Penitentiary.

1895– 1896

■ Goldman studies nursing and midwifery at Vienna General Hospital.

1901

■ **September 6**
Leon Czolgosz assassinates President William McKinley, and Goldman is implicated but released for lack of evidence.

1906

■ Goldman begins publication of New York City anarchist journal *Mother Earth.*

1910

■ Goldman publishes *Anarchism and Other Essays,* in which are included her essays "Anarchism: What It Really Stands For," "The Psychology of Political Violence," and "Marriage and Love."

1916

■ **February**
Goldman is arrested for violating the Comstock Laws—federal legislation that deemed the public discussion of birth control to be obscenity—by supporting the nurse and activist Margaret Sanger and lecturing on the topic of birth control.

---

that she addresses in "Marriage and Love." The exploitation of women within such capitalist institutions as marriage earned the ire of Goldman, who advocated the creative power of love beyond the sanctions of the state. The influential anthology of Goldman's political writings *Anarchism and Other Essays* was republished in 1917.

American entrance into World War I was opposed by Goldman as a capitalist conflict enriching bankers and munitions makers at the expense of the international working class. Her opposition to the war and conscription is well represented by her speech at Forward Hall in New York City, delivered on June 14, 1917. Goldman's antiwar activities resulted in her arrest and sentence to a two-year prison term under the Espionage Act. Following her imprisonment, Goldman was exiled to Russia, but she left the workers' paradise in 1921, settling in London three years later. Her denunciation of capitalism, as well as Bolshevism, led to increasing political isolation.

◆ "Anarchism: What It Really Stands For"

In her introduction to this essay, Goldman identifies anarchism as a progressive idea that is opposed by traditional society, which would choose to block a new dawn for humankind. It is worth noting that although Goldman was a champion of women's emancipation, in her language she employs the word *man* in a universal sense. Referring to anarchism as revolutionary and innovative, Goldman concludes that opposition to the philosophy was based upon the misperception that anarchism was beautiful but impractical or that it represented violence and destruction. Refuting the misunderstanding, Goldman argues that anarchism is the most practical of all philosophies, for it is based upon "building and sustaining new life." As for the assertion that anarchism encouraged only destruction and violence, Goldman maintains that anarchism attacks the influence of ignorance and seeks only to destroy the parasitic institutions—the weeds in the garden of society.

Goldman then proceeds to offer a definition of anarchism as "the philosophy of a new social order based on liberty unrestricted by man-made law; the theory that all forms of government rest on violence, and are therefore wrong and harmful, as well as unnecessary." She goes on to argue that mankind has been unable to attain the free social order envisioned by anarchism owing to the false dichotomy between the individual and social instincts. Goldman insists that out of free individuals comes a renewed sense of social cohesion. Goldman maintains that anarchism offers freedom for man and the blending of individual and social instincts by attacking the three major influences enslaving mankind: religion, property, and government.

Although she devotes far more attention to the denunciation of property and the state, Goldman supports the conclusion of Karl Marx that religion is the opiate of the masses. Referring to religion as a black monster, Goldman calls upon man to assert his supremacy over the false image of a supreme being. In this regard Goldman's thoughts are similar to Marx's argument that religion is a social construction by the ruling class to render the masses subservient.

The anarchist writer provides greater analysis of the role played by property in enslaving mankind, agreeing with Joseph Proudhon that ownership of property is theft. Writing with an angry flourish, Goldman describes property possession as fostering a lust for wealth and power while robbing workers of the product produced by their labor. But Goldman goes beyond the condemnation of monopolistic power concentrated in the hands of American captains of industry by addressing the alienation of labor, which is an important component in the Marxist critique of capitalism. Goldman describes the centralization of property in the factory system as limiting workers to dull and repetitious activities devoid of beauty and creativity. Anarchism, Goldman maintains, envisions a society in which the individual is free to select his or her working conditions and mode of labor. Accordingly, Goldman argues that in order to unleash labor as a creative force, economic arrangements must be governed by the actions of voluntary productive and distributive associations. Such voluntary associations, however, are prohibited by the forces of property backed by the coercive powers of the state.

Goldman thus concludes her powerful essay with a condemnation of the state. It is here that Goldman gains a degree of separation from Marxism, as she has little patience for a dictatorship of the proletariat or a withering away of the state. Goldman agrees with the American philosopher Ralph Waldo Emerson that "all government in essence is tyranny." In quoting Emerson and Henry David Thoreau, whom she describes as the "greatest American anarchist," Goldman is making an effort to place anarchism within the American strain and not construe it simply as an alien European ideology. She asserts that whether it is a monarchy or an ostensibly representative republic such as the United States, government has the goal of subordinating the individual to the powers of the state. To control the individual and protect property, the state employs legal and police terror because there is no social harmony in a society where property is held only by a few. Rather than preventing crime, Goldman proclaims that the state encourages criminal activity by perpetuating a system in which the individual is deprived of the opportunity to fully express joy and creativity in labor. She believes that anarchism promises "an order that will guarantee to every human being free access to the earth and full enjoyment of the necessities of life, according to individual desires, tastes, and inclinations."

The liberating possibilities of anarchism, however, will not be achieved through electoral politics. Instead, Goldman proclaims that anarchy assumes rebellion against the traditional order. She hedges, however, on calling for violent revolution. She concludes that in more mature political systems, such as that which exists in the United States, it may be possible to bring about an anarchist society through the direct action of labor organization or the general strike.

◆ **"The Psychology of Political Violence"**

In this essay Goldman expands upon her analysis of the role violence should play in bringing about an anarchist

Time Line

1917	■ **June 14** Goldman delivers an antiwar speech at Forward Hall in New York City.
	■ **June 15** Alexander Berkman and Goldman are arrested for violating the Espionage Act by opposing conscription and American participation in World War I.
1919	■ After being released from prison, Goldman is deported to Russia.
1921	■ **December** A disillusioned Goldman leaves Russia.
1931	■ Goldman publishes her autobiography, *Living My Life*.
1934	■ **February 2** Goldman begins a ninety-day lecture tour in the United States.
1936–1939	■ Goldman plays an active role in supporting the Spanish Republic.
1940	■ **May 14** Goldman dies in Toronto, Canada.

social order. Her arguments regarding violence are somewhat ambiguous and, her critics might say, disingenuous. She fails to address the ideas of her mentor Johann Most, who believed that the "propaganda of the deed," such as the political assassination of a tyrant, might spark the masses to undertake revolutionary action. Instead, Goldman discounts any connection between anarchism and political violence, arguing that capitalist authorities make false accusations and use anarchists as scapegoats to conceal their own destructive deeds.

Goldman commences her psychology of violence essay with the assertion that the *Attentäter*, a revolutionary committing an act of political violence, is not the lunatic or destructive monster constructed by the capitalist press. Instead, the revolutionary who takes up the gun or tosses a bomb is driven to such drastic means by watching the

Police charge rioters in Haymarket Square, Chicago. (Library of Congress)

suffering of humanity under capitalist oppression. She concludes that anarchists display such love and affection for their fellow man that they are willing to surrender their lives if such action will redeem humanity. Furthermore, the real perpetrators of violence are the many who silently witness exploitation and are unwilling to take any action to alter the economic suffering and oppression. Confronted with this conspiracy of silence, anarchists who love humanity are goaded into action by the capitalist system.

After celebrating those martyrs whose conscience propelled them to fight for humanity, Goldman then backs away from any association between violence and anarchism. She observes that many anarchists are blamed by the capitalist press for bombings and shootings initiated by the police. In support of her argument, she cites the Haymarket riot in Chicago on May 4, 1886. Following a day of labor agitation, someone tossed a bomb, resulting in the death of a policeman, Mathias J. Degan. A riot ensued, resulting in the deaths of seven more policemen and several civilians. In response, eight anarchists were arrested for murder. Following a trial appealing to the political and ethnic prejudices of the jury, the anarchists were convicted. Four were executed before Illinois Governor John Peter Altgeld pardoned the Haymarket defendants. The origins of

the actual bombing remain the subject of controversy, but Goldman makes it clear that she perceives the Haymarket affair as an example of police provocation.

Goldman next turns her attention to the assassination of President McKinley. She defends the assassin Leon Czolgosz by observing that the young man was driven to violence by a conscience that could no longer tolerate the republic of economic exploitation over which McKinley presided. Although many anarchist colleagues feared that her defense of Czolgosz would bring government repression, Goldman insisted upon holding the capitalist industrial order responsible for the assassination. She also defends the attempted assassination of Henry Clay Frick in 1893 by her friend Alexander Berkman, asserting that the brutal murder of eleven steel workers at Homestead had motivated Berkman, rather than the philosophy of anarchism.

Goldman concludes her argument by examining European political acts of violence attributed to anarchists. Focusing on the bombing of the Paris Chamber of Deputies in 1894 by Auguste Vaillant, the murder of the Spanish prime minister Canovas del Castillo by Michele Angiolillo, and Gaetano Bresci's assassination of the Italian king Umberto I, Goldman proclaims that these acts were the result of economic and political oppression that flamed the conscience of the perpetrators.

In a somewhat ambiguous conclusion to the essay, Goldman proclaims that anarchism is a philosophy that considers human life to be sacred, yet anarchism does not believe in submission of the human spirit. Compared with the tyranny of capitalism, the political violence of individuals motivated by conscience are minuscule. Thus, Goldman concludes that it is man's greatest obligation to resist tyranny. In "The Psychology of Violence," Goldman reveals the ambiguity of her thoughts on the relationship between violence and anarchy—a subject that produced controversy throughout her life.

◆ "Marriage and Love"

In her life as a political activist, Emma Goldman earned a well-deserved reputation as an advocate for women's emancipation. As an anarchist, however, she argued that women must assert more direct control over their lives rather than depend upon such bourgeois reforms as suffrage bestowed by an exploitive capitalist state. At the core of women's emancipation, according to Goldman, were the issues of marriage and love. Goldman associates the power of love with the liberating nature of anarchism, while the institution of marriage represents the coercive powers of the state seeking to enslave women by making them the property of a husband. Thus, the oppressive institution of marriage is a product of capitalist exploitation. Asserting that love and marriage are antagonistic, Goldman argues that marriage is primarily an economic arrangement in which women provide sexual favors in exchange for the husband's labor and financial support of the family. Marriage, in fact, becomes an insurance policy fostering female dependency.

Still, Goldman insists that owing to the puritanical restraints of American culture, women are rendered ignorant of the sexual role that they are expected to perform. In her embrace of female sexuality free from the restraints of marriage, Goldman was criticized for what respectable middle-class types often termed "free love." But Goldman argues that far greater tragedy and disappointment await young women who surrender their dreams of love to the mundane concerns of economic security.

Goldman scoffs at the idea that marriage is required to protect children, observing that child labor and abuse, along with orphanages, provide ample evidence that capitalist marriage fails to protect the interests of children. Instead, Goldman proclaims that women should be free to have fewer children and not be dictated to by church and state, seeking more sources of labor for the exploitation of capitalist society. Goldman concludes that women should be liberated from the tyranny of marriage and be free to pursue love, which she insists is the only hope for the world. In her personal life, Goldman sought independence from male domination through the liberating power of love and anarchism; however, she was often disappointed in her personal relationships.

◆ Speech against Conscription and War

On April 2, 1917, President Woodrow Wilson asked the Congress for a declaration of war against Germany, asserting that American participation in World War I would make the world "safe for democracy." Anarchists such as Emma Goldman denounced American entrance into the conflict, arguing that the powers of the state would be increased in pursuit of a war that would benefit bankers and munitions makers at the expense of the international working class whose blood would be shed to further imperialist and capitalist goals. Accompanying the declaration of war was a conscription act that forced young men into military service—the very sort of government oppression that Goldman proclaims led immigrants to flee the tyranny of czarist Russia.

Despite threats against her life, Goldman delivered a forceful speech on June 14, 1917, in Forward Hall in New York City, articulating her opposition to conscription and war. The meeting was convened following the convictions of two young anarchists, Morris Becker and Louis Kramer, for refusing conscription. Goldman began her address by telling her working-class immigrant audience that she would speak in English rather than her customary Yiddish so that the repressive forces of the state would understand her words. Appealing to the aspirations of immigrants who flocked to America's shores feeling the tyranny of European despotism, she scolds Americans for deserting the principles of liberty symbolized by the Statue of Liberty. She condemns President Wilson for sacrificing American lives in pursuit of a democracy "which has never yet existed in the United States of America."

Goldman asserts that the coercion pursued by the Wilson administration is yet another example of the imperialist and capitalist exploitation practiced by the American state. In her challenge to the nature of American democracy, she notes that Wilson was reelected to the presidency in 1916 for keeping the nation out of war, yet a year later Wilson led the country into war without the consent of the American people. In response to those who argued that Congress approved the declaration of war and conscription law, Goldman proclaims that she will only accept a legal order in which those "taking human life are going to be called before the bar of human justice and not before a wretched little court which is called your law of the United States."

Maintaining that conscription is unnecessary because Americans will support a war in which they believe, Goldman evokes the example of the Spanish-American War, seemingly ignoring the imperialistic ramifications of that conflict. Nevertheless, she continues to employ American history in the construction of her argument, insisting that the ruling class of the United States, in forcing war upon the American people, has departed from the principles enunciated by the nation's founders and contained in the Declaration of Independence.

In her conclusion, Goldman comes close to advocating revolution, asserting that the oppressive powers of prison and the state will not silence the anarchists. Warning Woodrow Wilson of the fate suffered by the ruling classes of Bourbon France and czarist Russia, Goldman proclaims that government suppression will only fan the flames of discontent and encourage the American people to establish a true

"Anarchism, then, really stands for the liberation of the human mind from the dominion of religion; the liberation of the human body from the dominion of property; and liberation from the shackles and restraint of government."

("Anarchism: What It Really Stands For")

"Anarchism stands for a social order based on the free grouping of individuals for the purpose of producing real social wealth; an order that will guarantee to every human being free access to the earth and full enjoyment of the necessities of life, according to individual desires, tastes, and inclinations."

("Anarchism: What It Really Stands For")

"It would say that resistance to tyranny is man's highest ideal. So long as tyranny exists, in whatever form, man's deepest aspiration must resist it as inevitably as man must breathe."

("The Psychology of Political Violence")

"The institution of marriage makes a parasite of women, an absolute dependent. It incapacitates her for life's struggle, annihilates her social consciousness, paralyzes her imagination, and then imposes its gracious protection, which is in reality a snare, a travesty on human character."

("Marriage and Love")

"If the world is ever to give birth to true companionship and oneness, not marriage, but love will be the parent."

("Marriage and Love")

"The only law that I recognize is the law which ministers to the needs of humanity, which makes men and women finer and better and more humane, the kind of law which teaches children that human life is sacred, and that those who aim for the purpose of taking human life are going to be called before the bar of human justice and not before a wretched little court which is called your law of the United States."

(Speech against Conscription and War)

democracy. While Goldman's call to action was unable to halt application of the conscription laws, she and other radicals certainly threatened the Wilson administration, which used the war emergency as an opportunity to silence the Industrial Workers of the World, anarchists, and Socialists. The day following her speech at Forward Hall, Goldman was arrested for violating the Espionage Act by inducing eligible young man to refuse registration for conscription.

Impact and Legacy

During the "red scare" following World War I, such government authorities as Attorney General A. Mitchell Palmer and the future director of the Federal Bureau of Investigation J. Edgar Hoover perceived Emma Goldman as a real and present danger to the United States. Largely self-educated, Goldman had left czarist Russia to pursue greater freedom in the United States, where she became disillusioned with the American ruling class and capitalist system.

Embracing the principles of anarchism in the period between 1893 and 1917, Goldman enjoyed a reputation as a public speaker and writer who challenged the American capitalist order. Urging that workers employ direct actions, such as the general strike, Goldman was an advocate for the syndicalism promoted by the Industrial Workers of the World. As a champion of women's rights, she questioned the institution of marriage and insisted that working-class women receive adequate birth control information. Her writing on anarchism and violence was more ambiguous, declaring that violent action against the ruling political order was primarily a reaction to exploitation rather than a reflection of anarchist principles.

After her death in 1940 Goldman's faith in the liberating possibilities of anarchism seemed anachronistic in a world increasingly dominated by ideological conflict. As the struggle against fascism of World War II disintegrated into the cold war between capitalism and Communism, Goldman's life and work were often ignored and forgotten. During the late 1960s and early 1970s, however, there was a renewed interest in Goldman's writings by political activists denouncing the excesses of American imperialism and capitalism while seeking to develop a participatory democracy more in line with the associational principles of anarchism.

Questions for Further Study

1. Do you agree with the presentation of anarchism and political violence that Goldman offers in the first two documents? Why or why not? Do great social ills, as she suggests, make it necessary for people of conviction to retaliate in extreme ways, or does the very act of choosing violence itself lead to corruption? When she says of Leon Czolgosz and others that "theirs was the attitude of the social student," is she making a valid point or simply excusing murder?

2. In her essay on marriage and love Goldman turns traditional concepts of sexuality on their heads: Thus, for instance, she uses the term "filthy" not to describe what others might have called lewd behavior but rather to identify marriage itself. What are the strongest arguments she makes for the abandonment of traditional family institutions, and what are some of her weaker points on this issue? To what extent was she reacting to the extreme sexual restraint that characterized the late nineteenth century, and to what extent was she responding to the rapid social changes taking place in the wake of World War I?

3. Research the Yiddish language, which has a rich history and great political significance. How did Goldman's background in Yiddish influence her as a writer? What are some of the peculiarities of the language that show up in her English works?

4. How did Goldman's experience in Soviet Russia change her political views? What did she see in the then newly established Communist state that disillusioned her? In what ways did this experience shape the political opinions of her later life, and how did she defend herself against fellow leftists who accused her of being a traitor to the radical cause?

5. Goldman's was a life filled with adventure. Discuss her biography and the major phases of her life. In what ways is she a role model for women, and what aspects of her life are less worthy of imitation?

The women's movement of the 1960s also found inspiration in Goldman's life and writings, and scholars devoted considerable new attention to her ideas. Her championing of personal liberation is appealing to many contemporary women and political activists, but her perceptions of political violence remain troubling for many attracted to her rhetoric of individual and social liberation.

Key Sources

The Emma Goldman Papers are available on seventy reels of microfilm from the publisher Chadwyck-Healey. Selections from the Emma Goldman Papers are also available online from the University of California Berkeley Digital Library (http://sunsite.berkeley.edu/Goldman/). Candace Falk has published two volumes from the Goldman Papers—*Emma Goldman: A Documentary History of the American Years*, Vol. 1: *Made for America, 1890–1902* (2003), and Vol. 2: *Making Speech Free, 1902–1909* (2005). Goldman's pieces for the anarchist journal *Mother Earth* are collected in *Anarchism and Other Essays*, which was originally published in 1910 and 1917, with a reprint in 1969. Essential reading for Goldman remains *My Disillusionment in Russia* (1923) and her autobiography, *Living My Life* (1931).

Further Reading

■ Articles
Fine, Sidney. "Anarchism and the Assassination of McKinley." *American Historical Review* 60 (July 1955): 777–799.

■ Books
Berkman, Alexander. *Prison Memoirs of an Anarchist*. 1912. Reprint. New York: Schocken Books, 1970.

Drinnon, Richard. *Rebel in Paradise: A Biography of Emma Goldman*. Chicago: University of Chicago Press, 1961.

Falk, Candace. *Love, Anarchy, and Emma Goldman*. New York: Holt, Rinehart and Winston, 1984.

Gelfant, Blanche H. "Speaking Her Own Piece: Emma Goldman and the Discursive Skeins of Autobiography." In *American Autobiography: Retrospect and Prospect*, ed. Paul John Eakin. Madison: University of Wisconsin Press, 1991.

Morton, Marian J. *Emma Goldman and the American Left: "Nowhere at Home."* New York: Twayne Publishers, 1992.

Wexler, Alice. *Emma Goldman: An Intimate Life*. New York: Pantheon Books, 1984.

———. *Emma Goldman in Exile: From the Russian Revolution to the Spanish Civil War*. Boston: Beacon Press, 1989.

—Ron Briley

"Anarchism: What It Really Stands For" (1917)

The history of human growth and development is at the same time the history of the terrible struggle of every new idea heralding the approach of a brighter dawn. In its tenacious hold on tradition, the Old has never hesitated to make use of the foulest and cruelest means to stay the advent of the New, in whatever form or period the latter may have asserted itself. Nor need we retrace our steps into the distant past to realize the enormity of opposition, difficulties, and hardships placed in the path of every progressive idea. The rack, the thumbscrew, and the knout are still with us; so are the convict's garb and the social wrath, all conspiring against the spirit that is serenely marching on....

What, then, are the objections? First, Anarchism is impractical, though a beautiful ideal. Second, Anarchism stands for violence and destruction, hence it must be repudiated as vile and dangerous. Both the intelligent man and the ignorant mass judge not from a thorough knowledge of the subject, but either from hearsay or false interpretation....

Anarchism is indeed practical. More than any other idea, it is helping to do away with the wrong and foolish; more than any other idea, it is building and sustaining new life....

Destruction and violence! How is the ordinary man to know that the most violent element in society is ignorance; that its power of destruction is the very thing Anarchism is combating? Nor is he aware that Anarchism, whose roots, as it were, are part of nature's forces, destroys, not healthful tissue, but parasitic growths that feed on the life's essence of society. It is merely clearing the soil from weeds and sagebrush, that it may eventually bear healthy fruit....

Anarchism urges man to think, to investigate, to analyze every proposition; but that the brain capacity of the average reader be not taxed too much, I also shall begin with a definition, and then elaborate on the latter.

ANARCHISM:—The philosophy of a new social order based on liberty unrestricted by man-made law; the theory that all forms of government rest on violence, and are therefore wrong and harmful, as well as unnecessary....

Anarchism is the only philosophy which brings to man the consciousness of himself; which maintains that God, the State, and society are non-existent, that their promises are null and void, since they can be fulfilled only through man's subordination. Anarchism is therefore the teacher of the unity of life; not merely in nature, but in man....

Anarchism is the great liberator of man from the phantoms that have held him captive; it is the arbiter and pacifier of the two forces for individual and social harmony. To accomplish that unity, Anarchism has declared war on the pernicious influences which have so far prevented the harmonious blending of individual and social instincts, the individual and society.

Religion, the dominion of the human mind; Property, the dominion of human needs; and Government, the dominion of human conduct, represent the stronghold of man's enslavement and all the horrors it entails. Religion! How it dominates man's mind, how it humiliates and degrades his soul. God is everything, man is nothing, says religion. But out of that nothing God has created a kingdom so despotic, so tyrannical, so cruel, so terribly exacting that naught but gloom and tears and blood have ruled the world since gods began. Anarchism rouses man to rebellion against this black monster. Break your mental fetters, says Anarchism to man, for not until you think and judge for yourself will you get rid of the dominion of darkness, the greatest obstacle to all progress.

Property, the dominion of man's needs, the denial of the right to satisfy his needs. Time was when property claimed a divine right, when it came to man with the same refrain, even as religion, "Sacrifice! Abnegate! Submit!" The spirit of Anarchism has lifted man from his prostrate position. He now stands erect, with his face toward the light. He has learned to see the insatiable, devouring, devastating nature of property, and he is preparing to strike the monster dead....

Just as religion has fettered the human mind, and as property, or the monopoly of things, has subdued and stifled man's needs, so has the State enslaved his spirit, dictating every phase of conduct. "All government in essence," says Emerson, "is tyranny." It matters not whether it is government by divine right or majority rule. In every instance its aim is the absolute subordination of the individual....

The most absurd apology for authority and law is that they serve to diminish crime. Aside from the fact that the State is itself the greatest criminal, breaking every written and natural law, stealing in the form of taxes, killing in the form of war and capital punishment, it has come to an absolute standstill in coping with crime. It has failed utterly to destroy or even minimize the horrible scourge of its own creation.

Crime is naught but misdirected energy. So long as every institution of today, economic, political, social, and moral, conspires to misdirect human energy into wrong channels; so long as most people are out of place doing the things they hate to do, living a life they loathe to live, crime will be inevitable, and all the laws on the statutes can only increase, but never do away with, crime....

Anarchism, then, really stands for the liberation of the human mind from the dominion of religion; the liberation of the human body from the dominion of property; liberation from the shackles and restraint of government. Anarchism stands for a social order based on the free grouping of individuals for the purpose of producing real social wealth; an order that will guarantee to every human being free access to the earth and full enjoyment of the necessities of life, according to individual desires, tastes, and inclinations....

Direct action, having proven effective along economic lines, is equally potent in the environment of the individual. There a hundred forces encroach upon his being, and only persistent resistance to them will finally set him free. Direct action against the authority in the shop, direct action against the authority of the law, direct action against the invasive, meddlesome authority of our moral code, is the logical, consistent method of Anarchism....

Anarchism, the great leaven of thought, is today permeating every phase of human endeavor. Science, art, literature, the drama, the effort for economic betterment, in fact every individual and social opposition to the existing disorder of things, is illumined by the spiritual light of Anarchism. It is the philosophy of the sovereignty of the individual. It is the theory of social harmony. It is the great, surging, living truth that is reconstructing the world, and that will usher in the Dawn.

Glossary

leaven	an element that improves the larger whole
rack…	
thumbscrew…knout	the first two being medieval torture devices, used respectively for stretching a victim's body and crushing his or her hands, and the third a particularly brutal type of whip that employs rawhide and sometimes even metal

"THE PSYCHOLOGY OF POLITICAL VIOLENCE" (1917)

The ignorant mass looks upon the man who makes a violent protest against our social and economic iniquities as upon a wild beast, a cruel, heartless monster, whose joy it is to destroy life and bathe in blood; or at best, as upon an irresponsible lunatic. Yet nothing is further from the truth. As a matter of fact, those who have studied the character and personality of these men, or who have come in close contact with them, are agreed that it is their supersensitiveness to the wrong and injustice surrounding them which compels them to pay the toll of our social crimes. The most noted writers and poets, discussing the psychology of political offenders, have paid them the highest tribute. Could anyone assume that these men had advised violence, or even approved of the acts? Certainly not. Theirs was the attitude of the social student, of the man who knows that beyond every violent act there is a vital cause....

That every act of political violence should nowadays be attributed to Anarchists is not at all surprising. Yet it is a fact known to almost everyone familiar with the Anarchist movement that a great number of acts, for which Anarchists had to suffer, either originated with the capitalist press or were instigated, if not directly perpetrated, by the police.

That the American police can perjure themselves with the same ease, that they are just as merciless, just as brutal and cunning as their European colleagues, has been proven on more than one occasion. We need only recall the tragedy of the eleventh of November, 1887, known as the Haymarket Riot....

When we approach the tragedy of September sixth, 1901, we are confronted by one of the most striking examples of how little social theories are responsible for an act of political violence. "Leon Czolgosz, an Anarchist, incited to commit the act by Emma Goldman." To be sure, has she not incited violence even before her birth, and will she not continue to do so beyond death? Everything is possible with the Anarchists.

Today, even, nine years after the tragedy, after it was proven a hundred times that Emma Goldman had nothing to do with the event, that no evidence whatsoever exists to indicate that Czolgosz ever called himself an Anarchist, we are confronted with the same lie, fabricated by the police and perpetuated by the press. No living soul ever heard Czolgosz make that statement, nor is there a single written word to prove that the boy ever breathed the accusation. Nothing but ignorance and insane hysteria, which have never yet been able to solve the simplest problem of cause and effect.

The President of a free Republic killed! What else can be the cause, except that the *Attentäter* must have been insane, or that he was incited to the act.

A free Republic! How a myth will maintain itself, how it will continue to deceive, to dupe, and blind even the comparatively intelligent to its monstrous absurdities. A free Republic! And yet within a little over thirty years a small band of parasites have successfully robbed the American people, and trampled upon the fundamental principles, laid down by the fathers of this country, guaranteeing to every man, woman, and child "life, liberty, and the pursuit of happiness."...

But, it is often asked, have not acknowledged Anarchists committed acts of violence? Certainly they have, always however ready to shoulder the responsibility. My contention is that they were impelled, not by the teachings of Anarchism, but by the tremendous pressure of conditions, making life unbearable to their sensitive natures. Obviously, Anarchism, or any other social theory, making man a conscious social unit, will act as a leaven for rebellion. This is not a mere assertion, but a fact verified by all experience. A close examination of the circumstances bearing upon this question will further clarify my position.

Let us consider some of the most important Anarchist acts within the last two decades. Strange as it may seem, one of the most significant deeds of political violence occurred here in America, in connection with the Homestead strike of 1892.

During that memorable time the Carnegie Steel Company organized a conspiracy to crush the Amalgamated Association of Iron and Steel Workers. Henry Clay Frick, then Chairman of the Company, was intrusted with that democratic task. He lost no time in carrying out the policy of breaking the Union, the policy which he had so successfully practiced during his reign of terror in the coke regions. Secretly, and while peace negotiations were being purposely prolonged, Frick supervised the military preparations, the fortification of the Homestead

Steel Works, the erection of a high board fence, capped with barbed wire and provided with loopholes for sharpshooters. And then, in the dead of night, he attempted to smuggle his army of hired Pinkerton thugs into Homestead, which act precipitated the terrible carnage of the steel workers. Not content with the death of eleven victims, killed in the Pinkerton skirmish, Henry Clay Frick, good Christian and free American, straightway began the hounding down of the helpless wives and orphans, by ordering them out of the wretched Company houses.

The whole country was aroused over these inhuman outrages. Hundreds of voices were raised in protest, calling on Frick to desist, not to go too far. Yes, hundreds of people protested,—as one objects to annoying flies. Only one there was who actively responded to the outrage at Homestead,—Alexander Berkman. Yes, he was an Anarchist. He gloried in that fact, because it was the only force that made the discord between his spiritual longing and the world without at all bearable. Yet not Anarchism, as such, but the brutal slaughter of the eleven steel workers was the urge for Alexander Berkman's act, his attempt on the life of Henry Clay Frick....

Anarchism, more than any other social theory, values human life above things. All Anarchists agree

Glossary

Amalgamated Association of Iron and Steel Workers	labor union founded in 1876, merged with the Steel Workers Organizing Committee in 1935, and absorbed into the United Steelworkers in 1942
Attentäter	a German word meaning "assassin" (that is, someone who targets political figures for murder)
Carnegie Steel Company	an industrial enterprise founded by Andrew Carnegie in the 1870s and sold in 1901 to the United States Steel Company
Henry Clay Frick	American industrialist (1849–1919) nicknamed "the most hated man in America" for actions such as the suppression of the Homestead Strike
Homestead strike of 1892	one of the most significant strikes in U.S. history, which occurred in Pittsburgh in June and July 1892
leaven	an element that improves the larger whole
Leon Czolgosz	young anarchist who shot President William McKinley in Buffalo, New York, and was later executed for the crime
nowise	in no way
small band of parasites have successfully robbed the American people	a reference to the so-called robber barons, industrialists and financiers (among them, Carnegie and Frick) who built vast fortunes in the late nineteenth century
Tolstoy	Russian novelist and political activist Leo Tolstoy (1828–1910), author of *War and Peace* and *Anna Karenina*
tragedy of September sixth, 1901	the assassination of President William McKinley
tragedy of the eleventh of November, 1887, known as the Haymarket Riot	not the actual Haymarket riot, in which eight policemen and many civilians were killed during a workers' demonstration in Chicago (May 4, 1886), but rather the execution of four anarchists charged with causing those deaths
the world without	the world outside himself

with Tolstoy in this fundamental truth: if the production of any commodity necessitates the sacrifice of human life, society should do without that commodity, but it can not do without that life. That, however, nowise indicates that Anarchism teaches submission. How can it, when it knows that all suffering, all misery, all ills, result from the evil of submission?

Has not some American ancestor said, many years ago, that resistance to tyranny is obedience to God? And he was not an Anarchist even. It would say that resistance to tyranny is man's highest ideal. So long as tyranny exists, in whatever form, man's deepest aspiration must resist it as inevitably as man must breathe.

Compared with the wholesale violence of capital and government, political acts of violence are but a drop in the ocean. That so few resist is the strongest proof how terrible must be the conflict between their souls and unbearable social iniquities.

High strung, like a violin string, they weep and moan for life, so relentless, so cruel, so terribly inhuman. In a desperate moment the string breaks. Untuned ears hear nothing but discord. But those who feel the agonized cry understand its harmony; they hear in it the fulfillment of the most compelling moment of human nature.

Such is the psychology of political violence.

"Marriage and Love" (1917)

The popular notion about marriage and love is that they are synonymous, that they spring from the same motives, and cover the same human needs. Like most popular notions this also rests not on actual facts, but on superstition.

Marriage and love have nothing in common; they are as far apart as the poles; are, in fact, antagonistic to each other. No doubt some marriages have been the result of love. Not, however, because love could assert itself only in marriage; much rather is it because few people can completely outgrow a convention. There are to-day large numbers of men and women to whom marriage is naught but a farce, but who submit to it for the sake of public opinion. At any rate, while it is true that some marriages are based on love, and while it is equally true that in some cases love continues in married life, I maintain that it does so regardless of marriage, and not because of it....

Marriage is primarily an economic arrangement, an insurance pact. It differs from the ordinary life insurance agreement only in that it is more binding, more exacting. Its returns are insignificantly small compared with the investments. In taking out an insurance policy one pays for it in dollars and cents, always at liberty to discontinue payments. If, however, woman's premium is a husband, she pays for it with her name, her privacy, her self-respect, her very life, "until death doth part." Moreover, the marriage insurance condemns her to life-long dependency, to parasitism, to complete uselessness, individual as well as social. Man, too, pays his toll, but as his sphere is wider, marriage does not limit him as much as woman. He feels his chains more in an economic sense....

From infancy, almost, the average girl is told that marriage is her ultimate goal; therefore her training and education must be directed towards that end. Like the mute beast fattened for slaughter, she is prepared for that. Yet, strange to say, she is allowed to know much less about her function as wife and mother than the ordinary artisan of his trade. It is indecent and filthy for a respectable girl to know anything of the marital relation. Oh, for the inconsistency of respectability, that needs the marriage vow to turn something which is filthy into the purest and most sacred arrangement that none dare question or criticize. Yet that is exactly the attitude of the average upholder of marriage. The prospective wife and mother is kept in complete ignorance of her only asset in the competitive field—sex. Thus she enters into life-long relations with a man only to find herself shocked, repelled, outraged beyond measure by the most natural and healthy instinct, sex. It is safe to say that a large percentage of the unhappiness, misery, distress, and physical suffering of matrimony is due to the criminal ignorance in sex matters that is being extolled as a great virtue. Nor is it at all an exaggeration when I say that more than one home has been broken up because of this deplorable fact.

If, however, woman is free and big enough to learn the mystery of sex without the sanction of State or Church, she will stand condemned as utterly unfit to become the wife of a "good" man, his goodness consisting of an empty head and plenty of money. Can there be anything more outrageous than the idea that a healthy, grown woman, full of life and passion, must deny nature's demand, must subdue her most intense craving, undermine her health and break her spirit, must stunt her vision, abstain from the depth and glory of sex experience until a "good" man comes along to take her unto himself as a wife? That is precisely what marriage means....

The woman considers her position as worker transitory, to be thrown aside for the first bidder. That is why it is infinitely harder to organize women than men. "Why should I join a union? I am going to get married, to have a home." Has she not been taught from infancy to look upon that as her ultimate calling? She learns soon enough that the home, though not so large a prison as the factory, has more solid doors and bars. It has a keeper so faithful that naught can escape him. The most tragic part, however, is that the home no longer frees her from wage slavery; it only increases her task....

But the child, how is it to be protected, if not for marriage? After all, is not that the most important consideration? The sham, the hypocrisy of it! Marriage protecting the child, yet thousands of children destitute and homeless. Marriage protecting the child, yet orphan asylums and reformatories over crowded, the Society for the Prevention of Cruelty to Children keeping busy in rescuing the little victims from "loving" parents, to place them under more loving care, the Gerry Society. Oh, the mockery of it!...

As to the protection of the woman—therein lies the curse of marriage. Not that it really protects her, but the very idea is so revolting, such an outrage and insult on life, so degrading to human dignity, as to forever condemn this parasitic institution.

It is like that other paternal arrangement—capitalism. It robs man of his birthright, stunts his growth, poisons his body, keeps him in ignorance, in poverty and dependence, and then institutes charities that thrive on the last vestige of man's self-respect.

The institution of marriage makes a parasite of woman, an absolute dependent. It incapacitates her for life's struggle, annihilates her social consciousness, paralyzes her imagination, and then imposes its gracious protection, which is in reality a snare, a travesty on human character.

Love, the strongest and deepest element in all life, the harbinger of hope, of joy, of ecstasy; love, the defier of all laws, of all conventions; love, the freest, the most powerful moulder of human destiny; how can such an all-compelling force be synonymous with that poor little State and Church-begotten weed, marriage?…

Some day, some day men and women will rise, they will reach the mountain peak, they will meet big and strong and free, ready to receive, to partake, and to bask in the golden rays of love. What fancy, what imagination, what poetic genius can foresee even approximately the potentialities of such a force in the life of men and women. If the world is ever to give birth to true companionship and oneness, not marriage, but love will be the parent.

SPEECH AGAINST CONSCRIPTION AND WAR (1917)

This is not the place to applaud or shout Hurrah for Emma Goldman. We have more serious things to talk about and some serious things to do. First of all I wish to say to you, all of you, workers, men and women from the East Side, that I regret deeply that I cannot speak to you in the language I have always spoken from this platform; that I cannot speak to you tonight in Yiddish. I shall speak English because I want those representing the State and Militarism and the Courts and Prisons to understand what I have to say....

Evidently, America has to learn a salutary lesson and it is going to pay a terrible price. It is going to shed oceans of blood, it is going to heap mountains of human sacrifices of men of this country who are able to create and produce, to whom the future belongs. They are to be slaughtered in blood and in sacrifice in the name of a thing which has never yet existed in the United States of America, in the name of democracy and liberty.

My friends, there are people who say and tell you that when they prophecy something the prophecy comes true. I am sorry to say that I am one such and I have to say the same. For thirty years we have pointed out to you that this democratic State which is a government supposedly of the people, by the people and for the people has now become one of the most Imperialistic that the world has ever laid its eyes upon....

If war is necessary, only the people must decide whether they want war or not, and as long as the people have not given their consent I deny that the President of the United States has any right to declare it; I deny that the President or those who back the President have any right to tell the people that they shall take their sons and husbands and brothers and lovers and shall conscript them in order to ship them across the seas for the conquest of militarism and the support of wealth and power in the United States. You say that is a law. I deny your law. I don't believe in it.

The only law that I recognize is the law which ministers to the needs of humanity, which makes men and women finer and better and more humane, the kind of law which teaches children that human life is sacred, and that those who arm for the purpose of taking human life are going to be called before the bar of human justice and not before a wretched little court which is called your law of the United States. And so, friends, the people have not yet decided whether they want war and the people are going to say, ultimately, whether they want war or not....

If the framers of the Declaration of Independence if Jefferson or Henry or the others, if they could look down upon the country and see what their offspring has done to it, how they have outraged it, how they have robbed it, how they have polluted it—why, my friends, they would turn in their graves. They would rise again and they would cleanse this country from its internal enemies, and that is the ruling class of the United States. There is a lesson you are going to learn and terrible as it is for us we nevertheless are glad that you will have to learn that lesson.

And now we come down to the tragedy that was committed in the United States Court in the State of New York yesterday, when two boys were sentenced. It is not only a tragedy because they were sentenced. Such things happen every day, hundreds, thousands of innocent working men are sent to the prison and the penitentiary, thousands of unfortunates throughout the world as well as here in so-called free America and nobody ever hears anything about it. It is an ordinary, commonplace thing to do. But the tragedy of yesterday is in the fact that a Judge, supported as you have been told by your money, protected by public opinion, protected by the President, the tragedy of it is that that Judge had the impudence and audacity to insult Kramer and Becker after he gave them the sentence of such horrible dimensions. Think of a man like that who sits there in judgment on other

Glossary

Yiddish	a language, whose name literally means "Jewish," that is based in German but uses elements of Hebrew and Aramaic

human beings. Think what must be his character, what must be his mind, what must be his soul, if he can spit human beings in the face, only because he has got the power....

I wish to say here, and I don't say it with any authority and I don't say it as a prophet, I merely tell you—I merely tell you the more people you lock up, the more will be the idealists who will take their place; the more of the human voice you suppress, the greater and louder and the profounder will be the human voice. At present it is a mere rumbling, but that rumbling is increasing in volume, it is growing in depth, it is spreading all over the country until it will be raised into a thunder and people of America will rise and say, we want to be a democracy, to be sure, but we want the kind of democracy which means liberty and opportunity to every man and woman in America.

Barry Goldwater (AP/Wide World Photos)

BARRY GOLDWATER 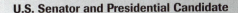 1909–1998

U.S. Senator and Presidential Candidate

Featured Documents
◆ Acceptance Speech for the Presidential Nomination of the Republican Party (1964)
◆ Address to the Republican National Convention (1984)

Overview

Barry Morris Goldwater was a U.S. senator from Arizona from 1953 to 1965 and again from 1969 to 1987. Leading into the hiatus, he made an unsuccessful run for the presidency in 1964, as the candidate of the Republican Party. At the time of his presidential campaign, Goldwater represented the far right wing of his party, and although he did not succeed in becoming president, he reshaped the Republican Party as a conservative institution and laid the foundation for its dominance of presidential politics in the last quarter of the twentieth century and the first decade of the twenty-first.

Goldwater's great rival, Lyndon B. Johnson, who defeated him to gain the presidency in 1964, often characterized the senator from Arizona as a child in private conversations—a seemingly strange description for such a tough-minded politician. But Johnson meant that he viewed Goldwater as primarily acting on principles, even ideals, and having little use for compromise or negotiation, rather than using the realpolitik approach that characterized Johnson's own style. Indeed, Goldwater was perfectly capable of holding political views and opinions that might well seem like unresolved mutual contradictions and did not necessarily base his ideas on rational analysis, favoring other sources of inspiration. He was more concerned with holding the "right" views, trusting that they would lead to beneficial outcomes. Goldwater expressed such a notion about himself in his 1964 campaign slogan: "In your heart you know he's right." He appealed to voters' moral sense rather than their reason.

One major theme of Goldwater's conservative ideology was opposition to Communism and Socialism. This meant not only a strong emphasis on defense against the cold war enemy of the Soviet bloc but also vigilance against Socialism in American political life. Though he himself never engaged in ideological investigations of government officials or others, Goldwater was one of the staunchest supporters of Senator Joseph McCarthy, who used the investigative power of Congress to help create a paranoid fear of Communist infiltration and subversion in the United States, ruining the lives or careers of many innocent individuals. Goldwater was one of the few not to vote to censure McCarthy after the press exposed his bullying tactics and demagoguery. Goldwater equally opposed what he viewed as socialistic government intervention in the economy through such programs as Social Security and Medicare. While he denounced such programs as early as

his speech announcing his first candidacy for the Senate, in the same speech he promised not to actually cut the very same programs from which voters directly benefited. His practical position throughout his career was simply to attempt to slow the growth of the welfare state.

Although he was an experienced pilot by the time World War II broke out, Goldwater's poor vision debarred him from combat duty. Instead, he acted as a flight instructor and eventually as an air-ferry pilot, flying aircraft from the United States to frontline combat units around the world. He also flew supplies from India over the difficult Himalayan route to Chinese troops fighting the Japanese. With this background, national defense was one of his primary concerns. Although he supported the peacetime expansion of the army during the cold war, he opposed the actual combat operations in Korea and Vietnam, considering them ill-advised wars entered into by Democratic administrations. He also opposed the space program and its original goal of landing on the moon as a purely scientific venture. He would have preferred to have the space program be run by the military for purely defensive purposes. Goldwater considered his lasting legacy to be two pieces of legislation passed during his last Senate term: the Goldwater-Nichols Act, reforming the command structure of the military to prevent interservice rivalry, and legislation requiring the nascent cable-television industry to allow free access to citizens so that political and other views could be voiced in an unfettered matter.

Explanation and Analysis of Documents

Goldwater was a leading political voice during the social transformations of the 1960s, the height of the cold war, and the drift of the country toward war in Vietnam. Besides the ordinary speeches of a politician, dealing with narrower political issues and the give-and-take of political campaigning, he made a number of magisterial speeches offering a conservative response to the broader issues facing the American republic at home and abroad. He also made his opinions known through occasional pieces in the *Los Angeles Times* that were syndicated throughout the country. Toward the end of his career, and especially after his political retirement, he made further use of the media, explaining his political views and the history of his campaigns in lengthy interviews with reporters, both in print and on television. Although the conservative movement that later

1909
- ■ **January 1**
  Barry Goldwater is born in Phoenix, Arizona Territory.

1941
- ■ **July**
  Goldwater becomes a training officer and later an air-ferry pilot in the U.S. Army Air Forces.

1949
- ■ Goldwater becomes a Phoenix city councilman.

1952
- ■ Goldwater is elected to the U.S. Senate.

1954
- ■ Goldwater votes against the censure of Senator Joseph McCarthy.

1960
- ■ Goldwater runs for the Republican presidential nomination, building a conservative political organization.

1964
- ■ **July 16**
  Goldwater delivers his acceptance speech for the presidential nomination of the Republican Party at the Republican National Convention; later that year, he is defeated in the presidential election.

1968
- ■ Goldwater is reelected to the U.S. Senate.

1981
- ■ Goldwater begins to strenuously criticize the political role of the religious right.

1984
- ■ **August 23**
  Nearing his retirement, Goldwater gives a speech at the Republican National Convention.

came to dominate presidential politics looked to Goldwater as an inspiration and owed its success to political strategies that he first implemented, he was not an especially important ideologue of that movement and in fact sharply criticized some aspects of it, such as the ascendency of evangelical Christianity as a political force. Goldwater's career is represented here by two documents, his acceptance speech for the presidential nomination at the 1964 Republican National Convention and his speech to the 1984 Republican National Convention, in which he supports Ronald Reagan's buildup of the armed forces and reflects on his own political impact on America.

◆ Acceptance Speech for the Presidential Nomination of the Republican Party

Goldwater did not originally expect to win the 1964 presidential race. Republicans generally assumed that the popular Democratic president John F. Kennedy would be unbeatable in his bid for a second term of office. Rather, Goldwater was hoping to work internal party politics and position himself for a run in 1968, when it seemed the Republicans might next have a serious chance of winning the presidency. Instead, Kennedy's assassination at the end of 1963 forced Goldwater to run against the far more vulnerable Lyndon B. Johnson. As a result, Goldwater was left in the precarious position of needing to shift what had begun as a purely ideological maneuver, where ultimate defeat did not matter, into a serious presidential campaign, a transition he never fully succeeded in making.

In 1964 America faced two dangers that seemed to threaten its long-term future. Cold war rivalry with the Soviet Union was a serious challenge to America's security. The development of nuclear weapons meant that all-out war between the two superpowers could result in the destruction of the United States, if not the end of human civilization and even life on the earth. Especially troubling were a series of Soviet provocations over the previous few years, such as the erection of the Berlin Wall (1961), which ended all freedom of movement between East and West Germany, and the Cuban missile crisis (1962), provoked by the Soviets' attempt to station nuclear armed missiles within ninety miles of the United States. All of these concerns and the already seemingly aimless war in Vietnam rightfully made Americans concerned about defense issues.

At the same time, America was undergoing a crisis of inequality at home, between rich and poor and between white and black Americans. It seemed increasingly questionable that such disparities could be allowed to exist in the most prosperous economy in history and in the nation that was the leader of the free world. Many initiatives begun to stimulate the economy during the Depression, such as Social Security, had been continued in order to address just this issue. Johnson proposed strengthening these efforts with his War on Poverty programs (including Medicare, Medicaid, and Head Start), which were announced in January 1964 and eventually implemented during his second term. Attempts to deal with legal barriers to racial equality in America had begun with the desegregation of the armed forces by Harry Truman's Executive Order 9981 (1948) and with judicial decisions such as *Brown v. Board of Education* (1954), which had desegregated public schools. The civil rights movement, with expanded focus on issues like black voting rights, was advanced by Johnson through legislation such as the Civil Rights Acts of 1964 and, in his second term, that of 1968.

Goldwater begins his 1964 speech by invoking the concept of the "whole man," to which he returns throughout the speech. This biblical concept views human beings as composites of spiritual and physical elements. This, along with his numerous other biblical references, should not be viewed as an admixture of Christian and even evangelical views into politics, as would become commonplace in much later conservative rhetoric; such a mixture contrasted sharply with Goldwater libertarianism and was to be roundly criticized by him throughout the 1980s both on the floor of the Senate and in newspaper columns. Rather, Goldwater is commenting on Democratic social policies, from the New Deal to Johnson's War on Poverty, that he feels are socialistic in nature and betray the traditional American view of humanity as a collection of free, autonomous individuals; these policies instead classify people as part of collectives such as class that have the potential to dehumanize individuals. Goldwater expands on this idea to set out his themes of opposition to Johnson's proposed reforms and his strong support for the cold war, and he ties the two together by labeling the War on Poverty as a form of "collectivism" akin to the Communism of America's enemy, being careful to evoke the emotional effect of the familiar language of the national anthem.

Goldwater moves on to criticize the foreign policy of the Kennedy-Johnson administration. He considers that their failure to adequately respond to Soviet provocations, such as the erection of the Berlin Wall, and their own misguided anti-Communist initiatives, such as the disastrous Bay of Pigs invasion of Cuba (actually an operation planned and approved by the administration of Dwight Eisenhower but executed under Kennedy) and the failure of the war in Southeast Asia to move toward a victorious conclusion, had humiliated the West and greatly enhanced Soviet power and influence in the world. He is equally critical of Democratic domestic policies, which he holds responsible for the growing trends through the 1960s of rioting and the countercultural youth movement.

Goldwater expresses the almost prophetic opinion that strong resistance to Communist aggression and expansion would produce a world, far from one in which Communism would bury the capitalist West (as the Soviet leader Nikita Khrushchev had predicted in 1956), in which a limited and constrained Communist bloc would wither and give way to a Europe reunited in freedom. This, "the flowering of an Atlantic civilization, the whole of Europe reunified and freed, trading openly across its borders, communicating openly across the world," Goldwater announces as the main policy he would pursue as president, characterizing it as an achievement far more laudable than the moon landing made the symbolic goal of the Kennedy and Johnson administrations. Goldwater also outlines his vision for overcoming

Time Line

1986

■ **October 1**
The Goldwater-Nichols Act, reforming the command structure of the U.S. Armed Forces, is signed into law by President Ronald Reagan.

1987

■ **January 3**
Goldwater retires from the U.S. Senate.

1998

■ **May 29**
Goldwater dies in Paradise Valley, Arizona.

the problems of poverty and discrimination in America. He expresses the wish to rely on an expanding economy, built on new technologies, to transform disadvantaged families into successful and self-reliant ones. His guiding principle was to preserve the independence of the individual and the family, which he felt were endangered by the welfare-state approach favored by Johnson's Great Society.

His preferred path to change was no doubt exemplified in his own practices running the Goldwater department stores. For that business, he paid much higher wages than his competitors, led the way in providing health insurance and retirement benefits to his workers, and began to desegregate the workforce as early as the 1930s, carrying out in miniature a program little different from Johnson's. But Goldwater insists that such reforms must be carried out on the initiative of individuals: "We must assure a society here which, while never abandoning the needy or forsaking the helpless, nurtures incentives and opportunities for the creative and the productive." In his view, as soon as even the most beneficial and benevolent reforms are compelled, whether by labor unions or by government, they become a tyrannical limitation of individual freedom and the right to private property.

In a coda to his acceptance speech, which was written the morning it was delivered, Goldwater added a line that would become the most famous he ever spoke and would be identified with him throughout the remainder of his career: "I would remind you that extremism in the defense of liberty is no vice." He wrote this line in response to a billboard rented outside the Cow Palace in San Francisco, where the Republican convention was being held. This contained a message satirizing Goldwater's campaign slogan, "In your heart you know he's right," with the text "In your guts you know he's nuts." Later in the campaign, this twisting of Goldwater's slogan in Democratic satire went further with the version "In your heart you know he might," meaning that he might provoke nuclear war with the Soviet Union. This point was emphasized also in a famous Johnson campaign ad that showed a young girl picking a

The actor Ronald Reagan leads an impromptu rally among fans of Senator Barry Goldwater outside San Francisco's Cow Palace on July 15, 1964. (AP/Wide World Photos)

flower in a field only to end with her and all of civilization being destroyed by a nuclear blast.

In the weeks before the election, the far left political journal *Fact* ran an issue devoted to Goldwater in which it was openly asserted that he was mentally unbalanced and hence likely to start a nuclear war out of sheer paranoia (an accusation over which Goldwater later successfully sued for libel). In the wake of the Cuban missile crisis, the fear of nuclear war was a pervasive national anxiety, as expressed in Eugene Burdick and Harvey Wheeler's novel *Fail-Safe*, in which the overly complicated procedures established by the militaries of both sides, meant to manage the possibility of nuclear war and create a credible deterrent, allow for a simple computer glitch to precipitate a crisis resulting in the nuclear bombing of New York and Moscow. A popular film version of this book (directed by Sidney Lumet) was released only a month before the election, while Stanley Kubrick's *Dr. Strangelove*, a satirical adaptation of the Peter George novel *Red Alert* released in January 1964, provided a darkly comic scenario in which the mental illness of an American military officer results in the complete extinction of human civilization in a nuclear war.

The prospect of the mass suicide of humankind through a nuclear war, which could thus not possibly serve to further any political agenda, seemed so mad (not coincidentally giving birth to the term *MAD*, for "mutual assured

destruction," to describe the doctrine of deterrence) and at the same time so palpable, almost inevitable, that it is not surprising that natural human fears were addressed by these films and novels. Nor is it surprising that these anxieties were projected onto the political figures who would actually have to manage the potential for nuclear war. By his famous embrace of extremism, Goldwater meant to show that he did not present a threat of the kind ascribed to him by his enemies but rather only loved liberty in the same way the Founding Fathers had, as something worth fighting or dying for, though certainly not as something worth destroying humankind for. Yet Goldwater left himself open to such stereotyping, which he unfairly received from his political opponents because, as a conservative, he played the role of the stern father quick to do what was right rather than what was pleasant, whereas Johnson's persona seemed kindly and giving, however far removed in reality both men were from such archetypal images.

It is hard to gauge the consequences of Goldwater's 1964 campaign and of this speech containing its guiding principles because of his eventual defeat. In any case, it is clear that his ideas could not yet persuade and compel the American people. Still, aside from the profound changes in the electoral politics of the Republican Party that Goldwater's campaign eventually brought about, his stated aim of resisting and destroying Communism by means other than out-right war did have a great effect on later history when it was taken up by the Reagan administration. Just as Goldwater's electoral strategy transformed American presidential politics, leading to an era of Republican domination, Goldwater was a prophet of the eventual American victory in the cold war.

◆ Address to the Republican National Convention

Goldwater delivered his speech to the 1984 Republican National Convention at the zenith of the cold war and, as he was fully aware, at the end of his career. One rhetorical purpose of the speech was for Goldwater to position himself within the framework of American history. He accomplish-es this by reciting several quotations from Thomas Paine, whose pamphlet *Common Sense* helped inspire the Ameri-can Revolution, and by arguing that his own career and the actions of the modern conservative Republican Party he helped to create flowed from the source of the Founding Fathers. He also recalls his own 1964 presidential cam-paign, giving new contexts to his famous slogans from that race. His more immediate purpose in giving the speech, however, was to defend the arms buildup then being con-ducted by President Ronald Reagan, who was in some sense Goldwater's protégé, since his switch from acting to a full-time political career had come about while he was working on behalf of Goldwater's 1964 campaign and since he had benefited from Goldwater's conservative reshaping of the Republican Party and its electoral strategy.

Goldwater begins this speech by recalling his 1964 acceptance speech and its famous line "Extremism in the defense of liberty is no vice." As he had often done before in explaining it, he places this quote in the context of the American Revolution and the difficult decision then made for liberty in rebelling against the British monarchy. The extremism of the Founding Fathers consisted in their will-ingness "to sacrifice, struggle and die for the ideal of liber-ty, while others sought more comfortable lives." Goldwater speaks of seeing this same dichotomy being played out in America again, between the Republicans, who under Rea-gan were willing to stand up for the freedom of the West against the Communist bloc, and the Democrats, whom he presents as betraying the American heritage in not realizing that a strong defense is necessary. In fact, he blames all the foreign wars of the twentieth century in which America became involved on weak Democratic administrations. "Every war in this century began and was fought under Democrat administrations. You doubt me? World War I, Woodrow Wilson, Democrat. World War II, Franklin Roo-sevelt, Democrat. Korea, Harry Truman, Democrat. Viet-nam, Jack Kennedy and Lyndon Johnson, both Democrats."

He complains that in the then-current cold war with the Soviet Union, the Democrats wanted to cut back military spending, in contrast to the large increases implemented and then further proposed by the Reagan administration. Goldwater goes on to dismiss claims that the soaring national budget deficit entailed by the Reagan defense buildup would be a grave danger to the United States on the argument that if the defense of the nation failed, its

economic condition would be irrelevant. He again quotes Thomas Paine in justification of his position: "Those who expect to reap the blessings of freedom must, like men, undergo the fatigue of supporting it."

Goldwater extends his argument for strengthening national defense by appealing to future generations who might be endangered by weakness shown in the present. He also appeals to elemental feelings of patriotism as a jus-tification for Reagan's policies, such as the emotions many Americans had recently felt upon seeing victorious Ameri-can Olympic athletes. Finally, he applies this emotional appeal directly to Reagan by transferring his old campaign slogan to the incumbent president: "And in your hearts, you know he's right."

The markedly partisan nature of this speech, with its constant personal attacks on the Democratic leaders of Congress, was meant not to further Reagan's reelection bid, which was not in much doubt, but to persuade voters to elect a new Republican Congress that would work toward the president's goals. Goldwater's speech, like much of the political rhetoric of the Reagan years, appealed to emotion and partisan feeling, tending to obscure the real geopolitical and economic issues involved rather than enlighten voters. Perhaps for this reason, among many other factors (includ-ing the generally local character of congressional politics), the Republican Party made no progress in changing the composition of the House of Representatives in 1984.

The American military buildup advanced by Goldwater in this speech indeed succeeded in its purpose of causing the collapse of the Communist bloc and eliminating the Soviet Union as a superpower rival of the United States. The Soviet military and the economy that supported it, drained by its unsuccessful invasion of Afghanistan, whose resistance was strongly supported by the United States, and by its own tremendous buildup of conventional forces in Europe in the 1970s and early 1980s, simply could not keep pace with the spending of the American military as supported by the more robust American economy. In par-ticular, the United States engaged the Strategic Defense Initiative, the so-called Star Wars program, utilizing cut-ting-edge technology that the Soviet Union had to keep pace with. Given the inherent weakness and small size of the Soviet economy compared with that of the United States, it could not bear up under the burden of increased military spending and eventually collapsed. This brought about the end of the Soviet Union as an imperialist power and the liberation of Eastern Europe, symbolized by the destruction of the Berlin Wall in a popular outpouring in 1989 that was really more of a celebration than an upris-ing. The Soviet Union itself quickly splintered into its con-stituent parts, with many of the new nations adopting con-stitutions and a public ethos based on those of the West.

Impact and Legacy

Goldwater completely transformed the character of the Republican Party and the dynamics of electoral politics in

"The good Lord raised this mighty Republic to be a home for the brave and to flourish as the land of the free—not to stagnate in the swampland of collectivism, not to cringe before the bullying of communism."

(Acceptance Speech for the Presidential Nomination of the Republican Party)

"We must, and we shall, return to proven ways—not because they are old, but because they are true."

(Acceptance Speech for the Presidential Nomination of the Republican Party)

"Now those who seek absolute power, even though they seek it to do what they regard as good, are simply demanding the right to enforce their own version of heaven on earth. They—and let me remind you, they are the very ones who always create the most hellish tyrannies."

(Acceptance Speech for the Presidential Nomination of the Republican Party)

"I would remind you that extremism in the defense of liberty is no vice. And let me remind you also that moderation in the pursuit of justice is no virtue."

(Acceptance Speech for the Presidential Nomination of the Republican Party)

"What, may I ask, was more extreme than our Revolutionary War? Our founding fathers pledged their lives, their fortunes and their sacred honor for that most honorable and noble cause, freedom."

(Address to the Republican National Convention)

"Indeed, they would have us ashamed of our freedom and our ability to defend it."

(Address to the Republican National Convention)

"Let me tell you, the proudest moments of my life have been those times when I wore the uniform of the United States of America."

(Address to the Republican National Convention)

"Now if we want to insure forces strong enough to protect our freedom— and we do—we must give them the tools to do the job."

(Address to the Republican National Convention)

the nation as a whole. On the foundation laid down as early as the 1960 campaign, "Goldwater Republicans" created a network of political activism that made conservatives more powerful than their numbers in party and national politics by increasing their proportional voter turnout. By 1964 this kind of organization had created a large conservative plurality within what had recently been a moderate Republican Party with a strong liberal wing based in the Northeast. This plurality (Goldwater won 38.33 percent of the primary vote in 1964) was enough to secure his nomination at the convention, since the remainder of the vote was divided between various factions. However, the general election revealed how weak conservative strength was in the nation as a whole, as the result was one of the most lopsided election defeats in American history, with Goldwater taking almost exactly the same percentage of the popular vote (38.5 percent) and carrying only five states, including his native Arizona. While this was a tremendous personal defeat for Goldwater, it had the paradoxical effect of strengthening the conservative control of the Republican Party over the long run.

While in 1968 the Republicans turned to the right-leaning moderate Richard Nixon so as not to repeat Goldwater's failed strategy, many well-established moderate and liberal Republicans had gone down to defeat with Goldwater in 1964. Their positions within the party were generally taken over by members of the well-organized conservative movement who would guide future developments. No one, however, had anticipated that factions of the "Solid South," which had been staunchly Democratic since Reconstruction, would rally to the Republican cause in 1964. The reason five southern states supported Goldwater was that their overwhelming white electorate feared that reforms being brought about by the Democratic Party would revolutionize southern society and race relations in America. They looked to such conservative platforms as states' rights and the limitation of the powers of the federal government as a bulwark of protection against change. Particularly after the disgrace of the centrist Nixon over the Watergate scandal, it became possible for Ronald Reagan in 1980 to revive Goldwater's base of activist ideological conservatives, to co-opt disaffected white voters in the South, and to add to this already uneasy alliance the previously largely apolitical community of evangelical Christians (with whose antilibertarian aims Goldwater personally had the gravest disagree-

Questions for Further Study

1. Although Goldwater was certainly a controversial figure, even his worst critics generally agreed that he was an honorable man. The same could not be said of Senator Joseph McCarthy, who was notorious for his intimidation tactics, deceptive claims, and outright bullying. Nevertheless, Goldwater supported McCarthy and remained loyal to him even after the senator went down in disgrace over his witch hunt for Communist sympathizers in government. Compare the styles of the two men as demonstrated in their writings and speeches. Was Goldwater a cynic like McCarthy or the opposite—a sincere idealist whose strong convictions ironically led him to support a dishonorable man? Alternatively, was Goldwater right about McCarthy?

2. Goldwater tended to appeal to his listeners' sense of morality rather than basing his arguments primarily on reasoned analysis. Yet in his later career, he distanced himself from the activist Christian element in the Republican Party and expressed deep misgivings regarding the influence of fundamentalists on politics. Did he change views, or is his later opposition to the influence of religion in the party actually consistent with his earlier position?

3. Lyndon B. Johnson won the 1964 presidential election against Goldwater largely because Americans believed that Goldwater would lead them into nuclear war. Yet Johnson went on to dramatically increase U.S. troop commitments in Vietnam, a war Goldwater opposed. How might America have been different if Goldwater had won? Consider not only Vietnam and other aspects of the cold war but also issues of civil rights and poverty, which also dominated the 1960s political landscape.

4. Near the end of his address to the 1964 Republican National Convention, Goldwater uttered what would prove to be the most oft-quoted—and damaging—words of his political career: "I would remind you that extremism in the defense of liberty is no vice.... Moderation in the pursuit of justice is no virtue." What did these words mean? How did Goldwater intend them to be understood, and how were they received? How did they affect his chances of winning the presidency, and was the response justified?

ments, for instance in his support for abortion rights and gay rights). Thus was created a conservative electoral coalition that triumphed in five of the seven presidential elections between 1980 and 2004.

Key Sources

No large collection of Goldwater's speeches and papers has yet been published, although in *Pure Goldwater* (2008), John W. Dean and Barry Goldwater, Jr., eds., provide a selection of archival material on Goldwater, including extracts from his journals, correspondence, and the *Fact* magazine libel trial. The principal collection of Barry Goldwater's papers is housed at the Arizona Historical Foundation at Arizona State University, in Tempe. A smaller collection is housed within the Eugene C. Barker Texas History Collection at the University of Texas at Austin. Additional material exists at the Barry Goldwater Center for the Southwest, located in Phoenix. All of Goldwater's speeches and activities on the Senate floor are documented in the *Congressional Record*; the Web site of the Arizona Historical Foundation (http://www.ahfweb.org/collections_search.htm) offers an index of its holdings. Goldwater himself has published extensively. *The Conscious of a Conservative* (1960) was an early statement of his political philosophy meant to help position him as a presidential candidate. *Where I Stand* reiterated his ideas in conjunction with his actual campaign in 1964. *With No Apologies: The Personal and Political Memoirs of United States Senator Barry M. Goldwater* (1979) marked the beginning of his criticism of the neoconservative moment for moving away from his own libertarian principles. *Goldwater*, a memoir written in conversation with the journalist Jack Casserly after Goldwater's retirement from the Senate in 1988, allowed him to give a characteristically unvarnished assessment of the political history and politicians he had known at first hand.

Further Reading

■ Articles

Crespi, Irving. "The Structural Basis for Right-Wing Conservatism: The Goldwater Case." *Public Opinion Quarterly* 29 (1965–1966): 523–543.

Schwartz, Morton. "The 1964 Presidential Elections through Soviet Eyes." *Western Political Quarterly* 19 (1966): 663–671.

Wingo, Walter. "Goldwater vs. Moon Shot." *Science News-Letter* 5 (1964): 77.

■ Books

Goldberg, Robert Alan. *Barry Goldwater*. New Haven, Conn.: Yale University Press, 1995.

Lokos, Lionel. *Hysteria 1964: The Fear Campaign against Barry Goldwater*. New Rochelle, N.Y.: Arlington House, 1967.

Middendorf, J. William. *A Glorious Disaster: Barry Goldwater's Presidential Campaign and the Origins of the Conservative Movement*. New York: Basic Books, 2006.

■ Web Sites

"Goldwater, Barry Morris (1909–1998)." Biographical Directory of the United States Congress Web site. http://bioguide.congress.gov/scripts/biodisplay.pl?index=G000267.

—Bradley Skeen

ACCEPTANCE SPEECH FOR THE PRESIDENTIAL NOMINATION OF THE REPUBLICAN PARTY (1964)

My good friend and great Republican, Dick Nixon, and your charming wife, Pat; my running mate, that wonderful Republican who has served us so well for so long, Bill Miller and his wife, Stephanie; to Thurston Morton who's done such a commendable job in chairmaning this Convention; to Mr. Herbert Hoover, who I hope is watching; and to that—that great American and his wife, General and Mrs. Eisenhower; to my own wife, my family, and to all of my fellow Republicans here assembled, and Americans across this great Nation.

From this moment, united and determined, we will go forward together, dedicated to the ultimate and undeniable greatness of the whole man. Together—Together we will win.

I accept your nomination with a deep sense of humility. I accept, too, the responsibility that goes with it, and I seek your continued help and your continued guidance. My fellow Republicans, our cause is too great for any man to feel worthy of it. Our task would be too great for any man, did he not have with him the hearts and the hands of this great Republican Party, and I promise you tonight that every fiber of my being is consecrated to our cause; that nothing shall be lacking from the struggle that can be brought to it by enthusiasm, by devotion, and plain hard work.

In this world no person, no Party can guarantee anything, but what we can do and what we shall do is to deserve victory, and victory will be ours.

The good Lord raised this mighty Republic to be a home for the brave and to flourish as the land of the free—not to stagnate in the swampland of collectivism, not to cringe before the bullying of communism.

Now, my fellow Americans, the tide has been running against freedom. Our people have followed false prophets. We must, and we shall, return to proven ways—not because they are old, but because they are true. We must, and we shall, set the tides running again in the cause of freedom. And this party, with its every action, every word, every breath, and every heartbeat, has but a single resolve, and that is freedom—freedom made orderly for this Nation by our constitutional government; freedom under a government limited by the laws of nature and of nature's God; freedom balanced so that order lacking liberty will not become the slavery of the prison cell; bal-anced so that liberty lacking order will not become the license of the mob and of the jungle.

Now, we Americans understand freedom. We have earned it; we have lived for it, and we have died for it. This Nation and its people are freedom's model in a searching world. We can be freedom's missionaries in a doubting world. But, ladies and gentlemen, first we must renew freedom's mission in our own hearts and in our own homes.

During four futile years, the administration which we shall replace has—has distorted and lost that vision. It has talked and talked and talked and talked the words of freedom, but it has failed and failed and failed in the works of freedom.

Now, failures cement the wall of shame in Berlin. Failures blot the sands of shame at the Bay of Pigs. Failures mark the slow death of freedom in Laos. Failures infest the jungles of Vietnam. And failures haunt the houses of our once great alliances and undermine the greatest bulwark ever erected by free nations—the NATO community. Failures proclaim lost leadership, obscure purpose, weakening will, and the risk of inciting our sworn enemies to new aggressions and to new excesses.

And because of this administration we are tonight a world divided; we are a Nation becalmed. We have lost the brisk pace of diversity and the genius of individual creativity. We are plodding along at a pace set by centralized planning, red tape, rules without responsibility, and regimentation without recourse.

Rather than useful jobs in our country, our people have been offered bureaucratic "make work"; rather than moral leadership, they have been given bread and circuses. They have been given spectacles, and, yes, they've even been given scandals.

Tonight, there is violence in our streets, corruption in our highest offices, aimlessness amongst our youth, anxiety among our elders, and there's a virtual despair among the many who look beyond material success for the inner meaning of their lives. And where examples of morality should be set, the opposite is seen. Small men, seeking great wealth or power, have too often and too long turned even the highest levels of public service into mere personal opportunity.

Now, certainly, simple honesty is not too much to demand of men in government. We find it in most. Republicans demand it from everyone. They demand it from everyone no matter how exalted or protected his position might be. Now—the growing menace in our country tonight, to personal safety, to life, to limb and property, in homes, in churches, on the playgrounds, and places of business, particularly in our great cities, is the mounting concern, or should be, of every thoughtful citizen in the United States.

Security from domestic violence, no less than from foreign aggression, is the most elementary and fundamental purpose of any government, and a government that cannot fulfill this purpose is one that cannot long command the loyalty of its citizens.

History shows us—it demonstrates that nothing, nothing prepares the way for tyranny more than the failure of public officials to keep the streets safe from bullies and marauders.

Now, we Republicans see all this as more, much more, than the result of mere political differences or mere political mistakes. We see this as the result of a fundamentally and absolutely wrong view of man, his nature, and his destiny. Those who seek to live your lives for you, to take your liberties in return for relieving you of yours, those who elevate the state and downgrade the citizen must see ultimately a world in which earthly power can be substituted for Divine Will, and this Nation was founded upon the rejection of that notion and upon the acceptance of God as the author of freedom.

Now those who seek absolute power, even though they seek it to do what they regard as good, are simply demanding the right to enforce their own version of heaven on earth. They—and let me remind you, they are the very ones who always create the most hellish tyrannies. Absolute power does corrupt, and those who seek it must be suspect and must be opposed. Their mistaken course stems from false notions, ladies and gentlemen, of equality. Equality, rightly understood, as our founding fathers understood it, leads to liberty and to the emancipation of creative differences. Wrongly understood, as it has been so tragically in our time, it leads first to conformity and then to despotism.

Fellow Republicans, it is the cause of Republicanism to resist concentrations of power, private or public,—which enforce such conformity and inflict such despotism. It is the cause of Republicanism to ensure that power remains in the hands of the people. And, so help us God, that is exactly what a Republican President will do with the help of a Republican Congress.

It is further the cause of Republicanism to restore a clear understanding of the tyranny of man over man in the world at large. It is our cause to dispel the foggy thinking which avoids hard decisions in the delusion that a world of conflict will somehow mysteriously resolve itself into a world of harmony, if we just don't rock the boat or irritate the forces of aggression—and this is hogwash.

It is further the cause of Republicanism to remind ourselves, and the world, that only the strong can remain free, that only the strong can keep the peace.

Now, I needn't remind you, or my fellow Americans regardless of party, that Republicans have shouldered this hard responsibility and marched in this cause before. It was Republican leadership under Dwight Eisenhower that kept the peace, and passed along to this administration the mightiest arsenal for defense the world has ever known. And I needn't remind you that it was the strength and the unbelievable will of the Eisenhower years that kept the peace by using our strength, by using it in the Formosa Straits and in Lebanon and by showing it courageously at all times.

It was during those Republican years that the thrust of Communist imperialism was blunted. It was during those years of Republican leadership that this world moved closer, not to war, but closer to peace, than at any other time in the last three decades.

And I needn't remind you—but I will—that it's been during Democratic years that our strength to deter war has stood still, and even gone into a planned decline. It has been during Democratic years that we have weakly stumbled into conflict, timidly refusing to draw our own lines against aggression, deceitfully refusing to tell even our people of our full participation, and tragically, letting our finest men die on battlefields, unmarked by purpose, unmarked by pride or the prospect of victory.

Yesterday, it was Korea. Tonight, it is Vietnam. Make no bones of this. Don't try to sweep this under the rug. We are at war in Vietnam. And yet the President, who is the Commander-in-Chief of our forces, refuses to say—refuses to say, mind you, whether or not the objective over there is victory. And his Secretary of Defense continues to mislead and misinform the American people, and enough of it has gone by.

And I needn't remind you—but I will—it has been during Democratic years that a billion persons were cast into Communist captivity and their fate cynically sealed.

Today—Today in our beloved country we have an administration which seems eager to deal with communism in every coin known—from gold to wheat, from consulates to confidences, and even human freedom itself.

Now the Republican cause demands that we brand communism as the principal disturber of peace in the world today. Indeed, we should brand it as the only significant disturber of the peace, and we must make clear that until its goals of conquest are absolutely renounced and its relations with all nations tempered, communism and the governments it now controls are enemies of every man on earth who is or wants to be free.

Now, we here in America can keep the peace only if we remain vigilant and only if we remain strong. Only if we keep our eyes open and keep our guard up can we prevent war. And I want to make this abundantly clear: I don't intend to let peace or freedom be torn from our grasp because of lack of strength or lack of will—and that I promise you, Americans.

I believe that we must look beyond the defense of freedom today to its extension tomorrow. I believe that the communism which boasts it will bury us will, instead, give way to the forces of freedom. And I can see in the distant and yet recognizable future the outlines of a world worthy of our dedication, our every risk, our every effort, our every sacrifice along the way. Yes, a world that will redeem the suffering of those who will be liberated from tyranny. I can see—and I suggest that all thoughtful men must contemplate—the flowering of an Atlantic civilization, the whole of Europe reunified and freed, trading openly across its borders, communicating openly across the world.

Now, this is a goal far, far more meaningful than a moon shot.

It's a—It's a truly inspiring goal for all free men to set for themselves during the latter half of the twentieth century.

I can also see—and all free men must thrill to—the events of this Atlantic civilization joined by its great ocean highway to the United States. What a destiny! What a destiny can be ours to stand as a great central pillar linking Europe, the Americas, and the venerable and vital peoples and cultures of the Pacific. I can see a day when all the Americas, North and South, will be linked in a mighty system, a system in which the errors and misunderstandings of the past will be submerged one by one in a rising tide of prosperity and interdependence. We know that the misunderstandings of centuries are not to be wiped away in a day or wiped away in an hour. But we pledge, we pledge that human sympathy—what our neighbors to the South call an attitude of "simpatico"—no less than enlightened self-interest will be our guide.

And I can see this Atlantic civilization galvanizing and guiding emergent nations everywhere.

Now I know this freedom is not the fruit of every soil. I know that our own freedom was achieved through centuries, by unremitting efforts of brave and wise men. And I know that the road to freedom is a long and a challenging road. And I know also that some men may walk away from it, that some men resist challenge, accepting the false security of governmental paternalism.

And I—And I pledge that the America I envision in the years ahead will extend its hand in health, in teaching and in cultivation, so that all new nations will be at least encouraged—encouraged!—to go our way, so that they will not wander down the dark alleys of tyranny or the dead-end streets of collectivism.

My fellow Republicans, we do no man a service by hiding freedom's light under a bushel of mistaken humility.

I seek an America proud of its past, proud of its ways, proud of its dreams, and determined actively to proclaim them. But our example to the world must, like charity, begin at home.

In our vision of a good and decent future, free and peaceful, there must be room, room for deliberation of the energy and the talent of the individual; otherwise our vision is blind at the outset.

We must assure a society here which, while never abandoning the needy or forsaking the helpless, nurtures incentives and opportunities for the creative and the productive. We must know the whole good is the product of many single contributions.

And I cherish a day when our children once again will restore as heroes the sort of men and women who, unafraid and undaunted, pursue the truth, strive to cure disease, subdue and make fruitful our natural environment and produce the inventive engines of production, science, and technology.

This Nation, whose creative people have enhanced this entire span of history, should again thrive upon the greatness of all those things which we, we as individual citizens, can and should do. And during Republican years, this again will be a nation of men and women, of families proud of their role, jealous of their responsibilities, unlimited in their aspirations—a Nation where all who can will be self-reliant.

We Republicans see in our constitutional form of government the great framework which assures the orderly but dynamic fulfillment of the whole man, and we see the whole man as the great reason for instituting orderly government in the first place.

We see—We see in private property and in economy based upon and fostering private property, the one way to make government a durable ally of the whole man, rather than his determined enemy. We see in the sanctity of private property the only durable foundation for constitutional government in a free society.

And—And beyond that, we see, in cherished diversity of ways, diversity of thoughts, of motives and accomplishments. We don't seek to lead anyone's life for him. We only seek—only seek to secure his rights, guarantee him opportunity—guarantee him opportunity to strive, with government performing only those needed and constitutionally sanctioned tasks which cannot otherwise be performed.

We Republicans seek a government that attends to its inherent responsibilities of maintaining a stable monetary and fiscal climate, encouraging a free and a competitive economy and enforcing law and order. Thus, do we seek inventiveness, diversity, and creative difference within a stable order, for we Republicans define government's role where needed at many, many levels—preferably, though, the one closest to the people involved.

Our towns and our cities, then our counties, then our states, then our regional compacts—and only then, the national government. That, let me remind you, is the ladder of liberty, built by decentralized power. On it also we must have balance between the branches of government at every level.

Balance, diversity, creative difference: These are the elements of the Republican equation. Republicans agree—Republicans agree heartily to disagree on many, many of their applications, but we have never disagreed on the basic fundamental issues of why you and I are Republicans.

This is a Party. This Republican Party is a Party for free men, not for blind followers, and not for conformists.

In fact, in 1858 Abraham Lincoln said this of the Republican Party—and I quote him, because he probably could have said it during the last week or so: "It was composed of strange, discordant, and even hostile elements"...in 1858. Yet—Yet all of these elements agreed on one paramount objective: To arrest the progress of slavery, and place it in the course of ultimate extinction.

Today, as then, but more urgently and more broadly than then, the task of preserving and enlarging freedom at home and of safeguarding it from the forces of tyranny abroad is great enough to challenge all our resources and to require all our strength.

Glossary

Bay of Pigs	a failed attempt by the administration of John F. Kennedy to overthrow the Communist government of Cuba's Fidel Castro in April 1961
bread and circuses	a reference to the Roman practice of giving poor people free bread and entertainment as a way of preventing revolt
collectivism	a political system, such as Communism or Nazism, that emphasizes the group, or collective, over individual rights
Formosa Straits	the narrow portion of sea separating mainland China, with its Communist government, from the pro-American regime on the island of Formosa (now Taiwan)
Herbert Hoover	president of the United States from 1929 to 1933, who died on October 20, 1964, just a few months after Goldwater's speech
Hiding…light under a bushel	a reference to Matthew 5:15 in the Bible; not sharing something good that should be shared
in every coin known	by every means possible
Laos	a Southeast Asian country that, like neighboring Vietnam, fought a long and ultimately unsuccessful war against Communist forces
"simpatico"	in sympathy or agreement
paternalism	a governmental policy of providing for citizens without expecting responsibilities from them; a "welfare state"
the wall of shame in Berlin	the wall erected in 1961 by East German government, with Soviet support, to separate East Berlin from West Berlin

Anyone who joins us in all sincerity, we welcome. Those who do not care for our cause, we don't expect to enter our ranks in any case. And—And let our Republicanism, so focused and so dedicated, not be made fuzzy and futile by unthinking and stupid labels.

I would remind you that extremism in the defense of liberty is no vice....

And let me remind you also that moderation in the pursuit of justice is no virtue.

Why the beauty of the very system we Republicans are pledged to restore and revitalize, the beauty of this Federal system of ours is in its reconciliation of diversity with unity. We must not see malice in honest differences of opinion, and no matter how great, so long as they are not inconsistent with the pledges we have given to each other in and through our Constitution.

Our Republican cause is not to level out the world or make its people conform in computer regimented sameness. Our Republican cause is to free our people and light the way for liberty throughout the world.

Ours is a very human cause for very humane goals.

This Party, its good people, and its unquenchable devotion to freedom will not fulfill the purposes of this campaign, which we launch here and now, until our cause has won the day, inspired the world, and shown the way to a tomorrow worthy of all our yesteryears.

I repeat, I accept your nomination with humbleness, with pride, and you and I are going to fight for the goodness of our land.

Thank you.

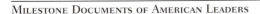

ADDRESS TO THE REPUBLICAN NATIONAL CONVENTION (1984)

First I want to thank John Tower for that most generous introduction. Frankly I didn't know it was going to happen. Knowing John as I do, I'm grateful he stopped when he did. I've known John all his political life and I hold him in the highest admiration.

Nancy Reagan, Mr. Chairman, delegates, ladies and gentlemen:

A month ago I sat in my den and watched the Democratic National Convention. Speaker after speaker promised the moon to every narrow, selfish interest group in the country. But they ignored the hopes and aspirations of the largest special interest group of them all, free men and free women.

So tonight I want to speak about freedom. And let me remind you that extremism in the defense of liberty is no vice.

What, may I ask, was more extreme than our Revolutionary War? Our founding fathers pledged their lives, their fortunes and their sacred honor for that most honorable and noble cause, freedom.

And I remind you, too, that these men and women who rebelled against tyranny did not have the unanimous support of even their friends, their neighbors or relatives. But they were willing to sacrifice, struggle and die for the ideal of liberty, while others sought more comfortable lives.

And since that time other Americans have fought, bled and died to protect those God-given privileges—because, as Tom Paine said in that day, tyranny, like hell, is not easily conquered.

But last month, those Democrat orators turned their backs on our own heritage. Indeed, they would have us ashamed of our freedom and our ability to defend it. And to me the worst part was that they said nicer things about the Soviet Union than about our own military services. And I would remind you that these are the men and women in uniform who are sworn to protect that very freedom that made our country so great.

Let me tell you, the proudest moments of my life have been those times when I wore the uniform of the United States of America. To have been privileged to join with the men and women in the defense of freedom was, to me, the ultimate expression of faith in our heritage.

I am also proud to be a veteran of the armed forces, and let me remind you veteran was a word you never heard from these Democrats on their podium. Let me say to the millions of veterans who are proud, proud, proud to have served our country, we will not forget you.

To those men and those women now in uniform, and to the veterans and the ones to come, I solemnly pledge that I will do all I can to see that you never are forsaken, as you were in San Francisco.

Now believe me what I'm going to say is not easy to say; but nonetheless, truth demands it. It has been the foreign policy and defense weakness of Democrat administrations that have led us to war in the past. And I will be as specific as the Democrats were unspecific in San Francisco.

Every war in this century began and was fought under Democrat administrations. You doubt me? World War I, Woodrow Wilson, Democrat. World War II, Franklin Roosevelt, Democrat. Korea, Harry Truman, Democrat. Vietnam, Jack Kennedy and Lyndon Johnson, both Democrats.

And let me further remind you that while we are decommissioning our old Polaris submarines, the Democrats would not allow us to build our new Trident submarines. And while our Air Force pilots are flying 30-year-old B-52 bombers, the Democrats want to take away the B-1 bomber.

The list goes on and on, while at home and abroad assaults continue on our basic principles of liberty and freedom. The Democrats and their special interest allies are trying to convince the American people that our own armed services are the biggest obstacle to peace and prosperity. They tell us that spending a small portion of our national resources for national defense is driving up deficits and hurting our economy. But let us never lose sight of this one fact: There is no more important step we can take to ensure a strong economy than to ensure a strong defense.

Again, let me give you Thomas Paine who said, "Those who expect to reap the blessings of freedom must, like men, undergo the fatigue of supporting it."

It's also a fact that the men and women in uniform are our first line of defense in the continuous struggle to maintain freedom. And it's a fact that the Democrat plan for defense would leave us ill-prepared for any sort of conflict.

Now a few short weeks ago the chairman of the House military appropriations subcommittee released a phony report, made several years ago, that our armed forces are weaker today than they were four years earlier. Yet every chief of staff of whom I have asked that question—and I have asked all of them—and every commander I asked around this world has said, "Never have we been so strong and never have we had such quality of men and women."

Now if we want to insure forces strong enough to protect our freedom—and we do—we must give them the tools to do the job. And I say thank God, we now have a Commander in Chief, our President, who is doing his utmost to provide this nation and our armed forces with those tools.

Now on the other hand, the chairman I just mentioned has not allowed his subcommittee to appropriate sufficient funds for our defense in years and years. He has refused to provide enough money for the military to protect our freedom. And at this very moment he is refusing to do the same thing again.

Now you want to look a little higher to poke some blame at? Okay let's take House leader Tip O'Neill. There's one. He will not allow the House Armed Services Committee to agree with the Senate on a military bill. Now why? He doesn't want a military bill until after the election.

Well, Tip, let me tell you something. You aren't going to win this election!

Now I suppose a lot of you are wondering why I chose to speak on this particular subject. It's true that defense is close to my heart. But that is not the reason.

What I am concerned about is our grandchildren and their children and grandchildren after that.

Wherever I may be, I do not want my grandchildren or their children asking, "Why didn't Paka—that's what they call me—do something so we would not have to go off to war now?"

If in the life left to me—and let me warn you that there's more life left in me than the Democrats like—if I can prevent that question from ever being asked, then I will have fulfilled my duty to my country and to freedom.

And let me warn those Democrats who made such a mockery out of freedom in San Francisco. Remember the millions of Americans who cheered, waved flags, and felt joy in their hearts and tears in their eyes at the success of the American men and women in the recent Olympics.

Don't you Democrat leaders try to tell me that Americans don't love and honor America. And don't you Democrat leaders poke fun at the progress America has made. And don't you Democrat leaders ever suggest we are not on the right path. And one more warning, quit trying to divide America. There are too many millions of Americans who just won't take that guff. I've cleaned that one up. Guff.

Members of the convention, we have a leader, a real leader, a great Commander in Chief: President Ronald Reagan. And in your hearts, you know he's right.

My friends, because we are in Dallas, delightful place, let me say vaya con Dios y buena suerte—'til we meet again.

Glossary

the recent Olympics	the 1984 Summer Olympics, held in Los Angeles
San Francisco	site of that year's Democratic National Convention

Samuel Gompers (Library of Congress)

SAMUEL GOMPERS   1850–1924

Union Organizer and Labor Activist

Featured Documents

◆ Address to Workers in Louisville, Kentucky (1890)
◆ Editorial on the Pullman Strike (1894)
◆ Editorial on the Supreme Court Ruling in the Danbury Hatters' Case (1908)
◆ Circular to the Organizers of the American Federation of Labor (1915)
◆ Address to the Annual Meeting of the National Civic Federation (1916)

Overview

Samuel Gompers was born on January 27, 1850, in London, England. In July 1863, his family immigrated to the United States, where Gompers and his father found employment in New York City as skilled cigar rollers. Although Gompers lacked formal education, he was introduced to the ideas of the political economists Karl Marx and Ferdinand Lassalle through the working-class self-education practiced by cigar makers, who hired a fellow worker to read aloud to those rolling cigars. This education helped convince Gompers of the necessity for trade unionism, and he became active in the Cigar Makers' International Union. Along with his friend Adolph Strasser, who assumed the presidency of the union in 1877, Gompers fostered a more centralized union model for skilled craft workers in response to the fragility of the labor movement during such troubled economic times as the Panic of 1873—a financial depression that led to losses of jobs.

As a trade unionist, Gompers believed that political action was premature prior to workers' forming a sense of class consciousness. Accordingly, he opposed political alignments with the Democrats and Republicans or parties of the left, such as the Socialists, in favor of direct action that would increase a sense of labor solidarity. Driven by these ideas, Gompers helped found the Federation of Organized Trades and Labor Unions in 1881. Although the federation was underfunded and organizationally weak, Gompers was successful in opposing the political orientation and influence of the Knights of Labor among the unions. In 1886, Gompers and supporters among organized skilled workers formed the American Federation of Labor (AFL), and Gompers was elected president. The AFL supported the independence of autonomous trade unions in the ordering of their internal affairs. Gompers and the AFL believed in voluntarism, rejecting an active role for the state in the regulation of industrial relations. In fact, with court decisions often overturning pro-labor legislation, Gompers was convinced that only collective action by workers, the essence of labor voluntarism, could protect the interests of labor and achieve such goals as the eight-hour workday. Gompers addressed workers across the nation to rally American workers to the forefront of an international campaign to allow labor more dignity by providing time for workers to cultivate their minds.

During the 1880s and 1890s Gompers worked tirelessly to establish the AFL's influence over skilled workers. Although he was often accused of fostering elitism within the labor movement, Gompers was a critic of the International Association of Machinists, which opposed black membership. Rejecting the Marxism and radicalism of his youth, Gompers attempted to distance himself from the influence of the Socialist and Populist parties. In an August 1894 editorial for the *American Federationist*, the newspaper organ of the AFL, Gompers opposed the actions of Eugene Debs and the American Railway Union (ARU) during the 1894 strike against the Pullman Palace Car Company. Debs, who would emerge as the leader of the Socialist Party of America in the early twentieth century, and the ARU were supporting striking workers at the Pullman company factory town where railroad sleeping cars were produced. Although Gompers condemned George Pullman's wage cuts for initiating the labor stoppage, he failed to support the call by Debs for a general strike by American labor. This stance led to Gompers's failure to win reelection as AFL president in 1895.

Regaining the presidency of the AFL the following year, Gompers soon attempted to offset employer opposition to unionization by cooperating with the National Civic Federation, a reform group composed of the nation's corporate leadership. Although this alliance produced few tangible benefits for the AFL, the organization's membership continued to grow, numbering nearly two million workers by 1904. Nevertheless, Gompers was troubled by the actions of the Supreme Court in the 1908 *Loewe v. Lawlor* decision, also referred to as the Danbury Hatters' Case. In a March 1908 editorial for the *American Federationist*, Gompers criticized the Court's declaration of the AFL's boycott against the hat manufacturer Dietrich Lowe, for its refusal to recognize the hatters' union, as an unlawful restraint of trade under the Sherman Antitrust Act (1890). In his editorial, Gompers displays frustration with the legal system, but his more conservative nature is apparent in his conclusion that the AFL must bow to the Court's ruling.

Gompers also came to rethink his organization's avoidance of political entanglements, and in 1906 he presented labor's Bill of Grievances to President Theodore Roosevelt and Congress. As the ruling Republican Party proved unsympathetic to Gompers, in 1912 the AFL executive abandoned nonpartisanship, supporting the presidential

Time Line

1850
- **January 27**
  Samuel Gompers is born in London, England.

1863
- **July 29**
  Gompers and his family arrive by ship in New York City.

1864
- Gompers joins Local 15 of the Cigar Makers' International Union.

1875
- Gompers is elected president of Local 144 of the Cigar Makers' International Union.

1881
- Gompers plays a leading role in the formation of the Federation of Organized Trades and Labor Unions.

1886
- The American Federation of Labor is formed, with Gompers as president.

1890
- **May 1**
  Gompers delivers an address to workers in Louisville, Kentucky, advocating an eight-hour workday.

1894
- **August**
  In the *American Federationist*, Gompers publishes an editorial concerning the Pullman strike.

1895
- Gompers loses the presidency of the American Federation of Labor for one year.

1906
- Gompers presents labor's Bill of Grievances to President Theodore Roosevelt.

1908
- **February 3**
  In the Danbury Hatters' Case—*Loewe v. Lawlor*—the Supreme Court rules that trade unions are subject to the Sherman Antitrust Act.

candidacy of the Democrat Woodrow Wilson, who prevailed. The Wilson administration honored labor's support by appointing a former coal miner, William B. Wilson, to head the Department of Labor and enacting legislation beneficial to labor. The 1914 Clayton Act, further antitrust legislation, was proclaimed by Gompers as labor's Magna Carta for exempting unions from the restraint of trade provisions of the Sherman Antitrust Act. Gompers's enthusiasm for both the Clayton Act and the Wilson administration is apparent in his 1915 circular letter dispatched to AFL organizers. Gompers concludes in that letter that working within the political system allowed labor to legislatively address the inequities of the Supreme Court decision in the 1908 Danbury Hatters' Case.

As the United States struggled with maintaining Wilson's policy of neutrality during World War I, Gompers spoke before the 1916 annual meeting of the National Civic Federation, asserting that labor would support national preparedness but needed to be a full participant in any plans for the nation to move to war footing. When the United States entered World War I in April 1917, Gompers supported the nation's effort, breaking with Eugene Debs and the Socialists, who opposed U.S. participation. Gompers also endorsed the National War Labor Board, which encouraged the cooperation of business and labor in the war effort, a relationship Gompers had advocated in his 1916 address before the National Civic Federation. Gompers also served the Wilson administration as an adviser on the labor sections of the Versailles Treaty. His influence waned with Wilson's failing health and the election of the Republican Warren G. Harding to the presidency in 1920. In December 1924, Gompers collapsed while participating in a meeting of the Pan-American Federation of Labor; he died a week later, on December 13, in San Antonio, Texas. While labor was on the defensive in the 1920s, Gompers's leadership of the AFL from 1886 until his death established a strong foundation for craft unionism in the United States.

Explanation and Analysis of Documents

After flirting with Marxism in his youth, Gompers played a leading role in developing craft trade unionism, serving as president of the American Federation of Labor for all but one year from its founding in 1886 until his death in 1924. An opponent of Socialism, Gompers advocated in his speeches and writings for the AFL a faith in voluntarism—a philosophy by which craft unions enjoyed considerable local autonomy. He also believed that better conditions for workers could be obtained through collective bargaining rather than legislative action. The nonpartisanship of Gompers and the AFL, however, was abandoned in 1912 with the endorsement of Woodrow Wilson. Labor's alliance with Wilson's Democratic administration, as well as cooperation with the National Civic Federation, provided Gompers with considerable influence on the national stage, although Gompers and labor played less of a role in the Republican administrations of the 1920s.

Although he was not a fiery orator, Gompers was an effective speaker and writer who worked tirelessly on behalf of labor during the late nineteenth and early twentieth centuries, establishing the AFL as an important national organization. In his address given in Louisville, Kentucky, in May 1890, Gompers demonstrated his devotion to collective bargaining in his campaign for the eight-hour workday. His August 1894 editorial made clear his opposition to what he considered the greed of the industrialist George Pullman, but he broke with Eugene Debs and the American Railway Union during the Pullman strike, becoming a critic of Debs's leadership of the Socialist Party. In reaction to the Supreme Court decision in the 1908 Danbury Hatters' Case, which placed labor under the restrictions of the Sherman Antitrust Act, Gompers penned an angry response urging labor to seek relief through congressional action. This shift in tactics was rewarded with the passage of the Clayton Act, which Gompers praised in a February 1915 circular to AFL organizers. Gompers was at the zenith of his political influence on the national stage when he gave his 1916 speech before the National Civic Federation, in which he embraced national preparedness for war while criticizing those on the political left advocating pacifism. The cooperative approach urged in this speech led Gompers and the AFL into participation with the National War Labor Board, but the alliance with business failed during the postwar period, as AFL membership declined.

◆ **Address to Workers in Louisville, Kentucky**

Gompers addressed working people of Louisville to advocate the eight-hour workday in a speech of nearly two hours on May 1, 1890; according to the *Louisville Courier*, the crowd never seemed to tire of listening to the labor leader. In the introduction to his speech, Gompers proclaims that workers throughout Western Europe are willing to join with their American counterparts in striking for the "limitation of hours of labor to eight hours for sleep, eight hours for work, and eight hours for what we will." Gompers ridicules the stereotype that workers will use their leisure time for debauchery and drink, observing that alcohol is usually abused by the wealthy who do not have to work, by the hopelessly unemployed, or by laborers who are worn thin because they are confined in factories for twelve- to sixteen-hour workdays. Seeking to foster a degree of cooperation between labor and management, Gompers argues that reduced hours of work will enhance the productivity and growth of the American economy. He contrasts the high standards of living in the United States and Great Britain, where labor hours are steadily declining, with the degradation of labor elsewhere, such as in China. Such comparisons were popular in the late nineteenth century among many workingmen, and here Gompers is appealing to the prejudice often displayed against the "yellow peril" (with reference to the color of Asians' skin) in driving down wages.

Gompers goes on to assert that exploited workers lack the energy for invention that allows for social and economic progress. He argues that with greater leisure at their disposal, working people will cultivate their minds through

Time Line	
1908	■ **March** Gompers presents an *American Federationist* editorial criticizing the Court's ruling in the Danbury Hatters' Case.
1912	■ Gompers and the American Federation of Labor abandon nonpartisanship and endorse the Democratic presidential candidacy of Woodrow Wilson.
1914	■ Upon its passage, the Clayton Act is lauded by Gompers as labor's version of the Magna Carta.
1915	■ **February 24** Gompers distributes a circular to organizers for the American Federation of Labor about the provisions of the Clayton Act.
1916	■ **January 18** Gompers delivers an address to the annual meeting of the National Civic Federation about labor's role in a potential U.S. war effort.
1917	■ **April** The United States enters World War I.
1918	■ **April** Gompers begins participating with the National War Labor Board.
1919	■ **June 28** Peace is secured by the Treaty of Versailles, for which Gompers served as an adviser on labor sections.
1924	■ **December 13** Gompers dies in San Antonio, Texas, after attending a meeting of the Pan-American Federation of Labor.

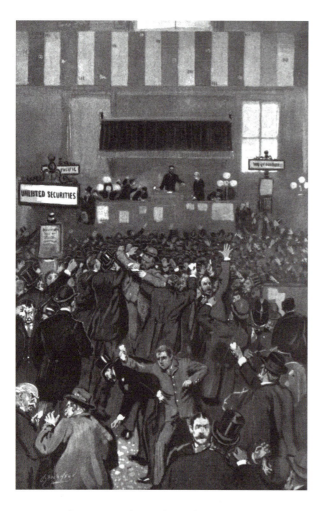

Panic at the New York Stock Exchange in May 1893
(Library of Congress)

activities such as the theater and reading. The laboring class will then contribute to the growth of American society through increased consumption. Gompers seems to envision a working class that will rise up to be absorbed into the middle class. But he proclaims that to achieve this mobility, workers must have time enough to devote energy to their own development; they must be working so as to live well rather than living only to work. He also insists that labor will continue to ask for its fair share of the wealth that high productivity has attained for the United States. In seeking the implementation of the eight-hour workday, Gompers returns to the principles of voluntarism; he insists that labor agitation rather than legislative fiat will advance reform and promote the interests of both labor and capital.

◆ Editorial on the Pullman Strike

In response to the declining economic conditions during the Panic of 1893, the industrialist George Pullman reduced wages but failed to lower rents for the workers in his company town outside Chicago. where railway sleeping cars were produced. The wildcat strike of Pullman Palace Car Company workers that began on May 11, 1894, was supported by the American Railway Union and its leader, Eugene Debs. The ARU launched a boycott of trains containing Pullman cars, which disrupted national railroad traffic. Arguing that the boycott interfered with mail delivery, the administration of President Grover Cleveland obtained an injunction against the ARU leadership, and troops were dispatched to quash the strike. In desperation, Debs appealed to Gompers and the AFL for a general strike on behalf of the beleaguered union. But at a meeting of the AFL executive board in Chicago on July 12, 1894, Gompers refused to call for a general strike, arguing that the ARU strike was impulsive and that it was in the best interest of working people for sympathy work stoppages to be halted. Gompers also believed that it was foolhardy to involve the AFL in a doomed strike. Debs, however, perceived Gompers as betraying industrial unionism in favor of the elite interests of skilled craft unions. Debs and Gompers would continue their antagonistic relationship into the early twentieth century as Debs assumed a leadership role within the Socialist Party.

While he considered the tactics of the ARU rash, Gompers makes clear in his August 1894 editorial for the *American Federationist* his sympathy for the Pullman workers and his antipathy for the industrialist himself. Declaring his working-class sensibilities, Gompers describes George Pullman as "the most consummate type of avaricious wealth absorber, tyrant and hypocrite this age, of that breed, has produced." Discrediting Pullman's brand of welfare capitalism, Gompers proclaims the purported living and health conditions of the factory company town to be a charade for media consumption. The reality of life for Pullman workers was subpar housing standards and increased exposure to disease. As for the claim by Pullman that he was forced to reduce wages because of his declining profits, Gompers concludes that the industrialist simply refused to justly arbitrate the dispute, because he was certainly financially capable of providing more equitable compensation for his workers. In a rhetorical finish to his editorial, Gompers seeks to refute Debs and others who accused him of abandoning labor's cause, asserting, "The end is not yet. Labor will not back down. It will triumph despite all the Pullmans combined; and as for Pullman, he has proven himself a public enemy." Criticism of Gompers for his perceived indifference to the Pullman strike deprived the union leader of his AFL presidency in 1895, but he regained office the following year.

◆ Editorial on the Supreme Court Ruling in the Danbury Hatters' Case

On February 3, 1908, the Supreme Court of the United States delivered its decision in the Danbury Hatters' Case. According to the Court, the boycott by the United Hatters of North America was an unlawful restraint of trade, and the manufacturer was entitled to triple damages under the Sherman Antitrust Act. In his *American Federationist* editorial of March 1908, Gompers asserts his opposition to the Court's ruling, although he concludes that the decision must be obeyed until Congress is able to bestow legislative relief for labor. In his advice to AFL organizers, Gompers makes it clear that as union president he is willing to accept the legal burdens that defiance of the Supreme Court's decision would entail. Nevertheless, he concludes that such a course of action would do little to avoid coercive actions by the state against other union officials and members. Gompers concludes that under the court's ruling all union officers would be liable for any violations committed by any AFL official or member. Thus, any individual action taken by Gompers would endanger the entire organization. Gompers goes on to argue that is almost inconceivable that the Court would make such a draconian decision. considering the services rendered by the AFL and labor movement to the economy and American civilization, but the Court is punishing labor while allowing big business, whose monopolistic policies the Sherman Act was passed to regulate, to remain unpunished.

Indeed, while finding the decision unjust, Gompers insists that labor must work within the system. He indicates, however, that he is willing to somewhat abandon his principles of voluntarism on this occasion, arguing that direct congressional action is necessary to protect organized labor, for the Court made the "natural and rational voluntary action of workmen unlawful and punishable by fine and imprisonment." Gompers recognizes the dangers of legislation generally in asserting that Congress did not intend that the Sherman Antitrust Act be applied to labor organizations. Nevertheless, the Court's ruling means that labor must seek relief from the legislative branch. Gompers concludes his editorial with a traditional call for continued organization to "promote the uplifting and noble work of our great cause of humanity."

◆ **Circular to the Organizers of the American Federation of Labor**

In 1912 Gompers officially abandoned the AFL policy of nonpartisanship by endorsing the Democratic candidacy of Woodrow Wilson. The support of Gompers and his labor organization was rewarded by the Wilson administration's passage of the Clayton Act (1914), which exempted labor unions from the restraint of trade provisions contained in the Sherman Antitrust Act. The Clayton Act, which effectively provided relief for labor following the Supreme Court decision in the 1908 Danbury Hatters' Case, was hailed by Gompers as labor's equivalent of the Magna Carta. Gompers begins his circular to AFL organizers by observing that opponents of the Wilson administration and organized labor were conducting a campaign of misinformation regarding the Clayton Act and its implications for labor. Gompers urges AFL organizers to ensure that union members are informed as to the great victory achieved by organized labor in this legislation, which guaranteed labor the right to engage in collective and direct action to influence employers. The Sherman Act, passed by Congress to control the monopolistic practices of big business, would no longer be applied by the courts to limit labor in seeking the redress of grievances from employers.

Gompers asserts that the focal point of the legislation is that "*the labor of a human being is not a commodity or article of commerce,*" distinguishing between the labor power of an individual and the product of that labor. Thus, labor is freed from the shadow of slavery in order to independently bargain with ownership—but Gompers certainly distances himself from any Marxist notions of labor owning the means of production. Gompers credits the Clayton Act with allowing labor the freedom to pursue organizing and the pressuring of businesses without fear of direct interference by the government. The earlier AFL policies of voluntarism are celebrated in Gompers's assertion that labor is now free to strike, boycott, picket, and assemble. He hails the fact that the bargaining tools that workers need to control their laboring lives are now protected. Gompers would continue to oppose legislation such as the Adamson Act (1916), which established the eight-hour workday for railroad employees, believing that such labor protection could be best assured through the type of direct labor action protected by the Clayton Act rather than by Congressional legislation.

◆ **Address to the Annual Meeting of the National Civic Federation**

As World War I raged on European battlefields in 1916, Americans were divided over whether the United States should participate in the conflict. While the Socialist Party, under the leadership of Eugene Debs, believed that entering the war would benefit only munitions makers and bankers at the expense of the working class, the Wilson administration advocated a policy of national preparedness that would allow the nation to build its strength while yet enjoying peace. Employing a slogan about how he kept the nation out of the war, Wilson defeated the Republican Charles Evans Hughes in the 1916 election—but in April 1917 the United States indeed entered World War I.

Gompers spoke of labor's stance with respect to the war in an address to the National Civic Federation on January 18, 1916, in Washington, D.C. After ruing the horrors of the war, Gompers proclaims his identification with the preparedness policies of the Wilson administration while suggesting that in a period of national emergency it is essential that labor and business cooperate in pursuit of national goals. Gompers informs his audience that he once shared pacifist notions of international brotherhood but that the European conflict has demonstrated that men must be willing to fight for freedom and to combat injustice. Preparedness and the defense of the nation are, accordingly, the obligations of all citizens, he says, and labor is at this point in time more than willing to do its patriotic duty.

Gompers recognized that modern warfare required the mobilization of natural resources, industry, commerce, and labor along with the allowance of increased power to the state. While many Socialists and anarchists on the political left feared the power of the war state, Gompers here expresses the belief that the need for national defense offers an opportunity for labor to make its rightful contributions to national preparedness. Labor, he asserts, will play an important role in the defense sphere if government and businesses embrace the democratic principles of trade

"In all industries where the hours of labor are long, there you will find the least development of the power of invention. Where the hours of labor are long, men are cheap, and where men are cheap there is no necessity for invention."

(Address to Workers in Louisville, Kentucky)

"The end is not yet. Labor will not back down. It will triumph despite all the Pullmans combined; and as for Pullman, he has proven himself a public enemy. His name and memory are excoriated to-day and will be forever."

(Editorial on the Pullman Strike)

"Under the court's construction of the Sherman law the voluntary and peaceful associations of labor that are organized for the uplifting of the workers, these unions I say, are made the greatest offenders under the anti-trust law."

(Editorial on the Supreme Court Decision in the Danbury Hatters' Case)

"In all the history of the working people of this or any other country, no such declaration has been enacted into law as was secured by the A.F. of L. in the enactment of the labor provisions of the Clayton Antitrust Act.... That law declares that the labor of a human being is not a commodity or article of commerce. It declares lawful the exercise of the normal activities of the labor movement of the United States."

(Circular to the Organizers of the American Federation of Labor)

"The labor movement has always been a leader in the case of democracy. The labor movement demands democracy in all things, including military organizations and institutions of the country. It holds that policies and methods of self-defense are best safe-guarded when there is equal opportunity for all to become members of whatever organizations and institutions, whether military or otherwise, exist throughout the country."

(Address to the Annual Meeting of the National Civic Federation) unionism. Thus, Gompers states his belief that laborers have earned the unquestioned right to assert their place as citizen-soldiers in the national preparedness state. In this instance Gompers is referring only to voluntary service, but in 1917 he supported conscription, which was opposed by Debs and the Socialist Party. As a result of this support, labor was included as a partner with business and government in the nation's democratic decision making with respect to the war. Asserting labor's preparedness to assume its role in the defense of the nation, Gompers perceives the bloodshed of World War I as offering an opportunity for labor to share in what Wilson would later call a war to make the world safe for democracy.

Impact and Legacy

As a young laboring man, Gompers was initially attracted to the ideas of Karl Marx, but his participation in the Cigar Makers' International Union convinced him that trade unionism offered the most viable option for working people to attain greater social equality. After assuming the presidency of the American Federation of Labor in 1886, Gompers advocated a policy of voluntarism and craft unionism that allowed the union movement to achieve such goals as the eight-hour workday through collective bargaining rather than legislative fiat. Gompers eschewed what he considered to be the premature industrial strike of the ARU against George Pullman's railroad car company. Following the Supreme Court's decision in the Danbury Hatters' Case, which placed labor within the restrictions of the Sherman Antitrust Act, Gompers compromised his

views on political engagement. The AFL's support of Woodrow Wilson was rewarded with the 1914 passage of the Clayton Act, which recognized labor's right to strike or boycott in support of collective bargaining agreements. Gompers, in turn, endorsed American entrance into the First World War, perceiving the crisis as an opportunity for labor to enhance its position in the national consensus. He vehemently opposed the antiwar stance of Eugene Debs and the Socialist Party and participated in the National War Labor Board. The expected gains in the status of organized labor in post–World War I America, however, failed to materialize during the Republican presidencies of Warren Harding and Calvin Coolidge. Although Gompers was disappointed by the political climate of the 1920s, his tireless efforts on behalf of organized labor during the late nineteenth and early twentieth centuries provided a solid foundation for labor's expansion during the turbulent 1930s.

Key Sources

Important archival collections of Samuel Gompers's writings are available in the Library of Congress, in the American Federation of Labor's Files of the Office of the President at the Wisconsin State Historical Society, and in the George Meany Memorial Archives in Silver Spring, Maryland. An invaluable source is Stuart B. Kaufman, ed., *The Samuel Gompers Papers*, 10 vols. (1987–2007). Gompers's autobiography, *Seventy Years of Life and Labor*, was published posthumously in 1925; an abridged version was published in 1984.

Questions for Further Study

1. Compare and contrast Gompers's views on the Pullman strike with those of Jane Addams (in "A Modern Lear") and Eugene V. Debs (in "Liberty"). Note that while all were identified as Progressives or leftists in their day, each—Addams the social reformer, Debs the Socialist, and Gompers the labor leader—had a distinctly different agenda.

2. Examine Gompers's 1890 Louisville address from the standpoint of his apparent views on humanity, individual rights and desires, and social organization. How does he move the discussion beyond a matter of mere hours and wages to higher issues of personal fulfillment for workers? (Note the third paragraph, for instance, in which he considers what workers might do with their time if their hours of labor were shortened.) How accurate do you believe he is in his observations about human motivation, particularly in the last paragraph, where he says that "a man generally wants more"?

3. Discuss Gompers's politics in relation to the spectrum of left to right. In what ways did he distance himself from the Socialists on the left and the racists on the right? Is it fair to say that in supporting U.S. entry into World War I he had shifted to the right? How would or did he respond to those in the international labor movement who maintained that the war was harmful to the workers' cause?

Further Reading

■ Books

Dick, William M. *Labor and Socialism in America: The Gompers Era*. Port Washington, N.Y.: Kennikat Press, 1972.

Kaufman, Stuart B. *Samuel Gompers and the Origins of the American Federation of Labor, 1848–1896*. Westport, Conn.: Greenwood Press, 1973.

Livesay, Harold C. *Samuel Gompers and Organized Labor in America*. Boston: Little, Brown, 1978.

Mandel, Bernard. *Samuel Gompers: A Biography*. New York: Penguin, 1963.

Taft, Philip. *The A.F. of L. in the Time of Gompers*. New York: Harper, 1957.

■ Web Sites

"Samuel Gompers (1850–1924)." American Federation of Labor–Congress of Industrial Organizations Web site. http://www.aflcio.org/aboutus/history/history/gompers.cfm.

—Ron Briley

ADDRESS TO WORKERS IN LOUISVILLE, KENTUCKY (1890)

My friends, we have met here today to celebrate the idea that has prompted the thousands of working-people of Louisville and New Albany to parade the streets of y[our city]; that prompts the toilers of Chicago to turn out by their fifty thousand or hundred thousand of men; that prompts the vast army of wage-workers in New York to demonstrate their enthusiasm and appreciation of the importance of this idea; that prompts the toilers of England, Ireland, Germany, France, Italy, Spain, and Austria to defy the manifestos of the autocrats of the world and say that on May the first, 1890, the wage-workers of the world will lay down their tools in sympathy with the wage-workers of America, to establish a principle of limitation of hours of labor to eight hours for sleep, eight hours for work, and eight hours for what we will.

It has been charged time and again that were we to have more hours of leisure we would merely devote it to debauchery, to the cultivation of vicious habits—in other words, that we would get drunk. I desire to say this in answer to that charge: As a rule, there are two classes in society who get drunk. One is that class who has no work to do in consequence of too much money; the other class, who also has no work to do, because it can't get any, and gets drunk on its face. I maintain that that class in our social life that exhibits the greatest degree of sobriety is that class who are able, by a fair number of hours of day's work to earn fair wages.... The man who works twelve, fourteen, and sixteen hours a day requires some artificial stimulant to restore the life ground out of him in the drudgery of the day....

Is it not a fact that we find laborers in England and the United States, where the hours are eight, nine and ten hours a day—do we not find that the employers and laborers are more successful? Don't we find them selling articles cheaper? We do not need to trust the modern moralist to tell us those things. In all industries where the hours of labor are long, there you will find the least development of the power of invention. Where the hours of labor are long, men are cheap, and where men are cheap there is no necessity for invention. How can you expect a man to work ten or twelve or fourteen hours at his calling and then devote any time to the invention of a machine or discovery of a new principle or force? If he be so fortunate as to be able to read a paper he will fall asleep before he has read through the second or third line.

Why, when you reduce the hours of labor, say an hour a day, just think what it means. Suppose men who work ten hours a day had the time lessened to nine, or men who work nine hours a day have it reduced to eight hours; what does it mean? It means millions of golden hours and opportunities for thought. Some men might say you will go to sleep. Well, some men might sleep sixteen hours in a day; the ordinary man might try that, but he would soon find he could not do it long. He would have to do something. He would probably go to the theater one night, to a concert another night, but he could not do that every night. He would probably become interested in some study and the hours that have been taken from manual labor are devoted to mental labor, and the mental labor of one hour will produce for him more wealth than the physical labor of a dozen hours....

Wherever men are cheap, there you find the least degree of progress. It has only been under the great influence of our great republic, where our people have exhibited their great senses, that we can move forward, upward and onward and are watched with interest in our movements of progress and reform....

The man who works the long hours has no necessities except the barest to keep body and soul together, so he can work. He goes to sleep and dreams of work; he rises in the morning to go to work; he takes his frugal lunch to work; he comes home again to throw himself down on a miserable apology for a bed so that he can get that little rest that he may be able to go to work again. He is nothing but a veritable machine. He lives to work instead of working to live.

My friends, the only thing the working people need besides the necessities of life is time. Time. Time with which our lives begin; time with which our lives close; time to cultivate the better nature within us; time to brighten our homes. Time, which brings us from the lowest condition up to the highest civilization; time, so that we can raise men to a higher plane....

We want eight hours and nothing less. We have been accused of being selfish, and it has been said that we will want more; that last year we got an advance of ten cents and now we want more. We do want more. You will find that a man generally wants more. Go and ask a tramp what he wants, and if he doesn't want a drink he will want a good, square meal. You ask a workingman, who is getting two dollars a day, and he will say that he wants ten cents more. Ask a man who gets five dollars a day and he will want fifty cents more. The man who receives five thousand dollars a year wants six thousand a year, and the man who owns eight or nine hundred thousand dollars will want a hundred thousand dollars more to make it a million, while the man who has his millions will want everything he can lay his hands on and then raise his voice against the poor devil who wants ten cents more a day. We live in the latter part of the nineteenth century. In the age of electricity and steam that has produced wealth a hundred fold, we insist that it has been brought about by the intelligence and energy of the workingmen, and while we find that it is now easier to produce it is harder to live. We do want more, and when it becomes more, we shall still want more. And we shall never cease to demand more until we have received the results of our labor.

Glossary

May the first	May Day, also known as International Workers' Day, a celebration of the labor movement
men are cheap	hourly wages are low

Editorial on the Pullman Strike (1894)

It is a lamentable fact that success does not always attend the right or those who struggle to achieve it. If any doubt existed as to the truth of this statement, the strike at Pullman, and the strike of the American Railway Union in support of it, has dispelled that doubt.

It is indeed difficult to conceive a cause in which right was more on the side of those who were defeated as in the one under consideration.

We present to our readers the true story of this contest, and the cause which led up to it; and we hope to add to the contumely and contempt which every earnest, honest, liberty loving man, woman and child in the country must feel for the most consummate type of avaricious wealth absorber, tyrant and hypocrite this age, of that breed, has furnished—Pullman.

In the language of the picture drawn by Pullman, the *philanthropist* of Pullman, the town, he says: "That it is bordered with bright beds of flowers and green velvety stretches of land, that [it] is shaded with trees and dotted with parks and pretty water vistas and glimpses here and there of artistic sweeps and landscape gardening, a town where the homes even of the most modest are bright and wholesome and filled with pure air and light, a town, in a word, from which all that is ugly, discordant and demoralizing is eliminated and all that inspires to self-respect, to thrift and to cleanliness of person and of being is generally provided."

This description is unquestionably true so far as it refers to the view which the passer by sees upon the train; but back where the workers live and die, what a pitiful, horrible condition prevails. In whole blocks entire families have for years lived in one room in order that they might eke out an existence. In no community in the world, except possibly China, was there such a small proportion of families living in family privacy....

In Pullman there was always an indefinable something telling the workers that their presence was not wanted where the flowers and Fountains and velvety lawns are. The houses are not healthy and the records show an unusual number of deaths by zymotic diseases.

During the terrible suffering last winter the Company insisted that there was no destitution nor suffering in the place and with much nonchalance declared that "there could be none because it was not contemplated in the theory upon which the town was founded and controlled."

When a number of charitable ladies organized to relieve the destitution they were not permitted to carry on the work, for that would be an acknowledgment that there was need of relief.

The town of Pullman covers 350 acres estimated to be worth $10,000,000. Buildings occupied by the workers are congested as the most thickly settled residence districts of Chicago, yet Pullman pays but

Glossary

capital stock	the total of all shares in a particular company that are authorized for sale by that company's charter
Carnegie	Scottish-born industrial and philanthropist Andrew Carnegie (1835–1919)
contumely	insolence or arrogance
Pullman	George Pullman (1831–1897), inventor of the Pullman sleeping car, which made overnight rail travel more comfortable
Pullman, the town	Pullman, Illinois, founded in the 1880s for Pullman company workers and later annexed to the city of Chicago
zymotic diseases	a term, since outmoded, for diseases such as typhoid fever and smallpox that were thought to be caused by fermentation

$15,000 on taxes. (Carnegie defrauds the government in his contracts; Pullman in taxes.)

Nor should it be imagined that the statement made by Pullman recently, that the reason he refused to arbitrate the matter in dispute with his employees was that the Company were producing cars at a loss. As a matter of fact last February, or two months before the strike commenced, the Company issued an official statement containing the following. "The day is near at hand when the $30,000,000 present capital of the Pullman Company will be covered and more than covered by the value of the 3,500 acres of land on which is built the town of Pullman." Coupled with this was the statement that the $30,000,000 capital stock had a market value of $60,000,000.

When the fact is borne in mind that Pullman has practically a monopoly in the building of his cars, is not the claim preposterous that he could not pay fair wages? Does anyone imagine that if Pullman's statement of his inability to pay the wage demanded was true that he would refuse to arbitrate? No arbitrator would make an award against him if he could prove his assertions; his refusal is the best evidence of his untruthfulness. In truth out of his own statements he convicts himself.

The end is not yet. Labor will not back down. It will triumph despite all the Pullmans combined; and as for Pullman, he has proven himself a public enemy. His name and memory are excoriated to-day and will be forever.

EDITORIAL ON THE SUPREME COURT RULING IN THE DANBURY HATTERS' CASE (1908)

TO ORGANIZED LABOR AND FRIENDS.

It has seldom occurred that I have found it necessary to use the first person in addressing my fellow-workers and the people through the editorial columns of the *American Federationist*. What follows here refers to such an extraordinary circumstance and affects the labor organizations, their members and our friends so fundamentally, that I am impelled to address them in the most direct manner. The Supreme Court of the United States on February 3, 1908, rendered a decision in the case of the hat manufacturer Loewe against the United Hatters of North America, and decreed that the Loewe suit for three-fold damages can be maintained under the Sherman anti-trust law. The Supreme Court holds that the action of the hatters, as described in the complaint, is a combination "in restraint of trade or commerce among the several states," in the sense in which those words are used in the Sherman law.

A decision by the Supreme Court, the highest tribunal of the country, is law and must be obeyed, regardless of whether or not we believe the decision to be a just one.

We protest that the trade unions of the country should not be penalized under the provisions of the Sherman anti-trust law. In fact, I know that Congress never intended the law to apply to the labor unions, but the Supreme Court rules that it shall apply to them; therefore, pending action by Congress to define our status and restore our rights by modifying or amending the Sherman law, there is no alternative for labor but to obey the mandate of the court....

I have no words adequate to express the regret I feel at being obliged to take this action, especially as in the opinion of competent lawyers—and their opinion is shared by many other laymen as well as myself—this decision by the Supreme Court is unwarranted and unjust, but until Congressional relief can be obtained it must undoubtedly be binding upon us all. Were it only myself personally who might suffer, for conscience sake I should not hesitate to risk every penalty, even unto the extreme, in defense of what I believe to be labor's rights. In this case of the adverse court decision, and indeed in every other circumstance which may arise, I think those who know me do not question my loyalty, devotion, and willingness to bear fully any responsibility involved in the forwarding of the cause to which my life is pledged; but unfortunately the terms of the decision are such that no one person, even though president of the American Federation of Labor and willing to assume entire responsibility, will be permitted to take upon himself the sole penalty of protest against what I and every member of every organization affiliated to the American Federation of Labor, and indeed every patriotic citizen, must feel to be a most sweeping drag-net decision making the natural and rational voluntary action of workmen unlawful and punishable by fine and imprisonment....

Glossary

Danbury Hatters' Case	*Loewe v. Lawlor*, a 1908 ruling in which the Supreme Court held that the boycott of D. E. Loewe & Company by the United Hatters of North America constituted a conspiracy in restraint of trade, a violation of the Sherman Antitrust Act
the hat manufacturer Loewe	Dietrich Loewe, whose refusal to allow unions to organize in his Danbury, Connecticut–based firm, D. E. Loewe & Company, resulted in a strike and boycott
laymen	nonprofessionals
met	dealt with
Sherman anti-trust law	an 1890 act of Congress, the first such law to limit the power of monopolies

Under the court's construction of the Sherman law the voluntary and peaceful associations of labor that are organized for the uplifting of the workers, these unions I say, are made the greatest offenders under the anti-trust law. It is almost unbelievable that our unions which perform so important a service in the interest of civilization and moral and material progress are to be accorded the treatment of malefactors. Yet the more carefully this decision is read the more absolutely clear does it become that our unions are to be penalized by it, as the most vicious of trusts were intended to be, yet the trusts still go unpunished.

I have a strong hope that Congress will promptly take heed of the injustice that has been done the workers, and will so amend or modify the Sherman anti-trust law, that the labor unions will be restored to the exercise of the powers and rights guaranteed to all our citizens under the constitution.

It is not conceivable that Congress will turn a deaf ear to the rightful demand of the workers of the country for relief from this most amazing decision, but until such time as relief is assured, I am compelled, for the safety of our men of labor, to obey literally the decision of the Supreme Court; but this situation created by the court must be met. It will be met.

While abiding by this decision, I urge most strongly upon my fellow unionists everywhere to be more energetic than ever before in organizing the yet unorganized, in standing together, in uniting and federating for the common good. Be more active than ever before in using every lawful and honorable means, not only to secure relief from the present situation at the hands of Congress, but in the doing of everything which may promote the uplifting and noble work of our great cause of humanity. Like all great causes it must meet temporary opposition, but in the end it will accomplish all the more on account of the trials endured.

CIRCULAR TO THE ORGANIZERS OF THE AMERICAN FEDERATION OF LABOR (1915)

To the Organizers of the American Federation of Labor:

Dear Sirs and Brothers:

There is an insidious and persistent attempt by the enemies of organized labor to minimize the importance of the labor sections of the Clayton Antitrust Act and to create the impression that the legislation has not secured for workers better protection in exercising their rights. Because the ultimate purpose of this attempt is to mislead the workers and to discourage efforts along the only lines from which progress can reasonably be expected and because many workers have not at hand sources of information by which they could inform themselves that the attacks upon the Clayton Antitrust Act are based upon un-truths, I am putting in your hands this simple concise statement. In your work among the rank and file of the workers you will find many opportunities to press home these truths and to counteract this attempt to mislead public opinion.

I urge upon you to let no misrepresentations go on unchallenged and unrefuted in regard to the great victory won by organized labor in the legislation embodied in the labor sections of the Clayton Act, which became law October 15, 1914.

The two sections of the act that are of greatest importance to labor are 6 and 20....

One of the reasons assigned by the Supreme Court of the United States for holding that the Sherman Antitrust Act applied in the case of the Danbury Hatters was that the hatters' organization had succeeded in establishing the union shop in seventy out of eighty-two hat manufacturing establishments.

The second sentence of Section 6 secured to labor organizations recognition as legal organizations, the right to exist and to carry out the legitimate purposes of organization. It exempts labor organizations and their members from the provision of trust legislation, when they are performing the duties for which the unions were instituted.

The activities which are the legitimate purposes of organized labor are of vital importance. Courts through abuse of the writ of injunction and by judicial interpretation have denied workers the right to do that which is necessary in order to promote their welfare and secure their protection against employers' greed and injustice. Section 20 specifically enumerates certain rights formerly denied by courts which are now lawful....

You will note that the second paragraph declares that workers have a right to quit work "singly or in concert"—that is, to strike. They have a right to ask others to join the strike movement. They have a right to "picket." They have a right to "withhold their patronage," or, in every-day English, to "boycott," and they have a right to recommend, advise or persuade others "to boycott." They have a right to pay strike benefits. They have the right of peaceful assemblage.

Glossary

the case of the Danbury Hatters	*Loewe v. Lawlor*, a 1908 ruling in which the Supreme Court held that the boycott of D. E. Loewe & Company by the United Hatters of North America constituted a conspiracy in restraint of trade, a violation of the Sherman Antitrust Act
Clayton Antitrust Act	a 1914 law that increased the scope of the Sherman Antitrust Act, thus further limiting monopolies
injunctive writ	a court order
organs	publications
Sherman Antitrust Act	an 1890 act of Congress, the first such law to limit the power of monopolies
union shop	a workplace in which unions are active

Then note particularly this significant clause:

"Nor shall any of the acts specified in this paragraph be considered or held to be violations of any law of the United States."

These rights enumerated here, now secured by the Clayton Act, have again and again been denied workers through the abuse of the injunctive writ. These injunctions were issued by the courts extending their jurisdiction and power, and then using this extended jurisdiction and power as precedents for further encroachment upon the workers' rights and liberties.

Now as to the decision in the Hatters' case, which occasioned the campaign of misrepresentation carried on through the daily press and organs of hostile employers. The Hatters' case was begun in 1903. That case and the decision of the Supreme Court in 1908 holding that the Sherman Antitrust law applied to organizations of labor were what convinced the A. F. of L. that legislation to prevent such litigation was necessary to protect the very existence of organized labor. It was the effort to secure such legislation that finally succeeded in the enactment of the labor provisions of the Clayton Act, which became law October 15, 1914....

In all the history of the working people of this or any other country, no such declaration has been enacted into law as was secured by the A. F. of L. in the enactment of the labor provisions of the Clayton Antitrust Act, which went into effect October 15, 1914. That law declares that *the labor of a human being is not a commodity or article of commerce.* It declares lawful the exercise of the normal activities of the labor movement of the United States. It gives freedom for the toilers of our country to work out their every-day problems of life, and to earnestly and persistently, as well as rationally, continue the struggle for a better and truer life for all.

ADDRESS TO THE ANNUAL MEETING OF THE NATIONAL CIVIC FEDERATION (1916)

For seventeen months war such as has never been known in the history of man has been devouring life and consuming the handiwork of man. Such a stupendous horror has compelled men to think deeply of the principles underlying our institutions and the spirit that makes for human progress and liberty....

The pacifists and those who hold to policies of non-resistance have failed, as I had failed, to understand and to evaluate that quality in the human race which makes men willing to risk their all for an ideal. Men worthy of the name will fight even for a "scrap of paper" when that paper represents ideals of human justice and freedom. The man who would not fight for such a scrap of paper is a poor craven who dares not assert his rights against the opposition and the demands of others. There is little progress made in the affairs of the world in which resistance of others is not involved. Not only must man have a keen sense of his own rights, but the will and the ability to maintain those rights with effective insistence. Resistance to injustice and tyranny and low ideals is inseparable from a virile fighting quality that has given purpose and force to ennobling causes, to all nations....

As the result of the European war there is hardly a citizen who has not in some degree modified his opinions upon preparedness and national defense. The belief prevails that there must be some policy of preparedness and national defense although there is wide diversion as to what policies ought to be adopted....

Constructive development must have consideration for every factor concerned in production and must secure to each equal opportunities that will result in the best service and in the conservation of the future service. Such a policy will involve thorough organization of all the factors of production. This organization must extend to the human element in production in order that there may be accorded to the workers proper consideration of their needs and proper conservation of their labor power.

Preparedness as viewed from this standpoint is a part of the larger problems of national development—physical, mental, economic. It is a civic, an economic, as well as a military problem. National development can be in accord with the highest ideals only when all citizens have the right to voluntary association to promote their own welfare and to activities necessary to carry out the purpose of such organizations.

This broad general policy includes associations of wage-earners—trade unions. These associations of the workers must be recognized by all agencies, whether private or governmental, that are concerned with the life and the work of the workers....

The labor movement has never advocated the abolition of agencies for the enforcement of right and justice, or for the abolition of the military arm of government, but it does demand that these shall be so organized as to prevent their misuse and abuse as a means of tyranny against the workers, and to prevent the development of pernicious results that have grown out of militarism, the building up of a separate military caste and the subversion of civic life to military government and military standards. When military institutions and military service are separated from the general life of the people they become subversive to the ideals of civic life, they become dangerous to the best development and the best interests of the nation.

The rights and privileges of citizenship impose a duty upon all who enjoy them. That duty involves service to the nation in all relations of the common life including its defense against attack and the maintenance of national institutions and ideals.

There are no citizens of our country who are more truly patriotic than the organized wage-earners—or all of the wage-earners, and we have done our share in the civic life of the nation as well as in the nation's wars. We have done our share to protect the nation against insidious attacks from within that were directed at the very heart of our national life and would have inevitably involved us in foreign complications.

The wage-earners stood unfalteringly for ideals of honor, freedom and loyalty. Their wisdom and their patriotism served our country in a time of great need. No one can question that the wage-earners of the United States are patriotic in the truest sense. No one can question their willingness to fight for the cause of liberty, freedom and justice. No one can question the value of the ideals that direct the labor movement.

The labor movement takes the position that plans and policies for national defense and preparedness must be in accord with the educated conscience which can discern values and is able and alert to distinguish the vital from the less important and willing to insist upon the ideals and standards of justice, equality and freedom.

Every observer knows that there is no peace—all of life is a struggle, physical and mental. Progress results only from the domination of the forces making for freedom and opportunity over the forces of repression....

The thoughts and suggestions I have submitted should commend themselves to the serious and favorable consideration and action of all of our people—all their groups and associations. Put into actual operation, they will make not only for immediate effective preparedness for defense, but will prove the potential means for permanent preparedness and defense, and at the same time make all our people more efficient in their every endeavor, and, in addition safeguard the spirit of justice, freedom, democracy and humanity.

Glossary

caste	social class
the European war	World War I, which the United States did not enter until April 1917

Al Gore (AP/Wide World Photos)

AL GORE   1948–

U.S. Congressman, Senator, Vice President, and Presidential Candidate

Featured Documents
- High-Performance Computing Act of 1991
- "From Red Tape to Results: Creating a Government That Works Better and Costs Less" (1993)
- Address to the 1996 Democratic National Convention
- 2000 Concession Speech

Overview

Albert Arnold Gore, Jr., was born on March 31, 1948, in Washington, D.C. His father, Albert, Sr., was elected to the House of Representatives in 1939, and in 1952 he began a Senate career that would last until 1970. The younger Al was raised in the elite circles of Washington, where his family groomed him for politics from an early age. He graduated from Harvard and shortly thereafter enlisted in the army, serving in Vietnam for five months of his two-year military service. Before he left for Vietnam, Gore married Mary Elizabeth (Tipper) Aitcheson. He was discharged from the army three months early in order to pursue religious studies at Vanderbilt University, and he also began a five-year career as a journalist for the *Nashville Tennessean*. In 1974 Gore enrolled in law school at Vanderbilt.

Raised as a senator's son, Gore eventually followed in his father's footsteps. In 1976 he left law school to run for the House of Representatives, winning the seat that represented the Gore family home in Carthage, Tennessee. In 1984 Gore successfully ran for a seat in the U.S. Senate. He built a reputation for being an articulate interrogator as a member of the Interstate and Foreign Commerce Committee, where he gained national attention for investigating the potential dangers of chemicals used in manufacturing flame-retardant children's pajamas and the public health threat posed by the Love Canal toxic waste site. He cosponsored the first Superfund Bill to finance cleanup of hazardous waste sites and helped pass the National Organ Transplant Act, which created a system to match organ donors with recipients. He also actively campaigned for arms reduction during the arms control debates of the Reagan administration.

Following a disastrous bid for the Democratic nomination for president in 1988, Gore redirected his political activities toward legislation affecting technology and the environment. In 1988 he traveled to the South Pole with atmospheric scientists and visited the Amazon a year later; both of these trips increased his concern about the impact of human activities on the environment. In response, Gore introduced a number of proposals in the Senate, including bills to develop alternative energy sources and to phase out the use of chlorofluorocarbons. In addition to his environmental bills, he also wrote the High-Performance Computing Act of 1991, which provided funding to expand a fledgling Internet.

Bill Clinton chose Al Gore as his running mate in 1992 based on his expertise in the environment, technology, and arms control along with his moderate position as a "New Democrat." The term *New Democrat* was used to describe leaders who sought to align the party's image not with the big government programs of its New Deal past but with a more global, modern constituency that embraced change. Gore and others associated with the New Democrats were open to importing techniques and ideas from the business sector in order to streamline government services and improve productivity.

As vice president, Gore worked to improve government efficiency and reduce bureaucracy, and he supported welfare reform. He led a massive reevaluation of federal government operations, detailed in his report titled "From Red Tape to Results: Creating a Government That Works Better and Costs Less," which called for a 12 percent reduction in the federal workforce over five years. Following his delivery of the successful keynote address at the 1996 Democratic National Convention, Gore established himself as a viable candidate for the 2000 Democratic presidential nomination. Facing George W. Bush in the 2000 election, Gore won the popular vote by approximately five hundred thousand votes but lost in a contested recount of Florida's twenty-five electoral votes, a fight that went to the U.S. Supreme Court. Gore conceded the election to Bush on December 13, 2000.

Once out of public office, Gore became a vocal critic of the Bush administration's environmental policies as well as its engagement in Iraq. Gore won the Nobel Peace Prize in 2007 for his work on publicizing global warming, as depicted in the film *An Inconvenient Truth*. He also continued to pursue his interests in technology; Gore served as an adviser to Google; joined the board of Apple Computer in 2005; and founded a television news network, Current, aimed at younger viewers.

Explanation and Analysis of Documents

Gore's political career as a senator and vice president occurred during an important shift in the American electorate's attitudes and voting habits. Following the "Reagan revolution" of the 1980s most voters, including those who identified themselves as Democrats, became more conser-

1948

■ **March 31**
Albert Arnold Gore, Jr., is born in Washington, D.C.

1969

■ **June 12**
Gore graduates from Harvard.

■ **August 8**
Gore enlists in the army.

1971

■ **Fall**
Gore enrolls in Vanderbilt University's School of Divinity and begins work as a journalist for the *Nashville Tennessean.*

1977

■ **January 4**
Gore takes the oath of office as member of the Ninety-fifth Congress.

1987

■ **April 10**
Gore launches an unsuccessful run for the Democratic presidential candidacy.

1991

■ **December 9**
House and Senate pass the High-Performance Computing Act, otherwise known as the Gore Bill.

1992

■ Gore publishes his first book, *Earth in the Balance.*

1993

■ **January 20**
Gore takes the oath of office as vice president.

■ **September 7**
Gore submits his National Performance Review, "From Red Tape to Results: Creating a Government That Works Better and Costs Less."

1996

■ **August 26**
Gore gives his acceptance address to the 1996 Democratic National Convention.

vative, favoring a smaller federal government. Groomed for politics from an early age, Gore molded himself as a different kind of Democrat, one whose agenda would resonate with centrist voters. Four documents illustrate Gore's meticulous attention to research and detail, his fascination with technology and innovation, and his often self-deprecating humor: the High-Performance Computing Act, his preface to the National Performance Review, his address to the 1996 Democratic National Convention, and his concession speech following his defeat in the 2000 presidential election.

◆ **High-Performance Computing Act of 1991**

In a 1999 television interview with CNN's Wolf Blitzer, Gore made one of the more unfortunate statements of his career: "During my service in the United States Congress, I took the initiative in creating the Internet" (qtd. in Turque, p. 22). Actually, the Internet began in the late 1960s as the Advance Research Projects Agency Network, a Department of Defense Advance Research Projects Agency program, but Gore was, in fact, instrumental in expanding its influence and use. On May 18, 1989, Gore introduced the National High-Performance Computer Technology Act, which would become the High-Performance Computing Act of 1991. This legislation mandated that the Defense Advance Research Projects Agency invest in the development of a national computer system that would connect government agencies as well as universities and libraries. At a time when such technology was known to only a few, Gore saw the potential for its use by a wide range of Americans.

At the time of this legislation, cooperative computer networks existed but were limited in speed, served only a few institutions, and were not funded by the government. The High-Performance Computing Act calls for the creation of a National Research and Education Network sponsored by the federal government that would link government, industry, and research and educational institutions. The National Research and Education Network was envisioned as an expansion of a limited network primarily used by research organizations. The legislation anticipates a number of challenges posed by an expanded Internet: security and copyright protections, means to allow entities to charge for using information posted on the Web, and the maintenance of a competitive marketplace.

Although the High-Performance Computing Act did not create the Internet, it did provide the funding to develop what was a very limited network into the familiar World Wide Web. Gore's legislation was a key document in implementing his vision for an information superhighway connecting government, business, academic and research institutions, and the public.

◆ **"From Red Tape to Results: Creating a Government That Works Better and Costs Less"**

Bill Clinton successfully defeated incumbent George H. W. Bush in the 1992 presidential election, in large part as a result of a campaign strategy that focused on the economy. Faced with a recession, the American public was also saddled with a soaring federal debt, which had grown during the Reagan and Bush administrations. Clinton's message of government and economic reform resonated with voters who no longer supported traditional Democratic social programs.

In March 1993, shortly after taking the oath of office, Clinton asked Gore to lead an evaluation of the federal government, known as the National Performance Review. In the preface to his report, Gore describes the review process using language similar to that used by businesspeople and management consultants. In doing so, he signals to the public that government is moving in the direction of the private sector: seeking greater efficiency in its use of resources.

Gore mentions Clinton's deficit reduction package of 1993, which included reductions in entitlement programs and tax increases as well as tax credits and business investment incentives. His primary message, however, is that government must serve the public and must drastically change in order to do so. Gore refers to "closing the trust deficit" to connect the reality of the government's deficit spending to declining public confidence in the federal government's ability to fulfill its obligations. He uses the term "customer service contract" to position the federal government as a service organization dedicated to the public.

Gore then describes the review process, again emphasizing the fact that the government must serve the public. He contrasts this review with past efforts to evaluate the government, which used external experts rather than people within the system. Gore's language reflects trends in the management practice of the time, which emphasized a bottom-up approach rather than a top-down strategy. Driven by the ideas of such theorists as Peter Drucker and W. Edwards Deming, management consultants encouraged businesses to involve employees and customers in decisions, using a team approach rather than a hierarchical, authoritative model. Emulating the private sector, Gore refers to "Reinvention Teams" of government employees; one of the best-selling business books in the late 1980s was *Re-Inventing the Corporation* by John Naisbitt and Patricia Aburdene, which popularized the concept of "reinvention" and led to other publications, including David Osborne and Ted Gaebler's *Reinventing Government: How the Entrepreneurial Spirit Is Transforming the Public Sector* (1993), an important influence on the Clinton campaign. Gore notes that the Performance Review involved input not just from employees but also citizens, state and local government leaders, business representatives, and members of the academic community. Well known for his tireless attention to detail and research, Gore collected information from many sources, and he highlights this widespread approach to differentiate his work from previous reviews that had relied on a handful of outside experts to evaluate government operations.

Gore's preface also reflects the changes that were taking place in American business during the late 1980s and early 1990s. As global competitors threatened American dominance in key industries, particularly automobile manufacturing, U.S. companies began to take measures to make their operations leaner and more efficient. Although the wave of downsizing would swell later in the 1990s, Gore's emphasis in 1993 on using innovative practices to create a more efficient government mirrors similar early efforts in the private sector. Given the substantial federal deficits at the time and the public sentiment that government should, like the private sector, learn to live within its means, Gore's emphasis on downsizing government, particularly through eliminating unnecessary staff and bureaucracy, appealed to the public, especially the business community.

Gore's recommendations led to some important changes in procurement practices as well as significant reductions in the number of government employees. In addition to the results it produced, the National Performance Review bears Gore's personal stamp: his interest in state-of-the-art technology or practices. In this case, Gore focused his attention on the most current management ideas of the time and sought to make those ideas function in the public sector. His interest in perpetuating those ideas beyond his report of September 1993 is clear; in 1997 Gore and Scott Adams published *Businesslike Government: Lessons Learned from America's Best Companies*, which described the interviews he conducted with business leaders as part of the National Performance Review. Although Gore did not eliminate all of the red tape in Washington, he brought into the open many of the more blatantly wasteful practices of the federal government, and his writings on reinventing government illustrate the important shift to the center that occurred in the Democratic Party during the Clinton administration. Gore's preface also shows the focus and clarity of message that is a strength of his writings and speeches.

Time Line

1999

■ **June 15**
Gore announces his candidacy for president.

2000

■ **December 13**
Gore gives his speech conceding the 2000 presidential election to George W. Bush.

2007

■ **February 25**
An Inconvenient Truth, a documentary covering Gore's campaign on global warming, wins the Academy Award for Best Documentary.

■ **December 10**
Gore delivers his Nobel lecture after receiving the Nobel Peace Prize for his work on global climate change.

◆ Address to the 1996 Democratic National Convention

Dogged by the Whitewater scandal, an investigation into allegedly improper real estate dealings by the Clintons, as well as by a failed attempt at health care reform and by the Paula Jones sexual harassment lawsuit against Bill Clinton, the Democrats suffered a historic defeat in the congressional election of 1994, losing control of both the House and the Senate. When President Clinton faced reelection in 1996 against the Republican contender Bob Dole, the incumbents appeared to have an uphill battle ahead of them; Clinton's and Gore's acceptance speeches at the Democratic National Convention would need to be memorable.

The vice presidential nominee typically delivers his acceptance speech before the presidential candidate does. In 1996 Gore was the keynote speaker on a separate evening, indicating that the party anticipated he would be a candidate for the Democratic presidential nomination in 2000. Gore needed to establish himself as an independent man, capable of taking on the executive office but also supportive of President Clinton, who was under attack by the Republican Party.

Gore immediately addresses one of his primary weaknesses: his stiff demeanor in public. He jokes about his "reputation for excitement," drawing laughter from the crowd. Gore then demonstrates his version of a popular dance at the time, the Macarena, at which point he stands absolutely rigid with a stony expression on his face, to the delight of the audience. Gore uses his ability to poke fun at himself in a masterful way to overcome a political obstacle to future higher office; he wins the audience over early in his speech by acknowledging his tendency to be uptight.

Gore then reviews the accomplishments of the Clinton administration, but emphasizes his own achievements. His list highlights improvements in the economy, technology, and the environment. Specifically, Gore mentions a "leaner re-invented government," a reference to his National Performance Review report; the information superhighway, a direct result of his work on the High-Performance Computing Act as a senator; and his priority of ensuring a clean environment. He also mentions foreign affairs in which he was involved, including negotiations with the Ukraine to disarm its nuclear warheads and diplomatic efforts to oust the military leader Raoul Cedras as ruler of Haiti and to respond to the growing crisis in Bosnia. By noting these specific instances of the Clinton administration's foreign policy accomplishments, Gore also highlights his own unusually active role in international affairs.

Gore then takes on Clinton's opponent in the upcoming election, Bob Dole. As majority leader of the Senate, Dole was a key figure during the acrimonious budget debate between Clinton and Congress that led to the shutdown of the federal government in 1995. Dole was wounded while serving in World War II and had been a member of the Senate for over thirty years. Thus, while Gore gives Dole credit for serving his country, he dubs him a "bridge to the past." By mentioning some specific policies Dole voted against, Gore makes the age difference between the candidates clear; Clinton would not yet have been twenty years old when Dole cast his vote against funding for the Apollo moon landing program.

Gore often refers to historical figures in his speeches and writings, and he does so in this speech to reinforce the dichotomy he is setting up between the past and the future. He mentions two American authors, Carl Sandburg and Ralph Waldo Emerson, both of whom are known for their poems and essays that portray America as a nation of optimism and progress. Gore dovetails the quotation from Emerson nicely into one about Clinton; Bill Clinton was born in Hope, Arkansas, and the phrase *man from Hope* had become a staple on the 1992 campaign trail.

Calling attention to the bipartisan tension of the time, Gore punctuates each of a string of charges against the Republican majority in Congress with the same words. This repetition serves as a rallying cry to the audience, and it also presents Gore as a leader; an important goal of this speech was to improve his image as a contender for the presidential nomination in 2000. Through his choice of words, Gore molds himself as the protector of Clinton's position, holding off the Republican threat.

The most controversial portion of this speech was Gore's emotional story about his sister, Nancy. According to his biographer Bill Turque, Gore wrestled with the text of this portion of the speech for days, inserting it at the last minute. Although some criticized him for exploiting his sister's death for political purposes and others took him to task for his own part in the tobacco industry (Gore received substantial campaign contributions from cigarette manufacturers and had long-standing ties to tobacco farmers in his home state), in using it Gore showed a more emotional side to the American public than he had before.

In this carefully crafted speech, Gore meets a number of political demands. He reminds the public of the administration's record, always calling attention to President Clinton's achievements but still making note of his own. He positions himself as a strong, capable leader, as presidential material in his own right; the rather angry partisan rhetoric is designed to counteract his image as a passive intellectual. Finally, through self-deprecating humor and the tragic example of his sister's death, Gore shows his emotional side to an American public that viewed him as too formal and guarded. No ordinary vice presidential nomination speech, Gore's 1996 address set the stage for his presidential run in 2000.

◆ 2000 Concession Speech

Setting a new record for voter participation, more than one hundred million Americans voted in the 2000 presidential election. As television networks began to predict which states George W. Bush and Al Gore had won, it became clear that the next president would have to win the state of Florida. At first, it appeared Bush had won Florida, and Gore called Bush to concede. However, an hour later, Gore had pulled within a few hundred votes of Bush. Gore called Bush to retract his concession. Because the race was so close, at Gore's request election officials began recounting the ballots by hand. Bush opposed the recount, charging that it was subject to human error.

The battle over the Florida recount went on through the month of November and eventually reached the United States Supreme Court. In its decision, *Bush v. Gore*, the Court ruled in favor of George W. Bush and declared him the winner of Florida and therefore the winner of the presidential election. According to the final certified results in Florida, Bush won by 537 votes. Although he publicly disagreed with the 5–4 Court decision, Gore conceded the election on December 13, 2000. The legal wrangling over the election results involved the exchange of strong words by both parties. Gore supporters felt that the election had been "stolen" from them, and, given how close the election was, the country was bitterly divided. Therefore Gore had to walk a fine line in his concession speech; he needed to assuage his supporters, but he also had a responsibility to help the nation move forward.

As he did in his 1996 address to the Democratic National Convention, Gore begins with humor; in this case, the humor serves to defuse some of the tension inherent in the situation. He refers to his earlier concession and retraction, which emphasizes the unusual nature and purpose of the speech, but in a nonthreatening way. He immediately remarks on the need to "heal the divisions" that face the nation. As he often does, Gore uses famous people from American history to illustrate points. In this case, he invokes Abraham Lincoln and Stephen Douglas, who debated each other in a contentious Senate campaign just before the Civil War. In 1860, when Lincoln defeated Douglas, the issue dividing the nation was slavery; Gore brings in the nation's history as a "house divided" to reinforce the fact that, although the rift between the parties is real, it must be healed.

Gore repeatedly reminds his listeners that they have an obligation to a higher authority than their own emotions. He asks for God's blessing on Bush and quotes a phrase engraved above Harvard's law library that places God and law above man. Gore also refers to the election turmoil as "one of God's unforeseen paths," indicating the potential for good to come out of the tumult. He also refers to the strength of American democracy and its institutions, invoking the Constitution, the Declaration of Independence, and the national hymn, "America the Beautiful."

Yet Gore peppers his speech with language that shows his disagreement with the election's outcome. He states very clearly that he disagrees with the Court's decision. Gore mentions "challenges to the popular will" in reference to the past, but his purpose is to call attention to the fact that he won the majority of the popular vote; Bush received fewer popular votes than Gore but won more electoral votes. Gore also notes that there will be opportunities to "debate our continuing differences," indicating that conceding the election does not necessarily mean that the parties will agree on matters of policy. Gore also voices his regret at not having a chance to "fight for the American people" as president and refers to "those who feel their voices have not been heard." There were charges

Judge Charles Burton, chairman of the Palm Beach County canvassing board, holds up the last ballot the board was able to consider in the manual recount of ballots as the Democratic lawyer Mark White, left, and the Republican lawyer John Bolton watch. (AP/Wide World Photos)

that, in some counties in Florida, voters had been unable to cast their ballots because of long lines at the polls, broken voting machines, or problems accessing polling sites. The issue of voting irregularities in Florida was a heated point of contention in the recount debate, and Gore addresses it here.

The narrow margin of victory, legal challenges, and ultimate Supreme Court decision made the 2000 presidential election a unique historical event. Faced with a bitter personal disappointment and a nation divided, Gore's 2000 concession speech allowed the nation to move forward yet conveyed his disagreement with the Supreme Court's final decision.

Impact and Legacy

Al Gore has created a wide range of documents as a politician and as a private citizen. His impact is greatest in three areas: the role and function of government, technology, and the environment. He wrote or helped develop key reform legislation while vice president, including the North American Free Trade Agreement, welfare reform, and the National Performance Report of 1993. He published several books on restructuring the federal government; in 1997, Gore co-authored *Businesslike Government: Lessons Learned from America's Best Companies* with Scott Adams. Out of office, Gore continued to write on ways to improve federal government efficiency, including *From Red Tape to Results: Creating a Government That*

Nobel Prize winner Al Gore and his wife, Tipper, with Crown Prince Haakon of Norway and Princess Mette-Mari at the Nobel Peace Prize Concert in Oslo, Norway. (AP/Wide World Photos)

Works Better and Costs Less in 2001. As a private citizen, Gore has been a vocal critic of government policies with which he disagrees, among them the United States' presence in Iraq. In 2007 Gore published *An Assault on Reason*, a book in which he severely criticizes the Bush administration's actions following the terrorist attacks of September 11, 2001.

Gore fostered the development of cutting-edge technologies throughout his career. As a senator, he advocated a freeze on new nuclear weapons development and the conversion of existing weapons to single warhead missiles, based on his knowledge of the destructive potential of this technology. The High-Performance Computing Act of 1991 provided funding for the Internet as it is known today. As vice president, Gore shepherded V-chip technology through Congress, which allowed parents to control their children's television viewing, and he created an interactive White House Web site for public use.

Gore is best known for his advocacy for environmental concerns. He was instrumental in passing the 1980 Superfund law and reauthorizing the Clean Air Act. His work on global warming, especially his 1992 book *Earth in the Balance* and the documentary *An Inconvenient Truth*, is enormously popular with the general public and earned Gore a Nobel Prize in 2007.

It is noteworthy that the qualities deemed negative early in Gore's career—among them, his serious demeanor—actually served him well later. His attention to detail and fascination with scientific data advanced his environmental causes, lending credibility to his speeches and writings. His interest in technology helped him develop new ways of communicating with the public, particularly his presentations on climate change shown in *An Inconvenient Truth.*

Gore's earnestness when discussing issues, particularly environmental topics, rankles some, who see it as evidence of his propensity to exaggerate the truth; some

liken his environmental cause to religious zealotry. Others see Gore as self-righteous and hypocritical in his critique of political wrongdoing. Gore himself was the target of an inquiry into illegal solicitation of campaign contributions while in the White House. As a political moderate, Gore managed to alienate those on both sides of the political aisle during his political career. Nevertheless, as public dissatisfaction with the Bush administration grew, Gore became increasingly popular. Some of his ardent supporters called on him to run again in the 2008 election, but Gore has remained a private citizen, active as a writer and speaker.

Both in and out of public office, Gore has generated a wealth of documents with far-reaching impact. He is a gifted writer who is remarkably focused and capable of organizing volumes of data into a coherent narrative. As evidenced by the range of his work, he can communicate with a wide variety of audiences, from the general public to lawmakers to the scientific and technical communities. Gore is able to develop highly technical arguments related to environmental or communications issues, and he can also craft a moving political speech. His writings are a testament to his mastery of detail, knowledge of the political process, and passion for the causes he believes in.

Key Sources

Gore has published several books on politics, the environment, and social issues. These include *Earth in the Balance: Ecology and the Human Spirit* (1992), *Joined at the Heart: The Transformation of the American Family* (2002, co-authored with Tipper Gore), and *The Assault on Reason* (2007). Selected speeches given by Gore as vice president can be found on the White House Web Site at http://clinton3.nara.gov/WH/EOP/OVP/speeches_bottom.html. Joseph Kaufmann has compiled a collection of Gore's writings and statements, published as *The World According to Al Gore: An A-to-Z Compilation of His Opinions, Positions, and Public Statements* (1999).

Further Reading

■ Books

Cockburn, Alexander, and Jeffrey St. Clair. *Al Gore: A User's Manual.* New York: Verso, 2000.

Hillin, Hank. *Al Gore Jr.: His Life and Career.* New York: Carol Publishing Group, 1988.

Maraniss, David, and Ellen Nakashima. *The Prince of Tennessee: The Rise of Al Gore.* New York: Simon & Schuster, 2000.

Sapet, Kerrily. *Al Gore.* Greensboro, N.C.: Morgan Reynolds Publishing, 2007.

Turque, Bill. *Inventing Al Gore.* New York: Houghton Mifflin, 2000.

"The President shall implement a National High-Performance Computing Program, which shall—(A) establish the goals and priorities for Federal high-performance computing research, development, networking, and other activities; and (B) provide for interagency coordination of Federal high-performance computing research, development, networking, and other activities undertaken pursuant to the Program."

(High-Performance Computing Act of 1991)

"The National Performance Review can reduce the deficit further, but it is not just about cutting spending. It is also about closing the trust deficit: proving to the American people that their tax dollars will be treated with respect for the hard work that earned them."

("From Red Tape to Results: Creating a Government That Works Better and Costs Less")

"Tradition holds that this speech be delivered tomorrow night. But President Clinton asked me to speak tonight. And you can probably guess the reason why. My reputation for excitement."

(Address to the 1996 Democratic National Convention)

"Tonight, Bill Clinton and I offer ourselves as a bridge to the future."

(Address to the 1996 Democratic National Convention)

"This has been an extraordinary election. But in one of God's unforeseen paths, this belatedly broken impasse can point us all to a new common ground, for its very closeness can serve to remind us that we are one people with a shared history and a shared destiny."

(2000 Concession Speech)

"While we yet hold and do not yield our opposing beliefs, there is a higher duty than the one we owe to political party. This is America and we put country before party; we will stand together behind our new president."

(2000 Concession Speech)

■ **Web Sites**

"Albert A. Gore, Jr., 45th Vice President (1993–2001)." U.S. Senate Web Site. http://www.senate.gov/artandhistory/history/common/generic/VP_Albert_Gore.htm.

"Biography of Vice President Al Gore." White House Web Site. http://clinton1.nara.gov/White_House/EOP/OVP/html/Bio.html.

—Karen Linkletter

Questions for Further Study

1. Although Gore became an object of ridicule for his claim to have "invented the Internet," does his authorship of the High-Performance Computing Act qualify him as a driving force behind the expansion of the "information superhighway"? Examine the specifics of his proposal, and compare them with resulting developments in computing and communications. To what extent should Gore be credited (or blamed) for those developments?

2. Discuss the principles underlying "From Red Tape to Results," in which Gore suggests that government should operate more like a business. Do you agree or disagree? Explain your position and give examples, including those Gore cites as well as others drawn from current or recent events.

3. Gore's 1996 address to the Democratic National Convention includes a poignant story about the death of his sister from lung cancer. Evaluate this portion of the speech from a number of standpoints, assessing its effectiveness in stirring emotion and recognizing the controversy and questions surrounding the fact that Gore himself had significant ties to the tobacco industry.

4. In what ways does Gore use humor in his 1996 Democratic National Convention address and other speeches? What objectives are behind this use of humor, much of which pokes fun at Gore himself? How well does he achieve those objectives?

High-Performance Computing Act of 1991

SEC. 101. NATIONAL HIGH-PERFORMANCE COMPUTING PROGRAM

(a) NATIONAL HIGH-PERFORMANCE COMPUTING PROGRAM—(1) The President shall implement a National High-Performance Computing Program, which shall—

(A) establish the goals and priorities for Federal high-performance computing research, development, networking, and other activities; and

(B) provide for interagency coordination of Federal high-performance computing research, development, networking, and other activities undertaken pursuant to the Program....

SEC. 102. NATIONAL RESEARCH AND EDUCATION NETWORK

(a) ESTABLISHMENT—As part of the Program, the National Science Foundation, the Department of Defense, the Department of Energy, the Department of Commerce, the National Aeronautics and Space Administration, and other agencies participating in the Program shall support the establishment of the National Research and Education Network, portions of which shall, to the extent technically feasible, be capable of transmitting data at one gigabit per second or greater by 1996. The Network shall provide for the linkage of research institutions and educational institutions, government, and industry in every State.

(b) ACCESS—Federal agencies and departments shall work with private network service providers, State and local agencies, libraries, educational institutions and organizations, and others, as appropriate, in order to ensure that the researchers, educators, and students have access, as appropriate, to the Network. The Network is to provide users with appropriate access to high-performance computing systems, electronic information resources, other research facilities, and libraries. The Network shall provide access, to the extent practicable, to electronic information resources maintained by libraries, research facilities, publishers, and affiliated organizations.

(c) NETWORK CHARACTERISTICS—The Network shall—

(1) be developed and deployed with the computer, telecommunications, and information industries;

(2) be designed, developed, and operated in collaboration with potential users in government, industry, and research institutions and educational institutions;

(3) be designed, developed, and operated in a manner which fosters and maintains competition and private sector investment in high-speed data networking within the telecommunications industry;

(4) be designed, developed, and operated in a manner which promotes research and development leading to development of commercial data communications and telecommunications standards, whose development will encourage the establishment of privately operated high-speed commercial networks;

(5) be designed and operated so as to ensure the continued application of laws that provide network and information resources security measures, including those that protect copyright and other intellectual property rights, and those that control access to data bases and protect national security;

(6) have accounting mechanisms which allow users or groups of users to be charged for their usage of copyrighted materials available over the Network and, where appropriate and technically feasible, for their usage of the Network;

(7) ensure the interoperability of Federal and non-Federal computer networks, to the extent appropriate, in a way that allows autonomy for each component network;

(8) be developed by purchasing standard commercial transmission and network services from vendors whenever feasible, and by contracting for customized services when not feasible, in order to minimize Federal investment in network hardware;

(9) support research and development of networking software and hardware; and

(10) serve as a test bed for further research and development of high-capacity and high-speed computing networks and demonstrate how advanced computers, high-capacity and high-speed computing networks, and data bases can improve the national information infrastructure.

(d) DEFENSE ADVANCED RESEARCH PROJECTS AGENCY RESPONSIBILITY—As part of the Program, the Department of Defense, through the Defense Advanced Research Projects Agency, shall support research and development of advanced fiber optics technology, switches, and protocols needed to develop the Network.

Glossary

gigabit	a unit of computer information storage
interoperability of	access between
protocols	standards for communication and data transfer between computers

"From Red Tape to Results: Creating a Government That Works Better and Costs Less" (1993)

The National Performance Review is about change—historic change—in the way the government works. The Clinton administration believes it is time for a new customer service contract with the American people, a new guarantee of effective, efficient, and responsive government. As our title makes clear, the National Performance Review is about moving from red tape to results to create a government that works better and costs less.

These are our twin missions: to make government work better and cost less. The President has already addressed the federal deficit with the largest deficit reduction package in history. The National Performance Review can reduce the deficit further, but it is not just about cutting spending. It is also about closing the trust deficit: proving to the American people that their tax dollars will be treated with respect for the hard work that earned them. We are taking action to put America's house in order.

The National Performance Review began on March 3, 1993, when President Clinton announced a 6-month review of the federal government and asked me to lead the effort. We organized a team of experienced federal employees from all corners of the government—a marked change from past efforts, which relied on outsiders.

We turned to the people who know government best—who know what works, what doesn't, and how things ought to be changed. We organized these people into a series of teams, to examine both agencies and cross-cutting systems, such as budgeting, procurement, and personnel. The President also asked all cabinet members to create Reinvention Teams to lead transformations at their departments, and Reinvention Laboratories, to begin experimenting with new ways of doing business. Thousands of federal employees joined these two efforts.

But the National Performance Review did not stop there. From the beginning, I wanted to hear from as many Americans as possible. I spoke with federal employees at every major agency and at federal centers across the country—seeking their ideas, their input, and their inspiration. I visited programs that work: a Miami school that also serves as a community center, a Minnesota pilot program that provides benefits more efficiently by using technology and debit cards, a Chicago neighborhood that has put community policing to work, a U.S. Air Force base that has made quality management a way of life.

We also heard from citizens all across America, in more than 30,000 letters and phone calls. We sought the views of hundreds of different organizations, large and small. We learned from the experience of state and local leaders who have restructured their organizations. And we listened to business leaders who have used innovative management practices to turn their companies around....

We have not a moment to lose. President Kennedy once told a story about a French general who asked his gardener to plant a tree. "Oh, this tree grows slowly," the gardener said. "It won't mature for a hundred years."

"Then there's no time to lose," the general answered. "Plant it this afternoon."

ADDRESS TO THE 1996 DEMOCRATIC NATIONAL CONVENTION

Four years ago, four years ago, you gave me your nomination to be vice president. And tonight I want to say, from the bottom of my heart: Thank you for the opportunity to serve our country, and for the privilege of working beside a president who has done so much to lift the lives of America's families.

Tradition holds that this speech be delivered tomorrow night. But President Clinton asked me to speak tonight. And you can probably guess the reason why.

My reputation for excitement....

This is some crowd. I've been watching you doing that macarena on television. And if I could have your silence, I would like to demonstrate for you the Al Gore version of the macarena.

Would you like to see it again?

Four years ago, America faced a set of problems our leaders had lost the courage to confront. Our nation was not creating jobs. Our jobs were not increasing pay. Our people were running in place. Our nation was falling behind.

Four years later, we meet in this great city of Chicago, the place Carl Sandburg called "the city of the big shoulders ... with lifted head so proud to be alive ... and strong." Four years later, Democrats are proud. Our hopes are alive. And America is strong.

Bill Clinton's leadership is paying off. How can you tell? By what the American people have achieved themselves. Just look at what all of us have created together these last four years:

Ten million new jobs; a deficit cut in half; a smaller, leaner re-invented government working better and costing less; unemployment and inflation both down; record exports; wages on the rise; an economy moving forward; empowerment zones bringing neighborhoods back to life; classrooms connected to the information superhighway; communities given the right to know about environmental dangers; toxic wastes being cleaned up; rivers and lakes reclaimed and thriving; an America not just better off, but better.

And our strength at home has led to renewed respect abroad, nuclear missiles no longer targeted at our cities, democracy replacing tyranny in Haiti, peace replacing war in Bosnia, leadership toward reconciliation in Northern Ireland and the Middle East. While our nation has made great progress, we have much more to do, and we are here to declare that the man who can help us fashion this better future is President Bill Clinton.

The president's opponent, Sen. Bob Dole, is a good and decent man. We honor his service to America, and his personal courage in fighting back from injuries sustained in battle. Though we disagree with his ideas, only the unknowing would deny him the respect he deserves.

But make no mistake: there is a profound difference in outlook between the president and the man who seeks his office. In his speech from San Diego, Sen. Dole offered himself as a bridge to the past. Tonight, Bill Clinton and I offer ourselves as a bridge to the future.

Ralph Waldo Emerson once said, "Humanity is divided between the past and the future ... between memory and hope." It is easy to understand the nostalgic appeal of the party of memory and the men who lead it. But let there be no doubt: the future lies with the party of hope and the man from Hope who leads it.

We Americans write our own history. And the chapters of which we're proudest are the ones where we had the courage to change. Time and again, Americans have seen the need for change, and have taken the initiative to bring that change to life. But always with a struggle. Always with opponents. Sen. Dole was there. We remember. We remember that he voted against the creation of Medicare, against the creation of Medicaid, against the Clean Air Act, against Head Start, against the Peace Corps in the '60s and AmeriCorps in the '90s. He even voted against the funds to send a man to the moon.

If he's the most optimistic man in America, I'd hate to see the pessimists.

That pessimistic view of America is very different from ours. And we saw it in the budget that Sen. Dole and Speaker Gingrich tried to slip past the American people last fall. Their budget doubled Medicare premiums while slashing benefits, wiped out nursing home care for seniors, ended the guarantee of decent medical care for disabled children, rolled back protections for our air and water, increased the cost of college while making student loans harder to get, terminated anti-drug programs for our schools, and raised taxes on the hardest-hit working families.

They passed their reckless plan, and then demanded that President Clinton sign it. They shut the government down. Twice. Because they thought Bill Clinton would buckle under the pressure, wither in the face of their attacks, cave in to their demands.

But they did not know the true measure of this man. He never flinched or wavered. He never stooped to their level. And, of course, he never attacked his opponent's wife.

Let me tell you what Bill Clinton did do. Bill Clinton took Speaker Newt Gingrich and Sen. Bob Dole into the Oval Office. I was there. I remember. And he said, President Clinton said: "As long as I occupy this office, you will never enact this plan. Because as long as I am president, I won't let you."

That's why they want to replace Bill Clinton. But we won't let them.

They want someone in that Oval Office who will rubber-stamp their plan. That's why they want to replace Bill Clinton. But we won't let them.

They want a president who will appoint the next three justices of the Supreme Court so they can control all three branches of government and take away a woman's right to choose. That's why they want to replace Bill Clinton. But we won't let them.

They want to give health insurance ripoff artists a license to change Medicare, to let this program for our seniors wither on the vine. That's why they want to replace Bill Clinton. But we won't let them.

They want to outlaw all affirmative action and many other measures to reach out to those who want to reach up. That's why they want to replace Bill Clinton. But we won't let them. They want to cut education and undermine our schools—put down teachers instead of lifting up students. That's why they want to replace Bill Clinton. But we won't let them.

They want to give free reign to lobbyists for the biggest polluters in America to rewrite our environmental laws allowing more poison in our air and water, and then auction off our natural wonders piece by piece. That's why they want to replace Bill Clinton. But we won't let them.

We will not; we cannot; we must not let them.

And you know what? We can make Bill Clinton's job a lot easier by making Dick Gephardt speaker of the House and Tom Daschle Senate majority leader.

You can judge a president by the enemies he is willing to make. You know that someone who's been attacked as much as Bill Clinton is doing something right. America has never changed without a president willing to confront the status quo and take on the forces of greed and indifference. It has changed only when we have had a president with the vision to tackle the real problems that really matter to our families. That's what this president has done.

Because families don't eat or breathe political slogans. They thrive or fail according to how they handle each day's challenges.

When your alarm goes off in the morning, if your family is like mine, everybody starts rushing around, getting ready for school and work. When one of your children reaches for cereal and fruit, you shouldn't have to worry about whether the food is safe. That's why just this month, President Clinton brought farmers and environmentalists together and signed an historic law to keep dangerous pesticides off our fruits and vegetables.

When you pour a glass of water for each member of the family at the table, you shouldn't have to wonder: "Should I buy bottled water? We really can't afford it." That's why President Clinton signed the Safe Drinking Water Act to give families more peace of mind that their water will be pure and safe.

When you notice your child staring at a television set, and watching violent and explicit images he or she is not old enough to handle, you shouldn't be forced to choose between throwing the TV out of the house and monitoring every second that child watches.

That is why, last month, the president persuaded the broadcasters to agree to air three hours of quality children's educational program—programming each week. And that's why we're giving parents a new tool, the V-chip, to keep violent and explicit programming out of their homes and away from their children. When our children turn on the TV, let them learn how to read and add and spell and think, not how to kill.

If one of your children has an operation, or some other serious health problem, you shouldn't have to choose between taking care of that child or keeping your job. That is why Bill Clinton fought to pass the Family and Medical Leave Act—so parents can get time off work to care for a sick child, bond with a newborn, or tend to an aging relative.

When your children do well in school and head toward graduation, they shouldn't have to wonder about whether their family can afford to send them to college. That's why President Clinton expanded scholarships, student loans, and Pell Grants. And that's why he wants to give a tax credit to pay $1,500 per year for tuition to make college more affordable for every single American family.

If the business where you work is changing in ways that cause you to think about getting a different kind of job, you ought to be able to get the training and education you need to learn new skills and plan for the future. That's why President Clinton is proposing a tax credit so if you go to a community college, you can take every single dollar you pay right off your taxes. If you take responsibility, President Clinton will give you the opportunity to learn.

And if you see an opportunity to move to a better job, you shouldn't feel forced to stay in your old job just because that's the only way you can keep because of your health insurance. Even if you have some pre-existing condition, you ought be able to change jobs and not lose your coverage. That is why President Clinton passed the Kennedy-Kassebaum law.

Americans shouldn't have to feel imprisoned in their homes because of crime. We have a right to streets and neighborhoods that are safe. That is why President Clinton fought for the Brady Bill and the assault weapons ban. And that is why President Clinton is putting 100,000 new community police officers on our streets and sidewalks.

These problems are real, and they must be addressed. It's been a long time since we've had a president so in tune with the issues that touch the real lives of America's families. It's been a long time since we've had a president willing to fight the powerful forces that often seem to stand in the way.

Some of the most powerful forces that do the most harm are often hard to see and even harder to understand. When I was a child, my family was attacked by an invisible force that was then considered harmless. My sister Nancy was older than me. There were only the two of us and I loved her more than life itself. She started smoking when she was 13 years old. The connection between smoking and lung cancer had not yet been established but years later the cigarettes had taken their toll.

It hurt very badly to watch her savaged by that terrible disease. Her husband, Frank, and all of us who loved her so much, tried to get her to stop smoking. Of course she should have, but she couldn't.

When she was 45, she had a lung removed. A year later, the disease had come back and she returned to the hospital. We all took turns staying with her. One day I was called to come quickly because things had taken a turn for the worse.

By then, her pain was nearly unbearable, and as a result, they used very powerful painkillers. And eventually it got so bad they had to use such heavy doses that she could barely retain consciousness. We sometimes didn't know if she could hear what we were saying or recognize us.

But when I responded to that call and walked into the hospital room that day, as soon as I turned the corner—someone said, "Al's here"—she looked up, and from out of that haze her eyes focused intensely right at me. She couldn't speak, but I felt clearly I knew she was forming a question: "Do you bring me hope?"

All of us had tried to find whatever new treatment or new approach might help, but all I could do was to say back to her with all the gentleness in my heart, "I love you." And then I knelt by her bed and held her hand. And in a very short time her breathing became labored and then she breathed her last breath.

Tomorrow morning another 13-year-old girl will start smoking. I love her, too. Three thousand young people in America will start smoking tomorrow. One thousand of them will die a death not unlike my sister's, and that is why, until I draw my last breath, I will pour my heart and soul into the cause of protecting our children from the dangers of smoking.

And that is also why I was intensely proud last week when President Clinton stood up for American

Brady Bill	the Brady Handgun Violence Prevention Act, signed into law by President Clinton in 1993
empowerment zones	specially designated urban and rural areas eligible for grants, tax incentives, and other programs
Kennedy-Kassebaum law	the Health Insurance Portability and Accountability Act, passed in 1996 to protect individuals' health insurance information
macarena	a dance based on a popular song of the same name, by the Spanish duo Los del Rio; dancing the macarena was a fad at the time of Gore's speech
man from Hope	a reference to Bill Clinton, who was born in Hope, Arkansas
San Diego	site of that year's Republican National Convention

families by standing up to tobacco advertising aimed at getting our children addicted. He proposed…the first-ever comprehensive plan to protect children from smoking; to ban tobacco advertising aimed at our children, and to ban it for good.

It took courage for Bill Clinton to take on the tobacco companies. I promise you it is no accident that no president has ever been willing to do it before.

But coming from him, that's no surprise. I've seen him get up day after day and make the toughest decisions, and always by asking, "What is right for the American people?"

As a result, with Bill Clinton's leadership, our nation is moving forward with confidence. Americans don't believe our best days are behind us. We see better days ahead because we have the courage to meet our challenges and protect our values. And now, once again, in pursuit of the American dream, we are crossing the bridge to the future.

By shepherding, guiding and protecting our children's souls, we build a better America. The American spirit lives within that child. The child grows up to believe in it, to add new vision to it.

It's not a vision of a distant future, nor of a remote past, but a constant accumulation of our best instincts and our noblest aspirations. From the spirit of our Founding Fathers, to the courage of today's families, it is one vision. It is an American vision. It is the vision of President Bill Clinton.

Thank you, God bless you, and God bless America.

2000 CONCESSION SPEECH

Good evening.

Just moments ago, I spoke with George W. Bush and congratulated him on becoming the 43rd president of the United States. And I promised him that I wouldn't call him back this time. I offered to meet with him as soon as possible so that we can start to heal the divisions of the campaign and the contest through which we've just passed.

Almost a century and a half ago, Senator Stephen Douglas told Abraham Lincoln, who had just defeated him for the presidency, "Partisan feeling must yield to patriotism. I'm with you, Mr. President, and God bless you." Well, in that same spirit, I say to President-elect Bush that what remains of partisan rancor must now be put aside, and may God bless his stewardship of this country. Neither he nor I anticipated this long and difficult road. Certainly neither of us wanted it to happen. Yet it came, and now it has ended, resolved, as it must be resolved, through the honored institutions of our democracy.

Over the library of one of our great law schools is inscribed the motto, "Not under man but under God and law." That's the ruling principle of American freedom, the source of our democratic liberties. I've tried to make it my guide throughout this contest, as it has guided America's deliberations of all the complex issues of the past five weeks.

Now the U.S. Supreme Court has spoken. Let there be no doubt, while I *strongly* disagree with the court's decision, I accept it. I accept the finality of this outcome which will be ratified next Monday in the Electoral College. And tonight, for the sake of our unity as a people and the strength of our democracy, I offer my concession. I also accept my responsibility, which I will discharge unconditionally, to honor the new President-elect and do everything possible to help him bring Americans together in fulfillment of the great vision that our Declaration of Independence defines and that our Constitution affirms and defends.

Let me say how grateful I am to all those who supported me and supported the cause for which we have fought. Tipper and I feel a deep gratitude to Joe and Hadassah Lieberman, who brought passion and high purpose to our partnership and opened new doors, not just for our campaign but for our country.

This has been an extraordinary election. But in one of God's unforeseen paths, this belatedly broken impasse can point us all to a new common ground, for its very closeness can serve to remind us that we are one people with a shared history and a shared destiny. Indeed, that history gives us many examples of contests as hotly debated, as fiercely fought, with their own challenges to the popular will. Other disputes have dragged on for weeks before reaching resolution. And each time, both the victor and the vanquished have accepted the result peacefully and in a spirit of reconciliation.

So let it be with us.

I know that many of my supporters are disappointed. I am too. But our disappointment must be overcome by our love of country.

And I say to our fellow members of the world community, let no one see this contest as a sign of American weakness. The strength of American democracy is shown most clearly through the difficulties it can overcome. Some have expressed concern that the unusual nature of this election might hamper the next president in the conduct of his office. I do not believe it need be so.

President-elect Bush inherits a nation whose citizens will be ready to assist him in the conduct of his large responsibilities. I, personally, will be at his disposal, and I call on all Americans—I particularly urge all who stood with us—to unite behind our next president. This is America. Just as we fight hard when the stakes are high, we close ranks and come together when the contest is done. And while there will be time enough to debate our continuing differences, now is the time to recognize that that which unites us is greater than that which divides us. While we yet hold and do not yield our opposing beliefs, there is a higher duty than the one we owe to political party. This is America and we put country before party; we will stand together behind our new president.

As for what I'll do next, I don't know the answer to that one yet. Like many of you, I'm looking forward to spending the holidays with family and old friends. I know I'll spend time in Tennessee and mend some fences, literally and figuratively.

Some have asked whether I have any regrets, and I do have one regret: that I didn't get the chance to stay and fight for the American people over the next four years, especially for those who need burdens lifted and barriers removed, especially for those who feel their voices have not been heard. I heard you. And I will not forget.

I've seen America in this campaign, and I like what I see. It's worth fighting for and that's a fight I'll never stop. As for the battle that ends tonight, I do believe, as my father once said, that "No matter how hard the loss, defeat might serve as well as victory to shape the soul and let the glory out."

So for me this campaign ends as it began: with the love of Tipper and our family; with faith in God and in the country I have been so proud to serve, from Vietnam to the vice presidency; and with gratitude to our truly tireless campaign staff and volunteers, including all those who worked so hard in Florida for the last 36 days.

Now the political struggle is over and we turn again to the unending struggle for the common good of all Americans and for those multitudes around the world who look to us for leadership in the cause of freedom.

In the words of our great hymn, "America, America": "Let us crown thy good with brotherhood, from sea to shining sea."

And now, my friends, in a phrase I once addressed to others: it's time for me to go.

Thank you, and good night, and God bless America.

Glossary

belatedly broken impasse	a stalemate that has taken too long to break
discharge unconditionally	perform without question or exception

Billy Graham (Library of Congress)

BILLY GRAHAM

1918–

Evangelist

Featured Documents
- ◆ "The Flame of Political Dilemma" (1965)
- ◆ "The Coming Storm" (1981)
- ◆ "The Winds of Change" (1992)
- ◆ "When Life Turns against Us" (2006)
- ◆ "A Final Word from Billy Graham" (2006)

Overview

William Franklin Graham, Jr., was born on November 7, 1918, on a dairy farm near Charlotte, North Carolina. His parents, zealous members of the Associate Reformed Presbyterian Church, enjoyed a reasonable standard of living and avoided many of the social and economic ills associated with the 1930s and the Great Depression. Graham's upbringing revolved around discipline, labor, and scriptural teachings. He graduated from Sharon High School in May 1936 and attended Bob Jones College, in Tennessee, and the Florida Bible Institute. It was at Wheaton College, in Illinois, in the early 1940s that Graham began to fulfill his religious calling and developed his unique style of lecturing, teaching, and preaching. Founded in 1860 by Wesleyan Methodists, Wheaton College established itself during and after Graham's student days as a robust center of neo-evangelicalism. Graham studied anthropology at Wheaton, graduating in 1943.

In his first official year as a minister (1943–1944) at First Baptist Church, in Western Springs, Illinois, Graham showed himself to be a compelling pulpit presence, captivating congregations. Through the 1940s Graham's reputation as an evangelist came to earn him the sort of celebrity recognition normally afforded a gifted musician or an athletic star. In 1949, with the support of the tycoon William Randolph Hearst, Graham gave a series of simply organized outdoor addresses in Los Angeles that put him on the front pages of American newspapers and further broadened his appeal.

In the 1950s Graham's touring revivals within the United States and around the world left him firmly positioned in the spotlight. During the 1960s and 1970s his reach and voice became thoroughly global. He was heard in countries behind the Soviet iron curtain; he spoke out against apartheid in South Africa in 1973; and a sermon in Seoul, South Korea, was delivered to an estimated live audience of one million. His early writing eagerly embraced all manner of political messages. He saw Communism as reprehensible and had no doubt that Western capitalism and the free market system represented the best avenue to achieve happiness and spiritual peace. In his later years he was less involved in political posturing, and his writings sought to promote social freedom, economic justice, and world peace through nuclear disarmament. Graham continued preaching into his eighties in the twenty-first century; his extraordinary longevity helps explain both his prolonged impact and the persistence of his role in American society.

Explanation and Analysis of Documents

For more than half a century Billy Graham was America's most well-known evangelist and a preacher who never failed to engage and embrace all manner of political, social, and polemic issues. The magic of Graham's persona was that while he began his career as a youthful and flamboyant regional conversion minister, he very quickly translated his message into an extraordinary outreach that made him a compelling world figure. He was a prolific writer and could easily and quickly turn out and deliver a dynamic sermon. The five book fragments presented here straddle and highlight his singular career. They stretch from 1965 to 2006 and were selected because they dramatically illustrate Graham's greatest talent, which was to powerfully address major American and global events—from the acme of the cold war with the Soviet Union in the 1960s to the modern-day concerns over global terrorism. The pieces also chart Graham's consistent moral foundation and core. It was the combination of Graham's close reading of the scriptures and a passionate belief in his own ability to communicate with people that shaped him as an iconic figure. The excerpts show Graham as a man of vision who relished crafting a Christian battle cry from his readings of the Bible from the middle of the twentieth century into the twenty first.

◆ "The Flame of Political Dilemma"

"The Flame of Political Dilemma" is an essay found in the opening portion of Graham's 1965 book titled, in accord with the tumultuous state of international affairs at the time, *World Aflame*. Graham was no stranger to over-the-top rhetoric. He was raised, after all, in an evangelical subculture that sought to champion Christianity against a powerfully secular world that was, according to Graham, peopled by groups committed to achieving a global, atheistic, totalitarian society. The world was indeed host to many antagonistic conflagrations in the 1960s, with the legacies of conflict and bloodshed affecting every continent even during stretches of peace. In March 1962 the cease-fire

1918

■ **November 7**
William Franklin Graham, Jr., is born near Charlotte, North Carolina.

1943

■ **June 14**
Graham graduates from Wheaton College.

1944

■ **January 2**
Graham takes over a leadership and management role in a freshly packaged version of the evangelical radio program *Songs in the Night.*

1948

■ **June 7**
Graham receives an honorary doctor of divinity degree at King's College, in New Castle, Delaware.

1950

■ **November 5**
Hour of Decision radio broadcasts, featuring Graham, begin in Atlanta, Georgia.

1955

■ **March 19**
Graham's six-week All-Scotland Crusade begins, in nine meetings drawing over 2.6 million people.

1965

■ Graham publishes *World Aflame*, which contains the essay "The Flame of Political Dilemma."

1981

■ Graham publishes *Till Armageddon: A Perspective on Suffering*, with the essay "The Coming Storm."

1984

■ **June 15**
A service in Adelaide, Australia, celebrates the twenty-fifth anniversary of the Australian branch of Graham's ministry.

between France and Algerian rebels finally ended a bloody seven-year war. In October 1962 border tensions led to the engagement of Chinese and Indian soldiers in fighting, while the world was left poised on the brink of a military nightmare as the United States and the Soviet Union faced off over the Soviet plan to install missile bases on Cuba; the latter crisis provided a stark reminder of the delicate global balance between peace and war. Less than a year after President John F. Kennedy's assassination in November 1963, Congress voted to support the Tonkin Gulf Resolution, which eventually saw the United States embroiled in the Vietnam War.

In light of a world if not at war, then certainly in states of conflagration and confrontation, Graham's greatest concern was, as he saw it, the inherently evil nature of Communism. While Graham's prose is repeatedly oriented as religious by his vision/version of the Antichrist—he speaks of a new devil appearing "with a charm and a cleverness never before known"—his writing has a directness and journalistic edge that can be objectively engaging. There is no political cant, polemic, or posturing when he speaks of a period of "crashing crowns and toppling thrones" or when he says, "Democracy began to blossom, but so did dictatorship.... Instability has entered into the changing political climate of the entire world until today the world is a seething political cauldron. Riots, demonstrations, and revolutions occur somewhere almost every day." Although it is set in this context, the narrative of "The Flame of Political Dilemma" is not limited to the political landscape. Since the mid-1960s marked the apotheosis of the cold war, Graham addresses the malevolence of the fabric of Communism, but he shifts to a sociological perspective when he focuses on the problems of crime and racism. Graham sees an America beset by nervous disorders and mental illnesses despite advances made by psychiatry and psychotherapy.

A consistent building block to be found in Graham's writings throughout his career is the crafting of a picture of doom, gloom, decay, and unpreparedness, along with a battle cry that some sort of redemption must take place. According to Graham, salvation will only happen if humankind stops grasping at straws and turns to the Bible. His concluding words are characteristic of his typical stance and tone; rather than being innovative or closing the monologue with a novel point, they feature a sort of muscular optimism and a sense of conviction: "I do not believe that all is black and hopeless. There is still time to return to the moral and spiritual principles that made the West great. There is still time for God to intervene."

◆ **"The Coming Storm"**

When *Till Armageddon: A Perspective on Suffering* was published in 1981, Graham's presence as a global figure had passed its zenith. Nevertheless, his status as a guiding light to common Americans remained undiminished. The tools of his trade continued to be fiery rhetoric supported by a reliance on biblical literature. In this book's preface Graham continues his lifelong embrace of the Bible as a source of illumination by which one can craft a personal road map. Always pragmatic, Graham justifies his text through its central message on suffering. His focus will be "to see what the Bible teaches us about suffering: how we should view it, and how should we prepare for it" (p. 8). His source of inspiration is the uncompromising and stern prose of the Old Testament, with its references to the time of Armageddon.

Critics of Graham have found him, in many respects, an easy target. His doom-and-gloom pronouncements and his repeated litanies on death, desolation, and destruction made him into a figure that lent itself to lampooning. His frequently pessimistic narratives and his incessant commentaries on moral decay, spiritual collapse, and physical disaster shaped a public perception of him that was arguably more about caricature than character. Nonetheless, Graham's opening line here—as headed by the words "The Coming Storm"—present dire predictions with a measure of accuracy about them. Graham writes, "The headlines of the eighties will continue to scream: war, violence, assassinations, torture, World War III—the real war, Armageddon." Indeed, through the 1980s and 1990s and into the twenty-first century, as with the decades before, war and violence persisted. Although the conflicts in Iraq and Afghanistan, as connected with the "war on terror" purveyed by President George W. Bush, had yet to balloon into World War III or Armageddon as of 2008, Graham makes a claim to being an acute observer of national ills and global stresses. In fact, a key facet of Graham's speech-making was his penchant for tying in natural disasters and headline-making news. Here, with his theme of a coming storm, Graham draws on the Mount Saint Helens eruption of 1980, using the metaphor of an exploding mountain in speaking of a God who is "going to shake the whole earth."

At the start of the 1980s, Graham was not cheered by feelings of international esprit de corps. He describes the repeated languishing of peace conferences and states categorically that hopes for and initiatives toward peace are illusory. Never an admirer of Hollywood and cinema, Graham vents about the manipulative bent of entertainment and popular culture: "Our movie theaters are jammed with the crowds who thrive on the disaster movies." Given his personal reliance on the entertainment value of disaster narratives, his issue here is presumably with the secular and noninstructive nature of the disaster movies in question. He goes on to discuss the issue of racial genocide under the subheading "Holocaust in the Wings." Here Graham again reveals a degree of prescience in identifying global ills, as the next two decades would bring the disintegration of Yugoslavia, marked by ethnic cleansing and barbaric conflict between Serbs and Bosnians, and the butchering of hundreds of thousands in Rwanda. After spotlighting racial concerns, Graham again frames a remark on current events in a prophetic manner, stating unequivocally, "Terrorist groups are growing more and more daring in their attacks on others." He goes on to write of nuclear weapons, germ warfare, and "precarious international relationships." While the 1980s and 1990s witnessed

Time Line

1991	■ **January 16** In comments about the war in the Persian Gulf, Graham notes that there are times when the only solution is to fight for peace.
1992	■ Graham publishes *Storm Warning*, with the chapter "The Winds of Change."
2001	■ **September 14** Graham heads up a special service at Washington National Cathedral to honor those killed in the terrorist attacks on the United States on September 11.
2006	■ Graham publishes *The Journey: How to Live by Faith in an Uncertain World,*" featuring the chapters "When Life Turns against Us" and "A Final Word from Billy Graham."
2007	■ **May 31** The dedication of the Billy Graham Library in Charlotte, North Carolina, takes place.

a remarkable degree of rapprochement between East and West and the effective dissolution of the iron curtain, strains and tensions between Israel and Palestine increased, and a series of new "hot spots" appeared all over the world.

In 2007 former Vice President Al Gore garnered the Nobel Peace Prize for a treatise in which he points out the colossal impact and appalling ramifications of global warming. Gore helped bring this issue to the center stage of political debates. In this essay, Graham demonstrates an early attunement to the warnings of environmental experts: "Our scientists are warning us that great climatic changes are in store in our world. We are told that the polar icecap seems to be slightly shifting, and this could affect our food-growing capabilities. Feeding the growing world population is an increasing burden."

Two-thirds of the way through "The Coming Storm," Graham reverts to a temper and a tone little different from those of his beginnings as a national voice in the 1940s and as a growing authority in the 1950s. He points out that drugs and alcohol are undermining American society, a

Thousands pack Houston's Domed Stadium as Billy Graham conducts his final service of a ten-day crusade in November 1965. (AP/Wide World Photos)

broadside few would disagree with. On the other hand, his railing against satanic cults and witchcraft and his perception of them as being widespread is open to criticism and skepticism. And while Graham always sought firm controls with respect to hedonism, he seems to be on less solid ground when he quotes an unnamed source who claims that "over 80 percent of modern novels center in perversion and the flouting of the moral law."

Graham's religious and political posture was always that of the fundamentalist. In a subsection of this chapter titled "The Root of the Problem," Graham turns to the spiritual tenets that are his hallmarks. The world is threatened with chaos, anarchy abounds, and the only way out of the confusion is to embrace and be energized by God, God's moral law, and the Bible. Through all his years Graham saw himself in a life-and-death battle with evil. His final commentary here, then, addresses the fate of communities and nations that reject Christian principles. Graham sees a stage being set for the establishment of "the Antichrist." In his conclusion Graham directly takes up the favorite theme of good and evil as titanic forces engaged in a massive and tempestuous contest. It is God against the Antichrist, and there will be global apocalyptic conflict on an unimaginable scale: "This massive upheaval will be the world's last war—the Battle of Armageddon."

◆ "The Winds of Change"

"The Winds of Change" is the opening section to a Graham book titled *Storm Warning*, published in 1992. The book's central thesis is that despite the collapse of Communism and the apparent decline of the nuclear threat, humankind should be prepared to combat all manners of evil. Graham perceives many storm clouds: debt, both personal and national, was soaring; crime statistics revealed much, such as how unsafe Washington, D.C., was at night; racial and ethnic hatred within and without the borders of the United States were increasing; moral values were in disarray; the AIDS epidemic was becoming a twentieth-century plague; and a cornerstone of American society, the traditional family unit, especially in African American communities, was in danger of collapse.

Turning to literal storm clouds, Graham focuses on Hurricane Andrew and the havoc that it wrought in southern Florida in August 1992, communicating his Christian message here as a reporting journalist. The hurricane's swath was thirty miles wide, with winds topping 164 miles per hour. Thirty-three people were left dead, sixty-three thousand homes were laid waste, over a million people found themselves without water and electricity, and damage estimates reached $30 billion. In describing the extent of the ravages brought about by Hurricane Andrew, Graham largely mutes the voices of the preacher, the moral guardian, and the religious zealot. For nearly four pages, he simply recounts in detail the extensive toll taken by Hurricane Andrew. This piece is a classic example of Graham's writing. He inspires a visceral response in the reader by invoking the power and majesty and destructive force of the hurricane, just as great biblical disasters allowed the Bible's authors to tell intimidating tales of suffering and, most important, the saving powers of God.

♦ "When Life Turns against Us"

When Graham writes and preaches about such topics as the Antichrist, he is providing grist for cynics who see such language and terminology as more fitting for a horror tale or a gothic novel. Nevertheless, Graham's prose is often clear, simple, and direct. He opens this chapter with a conundrum that has baffled and perplexed Christians through the ages: Why is there so much evil, and if God is so good and loving, why does he not do something about it? Bringing up the twenty-first century's most notoriously evil acts, Graham produces a single paragraph on the terrible events of September 11, 2001, that features a balanced pitch, with little sign of sentimentality or hyperbole. He opens the paragraph with the words "None of us will ever forget" and ends with an effort to connect with his audience, noting that one of those who died was a graduate of Wheaton College, the college home of both Graham and his wife, Ruth.

The events of September 11 were etched into the minds of Americans, with the graphic events captured by myriad television cameras. The attacks also irrevocably changed how the nation saw itself on the world stage, stunning Americans with the realization that they were now embroiled in a conflict taking place not only on foreign soil but at home as well. In 2001 Graham was in the twilight of his career and no longer a powerful figure. Still, when America needed to mourn those who perished on September 11, the man sought out to help heal and counsel the country was Billy Graham. Graham recalls that he was asked by President George W. Bush in mid-September 2001 to speak at a special service of prayer and remembrance at Washington National Cathedral. In his narrative he eschews images of violence, aggression, and conflict. His message is childlike in its simplicity: "I have been asked hundreds of times in my life why God allows tragedy and suffering....I really do not know the answer totally, even to my own satisfaction. I have to accept, by faith, that God is sovereign, and He is a God of love and mercy and compassion in the midst of suffering."

Graham goes on to carry out a biblical analysis of suffering and its allied mystery. He draws from the Old Testament (citing lines from Ecclesiastes, with life and work being full of pain and grief) and the New Testament (with Matthew offering up the symbolic optimism of the cup of wine that Jesus drank from prior to his arrest). According to Graham, Christ had to suffer on the cross, and, in so doing, he offered to shoulder "the sins of the whole human race...every murder, every adultery, every theft, every injus-

tice, every evil deed or thought—all the sins of the whole human race."

♦ "A Final Word from Billy Graham"

"A Final Word from Billy Graham" is the last chapter of *The Journey.* In his opening paragraph he asks a simple question, "One day your life's journey will be over.... But what kind of journey will it have been?" The chapter is not imbued with Graham's customary passion and zeal. The animation and theatrics needed to energize municipal stadiums and revival tabernacles are not summoned here, and Armageddon, Satan, and the Antichrist are not invoked. Rather, this chapter's charm stems from its bold directness and a clarity of content that make it a moving epilogue to the greater text. Graham's thesis is that life is an odyssey, and the tenor of his address is gentle. Graham shows himself to be a frail patriarch who is strongly sustained by a rock-solid personal faith. He ends by saying, "Some day this life will be over. I look forward to that day, because I know that beyond it is heaven. I pray you do too. But until that day God calls you home, make it your goal to live for Christ."

Impact and Legacy

Graham's legacy is that of a charming southerner who became the most famous evangelist of the twentieth century and then, not content with his role within the United States, established a commanding presence over several decades as a global preacher. In his life Graham preached in person to as many as two hundred million people across 185 countries. His international *Hour of Decision*, a weekly radio broadcast, endured successfully for more than half a century. Graham was a confidant of every incumbent of the White House from Harry S. Truman to George W. Bush. During these years, presidential dialogues afforded Graham opportunities to preach against Communism and to be an initial supporter of U.S. involvement in the Vietnam War; he often made the argument that fighting for peace was the correct course of action. He received America's two premier civilian honors, the Congressional Gold Medal and the Presidential Medal of Freedom.

Regarding his facility to connect and communicate with disparate audiences in America and around the world, Graham was a consummate showman. While he was the centerpiece of his religious gatherings, he was in reality a part of a traveling road show. He was the headliner of a package that also included an associate preacher, a gospel singer, a song leader, a uniformed choir, musicians, and a public relations director. The ensemble made much of its spiritual core but was constructed for secular consumption as well. Graham was also a master of mass media. He was equally at home communicating his message through radio, television, films, magazines, pamphlets, books, and newspaper columns.

Over the years Graham demonstrated a shrewd strategic mind-set. On the one hand he was a staunch archconservative, and yet on the other he realized the need to reach out

"*The modern world moves amidst its baffling dilemmas. While we know more economics than ever before, the world has more poverty and hunger than ever before. With our space program readying a flight to the moon, we have not yet solved the basic problems of earth.*"

("The Flame of Political Dilemma")

"*Modern man has become a spectator of world events, observing on his television screen without becoming involved. He watches the ominous events of our times pass before his eyes, while he sips his beer in a comfortable chair.*"

("The Flame of Political Dilemma")

"*Thousands of peace conferences have been held since World War II, and yet the headlines continue to shout about war, violence, death and streaming refugees. Governments of the world are rocked with assassinations and bloodshed.*"

("The Coming Storm")

"*Terrorist groups are growing more and more daring in their attacks on others. Almost daily reports of new atrocities fill our newspapers.*"

("The Coming Storm")

"*News reports later showed that the worst damage came at the little settlement of motels, go-go bars, and gambling houses known as Pass Christian, Mississippi, where some twenty people were killed at a hurricane party in the Richelieu Apartments. Nothing was left of that three-story structure but the foundation; the only survivor was a five-year-old boy found clinging to a mattress the following day.*"

("The Winds of Change")

"*None of us will ever forget September 11, 2001. Within minutes our world changed forever as two hijacked airlines plowed into the twin towers of America's tallest building, the World Trade Center in New York City, and a third slammed into the Pentagon in Washington, D.C. Thousands were killed in that merciless terrorist attack, including hundreds of heroic fire, police, and emergency personnel.*"

("When Life Turns Against Us")

to very different constituencies. For example, in the 1960s he opposed segregation but vigorously supported Martin Luther King, Jr. The case can be made that Graham moderated his political views as he aged. He was never a member of the Moral Majority, an evangelical Christian lobbying organization, and his faith, not politics, was both his passion and his life's focus. His uncanny ability, demonstrated in all varieties of settings, frequently in foreign lands, to compel people to come forward and embrace his vision of Christianity made him a unique religious icon.

Key Sources

The major repository for materials to do with Billy Graham is the Billy Graham Center Archives at Wheaton College, in Illinois. Graham published memoirs in 1997 titled *Just as I Am: The Autobiography of Billy Graham*. His books include *World Aflame* (1965), about conflagrations around the globe; *Till Armageddon* (1981), on the nature of suffering; *Storm Warning* (1992), an overview of contemporary issues such as abortion and AIDS; *The Journey* (2006), a biography of a busy and committed life; *America's Hour of Decision* (1951), the diary-like account of Graham's successful radio program, with a global following; *The Challenge* (1960), his defense of Christendom against Communism; and *Living in God's Love* (2005), gentle end-of-life reminiscences on God's companionly compassion.

Further Reading

■ Books

Ashman, Chuck. *The Gospel According to Billy*. Secaucus, N.J.: Lyle Stuart, 1977.

Cornwell, Patricia. *Ruth, a Portrait: The Story of Ruth Bell Graham*. New York: Doubleday, 1997.

Dullea, Charles W. *A Catholic Looks at Billy Graham*. New York: Paulist Press, 1973.

Pollock, John. *Billy Graham, Evangelist to the World: An Authorized Biography of the Decisive Years*. San Francisco: Harper & Row, 1979.

———. *To All the Nations: The Billy Graham Story*. San Francisco: Harper & Row, 1985.

Streiker, Lowell D., and Gerald S. Strober. *Religion and the New Majority: Billy Graham, Middle America, and the Politics of the 70s*. New York: Association Press, 1972.

■ Web Sites

"William (Billy) F. Graham." Billy Graham Evangelistic Association Web site. http://www.billygraham.org/MediaRelations_Bios.asp?id=0.

—Scott Crawford

Questions for Further Study

1. Billy Graham's audiences tended to be common, average people rather than theologians or highly educated people. After examining the documents, trace what you regard as the source of his appeal to those audiences.

2. During the height of his career, Graham enjoyed a great deal of influence with prominent politicians, notably American presidents. Why do you think Graham was popular with these leaders?

3. Graham saw a connection between modern Communism and the biblical account of the Antichrist. On what basis does he see this connection?

4. Was Billy Graham an optimist or a pessimist? Support your position with evidence from his writings.

5. How did Graham answer the age-old question about the existence of evil in a world that is ruled by a God that is regarded as loving? Both Graham and W. E. B. Du Bois rely heavily on biblical references and language in their works. Examine these references and compare how and for what purpose the two writers use them.

"The Flame of Political Dilemma" (1965)

A European statesman said recently: "If the devil could offer a panacea for the problems of the world, I would gladly follow the devil." This is precisely what the Bible predicts will someday happen. When the world can no longer solve its problems, the great Anti-Christ will appear with a charm and a cleverness never before known. The whole world will follow him and even worship him.

Meanwhile the modern political era is dominated by the events and changes that took place as a result of the First World War of 1914–1918. This marked the era of crashing crowns and toppling thrones. Democracy began to blossom, but so did dictatorship. We all remember when President Franklin Roosevelt promised the four freedoms for the entire world, yet today there is less freedom than ever. Instability has entered into the changing political climate of the entire world until today the world is a seething political cauldron. Riots, demonstrations, and revolutions occur somewhere almost every day. Even in Britain and America the people have become addicted to sitting, squatting, demonstrating, and striking for what they want!

History speaks with thundering words to say that no state or government devised by man can flourish forever. It is also true, as Will Durant said: "No great nation has ever been overcome until it has destroyed itself." Republics, kingdoms, and empires all live their uncertain lives and die. In America we are now on the verge of seeing a democracy gone wild. Freedom has become license. Moral law is in danger of being abandoned even by the courts. To what degree can we expect immunity from the inevitable law of regress that sets in when nations defy the laws of God?

This, then, is the modern international scene with its problems of population, crime, racism, Communism, science, and politics. These are complicating modern existence and making the world into which our young men and women are going one where personal liberties are hedged about by all sorts of limiting regulations. As the world gets smaller, our problems grow larger. Our freedoms disappear and our danger increases! Trouble and danger lie ahead. This present generation of young people can expect nothing but crisis, bloodshed, war, hate, greed, lust, and struggle as the world tries to readjust without the climate of peace.

The modern world moves amidst its baffling dilemmas. While we know more economics than ever before, the world has more poverty and hunger than ever before. With our space program readying a flight to the moon, we have not yet solved the basic problems of earth. The threat of war and revolution hangs over our heads like the sword of Damocles. While psychiatry and psychotherapy promise us a whole personality, there are more nervous disorders and mental illnesses than ever before.

What is the trouble? What is the answer to our problems? Without God, man is worse off than a flower severed from its stem. We forget that we are finite. We have paraded our arrogance to the very precipice of a tragic end. The problem now is Can we recover ourselves, clear our minds, regain our composure, and change our direction before it is too late?

Most of the current experts, analysts, historians, scientists, philosophers, and statesmen agree that man is sick. But the crucial question is Are we

Glossary

cacophony	a combination of unpleasant, harsh sounds
panacea	a cure-all
sword of Damocles	an impending disaster; based on an ancient Greek legend in which Damocles trades places with a king at a banquet, only to discover that a sword hung by a single horse hair is hanging above his head
Will Durant	a prominent American historian (1885–1981) whose extensive publications in history, philosophy, and religion were written for general audiences

beyond saving? Are we beyond hope? Some of our greatest minds privately agree that we have already passed the point of no return.

The people who ask these questions and express these forebodings are the experts, not the rank and file of the people. In a declining culture, one of its characteristics is that the ordinary people are unaware of what is happening. Only those who know and can read the signs of decadence are posing the questions that as yet have no answers. Mr. Average Man is comfortable in his complacency and as unconcerned as a silverfish ensconced in a carton of discarded magazines on world affairs. He is not asking any questions, because his social benefits from the government give him a false security. This is his trouble and his tragedy. Modern man has become a spectator of world events, observing on his television screen without becoming involved. He watches the ominous events of our times pass before his eyes, while he sips his beer in a comfortable chair. He does not seem to realize what is happening to him. He does not understand that his world is on fire and that he is about to be burned with it.

Into this cacophony of the voices of doom comes the Word of God. The Bible says that it is *not* too late. I do not believe that we have passed the point of no return. I do not believe that all is black and hopeless. There is still time to return to the moral and spiritual principles that made the West great. There is still time for God to intervene. But there is coming a time when it will be too late, and we are rapidly approaching that time!

"The Coming Storm" (1981)

Many writers are predicting that the headlines of the eighties will continue to scream: war, violence, assassinations, torture, World War III—the real war, Armageddon.

There is no doubt that global events are preparing the way for the final war of history—the great Armageddon! As the earthly time clock ticks off each second and the world approaches midnight, this planet, according to the Bible, is going to be plunged into suffering too horrible to imagine or comprehend. As the top of Mount St. Helens blew off early in 1980 and became one of the great disasters of that period, so the Bible teaches in Hebrews 12 that God is going to shake the whole earth. The Bible says, "Once more I will shake not only the earth but also the heavens" (Heb. 12:26). The tremors that are leading to the greatest earthquake of all time are now being felt throughout the world.

Holocaust in the Wings

The ancient prophets warned about a time toward the end of history when people would be saying "'Peace, peace,'…when there is no peace" (Jer. 6:14). Thousands of peace conferences have been held since World War II, and yet the headlines continue to shout about war, violence, death and streaming refugees. Governments of the world are rocked with assassinations and bloodshed.

Yet only a few years ago it was fashionable to write or suggest that the world was entering a great era of peace. We were told by many idealists that utopia would be ushered onto the scene, along with all the technological miracles of our time. The dream was an illusion. We should have learned from history. They dreamed of peace in the earlier part of the century, but that was shattered by World War I. They dreamed and planned for peace after World War I, but World War I was only a preparation for World War II. Now the signs are everywhere that the world is preparing feverishly for World War III, which could be the last war—Armageddon!

Permeating the media is the concentration on catastrophic titles. Our movie theaters are jammed with the crowds who thrive on the disaster movies. The list of titles in any major city, like London, New York or Los Angeles, is almost endless with titles suggesting the most fearsome, unreal—and sometimes real—fantasies.

Even the most cheerful optimists are predicting the probabilities of an increase in suffering in our wounded world. One of the most cheery programs on television is ABC's "Good Morning America." But sometime ago Rona Barrett was interviewing someone from the CIA who reported that germs capable of destroying nations have already been developed. There are new viruses, he said, that could cause a breakdown in the health of the populace of an entire continent. Chemical and germ warfare are part of the arms arsenal now being developed throughout the world. Articles and documentary films are constantly being released, reporting that before the end of the century insects could be in control of our planet. One major newspaper concluded an editorial with the words: "There is a feeling that one is seeing the world in its twilight."

Expressions like "racial suicide," "racial genocide," "the end of the world" and "the end of the human race" are cropping up in conversations, journals and motion pictures throughout the world.

Terrorist groups are growing more and more daring in their attacks on others. Almost daily reports of new atrocities fill our newspapers. The president of a West African government was killed, his son beheaded, and many members of his staff executed publicly by a firing squad. The story was a comparatively insignificant item buried in the back pages of the violence-filled daily newspaper that I read.

Nuclear weapons, germ warfare, and precarious international relationships are not the only indications of civilization on a collision course. Our scientists are warning us that great climatic changes are in store for our world. We are told that the polar icecap seems to be slightly shifting, and this could affect our food-growing capabilities. Feeding the growing world population is an increasing burden.

The statistics on the increase in earthquakes almost break the computer.

On the moral front, things look extremely bleak, especially through Judeo-Christian eyes. There is something of an explosion in the breakdown of marriages and the almost total rejection of moral law and guidelines. Drugs and alcohol are destroying the minds of millions. The emergence of satanic cults and witchcraft is especially widespread in America and Europe.

Pleasure has become the goal of millions. Hedonism is now almost in control. Pornography meets with little restraint. A publisher told me at Oxford that over 80 percent of modern novels center in perversion and the flouting of the moral law.

On every hand people are screaming for "liberation" and social justice. It seems the rich are getting richer and the poor are getting poorer. This is true of nations as well as individuals. The economic strength of the world has shifted to the oil-producing countries who have amassed billions they do not know how to spend. While Western Europe and America go deeper in debt, the Third World lives on the knife-edge of starvation.

The theory that the world is getting better and better, and solving its political, economic and social problems, is no longer taught with very much confidence. We are living in a day of serious turmoil and trouble, and most thinking people to whom I talk forecast that things are going to get worse instead of better.

The Root of the Problem

Today we see a world which is unparalleled in its unrest, whether it is the unrest of the individual human heart, or of the social, political, or even religious, situation. The world is in the confusion and mess it's in today because it has rejected God and His moral order. The Scriptures themselves make it clear that when God's law is discarded, the only intelligent, unifying principles for human life and conduct are also cast away.

With this rebellion against God, mankind has lost its sense of purpose and meaning in life and denied the worth of human personality, and the other values that make life worthwhile. Most people of the world have some belief in a supernatural being—but we act like atheists! We think like atheists! We live and plan as if there were no God. We are living in a world that does not recognize God. When everyone does what is right in his own eyes, there is no possibility of order and peace. There will be more and more confusion and turmoil as people follow their own wicked devices.

Man is a rebel, and a rebel is naturally in confusion. He is in conflict with every other rebel. For a rebel by his very nature is selfish. He is seeking his own good and not the good of others. Sometimes through rationalization there can emerge unbiblical goals that seem for a time to have a unifying effect upon man, even creating mob interest and unity for a time—but these goals are temporary. There is no depth or meaning to them, and therefore these elements cannot bring unity to society.

The Bible indicates that in rejecting God and His principles for governing life, the world is heading for a situation of tension, confusion and turmoil that will ultimately set the stage for a future evil world ruler or system—the Antichrist.

The Antichrist and Armageddon

While God has a plan for man's good, the devil also has a master plan. He will bring to power a counterfeit world ruler or system that will establish a false utopia for an extremely short time. The economic and political problems of the world will *seem* to be solved. But after a brief rule the whole thing will come apart. During the reign of Antichrist tensions will mount, and once again the world will explode—with a gigantic world war of overwhelming ferocity involving conflict and massacre on an unpar-

Glossary

Hebrews	a biblical book of the Christian New Testament
Judeo-Christian	the historical and religious tradition of Judaism and Christianity
Mount St. Helens	an active volcano about a hundred miles south of Seattle, Washington, the site of a devastating eruption on May 18, 1980
Third World	term used generally to refer to the world's poorest nations
utopia	an ideal or perfect world, from *Utopia*, a book by the English theologian Sir Thomas More (1478–1535)

alleled scale. Even the iron grip of the Antichrist will be unable to prevent it. This massive upheaval will be the world's last war—the Battle of Armageddon.

The Battle of Armageddon (and the events leading up to it) will usher in the most intensive suffering known to mankind. In the Bible we read that the earth will be ravaged by political, economic and ecological crises beyond the realm of our imagination. If it were not for the merciful intervention of God, the Bible teaches, the whole world would be destroyed.

"The Winds of Change" (1992)

All my experiences of disasters around the world, both manmade and natural, did not prepare me for what I saw in South Florida in September 1992. Hurricane Andrew had carved a path of devastation more than thirty miles wide, and it was a picture of absolute chaos for as far as the eye could see. Not a single house or building had been spared.

I had been asked by Florida Governor Lawton Chiles to come down to meet with the people in the hardest-hit areas of the state, especially Homestead and the other communities where Andrew had done such severe damage. On Saturday, September 5, we had the privilege of holding a religious service for those people who so desperately needed encouragement. Just a few days before these same people had been routinely going about their lives unconcerned with the swirls of small dark clouds that satellites had detected somewhere off the west coast of Africa.

At first it was just a typical tropical depression. But it began to grow in size and momentum and slowly moved westward across the sea. Weather forecasters worldwide noted the season's first hurricane but quickly added that it was too far from anything to cause concern.

That assessment changed radically over the next three days as the storm approached Caribbean waters. Each day the weather advisories were more pronounced: small craft warnings, gale warnings, tropical storm warnings, and—when the winds surged past forty-eight knots—hurricane warnings.

Andrew's first landfall was at 11 P.M. on Sunday, August 23, in the Bahamas. Four people were killed on the island of Eleuthera, and property damage was the most extensive in the island's history. Four hours later, the palm trees in South Florida began to dance in the wind with the first gusts from Andrew.

My daughter, GiGi, and her husband Stephan called us that evening from their home near Fort Lauderdale. "We're sitting here, waiting for Andrew," she said. "We aren't exactly sure where it's going to hit, but it should be here within the next four hours." They were taking what precautions they could, but they were going to stick it out at home. GiGi's words gave the storm a new sense of drama and urgency for Ruth and me.

Further south, near Florida City, Herman Lucerne was also preparing to ride the storm out. A former mayor of Florida City, Herman was a renowned outdoorsman and fishing guide. At the age of seventy-eight, he was known to many people as "Mr. Everglades," because that great swampland was his stomping ground. He had lived there all his life. When he heard the storm warnings, he took the usual precautions, just as he had done for countless other hurricanes. He had seen so many in the past, he was convinced he would weather another.

Andrew hit South Florida around 4 A.M.

During those long, deadly hours, Hurricane Andrew unleashed a fury of devastating proportions. For the first time, a storm passed directly over the National Hurricane Warning Service in Coral Gables, and it ripped the radar array from the top of the six-story structure. The center's anemometer was destroyed shortly after it recorded 164-mile-per-hour winds with wind gusts off the scale. The winds that blasted the tip of Florida left thirty-three people dead, destroyed more than sixty-three thousand homes, left 1.3 million people without water or electricity, and did more than $30 billion in damage. But it didn't stop there.

Nineteen hours later, the hurricane had crossed the Gulf of Mexico and struck the coast of Louisiana, where it killed again, leaving fifty thousand people homeless and hundreds of thousands without water or electricity.

The newspapers said that this was the greatest natural disaster ever to strike the United States.

As soon as Ruth and I could get through, we were on the phone with GiGi and Stephan. They said that 100-mile-an-hour winds had blasted their neighborhood, knocking down trees and light poles in the area. They survived unhurt, but they assured me that they would never try to ride out another hurricane. They had learned their lesson and were grateful to have a second chance.

Tragically in Florida City, Herman Lucerne would never get another chance. He didn't survive Andrew. He relied on his experience, but this time his usual precautions were not enough.

Twenty-three years earlier, in Pass Christian, Mississippi, a group of people were preparing to have a "hurricane party" in the face of a storm named Camille. Were they ignorant of the dangers? Could they have been overconfident? Did they let their egos and pride influence their decision? We'll never know.

What we do know is that the wind was howling outside the posh Richelieu Apartments when Police Chief Jerry Peralta pulled up sometime after dark. Facing the beach less than 250 feet from the surf, the apartments were directly in the line of danger. A man with a drink in his hand came out on the second-floor balcony and waved. Peralta yelled up, "You all need to clear out of here as quickly as you can. The storm's getting worse." But as others joined the man on the balcony, they just laughed at Peralta's order to leave. "This is my land," one of them yelled back. "If you want me off, you'll have to arrest me."

Peralta didn't arrest anyone, but he wasn't able to persuade them to leave either. He wrote down the names of the next of kin of the twenty or so people who gathered there to party through the storm. They laughed as he took their names. They had been warned, but they had no intention of leaving.

It was 10:15 P.M. when the front wall of the storm came ashore. Scientists clocked Camille's wind speed at more than 205 miles per hour, the strongest on record. Raindrops hit with the force of bullets, and waves off the Gulf Coast crested between twenty-two and twenty-eight feet high.

News reports later showed that the worst damage came at the little settlement of motels, go-go bars, and gambling houses known as Pass Christian, Mississippi, where some twenty people were killed at a hurricane party in the Richelieu Apartments. Nothing was left of that three-story structure but the foundation; the only survivor was a five-year-old boy found clinging to a mattress the following day.

anemometer	a device for measuring wind speed
knots	units of speed; one knot is equal to one nautical mile (1.15 standard miles) per hour

"WHEN LIFE TURNS AGAINST US" (2006)

It's the most-asked question in the world: *Why?* Why is there so much evil? Why do innocent children die from cancer and abuse and starvation? Why is the world wracked by natural disasters and war and disease? Why is there so much disappointment? Why do good people suffer just as much as bad people—and sometimes even more? If God is so loving and kind (we ask), why doesn't He do something? *Why?*

A Nation in Crisis

None of us will ever forget September 11, 2001. Within minutes our world changed forever as two hijacked airliners plowed into the twin towers of America's tallest building, the World Trade Center in New York City, and a third slammed into the Pentagon in Washington, D.C. Thousands were killed in that merciless terrorist attack, including hundreds of heroic fire, police, are emergency personnel. The attack would have been even more devastating had it not been for a courageous band of passenger who took control of a fourth hijacked plane, sacrificing then lives to keep it from reaching its intended target— probably the White House or the United States Capitol. (One of those fearless passengers had recently graduated from the college Ruth and I attended.)

I was invited by the president to speak three days later at a special service of prayer and remembrance in Washington's National Cathedral. I had participated in a similar event a few years earlier memorializing the victims of the bombing of the Federal Building in Oklahoma City—but this service was undoubtedly one of the hardest things I ever had to do. What could I say to bring comfort and hope to a nation in crisis? How could I possibly explain to those who were grieving why God hadn't intervened—when I didn't know the answer myself?

"I have been asked hundreds of times in my life why God allows tragedy and suffering," I told the congregation that day "I really do not know the answer totally, even to my own satisfaction. I have to accept, by faith, that God is sovereign, and He is a God of love and mercy and compassion in the midst of suffering."

Does that sound like a contradiction? Perhaps it does, at least to our limited minds. Yet both are true:

Evil is real—but so is God's power and love. And because He is all-powerful and loving we can cling to Him in trust and faith, even when we don't understand.

The Mystery of Suffering

Evil and suffering are real, whether we see them on our television screens or confront them in the privacy of our own lives. They aren't an illusion, nor are they simply an absence of good. None of us is immune from their grasp; suffering and tragedy touch us all, no matter who we are. The writer of Ecclesiastes asked, "What does a man get for all the toil and anxious striving with which he labors under the sun? All his days his work is pain and grief; even at night his mind does not rest" (Ecclesiastes 2:22–23). We are fallen creatures living in a fallen world that has been twisted and corrupted by sin, and we all share in its brokenness. Most of all, we share in its tragic legacy of disease and death.

But God is also real! He is just as real as our pain and heartache—and even more so, for someday they will vanish, but He will still remain. In the midst of life's tragedies, He wants to assure us of His presence and love—even if we don't understand why He allowed them to happen. He knows what we are going through, for He experienced evil's fiercest assault when His beloved Son suffered the pangs of death and hell. God understands our suffering, for Christ endured far greater suffering than we ever will. The Cross tells us that God understands our pain and confusion—but more than that, it tells us He loves us.

Can we believe this? Can we honestly believe God is loving and kind when there is so much suffering and sorrow in the world? Yes, we can—but not because we have all the answers, for we don't. We know God loves us for one reason: Christ died and rose again *for us*. Even when we don't understand why bad things happen, the cross tells us God loves us and cares for us. The greatest suffering in human history was Christ's suffering on the cross. Only hours before His arrest Jesus prayed, "My Father, if it is possible, may this cup be taken from me" (Matthew 26:39). The "cup" of which He spoke symbolized all the suffering He was about to endure. What was in that "cup"? It contained all the sins of the whole human race, and now He was about to partake of it. Think of what was in that "cup": every murder, every adultery, every theft, every injustice, every evil deed or thought—all the sins of the whole human race had been poured into that "cup." No wonder He asked the Father if there was any other way for our salvation to be won! But there was no other way. The sinless Son of God was about to have all our sins transferred to Him, so God's full judgment could fall on Him instead of us. Jesus' suffering wasn't simply that of a man dying a cruel and painful death—terrible as that was. His greatest suffering was the spiritual agony He endured as He took upon Himself the death and hell you and I deserve.

Yet by allowing His Son to suffer the pangs of death and hell, God demonstrated how much He loves us. If He didn't love us, He never would have allowed His Son to leave heaven's glory and die for us.

Glossary

America's tallest building	an incorrect statement, for the tallest was the Sears Tower in Chicago
bombing of the Federal Building in Oklahoma City	reference to the destruction of the Alfred P. Murrah Federal Building in Oklahoma City, Oklahoma, by the domestic terrorist Timothy McVeigh on April 19, 1995
Cross	in Christian tradition, a reference to the crucifix on which Christ died
Ecclesiastes	a book of "wisdom" literature in the Christian Old Testament

"A Final Word from Billy Graham" (2006)

One day your life's journey will be over, and you will enter eternity. But what kind of journey will it have been? At the end of your life, will you look back with sorrow and regret, realizing too late that you had traveled the wrong road? Or perhaps that the road you traveled was the right one—but you had allowed the troubles and temptations of this world to hold you back and keep you from reaching your full potential?

Instead, my prayer is that you would have been on the right road in life—and not only that, but that you would have reached the end of your journey with joy. My prayer is that you would have known God's presence the whole way, and that even in the midst of life's deepest trials you would have found your strength in Him.

If you and I could sit down and talk right now, I'd want to hear about your journey so far. On which road are you traveling? Is it the right road—the road God has set out for you? Or are you still on that broad road of which Jesus spoke—a road that looks deceptively inviting and easy, but in the end leads only to emptiness and sorrow and death?

Now is the time to decide which road you will follow. If you have never done so, I urge you to turn to Christ and by faith invite Him to come into your life today. No matter who you are or what your background has been, God still loves you, and Christ died and rose again so you could be on a new path in life—His path. God's promise is for you: "For God so loved the world that he gave his one and only Son, that whoever believes in him shall not perish but have eternal life" (John 3:16). Make your commitment to Jesus Christ today.

Then make it your goal to follow Him every day. As we have seen in this book, God has given us everything we need to see us through life's problems and hardships and to end our journey well. Don't waste your life, and don't be satisfied with anything less than God's plan.

Some day this life will be over. I look forward to that day, because I know that beyond it is heaven. I pray you do too. But until that day God calls you home, make it your goal to live for Christ.

ULYSSES S. GRANT,
LIEUTENANT-GENERAL, U.S.A.

Ulysses S. Grant (Library of Congress)

ULYSSES S. GRANT   1822–1885

Eighteenth President of the United States

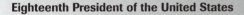

Featured Documents

◆ **Letter to William Tecumseh Sherman (1864)**
◆ **Final Report of Military Operations (1865)**
◆ **First Inaugural Address (1869)**
◆ **Special Message to Congress Announcing Ratification of the Fifteenth Amendment (1870)**
◆ **Sixth Annual Message to Congress (1874)**
◆ **Special Message to the Senate on Unrest in Louisiana (1875)**
◆ **Letter to Daniel H. Chamberlain (1876)**

Overview

As a military commander who rose to the position of general in chief of the armies of the United States during the American Civil War, Ulysses S. Grant helped preserve the Union and destroy slavery. In the last twenty years of his life he did what he could to define what victory meant, most notably as president of the United States from 1869 to 1877. Born in 1822 in southwestern Ohio, Grant was a shy boy who seemed most comfortable around horses. In 1839 he entered the U.S. Military Academy at West Point, graduating four years later in the middle of his class. The army, overlooking his skill with horses, commissioned him as a brevet second lieutenant of infantry. During the Mexican-American War (1846–1848) he distinguished himself several times on the field of battle; however, Grant found life in the peacetime army rather trying, especially when it meant he had to leave his family behind, so in 1854 he resigned his commission as captain. For the next seven years he struggled in civilian life in a variety of jobs; by 1861 he could be found working the desk of his father's general store in Galena, Illinois.

Commissioned colonel of an Illinois infantry regiment in 1861, Grant soon rose to the rank of brigadier general, and his rapid response in taking Paducah, Kentucky, in September 1861 established a launching point for future offensives. In February 1862 he captured Forts Henry and Donelson along the Tennessee-Kentucky border; two months later he fended off a Confederate counterattack at Shiloh, Tennessee, and survived subsequent criticism of his performance there. In 1863, after several failed efforts, he directed a masterful campaign that resulted in the capture of Vicksburg, Mississippi, and its garrison of thirty thousand on July 4; his triumph at Chattanooga that November made him the obvious choice to command the armies of the United States during the critical 1864 campaigns. In the year that followed, Grant drove Robert E. Lee's Army of Northern Virginia back to Richmond and Petersburg, while other forces under his direction captured Atlanta, secured the Shenandoah Valley, and penetrated the Confederate heartland through a series of marches. Union military success guaranteed the reelection of Abraham Lincoln as president in November 1864; the following April, Grant forced Lee first to evacuate Richmond and Petersburg and then to surrender his army on April 9, 1865, at Appomattox Court House, Virginia.

As a general, Grant was renowned for his coolness under fire and his ability to improvise in response to circumstances. He also displayed a knack for understanding how to work with his civil superiors and understood the relationship between how one wages war and why one is waging war. His ability to reduce complex problems to simple and understandable premises stood him in good stead as he mapped out ambitious campaign plans, including the one that most historians celebrate as his masterpiece, Vicksburg. His relentless determination proved valuable in weathering setbacks and pushing on. Documents he wrote during this time, including a letter to William Tecumseh Sherman and his final report of military operations, give historians insight into his generalship.

As general in chief during Reconstruction, Grant attempted to balance sectional reconciliation with justice for the newly freed blacks in the South. Over time he came to realize the seriousness of white violence against African Americans and their allies and supported enfranchising blacks as essential to giving them the means to protect themselves and become full partners in the national polity. In 1868 Republicans persuaded him to run for president as the best way to assure a Republican victory, which would safeguard the fruits of Union victory and serve to protect African Americans. Grant accepted the party's nomination, won the ensuing election, and during the next eight years served as president. Reconstruction proved to be his greatest challenge—as reflected in such documents as his first inaugural address, his special message to the Senate on unrest in Louisiana, and others. Endorsing the ratification of the Fifteenth Amendment, he came to sanction the use of federal force to protect blacks from violence and prevent white southerners from overthrowing Republican state governments in the South. Although his policies enjoyed some initial successes, over time white southern Democrats took over the South state by state, while a combination of limited enforcement tools, increasing apathy in the North, and political setbacks for Republicans limited what Grant could do to prevent the triumph of white supremacy. By 1876 he

Time Line

1822
- **April 27**
  Ulysses S. Grant is born Hiram Ulysses Grant in Point Pleasant, Ohio.

1843
- Grant graduates from the U.S. Military Academy at West Point, New York.

1846–1848
- Grant participates in the Mexican-American War.

1854
- Grant resigns from the army.

1861
- Grant rejoins the army as a colonel, advancing to brigadier general.

1862
- **February 16**
  Grant accepts Confederate surrender at Fort Donelson, Tennessee, for which he is made a major general of volunteers.

1863
- **July 4**
  Grant accepts the Confederate surrender at Vicksburg, Mississippi, for which he is promoted to major general in the regular army.

1864
- **March**
  Grant is promoted to lieutenant general and general in chief of the armies of the United States.
- **April 4**
  Grant outlines plan of the Overland campaign in a letter to William T. Sherman.

1865
- **April 9**
  Grant accepts the surrender of Robert E. Lee at Appomattox Court House, Virginia.
- **July 22**
  Grant submits report of operations during final year of the war.

conceded that he could do little to stop the retreat from Reconstruction, and after he left office in 1877 Democrats completed their resurgence in the South.

Following his presidency Grant took a trip around the world; upon his return to the United States in 1879 Republicans persuaded him to seek his party's nomination for a third term as president, but he lost that contest to James A. Garfield. He joined a private business firm run by his son in New York City but was swindled out of his earnings and investments in 1884. That same year he learned that he had throat cancer. Dying and destitute, he decided to compose his memoirs, which would be published by the American author Samuel Clemens, better known as Mark Twain. He completed the two-volume work just a week before his death at Mount McGregor, New York, on July 23, 1885. His autobiography was hailed as a masterpiece of American literature and proved to be a best seller.

Explanation and Analysis of Documents

As both general and president Grant played a major role in preserving the Union, destroying slavery, and battling for equal rights for blacks in the face of white supremacist terrorism. This selection of documents offers a glimpse at how he conceived of military strategy and how he confronted the challenge of Reconstruction. At the outset of the Civil War, Grant predicted the collapse of slavery, if for no other reason than that the wear and tear of military operations would erode the viability of the institution. At first he was reluctant to strike at slavery out of fear that doing so would deepen the resistance of white southerners. By 1862, however, he had come to accept the destruction of slavery as a critical part of the Union war effort, and by 1863 he had come to embrace emancipation and black enlistment as essential to Union victory, although he still defined that victory in terms of reunion. Equally important to achieving Union victory was the adoption of an approach to waging war against the Confederacy that targeted Confederate morale, logistics, and resources just as much as it aimed to destroy enemy armies. To achieve that goal, Grant believed that Union operations had to be coordinated and continuous. He explained his plan in a letter to William Tecumseh Sherman; he would revert to outlining that philosophy once more in his final report.

While the Confederacy was crushed under Grant's relentless and repeated blows, it remained an open question as to what the United States would look like after reunification, especially when it came to defining what freedom meant for some four million African Americans liberated by the results of the war. Although Grant wrestled with terrorism against blacks as general in chief during President Andrew Johnson's administration, as president he had to counter criticisms concerning federal intervention in the South. Initially he tried to appeal to Americans' sense of fair play and the need to accept the results of the war in order to move forward, but his repeated efforts to explain to the American people what was at stake and the need to treat blacks as equal citizens proved futile, even when he expressed his anger in blunt language. By the time he prepared to leave office, he showed signs that he had resigned himself to failure and frustration when it came to realizing black equality.

◆ Letter to William Tecumseh Sherman

In March 1864 Grant was promoted to the rank of lieutenant general and named general in chief of the armies of the United States. Within a month he had devised a plan of campaign for all the Union armies to pursue in 1864. In this letter he explains his strategic vision to his most able subordinate and close friend, William T. Sherman, whom Grant had named to replace him as commander of Union forces between the Appalachian Mountains and the Mississippi River. Grant would have preferred to have stayed in that theater, but his experiences during his trip east to accept his commission convinced him that only his physical presence could shield the eastern armies from excessive political meddling. In contrast, he had a great deal of confidence in Sherman, leaving his subordinate to devise his own plan of operations to achieve the objectives Grant has set forth.

By the spring of 1864, most of the great set-piece battles of the Civil War—Shiloh, Antietam, Gettysburg, Vicksburg—had already taken place. The remaining year of the war consisted of Union efforts to knock out the Confederacy's ability to wage war and to force surrender. Grant's letter details a series of military operations, all of which would be mounted simultaneously and each of which would place great pressure on a key Confederate stronghold. Some of his targets are Confederate armies, but others include important ports (Mobile, Alabama), cities (the Confederate capital at Richmond, Virginia), and critical railroads. It would be a massive operation that would have to be coordinated by messenger, letter, and telegraph. In commenting on the role of Major General Franz Sigel in western Virginia, moreover, Grant borrows (without attribution) an expression that President Abraham Lincoln had used when Grant explained his plan to the president: "If Sigel can't skin himself he can hold a leg while someone else skins."

In the campaigns that followed, not everything went according to plan. Nathaniel Banks never did make it to Mobile, although another general did later. Sherman never did destroy the enemy army blocking his way to Atlanta, although that army would nearly disintegrate by year's end after a disastrous campaign in Tennessee. Butler bobbled his advance against Richmond, and Sigel proved equally inept at holding and skinning. It was left to Grant to pin Lee against Richmond and then use another army under Major General Philip H. Sheridan to knock out the Shenandoah Valley to the west.

◆ Final Report of Military Operations

Some three months after the end of the war, Grant composed his final report detailing the military operations of 1864–1865. In that report, filled with details about various campaigns and battles, he offers a fairly concise summary of how he approached the strategic problem of defeating

Time Line

1866
- Grant is promoted to four-star general—the first man ever to gain this rank.

1868
- Grant wins presidential election as Republican nominee.

1869
- **March 4**
  Grant takes the oath of office as president and delivers his inaugural address.

1870
- **March 30**
  Grant celebrates ratification of the Fifteenth Amendment with a message to Congress.

1872
- **November 5**
  Grant is reelected for a second term.

1874
- **December 7**
  Grant defends Reconstruction policy in sixth annual message to Congress.

1875
- **January 13**
  Grant offers an extended discussion of Reconstruction in a message to the Senate on unrest in Louisiana.

1876
- **July 26**
  Grant shares his views on Reconstruction with South Carolina governor Daniel H. Chamberlain.

1880
- Grant fails to win nomination for a third term as president.

1885
- **July 23**
  After completing his memoirs, Grant dies at Mount McGregor, New York.

*Crowds surround the front of the capitol on March 4, 1869,
as Ulysses S. Grant takes the oath of office as president.* (AP/Wide World Photos)

the Confederacy. Some of its language, however, would come back to haunt him and damage his historical reputation. Grant explains that while Union forces enjoyed certain advantages, so did the Confederates. True, the Union might be able to draw upon more manpower, but the task confronting the Confederacy was challenging, and only if the Union armies managed to fight in coordinated fashion might they be able to make good use of their advantages while minimizing the impact of the Confederacy's strengths. That, Grant explains, involves targeting enemy resources and morale as well as the enemy's armies, and that is what he set out to do in 1864 by conducting campaigns that were coordinated and continuous.

Unfortunately, in his use of the term "mere attrition," Grant unwittingly gave support to some of his critics, who claimed that all he did was throw his men into a meat grinder that could not help but eventually erode enemy strength. In retrospect, that is what the Overland campaign of 1864 looked like in eventual outcome: tens of thousands of men killed, wounded, and captured in six weeks of continuous combat as Grant slowly forced Lee back to Richmond and Petersburg. In truth, Grant's original plan of campaign looked to slice apart the Confederate transporta-

tion network, damage the enemy's logistics and resources, and force the Confederates to come out and fight or face eventual destruction. However, several subordinates fumbled key aspects of the strategic plan, forcing Grant to adopt the approach he did at a much higher cost than he was hoping to pay. One can see Grant's own misgivings about this approach in the final paragraph quoted here, in which he says that he did the best he could do under the circumstances.

◆ First Inaugural Address

After the Civil War, Grant supervised the federal military forces that oversaw the implementation of federal Reconstruction policy. As committed as he was to reconciliation with former Confederates, he also believed that blacks had to be protected as they made the transition from slavery to freedom. During the next four years, he became more adamant about protecting blacks from terrorism and intimidation; he came to endorse giving blacks the right to vote and making them equal citizens before the law; he supported congressional Reconstruction initiatives; and he opposed President Andrew Johnson's efforts to obstruct the implementation of those measures.

Although at first he was skeptical about entering political life, by 1868 Grant had become convinced that only by running for president on the Republican ticket could he bring a successful end to Reconstruction, thus preserving in peace what had been won in war. He believed that it was time to remove issues of such national importance from the hands of scheming politicians. He was especially disturbed by Johnson's intemperate behavior as president. In the fall election, Grant and the Republicans prevailed, with his popular majority being secured by black votes—the first time African Americans had participated on a large scale in an American presidential contest.

In his inaugural address Grant outlines his conception of the office of the presidency and the approach he favored on a number of issues. In contrast to Johnson, who did what he could to block or thwart laws that he disliked, Grant assures Americans that "all laws will be faithfully executed, whether they meet my approval or not. I shall on all subjects have a policy to recommend, but none to enforce against the will of the people." His message is one of reassurance and a plea for Americans to set aside their passions and work together to address the outstanding issues facing the nation, including Reconstruction. He urges the ratification of the Fifteenth Amendment, which would remove the barrier of race, color, or previous condition of servitude from voting, as a way to resolve that outstanding issue so Americans could move forward. In short, Grant is looking forward to ending Reconstruction, and he believes this can be done if Americans obey the law and respect their fellow citizens.

◆ Special Message to Congress Announcing Ratification of the Fifteenth Amendment

Extending suffrage to large numbers of African American adult males became a key element of Republican Reconstruction policy after the war. At first Republicans were reluctant to mandate extending suffrage to blacks: The Fourteenth Amendment simply provided for a reduction in congressional representation for those states that denied the vote to any U.S. citizens. However, in the 1867 Reconstruction Acts, Congress provided for blacks' participation in voting for delegates to state constitutional conventions, which would reshape the constitutions of the ten former Confederate states it covered. (The Confederacy consisted of eleven states, but Tennessee had ratified the Fourteenth Amendment and was therefore readmitted to the Union, so the Reconstruction Acts did not apply to it.) Elsewhere, Republicans found it exceptionally hard to secure black suffrage, as a number of northern states defeated attempts to extend the right to vote to blacks. The importance of the black vote was evident in the 1868 presidential contest, in which black votes provided Grant with his slim majority in the popular vote; a majority of whites who voted preferred his Democratic rival, Horatio Seymour.

In the aftermath of the 1868 election, Republicans decided to embrace amending the Constitution as the best way to secure suffrage for black males. As state legislatures ratified proposed amendments, Republicans would be able to bypass the need to submit black suffrage proposals to direct popular vote and could rely on their control of state legislatures to prevail. Grant endorsed the amendment in his inaugural address. He had long thought that it was hypocritical to impose black suffrage in the South while leaving it optional in the North, and he had come to believe that enfranchising blacks offered them a means by which they could protect themselves in the political process. During the ratification process the president did what he could to promote the amendment's success, and he took the unusual step of celebrating its ratification in March 1870.

Grant believes that the enfranchisement of African Americans by constitutional amendment "completes the greatest civil change and constitutes the most important event that has occurred since the nation came into life." In celebrating this advance, he reminded Americans that it had been just thirteen years ago that the Supreme Court in *Dred Scott v. Sandford* had offered a far different assessment of blacks' position in the American republic, going so far as to quote Chief Justice Roger B. Taney's stark claim that "black men had no rights which the white man was bound to respect." The Fifteenth Amendment effectively struck the final blow at that claim, or so Grant believed. He calls upon blacks "to make themselves worthy of their new privilege"; he calls upon whites to "withhold no legal privilege of advancement to the new citizen." In an effort to secure the benefits of this fundamental revolution in the composition of the electorate, Grant also calls for measures to promote public education, but he did not charge Congress with seeking to legislate an economic foundation for equality or to pass new legislation to advance equality and integration. Unfortunately, many white Americans, especially in the South, did not heed the president's plea for fairness, and within the year Grant advocated measures that would allow him to suspend the writ of habeas corpus, declare martial law, and employ federal troops to quash white supremacist terrorist efforts to defeat black suffrage through intimidation, violence, and murder.

◆ Sixth Annual Message to Congress

Although Grant won reelection in 1872, his administration soon confronted several serious challenges, including economic depression and a continuing battle over Reconstruction in the South. In the fall of 1874 Democratic victories in the off-year elections gave that party control of the House of Representatives, meaning that once the new session of Congress convened in mid-1875, Republicans would no longer be able to pass Reconstruction measures through Congress. In his annual message in December 1874, Grant outlines once more why federal intervention in the South to protect black voters is necessary. He highlights the formation of new terrorist groups that intimidate black voters and use violence to secure Democratic victories in the South. Congress had passed legislation to enforce the Fifteenth Amendment, and if the government could not use force to protect blacks exercising the rights to vote, hold office, and participate in politics, "the whole scheme of colored enfranchisement is worse than mockery and little better than a crime."

Grant explains that he undertakes such intervention reluctantly and only because he views it as an absolute necessity. There would be no need for such intervention if white southerners took it upon themselves to end the terrorism and intimidation instead of claiming that they had nothing to do with it. No doubt there might be cause for unhappiness with the measures espoused by several Republican state governments in the South, he says, but violence was not the answer. As he reminds Americans, "Treat the negro as a citizen and a voter, as he is and must remain, and soon parties will be divided, not on the color line, but on principle."

◆ Special Message to the Senate on Unrest in Louisiana

Nearly a month after Grant sent his annual message to Congress, there was news of new trouble in Louisiana. Democrats had tried to take over the state legislature through a combination of trickery and force. Republicans regained the upper hand with the assistance of federal soldiers dispatched to the state house by General Philip H. Sheridan, who advocated treating white supremacist terrorists harshly. Sheridan's actions sparked criticism from people who were uneasy with the use of federal force in state political affairs. Grant felt compelled not only to defend his old wartime subordinate but also to remind Americans of the course of events in Louisiana over the past several years.

After outlining the events that had led to a disputed state election in 1872, Grant offers a blunt and explicit account of the Colfax massacre, where whites killed approximately a hundred blacks on April 13, 1873. Only a few of the whites were arrested and prosecuted, and in 1874 a federal district court decision challenged the ability of the federal government to intervene in such circumstances. State and local authorities failed to protect their black citizens: "Every one of the Colfax miscreants goes unwhipped of justice, and no way can be found in this boasted land of civilization and Christianity to punish the perpetrators of this bloody and monstrous crime." He employs the same blunt language in recalling the killing of several Republicans in Coushatta, Louisiana: "Some of them were Republicans and officeholders under Kellogg. They were therefore doomed to death.... No one has been punished, and the conservative press of the State denounced all efforts to that end and boldly justified the crime."

Grant reminds Americans that Democrats had used force in an effort to overthrow the Republican government in Louisiana in September 1874. That it is the federal government that draws criticism for intervening to stop bloodshed and protect blacks strikes him as reprehensible. Grant's 1875 message shows him at his angriest. However, lacking public support for continued intervention, Grant began to reassess the wisdom of undertaking such acts. Moreover, between court decisions that struck down key parts of congressional legislation and the ability of Democrats in the House of Representatives to block the passage of any new legislative initiatives, he felt increasingly helpless when it came to effecting lasting change.

◆ Letter to Daniel H. Chamberlain

During 1875 and 1876 Grant showed less willingness to authorize federal intervention in the South except in cases where it was a clear necessity. He declined to send troops to Mississippi in 1875, and in the elections that year the Democrats prevailed. However, elsewhere the Republicans regained ground. Declining to intervene might consign southern Republicans to oblivion, but it allowed Republicans to prevail on other grounds in the North and thus the nation. Even when white southerners committed acts of violence, as they did at Hamburg, South Carolina, on July 8, 1876, white northerners were hesitant to do very much about it, especially in a presidential election year that promised to be closely contested. That white supremacists had attacked the local militia, attempted to disarm it, shot down several blacks, and executed several blacks whom they had taken prisoner no longer made the impression it once did. White northerners were getting tired of such reports and wished for peace at virtually any price. The price white supremacists demanded was their return to power in the former Confederate states.

Grant's sense of resignation is evident in his reply to South Carolina governor Daniel H. Chamberlain's report of violence against Republicans in his state. "The scene at Hamburg, as cruel, blood-thirsty, wanton, unprovoked, and uncalled for, as it was, is only a repetition of the course which has been pursued in other Southern States within the last few years, notably in Mississippi and Louisiana," observes Grant. He adds: "Mississippi is governed to-day by officials chosen through fraud and violence, such as would scarcely be accredited to savages, much less to a civilized and Christian people." However, Grant says that he does not know when the violence will come to an end; he states that a government that cannot protect its citizens is a failure and that should the situation continue, he could see the day when blacks would retaliate.

Eventually, Grant sent soldiers to South Carolina, but he waited until the aftermath of the October state contests in several key northern states before acting. The following year, as Rutherford B. Hayes took office as president, the remaining Republican regimes in the South went the way of Mississippi, and Democrats regained control of the former Confederate states.

As he traveled around the world, Grant wondered whether the decision to restore civil government to the former Confederate states in the immediate aftermath of the war had been a mistake. Perhaps it would have been better for all concerned, he suggested, had there been a federally managed Reconstruction under military supervision. He doubted that most Americans would have stood for that, but he also doubted that they were ready to make equality under the law a reality. Union victory in the Civil War might have preserved the nation and destroyed slavery, but it had left unfinished defining what freedom meant.

Impact and Legacy

Had Ulysses S. Grant simply retired to private life in 1865, or had he declined to pursue the Republican presi-

"I therefore determined, first, to use the greatest number of troops practicable against the armed force of the enemy; preventing him from using the same force at different seasons against first one and then another of our armies, and the possibility of repose for refitting and producing necessary supplies for carrying on resistance."

(Final Report of Military Operations)

"I shall on all subjects have a policy to recommend, but none to enforce against the will of the people. Laws are to govern all alike—those opposed as well as those who favor them. I know no method to secure the repeal of bad or obnoxious laws so effective as their stringent execution."

(First Inaugural Address)

"To the race more favored heretofore by our laws I would say, Withhold no legal privilege of advancement to the new citizen."

(Message upon Ratification of Fifteenth Amendment)

"Complaints are made of this interference by Federal authority; but if said amendment and act do not provide for such interference under the circumstances as above stated, then they are without meaning, force, or effect, and the whole scheme of colored enfranchisement is worse than mockery and little better than a crime."

(Sixth Annual Message to Congress)

"Treat the negro as a citizen and a voter, as he is and must remain, and soon parties will be divided, not on the color line, but on principle. Then we shall have no complaint of sectional interference."

(Sixth Annual Message to Congress)

"A government that cannot give protection to life, property, and all guaranteed civil rights (in this country the greatest is an untrammeled ballot) to the citizen is, in so far, a failure, and every energy of the oppressed should be exerted, always within the law and by constitutional means, to regain lost privileges and protections. Too long denial of guaranteed rights is sure to lead to revolution—bloody revolution, where suffering must fall upon the innocent as well as the guilty."

(Letter to Daniel H. Chamberlain)

dential nomination in 1868, he would still be one of the pivotal figures in American history for his record of military success during the American Civil War. For it was Grant who led the way to a series of critical victories that resulted in the collapse of the Confederate defensive perimeter in Kentucky and Tennessee, sliced the Confederacy in half at Vicksburg, and positioned Union armies ready to strike at the Confederate heartland by the end of 1863. That at the same time he accepted the surrender of two enemy armies was of equal importance, given how much the Confederacy needed to conserve manpower, maintain morale, and preserve resources. By the end of 1863 Grant had emerged as the Union's preeminent general, one who worked well with his civilian superiors, recognized the importance of emancipation and enlisting blacks, and coordinated the movements of scattered military forces toward a common end. Those skills stood him in good stead in 1864, when he assumed the responsibilities of directing the armies of the United States. Some thirteen months to the day after he accepted his commission as lieutenant general, he accepted the surrender of Robert E. Lee.

However, Grant's historical reputation has suffered in part because he was not nearly as successful in guaranteeing black rights during Reconstruction. True, during Grant's administration Reconstruction largely came to a close, with the reestablishment of civilian state governments throughout the South; the Fifteenth Amendment sought to offer a stronger guarantee to blacks that their political rights would be respected and protected. However, during Reconstruction white supremacist terrorist groups waged a war against black equality. If Grant found this disappointing, he found equally discouraging the increasing criticism directed his way by a northern public that seemed increasingly apathetic when it came to the impact of such terrorism. Grant's complaints

grew louder as his efforts proved ever more ineffective. Thus, in peacetime Grant did not enjoy the success he attained in war. However, he remains important, in part because his generalship proved a model for subsequent military leaders, and in part because his impassioned declarations about Reconstruction remind us of what could—and should—have been.

Key Sources

The Ulysses S. Grant Papers at the Library of Congress are available on microfilm at many research libraries. Other collection of Grant papers are scattered throughout the country, including the Chicago History Museum (formerly the Chicago Historical Society), the Abraham Lincoln Presidential Library (formerly the Illinois State Historical Library), and the National Archives. *The Papers of Ulysses S. Grant* (1967–2009), edited by a team headed by John Y. Simon, will total some thirty-one volumes. Essential to understanding Grant is his *Personal Memoirs of U. S. Grant* (2 vols., 1885–1886), which concentrates on the first forty-three years of his life, through the end of the war; also helpful is Julia Dent Grant's *The Personal Memoirs of Julia Dent Grant* (1975). Several valuable interviews Grant gave after he left the presidency can be found in John Russell Young, *Around the World with General Grant* (2 vols., 1879).

Further Reading

■ Books

Bunting, Josiah, III. *Ulysses S. Grant*. New York: Times Books, 2004.

Catton, Bruce. *Grant Takes Command*. Boston: Little, Brown, 1969.

Questions for Further Study

1. Discuss the complicated details of the 1872 Louisiana gubernatorial elections and the resulting violence as well as the way that Grant—in part through his message to Congress—sought to deal with the aftermath.

2. Grant's description of the Colfax massacre makes powerful reading. Examine his ability as a storyteller and how he sought to influence Congress with his narrative. How does he display his anger through words?

3. One of the abiding themes in many documents associated with Grant is the issue of imposing federal power on the states. Today the influence of the federal government is taken for granted, but at that time the concept was still new, having only recently been put to the ultimate test in a bloody civil war. Address the principal issues involved in the extension of federal power to the states and how Grant sought to deal with these issues.

4. A number of terms used by Grant—"conservative," "Republican," "Democrat," and even "domestic violence"— have different meanings today than they did in his time. How have the definitions of these and other words that appear in his writings and speeches changed since the 1860s and 1870s?

———. *Grant Moves South 1861–1863*. Boston: Little, Brown, 1990.

Lewis, Lloyd. *Captain Sam Grant*. Boston: Little, Brown, 1950.

McFeely, William S. *Grant: A Biography*. New York: W. W. Norton, 1981.

Simpson, Brooks D. *Let Us Have Peace: Ulysses S. Grant and the Politics of War and Reconstruction, 1861–1868*. Chapel Hill: University of North Carolina Press, 1991.

———. *The Reconstruction Presidents*. Lawrence: University Press of Kansas, 1998.

———. *Ulysses S. Grant: Triumph over Adversity, 1822–1865*. Boston: Houghton Mifflin, 2000.

Smith, Jean Edward. *Grant*. New York: Simon and Schuster, 2001.

—Brooks D. Simpson

Grant, Ulysses S.

Letter to William Tecumseh Sherman (1864)

HEADQUARTERS ARMIES OF THE UNITED STATES, WASHINGTON, D.C., April 4, 1864.

MAJOR-GENERAL W. T. SHERMAN, Commanding Military Division of the Mississippi.

GENERAL:—It is my design, if the enemy keep quiet and allow me to take the initiative in the spring campaign, to work all parts of the army together, and somewhat towards a common centre. For your information I now write you my programme, as at present determined upon.

I have sent orders to Banks, by private messenger, to finish up his present expedition against Shreveport with all dispatch; to turn over the defence of Red River to General Steele and the navy and to return your troops to you and his own to New Orleans; to abandon all of Texas, except the Rio Grande, and to

Glossary

Banks	General Nathaniel Prentice Banks
Burnside	General Ambrose Burnside
Butler	General Benjamin Butler
Charleston on the Kanawha	Charleston, West Virginia
Crook	General George Crook
Department of West Virginia	the Army of West Virginia
Fortress Monroe	a military installation, now known as Fort Monroe, in Virginia
General Steele	Major General Frederick Steele
Gilmore	General Quincy Gilmore
if Sigel can't skin himself he can hold a leg while some one else skins	a reference to removing the skin from a dead animal, meaning "if Sigel can't get the job done himself, he can help somebody else to get it done"
inst.	instant—that is, of this month
of all arms	of all branches of service
Ord and Averell	Major General Edward Ord and Brigadier General William W. Averell
Saltville	a town in Virginia that provided the Confederacy with its principal source of salt, important at that time for preserving meat
Shreveport	capital of Louisiana at the time
Sigel	Major General Franz Sigel
Virginia and Tennessee Railroad	a rail line between Lynchburg, Virginia, and Bristol, Tennessee, that served as one of the principal supply routes for the Confederacy
W. F. Smith	Major General William Farrar Smith

hold that with not to exceed four thousand men; to reduce the number of troops on the Mississippi to the lowest number necessary to hold it, and to collect from his command not less than twenty-five thousand men. To this I will add five thousand men from Missouri. With this force he is to commence operations against Mobile as soon as he can. It will be impossible for him to commence too early.

Gillmore joins Butler with ten thousand men, and the two operate against Richmond from the south side of the James River. This will give Butler thirty-three thousand men to operate with, W. F. Smith commanding the right wing of his forces and Gillmore the left wing. I will stay with the Army of the Potomac, increased by Burnside's corps of not less than twenty-five thousand effective men, and operate directly against Lee's army, wherever it may be found.

Sigel collects all his available force in two columns, one, under Ord and Averell, to start from Beverly, Virginia, and the other, under Crook, to start from Charleston on the Kanawha, to move against the Virginia and Tennessee Railroad.

Crook will have all cavalry, and will endeavor to get in about Saltville, and move east from there to join Ord. His force will be all cavalry, while Ord will have from ten to twelve thousand men of all arms.

You I propose to move against Johnston's army, to break it up and to get into the interior of the enemy's country as far as you can, inflicting all the damage you can against their war resources.

I do not propose to lay down for you a plan of campaign, but simply lay down the work it is desirable to have done and leave you free to execute it in your own way. Submit to me, however, as early as you can, your plan of operations.

As stated, Banks is ordered to commence operations as soon as he can. Gillmore is ordered to report at Fortress Monroe by the 18th inst., or as soon thereafter as practicable. Sigel is concentrating now. None will move from their places of rendezvous until I direct, except Banks. I want to be ready to move by the 25th inst., if possible. But all I can now direct is that you get ready as soon as possible. I know you will have difficulties to encounter in getting through the mountains to where supplies are abundant, but I believe you will accomplish it.

From the expedition from the Department of West Virginia I do not calculate on very great results; but it is the only way I can take troops from there. With the long line of railroad Sigel has to protect, he can spare no troops except to move directly to his front. In this way he must get through to inflict great damage on the enemy, or the enemy must detach from one of his armies a large force to prevent it. In other words, if Sigel can't skin himself he can hold a leg while some one else skins.

I am, general, very respectfully, your obedient servant,

U. S. GRANT, Lieutenant-General

FINAL REPORT OF MILITARY OPERATIONS (1865)

From an early period in the rebellion I had been impressed with the idea that active and continuous operations of all the troops that could be brought into the field, regardless of season and weather, were necessary to a speedy termination of the war. The resources of the enemy and his numerical strength were far inferior to ours; but as an offset to this, we had a vast territory, with a population hostile to the government, to garrison, and long lines of river and railroad communications to protect, to enable us to supply the operating armies.

The armies in the East and West acted independently and without concert, like a balky team, no two ever pulling together, enabling the enemy to use to great advantage his interior lines of communication for transporting troops from East to West, reinforcing the army most vigorously pressed, and to furlough large numbers, during seasons of inactivity on our part, to go to their homes and do the work of producing, for the support of their armies. It was a question whether our numerical strength and resources were not more than balanced by these disadvantages and the enemy's superior position.

From the first, I was firm in the conviction that no peace could be had that would be stable and conducive to the happiness of the people, both North and South, until the military power of the rebellion was entirely broken.

I therefore determined, first, to use the greatest number of troops practicable against the armed force of the enemy; preventing him from using the same force at different seasons against first one and then another of our armies, and the possibility of repose for refitting and producing necessary supplies for carrying on resistance. Second, to hammer continuously against the armed force of the enemy and his resources, until by mere attrition, if in no other way, there should be nothing left to him but an equal submission with the loyal section of our common country to the constitution and laws of the land.

These views have been kept constantly in mind, and orders given and campaigns made to carry them out. Whether they might have been better in conception and execution is for the people, who mourn the loss of friends fallen, and who have to pay the pecuniary cost, to say. All I can say is that what I have done has been done conscientiously, to the best of my ability, and in what I conceived to be for the best interests of the whole country.

Glossary

balky team	a reference to horse or mule teams, described as "balky" when they proved difficult to command
the field	battle

First Inaugural Address (1869)

Citizens of the United States:

Your suffrages having elected me to the office of President of the United States, I have, in conformity to the Constitution of our country, taken the oath of office prescribed therein. I have taken this oath without mental reservation and with the determination to do to the best of my ability all that is required of me. The responsibilities of the position I feel, but accept them without fear. The office has come to me unsought; I commence its duties untrammeled. I bring to it a conscious desire and determination to fill it to the best of my ability to the satisfaction of the people.

On all leading questions agitating the public mind I will always express my views to Congress and urge them according to my judgment, and when I think it advisable will exercise the constitutional privilege of interposing a veto to defeat measures which I oppose; but all laws will be faithfully executed, whether they meet my approval or not.

I shall on all subjects have a policy to recommend, but none to enforce against the will of the people. Laws are to govern all alike—those opposed as well as those who favor them. I know no method to secure the repeal of bad or obnoxious laws so effective as their stringent execution.

The country having just emerged from a great rebellion, many questions will come before it for settlement in the next four years which preceding Administrations have never had to deal with. In meeting these it is desirable that they should be approached calmly, without prejudice, hate, or sectional pride, remembering that the greatest good to the greatest number is the object to be attained.

This requires security of person, property, and free religious and political opinion in every part of our common country, without regard to local prejudice. All laws to secure these ends will receive my best efforts for their enforcement....

The question of suffrage is one which is likely to agitate the public so long as a portion of the citizens of the nation are excluded from its privileges in any State. It seems to me very desirable that this question should be settled now, and I entertain the hope and express the desire that it may be by the ratification of the fifteenth article of amendment to the Constitution.

In conclusion I ask patient forbearance one toward another throughout the land, and a determined effort on the part of every citizen to do his share toward cementing a happy union; and I ask the prayers of the nation to Almighty God in behalf of this consummation.

Glossary

fifteenth article of amendment to the Constitution	the Fifteenth Amendment, ratified in 1870 and guaranteeing the right to vote regardless of race, color, or "previous condition of servitude" (that is, having been a slave)
suffrages	votes

SPECIAL MESSAGE TO CONGRESS ANNOUNCING RATIFICATION OF THE FIFTEENTH AMENDMENT (1870)

It is unusual to notify the two Houses of Congress by message of the promulgation, by proclamation of the Secretary of State, of the ratification of a constitutional amendment. In view, however, of the vast importance of the fifteenth amendment to the Constitution, this day declared a part of that revered instrument, I deem a departure from the usual custom justifiable. A measure which makes at once 4,000,000 people voters who were heretofore declared by the highest tribunal in the land not citizens of the United States, nor eligible to become so (with the assertion that at the time of the Declaration of Independence the opinion was fixed and universal in the civilized portion of the white race, regarded as an axiom in morals as well as in politics, that black men had no rights which the white man was bound to respect), is indeed a measure of grander importance than any other one act of the kind from the foundation of our free Government to the present day.

Institutions like ours, in which all power is derived directly from the people, must depend mainly upon their intelligence, patriotism, and industry. I call the attention, therefore, of the newly enfranchised race to the importance of their striving in every honorable manner to make themselves worthy of their new privilege. To the race more favored heretofore by our laws I would say, Withhold no legal privilege of advancement to the new citizen. The framers of our Constitution firmly believed that a republican government could not endure without intelligence and education generally diffused among the people. The Father of his Country, in his Farewell Address, uses this language:

> Promote, then, as an object of primary importance, institutions for the general diffusion of knowledge. In proportion as the structure of a government gives force to public opinion, it is essential that public opinion should be enlightened.

In his first annual message to Congress the same views are forcibly presented, and are again urged in his eighth message.

I repeat that the adoption of the fifteenth amendment to the Constitution completes the greatest civil change and constitutes the most important event that has occurred since the nation came into life. The change will be beneficial in proportion to the heed that is given to the urgent recommendations of Washington. If these recommendations were important then, with a population of but a few millions, how much more important now, with a population of 40,000,000, and increasing in a rapid ratio. I would therefore call upon Congress to take all the means within their constitutional powers to promote and encourage popular education throughout the country, and upon the people everywhere to see to it that all who possess and exercise political rights shall have the opportunity to acquire the knowledge which will make their share in the Government a blessing and not a danger. By such means only can the benefits contemplated by this amendment to the Constitution be secured.

Glossary

enfranchised	granted the right to vote
Fifteenth Amendment	the Fifteenth Amendment, ratified in 1870 and guaranteeing the right to vote regardless of race, color, or "previous condition of servitude" (that is, having been a slave)
promulgation	announcement
that revered instrument	the Constitution

SIXTH ANNUAL MESSAGE TO CONGRESS (1874)

I regret to say that with preparations for the late election decided indications appeared in some localities in the Southern States of a determination, by acts of violence and intimidation, to deprive citizens of the freedom of the ballot because of their political opinions. Bands of men, masked and armed, made their appearance; White Leagues and other societies were formed; large quantities of arms and ammunition were imported and distributed to these organizations; military drills, with menacing demonstrations, were held, and with all these murders enough were committed to spread terror among those whose political action was to be suppressed, if possible, by these intolerant and criminal proceedings. In some places colored laborers were compelled to vote according to the wishes of their employers, under threats of discharge if they acted otherwise; and there are too many instances in which, when these threats were disregarded, they were remorselessly executed by those who made them. I understand that the fifteenth amendment to the Constitution was made to prevent this and a like state of things, and the act of May 31, 1870, with amendments, was passed to enforce its provisions, the object of both being to guarantee to all citizens the right to vote and to protect them in the free enjoyment of that right. Enjoined by the Constitution "to take care that the laws be faithfully executed," and convinced by undoubted evidence that violations of said act had been committed and that a widespread and flagrant disregard of it was contemplated, the proper officers were instructed to prosecute the offenders, and troops were stationed at convenient points to aid these officers, if necessary, in the performance of their official duties. Complaints are made of this interference by Federal authority; but if said amendment and act do not provide for such interference under the circumstances as above stated, then they are without meaning, force, or effect, and the whole scheme of colored enfranchisement is worse than mockery and little better than a crime. Possibly Congress may find it due to truth and justice to ascertain, by means of a committee, whether the alleged wrongs to colored citizens for political purposes are real or the reports thereof were manufactured for the occasion....

The whole subject of Executive interference with the affairs of a State is repugnant to public opinion, to the feelings of those who, from their official capacity, must be used in such interposition, and to him or those who must direct. Unless most clearly on the side of law, such interference becomes a crime; with the law to support it, it is condemned without a hearing. I desire, therefore, that all necessity for Executive direction in local affairs may become unnecessary and obsolete. I invite the attention, not of Congress, but of the people of the United States, to the causes and effects of these unhappy questions. Is there not a disposition on one side to magnify wrongs and outrages, and on the other side to belittle them or justify them? If public opinion could be directed to a correct survey of what is and to rebuking wrong and aiding the proper authorities in punishing it, a better state of feeling would be inculcated, and the sooner we would have that peace which would leave the States free indeed to regulate their own domestic affairs. I believe on the part of our citizens of the Southern States—the better part of them—there is a disposition to be law abiding, and to do no violence either to individuals or to the laws existing. But do they do right in ignoring the existence of violence and bloodshed in resistance to constituted authority? I sympathize with their prostrate condition, and would do all in my power to relieve them, acknowledging that in some instances they have had most trying governments to live under, and very oppressive ones in the way of taxation for nominal improvements, not giving benefits equal to the hardships imposed. But can they proclaim themselves entirely irresponsible for this condition? They can not. Violence has been rampant in some localities, and has either been justified or denied by those who could have prevented it. The theory is even raised that there is to be no further interference on the part of the General Government to protect citizens within a State where the State authorities fail to give protection. This is a great mistake. While I remain Executive all the laws of Congress and the provisions of the Constitution, including the recent amendments added thereto, will be enforced with rigor, but with regret that they should have added one jot or tittle to Executive duties or powers. Let there be fairness in the discussion of Southern questions, the advocates of both or all political parties giving honest, truthful reports of occurrences, condemning the wrong and upholding the right, and soon all will be well. Under existing conditions the negro votes the Republican ticket because he knows his friends are of that party. Many a good citizen votes the opposite, not because he agrees with the great principles of state which separate parties, but because, generally, he is opposed to negro rule. This is a most delusive cry. Treat the negro as a citizen and a voter, as he is and must remain, and soon parties will be divided, not on the color line, but on principle. Then we shall have no complaint of sectional interference.

jot or tittle	a tiny detail
late	recent
nominal	in name only

SPECIAL MESSAGE TO THE SENATE ON UNREST IN LOUISIANA (1875)

I have the honor to make the following answer to a Senate resolution of the 8th instant, asking for information as to any interference by any military officer or any part of the Army of the United States with the organization or proceedings of the general assembly of the State of Louisiana, or either branch thereof; and also inquiring in regard to the existence of armed organizations in that State hostile to the government thereof and intent on overturning such government by force.

To say that lawlessness, turbulence, and bloodshed have characterized the political affairs of that State since its reorganization under the reconstruction acts is only to repeat what has become well known as a part of its unhappy history; but it may be proper here to refer to the election of 1868, by which the Republican vote of the State, through fraud and violence, was reduced to a few thousands, and the bloody riots of 1866 and 1868, to show that the disorders there are not due to any recent causes or to any late action of the Federal authorities.

Preparatory to the election of 1872 a shameful and undisguised conspiracy was formed to carry that election against the Republicans, without regard to law or right, and to that end the most glaring frauds and forgeries were committed in the returns, after many colored citizens had been denied registration and others deterred by fear from casting their ballots.

When the time came for a final canvass of the votes, in view of the foregoing facts William P. Kellogg, the Republican candidate for governor, brought suit upon the equity side of the United States circuit court for Louisiana, and against Warmoth and others, who had obtained possession of the returns of the election, representing that several thousand voters of the State had been deprived of the elective franchise on account of their color, and praying that steps might be taken to have said votes counted and for general relief. To enable the court to inquire as to the truth of these allegations, a temporary restraining order was issued against the defendants, which was at once wholly disregarded and treated with contempt by those to whom it was directed. These proceedings have been widely denounced as an unwarrantable interference by the Federal judiciary with the election of State officers; but it is to be remembered that by the fifteenth amendment to the Con-

stitution of the United States the political equality of colored citizens is secured, and under the second section of that amendment, providing that Congress shall have power to enforce its provisions by appropriate legislation, an act was passed on the 31st of May, 1870, and amended in 1871, the object of which was to prevent the denial or abridgment of suffrage to citizens on account of race, color, or previous condition of servitude; and it has been held by all the Federal judges before whom the question has arisen, including Justice Strong, of the Supreme Court, that the protection afforded by this amendment and these acts extends to State as well as other elections. That it is the duty of the Federal courts to enforce the provisions of the Constitution of the United States and the laws passed in pursuance thereof is too clear for controversy.

Section 15 of said act, after numerous provisions therein to prevent an evasion of the fifteenth amendment, provides that the jurisdiction of the circuit court of the United States shall extend to all cases in law or equity arising under the provisions of said act and of the act amendatory thereof. Congress seems to have contemplated equitable as well as legal proceedings to prevent the denial of suffrage to colored citizens; and it may be safely asserted that if Kellogg's bill in the above-named case did not present a case for the equitable interposition of the court, that no such case can arise under the act. That the courts of the United States have the right to interfere in various ways with State elections so as to maintain political equality and rights therein, irrespective of race or color, is comparatively a new, and to some seems to be a startling, idea, but it results as clearly from the fifteenth amendment to the Constitution and the acts that have been passed to enforce that amendment as the abrogation of State laws upholding slavery results from the thirteenth amendment to the Constitution....

Resulting from these proceedings, through various controversies and complications, a State administration was organized with William P. Kellogg as governor, which, in the discharge of my duty under section 4, Article IV, of the Constitution, I have recognized as the government of the State.

It has been bitterly and persistently alleged that Kellogg was not elected. Whether he was or not is not altogether certain, nor is it any more certain that his competitor, McEnery, was chosen. The election was a gigantic fraud, and there are no reliable returns of its result. Kellogg obtained possession of the office, and in my opinion has more right to it than his competitor....

Misinformed and misjudging as to the nature and extent of this report, the supporters of McEnery proceeded to displace by force in some counties of the State the appointees of Governor Kellogg, and on the 13th of April, in an effort of that kind, a butchery of citizens was committed at Colfax, which in bloodthirstiness and barbarity is hardly surpassed by any acts of savage warfare.

To put this matter beyond controversy I quote from the charge of Judge Woods, of the United States circuit court, to the jury in the case of The United States vs. Cruikshank and others, in New Orleans in March, 1874. He said:

In the case on trial there are many facts not in controversy. I proceed to state some of them in the presence and hearing of counsel on both sides; and if I state as a conceded fact any matter that is disputed, they can correct me.

After stating the origin of the difficulty, which grew out of an attempt of white persons to drive the parish judge and sheriff, appointees of Kellogg, from office, and their attempted protection by colored persons, which led to some fighting, in which quite a number of negroes were killed, the judge states:

Most of those who were not killed were taken prisoners. Fifteen or sixteen of the blacks had lifted the boards and taken refuge under the floor of the court-house. They were all captured. About thirty-seven men were taken prisoners. The number is not definitely fixed. They were kept under guard until dark. They were led out, two by two, and shot. Most of the men were shot to death. A few were wounded, not mortally, and by pretending to be dead were afterwards, during the night, able to make their escape. Among them was the Levi Nelson named in the indictment.

The dead bodies of the negroes killed in this affair were left unburied until Tuesday, April 15, when they were buried by a deputy marshal and an officer of the militia from New Orleans. These persons found fifty-nine dead bodies. They showed pistol-shot wounds, the great majority in the head, and most of them in the back of the head. In addition to the fifty-nine dead bodies found, some charred remains of dead bodies were discovered near the court-house. Six dead bodies were found under a warehouse, all shot in the head but one or two, which were shot in the breast....

To hold the people of Louisiana generally responsible for these atrocities would not be just, but it is a lamentable fact that insuperable obstructions were thrown in the way of punishing these murderers; and the so-called conservative papers of the State not only justified the massacre, but denounced as Federal tyranny and despotism the attempt of the United States officers to bring them to justice. Fierce denunciations ring through the country about office holding and election matters in Louisiana, while every one of the Colfax miscreants goes unwhipped of justice, and no way can be found in this boasted land of civilization and Christianity to punish the perpetrators of this bloody and monstrous crime.

Not unlike this was the massacre in August last. Several Northern young men of capital and enterprise had started the little and flourishing town of Coushatta. Some of them were Republicans and officeholders under Kellogg. They were therefore doomed to death. Six of them were seized and carried away from their homes and murdered in cold blood. No one has been punished, and the conservative press of the State denounced all efforts to that end and boldly justified the crime....

To say that the murder of a negro or a white Republican is not considered a crime in Louisiana would probably be unjust to a great part of the people, but it is true that a great number of such murders have been committed and no one has been punished therefor; and manifestly, as to them, the spirit of hatred and violence is stronger than law.

Representations were made to me that the presence of troops in Louisiana was unnecessary and irritating to the people, and that there was no danger of public disturbance if they were taken away. Consequently early in last summer the troops were all withdrawn from the State, with the exception of a small garrison at New Orleans Barracks. It was claimed that a comparative state of quiet had supervened. Political excitement as to Louisiana affairs seemed to be dying out. But the November election was approaching, and it was necessary for party purposes that the flame should be rekindled.

Accordingly, on the 14th of September D. P. Penn, claiming that he was elected lieutenant-governor in 1872, issued an inflammatory proclamation calling upon the militia of the State to arm, assemble, and drive from power the usurpers, as he designated the officers of the State. The White Leagues, armed and ready for the conflict, promptly responded.

On the same day the governor made a formal requisition upon me, pursuant to the act of 1795 and section 4, Article IV, of the Constitution, to aid in suppressing domestic violence. On the next day I issued my proclamation commanding the insurgents to disperse within five days from the date thereof; but before the proclamation was published in New Orleans the organized and armed forces recognizing a usurping governor had taken forcible possession of the statehouse and temporarily subverted the government. Twenty or more people were killed, including a number of the police of the city. The streets of the city were stained with blood. All that was desired in the way of excitement had been accomplished, and, in view of the steps taken to repress it, the revolution is apparently, though it is believed not really, abandoned, and the cry of Federal usurpation and tyranny in Louisiana was renewed with redoubled energy. Troops had been sent to the State under this requisi-tion of the governor, and as other disturbances seemed imminent they were allowed to remain there to render the executive such aid as might become necessary to enforce the laws of the State and repress the continued violence which seemed inevitable the moment Federal support should be withdrawn....

I have deplored the necessity which seemed to make it my duty under the Constitution and laws to direct such interference. I have always refused except where it seemed to be my imperative duty to act in such a manner under the Constitution and laws of the United States. I have repeatedly and earnestly entreated the people of the South to live together in peace and obey the laws; and nothing would give me greater pleasure than to see reconcil-

Glossary

bloody riots of 1866 and 1868	two uprisings in New Orleans to protest the Reconstruction Acts
brought suit upon the equity side	reference to the fact that under common law, modeled on the English system, regular lawsuits had to conform to very specific guidelines, whereas suits in equity allowed more freedom
circuit court	federal courts of appeals, which received their name in frontier days, when judges would "ride the circuit," or move from town to town, administering judgment
Colfax	reference to the Colfax massacre (or Colfax riot) on April 13, 1873, in Colfax, Louisiana, when disputes over the results of the state gubernatorial elections resulted in an outbreak of violence that claimed more than one hundred lives
Coushatta	a Louisiana town that in August 1874 saw an outbreak of violence by the White Leagues, resulting in some two dozen deaths
domestic violence	here referring to local terrorism
election of 1872	a scandalous incident in which the Louisiana governor Henry Clay Warmoth attempted to use his power to force the election of his handpicked successor
elective franchise	the right to vote
fifteenth amendment ...under the second section	the first section of the Fifteenth Amendment, ratified in 1870 and guaranteeing the right to vote regardless of race, color, or "previous condition of servitude," and the second section, providing Congress with power to enforce the amendment
Judge Woods	William Burnham Woods, a former Union officer appointed by Grant as the first judge of the newly reorganized Fifth Circuit, which included several former Confederate states
Justice Strong	William Strong, who served on the Supreme Court from 1870 to 1880
Levi Nelson	one of two African American men whose civil rights were allegedly violated by William Cruikshank and the Colfax mob and who was thus identified in *United States v. Cruikshank*
McEnery	John McEnery, Kellogg's Democratic opponent for the Louisiana governorship in 1872

iation and tranquillity everywhere prevail, and thereby remove all necessity for the presence of troops among them. I regret, however, to say that this state of things does not exist, nor does its existence seem to be desired, in some localities; and as to those it may be proper for me to say that to the extent that Congress has conferred power upon me to prevent it

neither Ku Klux Klans, White Leagues, nor any other association using arms and violence to execute their unlawful purposes can be permitted in that way to govern any part of this country; nor can I see with indifference Union men or Republicans ostracized, persecuted, and murdered on account of their opinions, as they now are in some localities.

Glossary

militia	a military force composed of citizens rather than full-time professional soldiers
obtained possession of the returns	illegally gained control of the ballots
parish	the equivalent of counties under Louisiana law
praying	calling for a court to make a ruling at a later time
previous condition of servitude	the situation of having formerly been a slave
reconstruction acts	four laws passed by Congress in 1867 and 1868 to reorganize the governments of the former Confederate states
restraining order	a court order demanding that one party stop bringing harm to another
section 4, Article IV	the constitutional guarantee that the states must have a republican government, or government by freely elected officials
suffrage	the vote
their attempted protection by colored persons	"their" referring to the judge and sheriff, not the people attempting to drive them from office
thirteenth amendment	the Thirteenth Amendment, ratified in December 1865, officially abolishing slavery in the United States
United States v. Cruikshank	an 1875 case, which resulted from the Colfax massacre and in which the Supreme Court addressed the question of extending Bill of Rights protections to the states
Warmoth	Henry Clay Warmoth, governor of Louisiana who, though he was a Republican, opposed Grant and therefore supported the Democrat John McEnery in the 1872 election
White Leagues	paramilitary groups, composed of white males opposed to Reconstruction, that operated in Louisiana from 1874 to the restoration of Democratic power in that state
William P. Kellogg	William Pitt Kellogg, whose tenure as governor of Louisiana (1873–1877) marked the last time a Republican held that office prior to 1980

Letter to Daniel H. Chamberlain (1876)

July 26, 1876
Executive Mansion, Washington, D.C.
Governor Daniel Chamberlain

Dear Sir: I am in receipt of your letter of the 22d of July, and all the inclosures enumerated therein, giving an account of the late barbarous massacre at the town of Hamburg, S.C. The views which you express as to the duty you owe to your oath of office and to citizens to secure to all their civil rights, including the right to vote according to the dictates of their own consciences, and the further duty of the Executive of the nation to give all needful aid, when properly called on to do so, to enable you to ensure this inalienable right, I fully concur in. The scene at Hamburg, as cruel, blood-thirsty, wanton, unprovoked, and uncalled for, as it was, is only a repetition of the course which has been pursued in other Southern States within the last few years, notably in Mississippi and Louisiana. Mississippi is governed to-day by officials chosen through fraud and violence, such as would scarcely be accredited to savages, much less to a civilized and Christian people. How long these things are to continue, or what is to be the final remedy, the Great Ruler of the universe only knows; but I have an abiding faith that the remedy will come, and come speedily, and I earnestly hope that it will come peacefully. There has never been a desire on the part of the North to humiliate the South. Nothing is claimed for one State that is not fully accorded to all the others, unless it may be the right to kill negroes and Republicans without fear of punishment and without loss of caste or reputation. This has seemed to be a privilege claimed by a few States. I repeat again, that I fully agree with you as to the measure of your duties in the present emergency, and as to my duties. Go on—and let every Governor where the same dangers threaten the peace of his State go on—in the conscientious discharge of his duties to the humblest as well as the proudest citizen, and I will give every aid for which I can find law or constitutional power. A government that cannot give protection to life, property, and all guaranteed civil rights (in this country the greatest is an untrammeled ballot) to the citizen is, in so far, a failure, and every energy of the oppressed should be exerted, always within the law and by constitutional means, to regain lost privileges and protections. Too long denial of guaranteed rights is sure to lead to revolution—bloody revolution, where suffering must fall upon the innocent as well as the guilty.

Expressing the hope that the better judgment and co-operation of citizens of the State over which you have presided so ably may enable you to secure a fair trial and punishment of all offenders, without distinction of race or color or previous condition of servitude, and without aid from the Federal Government, but with the promise of such aid on the conditions named in the foregoing, I subscribe myself, very respectfully, your obedient servant,

U.S. Grant.

Glossary

barbarous massacre at … Hamburg, S.C.	an outbreak of violence in a town across the Savannah River from Augusta, Georgia, on July 4, 1876
caste	social class
Daniel Chamberlain	Republican governor of South Carolina from 1874 to 1877
I subscribe myself	I sign below
late	recent
an untrammeled ballot	the right to vote in free and fair elections

Alexander Hamilton (Library of Congress)

ALEXANDER HAMILTON   CA. 1755–1804

Founding Father and First Secretary of the Treasury

Featured Documents
- ◆ Federalist 84 (1788)
- ◆ "First Report on Public Credit" (1790)
- ◆ "Against an Alliance with France" (1794)
- ◆ Letter to Harrison Gray Otis on Westward Expansion (1799)

Overview

The circumstances of Alexander Hamilton's early life are largely unknown. He was born in the West Indies and gave the year of his birth as 1757, but modern inquiries have established 1755 as more likely. In 1772 he was sent to New York City, and sometime in 1773 or 1774 he enrolled at King's College (now Columbia University). He was a fervent Revolutionary, and when the American Revolution broke out, he enlisted in the militia. In 1777 he was promoted to lieutenant colonel and served as General George Washington's aide-de-camp, though he persuaded Washington to allow him to lead a regiment of troops in the Battle of Yorktown in 1781. His fortunes took another turn for the better when he married a prominent and wealthy New York socialite in 1780.

Hamilton's career in politics began in 1782, when he was elected to the Continental Congress. There, and as a New York delegate to the Constitutional Convention in 1787, he advocated a strong federal government. He was not fully satisfied with the Constitution that the convention produced, but he believed that it was superior to the earlier Articles of Confederation, and he urged its ratification. To that end, he, along with James Madison and John Jay, wrote a series of papers that were later collected in a book called *The Federalist*; in Federalist 84, which he wrote in 1788, Hamilton argues that including a bill of rights in the Constitution was unnecessary.

President George Washington appointed Hamilton as the nation's first secretary of the treasury, an office he held from September 11, 1789, to January 31, 1795. He gained a reputation as a brilliant administrator who placed the new nation on a sound financial footing. He founded the nation's first public mint and the first national bank. His "First Report on Public Credit" in 1790, an example of his fiscal views, was in large part responsible for the emergence of political parties in the 1790s. As a member of the cabinet, Hamilton urged neutrality in France's disputes with England, a position he argued in 1794 in "Against an Alliance with France."

After leaving office, Hamilton entered private law practice, but he remained involved in the young nation's affairs. From 1798 to 1800 he was the inspector general of the army, and in a letter he wrote in 1799 to Representative

Harrison Gray Otis, he urged the use of the military to expand the nation westward. He also played a significant role in the 1800 presidential election. Although he was philosophically opposed to the republican views of the eventual winner, Thomas Jefferson, he believed that Jefferson's chief rival, Aaron Burr, was a man lacking in principle, so he lent his support to Jefferson. Over the next four years Burr's bitterness grew until he challenged Hamilton to a duel. The duel took place on July 11, 1804, in Weehawken, New Jersey. Hamilton, it appeared, fired into the air, but Burr did not, and Hamilton died of his gunshot wound the next day.

Explanation and Analysis of Documents

The chief mark that Alexander Hamilton left on the U.S. government in its early years was to consolidate power at the federal level. In this respect, he represented a point of view that contrasted sharply with that of Thomas Jefferson, who wanted to see more power in the hands of the states and individuals. Hamilton distrusted the masses, and he believed that the United States could survive only through the support of monied interests—those who had the greatest stake in the new nation. In his voluminous writings, Hamilton consistently urged this point of view.

◆ Federalist 84

The Constitutional Convention took place in Philadelphia from May 25 to September 17, 1787. The purpose of the convention was to amend the Articles of Confederation, the document under which the United States had been operating since independence from Great Britain. The articles, however, were not working. A considerable amount of interstate conflict had arisen, and it was apparent to the nation's leaders that the Articles of Confederation granted too much power to the individual states and not enough to the federal government. Many of the delegates to the convention, among them Alexander Hamilton and James Madison, arrived in Philadelphia with the intention not just of amending the articles but of creating an entirely new constitution. The convention, though, was marked by bitter debate. Some members of the convention left before the closing ceremonies. Three others refused to

1755(?)
- Hamilton is born on the island of Nevis in the West Indies.

1777–1781
- Hamilton serves as aide-de-camp to General George Washington during the American Revolution.

1782
- Hamilton is elected to the Continental Congress.

1787
- Hamilton attends the Constitutional Convention.

1788
- **May 28**
  Hamilton publishes Federalist 84.

1789
- **September 11**
  Hamilton is named President George Washington's secretary of the treasury, a post he holds until January 31, 1795.

1790
- **January 14**
  Hamilton issues the "First Report on Public Credit" to Congress.

1794
- **February 8**
  Hamilton publishes "Against an Alliance with France."

1798
- Hamilton begins service as inspector general of the army during the Quasi War with France, a post he held until 1800.

1799
- **January 26**
  In a letter to Harrison Gray Otis, Hamilton outlines his views on the nation's westward expansion.

1804
- **July 11**
  Hamilton fights a duel with his political rival Aaron Burr.
- **July 12**
  Hamilton dies from his wounds in New York City.

sign the new document. As the remainder of the delegates returned to their states to urge ratification, they knew that no one was entirely happy with the document.

A key sticking point in some states was the Constitution's omission of a bill of rights—provisions that would explicitly protect the rights of free speech, religion, freedom of the press, trial by jury, the bearing of arms, protection against self-incrimination, illegal search and seizures, cruel and unusual punishment, and the like. Even during the convention, many delegates argued that the Constitution was incomplete without provisions that would ensure the individual liberties of citizens. In the months after the Constitution was submitted to the states for ratification, debate in some of the states was intense. Although some states quickly ratified the Constitution, it was by no means certain that the necessary nine out of thirteen states would do so. Virginia, New York, and Massachusetts, in particular, were the scenes of contentious debate. Virginia, over the objections of Patrick Henry and others, finally ratified the Constitution on June 25, 1788, becoming the ninth of the thirteen, but the state submitted with its ratification a series of recommended amendments that were in effect a bill of rights. New Hampshire and New York took similar steps, as did Massachusetts, which insisted that the first U.S. Congress immediately pass a bill of rights.

In the debate over ratification, numerous pamphlets and newspaper articles appeared taking one position or the other. Among them were eighty-five papers, most of which were published in the *Independent Journal* and the *New York Packet* from October 1787 to August 1788. They were then collected in book form as *The Federalist* in 1788. These papers, the work principally of Hamilton and Madison (and, to a lesser extent, John Jay), were written in response to other published articles opposing ratification of the Constitution in New York. Collectively, the Federalist Papers provide historians with crucial insights into the theories of government held by the nation's Founders.

To take up the issue of a bill of rights, Hamilton wrote number 84, published on May 28, 1788, and titled "Certain General and Miscellaneous Objections to the Constitution Considered and Answered." Hamilton opposed the inclusion of a bill of rights—or at least opposed making ratification of the Constitution contingent on its inclusion. In this excerpt, Hamilton bases his opposition to a bill of rights on three major arguments. The first is that various articles of the Constitution contain provisions that protect individual liberties. He cites, for example, Article 1, Section 9, Clause 2, which protects the writ of habeas corpus—the right of a suspected criminal to have charges specified. Similar provisions in the Constitution protect individuals against bills of attainder (legislative acts that declare a person or classes of persons criminals without giving them the benefit of a trial) and "ex-post-facto laws" (laws that retroactively criminalize an act). In sum, Hamilton argues, a bill of rights is not needed because the structure of the Constitution itself protects people against "tyranny."

In his second argument, Hamilton takes up the history of such bills of rights in England, including the Magna

Carta, the Petition of Rights, and the Declaration of Right. These documents, Hamilton maintains, were created to protect individuals against arbitrary actions on the part of a monarch. The United States, however, is not governed by a monarch. The Constitution provides for a representative form of government, where power resides in the hands of the people through their elected representatives. Accordingly, a bill of rights is not necessary for people to preserve their rights in opposition to a king.

Hamilton's third argument is that a bill of rights would be "dangerous," for it "would contain various exceptions to powers not granted; and, on this very account, would afford a…pretext to claim more than were granted." If, he argues, a bill of rights grants freedom of the press when the Constitution contains no provision for curtailing such a freedom, then the question could arise whether such a right enumerated in a bill of rights implies that the government *could* under certain circumstances curtail freedom of the press—that granting freedom of the press could provide a "plausible pretense" for curtailing it. The excerpt concludes with Hamilton's assertion that the Constitution as written *is* a bill of rights and that "it is absurd to allege" that such rights are "not to be found in the work of the convention."

The Constitution was ratified without the inclusion of a bill of rights, but on June 8, 1789, Madison submitted, as amendments to the Constitution, a bill of rights to the first Congress. In doing so, he hoped to avoid the need for another constitutional convention that might undo the work of the first. On December 15, 1791, when Virginia ratified ten of the twelve amendments Madison had submitted, they became part of the U.S. Constitution.

◆ **"First Report on Public Credit"**

When Hamilton became the nation's first secretary of the treasury under President George Washington, he faced a number of difficulties. One was that the nation was still in debt from the Revolutionary War. He calculated that debt as $54 million on the part of the federal government, with individual states owing a further $25 million. Another was that he had no precedent for his duties as secretary of the treasury. In large measure, Hamilton shaped the activities of future treasury secretaries and other cabinet officials: investigating issues, writing reports, submitting those reports to Congress for action, and then taking measures to carry out plans for dealing with the issue. He dealt with both of these difficulties in the "First Report on Public Credit," which he submitted to Congress on January 14, 1790.

Hamilton wrote his report in the context of growing friction between the Federalists, who dominated the Washington administration and favored a strong federal government, and such Antifederalists as Thomas Jefferson, who distrusted a strong central government and wanted more power reserved to the states. Hamilton, though, recognized that ongoing debt is damaging American credit in foreign markets. He thus makes two proposals in his report. The first is to pay off the debt through the sale of government bonds. These bonds would be a perpetual debt; the nation could pay off foreign creditors and then use future revenues to pay continuing interest on the domestic debt. By paying off foreign creditors, Hamilton argues, "trade is extended," "agriculture and manufactures are also promoted," and "interest of money will be lowered" (that is, the interest rate the government is paying on its debt can be lowered).

Hamilton, however, anticipated objections to this proposal. At the time, debt instruments functioned as a form of currency. Often, creditors were strapped for money, so they sold the debt certificates they held, frequently at steep discounts, to wealthy speculators. The question would inevitably arise: Should the federal government redeem these certificates for their original face value or for what the speculator paid for them, thus assuring the speculators a healthy profit at the expense of the original owner of the certificate? As Hamilton puts it, "It is alledged that it would be unreasonable to pay twenty shillings in the pound to one who had not given more for it than three or four." Hamilton argues that such a debt certificate should be redeemed at face value because, like any other security (or any other property, for that matter), a seller sells it "for as much as it *may be worth in the market*, and that the buyer may be *safe* in the purchase."

The other proposal, which many observers found startling, was for the federal government to assume the debts of the states. This proposal met with intense opposition, primarily in the South. In the years after the Revolution, most of the southern states had paid off a substantial portion of their debts (an exception being South Carolina). They concluded that Hamilton's plan was at bottom a way to provide relief to the northern industrial states, which had lagged behind in their debt payments, at the expense of the southern states, which had not. In the end, Hamilton's plan was approved by Congress, U.S. credit abroad improved markedly, and foreign investors put their money into the U.S. economy. The resultant expansion was aided by a controversial proposal Hamilton made in 1791: the creation of a national bank.

Hamilton's proposals for funding the public debt put the nation on a firmer economic footing. They were motivated in large part by his belief that influential and wealthy people would act in their own self-interest by supporting the new nation. Hamilton believed that the federal government could tie the economic fortunes of such people to the fortunes of the nation, thus winning their support and loyalty. His actions with regard to both funding the debt and the creation of a national bank deepened the divisions between the Federalists and the Antifederalists, giving rise to the emergence of political parties: the Federalists and the Democratic-Republicans. Further, Hamilton's policies were embraced by the more commercial and industrial North— and opposed by the agricultural South—sowing the seeds of the division that would culminate in the Civil War.

◆ **"Against an Alliance with France"**

In the years following the Revolutionary War, the fledgling United States charted a perilous course in its relationships with two of the world's most powerful nations, England and France. During the Revolution, the United

This cartoon, titled "Mad Tom in a Rage," depicting Thomas Jefferson attempting to pull down the pillar of federal government, is described as "Typical of the Federalist attacks on Jefferson" at a time when he and Hamilton headed opposing political camps. (AP/Wide World Photos)

States had signed the Treaty of Alliance, also called the Franco-American Alliance, with France. Under the terms of this agreement made in 1778, the two nations pledged to come to the aid of each other in the event of a British attack. The Revolutionaries owed a debt of gratitude to the French, who had come to the Americans' aid against the British with troops under the command of the marquis de Lafayette and the comte de Rochambeau.

Matters became complicated when the French Revolution erupted in 1789 and replaced the monarchy with a revolutionary republican government. One consequence of the revolution was that the United States extinguished its debts to France from the American Revolution, arguing that the debts were owed to the monarchy, not to the new French Republic. Further complicating relations with France were two actions by the U.S. government. One was the Proclamation of Neutrality issued by President George Washington on April 22, 1793. In this proclamation, the United States declared itself neutral in the war between Britain and

France that had broken out in the wake of the French Revolution. It led to the passage of the Neutrality Act of 1794, which cemented the nation's position of neutrality between the belligerents and was consistent with Washington's distrust of "entangling" foreign alliances. The second action was the Jay Treaty, ratified by Congress in 1796. Negotiated by John Jay, the chief justice of the United States, and formulated primarily by Hamilton, the treaty settled a number of issues still outstanding from the Revolutionary War and ushered in a period of peaceful trade relations with Britain. From Britain's standpoint, the treaty was advantageous as a means of preventing the United States from allying itself with France in its war against Britain.

But the Neutrality Act and the Jay Treaty came later, after the publication of Hamilton's article on February 7, 1794, in *Dunlap and Claypoole's American Daily Advertiser* in which Hamilton argues against an alliance with France. The essay was one of a series of essays Hamilton wrote defending Washington's Proclamation of Neutrality. Some members of Congress, along with some members of Washington's cabinet, including Secretary of State Thomas Jefferson, believed that the president had exceeded his constitutional authority by issuing the proclamation; they would have preferred that the American government remain silent on the issue. Taking what today would be termed a "strict constructionist" view of the Constitution, they argued that matters of peace and war, and foreign affairs in general, were the purview of Congress, not the president. Jefferson was so opposed to the president's action that he resigned as secretary of state. Jefferson persuaded Hamilton's erstwhile ally James Madison to write a series of articles attacking Washington, Hamilton, and the Federalists who supported the president's actions. Madison went on the offensive, attacking the Federalists as secret "monarchists" out to undermine the principles of republicanism that had led to the American and French revolutions. Hamilton's position on this issue, in conjunction with his position on the nation's economic affairs, contributed to sharp divisions in the government and the emergence of political parties.

Hamilton does not address the constitutional issues. Rather, in these excerpts he focuses first on the economic consequences of an alliance with France that would draw the United States into its war with Britain. He points out that such an alliance would be particularly damaging to trade and that since the United States derived some 90 percent of its revenues from "commercial duties," or tariffs, war and disruption to trade would bankrupt the country. Additionally, Hamilton addresses the question of the threat to the United States that could result from the defeat of France. He dismisses this threat, arguing that the United States was so far removed from Europe that any effort on the part of Britain (or Spain) to harass the United States on its borders or to destroy the nation's republican form of government would be folly.

It is an irony that only five years later the United States was at war not with Britain but with France. This conflict, variously called the Quasi War, the Pirate Wars, the Half-War, and the Undeclared War with France, took place from

1798 to 1800. The Jay Treaty had angered the French in light of the earlier Treaty of Alliance. In 1796 French ships began seizing American merchant ships engaged in trade with Britain. President John Adams announced that the United States had to assume a posture of defense if negotiations with France broke down. Then in 1798 Adams revealed to Congress the so-called XYZ Affair, a demand by French diplomats for an immense bribe in exchange for normalizing relations with France. In the summer of 1798, Congress authorized U.S. Navy vessels to attack French ships. The Quasi War ended in the fall of 1800 after the French adopted a more conciliatory stance and signed the Convention of 1800.

◆ Letter to Harrison Gray Otis on Westward Expansion

Harrison Gray Otis was elected to the U.S. House of Representatives from Massachusetts in 1797. He was a staunch Federalist, so his views on the centralization of the federal government were compatible with Hamilton's. Throughout the late 1790s the United States faced the threat of war with revolutionary France, a threat that erupted into naval battles during the Quasi War of 1798–1800. In preparation for possible war with France on land, the United States maintained a large standing army. Many of Hamilton's contemporaries, including President John Adams, wanted to demobilize the army; Adams feared that such an army, with nothing to do, would turn unruly and pose a threat to domestic peace. In this letter to Otis written in 1799, Hamilton makes a startling proposal: The United States should maintain its army and use it to conquer western lands currently owned by France and Spain.

Hamilton begins by noting that the threat from France had not fully abated and that he would support Congress in passing a law authorizing the president to use force if necessary against France. He argues that in so doing, the nation could prepare itself for war if negotiations failed and "disable her [France] to do the mischief which she may meditate." He goes on to point out the possibility that the French had plans to occupy the "nation" of Louisiana. ("Louisiana" does not refer only to the modern-day U.S. state but also to the vast swath of territory west of the Mississippi River almost to the Rocky Mountains.) Hamilton goes on to argue that the United States should take possession of those lands for two reasons. One is to "obviate the mischief of their falling into the hands of an active foreign power"; the other is "to secure to the United States the advantage of keeping the key to the Western country." He is also concerned about Spain's ownership at the time of Florida. Hamilton believes that an "adequate military force" would enable the president to wrest control of these lands, box in Spain's empire in Mexico and South America, and hasten the nation's westward expansion.

It would be Hamilton's ideological opponent, Thomas Jefferson, who would acquire Louisiana in 1803 from the French through the Louisiana Purchase—accomplished without force of arms. Nevertheless, Hamilton's letter is noteworthy as one of the earliest indications of the belief that the new nation should pursue what would come to be called its "Manifest Destiny" to spread civilization across the North American continent.

Impact and Legacy

Throughout the twentieth century and beyond, attitudes toward Alexander Hamilton have undergone marked shifts. During the years of the Great Depression and President Franklin D. Roosevelt's New Deal, Hamilton was dismissed as a dangerous figure, one who was aristocratic, elitist, and antidemocratic. The New Dealers of the 1930s embraced Hamilton's ideological opponent, Thomas Jefferson, for his simple, agrarian values. And yet their position was odd, for it was Hamilton, not Jefferson, who was a proponent of a strong, activist federal government—the same type of government Roosevelt advocated in response to the Great Depression.

Historians after the New Deal resurrected Hamilton's image. They noted that in a very real sense, the United States retained the shape that Hamilton imposed on the country during his years as treasury secretary. While Jefferson envisioned an agricultural nation of simple, virtuous yeoman farmers, Hamilton saw the future of the country as one of trade, commerce, manufacturing and industrialization, high finance, and central banking—and many modern historians note that it is Hamilton's vision that won out. Further, Hamilton's views regarding the priority of the federal government over the states was ratified by the U.S. Supreme Court under the leadership of Chief Justice John Marshall in the early years of the nineteenth century.

More recent historians, however, dispute the view that Hamilton should be revered as one of the nation's "forgotten Founders." They note that he was high-handed and that in his later years he became obsessed with military force. They argue that he was not always supportive of constitutional rights but regarded as "right" any course of action that would benefit the commercial and industrial interests of the country. As one of the leaders of federal troops dispatched to put down the Whiskey Rebellion (an antitax revolt) in western Pennsylvania in 1794, Hamilton enacted policies, according to some historians, that were brutal and monarchical. Despite these reservations, though, it cannot be disputed that Alexander Hamilton had a profound and abiding impact on the development of the United States.

Key Sources

The most accessible one-volume edition of Alexander Hamilton's writings is *Alexander Hamilton: Writings*, edited by Joanne B. Freeman (2001). An online collection of his writings is available from the Online Library of Liberty: *The Works of Alexander Hamilton*, edited by Henry Cabot Lodge and originally published in twelve volumes in 1904 (http://oll.libertyfund.org/index.php?option=com_static xt&staticfile=show.php%3Fperson=201&Itemid=28). The

---

"*I go further, and affirm that bills of rights, in the sense and to the extent in which they are contended for, are not only unnecessary in the proposed Constitution, but would even be dangerous. They would contain various exceptions to powers not granted; and, on this very account, would afford a colorable pretext to claim more than were granted.*"

(Federalist 84)

"*The truth is, after all the declamations we have heard, that the Constitution is itself, in every rational sense, and to every useful purpose, A BILL OF RIGHTS.*"

(Federalist 84)

"*The Secretary, after mature reflection on this point, entertains a full conviction that an assumption of the debts of the particular states by the Union, and a like provision for them as for those of the Union, will be a measure of sound policy and substantial justice.*"

("First Report on Public Credit")

"*If there can be any danger to us, it must arise from our voluntarily thrusting ourselves into the war.*"

("Against an Alliance with France")

"*Indeed, if it is the policy of France to leave us in a state of semi-hostility, 'tis preferable to terminate it, and by taking possession of those countries [Florida and Louisiana] for ourselves, to obviate the mischief of their falling into the hands of an active foreign power, and at the same time to secure to the United States the advantage of keeping the key to the Western country.*"

(Letter to Harrison Gray Otis on Westward Expansion)

"*The reveries of some of the friends of the government are more injurious to it than the attacks of its declared enemies.*"

(Letter to Harrison Gray Otis on Westward Expansion)

essential collection of Hamilton's writings is the twenty-seven volumes of *The Papers of Alexander Hamilton* published under the general editorship of Harold C. Syrett (1961–1987).

Further Reading

■ Articles

Fatovic, Clement. "Constitutionalism and Presidential Prerogative: Jeffersonian and Hamiltonian Perspectives." *American Journal of Political Science* 48, no. 3 (2004): 429–444.

Martin, Robert W. T. "Reforming Republicanism: Alexander Hamilton's Theory of Republican Citizenship and Press Liberty." *Journal of the Early Republic* 25, no. 1 (2005): 21–46.

Sheehan, Colleen. "Madison v. Hamilton: The Battle over Republicanism and the Role of Public Opinion." *American Political Science Review* 98, no. 3 (2004): 405–424.

■ Books

Ambrose, Douglas, and Robert W. T. Martin. *The Many Faces of Alexander Hamilton: The Life and Legacy of America's Most Elusive Founding Father.* New York: New York University Press, 2006.

Brookhiser, Richard. *Alexander Hamilton, American.* New York: Free Press, 1999.

Chernow, Ron. *Alexander Hamilton.* New York: Penguin, 2004.

Ellis, Joseph J. *Founding Brothers: The Revolutionary Generation.* New York: Alfred A. Knopf, 2000.

Fleming, Thomas. *Duel: Alexander Hamilton, Aaron Burr, and the Future of America.* New York: Basic Books, 2002.

Flexner, James Thomas. *The Young Hamilton: A Biography.* New York: Fordham University Press, 1997.

McDonald, Forrest. *Alexander Hamilton: A Biography.* New York: W. W. Norton, 1982.

Miller, John Chester. *Alexander Hamilton: Portrait in Paradox.* Old Saybrook, Conn.: Konecky and Konecky, 1959.

Mitchell, Broadus. *Alexander Hamilton.* 2 vols. New York: Macmillan, 1957–1962.

Randall, Willard Sterne. *Alexander Hamilton: A Life.* New York: HarperCollins, 2003.

■ Web Sites

Hogeland, William. "Inventing Alexander Hamilton." *Boston Review* (November/December 2007). http://bostonreview.net/BR32.6/hogeland.php.

—Michael J. O'Neal

Questions for Further Study

1. In the debate between Hamilton and Jefferson, representing as they do two conflicting visions of the American government, whose side would you take? Would you support Jeffersonian democracy, with its emphasis on agriculture, rural regions, egalitarianism, and states' rights, or Hamiltonian federalism, which concentrated on industry, cities, elitism, and centralized federal government? Defend your position with reference to Hamilton's writings.

2. Examine Hamilton's arguments against the Bill of Rights, particularly his claim that such a document might actually threaten liberties. How valid is his case, and what are the most and least successful points he presents for it?

3. What are Hamilton's arguments for taking control of the Louisiana territory? Why did his vision not win out, and how did Jefferson succeed where Hamilton did not?

4. Compare and contrast Hamilton and Aaron Burr, the man whose pistol brought an end to his life. How were the two alike and how were they different? In what ways did these similarities and differences lead to their eventual conflict?

5. Discuss the changing views of Hamilton, with an emphasis on reinterpretations that occurred during the 1930s and later. What has been his standing with historians? Do you agree with the judgments on him? Why or why not?

FEDERALIST 84 (1788)

The most considerable of the remaining objections is that the plan of the convention contains no bill of rights. Among other answers given to this, it has been upon different occasions remarked that the constitutions of several of the States are in a similar predicament. I add that New York is of the number. And yet the opposers of the new system, in this state, who profess an unlimited admiration for its Constitution, are among the most intemperate partisans of a bill of rights. To justify their zeal in this matter, they allege two things: one is that, though the constitution of New York has no bill of rights prefixed to it, yet it contains in the body of it various provisions in favor of particular privileges and rights, which, in substance, amount to the same thing; the other is that the Constitution adopts, in their full extent, the common and statute law of Great Britain, by which many other rights, not expressed in it, are equally secured.

To the first I answer, that the Constitution proposed by the convention contains, as well as the constitution of this State, a number of such provisions.

Independent of those which relate to the structure of the government, we find the following: Article 1, section 3, clause 7—"Judgment in cases of impeachment shall not extend further than to removal from office, and disqualification to hold and enjoy any office of honor, trust, or profit under the United States; but the party convicted shall, nevertheless, be liable and subject to indictment, trial, judgment, and punishment according to law." Section 9, of the same article, clause 2—"The privilege of the writ of habeas corpus shall not be suspended, unless when in cases of rebellion or invasion the public safety may require it." Clause 3—"No bill of attainder or ex-post-facto law shall be passed." Clause 7—"No title of nobility shall be granted by the United States; and no person holding any office of profit or trust under them, shall, without the consent of the Congress, accept of any present, emolument, office, or title of any kind whatever, from any king, prince, or foreign state." Article 3, section 2, clause 3—"The trial of all crimes, except in cases of impeachment, shall be by jury; and such trial shall be held in the State where the said crimes shall have been committed; but when not committed within any state, the trial shall be at such place or places as the Congress may by law have directed." Section 3, of the same article—"Treason against the United States shall consist only in levying war against them, or in adhering to their enemies, giving them aid and comfort. No person shall be convicted of treason, unless on the testimony of two witnesses to the same overt act, or on confession in open court." And clause 3 of the same section—"The Congress shall have power to declare the punishment of treason; but no attainder of treason shall work corruption of blood, or forfeiture, except during the life of the person attainted."

It may well be a question, whether these are not, upon the whole, of equal importance with any which are to be found in the constitution of this state. The establishment of the writ of habeas corpus, the prohibition of ex post facto laws, and of TITLES OF NOBILTY, *to which we have no corresponding provision in our Constitution*, are perhaps greater securities to liberty and republicanism than any it contains. The creation of crimes after the commission of the fact, or, in other words, the subjecting of men to punishment for things which, when they were done, were breaches of no law, and the practice of arbitrary imprisonments have been, in all ages, the favorite and most formidable instruments of tyranny....

It has been several times truly remarked that bills of rights are, in their origin, stipulations between kings and their subjects, abridgments of prerogative in favor of privilege, reservations of rights not surrendered to the prince. Such was Magna Carta, obtained by the barons, sword in hand, from King John. Such were the subsequent confirmations of that charter by succeeding princes. Such was the Petition Of Right assented to by Charles I in the beginning of his reign. Such, also, was the Declaration of Right presented by the Lords and Commons to the Prince of Orange in 1688, and afterwards thrown into the form of an act of Parliament called the Bill of Rights. It is evident, therefore, that, according to their primitive signification, they have no application to constitutions professedly founded upon the power of the people, and executed by their immediate representatives and servants. Here, in strictness, the people surrender nothing; and as they retain every thing they have no need of particular reservations.

"We, the people of the United States, to secure the blessings of liberty to ourselves and our posterity, do *ordain and establish* this Constitution for the

United States of America." Here is a better recognition of popular rights, than volumes of those aphorisms which make the principal figure in several of our state bills of rights, and which would sound much better in a treatise of ethics than in a constitution of government....

I go further, and affirm that bills of rights, in the sense and to the extent in which they are contended for, are not only unnecessary in the proposed Constitution but would even be dangerous. They would contain various exceptions to powers not granted; and, on this very account, would afford a colorable pretext to claim more than were granted. For why declare that things shall not be done which there is no power to do? Why, for instance, should it be said that the liberty of the press shall not be restrained when no power is given by which restrictions may be imposed? I will not contend that such a provision would confer a regulating power; but it is evident that it would furnish to men disposed to usurp a plausible pretense for claiming that power. They might urge with a semblance of reason that the Constitution ought not to be charged with the absurdity of providing against the abuse of an authority which was not given, and that the provision against restraining the liberty of the press afforded a clear implication that a power to prescribe proper regulations concerning it was intended to be vested in the national government. This may serve as a specimen of the numerous handles which would be given to the doctrine of constructive powers by the indulgence of an injudicious zeal for bills of rights....

Glossary

abridgements of prerogative in favor of privilege	limitations on the power of rulers
adverting	calling attention to
bill of attainder	a legislative act declaring a party or parties guilty of a crime without trial
colorable	deceptive
common and statute law	laws that result from previous judicial rulings and laws passed by a legislative body
constructive powers	the ability to interpret laws broadly
corruption of blood	a penalty under English law, whereby relatives of an individual convicted of treason could not inherit property from that person
Declaration of Right	the English Bill of Rights, declared by Parliament in 1689
ex-post-facto law	a law that attempts to punish for offenses committed prior to the time that law was adopted
intemperate partisans	impassioned supporters of a particular position
Lords and Commons	the two houses of the English Parliament
Magna Carta	the "Great Charter," signed by King John of England in 1215, which granted specific rights to citizens and required the king to obey the law
Petition Of Right	a demand for civil liberties issued by the British Parliament to King Charles I in 1628
Prince of Orange	William of Orange, a Dutch nobleman who replaced James II as English monarch (and took the title William III) in the Glorious Revolution of 1688
republicanism	government by elected officials, rather than monarchs or dictators
writ of habeas corpus	a guarantee that individuals cannot be imprisoned without being formally charged in a court of law

There remains but one other view of this matter to conclude the point. The truth is, after all the declamations we have heard, that the Constitution is itself, in every rational sense and to every useful purpose, A BILL OF RIGHTS. The several bills of rights in Great Britain form its constitution, and, conversely, the constitution of each state is its bill of rights. And the proposed Constitution, if adopted, will be the bill of rights of the Union. Is it one object of a bill of rights to declare and specify the political privileges of the citizens in the structure and administration of the government? This is done in the most ample and precise manner in the plan of the convention; comprehending various precautions for the public security which are not to be found in any of the state constitutions. Is another object of a bill of rights to define certain immunities and modes of proceeding which are relative to personal and private concerns? This we have seen has also been attended to, in a variety of cases, in the same plan.

Adverting, therefore, to the substantial meaning of a bill of rights, it is absurd to allege that it is not to be found in the work of the Convention.

"First Report on Public Credit" (1790)

While the observance of that good faith, which is the basis of public credit, is recommended by the strongest inducements of political expediency, it is enforced by considerations of still greater authority. There are arguments for it which rest on the immutable principles of moral obligation. And in proportion as the mind is disposed to contemplate, in the order of Providence, an intimate connection between public virtue and public happiness will be its repugnancy to a violation of those principles.

This reflection derives additional strength from the nature of the debt of the United States. It was the price of liberty. The faith of America has been repeatedly pledged for it, and with solemnities that give peculiar force to the obligation. There is indeed reason to regret that it has not hitherto been kept; that the necessities of the war, conspiring with inexperience in the subjects of finance, produced direct infractions; and that the subsequent period has been a continued scene of negative violation, or non-compliance. But a diminution of this regret arises from the reflection that the last seven years have exhibited an earnest and uniform effort on the part of the government of the Union to retrieve the national credit by doing justice to the creditors of the nation; and that the embarrassments of a defective constitution, which defeated this laudable effort, have ceased....

It cannot but merit particular attention that, among ourselves, the most enlightened friends of good government, are those whose expectations are the highest.

To justify and preserve their confidence; to promote the increasing respectability of the American name; to answer the calls of justice; to restore landed property to its due value; to furnish new resources both to agriculture and commerce; to cement more closely the union of the states; to add to their security against foreign attack; to establish public order on the basis of an upright and liberal policy—these are the great and invaluable ends to be secured by a proper and adequate provision, at the present period, for the support of public credit.

To this provision we are invited, not only by the general considerations which have been noticed but by others of a more particular nature. It will procure to every class of the community some important advantages, and remove some no less important disadvantages. The advantage to the public creditors from the increased value of that part of their property which constitutes the public debt needs no explanation.

But there is a consequence of this, less obvious, though not less true, in which every other citizen is interested. It is a well known fact that in countries in which the national debt is properly funded, and an object of established confidence, it answers most of the purposes of money. Transfers of stock or public debt are there equivalent to payments in specie; or in other words, stock, in the principal transactions of business, passes current as specie. The same thing would, in all probability, happen here, under the like circumstances.

The benefits of this are various and obvious:

First, trade is extended by it, because there is a larger capital to carry it on, and the merchant can, at the same time, afford to trade for smaller profits; as his stock, which, when unemployed, brings him in an interest from the government, serves him also as money, when he has a call for it in his commercial operations.

Second, agriculture and manufactures are also promoted by it, for the like reason that more capital can be commanded to be employed in both, and because the merchant, whose enterprise in foreign trade gives to them activity and extension, has greater means for enterprise.

Third, the interest of money will be lowered by it, for this is always in a ratio to the quantity of money and to the quickness of circulation. This circumstance will enable both the public and individuals to borrow on easier and cheaper terms.

And from the combination of these effects, additional aids will be furnished to labor, to industry, and to arts of every kind. But these good effects of a public debt are only to be looked for when, by being well funded, it has acquired an adequate and stable value; till then, it has rather a contrary tendency. The fluctuation and insecurity incident to it in an unfunded state render it a mere commodity and a precarious one. As such, being only an object of occasional and particular speculation, all the money applied to it is so much diverted from the more useful channels of circulation, for which the thing itself affords no substitute, so that, in fact, one serious inconvenience of an unfunded debt is that it contributes to the scarcity of money....

Having now taken a concise view of the inducements to a proper provision for the public debt, the next enquiry which presents itself is: What ought to be the nature of such a provision? This requires some preliminary discussions.

It is agreed on all hands that that part of the debt which has been contracted abroad and is denominated the foreign debt ought to be provided for according to the precise terms of the contracts relating to it. The discussions which can arise, therefore, will have reference essentially to the domestic part of it, or to that which has been contracted at home. It is to be regretted that there is not the same unanimity of sentiment on this part as on the other.

The Secretary has too much deference for the opinions of every part of the community not to have observed one, which has more than once made its appearance in the public prints, and which is occasionally to be met with in conversation. It involves this question: Whether a discrimination ought not to be made between original holders of the public securities and present possessors by purchase. Those who advocate a discrimination are for making a full provision for the securities of the former at their nominal value but contend that the latter ought to receive no more than the cost to them and the interest. And the idea is sometimes suggested of making good the difference to the primitive possessor.

In favor of this scheme, it is alleged that it would be unreasonable to pay 20*s*. in the pound to one who had not given more for it than 3 or 4. And it is added that it would be hard to aggravate the misfortune of the first owner, who, probably through necessity, parted with his property at so great a loss, by obliging him to contribute to the profit of the person who had speculated on his distresses.

The Secretary, after the most mature reflection on the force of this argument, is induced to reject the doctrine it contains as equally unjust and impolitic; as highly injurious even to the original holders of public securities; as ruinous to public credit. It is inconsistent with justice, because, in the first place, it is a breach of contract; a violation of the rights of a fair purchaser. The nature of the contract in its origin is that the public will pay the sum expressed in the security to the first holder or his assignee. The intent in making the security assignable is that the proprietor may be able to make use of his property by selling it for as much as it may be worth in the market and that the buyer may be safe in the purchase.

capital	material wealth intended to be used for the production of more wealth
in the order of Providence	in the grand scheme of things
interest of money… always in a ratio to the quantity… and quickness	reference to the fact that the more money there is available and the more freely it is released by lending institutions, the lower will be the rate of interest on it
the last seven years	since the end of the Revolutionary War
negative violation, or non-compliance	failure to abide by a law through negligence or inaction, as opposed to actively undertaking to commit a crime
primitive	original
public credit	the confidence of the public in the basic financial soundness of its government
s.	abbreviation for shillings, a unit of English currency
security	a claim of partial ownership in a financial entity through stocks, bonds, or other instruments
specie	currency in the form of coins
stock	term used in a general sense to mean "units of value"
unfunded debt	short-term debt, or debt that is to be paid within a year

Every buyer, therefore, stands exactly in the place of the seller, has the same right with him to the identical sum expressed in the security, and, having acquired that right by fair purchase and in conformity to the original agreement and intention of the government, his claim cannot be disputed, without manifest injustice.

That he is to be considered as a fair purchaser results from this: whatever necessity the seller may have been under was occasioned by the government in not making a proper provision for its debts. The buyer had no agency in it and therefore ought not to suffer. He is not even chargeable with having taken an undue advantage. He paid what the commodity was worth in the market and took the risks of reimbursement upon himself. He of course gave a fair equivalent and ought to reap the benefit of his hazard; a hazard which was far from inconsiderable, and which, perhaps, turned on little less than a revolution in government....

The Secretary, concluding that a discrimination between the different classes of creditors of the United States cannot, with propriety, be made, proceeds to examine whether a difference ought to be permitted to remain between them and another description of public creditors: those of the states individually.

The Secretary, after mature reflection on this point, entertains a full conviction that an assumption of the debts of the particular states by the Union, and a like provision for them as for those of the Union, will be a measure of sound policy and substantial justice.

It would, in the opinion of the Secretary, contribute, in an eminent degree, to an orderly, stable, and satisfactory arrangement of the national finances.

"Against an Alliance with France" (1794)

All who are not willfully blind must see and acknowledge that this country at present enjoys an unexampled state of prosperity. That war would interrupt it need not be affirmed. We should then, by war, lose the advantage of that astonishing progress in which strength, wealth, and improvement which we are now making, and which, if continued for a few years, will place our national rights and interests upon immovable foundations. This loss alone would be of infinite moment; it is such a one as no prudent or good man would encounter but for some clear necessity or some positive duty. If, while Europe is exhausting herself in a destructive war, this country can maintain its peace, the issue will open to us a wide field of advantages, which even imagination can with difficulty compass.

But a check to the progress of our prosperity is not the greatest evil to be anticipated. Considering the naval superiority of the enemies of France, we cannot doubt that our commerce would in a very great degree be annihilated by a war. Our agriculture would of course with our commerce, receive a deep wound. The exportations which now continue to animate it could not fail to be essentially diminished. Our mechanics would experience their full share of the common calamity. That lively and profitable industry, which now spreads a smile over all of our cities and towns, would feel an instantaneous and rapid decay.

Nine-tenths of our present revenues are derived from commercial duties. Their declension must of course keep pace with that of the trade. A substitute cannot be found in other sources of taxation without imposing heavy burdens on the people. To support public credit and carry on the war would suppose exactions really grievous. To abandon public credit would be to renounce an important means of carrying on the war, besides the sacrifice of the public creditors and the disgrace of a national bankruptcy....

But we are told that our own liberty is at stake upon the event of the war against France—that if she falls, we shall be the next victim. The combined powers, it is said, will never forgive in us the origination of those principles which were the germs of the French Revolution. They will endeavor to eradicate them from the world. If this suggestion were ever so well-founded, it would perhaps be a sufficient answer to it to say that our interference is not likely to alter the case; that it would only serve prematurely to exhaust our strength....

To subvert, by force, republican liberty in this country, nothing short of entire conquest would suffice. This conquest, with our present increased population, greatly distant as we are from Europe, would either be impracticable, or would demand such exertions as, following immediately upon those which will have been requisite to the subversion of the

Glossary

commercial duties	taxes on imports
declension	decrease
glosses	false interpretations of facts or events
prosecute enterprises	undertake ventures or activities
public credit	the confidence of the public in the basic financial soundness of its government
republican	referring to government by elected officials, as opposed to monarchs or dictators
unexampled	unprecedented
would suppose exactions really grievous	would bring about extreme hardship

French Revolution, would be absolutely ruinous to the undertakers. It is against all probability that an undertaking, pernicious as this would be, even in the event of success, would be attempted against an unoffending nation, by its geographical position little connected with the political concerns of Europe....

If there can be any danger to us, it must arise from our voluntarily thrusting ourselves into the war. Once embarked, nations sometimes prosecute enterprises of which they would not otherwise have dreamed. The most violent resentment, as before intimated, would no doubt in such a case, be kindled against us for what would be called a wanton and presumptuous intermeddling on our part; what this might produce, it is not easy to calculate....

Let us content ourselves with lamenting the errors into which a great, a gallant, an amiable, a respectable nation has been betrayed, with uniting our wishes and our prayers that the Supreme Ruler of the world will bring them back from those errors to a more sober and more just way of thinking and acting; and will overrule the complicated calamities which surround them, to the establishment of a government under which they may be free, secure, and happy. But let us not corrupt ourselves by false comparisons or glosses, nor shut our eyes to the true nature of transactions which ought to grieve and warn us, nor rashly mingle our destiny in the consequences of the errors and extravagances of another nation.

LETTER TO HARRISON GRAY OTIS ON WESTWARD EXPANSION (1799)

TO HARRISON GRAY OTIS
NEW YORK, Jan. 26, 1799.
DEAR SIR:

You will recollect that I reserved for a future answer part of a letter which I had the pleasure of receiving from you some time since. These are my ideas on that subject.

I should be glad to see, before the close of the session, a law empowering the President, at his discretion, in case a negotiation between the United States and France should not be on foot by the 1st of August next, or being on foot should terminate without an adjustment of differences, to declare that a state of war exists between the two countries; and thereupon to employ the land and naval forces of the United States in such manner as shall appear to him most effectual for annoying the enemy, and for preventing and frustrating hostile designs of France, either directly or *indirectly through any of her allies.*

This course of proceeding, by postponing the event and giving time for the intervention of negotiation, would be a further proof of moderation in the government, and would tend to reconcile our citizens to the last extremity, if it shall ensue, gradually accustoming their minds to look forward to it.

If France be really desirous of accommodation, this plan will accelerate her measures to bring it about. If she have not that desire, it is best to antic-ipate her final vengeance, and to throw whatever weight we have into the scale opposed to her. This conduct may contribute to disable her to do the mischief which she may meditate.

As it is every moment possible that the project of taking possession of the Floridas and Louisiana, long since attributed to France, may be attempted to be put in execution, it is very important that the executive should be clothed with power to meet and defeat so dangerous an enterprise. Indeed, if it is the policy of France to leave us in a state of semihostility, it is preferable to terminate it, and, by taking possession of those countries for ourselves, to obviate the mischief of their falling into the hands of an active foreign power, and at the same time to secure to the United States the advantage of keeping the key to the western country. I have been long in the habit of considering the acquisition of those countries as essential to the permanency of the Union, which I consider as very important to the welfare of the whole.

If universal empire is still to be the pursuit of France, what can tend to defeat the purpose better than to detach South America from Spain, which is only the channel through which the riches of Mexico and Peru are conveyed to France? The executive ought to be put in a situation to embrace favorable conjunctures for effecting that separation. It is to be regretted that the preparation of an adequate mili-

Glossary

the Floridas and Louisiana	present-day Florida, at that time divided into the provinces of East and West Florida, and the entire territory later included in the Louisiana Purchase
on foot	in progress
reconcile … to the last extremity	prepare for the worst-case scenario
reveries	excessive or unfounded enthusiasm
Spain, which is only the channel through which … conveyed to France	reference to the fact that though it retained some of its colonies in the New World, Spain at that time was under the virtual control of France
universal empire	world conquest

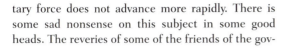
tary force does not advance more rapidly. There is some sad nonsense on this subject in some good heads. The reveries of some of the friends of the government are more injurious to it than the attacks of its declared enemies.

When will men learn to profit by experience?°

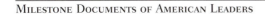

John Hancock (Library of Congress)

JOHN HANCOCK   1737–1793

Founding Father and First Governor of Massachusetts

Featured Documents
- ◆ **Boston Massacre Oration (1774)**
- ◆ **Address to the Ratification Convention of the Commonwealth of Massachusetts (1788)**
- ◆ **Address to the General Court of Boston (1788)**

Overview

Born on January 12, 1737, in Braintree (now Quincy), Massachusetts, John Hancock found his life altered by the death of his father in 1744. The following year young Hancock moved in with his affluent uncle, Thomas, who lived in Boston. This decision set Hancock's life on a course of wealth and privilege that afforded him the opportunity to be a generous public servant. His wealth and popularity in Boston made him a central figure in the American Revolutionary cause.

Educated at the Boston Latin School and Harvard College, Hancock began to work for his uncle in the mid-1750s. He spent the year 1760–1761 in England establishing business networks that no doubt helped when he took over his uncle's business a few years later. The same year that Hancock was put in charge of the House of Hancock, the events that eventually led to the separation of the colonies from Great Britain got under way with the Sugar Act of 1764. The subsequent Stamp Act (1765), Declaratory Act (1766), Townshend Revenue Act (1767), Boston Massacre (1770), Tea Act (1773), and finally the Intolerable (or Coercive) Acts (1774) brought tensions between the colonies and Great Britain to a head. Between 1764 and 1775 Boston became the epicenter of Revolutionary events in the power struggle between the colonies and Parliament. Hancock was at the center of that struggle as a private businessman who provided his funds when necessary and as a leader in an official capacity at both the local and state levels. When the Massachusetts General Court defiantly transformed itself into the Provincial Congress (1774), that Revolutionary body chose John Hancock as its president.

Hancock's name seemed always to be part of the Revolutionary controversy, whether it was when the British seized his ship *Liberty* in the late 1760s, when he delivered a fiery oration in 1774 commemorating the Boston Massacre of 1770 in the wake of the Boston Tea Party, when he became a target of British troops on that fateful April day in 1775 when the battles of Lexington and Concord became etched permanently in history, or when he sat as president of the Second Continental Congress and in that capacity was the first person to sign the Declaration of Independence. In fact, the British monarch perceived Hancock's role to be so central that King George III named him as one of only a few that the king would not pardon when or if the colonists came to their senses.

In 1780 Massachusetts approved its state constitution, and Hancock was elected the first governor of the Commonwealth. Hancock resigned the governorship in 1785 but was reelected to that position two years later and remained in it until his death. As governor he also served as the presiding officer at the state's ratifying convention. Hancock proved to be instrumental in persuading a divided convention to support the new federal Constitution, after suggesting a number of amendments. After years of poor health, Hancock died on October 8, 1793. For more than twenty years Hancock had been a committed public servant at the local, state, and national levels. He earned his credentials in the crucible of revolution, and he maintained them through war and government formation. When he died, Boston buried him like a hero.

Explanation and Analysis of Documents

In the three speeches presented here one gains a sense of Hancock's worldview as well as his contribution to both the American Revolution and the American Republic. Hancock's fiery speech in 1774, marking the anniversary of the Boston Massacre, reflects the mood of a people changing from protesters to Revolutionaries. His addresses to the ratification convention of the Commonwealth of Massachusetts and to the General Court came fourteen years later while he was serving as governor of Massachusetts. In these speeches he underscored his support for the proposed constitution that would ultimately replace the Articles of Confederation. Drawing on his leadership skills and his standing in the commonwealth, Hancock persuaded enough delegates to vote for a constitution with which they still had concerns. Once Massachusetts ratified, other states followed.

◆ Boston Massacre Oration

Before two of the Intolerable Acts of 1774 closed the port of Boston and changed the government of Massachusetts, the Boston Tea Party on December 16, 1773, had been one of the most dramatic moments yet in a period filled with drama. Just under three months after the Boston Tea Party, John Hancock, one of the richest men in North America, was scheduled to speak at the annual commemoration of the Boston Massacre. Bostonians had been marking the anniversary with a speech by a leading member of

Time Line

1737
- **January 12**
  John Hancock is born in Braintree, Massachusetts.

1754
- Hancock graduates from Harvard College and begins to work for his uncle Thomas.

1765
- Hancock is elected to serve as a selectman of Boston, a post he keeps until 1774.

1766
- Hancock becomes a member of the Massachusetts General Court.

1774
- **March 5**
  Hancock gives the annual Boston Massacre Day oration.
- **October 7**
  The Massachusetts General Court becomes the Provincial Congress, with Hancock as president.
- **December**
  Hancock is elected as delegate to the Second Continental Congress in Philadelphia.

1775
- **May**
  Hancock is elected president of the Second Continental Congress.

1776
- **July 4**
  Hancock becomes the first person to sign the Declaration of Independence.
- Hancock is appointed major general of the Massachusetts militia.

1777
- Hancock leaves the Continental Congress and returns to Massachusetts.

the community since that fateful day of March 5, 1770, when British regulars opened fire on those gathered around them, leaving five dead (including Crispus Attucks, the first African American casualty of the American Revolution). In March 1774, with people still aroused from the Boston Tea Party and waiting the inevitable response from Great Britain, Hancock gave the most important speech of his life up to that time. The speech was to take place at Faneuil Hall, but the immense crowd forced a move to the Old South Meeting House. There Hancock delivered a riveting speech that was universally recognized as a success.

It was a successful speech, but it was not unique as far as American Revolutionary rhetoric goes. Like others in Massachusetts and throughout the rebellious colonies, Hancock had to deal with the issue of separating himself from a long-standing and proud association with Great Britain. Historians have pointed out that speeches and sermons of the period were characterized by this need to disassociate the colonies from England and being American from being English. This was problematic, since there had been great pride in being English, in contributing to the empire, and in perpetuating English political traditions.

The first step in disconnecting was to question whether the government of Great Britain was doing its part. What was the purpose of government? Was the British government fulfilling that purpose? In answer to the question about the purpose of government, Hancock explains to his audience that "security to the persons and properties of the governed is so obviously the design and end of civil government, that to attempt a logical proof of it would be like burning tapers at noonday, to assist the sun in enlightening the world."

Hancock argues that to support a government that does not abide by first principles is unacceptable. He maintains that he is a friend of government that protects person and properties, but he is an enemy of tyranny. So, he finally asks the assembled crowd, "Is the present system, which the British administration have adopted for the government of the Colonies, a righteous government—or is it tyranny?" He points to the Declaratory Act of 1766, which asserted parliamentary authority over the colonies, and charges the king (who, Hancock argues, was given bad advice by his ministers) with failing to fulfill his protective duties while branding as traitors those colonials who aided the British in destroying American liberty. (By the time of the Declaration of Independence the king would be held fully responsible for the violations of rights, not just the Parliament or the king's ministers.)

Hancock and his fellow Bostonians, who had been at the center of political tensions and Revolutionary activity since the mid-1760s, believed that the British government had become tyrannical. A point of reference for Hancock and his audience alike was the presence and behavior of a standing army in their midst. Their shared experience created a bond and a common language. Hancock's discussion of the effect of the British troops stationed among them in Boston contrasted the crude and un-Christian behavior of the troops with the peaceful and virtuous way of life of Bostonians.

From the moment the troops arrived, their presence was menacing—from threatening governmental institutions and buildings with cannon to the raucous noise that rang through the normally quiet nighttime streets of Boston, from the interruption of worship services to the foul language that was subsequently picked up by the youth of the town. Hancock pays particular attention to the negative effect that the troops' presence was having on Boston's youth. Males, Hancock observed, were acquiring bad habits from the soldiers as well as becoming less industrious—a hallmark of societal decline for many eighteenth-century Americans—while females were vulnerable to seduction and becoming victims of rape. Hancock laments that the innocence of youth has made them "prey to wretches" who were enemies to both God and country. Clearly these evil instances have taken place—why else, Hancock asks, is "an honest father clothed with shame; or why a virtuous mother drowned in tears?"

Hancock continues by comparing the standing army with the New England militia. His critique draws on his classical republican worldview, in which duty to community is more virtuous than personal enrichment for one's own sake. Between 1720 and 1723, John Trenchard and Thomas Gordon had written a series of articles called *Cato's Letters*—subtitled "Essays on Liberty, Civil and Religious, and Other Important Subjects"—that had had a tremendous influence on the way Americans viewed their relationship to government. One important feature of those letters was a stern warning regarding standing armies in peacetime. Standing armies in times of peace could mean only one thing—tyranny. Knowing that his audience was just as cognizant as he of the dangers of a such a permanent army of paid soldiers, Hancock continues to distinguish the differences between the Americans and the British by contrasting the motives of a standing army with those of a militia.

The soldiers of a standing army, Hancock contends, are uncivilized and are driven by a quest to gratify neither God nor country but only themselves. They work for the highest bidder—no matter the king or the religious symbol depicted on a standard. Unlike other fighting forces in history, the American militias, he claims, are motivated by a love of country, of community, of family, and of God. To an approving audience, Hancock cries that the militia "fight for their houses, their lands, for their wives, their children; for all who claim the tenderest names, and are held dearest in their hearts; they fight pro aris et focis, for their liberty, and for themselves, and for their God." In short, the militia is a strong, virtuous, and effective fighting force. The Americans, as intrepid and virtuous citizens, have no need for a standing army.

Throughout his speech, Hancock draws on religious rhetoric to stress his points regarding the British government, British soldiers, and British deeds. When discussing British soldiers, he argues that these "are the men whom sceptred robbers now employ to frustrate the designs of God, and render vain the bounties which his gracious hand pours indiscriminately upon his creatures." The contrast could not be clearer between the offensive British and the righteous Bostonians, the descendants of New England Puritans. Hancock publicly worries that the emulation of

Time Line

1780
- Massachusetts approves a state constitution, and Hancock is elected first governor of the commonwealth.

1785
- **January 29**
  Hancock resigns the governorship.
- **November 23**
  Hancock is elected president of Congress.

1786
- **May 29**
  Owing to poor health, Hancock resigns as president of Congress without having attended a session.

1787
- Hancock is reelected governor, a post he holds until his death.

1788
- **January 2**
  Hancock is elected to serve as president of the state ratifying convention.
- **January 31**
  Hancock submits amendments for consideration.
- **February 6**
  Hancock delivers an oration to the ratification convention of the Commonwealth of Massachusetts before the final vote.
- **February 27**
  Hancock reasserts his support for the Constitution and advocates state laws centered on morality in a speech to the General Court in Boston.

1793
- **September 16**
  Hancock makes his last appearance before the Massachusetts General Court.
- **October 8**
  Hancock dies in Braintree, Massachusetts.

The Boston Massacre of March 5, 1770 (Library of Congress)

the poor behavior of the British army by the youth of Boston could bring destruction upon the community—a sentiment quite similar to that of John Winthrop, the colony's first governor. Hancock's audience of Puritan descendants would not have blinked when Hancock fused heritage and religion in his rallying cry: "Let not a meanness of spirit, unknown to those whom you boast of as your fathers, excite a thought to the dishonor of your mothers I conjure you, by all that is dear, by all that is honorable, by all that is sacred, not only that ye pray, but that ye act; that, if necessary, ye fight, and even die, for the prosperity of our Jerusalem."

As had become increasingly common since the 1750s, Hancock refers to himself and his fellow citizens as Americans. Unlike earlier uses—and periods—the moment had arrived when a sense of identity divorced from the British Empire and from the rights of the English needed to be forged. Hancock's speech commemorating the Boston Massacre contributed mightily to creating a sense of national American identity.

◆ Address to the Ratification Convention of the Commonwealth of Massachusetts

When the Constitutional Convention came to a close on September 17, 1787, the document was sent to ratifying conventions throughout the Union. Scenes of intense debate and division were played out at the different conventions, including the one held in Massachusetts. On January 31, 1788, Hancock, the president of the convention, proposed nine amendments to the Constitution that he felt would ameliorate the concerns of those who had issues with the proposed form of government. The amendments submitted by Governor Hancock are widely considered to mark a turning point for the deeply divided convention in Massachusetts. While they were an important development in the debate, the amendments themselves were not enough to change the tide. That moment arrived nearly a week later, on February 6, when Hancock, who had been present for the entire debate, addressed the convention for the first time, just before the final vote.

At a moment when the supporters of the Constitution at the Massachusetts ratifying convention were still shy of the necessary votes, Hancock made clear his commitment to the proposed form of government. He believed that it would bring greater political freedom and national dignity to the new country. At a time when armed rebellion in Massachusetts was still fresh in people's memories and when the knowledge that the United States could not pay its debt weighed heavily on the public mind, Hancock's points resonated with enough of the men present to make a difference. The vote to ratify the Constitution was 187 votes in support and 168 against.

Just as powerful—and persuasive—as his argument for ratification is Hancock's use of empathy for those who were wary of certain features of the federal constitution. Hancock echoes the observation made earlier by a convention delegate that it would be impossible to achieve a perfect consensus in a geographic space as large and diverse as the United States. Hancock tries to assuage the myriad concerns of the delegates by reminding them that should the need arise to adjust the Constitution, there would be constitutional means available to the citizenry to make such changes.

In addition to the ability to amend the Constitution, Hancock acknowledges the overarching concern of the critics of the Constitution about civil rights by directly addressing the issue. He underscores the fact that "the powers reserved by the people render them secure." This security would be achieved in two ways. First, frequent elections would keep alive a spirit of accountability to the citizenry. As such, if civil rights were threatened, Hancock implies that the responsibility would lie with the voter. Before the leaders fail to represent their constituents and encroach on their rights, the citizenry first must become corrupted. Once again, Hancock utilizes classic republican rhetoric, emphasizing virtue and community and suggesting that liberty is lost when love of luxury compromises the necessary vigilance to maintain a free and virtuous society. Moreover, Hancock exudes a Jeffersonian confidence in the ability of the people to rule themselves.

Second, the ultimate protection is the desire of a community to live happily and peacefully. He reminds the rulers that their interests are not distinct from their constituents' interests; to protect their own rights and interests is thus to protect the rights and interests of their constituents. The people of Massachusetts, Hancock explains, "know that we have none of us an interest separate from theirs—that it must be our happiness to conduce to theirs—and that we must all rise or fall together." Consequently, he is confident that whether one side wins the ratification vote or loses, the "first principle of society," that is, that the majority rules, will guide the response after the vote.

The vote was taken immediately following Hancock's speech. The crucial votes that were needed were won over by Hancock's empathetic speech to a divided convention. Hancock demonstrated his leadership by bringing the ratification in support of the Constitution to a successful conclusion. If Massachusetts had failed to support the Constitution, it is highly likely that other key states would have failed to support it, too.

◆ Address to the General Court of Boston

Twenty-one days after his influential speech before the final vote to ratify the federal Constitution, Hancock stood before the General Court. Some members of that body had also been members of the ratification convention, but others had not. While Hancock strikes themes similar to the ones he had struck on February 6, his comments provide more explicit insight into his opinions regarding the Articles of Confederation, his motives for proposing and ratifying a new form of government, his hope for the future under the Constitution, and his views of the relationship between church and state.

After bringing the General Court up to date on routine business and issues of government—such as debt and taxes—Hancock launches into a discussion of the not-so-routine business that had recently transpired. He describes the articles as an "obvious imbecility" that troubled the friends of America and pleased its enemies. He explains that the fear of losing "our national existence" acted as the key motivator to bring people together for such a momentous task.

In this speech Hancock reveals his belief that the Union is the strength of all the states and that to truly be a nation there is a need for coercive force in order to protect Americans from foreign enemies and to maintain peace at home so people could live happily. Obviously Hancock's spirits were high following the successful ratification of the Constitution. The differences that remained did not discourage him. In fact, the spirit of public service that infused the debate and the "spirit of Conciliation" that followed the vote impressed the governor and gave him great confidence in the future. He understood that in the General Court, as in the ratifying convention, there were individuals who remained concerned about the new form of government. Hancock once again brings their attention to the amendments and assures them that the protective measures would soon become part of the Constitution. Once they were, he contends, the United States government would indeed be "more perfect."

As is customary in his speeches, he closes with an acknowledgement of the power of God, especially over the affairs of humankind. In this speech he goes a step further

and calls for the support of institutions that promote "the Arts & Sciences" but also asks the legislature to establish "Laws for the support of piety, Religion & Morality" as well as those that punish unacceptable behavior. These laws, he contends, will bring more dignity to a sovereign people than crown jewels bring to princes. In this speech Hancock comes across as a nationalist who emphasizes the benefits of a stronger union and federal government. At the same time his provincialism and the Puritan roots of Massachusetts come through in his reaffirmation of the role of the state and the church as guardians of order in the commonwealth—a trend that would continue in the Bay State as well as in other New England states just as it was disappearing in other places, such as Virginia.

Impact and Legacy

Not a great producer of speeches (thirty-one in total), Hancock nonetheless remains in the pantheon of Founding Fathers. He does so because he was always in the thick of it. Hancock had an uncanny talent for being in the right place at the right time. He was most effective when he was in a position to bring different sides together. Although he was a businessman, Hancock's true passion was politics. He demonstrated elite support for the Revolutionary cause and provided leadership in a society ordered by deference. As his speeches in different locations and at different times reveal, he believed that the interests of the leaders and the people were one and the same. He clearly had a talent for bringing people with diverse interests and opinions together. That talent explains why Hancock always seemed to be in the presiding chair—whether it was at the Revolutionary Provincial Congress in Boston or the Second Continental Congress in Philadelphia or as governor of the Commonwealth of Massachusetts. A great deal of his life was spent bringing people together during trying, and sometimes, desperate times.

Hancock's outlook personified the new American. He was clearly a product of his state. His pride in the militia and his commitment to community as well as his sense of the relationship between God and human events characterized him as an old-school Massachusetts man. His belief in the role of the church in providing an orderly society that maintained liberty was characteristic of New Englanders and of Federalists. However, his love of and confidence in the people resembled Thomas Jefferson's confidence in the ability of humankind to rule itself. His speeches reveal a pride of place. This pride of place stemmed from his having observed his community of Boston and his larger community of the United States perform their patriotic duties heroically. In this sense, he saw a reflection of himself in the patriotic and Revolutionary commitment of others. His ability to lead and to empathize with his fellow citizens during the Revolutionary era is best captured when an elderly shoemaker and former Son of Liberty, remembered that he, a poor man, threw tea overboard with John Hancock, a rich man, in a shared Revolutionary moment. That he misre-

"Some boast of being friends to government; I am a friend to righteous government, to a government founded upon the principles of reason and justice; but I glory in publicly avowing my eternal enmity to tyranny."

(Boston Massacre Oration)

"Tell me, ye bloody butchers! ye villains high and low! ye wretches who contrived, as well as you who executed the inhuman deed! do you not feel the goads and stings of conscious guilt pierce through your savage bosoms?"

(Boston Massacre Oration)

"That people who pay greater respect to a wealthy villain than to an honest, upright man in poverty, almost deserve to be enslaved; they plainly show that wealth, however it may be acquired, is, in their esteem, to be preferred to virtue."

(Boston Massacre Oration)

"But I thank God that America abounds in men who are superior to all temptation, whom nothing can divert from a steady pursuit of the interest of their country, who are at once its ornament and safeguard."

(Boston Massacre Oration)

"The question now before you is such as no nation on earth, without the limits of America, has ever had the privilege of deciding upon."

(Address to the Ratification Convention of the Commonwealth of Massachusetts)

"To pretend to exist as a nation without possessing those powers of Coerce, which are necessarily incident to the national Character, would prove a fatal solecism in politicks."

(Address to the General Court of Boston)

"And although when the momentous Question was decided, there was a greater division than some expected, yet there appeared a candor, & a spirit of Conciliation, in the Minority, which did them great honor, & afforded an happy presage of unanimity amongst the people at large."

(Address to the General Court of Boston)

membered is of no consequence, for John Hancock made sure he was conspicuously seen elsewhere. The old man's memory is nonetheless important for what it says not only about attitudes about the American Revolution but also about the memories about one of its key Patriots. So while Hancock lived a life of wealth and privilege that was beyond the experience of most Americans, he nonetheless demonstrated to a freethinking people that he was truly a man of the people—and herein lies Hancock's revolutionary contribution to the American experience.

Key Sources

John Hancock's papers can be found at the New England Historic Genealogical Society and at the Massachusetts Historical Society. The *Letters of Delegates to Congress, 1774–1789* are available at many academic libraries. The twenty-six volumes of letters that make up the collection are accessible via the Library of Congress's Web site (http://memory.loc.gov/ammem/amlaw/lwdg.html).

Further Reading

■ Articles

Young, Alfred F. "George Robert Twelves Hewes (1742–1840): A Boston Shoemaker and the Memory of the American Revolution." *William and Mary Quarterly*, 3d ser., 38 (1981): 562–623.

■ Books

Brandes, Paul D. *John Hancock's Life and Speeches: A Personalized Vision of the American Revolution, 1763–1793.* Lanham, Md.: Scarecrow Press, 1996.

Fowler, William M., Jr. *The Baron of Beacon Hill: A Biography of John Hancock.* Boston: Houghton Mifflin, 1980.

Jensen, Merrill, John P. Kaminski, and Gaspare J. Saladino, eds. *The Documentary History of the Ratification of the Constitution: Ratification of the Constitution by the States: Massachusetts*, vol. 6. Madison: State Historical Society of Wisconsin, 2000.

Maier, Pauline. *From Resistance to Revolution: Colonial Radicals and the Development of American Opposition to Britain, 1765–1776.* New York: W. W. Norton., 1991.

Ritter, Karl W., and James R. Andrews. *The American Ideology: Reflections of the Revolution in American Rhetoric.* Falls Church, Va.: Speech Communication Association, 1978.

—Christopher J. Young

Questions for Further Study

1. Is the language Hancock uses in his discussion of the Boston Massacre—for instance, his references to devils and hell with regard to the actions of the British—too extreme? Examine several of his strongest statements or references, and discuss whether you think these figures of speech are too strong (or not strong enough or just right) for the situation he was addressing.

2. Why did Hancock fear the development of standing armies? What are the main points of his argument against them? How would he view the subsequent development of a large professional military force in the United States?

3. Whereas people today take for granted the vast size of the United States, in terms of both population and area, such an enormous nation would have been very difficult to comprehend in Hancock's day. How does he view the size of the country at that time, and how might he have responded to its considerable later growth?

BOSTON MASSACRE ORATION (1774)

The attentive gravity; the venerable appearance of this crowded audience; the dignity which I behold in the countenances of so many in this great assembly; the solemnity of the occasion upon which we have met together, joined to a consideration of the part I am to take in the important business of this day, fill me with an awe hitherto unknown....

I have always, from my earliest youth, rejoiced in the felicity of my fellow-men; and have ever considered it as the indispensable able duty of every member of society to promote, as far as in him lies, the prosperity of every individual, but more especially of the community to which he belongs; and also, as a faithful subject of the State, to use his utmost endeavors to detect, and having detected, strenuously to oppose every traitorous plot which its enemies may devise for its destruction. Security to the persons and properties of the governed is so obviously the design and end of civil government, that to attempt a logical proof of it would be like burning tapers at noonday, to assist the sun in enlightening the world; and it cannot be either virtuous or honorable to attempt to support a government of which this is not the great and principal basis; and it is to the last degree vicious and infamous to attempt to support a government which manifestly tends to render the persons and properties of the governed insecure. Some boast of being friends to government; I am a friend to righteous government, to a government founded upon the principles of reason and justice; but I glory in publicly avowing my eternal enmity to tyranny. Is the present system, which the British administration have adopted for the government of the Colonies, a righteous government—or is it tyranny?... They have declared that they have ever had, and of right ought ever to have, full power to make laws of sufficient validity to bind the Colonies in all cases whatever. They have exercised this pretended right by imposing a tax upon us without our consent; and lest we should show some reluctance at parting with our property, her fleets and armies are sent to enforce their mad pretensions. The town of Boston, ever faithful to the British Crown, has been invested by a British fleet; the troops of George III have crossed the wide Atlantic, not to engage an enemy, but to assist a band of traitors in trampling on the rights and liberties of his most loyal subjects in America—those rights and liberties which, as a father, he ought ever to regard, and as a king, he is bound, in honor, to defend from violation, even at the risk of his own life....

Let not the history of the illustrious house of Brunswick inform posterity that a king, descended from that glorious monarch George II, once sent his British subjects to conquer and enslave his subjects in America. But be perpetual infamy entailed upon that villain who dared to advise his master to such execrable measures; for it was easy to foresee the consequences which so naturally followed upon sending troops into America to enforce obedience to acts of the British Parliament, which neither God nor man ever empowered them to make. It was reasonable to expect that troops, who knew the errand they were sent upon, would treat the people whom they were to subjugate, with a cruelty and haughtiness which too often buries the honorable character of a soldier in the disgraceful name of an unfeeling ruffian. The troops, upon their first arrival, took possession of our Senate House, and pointed their cannon against the judgment hall, and even continued them there whilst the supreme court of judicature for this province was actually sitting to decide upon the lives and fortunes of the King's subjects. Our streets nightly resounded with the noise of riot and debauchery; our peaceful citizens were hourly exposed to shameful insults, and often felt the effects of their violence and outrage. But this was not all: as though they thought it not enough to violate our civil rights, they endeavored to deprive us of the enjoyment of our religious privileges, to vitiate our morals, and thereby render us deserving of destruction. Hence, the rude din of arms which broke in upon your solemn devotions in your temples, on that day hallowed by heaven, and set apart by God himself for his peculiar worship. Hence, impious oaths and blasphemies so often tortured your unaccustomed ear. Hence, all the arts which idleness and luxury could invent were used to betray our youth of one sex into extravagance and effeminacy, and of the other to infamy and ruin....Did not our youth forget they were Americans, and, regardless of the admonitions of the wise and aged, servilely copy from their tyrants those vices which finally must overthrow the empire of Great Britain?... When virtue has once erected her throne within the female breast, it is upon so solid a basis that nothing is able to expel the heavenly inhabitant. But have there not been some few, indeed, I hope, whose youth and inexperience have rendered them a prey to wretches, whom, upon the least reflection, they would have despised and hated as foes to God and their country? I fear there have been some such unhappy instances, or why have I seen an honest father clothed with shame; or why a virtuous mother drowned in tears?

But I forbear, and come reluctantly to the transactions of that dismal night, when in such quick succession we felt the extremes of grief, astonishment, and rage; when heaven in anger, for a dreadful moment, suffered hell to take the reins; when Satan, with his chosen band, opened the sluices of New England's blood, and sacrilegiously polluted our land with the dead bodies of her guiltless sons! Let this sad tale of death never be told without a tear; let not the heaving bosom cease to burn with a manly indignation at the barbarous story, through the long tracts of future time; let every parent tell the shameful story to his listening children until tears of pity glisten in their eyes, and boiling passions shake their tender frames; and whilst the anniversary of that ill-fated night is kept a jubilee in the grim court of pandemonium, let all America join in one common prayer to heaven that the inhuman, unprovoked murders of the fifth of March, 1770, planned by Hillsborough, and a knot of treacherous knaves in Boston, and executed by the cruel hand of Preston and his sanguinary coadjutors, may ever stand in history without a parallel. But what, my countrymen, withheld the ready arm of vengeance from executing instant justice on the vile assassins? Perhaps you feared promiscuous carnage might ensue, and that the innocent might share the fate of those who had performed the infernal deed. But were not all guilty? Were you not too tender of the lives of those who came to fix a yoke on your necks? But I must not too severely blame a fault, which great souls only can commit. May that magnificence of spirit which scorns the low pursuits of malice, may that generous compassion which often preserves from ruin, even a guilty villain, forever actuate the noble bosoms of Americans! But let not the miscreant host vainly imagine that we feared their arms. No; them we despised; we dread nothing but slavery. Death is the creature of a poltroon's brains; 'tis immortality to sacrifice ourselves for the salvation of our country. We fear not death. That gloomy night, the pale-faced moon, and the affrighted stars that hurried through the sky, can witness that we fear not death. Our

hearts which, at the recollection, glow with rage that four revolving years have scarcely taught us to restrain, can witness that we fear not death; and happy it is for those who dared to insult us, that their naked bones are not now piled up an everlasting lasting monument of Massachusetts' bravery. But they retired, they fled, and in that flight they found their only safety. We then expected that the hand of public justice would soon inflict that punishment upon the murderers, which, by the laws of God and man, they had incurred. But let the unbiased pen of a Robertson, or perhaps of some equally famed American, conduct this trial before the great tribunal of succeeding generations. And though the murderers may escape the just resentment of an enraged people; though drowsy justice, intoxicated by the poisonous draught prepared for her cup, still nods upon her rotten seat, yet be assured such complicated crimes will meet their due reward. Tell me, ye bloody butchers! ye villains high and low! ye wretches who contrived, as well as you who executed the inhuman deed! do you not feel the goads and stings of conscious guilt pierce through your savage bosoms? Though some of you may think yourselves exalted to a height that bids defiance to human justice, and others shroud yourselves beneath the mask of hypocrisy, and build your hopes of safety on the low arts of cunning, chicanery, and falsehood, yet do you not sometimes feel the gnawings of that worm which never dies? Do not the injured shades of Maverick, Gray, Caldwell, Attucks, and Carr attend you in your solitary walks, arrest you even in the midst of your debaucheries, and fill even your dreams with terror?

Ye dark designing knaves, ye murderers, parricides! how dare you tread upon the earth which has drunk in the blood of slaughtered innocents, shed by your wicked hands? How dare you breathe that air which wafted to the ear of heaven the groans of those who fell a sacrifice to your accursed ambition?... The eye of heaven penetrates the darkest chambers of the soul, traces the leading clue through all the labyrinths which your industrious folly has devised; and you, however you may have screened yourselves from human eyes, must be arraigned, must lift your hands, red with the blood of those whose death you have procured, at the tremendous bar of God!

But I gladly quit the gloomy theme of death, and leave you to improve the thought of that important day when our naked souls must stand before that Being from whom nothing can be hid. I would not dwell too long upon the horrid effects which have already followed from quartering regular troops in this town. Let our misfortunes teach posterity to guard against such evils for the future. Standing armies are sometimes (I would by no means say generally, much less universally) composed of persons who have rendered themselves unfit to live in civil society; who have no other motives of conduct than those which a desire of the present gratification of their passions suggests; who have no property in any country; men who have given up their own liberties, and envy those who enjoy liberty; who are equally indifferent to the glory of a George or a Louis; who, for the addition of one penny a day to their wages, would desert from the Christian cross and fight under the crescent of the Turkish Sultan. From such men as these, what has not a State to fear?…These are the men whom sceptred robbers now employ to frustrate the designs of God, and render vain the bounties which his gracious hand pours indiscriminately upon his creatures. By these the miserable slaves in Turkey, Persia, and many other extensive countries, are rendered truly wretched, though their air is salubrious, and their soil luxuriously fertile. By these, France and Spain, though blessed by nature with all that administers to the convenience of life, have been reduced to that contemptible state in which they now appear; and by these, Britain,—but if I were possessed of the gift of prophesy, I dare not, except by divine command, unfold the leaves on which the destiny of that once powerful kingdom is inscribed.

But since standing armies are so hurtful to a State, perhaps my countrymen may demand some substitute, some other means of rendering us secure against the incursions of a foreign enemy.…Will not a well-disciplined militia afford you ample security

Glossary

"Although the fig tree shall not blossom,… we will joy in the God of our salvation"	a quote from the Bible, Habbukuk 3:17–18
as a father	a reference to the king's symbolic role as "father of his people"
at once its ornament and safeguard	its pride and protector at the same time
be perpetual infamy entailed upon that villain	that villain's name should be cursed forever
Boston Massacre	an incident on March 5, 1770, in which tension between Bostonians and British troops led to the deaths of five civilians
clue…labyrinth	a reference to the Greek myth of Theseus, who found his way out of the cave controlled by a monster known as the Minotaur by using a "clue," or ball of yarn, to retrace his steps
conjure	call upon
death is the creature of a poltroon's brains	only cowards fear death
effrontive of the tutelar deity	disrespectful to the god who acts as guardian
ever appeared in more flourishing condition than that of this province now cloth	was ever more well dressed
fifth of March, 1770	date of the Boston Massacre

against foreign foes? We want not courage; it is discipline alone in which we are exceeded by the most formidable troops that ever trod the earth. Surely our hearts flutter no more at the sound of war than did those of the immortal band of Persia, the Macedonian phalanx, the invincible Roman legions, the Turkish janissaries, the gens d'armes of France, or the well-known grenadiers of Britain. A well-disciplined militia is a safe, an honorable guard to a community like this, whose inhabitants are by nature brave, and are laudably tenacious of that freedom in which they were born. From a well-regulated militia we have nothing to fear; their interest is the same with that of the State. When a country is invaded, the militia are ready to appear in its defense; they march into the field with that fortitude which a consciousness of the justice of their cause inspires; they do not jeopardy their lives for a master who considers them only as the instruments of his ambition, and whom they regard only as the daily dispenser of the scanty pittance of bread and water. No; they fight for their houses, their lands, for their wives, their children; for all who claim the tenderest names, and are held dearest in their hearts; they fight pro aris et focis, for their liberty, and for themselves, and for their God. And let it not offend if I say that no militia ever appeared in more flourishing condition than that of this province now cloth; and pardon me if I say, of this town in particular. I mean not to boast; I would not excite envy, but manly emulation. We have all one common cause; let it, therefore, be our only contest, who shall most contribute to the security of the liberties of America. And may the same kind Providence which has watched over this country

Glossary

George II	English king (1683–1760) and grandfather of George III
a George or a Louis	a reference to the kings of England and France, respectively
the great tribunal of succeeding generations	the judgment of later generations
Hillsborough	Lord Hillsborough, parliamentary minister for American affairs
house of Brunswick	the family, also known as the House of Hanover, who controlled the English throne from 1714 to 1901
I dare not…unfold the leaves on which the destiny of that…kingdom is inscribed	I will not even try to predict England's sad future
the immortal band of Persia…	a list of notable armies from history, beginning with the "Immortals" of the Persian Empire who attacked Greece in the fifth century BCE
in sunder	apart
invested	attacked
judicature	the administration of justice
kept a jubilee in the grim court of pandemonium	celebrated in hell
manifestly tends to render the persons and properties of the governed insecure	obviously fails to protect its citizens' life, liberty, and property

from her infant state still enable us to defeat our enemies! I cannot here forbear noticing the signal manner in which the designs of those who wish not well to us have been discovered. The dark deeds of a treacherous cabal have been brought to public view.... But the representatives of the people have fixed a mark on these ungrateful monsters, which, though it may not make them so secure as Cain of old, yet renders them, at least, as infamous. Indeed, it would be effrontive to the tutelar deity of this country even to despair of saving it from all the snares which human policy can lay....

Remember, my friends, from whom you sprang. Let not a meanness of spirit, unknown to those whom you boast of as your fathers, excite a thought to the dishonor of your mothers I conjure you, by all that is dear, by all that is honorable, by all that is sacred, not only that ye pray, but that ye act; that, if necessary, ye fight, and even die, for the prosperity of our Jerusalem. Break in sunder, with noble disdain, the bonds with which the Philistines have bound you. Suffer not yourselves to be betrayed, by the soft arts of luxury and effeminacy, into the pit digged for your destruction. Despise the glare of wealth. That people who pay greater respect to a wealthy villain than to an honest, upright man in poverty, almost deserve to be enslaved; they plainly show that wealth, however it may be acquired, is, in their esteem, to be preferred to virtue.

But I thank God that America abounds in men who are superior to all temptation, whom nothing can divert from a steady pursuit of the interest of their country, who are at once its ornament and safeguard. And sure I am...if I paid a respect, so justly

Glossary

Maverick, Gray, Caldwell, Attucks, and Carr	the five civilians who died as a result of the Boston Massacre: Samuel Maverick, Samuel Gray, James Caldwell, Crispus Attucks, and Patrick Carr
miscreant	lawbreaker, wrongdoer
no property in any country	no stake in any country
parricides	killers of their fathers
the Philistines	enemies of the Israelites in the Old Testament
play the man for our God	obey and honor our God
Preston	British captain Thomas Preston, who was charged with giving his soldiers the order to fire on the Boston crowd
pro aris et focis	in Latin, literally, "for altars and firesides," meaning "for God and country"
promiscuous carnage	unrestrained killing
quartering	stationing
sanguinary coadjutors	bloody assistants
signal	unusual
standing armies	full-time, professional military forces, as opposed to militias composed of civilians called up in the event of an emergency
that day hallowed by heaven	Sunday
that worm which never dies	a reference to a statement by Jesus regarding the agonies of souls tortured in hell

due to their much-honored characters, in this place. But when I name an Adams, such a numerous host of fellow-patriots rush upon my mind, that I fear it would take up too much of your time, should I attempt to call over the illustrious roll. But your grateful hearts will point you to the men; and their revered names, in all succeeding times, shall grace the annals of America. From them let us, my friends, take example; from them let us catch the divine enthusiasm; and feel, each for himself, the godlike pleasure of diffusing happiness on all around us; of delivering the oppressed from the iron grasp of tyranny; of changing the hoarse complaints and bitter moans of wretched slaves into those cheerful songs, which freedom and contentment must inspire. There is a heartfelt satisfaction in reflecting on our exertions for the public weal, which all the sufferings an enraged tyrant can inflict will never take away; which the ingratitude and reproaches of those whom we have saved from ruin cannot rob us of. The virtuous asserter of the rights of mankind merits a reward, which even a want of success in his endeavors to save his country, the heaviest misfortune which can befall a genuine patriot, cannot entirely prevent him from receiving.

I have the most animating confidence that the present noble struggle for liberty will terminate gloriously for America. And let us play the man for our God, and for the cities of our God; while we are using the means in our power, let us humbly commit our righteous cause to the great Lord of the Universe, who loveth righteousness and hateth iniquity. And having secured the approbation of our hearts, by a faithful and unwearied discharge of our duty to our country, let us joyfully leave our concerns in the hands of him who raiseth up and pulleth down the empires and kingdoms of the world as he pleases; and with cheerful submission to his sovereign will, devoutly say: "Although the fig tree shall not blossom, neither shall fruit be in the vines; the labor of the olive shall fail, and the field shall yield no meat; the flock shall be cut off from the fold, and there shall be no herd in the stalls; yet we will rejoice in the Lord, we will joy in the God of our salvation."

Glossary

too tender of the lives	too eager to spare the lives
transactions	events
the tremendous bar of God	God's final judgment
vitiate	corrupt or reduce the value or effectiveness of
weal	the common good

ADDRESS TO THE RATIFICATION CONVENTION OF THE COMMONWEALTH OF MASSACHUSETTS (1788)

Being now called upon to bring the subject under debate to a decision, by bringing forward the question—I beg your indulgence to close the business with a few words. I am happy that my health has been so far restored, that I am rendered able to meet my fellow citizens, as represented in this Convention. I should have considered it as one of the most distressing misfortunes of my life, to be deprived of giving my aid and support to a system, which if amended (as I feel assured it will be) according to your proposals, cannot fail to give the people of the United States a greater degree of political freedom, and eventually as much national dignity, as falls to the lost of any nation on the earth. I have not since I had the honor to be in this place, said much on the important subject before us: All the ideas appertaining to the system, as well as those which are against as for it, have been debated upon with so much learning and ability, that the subject is quite exhausted.

But you will permit me, Gentlemen, to close the whole with one or two general observations. This I request, not expecting to throw any new light upon the subject, but because it may possibly prevent uneasiness and discordance from taking place amongst us and amongst our constituents.

That a general system of government is indispensably necessary to save our country from ruin is agreed upon all sides.—That the one now to be decided upon has its defects all agree,—but when we consider the variety of interests, and the different habits of the men it is intended for, it would be very singular to have an entire union of sentiment respecting it. Were the people of the United States to delegate the powers proposed to be given, to men who were not dependent on them frequently for elections—to men whose interests, either from rank, or title, would differ from that of their fellow-citizens in common, the tasks of delegating authority would be vastly more difficult; but as the matter now stands, the powers reserved by the people render them secure, and until they themselves become corrupt, they will always have upright and able rulers. I give my assent to the Constitution in full confidence that the amendments proposed will soon become a part of the system—these amendments being in no wise local, but calculated to give security and ease alike to all the States....

Suffer me to add that let the question be decided as it may, there can be no triumph on the one side, or chagrin on the other—Should there be a great division, every good man, every one who loves his country, will be so far from exhibiting extraordinary marks of joy, that he will sincerely lament the want of unanimity, and strenuously endeavor to cultivate a spirit of conciliation, both in Convention, and at home.

The people of this Commonwealth are a people of great light—of great intelligence in publick business— They know that we have none of us an interest separate from theirs—that it must be our happiness to conduce to theirs—and that we must all rise or fall together—They will never, therefore, forsake the first principle of society, that of being governed by the voice of the majority—and should it be that the proposed form of government should be rejected, they will zealously attempt another.—Should it, by the vote now to be taken be ratified, they will quietly acquiesce, and

Glossary

constituents	persons represented by a political leader
an entire union of sentiment respecting it	total agreement of feelings about it
in Convention	at the Constitutional Convention
in no wise	in no sense
without the limits	outside the boundaries

where they see a want of perfection in it, endeavor in a constitutional way to have it amended.

The question now before you is such as no nation on earth, without the limits of America, has ever had the privilege of deciding upon. As the Supreme Ruler of the Universe has seen fit to bestow upon us this glorious opportunity, let us decide upon it—appealing to him for the rectitude of our intentions—and in humble confidence that he will yet continue to bless and save our country.

ADDRESS TO THE GENERAL COURT OF BOSTON (1788)

Gentlemen of the Senate & Gentlemen of the House of Representatives—

...In the beginning of your last Session, I laid before you the Constitution & Frame of Government for the United States of America, agreed upon by the late General Convention, & transmitted to me by Congress. As the System was to be submitted to the people, & to be decided upon by their Delegates in Convention, I forbore to make any remarks upon it. The Convention which you appointed to deliberate upon that important subject, have concluded their Session, after having adopted & ratified the proposed plan, according to their resolution, a copy whereof, I have directed the Secretary to lay before you.

The obvious imbecility of the Confederation of the United States, has too long given pain to our friends, & pleasure to our enemies; but the forming a new System of Government, for so numerous a people, of very different views, & habits, spread upon such a vast extent of Territory, containing such a great variety of Soils, & under such extremes of climate, was a task, which nothing less than the dreadful apprehension of loosing our national existence could have compelled the people to undertake.

We can be known to the World, only under the appellation of the United States, if we are robbed of the idea of our Union, we immediately become separate nations, independent of each other, & no less liable to the depredations of foreign powers, than to Wars, & bloody contentions amongst ourselves. To pretend to exist as a nation without possessing those powers of Coerce, which are necessarily incident to the national Character, would prove a fatal solecism in politicks. The objects of the proposed Constitution, are defence against external enemies, & the promotion of tranquility, & happiness amongst the States—Whether it is well calculated for those important purposes, has been the subject of extensive & learned discussion in the Convention which you appointed—I believe there was never a Body of Men assembled, with greater purity of intention, or with higher zeal for the public interest. And although when the momentous Question was decided, there was a greater division than some expected, yet there appeared a candor, & a spirit of Conciliation, in the Minority, which did them great honor, & afforded an happy presage of unanimity amongst the people at large. Tho' so many of the Members of the late Convention could not feel themselves convinced that they ought to vote for the ratification of this System, yet their opposition was conducted with a candid & manly firmness & with such marks of integrity & real regard to the publick interest, did them the highest honor, & leaves no reason to suppose that the peace, & good order of the Government is not their object.—

The amendments proposed by the Convention are intended to obtain a Constitutional security of the principles to which they refer themselves, & must meet the wishes of all the States, I feel myself assured that they will very early become a part of the Constitution, & when they shall be added to the purposed plan, I shall consider it as the most perfect System of Government, as to the objects it embraces, that has been known amongst mankind.—

Glossary

the Confederation of the United States	the state of government under the Articles of Confederation, the charter of the newly independent American nation prior to the ratification of the Constitution in 1787
late General Convention	the recent constitutional convention
Sovereign	self-ruling
those powers of Coerce	the ability to bring force to bear

Gentlemen,

As that Being, in whose hands is the government of all the Nations of the Earth, & who putteth down one, & raiseth up another according to His Sovereign Pleasure, has given to the people of these States a rich & an extensive Country; has in a marvellous manner given them a name & a standing among the Nations of the World, has blessed them with external peace & internal tranquility; I hope & pray that the gratitude of their hearts may be expressed by a proper use of those inestimable blessings, by the greatest exertions of patriotism, by forming & supporting institutions for cultivating the human understanding & for the greatest progress of the Arts & Sciences, by establishing Laws for the support of piety, Religion & Morality, as well as for punishing vice & wickedness, & by exhibiting on the great Theatre of the World, those social, public & private virtues, which give more Dignity to a people possessing their own Sovereignty, than Crowns & Diadems afford to Sovereign Princes....

John Marshall Harlan (Library of Congress)

JOHN MARSHALL HARLAN   1833–1911

Supreme Court Justice

Featured Documents
- ◆ Civil Rights Cases (1883)
- ◆ *Hurtado v. California* (1884)
- ◆ *Pollock v. Farmers' Loan & Trust Co.* (1895)
- ◆ *Plessy v. Ferguson* (1896)

Overview

Named for the "Great Chief Justice" of the United States and ardent Federalist John Marshall, John Marshall Harlan was born into a prominent Kentucky family with Whig Party affiliations. Harlan was the first U.S. Supreme Court justice to earn a law degree, which he received from Transylvania University in 1853, after graduating from Centre College in 1850. Harlan joined his father's Frankfort, Kentucky, law practice and his father's political party. The elder Harlan was a slaveholder and crony of the Whig leader Henry Clay, who supported gradual emancipation. John Marshall Harlan inherited James Harlan's paternalistic attitude toward slavery as well as some of his father's slaves. He would have inherited his father's position among the Whigs had the party not come apart in the 1850s over the issue of whether slavery should be allowed to expand into the American territories. Instead, father and son joined the nativist Know-Nothings, a short-lived political party in the 1850s that was fueled by fear that the nation was being overrun by Irish Catholic immigrants.

In 1858, Harlan, running as a Know-Nothing, was elected county judge. Over the next few years he voiced a number of racist and states' rights opinions that would later come back to haunt him. With the advent of the Civil War in 1861, however, Harlan discovered his true political orientation. A staunch supporter of the Union, he raised a company of infantry volunteers and joined the Union army. He did so out of unswerving loyalty to the Constitution, not any abolitionist sentiments. He threatened to resign his colonel's commission if President Abraham Lincoln signed the Emancipation Proclamation, but he did not do so until James Harlan's death in 1863 obliged him to take over his father's unfinished business. The same year, running as a Constitutional Unionist, Harlan won election as Kentucky's attorney general. After the war ended, the party, made up largely of conservative former Whigs who wanted to avoid disunion over slavery, lost its reason for being. In 1868, like many former Whigs, Harlan joined the Republicans, where he quickly embraced his new party's antislavery platform.

Despite failing to win the governorship of Kentucky in 1871 and 1875, Harlan remained active in Republican political circles. In 1876, heading up the Kentucky delegation, he attended the Republican National Convention, where his support for Rutherford B. Hayes helped the lat-ter secure the party's nomination. The close presidential contest in 1876 between Hayes and Samuel J. Tilden dragged on for months, but shortly after it was settled in Hayes's favor, the new president appointed Harlan to head a commission charged with ending Republican rule in Louisiana, thus enforcing the political compromise that had resulted in Hayes's election. Consistent with his policy of ending Reconstruction and promoting North-South recon-ciliation, in 1877 Hayes nominated Harlan, a Unionist son of border-state Kentucky, to serve on the Supreme Court. Important documents from Harlan's tenure on the Supreme Court include his dissents in a number of landmark cases.

Explanation and Analysis of Documents

John Marshall Harlan served thirty-three years, ten months, and four days on the U.S. Supreme Court, one of the longest tenures of all who have sat on the high bench. During that period, he wrote his share of opinions for the Court majority. Yet he is best remembered for his dissents—for their passion, for their prescience, and for the sheer fact that the most significant among them, those concerning civil rights, were written by a southerner and former slave-holder. Harlan's passion for the Constitution led him to fight for the Union during the Civil War; it may also have accounted for his expansive reading of the Civil War Amendments, particularly the Fourteenth Amendment.

Harlan had the foresight to maintain in his dissent in the Civil Rights Cases that the "colored race" was entitled to the same right in public accommodations as any other member of the public. But in 1883 what most impressed his audience was the former slaveholder's willingness to stand alone as the voice of conscience, delivering his opin-ion with passion and directness. As one eyewitness recalled, "His great voice rang through the little court room ...filled with tones of feeling, while from time to time he gesticulated and even struck the desk before him in his earnestness" (Przybyszewski, p. 95). In one of the Court's most infamous decisions, *Plessy v. Ferguson* (1896), he once again argued—and again argued alone—that separate but equal public accommodations for black and white were unconstitutional. Dissenting in *Hurtado v. California* (1884), he laid out the rudiments of the incorporation doc-trine (the theory that the Fourteenth Amendment incorpo-

Time Line

1833

■ **June 1**
John Marshall Harlan is born in Boyle County, Kentucky.

1850

■ Harlan graduates with an AB degree from Centre College in Danville, Kentucky.

1853

■ Harlan graduates with a law degree from Transylvania University in Lexington, Kentucky.

1854

■ Harlan is elected city attorney for Frankfort, Kentucky.

1858

■ Harlan, running as a Know-Nothing candidate, is elected county judge for Franklin County, Kentucky.

1859

■ Harlan, running as a member of the Opposition Party, loses the contest for Henry Clay's former congressional seat in Kentucky.

1860

■ Harlan serves as a delegate to the Constitutional Union Party's Kentucky state conclave, pledging support to the Union and opposition to both northern republicanism and southern secession.

1861

■ **September 27**
Harlan announces the formation of a company of volunteer infantrymen to join the Union army.

1863

■ **February 23**
Harlan's father dies, forcing him to resign his colonel's commission and return to civilian life.

■ Harlan, running on the Union Party ticket, is elected as Kentucky's attorney general.

---

rates most of the Bill of Rights, making it applicable at the state level); more than fifty years passed before Justice Hugo Black developed the doctrine into mainstream constitutional law. And Harlan's support for the federal income tax in *Pollock v. Farmers' Loan & Trust Co.* (1895) was validated not by the Court but by the Sixteenth Amendment to the Constitution, passed two years after Harlan's death.

◆ **Civil Rights Cases**

The Civil Rights Cases actually consisted of five separate cases grouped together for decision: *United States v. Stanley, United States v. Ryan, United States v. Nichols, United States v. Singleton,* and *Robinson and Wife v. Memphis & Charleston Railroad Co.* Each of the cases presented the same basic issue: Do the Thirteenth and Fourteenth Amendments (two of the three so-called Civil War Amendments), together with their enabling legislation, the Civil Rights Act of 1875, grant the federal government power to protect African Americans from private as well as state-sponsored discrimination?

Abolition of slavery was accomplished by ratification of the Thirteenth Amendment in 1865. In reaction, states and localities enacted so-called Black Codes, modeled on earlier laws intended to counter those wishing to help fugitive slaves and now regulating the conduct of newly freed African Americans living within their borders. These were the sorts of restrictions complained of by litigants, who had been, variously, excluded from a hotel dining room in Topeka, Kansas; expelled from an opera in New York City; kept away from the better seats in a San Francisco theater; and removed from a train car that had been reserved for ladies. Such actions with respect to what are known as public accommodations were one of the targets of the Fourteenth Amendment, ratified in 1868, and—more particularly—of the Civil Rights Act of 1875, the enabling legislation enabling provided for in the Fourteenth Amendment.

Eight Supreme Court justices chose to read the Civil War Amendments narrowly. Joseph P. Bradley, on behalf of the majority, wrote that the Thirteenth Amendment merely abolished slavery and that the prohibitions of the Fourteenth Amendment were intended only to prohibit state action abridging individuals' rights. Literally, he was right: The amendment states only that "no state shall make or enforce any law which shall abridge the privileges or immunities of citizens of the United States." The majority agreed that the Civil War Amendments did not, therefore, control the actions of private individuals or institutions and that the Civil Rights Act of 1875 was unconstitutional. Adding insult to injury, Bradley said that individuals whose rights had been violated by private concerns were obliged to look to their individual states for redress.

Harlan, the youngest member of the Court, alone spoke out against the ruling. He did so passionately and at length—his dissent more than doubling the length of the majority's opinion. His opinion begins by emphasizing the spirit rather than the letter of the law. The purpose of the Civil Rights Act, he declares, is to prevent racial discrimination. As justification for this statement, Harlan examines the history of slavery, beginning with the drafting of the Constitution, where the inferiority of the black race was accepted, such that for purposes of enumeration, a black man was counted as three-fifths of a person. In addition, he says, Article IV, Section 2, clearly spells out the African American's status as property. Such provisions inevitably led to fugitive slave laws and such decisions as *Dred Scott v. Sandford* (1857), in which the Court declared that blacks were not citizens. Harlan quotes the author of that case, Chief Justice Roger B. Taney, who recognized even then that whether emancipated or not, blacks had no rights or privileges other than those granted by white men. The Thirteenth Amendment, Harlan allows, was intended to rectify this situation, establishing "universal civil freedom," meaning an end not only to slavery per se but also to discrimination on the part of the state. The ban on such discrimination, Harlan goes on to say, reaches public accommodations: "The authority to establish and maintain them [public accommodations] comes from the public. The black race is a part of that public."

Harlan is similarly unwilling to limit the scope of the Fourteenth Amendment: The first clause, granting citizenship, was meant to apply to private acts. Pointing once again to legislative history, he observes: "It was perfectly well known that the great danger to the equal enjoyment by citizens of their rights, as citizens, was to be apprehended, not altogether from unfriendly state legislation, but from the hostile action of corporations and individuals in the states." Legislation intended to curtail hostile private action does not, as the majority holds, make the black race into "the special favorite of the laws"; rather, the Civil Rights Act upholds blacks' rights and privileges as citizens. In finding otherwise, the Court now risks making as big a mistake as it did a quarter century earlier in *Dred Scott*.

Harlan would soon be proved right. In the wake of the Civil Rights Cases decision, the federal government withdrew from enforcement of civil rights, ushering in an age of "Jim Crow" laws and customs that led to widespread, sanctioned discrimination in all aspects of public life, including housing, employment, and public accommodations.

◆ Hurtado v. California

Hurtado is a case about due process as it applies to a state criminal trial. The defendant, Joseph Hurtado, was accused of having fatally shot his wife's lover. Despite being accused of a capital crime, Hurtado was not indicted by a grand jury. The rules operating in California criminal courts at the time allowed him to be tried simply on the basis of "information"—in essence, a charge filed by the district attorney acting on his own authority. After the information was examined by a magistrate, who found it sufficient to permit the trial to move forward, Hurtado was tried, found guilty, and sentenced to death. Hurtado appealed his sentence, first to the California Supreme Court and then to the U.S. Supreme Court, on the ground that it violated his right under the Fifth Amendment to a hearing before a grand jury. The mechanism whereby this protection applied to him, he argued, could be found in the

Time Line

1871	■ Harlan, running on the Republican ticket, is defeated in his bid to become governor of Kentucky.
1872	■ Harlan, running as a Republican, loses a bid for a U.S. Senate seat.
1873	■ Harlan is appointed special counsel for federal prosecution of the Fourteenth Amendment Enforcement Acts, making him a champion of civil rights.
1875	■ Harlan's second bid for the Kentucky governorship is defeated.
1876	■ Harlan, a delegate to the Republican National Convention, switches his support from his law partner, Benjamin Bristow, to Rutherford B. Hayes, thereby becoming a kingmaker.
1877	■ **October 16** Rutherford Hayes nominates Harlan to the U.S. Supreme Court.
1883	■ **October 15** Harlan delivers the lone dissent in the Civil Rights Cases.
1884	■ **March 3** Harlan dissents alone in *Hurtado v. California*.
1895	■ **May 20** Harlan dissents in *Pollock v. Farmers' Loan & Trust Co.*.
1896	■ **May 18** Harlan is the lone dissenter in *Plessy v. Ferguson*.
1911	■ **October 14** Still a member of the Court, Harlan dies in Washington, D.C.

Illustration of "Jim Crow" (Library of Congress)

due process clause of the Fourteenth Amendment, which made this Fifth Amendment protection applicable to state as well as federal trials for capital crimes.

Writing for the Court majority, Justice Stanley Matthews declared that the framers of the Fourteenth Amendment had not intended to guarantee a grand jury to state criminal defendants; if such had been their intent, they would have specified as much. What is more, Matthews wrote, Hurtado's right to due process had not been violated, as presenting information is a preliminary proceeding. The actual trial where Hurtado had been found guilty had been fair.

Harlan, once again voicing a lone dissent, objected to the majority's interpretation of the framers' intent. Diluting the requirement of a grand jury in circumstances such as Hurtado's to any legal proceeding enforced by public authority did not square with Harlan's sense of constitutional integrity. The only change to the Founders' plan for the nation was fulfillment of their vision by nationalizing the Constitution's standard of rights. At the time *Hurtado* was making its way through the courts, a movement among legal professionals was calling for an end to the cumbersome grand jury system. For Harlan, this notion had the

potential to undermine the whole structure of republican government, with its emphasis on popular participation in decision making.

As a foundation for his argument, Harlan opens with a thorough rehearsal of the history of due process in English law, beginning with the Magna Carta in the thirteenth century. He illustrates that participation of the people in the administration of justice is a time-honored and indispensable part of English common law, which provided the drafters of the Constitution with their frame of reference. Informal instruments such as the information used to bring Hurtado to trial were, Harlan shows, traditionally frowned upon in the context of capital crimes. If the right to a grand jury were not fundamental in serious criminal cases, he says, the Fifth Amendment would not have required the federal government to provide one for federal defendants suspected, like Hurtado, of having committed heinous crimes. Substituting information for a grand jury was not progress, not an acceptable new method of ensuring due process, but a violation of the Founders' original vision for the Republic.

Harlan's argument was sound, but it was subject to one obvious objection: From the beginning, American criminal procedure had been almost exclusively a state matter. And well into the next century, the majority's position in *Hurtado*—that the Fourteenth Amendment did not oblige the states to honor Fifth Amendment guarantees—was not questioned. Eventually, however, because of events such as the red scare (the fear of Communism) during World War I and an epidemic of lynchings of blacks in the South, the American public became uncomfortable with the justice system's lack of federal oversight. With the burgeoning of the civil rights movement at midcentury, pressure to nationalize the Bill of Rights—as Harlan had argued for—increased. With the Court's adoption and expansion of the incorporation doctrine under the leadership of Chief Justice Earl Warren in the 1950s and 1960s, most of the guarantees of the Bill of Rights were, in fact, applied to the states. *Hurtado* itself remains good law, such that criminal defendants—even those accused of capital offenses—can still be tried in state courts without having first been indicted by grand jury. Nonetheless, it can be argued that Justice Harlan's dissent in the case contributed greatly to the national debate that led to what has come to be known as the "due process revolution."

◆ *Pollock v. Farmers' Loan & Trust Co.*

Pollock was unquestionably the most controversial case of its day. It was in fact a contrived case, conjured up in the wake of passage of the income tax law of 1894, the nation's first peacetime attempt to tax income. The tax did not amount to much, as it was limited to 2 percent of income over $4,000, but it was laid against not only earned income (the so-called indirect tax) but also against income derived from property, such as interest, dividends, and rent. The New York–based Farmers' Loan & Trust Co. accordingly informed its shareholders that it was obligated to pay the tax, adding that it also intended to inform the Department of the

Treasury of the names of its shareholders, who were liable for the tax. Charles Pollock owned a mere ten shares of the company's stock, but he was prevailed upon to sue the bank to enjoin it from paying a tax it wished to avoid in any event.

The Supreme Court heard oral argument in the case twice and decided it twice in 1895. The first decision divided the new tax law into three parts, with the result that (1) tax on income from state or local municipal bonds was found to violate state sovereignty; (2) tax on income from real property was found to be a "direct" tax, which the Constitution required to be apportioned among the states; and (3) with only six of the justices participating, the Court equally divided on the question of whether a tax on individual and corporate income was a direct tax. After such a muddled decision, the Court decided almost immediately to rehear the *Pollock* case, with the ultimate result that by a decision of five to four, the entire law was invalidated as imposing a direct tax, requiring apportionment among the states by population.

The Wilson-Gorman Tariff Act of 1894 had been passed by Congress in an attempt to redistribute the tax burden during an economic depression following the Panic of 1893. It was the end of the Gilded Age, an era of extravagant displays of wealth, and although popular sentiment was running strongly against millionaires and monopolies, the Court, committed to a philosophy of economic laissez-faire, remained above the fray. The decision in *Pollock* proved highly unpopular with the public and the press and was even held up for special criticism in the Democratic platform during the 1896 general election. Eventually, with adoption of the Sixteenth Amendment—legitimizing federal taxation on income from "whatever source derived, without apportionment among the several states" and proposed specifically in response to *Pollock*—the decision became moot.

Harlan dissented both times in *Pollock*. For him, the experience of hearing and deciding the case was exceptionally emotional. As he confided privately at the time, "I feel more strongly about this recent decision than any which ever emanated from this court" (Przybyszewski, p. 171). Harlan saw the issue in the case as essentially the same as that which had motivated him to pen his dissent in the Civil Rights Cases, but instead of slaveholders living off the free labor of their human chattel, now investors and landholders were taking advantage of those who worked for a living. As during the Civil War, for Harlan, the forces of tyranny were pitted against those wishing to uphold the nation, and once again, as it had in *Dred Scott*, the Court was on the wrong side of the battle. He takes great offense at the majority's implication that the income tax passed during the war as an emergency measure was somehow unconstitutional: "The supremacy of the nation was re-established against armed rebellion seeking to destroy its life, but it seems that that consummation, so devoutly wished, and to effect which so many valuable lives were sacrificed, was attended with a disregard of the constitution by which the Union was ordained." He fears that with its decision, the Court is once more threatening to divide the American people and expresses a "deep, abiding convic-

tion" that in *Pollock* the majority has arrived at the worst judgment. The only solution, he declares, is for Congress to amend the Constitution as soon as possible to clarify what he sees as the Founders' original intention of permitting federal taxation of income, regardless of source. The Sixteenth Amendment was ratified in 1913, vindicating Harlan—if only posthumously.

◆ **Plessy v. Ferguson**

Plessy was essentially a test case. After the Supreme Court ruled in the Civil Rights Cases that the Fourteenth Amendment did not outlaw racial discrimination on the part of private individuals or entities, southern states began adopting a whole series of Jim Crow laws aimed at segregating whites and blacks. One of these laws was Louisiana's Separate Car Act, which relegated black train passengers to separate cars. In response, a New Orleans group of African Americans and Creoles—with tacit support from the railroads, burdened with extra expense—organized the Citizens' Committee to Test the Constitutionality of the Separate Car Law. Homer Plessy, a light-skinned individual classified as black because he was one-eighth African American, was enlisted to test the law on behalf of the committee. Because an earlier state court decision had stipulated that the law in question could not be applied to interstate commerce, Plessy was careful to purchase a ticket for travel only within Louisiana. He also ensured that the conductor knew of his mixed race. After he refused to move to the "colored only" car, Plessy was duly arrested and tried. When, as expected, the state courts rejected his argument that the Separate Car Act violated his rights under the Thirteenth and Fourteenth Amendments, Plessy appealed to the U.S. Supreme Court.

The Court majority similarly rejected Plessy's Thirteenth and Fourteenth Amendment arguments, declaring that the former barred only actions intended to impose slavery and that the Separate Car Act did not violate the latter—not even with its implication that blacks are inferior. What is more, the majority proclaimed, it was fruitless for the Court to try to mandate racial integration when, as manifested by laws such as the one under consideration, society was so strongly opposed to race mixing. Transportation was like schooling, the Court opined: Racial segregation in both settings was a social right.

Harlan, once again a solitary dissenter, lays out quite a different definition of equality. For Harlan, segregation is in itself an incident of slavery and a violation of personal liberty. The Thirteenth Amendment barred not only slavery per se but also all "badges of … servitude." "Separate but equal" public accommodations simply could not exist in a society governed by a Constitution that is "color-blind, and neither knows nor tolerates classes among citizens." The white race, which dominated society, could remain dominant only if it fulfilled its destiny by acknowledging and yielding to its better instincts by adhering to the law.

In the end, Homer Plessy paid a fine and "separate but equal" remained the law of the land for another half century. In 1954, however, yet another African American organization, the National Association for the Advancement of Colored People, chose yet another representative plaintiff—Oliver Brown, the parent of a third-grader obliged to attend an inconvenient segregated school in Topeka, Kansas—to challenge the constitutionality of "separate but equal" in public accommodations. *Brown v. Board of Education* overturned *Plessy*, thereby placing the civil rights movement center stage in American life and proving the aptness of Harlan's assertion that our Constitution is color-blind.

Impact and Legacy

During a banquet to celebrate Harlan's twenty-fifth year of service on the Court, his colleague David J. Brewer jocularly remarked that Harlan "goes to bed every night with one hand on the Constitution and the other on the Bible, and so sleeps the sweet sleep of justice and righteousness" (Przybyszewski, p. 54). Justice Brewer's joke was not wide of the mark—either philosophically or practically—for although many commentators have remarked on the close connections between Harlan's jurisprudence and his faith, throughout the period when he sat on the high bench, Harlan also taught both constitutional law and Sunday school, activities that constantly reinforced his core beliefs. His reputation as one of the Court's great dissenters and latter-day prophets stems as much from his attitude—his outspokenness and rectitude—as from his legal prescience.

In his day, John Marshall Harlan was viewed as an eccentric. This reputation owed something, no doubt, to his shifting political alliances and to certain biographical anomalies. A southerner and onetime slaveholder, he fought for the North during the Civil War, mainly to save the Union but also—at least in part—to preserve the institution of slavery. He freed his own slaves and went on to support equal rights for African Americans with a ferocity and eloquence unmatched by any of his peers. His confidence in the rightness of his opinions was similarly unequaled. Friends viewed his certitude with humor and respect, but detractors such as the redoubtable Supreme Court justice Oliver Wendell Holmes, Jr., thought Harlan possessed of a powerful will but only a second-rate intellect.

Formalist legal scholars of the time criticized Harlan for his habit of bringing extraneous matters into his opinions, but Harlan's convictions grew out of his sense of the long perspective, and he regularly pointed out the consequences of Court decisions he thought ill advised. Ironically perhaps, he was, after a fashion, a strict constructionist who never tired of objecting to others' legal interpretations he thought at odds with the framers' original intent. His own view of what those who drafted the Constitution had in mind, however, was infinitely more expansive than the views held by his contemporaries. Harlan has frequently been referred to as a prophet; it is certainly true that in his constitutional liberalism he was far ahead of his time.

Harlan's attitude toward the Constitution has been said to have bordered on religious reverence, and there is little doubt that his own devout Presbyterianism colored both his view of the law and his manner of expressing it. Harlan wrote and spoke simply and directly, and his opinions are eloquent not because of rhetorical flourishes but because they carry the ring of truth, expressed by a man who lived what he believed. He is best remembered for his dissent in one of the Supreme Court's most infamous decisions, *Plessy v. Ferguson*, which clearly illustrates Harlan's continuing appeal. The language carries gospel overtones; it is altogether fitting that it proved prophetic. The same can be said of many of Harlan's justly famous dissents, including the Civil Rights Cases, concerning the disenfranchisement of African Americans, as well as *Hurtado v. California*, where he can be seen advocating powerfully on behalf of the criminally accused. Perhaps the classic Harlan dissent appears in the context of the debate over a federal income tax in *Pollock v. Farmers' Loan & Trust Co.*, where he is fully engaged in the archetypal battle between haves and have-nots. In this instance, too, Harlan proved prophetic, calling like a voice in the wilderness for a constitutional amendment that eventually followed. Harlan is an American hero precisely because his career describes a paradigmatic course, proving that in the United States, one individual indeed can change the course of history.

At Harlan's memorial service in 1911, Attorney General George W. Wickersham remarked that "[Harlan] could lead but he could not follow.... His was not the temper of a negotiator" (Hall, p. 363). Harlan's differences with Court majorities have not all stood the test of time. For example, writing separately (in the first instance concurring and in the second concurring and dissenting) in two antitrust cases decided in 1911, *Standard Oil Co. v. United States* and *United States v. American Tobacco Co.*, Harlan expressed the view that monopolies are not inherently malignant. These opinions made him popular at the time but have since proved outmoded. Harlan is best remembered for those solitary—some called them eccentric—dissents that reflected both his own volatile nature and his most deeply held beliefs, legal and spiritual.

Key Sources

The majority of Harlan's private papers, consisting mainly of correspondence, business records, and scrapbooks, are located in the John Marshall Harlan Collection at the Louis D. Brandeis School of Law at the University of Louisville in Kentucky. The papers date from 1835 to 1911, with the bulk having been written during Harlan's Court tenure. Harlan's official writings are housed with other Supreme Court records in the National Archives in Washington, D.C.

Further Reading

■ Articles

Abraham, Henry J. "John Marshall Harlan: A Justice Neglected." *Virginia Law Review* 41 (1955): 871–891.

"That there are burdens and disabilities which constitute badges of slavery and servitude, and that the express power delegated to congress to enforce, by appropriate legislation, the thirteenth amendment, may be exerted by legislation of a direct and primary character, for the eradication, not simply of the institution, but of its badges and incidents, are propositions which ought to be deemed indisputable."

(Civil Rights Cases)

"It is, I submit, scarcely just to say that the colored race has been the special favorite of the laws. What the nation, through congress, has sought to accomplish in reference to that race is, what had already been done in every state in the Union for the white race, to secure and protect rights belonging to them as freemen and citizens; nothing more."

(Civil Rights Cases)

"The real friends of property are not those who would exempt the wealth of the country from bearing its fair share of the burdens of taxation....There is nothing in the nature of an income tax per se that justifies judicial opposition to it upon the ground that it illegally discriminates against the rich, or imposes undue burdens upon that class. There is no tax which, in its essence, is more just and equitable than an income tax."

(Pollock v. Farmers' Loan & Trust Co.)

"In view of the constitution, in the eye of the law, there is in this country no superior, dominant, ruling class of citizens. There is no caste here. Our constitution is color-blind, and neither knows nor tolerates classes among citizens. In respect of civil rights, all citizens are equal before the law."

(Plessy v. Ferguson)

"The arbitrary separation of citizens, on the basis of race, while they are on a public highway, is a badge of servitude wholly inconsistent with the civil freedom and the equality before the law established by the constitution. It cannot be justified upon any legal grounds."

(Plessy v. Ferguson)

Gressman, Eugene. "The Unhappy History of Civil Rights Legislation." *Michigan Law Review* 50 (1952): 1323–1358.

■ **Books**

Beth, Loren P. *John Marshall Harlan: The Last Whig Justice*. Lexington: University Press of Kentucky, 1992.

Bodenhamer, David J., and James W. Ely, eds. *The Bill of Rights in Modern America*. Bloomington: Indiana University Press, 2008.

Hall, Kermit L., et al., eds. *The Oxford Companion to the Supreme Court of the United States*. New York: Oxford University Press, 1992.

Harlan, Malvina Shaklin, and Linda Przybyszewski. *Some Memories of a Long Life, 1854–1911*. New York: Modern Library, 2003.

Lofgren, Charles A. *The* Plessy *Case: A Legal-Historical Interpretation*. New York: Oxford University Press, 1988.

Medley, Keith Weldon. *We as Free Men*: Plessy v. Ferguson. Greta, La.: Pelican Publishing, 2003.

Przybyszewski, Linda. *The Republic According to John Marshall Harlan*. Chapel Hill: University of North Carolina Press, 1999.

—Lisa Paddock

Questions for Further Study

1. How did Justice Harlan's reading of the Fourteenth Amendment to the Constitution differ from that of the other members of the Supreme Court? Why was this different reading significant?

2. The Civil Rights Cases and *Hurtado v. California* would appear to be about very different issues—one involving racial discrimination and the other involving the rights of criminal defendants. On what constitutional basis are the cases similar in Justice Harlan's opinion? What fundamental constitutional issue is raised in both cases?

3. Similarly, Justice Harlan's decision in *Pollock v. Farmers' Loan & Trust Co.* was motivated in part by the same considerations he applied in his dissent in the Civil Rights Cases. Fundamentally, how were the two cases similar in Harlan's view?

4. The majority opinion in *Plessy v. Ferguson* is one of the most infamous in American judicial history. On what basis did Justice Harlan dissent from the majority? Explain how a former slave owner such as Harlan could in time come to argue so passionately for racial equality.

5. Compare Harlan's views on racial issues in *Hurtado v. California* and *Plessy v. Ferguson* with those enunciated by Salmon Chase in *Reclamation of Fugitives from Service* and by Stephen Field in *Ho Ah Kow v. Nunan*.

6. To what extent did Harlan's view anticipate those of Earl Warren in the 1954 case *Brown v. Board of Education*?

Civil Rights Cases (1883)

Harlan dissent

The opinion in these cases proceeds ... upon grounds entirely too narrow and artificial. The substance and spirit of the recent amendments of the constitution have been sacrificed by a subtle and ingenious verbal criticism. "It is not the words of the law but the internal sense of it that makes the law. The letter of the law is the body; the sense and reason of the law is the soul." Constitutional provisions, adopted in the interest of liberty, and for the purpose of securing, through national legislation, if need be, rights inhering in a state of freedom, and belonging to American citizenship, have been so construed as to defeat the ends the people desired to accomplish, which they attempted to accomplish, and which they supposed they had accomplished by changes in their fundamental law. By this I do not mean that the determination of these cases should have been materially controlled by considerations of mere expediency or policy. I mean only, in this form, to express an earnest conviction that the court has departed from the familiar rule requiring, in the interpretation of constitutional provisions, that full effect be given to the intent with which they were adopted.

The purpose of the first section of the act of congress of March 1, 1875, was to prevent race discrimination. It does not assume to define the general conditions and limitations under which inns, public conveyances, and places of public amusement may be conducted, but only declares that such conditions and limitations, whatever they may be, shall not be applied, by way of discrimination, on account of race, color, or previous condition of servitude. The second section provides a penalty against any one denying, or aiding or inciting the denial, to any citizen that equality of right given by the first section, except for reasons by law applicable to citizens of every race or color, and regardless of any previous condition of servitude.

There seems to be no substantial difference between my brethren and myself as to what was the purpose of congress; for they say that the essence of the law is, not to declare broadly that all persons shall be entitled to the full and equal enjoyment of the accommodations, advantages, facilities, and privileges of inns, public conveyances, and theaters, but that such enjoyment shall not be subject to any conditions applicable only to citizens of a particular race or color, or who had been in a previous condition of servitude. The effect of the statute, the court says, is that colored citizens, whether formerly slaves or not, and citizens of other races, shall have the same accommodations and privileges in all inns, public conveyances, and places of amusement as are enjoyed by white persons, and vice versa.

The court adjudges that congress is without power, under either the thirteenth or fourteenth amendment, to establish such regulations, and that the first and second sections of the statute are, in all their parts, unconstitutional and void....

The terms of the thirteenth amendment are absolute and universal.... No race, as such, can be excluded from the benefits or rights thereby conferred. Yet it is historically true that that amendment was suggested by the condition, in this country, of that race which had been declared by this court to have had, according to the opinion entertained by the most civilized portion of the white race at the time of the adoption of the constitution, "no rights which the white man was bound to respect," none of the privileges or immunities secured by that instrument to citizens of the United States. It had reference, in a peculiar sense, to a people which (although the larger part of them were in slavery) had been invited by an act of congress to aid, by their strong right arms, in saving from overthrow a government which, theretofore, by all of its departments, had treated them as an inferior race, with no legal rights or privileges except such as the white race might choose to grant them....

That there are burdens and disabilities which constitute badges of slavery and servitude, and that the express power delegated to congress to enforce, by appropriate legislation, the thirteenth amendment, may be exerted by legislation of a direct and primary character, for the eradication, not simply of the institution, but of its badges and incidents, are propositions which ought to be deemed indisputable. They lie at the very foundation of the civil rights act of 1866. Whether that act was fully authorized by the thirteenth amendment alone, without the support which it afterwards received from the fourteenth amendment, after the adoption of which it was re-enacted with some additions, the court, in its opinion, says it is unnecessary to inquire. But I submit,...that its constitutionality is conclusively shown by other portions of their opinion. It is expressly conceded by them that the thirteenth amendment established freedom; that there are burdens and disabilities, the necessary incidents of slavery, which constitute its substance and visible form; that congress, by the act of 1866, passed in view of the thirteenth amendment, before the fourteenth was adopted, undertook to remove certain burdens and disabilities, the necessary incidents of slavery, and to secure to all citizens of every race and color, and without regard to previous servitude, those fundamental rights which are the essence of civil freedom, namely, the same right to make and enforce contracts, to sue, be parties, give evidence, and to inherit, purchase, lease, sell, and convey property as is enjoyed by white citizens; that under the thirteenth amendment congress has to do with slavery and its incidents; and that legislation, so far as necessary or proper to eradicate all forms and incidents of slavery and involuntary servitude, may be direct and primary, operating upon the acts of individuals, whether sanctioned by state legislation or not. These propositions being conceded, it is impossible, as it seems to me, to question the constitutional validity of the civil rights act of 1866. I do not contend that the thirteenth amendment invests congress with authority, by legislation, to regulate the entire body of the civil rights which citizens enjoy, or may enjoy, in the several states. But I do hold that since slavery,...was the moving or principal cause of the adoption of that amendment, and since that institution rested wholly upon the inferiority, as a race, of those held in bondage, their freedom necessarily involved immunity from, and protection against, all discrimination against them, because of their race, in respect of such civil rights as belong to freemen of other races. Congress, therefore, under its express power to enforce that amendment, by appropriate legislation, may enact laws to protect that people against the deprivation, on account of their race, of any civil rights enjoyed by other freemen in the same state; and such legislation may be of a direct and primary character, operating upon states, their officers and agents, and also upon, at least, such individuals and corporations as exercise public functions and wield power and authority under the state....

What has been said is sufficient to show that the power of congress under the thirteenth amendment is not necessarily restricted to legislation against slavery as an institution upheld by positive law, but

may be exerted to the extent at least of protecting the race, so liberated, against discrimination, in respect of legal rights belonging to freemen, where such discrimination is based upon race....

As to places of public amusement. It may be argued that the managers of such places have no duties to perform with which the public are, in any legal sense, concerned, or with which the public have any right to interfere; and that the exclusion of a black man from a place of public amusement on account of his race, or the denial to him, on that ground, of equal accommodations at such places, violates no legal right for the vindication of which he may invoke the aid of the courts. My answer to that argument is that places of public amusement, within the meaning of the act of 1875, are such as are established and maintained under direct license of the law. The authority to establish and maintain them comes from the public. The colored race is a part of that public....

But of what value is this right of locomotion, if it may be clogged by such burdens as congress intended by the act of 1875 to remove? They are burdens which lay at the very foundation of the institution of slavery as it once existed. They are not to be sustained, except upon the assumption that ... that, deprived of their enjoyment, in common with others, a freeman is not only branded as one inferior and infected, but, in the competitions of life, is robbed of some of the most necessary means of existence; and all this solely because they belong to a particular race which the nation has liberated. The thirteenth amendment alone obliterated the race line, so far as all rights fundamental in a state of freedom are concerned.

I am of opinion that such discrimination is a badge of servitude, the imposition of which congress may prevent under its power...to enforce the thirteenth amendment; and consequently, without reference to its enlarged power under the fourteenth amendment, the act of March 1, 1875, is not, in my judgment, repugnant to the constitution.

It remains now to consider these cases with reference to the power congress has possessed since the adoption of the fourteenth amendment.

Before the adoption of the recent amendments it had become...the established doctrine of this court that negroes, whose ancestors had been imported and sold as slaves, could not become citizens of a state, or even of the United States, with the rights and privileges guaranteed to citizens by the national constitution; further, that one might have all the rights and privileges of a citizen of a state without being a citizen in the sense in which that word was used in the national constitution, and without being entitled to the privileges and immunities of citizens of the several states. Still further, between the adoption of the thirteenth amendment and the proposal by congress of the fourteenth amendment, on June 16, 1866, the statute-books of several of the states … had become loaded down with enactments which, under the guise of apprentice, vagrant, and contract regulations, sought to keep the colored race in a condition, practically, of servitude. It was openly announced that whatever rights persons of that race might have as freemen, under the guaranties of the national constitution, they could not become citizens of a state, with the rights belonging to citizens, except by the consent of such state; consequently, that their civil rights, as citizens of the state, depended entirely upon state legislation. To meet this new peril to the black race, that the purposes of the nation might not be doubted or defeated, and by way of further enlargement of the power of congress, the fourteenth amendment was proposed for adoption.…

The citizenship thus acquired by that race … may be protected, not alone by the judicial branch of the government, but by congressional legislation of a primary direct character; this, because the power of congress is not restricted to the enforcement of prohibitions upon state laws or state action. It is, in terms distinct and positive, to enforce "the provisions of this article" of amendment; not simply those of a prohibitive character, but the provisions,… affirmative and prohibitive, of the amendment. It is, therefore, a grave misconception to suppose that the fifth section of the amendment has reference exclusively to express prohibitions upon state laws or state action. If any right was created by that amendment, the grant of power, through appropriate legislation, to enforce its provisions authorizes congress, by means of legislation operating throughout the entire Union, to guard, secure, and protect that right.

It is, therefore, an essential inquiry what, if any, right, privilege, or immunity was given by the nation to colored persons when they were made citizens of the state in which they reside?…That they became entitled, upon the adoption of the fourteenth amendment, "to all privileges and immunities of citizens in the several states,"… no one, I suppose, will for a moment question. What are the privileges and immunities to which, by that clause of the constitution, they became entitled? To this it may be answered, generally, upon the authority of the adjudged cases, that they are those which are fundamental in citizenship in a free government, "common to the citizens in the latter states under their consti-

tutions and laws by virtue of their being citizens." Of that provision it has been said, with the approval of this court, that no other one in the constitution has tended so strongly to constitute the citizens of the United States one people.…

Although this court has wisely forborne any attempt, by a comprehensive definition, to indicate all the privileges and immunities to which the citizens of each state are entitled of right to enjoy in the several states, I hazard nothing,… in saying that no state can sustain her denial to colored citizens of other states, while within her limits, of privileges or immunities, fundamental in republican citizenship, upon the ground that she accords such privileges and immunities only to her white citizens and withholds them from her colored citizens. The colored citizens of other states, within the jurisdiction of that state, could claim, under the constitution, every privilege and immunity which that state secures to her white citizens. Otherwise, it would be in the power of any state, by discriminating class legislation against its own citizens of a particular race or color, to withhold from citizens of other states, belonging to that proscribed race, when within her limits, privileges and immunities of the character regarded by all courts as fundamental in citizenship; and that, too, when the constitutional guaranty is that the citizens of each state shall be entitled to "all privileges and immunities of citizens of the several states." No state may, by discrimination against a portion of its own citizens of a particular race, in respect of privileges and immunities fundamental in citizenship, impair the constitutional right of citizens of other states, of whatever race, to enjoy in that state all such privileges and immunities as are there accorded to her most favored citizens. A colored citizen of Ohio or Indiana, being in the jurisdiction of Tennessee, is entitled to enjoy any privilege or immunity, fundamental in citizenship, which is given to citizens of the white race in the latter state.…

But what was secured to colored citizens of the United States…by the grant to them of state citizenship? With what rights, privileges, or immunities did this grant from the nation invest them? There is one, if there be no others—exemption from race discrimination in respect of any civil right belonging to citizens of the white race in the same state. That, surely, is their constitutional privilege when within the jurisdiction of other states.… Citizenship in this country necessarily imports equality of civil rights among citizens of every race in the same state. It is fundamental in American citizenship that, in respect of such rights, there shall be no discrimination by the state, or its officers, or by individuals, or corporations exercising public functions or authority, against any citizen because of his race or previous condition of servitude.... If, then, exemption from discrimination in respect of civil rights is a new constitutional right, secured by the grant of state citizenship to colored citizens of the United States, why may not the nation, by means of its own legislation of a primary direct character, guard, protect, and enforce that right? It is a right and privilege which the nation conferred. It did not come from the states in which those colored citizens reside. It has been the established doctrine of this court during all its history, accepted as vital to the national supremacy, that congress, in the absence of a positive delegation of power to the state legislatures, may by legislation enforce and protect any right derived from or created by the national constitution....

It was perfectly well known that the great danger to the equal enjoyment by citizens of their rights, as citizens, was to be apprehended, not altogether from unfriendly state legislation, but from the hostile action of corporations and individuals in the states....

My brethren say that when a man has emerged from slavery, and by the aid of beneficent legislation has shaken off the inseparable concomitants of that state, there must be some stage in the progress of his elevation when he takes the rank of a mere citizen, and ceases to be the special favorite of the laws, and when his rights as a citizen, or a man, are to be protected in the ordinary modes by which other men's rights are protected. It is, I submit, scarcely just to say that the colored race has been the special favorite of the laws. What the nation, through congress, has sought to accomplish in reference to that race is, what had already been done in every state in the Union for the white race, to secure and protect rights belonging to them as freemen and citizens; nothing more. The one underlying purpose of congressional legislation has been to enable the black race to take the rank of mere citizens. The difficulty has been to compel a recognition of their legal right to take that rank, and to secure the enjoyment of privileges belonging, under the law, to them as a component part of the people for whose welfare and happiness government is ordained. At every step in this direction the nation has been confronted with class tyranny, which a contemporary English historian says is, of all tyrannies, the most intolerable.... To-day it is the colored race which is denied, by corporations and individuals wielding public authority, rights fundamental in their freedom and citizenship. At some future time it may be some other race that will fall under the ban. If the constitutional amendments be enforced, according to the intent with which, as I conceive, they were adopted, there cannot be, in this republic, any class of human beings in practical subjection to another class, with power in the latter to dole out to the former just such privileges as they may choose to grant. The supreme law of the land has decreed that no authority shall be exercised in this country upon the basis of discrimination, in respect of civil rights, against freemen and citizens because of their race, color, or previous condition of servitude. To that decree ... every one must bow, whatever may have been, or whatever now are, his individual views as to the wisdom or policy, either of the recent changes in the fundamental law, or of the legislation which has been enacted to give them effect.

Glossary

beneficent	kind, producing good
concomitants	things that accompany or are related to something else
forborne	refrained
incidents	accompaniments
previous condition of servitude	slavery; used to refer to the status of former slaves
privileges and immunities	a legal term referring to Article IV of the Constitution, which requires that a citizen in one state be considered equal to a citizen in any other state with regard to U.S. citizenship rights

HURTADO V. CALIFORNIA (1884)

Harlan dissent

According to the settled usages and modes of proceeding existing under the common and statute law of England at the settlement of this country, information in capital cases was not consistent with the "law of the land" or with "due process of law." Such was the understanding of the patriotic men who established free institutions upon this continent. Almost the identical words of Magna Charta were incorporated into most of the state constitutions before the adoption of our national constitution. When they declared, in substance, that no person shall be deprived of life, liberty, or property except by the judgment of his peers or the law of the land, they intended to assert his right to the same guaranties that were given in the mother country by the great charter and the laws passed in furtherance of its fundamental principles.

My brethren concede that there are principles of liberty and justice lying at the foundation of our civil and political institutions which no state can violate consistently with that due process of law required by the fourteenth amendment in proceedings involving life, liberty, or property. Some of these principles are enumerated in the opinion of the court. But for reasons which do not impress my mind as satisfactory, they exclude from that enumeration the exemption from prosecution, by information, for a public offense involving life. By what authority is that exclusion made?…If it be supposed that immunity from prosecution for a capital offense, except upon the presentment or indictment of a grand jury, was regarded at the common law any less secured by the law of the land, or any less valuable, or any less essential to due process of law, than the personal rights and immunities just enumerated, I take leave to say that no such distinction is authorized by any adjudged case, determined in England or in this country prior to the adoption of our constitution, or by any elementary writer upon the principles established by Magna Charta and the statutes subsequently enacted in explanation or enlargement of its provisions.

But it is said that the framers of the constitution did not suppose that due process of law necessarily required for a capital offense the institution and procedure of a grand jury, else they would not in the same amendment prohibiting the deprivation of life, liberty, or property without due process of law, have made specific and express provision for a grand jury where the crime is capital or otherwise infamous; therefore, it is argued, the requirement by the fourteenth amendment of due process of law in all proceedings involving life, liberty, and property, without specific reference to grand juries in any case whatever, was not intended as a restriction upon the power which it is claimed the states previously had, so far as the express restrictions of the national constitution are concerned, to dispense altogether with grand juries. This line of argument…would lead to results which are inconsistent with the vital principles of republican government. If the presence in the fifth amendment of a specific provision for grand juries in capital cases…is held to prove that "due process of law" did not, in the judgment of the framers of the constitution, necessarily require a grand jury in capital cases, inexorable logic would require it to be likewise held that the right not to be put twice in jeopardy of life and limb, for the same offense, nor compelled in a criminal case to testify against one's self,—rights and immunities also specifically recognized in the fifth amendment—were not protected by that due process of law required by the settled usages and proceedings existing under the common and statute law of England at the settlement of this country.…It seems to me that too much stress is put upon the fact that the framers of the constitution made express provision for the security of those rights which at common law were protected by the requirement of due process of law, and, in addition, declared, generally, that no person shall "be deprived of life, liberty, or property without due process of law." The rights, for the security of which these express provisions were made, were of a character so essential to the safety of the people that it was deemed wise to avoid the possibility that congress…would impair or destroy them. Hence, their specific enumeration in the earlier amendments of the constitution, in connection with the general requirement of due process of law.…

It is said by the court that the constitution of the United States was made for an undefined and expanding future, and that its requirement of due process of law, in proceedings involving life, liberty, and property, must be so interpreted as not to deny to the law the capacity of progress and improvement; that the greatest security for the fundamental principles of justice resides in the right of the people to make their own laws and alter them at pleasure. It is difficult, however, to perceive anything in the system of prosecuting human beings for their lives, by information, which suggests that the state which adopts it has entered upon an era of progress and improvement in the law of criminal procedure....

When the fourteenth amendment was adopted all the states of the Union…declared, in their constitution, that no person shall be deprived of life, liberty, or property otherwise than "by the judgment of his peers or the law of the land," or "without due process of law." When that amendment was adopted the constitution of each state, with few exceptions, contained, and still contains, a bill of rights, enumerating the rights of life, liberty, and property, which cannot be impaired or destroyed by the legislative department.... It may be safely affirmed that, when that amendment

was adopted, a criminal prosecution, by information, for a crime involving life, was not permitted in any one of the states composing the Union. So that the court, in this case, while conceding that the requirement of due process of law protects the fundamental principles of liberty and justice, adjudges, in effect, that an immunity or right, recognized at the common law to be essential to personal security, jealously guarded by our national constitution against violation by any tribunal or body exercising authority under the general government, and expressly or impliedly recognized, when the fourteenth amendment was adopted, in the bill of rights or constitution of every state in the Union, is yet not a fundamental principle in governments established, as those of the states of the Union are, to secure to the citizen liberty and justice, and therefore is not involved in due process of law as required by that amendment in proceedings conducted under the sanction of a state. My sense of duty constrains me to dissent from this interpretation of the supreme law of the land.

POLLOCK V. FARMERS' LOAN & TRUST CO. (1895)

Harlan dissent

It is appropriate now to say that, however objectionable the law would have been, after the provision for taxing incomes arising from rents was stricken out, I did not then, nor do I now, think it within the province of the court to annul the provisions relating to incomes derived from other specified sources, and take from the government the entire revenue contemplated to be raised by the taxation of incomes, simply because the clause relating to rents was held to be unconstitutional....

It thus appears that the primary object of all taxation by the general government is to pay the debts and provide for the common defense and general welfare of the United States, and that, with the exception of the inhibition upon taxes or duties on articles exported from the states, no restriction is in terms imposed upon national taxation, except that direct taxes must be apportioned among the several states on the basis of numbers,...while duties, imposts, and excises must be uniform throughout the United States....

Since the Hylton Case was decided this country has gone through two great wars, under legislation based on the principles of constitutional law previously announced by this court. The recent Civil War, involving the very existence of the nation, was brought to a successful end, and the authority of the Union restored, in part, by the use of vast amounts of money raised under statutes imposing duties on incomes derived from every kind of property, real and personal, not by the unequal rule of apportionment among the states on the basis of numbers, but by the rule of uniformity, operating upon individuals and corporations in all the states. And we are now asked to declare...that the enormous sums thus taken from the people...were taken in violation of the supreme law of the land. The supremacy of the nation was re-established against armed rebellion seeking to destroy its life, but it seems that that consummation, so devoutly wished, and to effect which so many valuable lives were sacrificed, was attended with a disregard of the constitution by which the Union was ordained....It is necessary that the power of the general legislature should extend to all the objects of taxation; that government should be able to command

all the resources of the country,—because no man can tell what our exigencies may be....

I have a deep, abiding conviction, which my sense of duty compels me to express, that it is not possible for this court to have rendered any judgment more to be regretted than the one just rendered.

In my judgment ... this decision may well excite the gravest apprehensions. It strikes at the very foundations of national authority, in that it denies to the general government a power which is or may become vital to the very existence and preservation of the Union in a national emergency....

Why do I say that the decision just rendered impairs or menaces the national authority?... In its practical operation this decision withdraws from national taxation not only all incomes derived from real estate, but tangible personal property, "invested personal property, bonds, stocks, investments of all kinds," and the income that may be derived from such property. This results from the fact that, by the decision of the court, all such personal property and all incomes from real estate and personal property are placed beyond national taxation otherwise than by apportionment among the states on the basis simply of population. No such apportionment can possibly be made without doing gross injustice to the many for the benefit of the favored few in particular states.... When, therefore, this court adjudges, as it does now adjudge, that congress cannot impose a duty or tax upon personal property, or upon income arising either from rents of real estate or from personal property, including invested personal property, bonds, stocks, and investments of all kinds, except by apportioning the sum to be so raised among the states according to population, it practically decides that, without an amendment of the constitution,...such property and incomes can never be made to contribute to the support of the national government....

The decision now made may provoke a contest in this country from which the American people would have been spared if the court had not overturned its former adjudications, and had adhered to the principles of taxation under which our government, following the repeated adjudications of this court, has always been administered....By its present construction of the constitution, the court, for the first time in all its history, declares that our government has been so framed that, in matters of taxation for its support and maintenance, those who have incomes derived from the renting of real estate, or from the leasing or using of tangible personal property, or who own invested personal property, bonds, stocks, and investments of whatever kind, have privileges that cannot be accorded to those having incomes derived from the labor of their hands, or the exercise of their skill, or the use of their brains....And it is now the law, as this day declared, that under the constitution, however urgent may be the needs of the government,...congress cannot tax the personal property of the country, nor the income arising either from real estate or from invested personal property, except by a tax apportioned among the states, on the basis of their population, while it may compel the merchant, the artisan, the workman, the artist, the author, the lawyer, the physician, even the minister of the Gospel, no one of whom happens to own real estate, invested personal property, stocks, or bonds, to contribute directly from their respective earnings, gains, and profits, and under the rule of uniformity or equality, for the support of the government....

It was said in argument that the passage of the statute imposing this income tax was an assault by the poor upon the rich, and by much eloquent speech this court has been urged to stand in the breach for the protection of the just rights of property against the advancing hosts of socialism. With the policy of legislation of this character the court has nothing to do. That is for the legislative branch of the government.... With that determination, so far as it rests upon grounds of expediency or public policy, the courts can have no rightful concern....There is no foundation for the charge that this statute was framed in sheer hostility to the wealth of the country. The provisions most liable to objection are those exempting from taxation large amounts of accumulated capital, particularly that represented by savings banks, mutual insurance companies, and loan associations. Surely, such exemptions do not indicate sympathy on the part of the legislative branch of the government with the pernicious theories of socialism, nor show that congress had any purpose to despoil the rich....

I may say ... that the real friends of property are not those who would exempt the wealth of the country from bearing its fair share of the burdens of taxation, but rather those who seek to have every one, without reference to his locality contribute from his substance, upon terms of equality with all others, to the support of the government. There is nothing in the nature of an income tax per se that justifies judicial opposition to it upon the ground that it illegally discriminates against the rich, or imposes undue burdens upon that class. There is no tax which, in its essence, is more just and equitable than an income tax....

The vast powers committed to the present government may be abused, and taxes may be imposed by congress which the public necessities do not in fact require, or which may be forbidden by a wise policy. But the remedy for such abuses is to be found at the ballot box, and in a wholesome public opinion, which the representatives of the people will not long, if at all, disregard, and not in the disregard by the judiciary of powers that have been committed to another branch of the government....

I cannot assent to an interpretation of the constitution that impairs and cripples the just powers of the national government in the essential matter of taxation, and at the same time discriminates against the greater part of the people of our country.

Glossary

adjudications	judgments by a court
construction	interpretation
consummation, so devoutly wished	an allusion to the monologue of Hamlet in William Shakespeare's play of that title
direct taxes	taxes levied directly on individuals and business
duties, imposts, and excises	taxes on imported goods
exigencies	emergencies, urgent needs
hosts of socialism	multitudes of people who support Socialist views, such as the abolition of private property, redistribution of wealth, and opposition to the monied classes

PLESSY V. FERGUSON (1896)

Harlan dissent

In respect of civil rights, common to all citizens, the constitution of the United States does not, I think, permit any public authority to know the race of those entitled to be protected in the enjoyment of such rights. Every true man has pride of race, and under appropriate circumstances, when the rights of others, his equals before the law, are not to be affected, it is his privilege to express such pride and to take such action based upon it as to him seems proper. But I deny that any legislative body or judicial tribunal may have regard to the race of citizens when the civil rights of those citizens are involved. Indeed, such legislation as that here in question is inconsistent not only with that equality of rights which pertains to citizenship, national and state, but with the personal liberty enjoyed by every one within the United States.

The thirteenth amendment does not permit the withholding or the deprivation of any right necessarily inhering in freedom. It not only struck down the institution of slavery as previously existing in the United States, but it prevents the imposition of any burdens or disabilities that constitute badges of slavery or servitude. It decreed universal civil freedom in this country....But, that amendment having been found inadequate to the protection of the rights of those who had been in slavery, it was followed by the fourteenth amendment, which added greatly to the dignity and glory of American citizenship, and to the security of personal liberty, by declaring that "all persons born or naturalized in the United States, and subject to the jurisdiction thereof, are citizens of the United States and of the state wherein they reside," and that "no state shall make or enforce any law which shall abridge the privileges or immunities of citizens of the United States; nor shall any state deprive any person of life, liberty or property without due process of law, nor deny to any person within its jurisdiction the equal protection of the laws." These two amendments, if enforced according to their true intent and meaning, will protect all the civil rights that pertain to freedom and citizenship....

It was said in argument that the statute of Louisiana does not discriminate against either race, but prescribes a rule applicable alike to white and colored citizens. But this argument does not meet the difficulty. Every one knows that the statute in question had its origin in the purpose, not so much to exclude white persons from railroad cars occupied by blacks, as to exclude colored people from coaches occupied by or assigned to white persons.... The thing to accomplish was, under the guise of giving equal accommodation for whites and blacks, to compel the latter to keep to themselves while traveling in railroad passenger coaches.... The fundamental objection, therefore, to the statute, is that it interferes with the personal freedom of citizens. "Personal liberty," it has been well said, "consists in the power of locomotion, of changing situation, or removing one's person to whatsoever places one's own inclination may direct, without imprisonment or restraint, unless by due course of law."... If a white man and a black man choose to occupy the same public conveyance on a public highway, it is their right to do so; and no government, proceeding alone on grounds of race, can prevent it without infringing the personal liberty of each.

It is one thing for railroad carriers to furnish, or to be required by law to furnish, equal accommodations for all whom they are under a legal duty to carry. It is quite another thing for government to forbid citizens of the white and black races from traveling in the same public conveyance, and to punish officers of railroad companies for permitting persons of the two races to occupy the same passenger coach. If a state can prescribe, as a rule of civil conduct, that whites and blacks shall not travel as passengers in the same railroad coach, why may it not so regulate the use of the streets of its cities and towns as to compel white citizens to keep on one side of a street, and black citizens to keep on the other?...

The white race deems itself to be the dominant race in this country. And so it is, in prestige, in achievements, in education, in wealth, and in power....But in view of the constitution, in the eye of the law, there is in this country no superior, dominant, ruling class of citizens. There is no caste here. Our constitution is color-blind, and neither knows nor tolerates classes among citizens. In respect of civil rights, all citizens are equal before the law....In my opinion, the judgment this day rendered will, in time, prove to be quite as pernicious as the decision made by this tribunal in the *Dred Scott* Case....

The recent amendments of the constitution, it was supposed, had eradicated these principles from our institutions. But it seems that we have yet, in some of the states, a dominant race…which assumes to regulate the enjoyment of civil rights, common to all citizens, upon the basis of race. The present decision… will not only stimulate aggressions, more or less brutal and irritating, upon the admitted rights of colored citizens, but will encourage the belief that it is possible, by means of state enactments, to defeat the beneficent purposes which the people of the United States had in view when they adopted the recent amendments of the constitution, by one of which the blacks of this country were made citizens of the United States and of the states in which they respectively reside, and whose privileges and immunities, as citizens, the states are forbidden to abridge.…The destinies of the two races, in this country, are indissolubly linked together, and the interests of both require that the common government of all shall not permit the seeds of race hate to be planted under the sanction of law.…

The arbitrary separation of citizens, on the basis of race, while they are on a public highway, is a badge of servitude wholly inconsistent with the civil freedom and the equality before the law established by the constitution. It cannot be justified upon any legal grounds.

I am of opinion that the state of Louisiana is inconsistent with the personal liberty of citizens, white and black, in that state, and hostile to both the spirit and letter of the constitution of the United States. If laws of like character should be enacted in the several states of the Union, the effect would be in the highest degree mischievous. Slavery, as an institution tolerated by law, would, it is true, have disappeared from our country; but there would remain a power in the states, by sinister legislation, to interfere with the full enjoyment of the blessings of freedom, to regulate civil rights, common to all citizens, upon the basis of race, and to place in a condition of legal inferiority a large body of American citizens, now constituting a part of the political community, called the "People of the United States," for whom, and by whom through representatives, our government is administered. Such a system is inconsistent with the guaranty given by the constitution to each state of a republican form of government, and may be stricken down by congressional action, or by the courts in the discharge of their solemn duty to maintain the supreme law of the land, anything in the constitution or laws of any state to the contrary notwithstanding.

Glossary

caste	a system of laws or customs that divides people on the basis of prestige or social class
***Dred Scott* Case**	the U.S. Supreme Court case *Dred Scott v. Sandford* (1857), in which the Court ruled that African Americans were not citizens of the United States
pernicious	tending toward evil

Patrick Henry (AP/Wide World Photos)

PATRICK HENRY   1736–1799

Orator and Founding Father

Featured Documents
◆ Resolutions in Opposition to the Stamp Act (1765)
◆ Letter to Robert Pleasants, a Quaker, Concerning Slavery (1773)
◆ Speech to the First Continental Congress (1774)
◆ Speech to the Virginia Revolutionary Convention in Opposition to the Intolerable Acts (1775)
◆ Speech to the Virginia Convention Opposing the Constitution (1788)
◆ Election Speech at Charlotte Court House (1799)

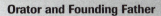

Overview

Patrick Henry was one of the most admired leaders of the American Revolution, considered by contemporaries as an indispensible instigator of revolution. He is remembered best for his passionate speeches calling his countrymen to defense of liberty against what he saw as British oppression. Both contemporary and modern observers have noted that Henry's style tended to mimic that of the "New Light" evangelical ministers who were making progress against Virginia's established Anglican Church in the mid-eighteenth century. Unfortunately, Henry does not enjoy the reputation that he probably deserves as a Founding Father for two reasons. First, since Henry's greatest influence was in his dramatic oratory and his speeches were at best imperfectly recorded—and by all accounts even a full transcript could not do justice to his eloquence—the warp and woof of his contribution began to dissipate with his words. Second, and perhaps even more important, when the Philadelphia Convention drafted the Constitution in 1787 to address growing fiscal and administrative problems under the Articles of Confederation, Henry opposed the Constitution in its excessive concentration of power (declaring, so it is said, that he refused a seat in the Convention because "I smelt a rat"). He never served in a national office under the Constitution, although he was offered a position in George Washington's cabinet and on the Supreme Court. With the new nation's success, Henry's opposition seemed anachronistic. Yet, even in this role, his contribution was significant, with the opposition of Henry and others to the new Constitution playing a key part in encouraging adoption of the Bill of Rights in 1791.

Henry was born on May 29, 1736, the second son of John Henry, a member of the lesser gentry. John Henry's success never matched his ambition, and Patrick grew up without a formal education and with a persistent aspiration to maintain himself in the manner of Virginia's landed gentry but also a deep sympathy for the common man. Henry initially failed as a merchant and farmer, spending some time keeping tavern with his father-in-law before he read the law and recognized his oratorical genius. In later life, as a successful planter, Henry was a slave owner, but as his 1773 letter to Robert Pleasants makes clear, he recognized

the moral reprehensibility of the practice and its inconsistency with the professed principles of the Revolution. Still, like many of his fellow gentry, Henry only bewailed his own failure to address slavery.

As an unknown lawyer, Henry came to fame in 1763 in his statement to the jury in the Parson's Cause by arguing against an Anglican minister seeking compensation for back pay under Virginia's system of state-supported religion. Using the philosopher John Locke's "social compact" theory, Henry urged that a king who acted against his people's interest by refusing consent to a law that limited clergy salaries in times of economic distress was a "Tyrant"— not for the last time to cries of "treason" from the assembled audience—and ministers who demanded excessive pay were "rapacious harpies." Henry persuaded the jury to award one penny in damages. This populist success launched Henry's political career. In 1765, in his first term in office, Henry led the effort to introduce resolutions in the Virginia House of Burgesses condemning the Stamp Act. The Stamp Act, passed by the British Parliament, required that any formally written or printed document appear on stamped paper issued by English agents. While only five of the seven resolutions Henry had prepared were adopted (the most vehement not being considered) and the next day, after Henry departed, the House withdrew the fifth resolution as excessive, all or most of the resolutions were published throughout the colonies, propelling Henry to even greater prominence.

Henry joined Virginia's delegation to the First Continental Congress in 1774 and there unsuccessfully urged military preparedness. Back in Virginia, he renewed that theme in early 1775 with his famous "give me liberty or give me death" speech. Henry played a key role in formation of the Commonwealth of Virginia and, as Virginia's first governor, from 1776 to 1779, was forced to grapple with the difficulty of mobilizing America's most populous state for a strenuous war effort. After the war, when the new Constitution was proposed to remedy defects in the Articles of Confederation, Henry opposed it as an excessive consolidation of power and urged at least that amendments be adopted to protect individual freedoms. Henry was called out of retirement in 1799 by George Washington to counter threats to the union posed by the opposition of radical Republicans—

1736

■ **May 29**
Patrick Henry is born in
Hanover County, Virginia.

1760

■ Henry passes an oral
examination to be licensed
to practice law.

1763

■ **December 1**
Henry successfully
represents the Louisa
County (Virginia) vestry in
the Parson's Cause; the
Reverend James Maury,
seeking back pay, is
awarded one penny in
damages.

1765

■ **May**
Louisa County elects
Henry to the Virginia
House of Burgesses.

■ **May 29–30**
Henry offers resolutions in
opposition to the Stamp
Act and makes his "Caesar
had his Brutus" speech to
cries of "Treason."

1774

■ **September 5**
Henry, a member of
Virginia's delegation to the
First Continental Congress,
urges united opposition to
Britain, declaring "I am not
a Virginian, but an
American."

1775

■ **March 23**
Calling for military
preparedness, Henry
delivers his "give me
liberty or give me death"
speech to the Virginia
Convention meeting in
Saint John's Church in
Richmond.

■ **May**
Hanover and other militia
under the command of
Henry march on
Williamsburg to demand
return of gunpowder
seized by British Governor
Lord Dunmore or
compensation.

including Thomas Jefferson and James Madison—to Federalist policies, particularly the Alien and Sedition Acts, enacted during the so-called Quasi War with France precipitated by French attacks on U.S. shipping, at a time of international crisis in a climate of fear of domestic subversion. The acts gave the president the authority to deport "dangerous" aliens and imposed criminal penalties for scandalous or false writings against the government. Henry died before he could again take his seat in the Assembly. After his death, a note was found with Henry's papers giving his last admonition to the American people: "Whether this [American independence] will prove a blessing or a curse, will depend upon the use our people make of the blessings which a gracious God hath bestowed on us.... Righteousness alone can exalt them as a nation. Reader! whoever thou art, remember this; and in thy sphere practise virtue thyself, and encourage it in others" (Henry, 1891, vol. 2, p. 632).

Explanation and Analysis of Documents

Henry rose to prominence in Virginia during a period when conflicts between the colony (and its sister colonies) and Great Britain were growing increasingly heated. Almost always championing the cause of the common man, Henry insisted both that government owed a duty to its citizens and that excessive government threatened individual liberty. With his unparalleled oratorical skills, Henry became a key defender of religious liberty, freedom of speech, and government responsiveness to citizen interests and violently opposed anything that he saw as government tyranny; as such, many contemporaries credit Henry as being among the key instigators of revolution. After the war, he led opposition to consolidation of power in a national government and refused various proffered offices under the U.S. government. In 1799 Henry was called out of retirement by George Washington in the face of a threat of disunion brought on by the opposition of Thomas Jefferson's supporters to the Federalist Alien and Sedition Acts. In each of his important contributions, his speeches—rather than written documents or letters—take pride of place and evidence a consistent theme of the preservation of liberty.

◆ **Resolutions in Opposition to the Stamp Act**

Based largely on his popularity arising from the Parson's Cause, Henry was first elected to the House of Burgesses in 1765. The timing was auspicious. After Britain had won the Seven Years' War in 1763, it faced a massive burden of debt and sought to retrieve some of its cost from the American colonies without waiting for the colonies to grant funds, as had occurred in the past. British imposition of a "stamp tax" in 1765 on all legal documents, commercial shipping documents, newspapers and even playing cards, led to an outcry against "taxation without representation."

Senior members of Virginia's hierarchy had supported staid petitions to Parliament asking that the proposed Stamp Act not be adopted, but word arrived during the

1765 assembly session that their protests had not been heard and taxes would be imposed. Henry, having joined the House of Burgesses on May 20, waited until late in the legislative session and then brought to the Committee of the Whole House on May 29, 1765, a set of resolutions building upon the petition that had been adopted in December 1764 and forcefully challenging Parliament's authority (and implicitly challenging control of the House by its senior members). After a heated debate, Henry's proposed preamble was deleted, but five of seven resolutions were adopted by the House on May 30, the last by a single vote, reportedly leading the conservative speaker of the House, Peyton Randolph, to declare "By God, I would have given 500 guineas for a single vote" (Morgan and Morgan, p. 125). Henry left for home that evening, and the next day a further reduced House withdrew the fifth resolution.

Before the final vote in Virginia, Henry and his allies apparently sent copies of the draft resolutions to newspapers throughout the colonies. The result was that several newspapers printed all seven resolutions (including two so violently opposed to parliamentary authority that Henry had not even offered them in the Virginia House), and a number of newspapers printed six or five resolutions; few people recognized that Virginia ultimately supported only four. The net effect was to inflame colonial opposition to Britain, encourage similar resolutions in several colonies, and feed Henry's fame as a defender of American liberty.

Even today, the lineage of the resolutions is somewhat unclear. While resolutions closely resembling the first four resolutions published in the *Maryland Gazette* (those given here) were adopted by the Virginia House of Burgesses, there is some question as to the nature of the fifth resolution initially adopted and as to the origin of the two additional resolutions (in light of the fact that a document in Henry's hand found with his papers refers to only the first five resolutions). The best surmise is that the fifth resolution was adopted and withdrawn the next day, after Henry's departure, and that Henry was prepared to offer the even more strident sixth and seventh resolutions but decided not to do so given that the fifth had barely passed. (Governor Francis Fauquier reported to authorities in England that the radicals had two additional, more violent resolutions that they had decided to withhold.)

Of course, Henry supported his proposed resolves with another passionate speech. While there is no official report of his speech, and accounts vary, by all accounts Henry spellbound the burgesses. John Tyler, Sr. (father of the future president John Tyler, Jr.) made this report of Henry's speech:

> While descanting on the tyranny of the obnoxious Act, [he] exclaimed in a voice and with a gesture which startled the House: "Tarquin and Caesar had each his Brutus, Charles the First his Cromwell, and George the Third"—"Treason!" shouted the Speaker. "Treason! Treason!" echoed from every part of the House. Without faltering for an instant, but rising to a loftier attitude, and fixing on the Speaker an eye which seemed to flash fire, Mr. Henry added, with

	Time Line
1776	■ **June–July** Henry is a member of the convention drafting Virginia's Declaration of Rights and constitution and is elected first governor of the Commonwealth of Virginia.
1784	■ Henry leads an unsuccessful effort in the Virginia General Assembly for adoption of a general assessment to benefit all Christian religious sects.
1788	■ **June** Opposition to the proposed U.S. Constitution in the Virginia Convention is led by Henry.
1799	■ **March** Henry comes out of retirement at the behest of George Washington to oppose radical republican opposition to federal authority in Virginia and Kentucky. ■ **June 6** Henry dies at Red Hill in Charlotte County, Virginia.

the most thrilling emphasis—"may profit by their example! If this be treason, make the most of it." (Henry, 1891, vol. 1, p. 86).

It also seems likely from several sources that Henry apologized to the House if the heat of his words offended, but this was an old lawyer's tactic—the message had been conveyed. At this point Henry was the unquestioned champion of the young faction of radicals rising in the House of Burgesses and insisting on protection of American liberties.

◆ Letter to Robert Pleasants, a Quaker, Concerning Slavery

As with most of the Virginia gentry in the latter part of the eighteenth century, Henry was a slave owner. He recognized that slavery was unjustifiable on principle, and he was well aware of the inconsistency of insisting upon civil liberties for some while denying them to others. At the same time, Henry recognized his own unwillingness to make the difficult financial sacrifices that would be necessary to do away with slavery.

Others, most notably Quakers, were beginning to raise an outcry against both the slave trade and slave ownership

Bostonians paying the excise man by tarring and feathering him; a sign with "Stamp Act" written upside down is posted on the tree. (Library of Congress)

in general. In a letter written on January 18, 1773, to a Quaker friend, Robert Pleasants, Henry recognized the moral reprehensibility of slavery while acknowledging his own failings. While he would never take action to discourage the institution, Henry's letter is an excellent example of the growing tension felt by many Patriot leaders as they fought for their own liberty from Britain while most grossly denying liberty to others. As Henry explained, it was "amazing" that the practice could continue in Virginia, "a Country above all others fond of Liberty." The exchange with Robert Pleasants followed Henry's successful effort to obtain an exemption from militia muster for Quakers, a success that was compromised during the difficult war years of the Revolution. While Henry recognized the problems with slavery, he continued to own slaves and years later, during the debates over the adoption of the Constitution, used the specter of federal authority over slavery and the threat of federal emancipation in an effort to encourage slaveholders to oppose the Constitution.

◆ Speech to the First Continental Congress

When the First Continental Congress met in Philadelphia in September 1774, delegates from across the colonies grappled with the question of how to coordinate colonial opposition to British policies, in particular, the Intolerable (or Coercive) Acts that Britain had adopted in

response to the Boston Tea Party in December 1773. These acts—passed to punish Massachusetts for the Boston Tea Party—closed the port of Boston and revoked key provisions of the Massachusetts charter. Most delegates were still far from supporting any notion of independence, and their suspicions of their sister colonies ran perhaps deep as or even deeper than their suspicions of British action. Henry potentially exacerbated this problem when he proposed that voting in the Congress should be based upon the population or wealth of a colony, rather than the less democratic one vote per colony. This proposal was, of course, an anathema to the smaller colonies. Recognizing that this issue could undermine Congress's efforts at coordinating colonial action, Henry rose on September 5 to note the legitimacy of his point but to accept the reality that voting could be by colony. He rallied the delegates to a common cause by urging them that "the distinctions between Virginians, Pennsylvanians, New Yorkers, and New Englanders, are no more. I am not a Virginian, but an American." Voting by colony was adopted and, as Henry had suspected, would prove to vex the Continental Congress and Confederation Congress, only to become a key issue of dispute in the Constitutional Convention.

◆ Speech to the Virginia Revolutionary Convention in Opposition to the Intolerable Acts

Henry was unsuccessful in 1774 in Philadelphia in urging the other colonies to support military preparedness as moderates continued to petition Britain and felt that such aggressive action would only provoke British wrath. Back in Virginia, at the Virginia Convention (formed after the royal governor had dissolved the House of Burgesses) held several weeks before the battles of Lexington and Concord, Henry rejoined the theme by introducing resolutions for arming and training the militia and admonished his colleagues that Britain had sent troops and fleets to deny colonists their liberties and enforce tyranny. Still, moderates in Virginia also hoped for a peaceful resolution to the conflict.

When his resolutions were debated on March 23, 1775, Henry's frustration, anger, and passion poured forth in his most famous speech. Warning that men were grasping at the "illusions of hope" while Britain prepared for war, an exasperated Henry declared that "war is actually begun!" and prophetically said, "The next gale that sweeps from the north will bring to our ears the clash of resounding arms!" His voice rising with a demand that Virginia support its New England brethren who were facing British guns, Henry grasped an ivory letter opener and stormed "give me liberty," thrusting the apparent knife toward his breast, "or give me death." Henry stood silent amid a stunned convention and audience. His speech had its intended effect, and the Virginia Convention adopted Henry's resolutions calling for the arming of voluntary companies.

Shortly after Henry's speech, British Governor Dunmore seized gunpowder from the public magazine in Williamsburg (April 20), and word of the battle of Lexington and Concord (fought on April 19) arrived in Virginia. As a result, Henry's words became a battle cry. Some newly

An illustration of Patrick Henry's speech to the Virginia Revolutionary Convention in 1775 (Library of Congress)

formed Minutemen emblazoned their hunting shirts with the motto "Liberty or Death," as did a number of assembly-men. The same slogan appeared on flags and broadsides. Henry's speech had given the Patriot cause a new motto, which was quickly embraced by the populace.

◆ Speech to the Virginia Convention Opposing the Constitution

After the Revolution, the new American government operated for several years under the Articles of Confeder-ation, but a number of systemic problems interfered with national policies. Most notably, the Confederation was unable to impose taxes and could make only "requisitions" of funds from the states—requisitions that were often ignored or delayed. The very limited authority of the Con-federation Congress also prevented the national govern-ment from effectively regulating commerce or even enforcing the terms of the Treaty of Paris, which had ended the Revolution. These difficulties fed serious finan-cial problems, not the least of which was the deep depre-ciation in Continental bills issued during the war. Com-mercial interests, in particular, found continuation under the Articles of Confederation unacceptable; by 1787 a convention of the states took on the task of drafting a national constitution.

Henry was deeply suspicious of the Philadelphia Con-vention and declined to attend, even though he was elect-ed a delegate from Virginia. When the convention pro-duced a wholly new form of government, rather than pro-posing amendments—as had been its stated purpose—Henry joined George Mason in opposing the adoption of the Constitution. Unfortunately for their efforts, by the time the Virginia Convention to consider the Constitution convened in June 1788, eight other states (of the requisite nine) had already ratified it; unbeknownst to Virginia dele-gates, New Hampshire would ratify during their conven-tion. By that time, too, the "Federalists" in Virginia, who supported its adoption, were well organized under James Madison, Edmund Pendleton, John Marshall, and, after an initial refusal to sign the document in Philadelphia, the popular governor, Edmund Randolph. Of perhaps even greater significance, George Washington had chaired the Philadelphia Convention and, while he did not attend the ratifying convention in Virginia, he lent his enormous pop-ularity to the cause.

Henry and other opponents of the Constitution focused on the power of the Congress to tax, the overall power of the president, control of the treaty process by the undemo-cratic Senate and the president, the control of commerce by the Congress, and the lack of a declaration of rights.

With perfect hindsight it is clear that Henry's effort to demand a second constitutional convention or amendments before adoption was doomed. But his forceful insistence that excessive power had been granted to the federal government, while it failed to evoke any of the structural changes he sought, did have an important impact in encouraging adoption of the Bill of Rights.

In what became known as his "Liberty or Empire?" speech, delivered on June 5, Henry expressed deep regret that Americans seemed to be choosing the power of a national empire over the blessings of liberty for which he and his compatriots had fought the Revolution. Henry introduced this speech by reading Article 3 of the Virginia Declaration of Rights, which provides that government is to benefit the people and the community and that community has a right to "reform, alter, or abolish it." His plea for liberty and local control is still a classic text for those seeking limited government. As the end of the convention approached, Henry vowed to live peaceably under its terms should it be adopted.

◆ Election Speech at Charlotte Court House

Henry had opposed adoption of the Constitution, but he looked with concern upon the rise of partisan politics in the 1790s. As he had predicted, government quickly sought to expand its power. Alexander Hamilton and other Federalists successfully encouraged assumption of state debt and creation of a new national bank based upon implied powers; this raised concern among key supporters of the Constitution, most notably Jefferson and Madison. Adding to these difficulties was a growing controversy with republican France, exacerbated by French seizure of American ships trading with Britain. America's new Republican Party supported French interests, while Federalists (including John Adams after 1796) seemed to promote British interests. Henry's political tendencies leaned toward the principles of the new Republican Party (led by Jefferson and Madison), but he was deeply concerned about the French Terror accompanying the French Revolution and could not avoid some long-standing personal animosity toward Jefferson (and, to a lesser extent, Madison).

In 1798 the Federalists forced through the Congress the Alien and Sedition Acts in an effort to strengthen their hand in dealing with a growing political opposition. While several Republican newspaper editors were jailed, the acts had the opposite of their intended effect. Kentucky and Virginia adopted resolutions declaring the laws unconstitutional and insisting upon a state's right to nullify such federal action (the first of these resolutions drafted by Jefferson and the second by Madison). Adding to the complex milieu, a delegation that Adams had sent to France to negotiate a new treaty (Charles Pinckney, John Marshall, and Elbridge Gerry) had been asked for a bribe, a request that was angrily rejected; this became known as the notorious XYZ Affair. As a result, war with France loomed, and disunion appeared to be a real possibility.

It was in this circumstance that George Washington persuaded Henry to come out of retirement as an unlikely pro-tector of the union. Henry, in his last public address, an election speech at the Charlotte Court House in March 1799, warned Republican radicals that the cost of disunion might be civil war, with the venerable Washington leading federal troops. Moreover, while he certainly supported an individual's or state's right to oppose tyranny, Virginia should consider carefully whether its grievances justified such a portentous step. When a drunk in the audience vowed that he would oppose even Washington, Henry reportedly erupted: "No,…you dare not do it: in such a parricidal attempt, the steel would drop from your nerveless arm!" (qtd. in Tyler, p. 418). Henry, however, died before he could again take a seat in the Virginia legislature. The boiling national controversy was quieted when Jefferson was elected president in 1800 and a second delegation sent by Adams returned in early 1801 with a new treaty with France.

Impact and Legacy

Henry's legacy is difficult for contemporary Americans to evaluate both because his most important contributions were in the spoken word and because he eschewed national office based upon principled opposition to what he perceived as an unhealthy consolidation of power in the new Constitution. Contemporaries, however, saw Henry as a crucial personage who rallied the populace to the American cause, explaining British infringements of American liberty in terms that were understood and embraced by the common man. Even Jefferson, in later life a Henry detractor, acknowledged the important role played by Henry, saying that "it is not now easy to say what we would have done without" him (qtd. in Meade, vol. 1, p. 268). His oratory was a spark that other leaders of the Patriot movement relied upon.

While Henry's opposition to the Constitution failed, his popularity was an important factor in encouraging adoption of the Bill of Rights. Henry believed that these amendments were inadequate to the task of limiting federal power, but the importance of this contribution today cannot be underestimated. His opposition resonates today in the libertarian movement. Having refused national offices and spent his career primarily in Virginia politics and courts, Henry's legacy is largely limited to schoolhouse quotations, especially his most famous "I know not what course others may take; but as for me, give me liberty or give me death!" Even so, it is no small legacy.

Key Sources

Henry's speeches were imperfectly recorded and transmitted to posterity, and his official memoranda and correspondence are limited. As a result, modern scholars legitimately question the reported texts handed down by tradition, although some of that criticism has been excessive and at least as speculative as the traditions that provide the texts. Still, the general tone and content of Henry's speech-

Henry, Patrick

"*Is it not amazing, that at a time, when the Rights of Humanity are defined & understood with precision, in a Country above all others fond of Liberty; that in such an Age, & such a Country we find Men, professing a Religion the most humane, mild, meek, gentle, & generous; adopting a Principle as repugnant to humanity as it is inconsistent with the Bible and destructive to Liberty.*"

(Letter to Robert Pleasants, a Quaker, Concerning Slavery)

"*The distinctions between Virginians, Pennsylvanians, New Yorkers, and New Englanders, are no more. I am not a Virginian, but an American.*"

(Speech to the First Continental Congress)

"*It is natural to man to indulge in the illusions of hope. We are apt to shut our eyes against a painful truth, and listen to the song of that siren till she transforms us into beasts. Is this the part of wise men, engaged in a great and arduous struggle for liberty?*"

(Speech to the Virginia Revolutionary Convention in Opposition to the Intolerable Acts)

"*Gentlemen may cry, Peace, Peace—but there is no peace. The war is actually begun! The next gale that sweeps from the north will bring to our ears the clash of resounding arms! Our brethren are already in the field! Why stand we here idle?*"

(Speech to the Virginia Revolutionary Convention in Opposition to the Intolerable Acts)

"*Is life so dear, or peace so sweet, as to be purchased at the price of chains and slavery? Forbid it, Almighty God! I know not what course others may take; but as for me, give me liberty or give me death!*"

(Speech to the Virginia Revolutionary Convention in Opposition to the Intolerable Acts)

"*If we admit this consolidated government, it will be because we like a great, splendid one. Some way or other we must be a great and mighty empire; we must have an army, and a navy, and a number of things. When the American spirit was in its youth, the language of America was different; liberty, sir, was then the primary object.*"

(Speech to the Virginia Convention Opposing the Constitution) es cannot be questioned, and the texts that have been utilized serve as excellent indicators of his principles and his oratorical styles. Adding to the difficulty, there is no modern edition of Henry's papers. Henry's first biography, published in 1817 and again in 1852, continues to be an important source: William Wirt, *Sketches of the Life and Character of Patrick Henry*. A new edition was published in 2002. The seminal work on Henry's papers, in three volumes, was prepared by his grandson, William Wirt Henry, as *Patrick Henry: Life, Correspondence and Speeches* (1891). A new edition came out in 2004. See also H. R. McIlwaine, ed., *Official Letters of the Governors of the State of Virginia*, Vol. 1: *The Letters of Patrick Henry* (1926).

Further Reading

■ Books

Elliot, Jonathan, ed., *The Debates in the Several State Conventions on the Adoption of the Federal Constitution*, vol. 3. Philadelphia: J. B. Lippincott, 1861.

Elson, James M., comp. *Patrick Henry in His Speeches and Writings and in the Words of His Contemporaries*. Lynchburg, Va.: Warwick House Publishers, 2007.

McCants, David A. *Patrick Henry, the Orator* New York: Greenwood Press, 1990.

Meade, Robert Douthat, *Patrick Henry*, 2 vols. Philadelphia: J. B. Lippincott, 1957–1969.

Morgan, Edmund S., and Helen M. Morgan. *The Stamp Act Crisis: Prologue to Revolution*. New York: Collier Books, 1965.

Tyler, Moses Coit, *Patrick Henry*. New York: Houghton, Mifflin, 1975.

—John A. Ragosta

Questions for Further Study

1. Critique Henry's comments on slavery in his letter to Robert Pleasants. Was he sincere in his opposition to it?

2. Discuss the pros and cons of Henry's idea, expressed in his speech to the First Continental Congress, that the legislative influence of a state should be based on wealth and population.

3. Henry's speech to the Virginia Revolutionary Convention on the Intolerable Acts is most famous for its last seven words: "Give me liberty or give me death!" Yet the address is full of scriptural imagery as well as allusions to classical mythology. Discuss these images from the Christian and Greco-Roman traditions and how Henry uses them.

4. Although he is remembered as one of the Founders, Henry had his problems with the nation's Constitution, as evidenced in his speech opposing it before the Virginia Convention. What are his reasons for rejecting the Constitution?

RESOLUTIONS IN OPPOSITION TO THE STAMP ACT (1765)

RESOLVES of the House of Burgesses in Virginia, *June* 1765.

That the first Adventurers & Settlers of this his Majesty's Colony and Dominion of *Virginia*, brought with them, and transmitted to their Posterity, and all other his Majesty's Subjects since inhabiting in this his Majesty's Colony, all the Liberties, Privileges, Franchises, and Immunities, that at any Time been held, enjoyed, and possessed, by the people of *Great Britain*.

That by Two Royal Charters, granted by King *James* the First, the Colonists aforesaid are Declared Entitled, to all Liberties, Privileges and Immunities, of Denizens and Natural Subjects (to all Intents and Purposes) as if they had been Abiding and Born within the Realm of *England*.

That the Taxation of the People by Themselves, or by Persons Chosen by Themselves to Represent them, who can only know what Taxes the People are able to bear, or the easiest Method of Raising them, and must themselves be affected by every Tax laid upon the People, is the only Security against a Burthensome Taxation; and the distinguishing Characteristic of *British* FREEDOM; and, without which, the ancient Constitution cannot exist.

That his Majesty's Liege People of this most Ancient and Loyal Colony, have, without Interruption, the inestimable Right of being Governed by such Laws, respecting their internal Policy and Taxation, as are derived from their own Consent, with the Approbation of their Sovereign, or his Substitute; which Right hath never been Forfeited, or Yielded up; but hath been constantly recognized by the Kings and People of *Great Britain*.

Resolved therefore, That the General Assembly of this Colony, with the consent of his Majesty, or his Substitute, HAVE the Sole Right and Authority to lay Taxes and Impositions upon Its Inhabitants: And, That every Attempt to vest such Authority in any other Person or Persons whatsoever, has a Manifest Tendency to Destroy AMERICAN FREEDOM.

That his Majesty's Liege People, Inhabitants of this Colony, are not bound to yield Obedience to any Law or Ordinance whatsoever, designed to impose any Taxation upon them, other than the Laws or Ordinances of the General Assembly as aforesaid.

That any Person who shall, by Speaking, or Writing, assert or maintain, That any Person or Persons, other than the General Assembly of this Colony, with such Consent as aforesaid, have any Right or Authority to lay or impose any Tax whatever on the Inhabitants therof, shall be Deemed, AN ENEMY TO THIS HIS MAJESTY'S COLONY.

Glossary

Burthensome	burdensome
House of Burgesses	the Virginia house of representatives, the first elected lower-house assembly in the New World
Liege	loyal

LETTER TO ROBERT PLEASANTS, A QUAKER, CONCERNING SLAVERY (1773)

Dear Sir,

I take this opportunity to acknowledge the receipt of A[nthony] Benezets Book against the Slave Trade. I thank you for it. It is not a little surprising that Christianity, whose chief excellence consists in softening the human heart, in cherishing & improving its finer Feelings, should encourage a Practice so totally repugnant to the first Impression of right & wrong. What adds to the wonder is that this Abominable Practice has been introduced in the most enlightened Ages, Times that seem to have pretensions to boast of high Improvements in the Arts, Sciences, & Refined Morality, h[ave] brought into general use, & guarded by many Laws, a Species of Violence & Tyranny, which our more rude & barbarous, but more honest Ancestors detested. Is it not amazing, that at a time, when the Rights of Humanity are defined & understood with precision, in a Country above all others fond of Liberty; that in such an Age, & such a Country we find Men, professing a Religion the most humane, mild, meek, gentle, & generous; adopting a Principle as repugnant to humanity as it is inconsistent with the Bible and destructive to Liberty.

Every thinking honest Man rejects it in Speculation; how few in Practice from conscientious Motives?…

Would any one believe that I am Master of Slaves of my own purchase! I am drawn along by the general inconvenience of living without them, I will not, I cannot justify it. However culpable my Conduct, I will so far pay my devoir to Virtue, as to own the excellence and rectitude of her Precepts, & to lament my want of conforming to them.—

I believe a time will come when an opportunity will be offered to abolish this lamentable Evil.— Every thing we can do is to improve it, if it happens in our day, if not, let us transmit to our descendants together with our Slaves, a pity for their unhappy Lot, & an abhorrence for Slavery. If we cannot reduce this wished for Reformation to practice, let us treat the unhappy victims with lenity, it is the furthest advance we can make toward Justice.…

Excuse this Scrawl, and believe me with esteem, Your humble servant, Patrick Henry, Junior

Glossary

A[nthony] Benezet	American abolitionist leader (1713–1784)
devoir	respect or honor
in Speculation	as a philosophical idea
lament my want of conforming	regret my inability to conform
lenity	the quality of lenience, or mercy

Speech to the First Continental Congress (1774)

Government is dissolved. Fleets and armies and the present state of things show that government is dissolved....We are in a state of nature, sir. I did propose that a scale should be laid down; that part of North America which was once Massachusetts Bay, and that part which was once Virginia, ought to be considered as having a weight. Will not people complain? Ten thousand Virginians have not outweighed one thousand others.

I will submit, however; I am determined to submit, if I am overruled....

The distinctions between Virginians, Pennsylvanians, New Yorkers, and New Englanders, are no more. I am not a Virginian, but an American.

Glossary

weight	the population and wealth of each colony

Speech to the Virginia Revolutionary Convention in Opposition to the Intolerable Acts (1775)

No man thinks more highly than I do of the patriotism, as well as abilities, of the very worthy gentlemen who have just addressed the House. But different men often see the same subject in different lights; and, therefore, I hope it will not be thought disrespectful to those gentlemen if, entertaining as I do opinions of a character very opposite to theirs, I shall speak forth my sentiments freely and without reserve. This is no time for ceremony. The question before the House is one of awful moment to this country. For my own part, I consider it as nothing less than a question of freedom or slavery; and in proportion to the magnitude of the subject ought to be the freedom of the debate. It is only in this way that we can hope to arrive at truth, and fulfill the great responsibility which we hold to God and our country. Should I keep back my opinions at such a time, through fear of giving offense, I should consider myself as guilty of treason towards my country, and of an act of disloyalty toward the Majesty of Heaven, which I revere above all earthly kings.

Mr. President, it is natural to man to indulge in the illusions of hope. We are apt to shut our eyes against a painful truth, and listen to the song of that siren till she transforms us into beasts. Is this the part of wise men, engaged in a great and arduous struggle for liberty? Are we disposed to be of the number of those who, having eyes, see not, and, having ears, hear not, the things which so nearly concern their temporal salvation? For my part, whatever anguish of spirit it may cost, I am willing to know the whole truth; to know the worst, and to provide for it. I have but one lamp by which my feet are guided, and that is the lamp of experience. I know of no way of judging the future but by the past. And judging by the past, I wish to know what there has been in the conduct of the British ministry for the last ten years to justify those hopes with which gentlemen have been pleased to solace themselves and the House. Is it that insidious smile with which our petition has been lately received? Trust it not, sir; it will prove a snare to your feet. Suffer not yourselves to be betrayed with a kiss. Ask yourselves how this gracious reception of our petition comports with those warlike preparations which cover our waters and darken our land. Are fleets and armies necessary to a work of love and reconciliation? Have we shown ourselves so unwilling to be reconciled that force must be called in to win back our love? Let us not deceive ourselves, sir. These are the implements of war and subjugation; the last arguments to which kings resort. I ask gentlemen, sir, what means this martial array, if its purpose be not to force us to submission? Can gentlemen assign any other possible motive for it? Has Great Britain any enemy, in this quarter of the world, to call for all this accumulation of navies and armies? No, sir, she has none. They are meant for us: they can be meant for no other. They are sent over to bind and rivet upon us those chains which the British ministry have been so long forging. And what have we to oppose to them? Shall we try argument? Sir, we have been trying that for the last ten years. Have we anything new to offer upon the subject? Nothing. We have held the subject up in every light of which it is capable; but it has been all in vain. Shall we resort to entreaty and humble supplication? What terms shall we find which have not been already exhausted? Let us not, I beseech you, sir, deceive ourselves. Sir, we have done everything that could be done to avert the storm which is now coming on. We have petitioned; we have remonstrated; we have supplicated; we have prostrated ourselves before the throne, and have implored its interposition to arrest the tyrannical hands of the ministry and Parliament. Our petitions have been slighted; our remonstrances have produced additional violence and insult; our supplications have been disregarded; and we have been spurned, with contempt, from the foot of the throne! In vain, after these things, may we indulge the fond hope of peace and reconciliation. There is no longer any room for hope. If we wish to be free—if we mean to preserve inviolate those inestimable privileges for which we have been so long contending—if we mean not basely to abandon the noble struggle in which we have been so long engaged, and which we have pledged ourselves never to abandon until the glorious object of our contest shall be obtained—we must fight! I repeat it, sir, we must fight! An appeal to arms and to the God of hosts is all that is left us!

They tell us, sir, that we are weak; unable to cope with so formidable an adversary. But when shall we be stronger? Will it be the next week, or the next year? Will it be when we are totally disarmed, and when a

British guard shall be stationed in every house? Shall we gather strength by irresolution and inaction? Shall we acquire the means of effectual resistance by lying supinely on our backs and hugging the delusive phantom of hope, until our enemies shall have bound us hand and foot? Sir, we are not weak if we make a proper use of those means which the God of nature hath placed in our power. The millions of people, armed in the holy cause of liberty, and in such a country as that which we possess, are invincible by any force which our enemy can send against us. Besides, sir, we shall not fight our battles alone. There is a just God who presides over the destinies of nations, and who will raise up friends to fight our battles for us. The battle, sir, is not to the strong alone; it is to the vigilant, the active, the brave. Besides, sir, we have no election. If we were base enough to desire it, it is now too late to retire from the contest. There is no retreat but in submission and slavery! Our chains are forged! Their clanking may be heard on the plains of Boston! The war is inevitable—and let it come! I repeat it, sir, let it come.

It is in vain, sir, to extenuate the matter. Gentlemen may cry, Peace, Peace—but there is no peace. The war is actually begun! The next gale that sweeps from the north will bring to our ears the clash of resounding arms! Our brethren are already in the field! Why stand we here idle? What is it that gentlemen wish? What would they have? Is life so dear, or peace so sweet, as to be purchased at the price of chains and slavery? Forbid it, Almighty God! I know not what course others may take; but as for me, give me liberty or give me death!

Glossary

already in the field	already at war and prepared for battle
awful moment	grave importance
British ministry	the king's government in general, but particularly its representatives responsible for administering the American colonies
extenuate	attempt to reduce an offense by providing explanations or excuses
the last arguments to which kings resort	violence

SPEECH TO THE VIRGINIA CONVENTION OPPOSING THE CONSTITUTION (1788)

This [Article 3 of the Virginia Declaration of Rights], sir, is the language of democracy—that a majority of the community have a right to alter government when found to be oppressive. But how different is the genius of your new Constitution from this! How different from the sentiments of freemen that a contemptible minority can prevent the good of the majority! If, then, gentlemen standing on this ground are come to that point, that they are willing to bind themselves and their posterity to be oppressed, I am amazed and inexpressibly astonished. If this be the opinion of the majority, I must submit; but to me, sir, it appears perilous and destructive....

A standing army we shall have, also, to execute the execrable commands of tyranny; and how are you to punish them? Will you order them to be punished? Who shall obey these orders? Will your mace-bearer be a match for a disciplined regiment? In what situation are we to be? The clause before you gives a power of direct taxation, unbounded and unlimited—an exclusive power of legislation, in all cases whatsoever, for ten miles square, and over all places purchased for the erection of forts, magazines, arsenals, dockyards, etc. What resistance could be made? The attempt would be madness. You will find all the strength of this country in the hands of your enemies; their garrisons will naturally be the strongest places in the country. Your militia is given up to Congress, also, in another part of this plan; they will therefore act as they think proper; all power will be in their own possession. You can not force them to receive their punishment: of what service would militia be to you, when, most probably, you will not have a single musket in the State? For as arms are to be provided by Congress, they may or may not furnish them....

If we admit this consolidated government, it will be because we like a great, splendid one. Some way or other we must be a great and mighty empire; we must have an army, and a navy, and a number of things. When the American spirit was in its youth, the language of America was different; liberty, sir, was then the primary object.

We are descended from a people whose government was founded on liberty; our glorious forefathers of Great Britain made liberty the foundation of everything. That country is become a great, mighty, and splendid nation; not because their government is strong and energetic, but, sir, because liberty is its direct end and foundation. We drew the spirit of liberty from our British ancestors; by that spirit we have triumphed over every difficulty. But now, sir, the American spirit, assisted by the ropes and chains of consolidation, is about to convert this country into a powerful and mighty empire. If you make the citizens of this country agree to become the subjects of one great consolidated empire of America, your government will not have sufficient energy to keep them together. Such a government is incompatible with the genius of republicanism. There will be no checks, no real balances, in this government. What can avail your specious, imaginary balances, your rope-dancing, chain-rattling, ridiculous ideal checks and contrivances? But, sir, "we are not feared by foreigners; we do not make nations tremble." Would this constitute happiness or secure liberty? I trust, sir, our political hemisphere will ever direct their operations to the security of those objects.

Consider our situation, sir; go to the poor man and ask him what he does. He will inform you that he enjoys the fruits of his labor, under his own fig tree, with his wife and children around him, in peace and security. Go to every other member of society; you will find the same tranquil ease and content; you will find no alarms or disturbances. Why, then, tell us of danger, to terrify us into an adoption of this new form of government? And yet who knows the dangers that this new system may produce? They are out of sight of the common people; they can not foresee latent consequences. I dread the operation of it on the middling and lower classes of people; it is for them I fear the adoption of this system....

The voice of tradition, I trust, will inform posterity of our struggles for freedom. If our descendants be worthy the name of Americans they will preserve and hand down to their latest posterity the transactions of the present times;... for I never will give up the power of direct taxation but for a scourge. I am willing to give it conditionally—that is, after noncompliance with requisitions. I will do more, sir, and what I hope will convince the most skeptical man that I am a lover of the American Union; that, in case Virginia shall not make punctual payment, the control of our customhouses and the whole regulation of trade shall be given to Congress, and that Virginia shall depend on Congress even for passports, till Virginia shall have paid the last farthing and furnished the last soldier.

Nay, sir, there is another alternative to which I would consent; even that they should strike us out of the Union and take away from us all federal privileges till we comply with federal requisitions; but let it depend upon our own pleasure to pay our money in the most easy manner for our people. Were all the States, more terrible than the mother country, to join against us, I hope Virginia could defend herself; but, sir, the dissolution of the Union is most abhorrent to my mind. The first thing I have at heart is American liberty; the second thing is American union; and I hope the people of Virginia will endeavor to preserve that union. The increasing population of the Southern States is far greater than that of New England; consequently, in a short time, they will be far more numerous than the people of that country. Consider this and you will find this State more particularly interested to support American liberty and not bind our posterity by an improvident relinquishment of our rights. I would give the best security for a punctual compliance with requisitions; but I beseech gentlemen, at all hazards, not to give up this unlimited power of taxation. The honorable gentleman has told us that these powers given to Congress are accompanied by a judiciary which will correct all. On examination you will find this very judiciary oppressively constructed, your jury trial destroyed, and the judges dependent on Congress.

This Constitution is said to have beautiful features; but when I come to examine these features, sir, they appear to me horribly frightful. Among other deformities, it has an awful squinting; it squints toward monarchy, and does not this raise indignation in the breast of every true American? Your president may easily become king. Your Senate is so imperfectly constructed that your dearest rights may be sacrificed to what may be a small minority; and a very small minority may continue for ever unchangeably this government, altho horridly defective....It is on a supposition that your American governors shall be honest that all the good qualities of this government are founded; but its defective and imperfect construction puts it in their power to perpetrate the worst of mischiefs should they be bad men; and, sir, would not all the world, blame our distracted folly in

Glossary

checks...balances	procedures and institutions within a government that prevent one party, group, or individual from gaining too much power
contrivances	creations, fabrications, inventions—all in a negative sense, meaning something very close to lies or untruths
democracy	government by popular vote
execute the execrable	put into action the horrible
farthing	a very small denomination of money in the British currency of that time, meant to represent an insignificant amount
genius of	idea behind
magazines	ammunition storage areas
man of address	someone of importance and influence
militia	a military force composed of citizen-soldiers, as opposed to a standing army
republicanism	a system of rule by elected leaders, as opposed to monarchs or dictators
requisitions	demands for soldiers and military supplies
scourge	whip; more generally, curse
standing army	a full-time military force, as opposed to a citizen militia
terrible	powerful

resting our rights upon the contingency of our rulers being good or bad? Show me that age and country where the rights and liberties of the people were placed on the sole chance of their rulers being good men without a consequent loss of liberty! I say that the loss of that dearest privilege has ever followed, with absolute certainty, every such mad attempt.

If your American chief be a man of ambition and abilities, how easy is it for him to render himself absolute! The army is in his hands, and if he be a man of address, it will be attached to him, and it will be the subject of long meditation with him to seize the first auspicious moment to accomplish his design, and, sir, will the American spirit solely relieve you when this happens?…If ever he violate the laws, one of two things will happen: he will come at the head of the army to carry everything before him, or he will give bail, or do what Mr. Chief Justice will order him. If he be guilty, will not the recollection of his crimes teach him to make one bold push for the American throne? Will not the immense difference between being master of everything and being ignominiously tried and punished powerfully excite him to make this bold push? But, sir, where is the existing force to punish him? Can he not, at the head of his army, beat down every opposition? Away with your president! We shall have a king: the army will salute him monarch; your militia will leave you, and assist in making him king, and fight against you: and what have you to oppose this force? What will then become of you and your rights? Will not absolute despotism ensue?

ELECTION SPEECH AT CHARLOTTE COURT HOUSE (1799)

They [the Alien and Sedition Acts] were passed by Congress, Congress is a wise body—too deep for me. They may be right—they may be wrong. But this much I know—you are wrong—you are now progressing to civil war, and when you reach the field, who will you meet—Washington—the father of his country; and you will see when you face him your steel will turn.

Glossary

your steel will turn	you will lose your courage

Oliver Wendell Holmes, Jr. (Library of Congress)

OLIVER WENDELL HOLMES, JR.   1841–1935

Supreme Court Justice

Featured Documents
- "Early Forms of Liability" (1881)
- *Lochner v. New York* (1905)
- *Schenck v. United States* (1919)
- *Abrams v. United States* (1919)
- *Buck v. Bell* (1927)

Overview

Oliver Wendell Holmes, Jr., like many before him, believed John Marshall, the "Great Chief Justice," to be the one person who best embodied American law. But Holmes, for his part, so profoundly influenced American law during his own lifetime that many others, like the noted Court historian Bernard Schwartz, believe that "it was Holmes, more than any other legal thinker, who set the agenda for modern Supreme Court jurisprudence" (Schwartz, p. 190).

Born in 1841 into what Oliver Wendell Holmes, Sr.— himself a celebrated physician and writer—called "the Brahmin caste of New England" (Schwartz, p. 191), the younger Holmes spent much of his life struggling to free himself from the large shadow cast by his father. The Civil War presented him with an opportunity both to leave home and to distinguish himself in an endeavor outside his father's sphere. Holmes served with great distinction in the Union army. Seriously wounded three times, he was discharged after three years with the rank of brevet lieutenant colonel. He then returned to his father's home and, against the elder Holmes's wishes, enrolled in law school at Harvard University.

Holmes continued to live under his father's roof even after marrying at the relatively advanced age of thirty-one. During that period, Holmes assiduously applied himself to gaining distinction in the legal field, practicing as a litigator while at the same time pursuing legal scholarship as coeditor of the *American Law Review*. With the successful publication of his newly edited twelfth edition of James Kent's *Commentaries on American Law* in 1873, Holmes and his wife, Fanny, were finally able to move into a home of their own. Invited to deliver the prestigious Lowell Institute lectures in 1880, Holmes published them to great acclaim the following year as *The Common Law*, earning him such renown that he was soon invited to teach at Harvard Law School.

Holmes had been lecturing at Harvard for less than a year when he abruptly tendered his resignation. He had been appointed to the Supreme Judicial Court of Massachusetts a month earlier, but his university colleagues and students learned of his new position only upon reading about it in the newspapers. Holmes served as an associate justice of the state's highest tribunal for the next sixteen years. During much of that period he found the work trivial and repetitive, but he used the time to hone his style into the taut, epigrammatic form that would eventually earn him a place in the American legal pantheon. He also delivered a number of important public speeches, the most significant of which, "The Path of the Law" (1897) and "Law in Science and Science in Law" (1899), cemented his position as a pathbreaking legal realist who believed that law should be based on experience rather than on abstract principles and logic. In July 1899, when the chief justice of the Massachusetts supreme court died, Holmes was tapped to be his successor.

Holmes was not universally popular. His personal style was often characterized as combative, and in 1896 he had issued a notorious dissenting opinion in *Vegelahn v. Guntner*, arguing that furniture workers had a right to strike for better wages and hours, even at the expense of their employer, so long as they did so peacefully and without malice. Holmes's "actual malice" standard would later become a cornerstone of First Amendment law, but in 1902 his *Vegelahn* dissent threatened to derail a possible appointment to the U.S. Supreme Court. Finally, however, President Theodore Roosevelt overcame his qualms, and in August of that year, Holmes was nominated to succeed Horace Gray (who, like Holmes, had previously served on the Massachusetts supreme court) in occupying the Court's "Massachusetts seat." Once again, Holmes declined to resign his previous post until the eleventh hour.

Holmes would serve on the Court for thirty years, during which he authored 873 opinions—more than any other Supreme Court justice has yet to write. The number of his dissents was proportionally low, but they were so eloquently and powerfully written that they have led to Holmes being dubbed the "Great Dissenter." In what is perhaps his most celebrated opinion, his dissent in *Lochner v. New York* (1905), Holmes, joined by the maverick John Marshall Harlan, voted against the Court's long-standing deference to the doctrine of substantive due process, arguing for New York State's right to enact legislation limiting work hours and against unbridled freedom of contract. Writing for the majority in *Schenck v. United States* (1919), Holmes declared that the right of free speech was not absolute, but that same year he refined his restrictive "clear and present danger" standard in his dissenting opinion in

1841

■ **March 8**
Oliver Wendell Holmes, Jr., is born in Boston, Massachusetts.

1861

■ **June 21**
Holmes graduates from Harvard College, where he served as class poet.

■ **July 10**
Holmes receives his commission as first lieutenant in the Twentieth Regiment of Massachusetts Volunteer Infantry.

■ **October 21**
Holmes is seriously wounded at the Battle of Ball's Bluff in Virginia.

1862

■ **September 17**
Holmes is again seriously wounded, this time while leading a battle charge at Antietam.

1864

■ **January 29**
Holmes becomes General Horatio Wright's aide-de-camp.

■ **July 17**
Holmes is discharged from military service.

1866

■ **June 30**
Holmes graduates from Harvard Law School.

1870

■ **October**
The first volume of the *American Law Review* coedited by Holmes is published.

1873

■ **December**
Holmes publishes his new edition of James Kent's *Commentaries on American Law*.

1881

■ **March**
The Common Law, Holmes's series of Lowell Institute lectures, is published.

Abrams v. United States, excluding most political dissent from government suppression.

Holmes's reputation is not unblemished. He was farsighted, to be sure, but he was also very much a creature of his times. A disciple of social Darwinism—a theory adapted to human society from Charles Darwin's "survival of the fittest" theory of evolution—he also absorbed principles of eugenics, popular in his day. He may have believed that jurists were obliged to set personal prejudices aside when deciding cases, but all indications are that Holmes contentedly upheld, in *Buck v. Bell* (1927), the Virginia statute mandating the sterilization of "feeble-minded" individuals.

In April 1929, Holmes's wife of fifty-seven years died. Holmes stayed on the Court, publicly celebrating his ninetieth birthday two years later, but then began to fail. Colleagues and friends hinted that it was time for him to leave, and on January 11, 1932, he did so, announcing only, "I won't be in tomorrow" (Aichele, p. 159); he submitted his resignation the following day. In 1935, two days before his ninety-fourth birthday, Holmes died of pneumonia in his home.

Explanation and Analysis of Documents

Holmes remains one of the most influential of American legal philosophers. His legal tutorial *The Common Law*, well represented by the opening lecture "Early Forms of Liability," remains a classic of the genre. His dissent in one of the Court's most notorious opinions, *Lochner v. New York*, proved prophetic with its brief polemic against the misuse of the doctrine of substantive due process to prioritize property rights over individual rights. Holmes's formulation of the "clear and present danger" test regarding the right to free speech in *Schenck v. United States*, further refined in his dissent in *Abrams v. United States*, set the stage for the development of free speech law. And despite the recognition of the odiousness of forced sterilization in contemporary American law and society, in its day Holmes's majority opinion supporting the practice in *Buck v. Bell* effectively condoned the practice nationwide.

◆ "Early Forms of Liability"

It is not an exaggeration to say that *The Common Law* changed the course of American jurisprudence. Holmes's thinking about law—indeed, about much of life—was forged, in a sense, in the heat of battle. At twenty-three, he emerged from the Union army after three years, during which he experienced three life-threatening injuries, with a profound sense of the essential brutality of existence. His study of social Darwinism—in particular, the works of Herbert Spencer—after the Civil War helped refine his thinking about law and society into a quasi-scientific approach through which he debunked the notion that the essence of law is an ordered system. "The life of the law has not been logic: it has been experience," he announces at the outset of the first lecture, or chapter, of *The Common Law*, titled "Early Forms of Liability." This was a revolutionary notion at a time when the legal establishment saw the development of law as a stately and preordained progression rather than as an evolutionary process governed by what Holmes memorably labels "the felt necessities of the time."

It is hardly surprising that nineteenth-century society thought of common law, also known as judge-made law, as formalistic and based in tradition: Even today, the notion of stare decisis, or adherence to precedent, continues to define common law. Holmes's revolutionary idea, however, is that judges actually decide individual cases first and only afterward find principles to support their decisions. Whether or not they are conscious of doing so, judges rely on external perspectives—contemporary concerns of their respective communities—in arriving at outcomes.

It is fitting that Holmes's first chapter should be devoted to a history of liability, for he came to believe that liability itself is the organizing principle behind common law: The concern in every case is not the fault per se but whether or not the fault accounts for liability. This insight provides the basis for a theoretical framework that has been called legal realism, which upon its establishment paved the way for an economic model of legal analysis that shaped Holmes's Supreme Court career and has dominated American law ever since.

Holmes was a legal historian before becoming a judge, and his research into the foundations of law jibed with his own experience. Incipient forms of legal procedure, he tells us, are warlike, grounded in vengeance. When law intervenes in disputes, it imposes order by effectively buying off the injured party, determining guilt by weighing questions of actual intent and actual responsibility. As law has advanced from "barbarism to civilization," its form has evolved in a consistent fashion, "but just as the clavicle in the cat only tells of the existence of some earlier creature to which a collar-bone was useful, precedents survive in the law long after the use they once served is at an end." That is, the substance of the law is often divorced from its formal aspects, particularly the purported logical progression of precedents. Instead, Holmes asserts, "The growth of the law is legislative," by which he means that justices address contemporary public policy and opinion rather than paying obeisance to tradition. He proceeds to note that reality demands that judges acknowledge as much about the role of their profession. Eventually they would—but only after Holmes put his theory to work in the Supreme Court in ringing dissents that demanded judicial deference to those elected to carry out the will of the people.

◆ Lochner v. New York

After *Dred Scott v. Sandford* (1857), in which the Supreme Court upheld the institution of slavery, *Lochner v. New York* (1905) is considered one of the Court's most infamous decisions. This high-water mark of laissez-faire capitalism represented the beginning of an era that elevated the freedom to contract into a constitutional mandate, an era that lasted until President Franklin D. Roosevelt's New Deal.

Lochner concerned a New York state law limiting bakers to a sixty-hour workweek, with no more than ten hours to be

Time Line	
1882	■ **February 11** Holmes joins the faculty of Harvard Law School.
1883	■ **January 3** Holmes submits his resignation to Harvard and is sworn in as associate justice of the Supreme Judicial Court of Massachusetts.
1899	■ **August 2** Holmes is elevated to chief justice of the Massachusetts supreme court.
1902	■ **December 8** Holmes is sworn in as associate justice of the U.S. Supreme Court.
1905	■ **April 17** Holmes dissents in *Lochner v. New York.*
1919	■ **March 3** Holmes writes the opinion of the Court in *Schenck v. United States.*
1919	■ **November 10** Holmes dissents in *Abrams v. United States.*
1927	■ **May 2** Holmes writes the majority opinion in *Buck v. Bell.*
1932	■ **January 12** Holmes resigns from the Court.
1935	■ **March 6** Holmes dies in Washington, D.C.

worked in a given day. Wage and hour laws have traditionally fallen under the rubric of police powers, which grant states the ability to enact legislation out of concern for citizens' health and welfare. Joseph Lochner, a bakery owner in Utica, New York, challenged a fine imposed on him for overworking an employee under New York's Bakeshop Act, arguing that the legislation violated his due process rights, specifically the right to contract, as guaranteed by the Fourteenth Amendment. Following the 1868 ratification of the Fourteenth Amendment, which served to overrule *Dred Scott*, the Court had adhered to an interpretation of that amendment's due process clause that made it something more than a procedural protection; instead, due process was said, in this context, to be a substantive limitation on the government's control of individuals. Initially, a bare majority of the justices agreed with Lochner's argument, and Justice John Marshall Harlan drafted an opinion for the Court. Before the decision was announced, however, one of the justices changed his vote, and the majority opinion was rewritten by Justice Rufus Peckham, a strong advocate of what he viewed as venerable "sacred rights of property and the individual right of contract." Thus, what had been enacted as a health law was styled, in *Lochner*, an unconstitutional interference in the right of employer and employee—despite their unequal status—to make labor contracts.

Holmes's opposing opinion, only two paragraphs long, is arguably the most famous dissent ever written. Filled with quotable epigrams, it is short on conventional case citation and legal argument. Richard Posner, a judge on the U.S. Court of Appeals for the Seventh Circuit and a proponent of the conservative Chicago economic school of legal theory, sums up Holmes's *Lochner* dissent—which he terms not "a *good* judicial opinion"—this way: "It is merely the greatest judicial opinion of the last hundred years. To judge it by [the usual] standards is to miss the point. It is a rhetorical masterpiece" (qtd. in Schwartz, p. 197).

Besides being revolutionary in form, Holmes's dissent argues for a radical departure from the customary view that cases are to be decided according to legal precepts and facts deemed objective by the Court. Yet justices, Holmes warns, should not substitute their judgment for that of legislatures. The *Lochner* Court struck down the Bakeshop Act because it did not conform to the majority's economic theories, but as Holmes mordantly remarks, "The 14th Amendment does not enact Mr. Herbert Spencer's Social Statics." The question of whether or not a given law is constitutional, he asserts, should instead be decided according to more subjective, immediate criteria based on reasonableness. Instead of substituting their own views for those of elected lawmakers, judges should be obliged merely to consider whether legislatures could reasonably have enacted the legislation being challenged. To do otherwise in a case like *Lochner* is to provide legal sanction for social Darwinism, a theory far removed from the practical applications intended by the framers of the Fourteenth Amendment.

For the next thirty-five years, however, the Court did exactly that, embracing the doctrine of substantive due process and employing it repeatedly to strike down economic and labor regulations. Judicial restraint gave way to judicial activism, with majorities of justices striking down even legislation aimed at social advancement when it did not conform to their notions of laws appropriate to the promotion of free enterprise. Then, in 1937, one justice changed his vote in *West Coast Hotel Co. v. Parrish*, and the Supreme Court finally upheld a minimum-wage law for women. Called "the switch in time that saved nine," this single vote change—which occurred just two months after President Roosevelt proposed to pack the Court to promote New Deal legislation—represented a dramatic Court reorientation that changed the course of history. The Court has never expressly overruled *Lochner*, but henceforth due process became more of a tool for advancing rights legislation rather than a bulwark for economic laissez-faire.

◆ Schenck v. United States

Charles Schenck, secretary-general of the Socialist Party of America, was charged with printing and distributing literature urging American men to resist the draft during World War I. A federal district court found Schenck guilty of having violated the 1917 Espionage Act, which outlawed interference with conscription. Schenck appealed his criminal conviction to the U.S. Supreme Court, questioning the constitutionality of the Espionage Act on First Amendment grounds. There was, he argued, a tradition in Anglo-American law of distinguishing between opinion and incitement to illegal action. His leaflet was a reflection of the debate then raging in American society about the justness of the war and, as such, was an expression of opinion. Rather than violence, it urged that those subject to the draft assert their rights by signing an anticonscription petition that would be forwarded to Congress.

Writing for a unanimous Court, Justice Holmes upheld the constitutionality of the Espionage Act and Schenck's conviction. In considering First Amendment protection for any speech, he states, the Court must consider not only the content of the speech but also its context. Whereas in some circumstances banning speech such as Schenck's leaflet might amount to prohibited prior restraint, in the context of wartime, such speech is akin to shouting "fire" in a crowded theater. In distributing his leaflets Schenck plainly intended to interfere with the draft, and such interference plainly violates the nation's settled right to draft citizens during time of war. Furthermore, the Espionage Act plainly applies to conspiracies as well as to actual obstruction of military activities; the intended action need not have actually succeeded to be prohibited. The test, Holmes memorably declares, is whether the words at issue present a "clear and present danger" of provoking "substantive evils" that Congress is empowered to prevent.

Decided in 1919, *Schenck* was the Court's first significant attempt to define what constitutes free speech under the First Amendment. Two schools of thought about the subject grew directly out of this case: Absolutists hold that the framers meant, literally, that "Congress shall make no law ... abridging the freedom of speech," while others believe that an individual's right to be left alone must be balanced against compelling public necessity. For his part, Holmes's subsequent refinement of the "clear and present danger" test seems to indicate that his use of the phrase in *Schenck* had been casual. In two companion unanimous decisions to *Schenck*, *Frohwerk v. United States* and *Debs v. United States*, Holmes used the same traditional "bad tendency" test—judging the legality of speech according to its tendency to provoke illegal acts—that he had employed in earlier free speech cases. It is arguable, then, that in *Schenck* he intended to equate the "clear and present danger" test with the "bad tendency" test. Within a few months, however, Holmes, together with Justice Louis D. Brandeis, would begin the process of refining the "clear and present danger" test in *Abrams v. United States* so that it would reflect his intention of providing greater legal latitude for dissident speech.

◆ Abrams v. United States

Jacob Abrams was a Russian immigrant and anarchist living in New York City, where, amid the clamor of debate over U.S. involvement in World War I, he was arrested in August 1918. Abrams and several associates were charged with violating the Sedition Act of 1918 (an amendment to the 1917 Espionage Act) by writing, printing, and distributing two leaflets—one in English, one in Yiddish—denouncing President Woodrow Wilson for sending troops to fight in Soviet Russia. The Yiddish version also included a call for a general strike to protest U.S. interventionist policy. At trial in federal court, the leaflets were found to violate the Sedition Act's ban against language abusive to the government as well as its prohibition of speech intended to curtail the production of materials essential to the prosecution of the war.

Upon appeal, a seven-member majority of the Supreme Court voted to uphold Abrams's criminal conviction. Justice John H. Clarke, writing for the Court, cited the "clear and present danger" test that Holmes had announced only months before in his opinion for the unanimous Court in *Schenck v. United States*. But during the intervening period, Holmes had modified his perception of his own test, as spurred by the persecution of dissidents during the "red scare" that followed World War I as well as by a *Harvard Law Review* article. The article in question, by Zechariah Chafee, Jr., mistakenly claimed that Holmes had intended his new test to make punishment for the "bad tendency" of words to be impossible; but Holmes, in turn, used Chafee's argument to buttress his refinement of what constitutes "clear and present danger" in his *Abrams* dissent, in which he was joined by Justice Brandeis.

Although the questions of law presented in *Schenck* were rightly decided, Holmes asserts, the basic principle of free speech is the same during war as it is in times of peace: Congress can prohibit speech only when it threatens to provoke immediate danger. In this case, "the surreptitious publishing of a silly leaflet by an unknown man" cannot be construed as threatening immediate danger—even in wartime, when the government does have, of necessity, greater latitude in prohibiting certain kinds of speech. The Sedition Act, meanwhile, requires that the same party responsible for performing a prohibited act also be responsible for forming the criminal intent behind the act; the kind of conspiracy of words outlawed in *Abrams* under the original Espionage Act cannot be a consideration here. Holmes goes on to say that persecution for the expression of opinion may make sense logically, but history has undone many "fighting faiths," and society has come to understand that the validity of any belief can best be tested by free exchange in the marketplace of ideas. This, he says, is the theory behind the nation's very Constitution, which is itself a grand experiment. Holmes concludes that the First Amendment trumps common law with respect to seditious libel, such that neither expression of belief nor mere exhortation to action qualifies as criminal offense.

For the next decade, Holmes and Brandeis continued to develop their notion of what would constitute clear and present danger sufficient to allow government prohibition of speech. The Court eventually adopted their libertarian view of First Amendment protection for political dissent, and many aspects of the "clear and present danger" test remain at the heart of First Amendment law today. Holmes's *Abrams* dissent is generally accounted his most influential opinion.

◆ Buck v. Bell

The eugenics movement was an integral part of the Progressive Era, a period spanning roughly the first two decades of the twentieth century, during which American institutions attempted to adapt to wholesale social and economic reforms. The first state law authorizing sterilization on eugenics grounds—viewed as a valid exercise of state police powers—was passed in Indiana in 1907; other states soon followed suit. In 1914, Harry Laughlin, director of the Eugenics Record Office in Cold Spring Harbor, New York, published a "Model Eugenical Sterilization Law" that proposed sterilization of "socially inadequate" groups, classified as the "feebleminded," "insane," "criminalistic," "epileptic," "inebriate," "diseased," "blind," "deaf," "deformed," and "dependent"; as such laws were aimed at relieving society of the burden of supporting the less fortunate, the last category included "orphans, ne'er-do-wells, the homeless, tramps and paupers." In 1924 Virginia passed a Eugenical Sterilization Act based on Laughlin's model that was eagerly embraced by Albert Priddy, superintendent of the State Colony for Epileptics and Feebleminded in Lynchburg, Virginia. Priddy had performed forced sterilization at the colony for a number of years, until he was cautioned that the practice could place both him and the colony in legal jeopardy.

In March 1924, Carrie Buck, a seventeen-year-old inmate of the Lynchburg colony, was chosen as the first person to be legally sterilized under the new law. Buck, the mother of a newborn illegitimate daughter, was herself the illegitimate daughter of another colony inmate. Priddy recommended Buck for sterilization because, he said, she had inherited feeblemindedness and moral delinquency from her mother; she was the perfect test case. In order to test the law in court, the colony proceeded to hire two accomplished and respected attorneys: Aubrey Strode, who had

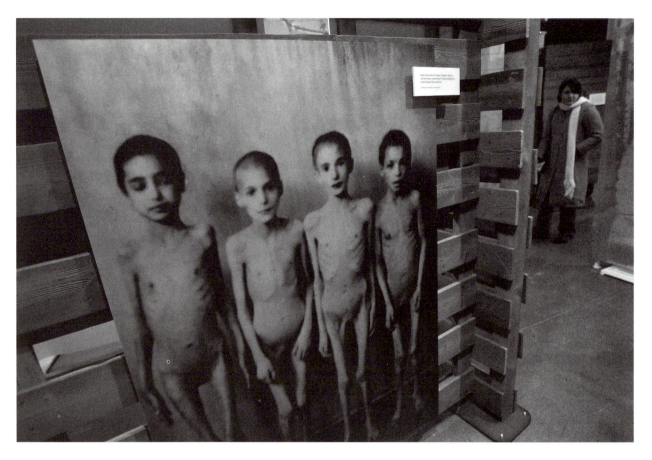

Photograph of a group of Gypsy children who were subjects of Dr. Josef Mengele's research at Auschwitz between 1943 and 1945 as part of the Nazi eugenics program (AP/Wide World Photos)

helped to push the sterilization law through the Virginia legislature, represented the colony, and Irving Whitehead, a former member of the colony's board and a friend of Strode's, represented Buck, a ward of the state.

At trial, numerous witnesses—some of whom had never even seen Buck—offered evidence of her, her mother's, and her daughter's supposed defects of mind and character. In contrast, Whitehead made no attempt to defend his client, owing to what clearly was conflict of interest. After the trial court upheld the Virginia statute, however, Whitehead appealed the case (now named *Buck v. Bell*, as John H. Bell had replaced Priddy as superintendent of the colony), which eventually made it to the U.S. Supreme Court, where Whitehead argued against the state law on equal protection grounds.

Holmes, a longtime student of eugenics, wrote the opinion for the eight-member Court majority. Procedural guarantees, he writes, had been scrupulously followed in Buck's case. Substantively, public welfare interests outweigh those of individuals who "sap the strength" of the state. If the nation's "best citizens" can legitimately be called upon to sacrifice their lives during time of war, he holds, the rights of the "unfit" are not violated by a mandate preventing them from reproducing their kind. "Three generations of imbeciles are enough," Holmes infamously concludes.

After the Court handed down its ruling, Carrie Buck was sterilized. In 1985 the historian Paul Lombardo convincingly argued that Buck was not, in fact, "feebleminded" but that her foster family had concocted the case against her after she was raped by one of their relatives. In the interim, *Buck v. Bell* cleared the way for numerous states to pass their own involuntary sterilization laws. In 1933 the German Nazi government borrowed from Laughlin's model law to create its own justification for sterilizing some 350,000 individuals against their will. The Supreme Court did not hear another eugenics case until 1942, when in *Skinner v. Oklahoma* the Court struck down a statute prescribing involuntary sterilization of repeat criminals while exempting those convicted of embezzlement. In his opinion for the Court, Justice William O. Douglas underscored the dangers of endorsing pseudosciences such as eugenics:

We have not the slightest basis for inferring that that line has any significance in eugenics nor that the inheritability of criminal traits follows the neat legal distinctions which the law has marked between those two offenses. In terms of fines and imprisonment the crimes of larceny and embezzlement rate the same under the Oklahoma code. Only when it comes to sterilization are the pains and penalties of the law different. The equal protection clause would indeed be a formula of empty words if such conspicuously artificial lines could be drawn.

But *Skinner* did not overturn *Buck* (which has never been officially overruled), and forced sterilization of the mentally ill and mentally retarded continued into the 1970s. Virginia's compulsory sterilization law was finally repealed in 1974.

Impact and Legacy

In March 1931, the Court and the nation celebrated Holmes's ninetieth birthday, with Holmes delivering a radio address to the whole country. After almost thirty years on the high bench, he was widely considered a national treasure. When he died four years later, Holmes returned the compliment, so to speak, by willing his considerable estate to the United States, an act that only added to his growing legendary status. Through his friend Felix Frankfurter, a confidant of Franklin Roosevelt and later also a Supreme Court justice, Holmes helped to inform the policies of the New Deal. Frankfurter's jurisprudence emphasized Holmes's commitment to legislative power, although others used Holmes's acceptance of judges' ability to advance the law as justification for a new sort of judicial activism. Emphasizing his memorable dissents, in particular, this camp saw Holmes—incorrectly—as the chief liberal of the Court.

Holmes was not, of course, without his detractors. The distinguished literary and social critic H. L. Mencken frequently debunked the "myth" of Holmes's liberalism, also declaring the justice to be more distinguished as a writer than as a legal thinker. Catholics objected to what they saw as Holmes's moral relativeness and legal pragmatism, which they equated with the forces that gave rise to Nazism. And in the aftermath of World War II Holmes's reputation was seriously battered by charges that he had never been a champion of individual rights.

Holmes's epigrammatic style made his opinions memorable while at the same time contributing to the sense of inconsistency that dogs his legacy. For Richard Posner, Holmes's two-paragraph dissent in *Lochner v. New York* is both "the greatest judicial opinion of the last hundred years" and yet not really a "*good*" opinion. The same man who wrote expansively in the free speech case *Abrams v. United States* that the Constitution "is an experiment, as all life is an experiment," was also capable of abruptly turning his back on equal protection for fundamental rights in *Buck v. Bell* with a curt, dismissive "Three generations of imbeciles are enough." The same justice who argued persuasively for curtailing substantive due process and expanding First Amendment protections can also be fingered as the party responsible, in large part, for inserting eugenics into American legal discourse. Holmes's contradictions have made him—perhaps more than anyone else who has served on the Supreme Court—a constant source of legal debate and of public fascination.

Key Sources

Collections of Holmes's private papers are available at Harvard Law School in Cambridge, Massachusetts, and in the Library of Congress in Washington, D.C. Holmes's correspondence with the Michigan chief justice Thomas M. Cooley is located in the Cooley papers at the University of Michigan Law School in Ann Arbor. Even excluding legal opinions, Holmes's published works are numerous. In addition to his edition of James Kent's *Commentaries on American Law* (1873) and the lectures collected as *The Common Law* (1881), notable Holmes works include Mark D. Howe's edition of *The Occasional Speeches of Justice Oliver Wendell Holmes* (1962); Holmes's extrajudicial legal statements, published as *Collected Legal Papers* (1920); Edward J. Bander's edition of famous statements by and about Holmes, *Justice Holmes, Ex Cathedra* (1966); Howe's *Touched with Fire: Civil War Letters and Diary of Oliver Wendell Holmes, Jr., 1861–1864* (1969); and Howe's two-volume edition of Holmes's candid observations about the Supreme Court, *Holmes-Laski Letters: The Correspondence of Mr. Justice Holmes and Harold J. Laski, 1916–1935* (1953).

Further Reading

■ Articles

Chafee, Zechariah. "Freedom of Speech in Wartime." *Harvard Law Review* 32 (June 1919): 932–973.

Frankfurter, Felix. "The Constitutional Opinions of Justice Holmes." *Harvard Law Review* 29 (April 1916): 683–702.

■ Books

Aichele, Gary J. *Oliver Wendell Holmes, Jr.: Soldier, Scholar, Judge*. Boston: Twayne, 1989.

Alschuler, Albert W. *Law without Values: The Life, Work, and Legacy of Justice Holmes*. Chicago: University of Chicago Press, 2000.

Howe, Mark DeWolfe. *Justice Oliver Wendell Holmes*. Vol. 1: *The Shaping Years, 1841–1870*. Cambridge, Mass.: Harvard University Press, 1957; Vol. 2: *The Proving Years, 1870–1882*. Cambridge, Mass.: Harvard University Press, 1963.

Kellogg, Frederic R. *Oliver Wendell Holmes, Jr., Legal Theory, and Judicial Restraint*. New York: Cambridge University Press, 2006.

Kens, Paul. Lochner v. New York: *Economic Regulation on Trial*. Lawrence: University Press of Kansas, 1998.

Lewis, Anthony. *Freedom for the Thought That We Hate: A Biography of the First Amendment*. New York: Basic Books, 2008.

Lombardo, Paul A. *Three Generations, No Imbeciles: Eugenics, the Supreme Court, and* Buck v. Bell. Baltimore: Johns Hopkins University Press, 2008.

"The law embodies the story of a nation's development through many centuries, and it cannot be dealt with as if it contained only the axioms and corollaries of a book of mathematics."

("Early Forms of Liability")

"A Constitution is not intended to embody a particular economic theory, whether of paternalism and the organic relation of the citizen to the state or of laissez faire. It is made for people of fundamentally differing views, and the accident of our finding certain opinions natural and familiar, or novel, and even shocking, ought not to conclude our judgment upon the question whether statutes embodying them conflict with the Constitution of the United States."

(*Lochner v. New York*)

"The most stringent protection of free speech would not protect a man in falsely shouting fire in a theatre and causing a panic."

(*Schenck v. United States*)

"But when men have realized that time has upset many fighting faiths, they may come to believe even more than they believe the very foundations of their own conduct that the ultimate good desired is better reached by free trade in ideas—that the best test of truth is the power of the thought to get itself accepted in the competition of the market, and that truth is the only ground upon which their wishes safely can be carried out."

(*Abrams v. United States*)

"It is better for all the world, if instead of waiting to execute degenerate offspring for crime, or to let them starve for their imbecility, society can prevent those who are manifestly unfit from continuing their kind.... Three generations of imbeciles are enough."

(*Buck v. Bell*)

Novick, Sheldon M. *Honorable Justice: The Life of Oliver Wendell Holmes*. Boston: Little, Brown, 1989.

Polenberg, Richard. *Fighting Faiths: The Abrams Case, the Supreme Court, and Free Speech*. Ithaca, N.Y.: Cornell University Press, 1999.

Schwartz, Bernard. *A History of the Supreme Court*. New York: Oxford University Press, 1993.

White, G. Edward. *Justice Oliver Wendell Holmes: Law and the Inner Self*. New York: Oxford University Press, 1993.

■ **Web Sites**

"Oliver Wendell Holmes, Jr." Arlington National Cemetery Web site. http://www.arlingtoncemetery.net/owholmes.htm.

"Oliver Wendell Holmes, Jr." Harvard Regiment Web site. http://harvardregiment.org/holmes.html.

—Lisa Paddock

Questions for Further Study

1. Oliver Wendell Holmes, Jr., makes a distinction between "logic" and "experience" in his judicial thinking. What did he mean by this distinction, and how did it affect his judicial opinions?

2. Holmes also calls attention to the distinction between "substantive due process" and "procedural due process." What is the distinction between the two forms of due process, and how did Holmes apply this distinction in such cases as *Lochner v. New York*?

3. Arguably, the most famous expression that survives from Holmes's work is his statement about shouting "fire" in a crowded theater. What is the significance of this statement, and how did its meaning influence Holmes's views regarding free speech?

4. Similarly, a famous expression that Holmes used is the "clear and present danger test" in connection with speech. What is the meaning of this expression, and how did it become a factor in Holmes's jurisprudence regarding free speech?

5. In the twenty-first century, a contentious political issue concerns "judicial activism," or the notion that judges sometimes use their own opinions to, in effect, make law. Opponents of judicial activism argue that law should be made by the people through their elected representatives and that the role of the judiciary is to interpret the law as written. To what extent was Holmes a proponent of judicial activism? Provide evidence from the documents.

6. Holmes served on the Supreme Court during World War I. To what extent did the demands of war influence Holmes's jurisprudence, particularly as it extended to free speech?

"Early Forms of Liability" (1881)

The object of this book is to present a general view of the Common Law. To accomplish the task, other tools are needed besides logic. It is something to show that the consistency of a system requires a particular result, but it is not all. The life of the law has not been logic: it has been experience. The felt necessities of the time, the prevalent moral and political theories, intuitions of public policy, avowed or unconscious, even the prejudices which judges share with their fellow-men, have had a good deal more to do than the syllogism in determining the rules by which men should be governed. The law embodies the story of a nation's development through many centuries, and it cannot be dealt with as if it contained only the axioms and corollaries of a book of mathematics. In order to know what it is, we must know what it has been, and what it tends to become. We must alternately consult history and existing theories of legislation. But the most difficult labor will be to understand the combination of the two into new products at every stage. The substance of the law at any given time pretty nearly corresponds, so far as it goes, with what is then understood to be convenient; but its form and machinery, and the degree to which it is able to work out desired results, depend very much upon its past.

In Massachusetts today, while, on the one hand, there are a great many rules which are quite sufficiently accounted for by their manifest good sense, on the other, there are some which can only be understood by reference to the infancy of procedure among the German tribes, or to the social condition of Rome under the Decemvirs.

I shall use the history of our law so far as it is necessary to explain a conception or to interpret a rule, but no further. In doing so there are two errors equally to be avoided both by writer and reader. One is that of supposing, because an idea seems very familiar and natural to us, that it has always been so. Many things which we take for granted have had to be laboriously fought out or thought out in past times. The other mistake is the opposite one of asking too much of history. We start with man full grown. It may be assumed that the earliest barbarian whose practices are to be considered had a good many of the same feelings and passions as ourselves.

The first subject to be discussed is the general theory of liability civil and criminal. The Common Law has changed a good deal since the beginning of our series of reports, and the search after a theory which may now be said to prevail is very much a study of tendencies. I believe that it will be instructive to go back to the early forms of liability, and to start from them.

It is commonly known that the early forms of legal procedure were grounded in vengeance. Modern writers have thought that the Roman law started from the blood feud, and all the authorities agree that the German law begun in that way. The feud led to the composition, at first optional, then compulsory, by which the feud was bought off. The gradual encroachment of the composition may be traced in the Anglo-Saxon laws, and the feud was pretty well broken up, though not extinguished, by the time of William the Conqueror. The killings and house-burnings of an earlier day became the appeals of mayhem and arson. The appeals de pace et plagis and of mayhem became, or rather were in substance, the action of trespass which is still familiar to lawyers. But as the compensation recovered in the appeal was the alternative of vengeance, we might expect to find its scope limited to the scope of vengeance. Vengeance imports a feeling of blame, and an opinion, however distorted by passion, that a wrong has been done. It can hardly go very far beyond the case of a harm intentionally inflicted: even a dog distinguishes between being stumbled over and being kicked.

Whether for this cause or another, the early English appeals for personal violence seem to have been confined to intentional wrongs....

It will be seen that this order of development is not quite consistent with an opinion which has been held, that it was a characteristic of early law not to penetrate beyond the external visible fact.... It has been thought that an inquiry into the internal condition of the defendant, his culpability or innocence, implies a refinement of juridical conception equally foreign to Rome before the Lex Aquilia, and to England when trespass took its shape. I do not know any very satisfactory evidence that a man was generally held liable either in Rome or England for the accidental consequences even of his own act. But whatever may have been the early law, the foregoing account shows the starting-point of the system with which we have to deal. Our system of private liability for the consequences of a man's own acts, that is, for his trespasses, started from the notion of actual intent and actual personal culpability.

The original principles of liability for harm inflicted by another person or thing have been less carefully considered hitherto than those which governed trespass, and I shall therefore devote the rest of this Lecture to discussing them. I shall try to show that this liability also had its root in the passion of revenge, and to point out the changes by which it reached its present form. But I shall not confine myself strictly to what is needful for that purpose, because it is not only most interesting to trace the transformation throughout its whole extent, but the story will also afford an instructive example of the mode in which the law has grown, without a break, from barbarism to civilization. Furthermore, it will throw much light upon some important and peculiar doctrines which cannot be returned to later.

A very common phenomenon, and one very familiar to the student of history, is this. The customs, beliefs, or needs of a primitive time establish a rule or a formula. In the course of centuries the custom, belief, or necessity disappears, but the rule remains. The reason which gave rise to the rule has been forgotten, and ingenious minds set themselves to inquire how it is to be accounted for. Some ground of policy is thought of, which seems to explain it and to reconcile it with the present state of things; and then the rule adapts itself to the new reasons which have been found for it, and enters on a new career. The old form receives a new content, and in time even the form modifies itself to fit the meaning which it has received....

The reader may begin to ask for the proof that all this has any bearing on our law of today. So far as concerns the influence of the Roman law upon our own, especially the Roman law of master and servant, the evidence of it is to be found in every book which has been written for the last five hundred years. It has been stated already that we still repeat the reasoning of the Roman lawyers, empty as it is, to the present day. It will be seen directly whether the German folk-laws can also be followed into England....

We will now follow the history of that branch of the primitive notion which was least likely to survive,—the liability of inanimate things....

I now come to what I regard as the most remarkable transformation of this principle, and one which is a most important factor in our law as it is today. I must for the moment leave the common law and take up the doctrines of the Admiralty. In the early books

which have just been referred to, and long afterwards, the fact of motion is adverted to as of much importance. A maxim of Henry Spigurnel, a judge in the time of Edward I., is reported, that "where a man is killed by a cart, or by the fall of a house, or in other like manner, and the thing in motion is the cause of the death, it shall be deodand."... The reader sees how motion gives life to the object forfeited....

A ship is the most living of inanimate things. Servants sometimes say "she" of a clock, but every one gives a gender to vessels. And we need not be surprised, therefore, to find a mode of dealing which has shown such extraordinary vitality in the criminal law applied with even more striking thoroughness in the Admiralty. It is only by supposing the ship to have been treated as if endowed with personality, that the arbitrary seeming peculiarities of the maritime law can be made intelligible, and on that supposition they at once become consistent and logical....

Those great judges, although of course aware that a ship is no more alive than a mill-wheel, thought that not only the law did in fact deal with it as if it were alive, but that it was reasonable that the law should do so. The reader will observe that they do not say simply that it is reasonable on grounds of policy to sacrifice justice to the owner to security for somebody else but that it is reasonable to deal with the vessel as an offending thing. Whatever the hidden ground of policy may be, their thought still clothes itself in personifying language....

We have now followed the development of the chief forms of liability in modern law for anything other than the immediate and manifest consequences of a man's own acts. We have seen the parallel course of events in the two parents,—the Roman law and the German customs, and in the offspring of those two on English soil with regard to servants, animals, and inanimate things. We have seen a single germ multiplying and branching into products as different from each other as the flower from the root. It hardly remains to ask what that germ was. We have seen that it was the desire of retaliation against the offending thing itself. Undoubtedly, it might be argued that many of the rules stated were derived from a seizure of the offending thing as security for reparation, at first, perhaps, outside the law. That explanation, as well as the one offered here; would show that modern views of responsibility had not yet been attained, as the owner of the thing might very well not have been the person in fault. But such has not been the view of those most competent to judge. A consideration of the earliest instances will show, as might have been expected, that vengeance, not compensation, and vengeance on the offending thing, was the original object. The ox in Exodus was to be stoned. The axe in the Athenian law was to be banished. The tree, in Mr. Tylor's instance, was to be chopped to pieces. The slave under all the systems was to be surrendered to the relatives of the slain man, that they might do with him what they liked. The deodand was an accursed thing. The original limitation of liability to surrender, when the owner was before the court, could not be accounted for if it was his liability, and not that of his property, which was in question. Even where, as in some of the cases, expiation seems to be intended rather than vengeance, the object is equally remote from an extrajudicial distress.

The foregoing history, apart from the purposes for which it has been given, well illustrates the paradox of form and substance in the development of law. In form its growth is logical. The official theory is that each new decision follows syllogistically from existing precedents. But just as the clavicle in the cat only tells of the existence of some earlier creature to which a collar-bone was useful, precedents survive in the law long after the use they once served is at an end and the reason for them has been forgotten. The result of following them must often be failure and confusion from the merely logical point of view.

On the other hand, in substance the growth of the law is legislative. And this in a deeper sense than that what the courts declare to have always been the law is in fact new. It is legislative in its grounds. The very considerations which judges most rarely mention, and always with an apology, are the secret root from which the law draws all the juices of life. I mean, of course, considerations of what is expedient for the community concerned. Every important principle which is developed by litigation is in fact and at bottom the result of more or less definitely understood views of public policy; most generally, to be sure, under our practice and traditions, the unconscious result of instinctive preferences and inarticulate convictions, but none the less traceable to views of public policy in the last analysis. And as the law is administered by able and experienced men, who know too much to sacrifice good sense to a syllogism, it will be found that, when ancient rules maintain themselves in the way that has been and will be shown in this book, new reasons more fitted to the time have been found for them, and that they gradually receive a new content, and at last a new form, from the grounds to which they have been transplanted.

But hitherto this process has been largely unconscious. It is important, on that account, to bring to mind what the actual course of events has been. If it were only to insist on a more conscious recognition of the legislative function of the courts, as just explained, it would be useful, as we shall see more clearly further on.

What has been said will explain the failure of all theories which consider the law only from its formal side; whether they attempt to deduce the corpus from a priori postulates, or fall into the humbler error of supposing the science of the law to reside in the elegantia juris, or logical cohesion of part with part. The truth is, that the law is always approaching, and never reaching, consistency. It is forever adopting new principles from life at one end, and it always retains old ones from history at the other, which have not yet been absorbed or sloughed off. It will become entirely consistent only when it ceases to grow.

The study upon which we have been engaged is necessary both for the knowledge and for the revision of the law. However much we may codify the law into a series of seemingly self-sufficient propositions, those propositions will be but a phase in a continuous growth. To understand their scope fully, to know how they will be dealt with by judges trained in the past which the law embodies, we must ourselves know something of that past. The history of what the law has been is necessary to the knowledge of what the law is.

Again, the process which I have described has involved the attempt to follow precedents, as well as to give a good reason for them. When we find that in large and important branches of the law the various grounds of policy on which the various rules have been justified are later inventions to account for what are in fact survivals from more primitive times, we have a right to reconsider the popular reasons, and, taking a broader view of the field, to decide anew whether those reasons are satisfactory. They may be, notwithstanding the manner of their appearance. If truth were not often suggested by error, if old implements could not be adjusted to new uses, human progress would be slow. But scrutiny and revision are justified.

But none of the foregoing considerations, nor the purpose of showing the materials for anthropology contained in the history of the law, are the immediate object here. My aim and purpose have been to show that the various forms of liability known to modern law spring from the common ground of revenge. In the sphere of contract the fact will hardly be material outside the cases which have been stated in this Lecture. But in the criminal law and the law of torts it is of the first importance. It shows that they have started from a moral basis, from the thought that some one was to blame.

It remains to be proved that, while the terminology of morals is still retained, and while the law does still and always, in a certain sense, measure legal liability by moral standards, it nevertheless, by the very necessity of its nature, is continually transmuting those moral standards into external or objective ones, from which the actual guilt of the party concerned is wholly eliminated.

Glossary

Admiralty	the court having jurisdiction over maritime affairs
Anglo-Saxon	reference to the Germanic tribes that invaded England in the fifth century
Common Law	law that evolves through court decisions, as opposed to statutory law, or law made by the legislature
Decemvirs	literally, "Ten Men"; any commission of ten men in the ancient Roman Republic
deodand	in law, an object that its owner must forfeit if it has caused the death of another
de pace et plagis	Latin for "of breach of the peace and wounding"
Exodus	the second book of the Bible
Lex Aquilia	in ancient Rome, a law that provided for compensation to the owner of property damaged through another's fault
Mr. Tylor	Edward B. Tylor (1832–1917), English anthropologist
syllogism	a logical argument in which a conclusion flows from two premises
torts	civil wrongs or breaches of duty to another, for which a person can be held liable
William the Conqueror	leader of the Norman (French) conquest of England beginning in 1066 and king of England from that date until his death (1027–1087)

LOCHNER V. NEW YORK (1905)

Holmes dissent

This case is decided upon an economic theory which a large part of the country does not entertain. If it were a question whether I agreed with that theory, I should desire to study it further and long before making up my mind. But I do not conceive that to be my duty, because I strongly believe that my agreement or disagreement has nothing to do with the right of a majority to embody their opinions in law. It is settled by various decisions of this court that state constitutions and state laws may regulate life in many ways which we as legislators might think as injudicious, or if you like as tyrannical, as this, and which, equally with this, interfere with the liberty to contract. Sunday laws and usury laws are ancient examples. A more modern one is the prohibition of lotteries. The liberty of the citizen to do as he likes so long as he does not interfere with the liberty of others to do the same, which has been a shibboleth for some well-known writers, is interfered with by school laws, by the Post Office, by every state or municipal institution which takes his money for purposes thought desirable, whether he likes it or not. The 14th Amendment does not enact Mr. Herbert Spencer's Social Statics. The other day we sustained the Massachusetts vaccination law.…Two years ago we upheld the prohibition of sales of stock on margins, or for future delivery, in the Constitution of California.…The decision sustaining an eight-hour law for miners is still recent.…Some of these laws embody convictions or prejudices which judges are likely to share. Some may not. But a Constitution is not intended to embody a particular economic theory, whether of paternalism and the organic relation of the citizen to the state or of laissez faire. It is made for people of fundamentally differing views, and the accident of our finding certain opinions natural and familiar, or novel, and even shocking, ought not to conclude our judgment upon the question whether statutes embodying them conflict with the Constitution of the United States.

General propositions do not decide concrete cases. The decision will depend on a judgment or intuition more subtle than any articulate major premise. But I think that the proposition just stated, if it is accepted, will carry us far toward the end. Every opinion tends to become a law. I think that the word "liberty," in the 14th Amendment, is perverted when it is held to prevent the natural outcome of a dominant opinion, unless it can be said that a rational and fair man necessarily would admit that the statute proposed would infringe fundamental principles as they have been understood by the traditions of our people and our law. It does not need research to show that no such sweeping condemnation can be passed upon the statute before us. A reasonable man might think it a proper measure on the score of health. Men whom I certainly could not pronounce unreasonable would uphold it as a first instalment of a general regulation of the hours of work. Whether in the latter aspect it would be open to the charge of inequality I think it unnecessary to discuss.

Glossary

Herbert Spencer	English social theorist and originator of the expression "survival of the fittest," who, in his 1851 book *Social Statics*, predicted that humanity would evolve sufficiently so that the need for a state would wither away (1820–1903)
laissez faire	a French expression meaning "to leave alone," often used to refer to an economic system with minimal regulation or government interference in free markets
shibboleth	a widely held belief, particularly among members of a political group or sect
Sunday laws	laws prohibiting work or commerce on Sunday
usury laws	laws against charging excessive interest on loans

SCHENCK V. UNITED STATES (1919)

The document in question, upon its first printed side, recited the first section of the Thirteenth Amendment, said that the idea embodied in it was violated by the Conscription Act, and that a conscript is little better than a convict. In impassioned language, it intimated that conscription was despotism in its worst form, and a monstrous wrong against humanity in the interest of Wall Street's chosen few. It said "Do not submit to intimidation," but in form, at least, confined itself to peaceful measures such as a petition for the repeal of the act. The other and later printed side of the sheet was headed "Assert Your Rights." It stated reasons for alleging that anyone violated the Constitution when he refused to recognize "your right to assert your opposition to the draft," and went on "If you do not assert and support your rights, you are helping to deny or disparage rights which it is the solemn duty of all citizens and residents of the United States to retain."

It described the arguments on the other side as coming from cunning politicians and a mercenary capitalist press, and even silent consent to the conscription law as helping to support an infamous conspiracy. It denied the power to send our citizens away to foreign shores to shoot up the people of other lands, and added that words could not express the condemnation such cold-blooded ruthlessness deserves,... winding up, "You must do your share to maintain, support and uphold the rights of the people of this country." Of course, the document would not have been sent unless it had been intended to have some effect, and we do not see what effect it could be expected to have upon persons subject to the draft except to influence them to obstruct the carrying of it out. The defendants do not deny that the jury might find against them on this point.

But it is said, suppose that that was the tendency of this circular, it is protected by the First Amendment to the Constitution. Two of the strongest expressions are said to be quoted respectively from well-known public men. It well may be that the prohibition of laws abridging the freedom of speech is not confined to previous restraints, although to prevent them may have been the main purpose, as intimated in *Patterson v. Colorado*.... We admit that in many places and in ordinary times the defendants in saying all that was said in the circular would have been within their constitutional rights. But the character of every act depends upon the circumstances in which it is done.... The most stringent protection of free speech would not protect a man in falsely shouting fire in a theatre and causing a panic. It does not even protect a man from an injunction against uttering words that may have all the effect of force.... The question in every case is whether the words used are used in such circumstances and are of such a nature as to create a clear and present danger that they will bring about the substantive evils that Congress has a right to prevent. It is a question of proximity and degree. When a nation is at war many things that might be said in time of peace are such a hindrance to its effort that their utterance will not be endured so long as men fight and that no Court could regard them as protected by any constitutional right. It seems to be admitted that if an actual obstruction of the recruiting service were proved, liability for words that produced that effect might be enforced. The statute of 1917 in section 4...punishes conspiracies to obstruct as well as actual obstruction. If the act, (speaking, or circulating a paper,) its tendency and the intent with which it is done are the same, we perceive no ground for saying that success alone warrants making the act a crime.... Indeed that case might be said to dispose of the present contention if the precedent covers all media concludendi. But as the right to free speech was not referred to specially, we have thought fit to add a few words.

Glossary

media concludendi	grounds for asserting a right
Wall Street	a street in New York City where the New York Stock Exchange is located; more generally, the investment industry as a whole

It was not argued that a conspiracy to obstruct the draft was not within the words of the Act of 1917. The words are "obstruct the recruiting or enlistment service," and it might be suggested that they refer only to making it hard to get volunteers. Recruiting heretofore usually having been accomplished by getting volunteers, the word is apt to call up that method only in our minds. But recruiting is gaining fresh supplies for the forces, as well by draft as otherwise. It is put as an alternative to enlistment or voluntary enrollment in this act.

ABRAMS V. UNITED STATES (1919)

Holmes dissent

I am aware, of course, that the word intent as vaguely used in ordinary legal discussion means no more than knowledge at the time of the act that the consequences said to be intended will ensue. Even less than that will satisfy the general principle of civil and criminal liability. A man may have to pay damages, may be sent to prison, at common law might be hanged, if, at the time of his act, he knew facts from which common experience showed that the consequences would follow, whether he individually could foresee them or not. But, when words are used exactly, a deed is not done with intent to produce a consequence unless that consequence is the aim of the deed. It may be obvious, and obvious to the actor, that the consequence will follow, and he may be liable for it even if he regrets it, but he does not do the act with intent to produce it unless the aim to produce it is the proximate motive of the specific act, although there may be some deeper motive behind.

It seems to me that this statute must be taken to use its words in a strict and accurate sense. They would be absurd in any other. A patriot might think that we were wasting money on aeroplanes, or making more cannon of a certain kind than we needed, and might advocate curtailment with success, yet, even if it turned out that the curtailment hindered and was thought by other minds to have been obviously likely to hinder the United States in the prosecution of the war, no one would hold such conduct a crime. I admit that my illustration does not answer all that might be said, but it is enough to show what I think, and to let me pass to a more important aspect of the case. I refer to the First Amendment to the Constitution, that Congress shall make no law abridging the freedom of speech.

I never have seen any reason to doubt that the questions of law that alone were before this Court in the Cases of Schenck, Frohwerk, and Debs were rightly decided. I do not doubt for a moment that by the same reasoning that would justify punishing persuasion to murder, the United States constitutionally may punish speech that produces or is intended to produce a clear and imminent danger that it will bring about forthwith certain substantive evils that the United States constitutionally may seek to prevent. The power undoubtedly is greater in time of war than in time of peace because war opens dangers that do not exist at other times.

But as against dangers peculiar to war, as against others, the principle of the right to free speech is always the same. It is only the present danger of immediate evil or an intent to bring it about that warrants Congress in setting a limit to the expression of opinion where private rights are not concerned. Congress certainly cannot forbid all effort to change the mind of the country. Now nobody can suppose that the surreptitious publishing of a silly leaflet by an unknown man, without more, would present any immediate danger that its opinions would hinder the success of the government arms or have any appreciable tendency to do so. Publishing those opinions for the very purpose of obstructing, however, might indicate a greater danger and at any rate would have the quality of an attempt. So I assume that the second leaflet if published for the purposes alleged in the fourth count might be punishable. But it seems pretty clear to me that nothing less than that would bring these papers within the scope of this law. An actual intent in the sense that I have explained is necessary to constitute an attempt, where a further act of the same individual is required to complete the substantive crime.... It is necessary where the success of the attempt depends upon others because if that intent is not present the actor's aim may be accomplished without bringing about the evils sought to be checked....

In this case sentences of twenty years imprisonment have been imposed for the publishing of two leaflets that I believe the defendants had as much right to publish as the Government has to publish the Constitution of the United States now vainly invoked by them. Even if I am technically wrong and enough can be squeezed from these poor and puny anonymities to turn the color of legal litmus paper; I will add, even if what I think the necessary intent were shown; the most nominal punishment seems to me all that possibly could be inflicted, unless the defendants are to be made to suffer not for what the indictment alleges but for the creed that they avow....

Persecution for the expression of opinions seems to me perfectly logical. If you have no doubt of your premises or your power and want a certain result with all your heart you naturally express your wishes in law and sweep away all opposition. To allow opposition by speech seems to indicate that you think the speech impotent, as when a man says that he has squared the circle, or that you do not care whole heartedly for the result, or that you doubt either your power or your premises. But when men have realized that time has upset many fighting faiths, they may come to believe even more than they believe the very foundations of their own conduct that the ultimate good desired is better reached by free trade in ideas—that the best test of truth is the power of the thought to get itself accepted in the competition of the market, and that truth is the only ground upon which their wishes safely can be carried out. That at any rate is the theory of our Constitution. It is an experiment, as all life is an experiment. Every year if not every day we have to wager our salvation upon some prophecy based upon imperfect knowledge. While that experiment is part of our system I think that we should be eternally vigilant against attempts to check the expression of opinions that we loathe and believe to be fraught with death, unless they so imminently threaten immediate interference with the lawful and pressing purposes of the law that an immediate check is required to save the country. I wholly disagree with the argument of the Government that the First Amendment left the common law as to seditious libel in force. History seems to me against the notion. I had conceived that the United States through many years had shown its repentance for the Sedition Act of 1798, by repaying fines that it imposed. Only the emergency that makes it immediately dangerous to leave the correction of evil counsels to time warrants making any exception to the sweeping command, "Congress shall make no law abridging the freedom of speech." Of course I am speaking only of expressions of opinion and exhortations, which were all that were uttered here, but I regret that I cannot put into more impressive words my belief that in their conviction upon this indictment the defendants were deprived of their rights under the Constitution of the United States.

Glossary

Debs	Eugene V. Debs, a Socialist American labor leader who was imprisoned for antiwar statements during World War I
Frohwerk	Jacob Frohwerk, who was fined and imprisoned for helping to prepare antidraft articles during World War I and whose appeal was denied in *Frohwerk v. United States*
litmus paper	paper that turns various colors to indicate the acidity or baseness of a substance

BUCK V. BELL (1927)

Carrie Buck is a feeble-minded white woman who was committed to the State Colony above mentioned in due form. She is the daughter of a feeble-minded mother in the same institution, and the mother of an illegitimate feeble-minded child. She was eighteen years old at the time of the trial of her case in the Circuit Court in the latter part of 1924. An Act of Virginia approved March 20, 1924…recites that the health of the patient and the welfare of society may be promoted in certain cases by the sterilization of mental defectives, under careful safeguard, etc.; that the sterilization may be effected in males by vasectomy and in females by salpingectomy, without serious pain or substantial danger to life; that the Commonwealth is supporting in various institutions many defective persons who if now discharged would become a menace but if incapable of procreating might be discharged with safety and become self-supporting with benefit to themselves and to society; and that experience has shown that heredity plays an important part in the transmission of insanity, imbecility, etc. The statute then enacts that whenever the superintendent of certain institutions including the above-named State Colony shall be of opinion that it is for the best interest of the patients and of society that an inmate under his care should be sexually sterilized, he may have the operation performed upon any patient afflicted with hereditary forms of insanity, imbecility, etc., on complying with the very careful provisions by which the act protects the patients from possible abuse.

The superintendent first presents a petition to the special board of directors of his hospital or colony, stating the facts and the grounds for his opinion, verified by affidavit. Notice of the petition and of the time and place of the hearing in the institution is to be served upon the inmate, and also upon his guardian, and if there is no guardian the superintendent is to apply to the Circuit Court of the County to appoint one. If the inmate is a minor notice also is to be given to his parents, if any, with a copy of the petition. The board is to see to it that the inmate may attend the hearings if desired by him or his guardian. The evidence is all to be reduced to writing, and after the board has made its order for or against the operation, the superintendent, or the inmate, or his guardian, may appeal to the Circuit Court of the

County. The Circuit Court may consider the record of the board and the evidence before it and such other admissible evidence as may be offered, and may affirm, revise, or reverse the order of the board and enter such order as it deems just. Finally any party may apply to the Supreme Court of Appeals, which, if it grants the appeal, is to hear the case upon the record of the trial in the Circuit Court and may enter such order as it thinks the Circuit Court should have entered. There can be no doubt that so far as procedure is concerned the rights of the patient are most carefully considered, and as every step in this case was taken in scrupulous compliance with the statute and after months of observation, there is no doubt that in that respect the plaintiff in error has had due process at law.

The attack is not upon the procedure but upon the substantive law. It seems to be contended that in no circumstances could such an order be justified. It certainly is contended that the order cannot be justified upon the existing grounds. The judgment finds the facts that have been recited and that Carrie Buck "is the probable potential parent of socially inadequate offspring, likewise afflicted, that she may be sexually sterilized without detriment to her general health and that her welfare and that of society will be promoted by her sterilization," and thereupon makes the order. In view of the general declarations of the Legislature and the specific findings of the Court obviously we cannot say as matter of law that the grounds do not exist, and if they exist they justify the result. We have seen more than once that the public welfare may call upon the best citizens for their lives. It would be strange if it could not call upon those who already sap the strength of the State for these lesser sacrifices, often not felt to be such by those concerned, in order to prevent our being swamped with incompetence. It is better for all the world, if instead of waiting to execute degenerate offspring for crime, or to let them starve for their imbecility, society can prevent those who are manifestly unfit from continuing their kind. The principle that sustains compulsory vaccination is broad enough to cover cutting the Fallopian tubes…. Three generations of imbeciles are enough. But, it is said, however it might be if this reasoning were applied generally, it fails when it is confined to the small number who are in the institutions named and is not applied to the multitudes outside. It is the usual last resort of constitutional arguments to point out shortcomings of this sort. But the answer is that the law does all that is needed when it does all that it can, indicates a policy, applies it to all within the lines, and seeks to bring within the lines all similarly situated so far and so fast as its means allow. Of course so far as the operations enable those who otherwise must be kept confined to be returned to the world, and thus open the asylum to others, the equality aimed at will be more nearly reached.

Glossary

salpingectomy	a method of sterilizing females by removal of the fallopian tubes, which carry eggs from the ovary to the uterus
vasectomy	a method of sterilizing males by removing a small section of the vas deferens, the duct through which sperm cells flow

Herbert Hoover (Library of Congress)

HERBERT HOOVER   1874–1964

Thirty-first President of the United States

Featured Documents
◆ "Rugged Individualism" Campaign Speech (1928)
◆ Inaugural Address (1929)
◆ Kellogg-Briand Pact Proclamation (1929)
◆ Annual Message to Congress (1931)
◆ "The Consequences of the Proposed New Deal" (1932)

Overview

Herbert Hoover was born in Iowa and moved to Oregon at age eleven. Hoover attended Stanford University, gained a degree in geology, and had a successful career in mining, becoming a millionaire at age forty. During World War I, Hoover gained international fame for his humanitarian efforts on behalf of the people of Belgium. In 1917 he was appointed the head of the U.S. government's Food Administration. Following the war, his stature grew as he oversaw relief programs for Europe. Hoover declined efforts by figures in the Democratic Party to entice him to run for office. A registered Republican, Hoover instead served as secretary of commerce in the administrations of Warren G. Harding and Calvin Coolidge. He won the presidential election in 1928, but the increasing economic strains of the Great Depression undermined his popularity, and he was defeated by Franklin D. Roosevelt in 1932. He remained active in party politics and later served as an adviser on humanitarian issues and government reform.

Hoover's foreign policy reflected his Quaker roots and his firsthand experiences with the devastation of World War I. He supported the Kellogg-Briand Pact, an international agreement designed to end armed conflict by banning aggressive war. The London Naval Conference of 1930 produced an accord that limited the number and size of naval warships. The president withdrew American troops from Haiti and Nicaragua and initiated an arms embargo on South America. In response to the Japanese invasion of Manchuria in 1931, the administration issued the Hoover-Stimson Doctrine, which declared that the United States would not recognize any territorial expansion that occurred through the use of force. As the global economic crisis worsened, Hoover suspended reparations from Germany.

The progressive Hoover entered office determined to reform the government. His administration undertook a range of progressive actions. Reforms were enacted at the Bureau of Indian Affairs and within both federal prisons and the veterans' hospital system. The government also initiated numerous public works projects, including the Oakland Bay Bridge (near San Francisco) and Boulder Dam (later named in Hoover's honor). However, most of the president's proposed reforms, such as old-age pensions and

tax relief for lower-income Americans, failed to win passage in Congress. More significant, Hoover initially moved slowly to counter the onset of the Great Depression. Furthermore, his support for protective tariffs accelerated the country's economic decline. The president preferred laissez-faire solutions to the worsening economic and social problems, although he endorsed more government action and intervention than had any of his predecessors. Democrats, who gained control of the House of Representatives in 1930, prevented many of the president's initiatives and voraciously criticized the restrained nature of the administration's economic policies. Meanwhile, Hoover angered conservatives by endorsing the largest tax increase in U.S. history up to that point in 1932. He left office unpopular, but his public perception was rehabilitated over time. Hoover emerged as one of the most prominent critics of government expansion during the New Deal years and was one of the leaders of the isolationist wing of the Republican Party in the aftermath of World War II.

Explanation and Analysis of Documents

Hoover was an honest public servant who entered politics reluctantly. He lacked the personal ambition of many of his contemporaries and truly believed his role in government was to serve the American people. Nonetheless, history initially unfairly portrayed the president as cold and uncaring, and Hoover became forever identified with the misery and suffering of the Great Depression. Hoover was not a dynamic speaker. His public addresses tend to contain a high degree of technical and policy information, but they lack dynamism. Hoover believed that the public could be swayed through logic and detail, and he looked down on other politicians who adopted a populist tone or who appealed to emotion in their messages. Consequently, many of his speeches and messages were intended to persuade people through the recitation of facts and figures, not necessarily to inspire. Five documents highlight Hoover's style and political beliefs: his 1928 campaign speech on rugged individualism, the president's 1929 inaugural address, an address on the Kellogg-Briand Pact that conveys Hoover's pacifism, his 1931 annual message to Congress that provides an overview of Hoover's efforts to

Time Line

deal with the Great Depression, and a 1932 campaign speech that criticizes Roosevelt's New Deal initiatives.

◆ "Rugged Individualism" Campaign Speech

In 1928 Hoover was arguably the most popular Republican in the country, and he easily secured the Republican nomination for the presidency after President Calvin Coolidge announced that he would not seek another term. Hoover had not developed a large or influential political machine, as had his rivals in the Republican presidential race or, indeed, as had Al Smith, his Democratic opponent in the general election. Smith, the governor of New York, was a populist who opposed Prohibition and whose Catholicism alienated southern Democrats. Most Americans perceived Hoover as a safe, competent administrator with a background in humanitarian causes who would continue the nation's postwar economic expansion. Indeed, in his acceptance speech at the party's convention in Kansas City, Hoover promised that his administration would achieve a final victory over poverty. His campaign slogan pledged a chicken in every pot and a car in every garage.

During the general campaign Hoover delivered seven radio addresses and made only select campaign appearances. His campaign did release an emotional film on Hoover that highlighted his background and his contributions during the great Mississippi flood of 1927, when he oversaw federal relief efforts. On October 22, 1928, at Madison Square Garden in New York City, Hoover delivered his best campaign speech and outlined his personal and political philosophy for the American people. Unlike many of his other addresses, the speech was based on broad themes and was an effort to draw Americans to him by tying the election to a larger ideological battle between the two parties.

Hoover begins by arguing that Americans had developed a unique governmental and economic system based on personal liberty. He notes that during World War I the government assumed a greater role in the economy and that it had curtailed individual freedom in order to protect national security. Hoover contends that when Republicans took control of Congress and the presidency in 1920, they endeavored to reverse this trend toward centralization and return the "government to its position as an umpire instead of a player in the economic game."

The Republican nominee argues that the Democrats were campaigning on a platform that would lead to the "abandonment of our American system and a surrender to the destructive operation of governmental conduct of commercial business." Hoover also accuses the Democrats of abandoning their own political ideals to embrace government in an effort to find solutions for the nation's problems. In many ways, Hoover's arguments foreshadowed the main ideological differences between the Republican and Democratic Parties for the rest of the twentieth century. The candidate declares that "every step of bureaucratizing of the business of our country poisons the very roots of liberalism" and that "liberalism should be found not striving to spread bureaucracy but striving to set bounds to it."

Hoover qualifies his support for individualism and limited government by noting that Washington had a role to play in regulating and protecting the nation's natural resources on behalf of the people. In addition, he acknowledges that true liberty required "economic justice as well as political and social justice" and that government had a responsibility to prevent any one group from dominating others. Hoover ends his address by describing how the American system prompted a "degree of well-being unparalleled in all the world" and asserts that the United States had come closer to "the abolition of poverty" than any other civilization.

Hoover was a progressive Republican who believed that government bureaucracies had to be carefully and routinely scrutinized to prevent graft, corruption, and inefficiency. He wanted to develop a balance between regulation and unfettered laissez-faire competition. He believed this was the best way to prevent the boom-and-bust cycle of the U.S. economy and gain higher, long-term rates of economic growth. Hoover's message resonated with most Americans at a time when the majority of the country remained prosperous. In the presidential balloting, Hoover easily defeated Smith. The Republican secured 58.2 percent of the popular vote to his opponent's 40.9 percent (and 444 electoral votes to 87).

◆ **Inaugural Address**

Hoover was inaugurated on March 4, 1929. His address contained many of the themes present in his campaign addresses, and it outlined the new president's priorities. The new president begins by noting some of the achievements of the past decade and thanking Calvin Coolidge, his predecessor. Hoover then presents an overview of the main challenges facing the nation and a brief summary of his plans to deal with those issues. He discusses crime and acknowledges that many Americans were increasingly dissatisfied with the criminal justice system. Hoover notes that the Eighteenth Amendment created new enforcement duties for the nation's justice system and provided new opportunities for criminals; however, he contends that most of the problems existed before the ratification of Prohibition. He proposes reforms to both the judicial and law enforcement systems. Once in office, these would culminate in increased efforts by federal agents to investigate and prosecute leading organized crime figures, such as the Chicago gangster Al Capone. Concurrently, Hoover also instituted reforms to the federal prison system.

The new president declares that his victory was an endorsement of his opposition to an increased government role in the economy, in that it showed "the determination of the American people that regulation of private enterprise and not Government ownership or operation is the course rightly to be pursued in our relation to business." He differentiates between public utilities and companies that produce or provide consumer goods and services. The latter should be generally free of significant government oversight, but the former, including power and sewage or water companies, were granted a degree of monopoly in provid-

Time Line

1932

■ **October 21**
Hoover delivers a speech on the eve of the election for his second term that defends his four years in office and attacks Franklin D. Roosevelt, his Democratic opponent, and Roosevelt's proposed New Deal.

■ **November 8**
Hoover is defeated by Roosevelt in the presidential election.

1947

■ Hoover is selected to chair a commission on government reform that became known as the Hoover Commission, with its main purpose to reorganize the executive departments.

1964

■ **October 20**
Hoover dies in New York City.

ing their services and therefore should have a higher degree of government regulation.

In previewing his foreign policy, Hoover praises the Kellogg-Briand Pact, which sought to outlaw war. He hoped that the accord would lead to disarmament and better relations between states. Hoover also expresses a desire for the United States to play a greater role in global peace efforts and pledges that the country would adopt a less forceful or aggressive foreign policy. The incoming president speaks at length about relations with Latin America and the Caribbean. In the period between his election and the inauguration, Hoover went on a goodwill tour of the region. In his inaugural address Hoover notes that the United States and the other nations of the Western Hemisphere shared a common history and that America had "particular bonds of sympathy and common interest with them." His remarks foreshadowed efforts by his administration to decrease hostility toward the United States by ending ongoing military interventions and taking a more active role to promote regional peace and stability. For instance, he mediated a territorial dispute between Chile and Peru that resulted in the Treaty of Lima in 1929.

Hoover closes his address by reciting a list of what he perceived to be "mandates" from the election. He declares that the American people wanted to preserve the "integrity of the Constitution" and limit government interference in the economy. He reiterates the need to address the rising crime rate through the "vigorous enforcement" of existing statutes and laws. Hoover also claims that the election was

French Foreign Minister Aristide Briand (center standing) gives his address in the Palais D'Orsay, Paris, on August 27, 1928, before the signing of the Pact of Paris; Frank Kellogg is seated to his left. (AP/Wide World Photos)

a referendum on the desire of the American people to limit government programs and expenditures, but he pledges to expand public works. The speech succinctly outlines how Hoover would govern for the next four years.

◆ Kellogg-Briand Pact Proclamation

In 1927 Secretary of State Frank Kellogg and French Foreign Minister Aristide Briand proposed an international agreement to renounce war. The two hoped that their initiative would prevent another world war and compel states to seek peaceful means to resolve conflicts. The resulting accord, signed in 1928, was known as the Pact of Paris and commonly referred to as the Kellogg-Briand Pact. Hoover was an enthusiastic supporter of the agreement when he was secretary of commerce and hoped that the accord would serve as a cornerstone of U.S. foreign policy when he became president.

Hoover announced in a short address from the East Room of the White House, during a ceremony on July 29, 1929, that the pact had entered into force. In attendance

were former President Coolidge, Kellogg, and representatives from the countries that had ratified the pact. The event was broadcast over the radio. The pact itself was very simple and straightforward. It contained only two substantive articles, and Hoover quotes both in their entirety during his remarks (a third article dealt with the treaty's ratification process). The first article denounced the use of force to resolve disagreements and declared that the signatory nations renounced force "as an instrument of national policy in their relations with one another." The second article reiterated its predecessor by pledging that the signatories agreed that only peaceful means would be used to settle disputes.

In his address Hoover describes the pact as a new page in world history and says that it embodied the "conscience and idealism of civilized nations." He also declares that the accord would have "instant appeal" for the people of the world. The president notes that fifteen nations had originally signed the pact and an additional thirty-one states had signed and ratified the agreement. Hoover goes on to praise the nations that adopted the pact, and he commended Kellogg and Briand for their roles in negotiating the agreement that bore their name. The president also praises his predecessor and the leaders of the Senate who guided the pact through the ratification process. (It passed the Senate on a vote of eighty-five to one on January 16, 1929.) He declares that the pact gave the world a "magnificent opportunity" to usher in a new era in human history in which war no longer existed. However, he also warns that the signatory nations had a "compelling duty" to ensure compliance with the Pact and to attempt to spread its influence by convincing other nations to sign.

Hoover's vision of world peace collapsed when Japan, one of the original signatories of the Kellogg-Briand Pact, invaded Manchuria in September 1931. By February of the following year the Japanese had seized control of all of Manchuria. On January 7, 1932, Secretary of State Henry Stimson sent diplomatic notes to both China and Japan in which he declared that the policy of the United States would be not to recognize territorial acquisitions if they occurred through the use of force. The notes became known as the Stimson Doctrine (sometimes referred to as the Hoover-Stimson Doctrine). The administration was criticized at home and abroad for not undertaking a more assertive response, but with the growing economic depression in the United States, the government's focus was increasingly on domestic issues. Stimson initially sought to institute economic sanctions against Japan, but Hoover demurred because of the potential impact on the domestic economy. The Stimson Doctrine would be employed again during events such as the Soviet invasion of Estonia, Latvia, and Lithuania in 1940.

◆ **Annual Message to Congress**

By December 1931 the United States was in a severe economic recession. Over the previous year, more than 2,200 banks had failed. Since Hoover entered office in 1929, the stock market lost more than 80 percent of its value, agricultural prices had fallen by 40 percent, and unemployment had grown from four million to eleven million. In an effort to protect domestic industries, Hoover signed the Smoot-Hawley Tariff Act in 1930. The tariff was the most restrictive in U.S. history and led to higher prices and reduced exports as other countries enacted retaliatory restrictions on U.S. products. In addition, the international financial and credit system had essentially collapsed. Hoover responded by proposing a moratorium on international debt and reparations payments. The president also increased spending on public works projects in an effort to reduce domestic unemployment and supported reforms in the banking system. However, Hoover continued to believe that the government should have only a limited role in the economy. The president sincerely believed that private groups, with appropriate support from the federal government, could provide relief and assistance for Americans facing hard economic times. He launched a number of public-private programs. Hoover also remained determined to minimize government spending in order to prevent a

large federal deficit. Many Americans wanted more government action, and Hoover's political opponents were able to successfully portray the president as remote and uncaring. As the unemployed and destitute created shanty camps, these areas became known as "Hoovervilles."

In his annual message to Congress, which was transmitted in written form on December 8, 1931, Hoover outlines the most ambitious program of government action in U.S. history outside wartime. The president did not betray his belief in the need to limit government intervention, but he proposed a broad agenda that foreshadowed the New Deal. Hoover begins the message by noting the extraordinary times that the nation faced, but he tells Americans that economic downturns "have been recurrent in the life of our country and are but transitory." He goes on to declare, "The nation has emerged from each of them with increased strength and virility." The president also reminds the nation that it had been free of the wide-scale labor strife and social revolution that other countries around the globe faced. Hoover was correct at the time, but in the summer of 1932 a group of war veterans, the Bonus Army, descended on Washington, D.C. The fifteen hundred veterans and their families demanded the immediate payment of bonus certificates that had been issued to them for their service and established a camp in the nation's capital. When police tried to disperse the marchers, fighting broke out, and Hoover ordered the military to scatter the protesters. The event further undermined the president's credibility and standing with average Americans.

To ameliorate unemployment, Hoover informs Congress that the federal government had embarked on the largest public works program in U.S. history. He also notes that he had taken action to curb immigration so as to lessen competition for jobs. The president also highlights his public-private partnerships, developed to provide assistance to the poor and unemployed without the creation of new federal bureaucracies. He then attempts to argue that the economic fundamentals of the United States were sound and that the country was in far better shape than most other states because of the nation's balance of trade and gold reserves. He argues against expanding the deficit and asserts that the nation needed to impose "a temporary increase in taxes" so that the budget would be balanced by 1933. The resultant tax increases further constrained economic growth. Hoover proposes that the federal bureaucracy be reformed and streamlined in an effort to reduce waste and redundancy and to direct more resources toward relief efforts.

The bulk of Hoover's message is devoted to specific policy prescriptions. For instance, he asks Congress to enact legislation to allow those who lost their savings in bank failures to recover some portion of the lost monies. Hoover also recommends the creation of a system of discount home-loan banks to make it easier to purchase homes or borrow money for farm operations. The president proposes that Congress create a public works administration to coordinate all construction and public works activities within the federal government. He also asks for the establishment of a reconstruction corporation to oversee the nation's efforts to recover. This proposal was implemented in 1932 with the creation of the Reconstruction Finance Corporation, which oversaw the dispersal of more than $2 billion in assistance to state and local governments and almost $10 billion in loans and assistance to businesses, banks, and farms.

Hoover argues strongly against the creation of government programs that would take employment away from private firms. He also states that he opposed revisions to the nation's tariffs and contends that any effort to revise the system "would prolong the depression." Hoover declares, "If the individual surrenders his own initiative and responsibilities, he is surrendering his own freedom and his own liberty." Instead, he contends, the federal government should take appropriate action to ensure that individuals were able to achieve success through their own efforts and initiative.

Hoover's annual message and his general theme of individual responsibility did not resonate with the American people. Most sought more government action to resolve the country's economic woes, and an increasing number wanted direct government intervention in the economy. In addition, Hoover's likely opponent in the upcoming 1932 presidential election, Franklin Roosevelt, increasingly called for an expansion of government programs that he labeled as a New Deal for the American people.

◆ **"The Consequences of the Proposed New Deal"**

On the eve of the 1932 presidential balloting, Hoover was extremely unpopular and personally disenchanted with the office. However, he deeply feared that politicians from either party were far too willing to compromise in efforts to garner public support. Hoover initially planned only a limited campaign, since he wanted to devote his attention to the Depression. As Roosevelt's popularity steadily increased and his own standing diminished, Hoover became more aggressive on the campaign trail. In a speech at Madison Square Garden on October 21, 1932, Hoover passionately defended his administration while attacking his opponent and the Democrats in general.

Hoover endeavored to cast the election in ideological terms. He declares at the beginning of his address that the upcoming balloting would be a "contest between two philosophies of government." Through the speech, Hoover criticizes many of Roosevelt's campaign promises and various plans put forth by congressional Democrats. For instance, the incumbent derides a proposal passed by Democrats in the House whereby the government would issue $2.3 billion in paper currency without backing. Hoover claims the initiative would create high inflation and notes that when the government did this after the Civil War, it created financial havoc. (Roosevelt took the nation off the gold standard after he was elected.)

The president also points out differences with his opponent on the government's role in public utilities. Hoover steadfastly maintains that private companies should manage electric power or water services and vetoed a bill that would have launched a large program to expand electricity through rural areas of the South. He believed that the government's role was to create favorable conditions that would prompt private companies to expand, but he argues that a government-run utility company would be more expensive than its private-sector counterpart and prone to waste and inefficiency. Roosevelt supported government-run efforts to provide electricity to areas that did not have service. Once in office, his administration created the Tennessee Valley Authority, which was responsible for expanding electrical service through many areas of the Deep South.

Throughout his campaign speech Hoover stresses the inappropriateness of government involvement in the private sector. He notes that as elected officials, members of Congress were under constant pressure from their constituents to secure privileges and benefits, and such pressure could undermine the effectiveness of corporations or firms if they were subject to significant government oversight. Hoover states that when the government becomes involved in a business or corporation, "531 Senators and Congressmen become actual boards of directors of that business."

Hoover argues that during times of prosperity, people tended to pay little attention to the importance of rights and liberties. Furthermore, during difficult times, people often sought immediate government action to solve problems, even at the expense of individual rights and freedom. The result was a steady erosion of liberties and freedoms. He reminds people, "It is men who do wrong, not our institutions."

In the 1932 election Roosevelt defeated Hoover with 57.4 percent to 39.7 percent of the popular vote. In addition, in the House, Democrats increased their majority to 313 seats, to 117 for the Republicans. (The Farmer-Labor Party secured five seats.) Republicans lost control of the Senate as the Democrats gained twelve seats. Hoover sought to work with the incoming administration in the interregnum between the election and the inauguration; however, Roosevelt rebuffed his predecessor's offers and instead developed an ambitious agenda, which he launched during his first one hundred days in office. Meanwhile, Hoover left office disgraced and determined to avoid public life.

Impact and Legacy

Hoover was in many ways one of the most qualified men to become the nation's chief executive. He had substantial experience and highly successful careers in both the private and public sectors. He also had a keen analytical mind and enjoyed the intricacies of formulating and implementing public policy. He foreshadowed later presidents with his tendency to discuss in great detail public policy in speeches. He enjoyed speaking on the radio and set the stage for the effective use of the medium by his successor, Roosevelt.

Hoover was highly principled and ultimately it was his strong belief in individualism and limited government that constrained his openness to government action during the Great Depression. He articulated a view of American politics and values that could not withstand the onslaught of the Great Depression and the New Deal. Hoover's stance

"*Liberalism should be found not striving to spread bureaucracy but striving to set bounds to it.*"

("Rugged Individualism" Campaign Speech)

"*We aspire to distinction in the world, but to a distinction based upon confidence in our sense of justice as well as our accomplishments within our own borders and in our own lives.*"

(Inaugural Address)

"*I covet for this administration a record of having further contributed to advance the cause of peace.*"

(Inaugural Address)

"*That was a proposal to the conscience and idealism of civilized nations. It suggested a new step in international law, rich with meaning, pregnant with new ideas in the conduct of world relations.*"

(Kellogg-Briand Pact Proclamation)

"*Business depressions have been recurrent in the life of our country and are but transitory. The nation has emerged from each of them with increased strength and virility because of the enlightenment they have brought, the readjustments and the larger understanding of the realities and obligations of life and work which come from them.*"

(Annual Message to Congress)

"*I am opposed to any direct or indirect government role. The breakdown and increased unemployment in Europe is due in part to such practices.*"

(Annual Message to Congress)

"*It is men who do wrong, not our institutions. It is men who violate the laws and public rights. It is men, not institutions, who must be punished.*"

("The Consequences of the Proposed New Deal")

on most issues, including government intervention in the economy, formed the mainstream of the Republican Party until the election of Dwight D. Eisenhower in 1952. His emphasis on limited government remained a core principle of the party through the twentieth century.

Key Sources

The Herbert Hoover Presidential Library and Museum has an extensive collection of papers, some available online at http://www.ecommcode2.com/hoover/research/index.html. *The Memoirs of Herbert Hoover* were published in three volumes (1951). The National Archives has published a four-volume collection of Hoover's presidential papers, *The Public Papers of the Presidents: Herbert Hoover (1929–1933)* and a two-volume set of his proclamations and exec-

utive orders, *Proclamations and Executive Orders: Herbert Hoover*. These collections and editions of Hoover's press conferences and other public addresses are available online through the American Presidency Project at the University of California, Santa Barbara, at http://www.presidency.ucsb.edu/.

Further Reading

■ Articles

Clements, Kendrick A. "Herbert Hoover and Conservation, 1921–1933." *American Historical Review* 89, no. 3 (June 1984): 67–88.

Nash, Gerald D. "Herbert Hoover and the Origins of the Reconstruction Finance Corporation." *Mississippi Valley Historical Review* 46, no. 3 (December 1959): 455–468.

Questions for Further Study

1. Although the Kellogg-Briand Pact promised an end to war, this hope was not to be achieved. Within two years of Hoover's proclamation regarding the agreement, Japan invaded Manchuria, and two years after that the Nazis took power in Germany. Why did the pact fail to prevent war, and in what ways did Hoover himself fall victim to the very same tragic optimism embodied in the agreement? One fruitful line of discussion in this vein is a consideration of his early reputation as "the Boy Wonder" who could solve virtually any problem with the application of modern ideas—an example of the naive belief in progress that did not survive the tragedies of the mid-twentieth century.

2. Hoover's reputation and legacy remain a matter of debate among historians. Although he was dismissed at the time as a do-nothing president whose inaction helped to worsen the Great Depression, that reality is far more complicated. Discuss assessments of Hoover and how opinions have changed.

3. Conventional wisdom maintains that Hoover was an old-style conservative, whereas Franklin D. Roosevelt represented a sharp break from the past. This simplistic evaluation is not likely to survive careful study of the two men and their policies. For example, in his 1931 message to Congress, Hoover calls for the creation of a Public Works Administration—an idea that history associates with Roosevelt, who actually put it into place. Compare the political views of the two leaders, noting similarities as well as crucial differences. In what ways did they agree on the role of government in economics; given that similarity, why did Roosevelt prove to be so much more successful in terms of his public image and legacy?

4. If Hoover were alive and active today, how would he fit into the political landscape? Would he still be a Republican? If so, would he be considered a liberal, moderate, or conservative? Use examples from his speeches to support your position.

5. Early in the twenty-first century, another Hoover appeared on the American political landscape: Margaret, Herbert's great-granddaughter, who became a prominent political commentator and media figure. Research and discuss the politics of Margaret Hoover (a blogger and active presence on the Internet) and her efforts to maintain her ancestor's legacy. In what ways is she "a chip off the old block" and in what ways do her views differ from those of her great-grandfather? Are those differences rooted in cultural and social changes that have occurred since Herbert Hoover's time, or do they result from other influences?

■ Books

Barber, William. *From New Era to New Deal: Herbert Hoover, the Economists, and American Economic Policy, 1921–1933*. New York: Cambridge University Press, 1985.

Best, Gary Dean. *Herbert Hoover: The Postpresidential Years, 1933–1964*. Stanford, Calif.: Hoover Institution Press, 1983.

Brandes, Joseph. *Herbert Hoover and Economic Diplomacy*. Pittsburgh, Pa.: University of Pittsburgh Press, 1962.

Burner, David. *Herbert Hoover: A Public Life*. New York: Alfred A. Knopf, 1979.

Ferrell, Robert H. *American Diplomacy in the Great Depression: Hoover-Stimson Foreign Policy, 1929–1933*. New Haven, Conn.: Yale University Press, 1957.

Krog, Carl E., and William R. Tanner, eds. *Herbert Hoover and the Republican Era: A Reconsideration*. Lanham, Md.: University Press of America, 1984.

Lisio, Donald J. *Hoover, Blacks, and Lily-Whites: A Study of Southern Strategies*. Chapel Hill: University of North Carolina Press, 1985.

Nash, Lee, ed. *Understanding Herbert Hoover: Ten Perspectives*. Stanford, Calif.: Hoover Institution Press, 1987.

—Tom Lansford

"RUGGED INDIVIDUALISM" CAMPAIGN SPEECH (1928)

After the war, when the Republican Party assumed administration of the country, we were faced with the problem of determination of the very nature of our national life. During one hundred and fifty years we have builded up a form of self-government and a social system which is peculiarly our own. It differs essentially from all others in the world. It is the American system. It is just as definite and positive a political and social system as has ever been developed on earth. It is founded upon a particular conception of self-government in which decentralized local responsibility is the very base. Further than this, it is founded upon the conception that only through ordered liberty, freedom, and equal opportunity to the individual will his initiative and enterprise spur on the march of progress. And in our insistence upon equality of opportunity has our system advanced beyond all the world.

During the war we necessarily turned to the government to solve every difficult economic problem. The government having absorbed every energy of our people for war, there was no other solution. For the preservation of the state the Federal Government became a centralized despotism which undertook unprecedented responsibilities, assumed autocratic powers, and took over the business of citizens. To a large degree we regimented our whole people temporarily into a socialistic state. However justified in time of war if continued in peace-time it would destroy not only our American system but with it our progress and freedom as well.

When the war closed, the most vital of all issues both in our own country and throughout the world was whether governments should continue their wartime ownership and operation of many instrumentalities of production and distribution. We were challenged with a peace-time choice between the American system of rugged individualism and a European philosophy of diametrically opposed doctrines—doctrines of paternalism and state socialism. The acceptance of these ideas would have meant the destruction of self-government through centralization of government. It would have meant the undermining of the individual initiative and enterprise through which our people have grown to unparalleled greatness.

When the Republican Party came into full power it went at once resolutely back to our fundamental conception of the state and the rights and responsibilities of the individual. Thereby it restored confidence and hope in the American people, it freed and stimulated enterprise; it restored the government to its position as an umpire instead of a player in the economic game.... If anyone will study the causes of retarded recuperation in Europe, he will find much of it due to stifling of private initiative on one hand, and overloading of the government with business on the other.

There has been revived in this campaign, however, a series of proposals which, if adopted, would be a long step toward the abandonment of our American system and a surrender to the destructive operation of governmental conduct of commercial business. Because the country is faced with difficulty and doubt over certain national problems—that is prohibition, farm relief, and electrical power—our opponents propose that we must thrust government a long way into the businesses which give rise to these problems. In effect, they abandon the tenets of their own party and turn to state socialism as a solution for the difficulties presented by all three. It is proposed that we shall change from prohibition to the state purchase and sale of liquor. If their agriculture relief program means anything, it means the government shall directly or indirectly buy and sell and fix prices of agriculture products. And we are to go into the hydro electric power business. In other words, we are confronted with a huge program of government in business....

I should like to state to you the effect that this projection of government in business would have upon our system of self-government and our economic system. That effect would reach to the daily life of every man and woman. It would impair the very basis of liberty and freedom not only for those left outside the fold of expanded bureaucracy but for those embraced within it.

Let us first see the effect upon self-government. When the Federal Government undertakes to go into commercial business it must at once set up the organization and administration of that business, and it immediately finds itself in a labyrinth, every alley of which leads to the destruction of self-government.

Commercial business requires a concentration of responsibility. Self-government requires decentralization and many checks and balances to safeguard liberty. Our government to succeed in business would need to become in effect a despotism. There at once begins the destruction of self-government.

It is a false liberalism that interprets itself into the government operation of commercial business. Every step of bureaucratizing of the business of our country poisons the very roots of liberalism—that is, political equality, free speech, free assembly, free press, and equality of opportunity. It is the road not to more liberty, but to less liberty. Liberalism should be found not striving to spread bureaucracy but striving to set bounds to it. True liberalism seeks all legitimate freedom first in the confident belief that without such freedom the pursuit of all other blessings and benefits is vain. That belief is the foundation of all American progress, political as well as economic.

Liberalism is a force truly of the spirit, a force proceeding from the deep realization that economic freedom cannot be sacrificed if political freedom is to be preserved. Even if governmental conduct of business could give us more efficiency instead of less efficiency, the fundamental objection to it would remain unaltered and unabated. It would destroy political equality. It would increase rather than decrease abuse and corruption. It would stifle initiative and invention. It would undermine the development of leadership. It would cramp and cripple the mental and spiritual energies of our people. It would extinguish equality and opportunity. It would dry up the spirit of liberty and progress. For these reasons primarily it must be resisted. For a hundred and fifty years liberalism has found its true spirit in the American system, not in the European systems.

I do not wish to be misunderstood in this statement. I am defining a general policy. It does not mean that our government is to part with one iota of its national resources without complete protection to the public interest. I have already stated that where the government is engaged in public works for purposes of flood control, of navigation, of irrigation, of scientific research or national defense, or in pioneering a new art, it will at times necessarily produce power or commodities as a by-product. But they must be a by-product of the major purpose, not the major purpose itself.

Nor do I wish to be misinterpreted as believing that the United States is free-for-all and devil-take-the-hindmost. The very essence of equality of opportunity and of American individualism is that there shall be no domination by any group or combination in this republic, whether it be business or political. On the contrary, it demands economic justice as well as political and social justice. It is no system of laissez faire....

And what have been the results of the American system? Our country has become the land of opportunity to those born without inheritance, not merely because of the wealth of its resources and industry but because of this freedom of initiative and enterprise. Russia has natural resources equal to ours. Her people are equally industrious, but she has not had the blessings of one hundred and fifty years of our form of government and our social system.

By adherence to the principles of decentralized self-government, ordered liberty, equal opportunity, and freedom to the individual, our American experiment in human welfare has yielded a degree of well-being unparalleled in all the world. It has come nearer to the abolition of poverty, to the abolition of fear

Glossary

checks and balances	safeguards, in the form of laws and organizational structures, that balance the power among branches of government by placing controls on their influence and authority
devil-take-the-hindmost	an expression meaning "every man for himself," implying that those who are not fast enough to get themselves out of the devil's way will become his victims
interprets itself	inserts itself
laissez faire	French term, meaning "let do," for a policy of allowing events, especially in economics, to run their course with a minimum of government intervention
paternalism	a policy of providing for citizens as though they were children and the government a father, the implication being that people are incapable of caring for themselves
retarded recuperation	slowed recovery from World War I
state socialism	any variety of Socialism in which the state controls factories and other means of production

of want, than humanity has ever reached before. Progress of the past seven years is the proof of it. This alone furnishes the answer to our opponents, who ask us to introduce destructive elements into the system by which this has been accomplished.

INAUGURAL ADDRESS (1929)

If we survey the situation of our Nation both at home and abroad, we find many satisfactions; we find some causes for concern. We have emerged from the losses of the Great War and the reconstruction following it with increased virility and strength. From this strength we have contributed to the recovery and progress of the world. What America has done has given renewed hope and courage to all who have faith in government by the people. In the large view, we have reached a higher degree of comfort and security than ever existed before in the history of the world. Through liberation from widespread poverty we have reached a higher degree of individual freedom than ever before. The devotion to and concern for our institutions are deep and sincere. We are steadily building a new race—a new civilization great in its own attainments. The influence and high purposes of our Nation are respected among the peoples of the world. We aspire to distinction in the world, but to a distinction based upon confidence in our sense of justice as well as our accomplishments within our own borders and in our own lives. For wise guidance in this great period of recovery the Nation is deeply indebted to Calvin Coolidge.

The most malign of all these dangers today is disregard and disobedience of law. Crime is increasing. Confidence in rigid and speedy justice is decreasing. I am not prepared to believe that this indicates any decay in the moral fiber of the American people. I am not prepared to believe that it indicates an impotence of the Federal Government to enforce its laws.

It is only in part due to the additional burdens imposed upon our judicial system by the eighteenth amendment. The problem is much wider than that. Many influences had increasingly complicated and weakened our law enforcement organization long before the adoption of the eighteenth amendment.

To reestablish the vigor and effectiveness of law enforcement we must critically consider the entire Federal machinery of justice, the redistribution of its functions, the simplification of its procedure, the provision of additional special tribunals, the better selection of juries, and the more effective organization of our agencies of investigation and prosecution that justice may be sure and that it may be swift....

The election has again confirmed the determination of the American people that regulation of private enterprise and not Government ownership or operation is the course rightly to be pursued in our relation to business. In recent years we have established a differentiation in the whole method of business regulation between the industries which produce and distribute commodities on the one hand and public utilities on the other. In the former, our laws insist upon effective competition; in the latter, because we substantially confer a monopoly by limiting competition, we must regulate their services and rates....

The recent treaty for the renunciation of war as an instrument of national policy sets an advanced standard in our conception of the relations of nations. Its acceptance should pave the way to greater limitation of armament, the offer of which we sincerely extend to the world. But its full realization also implies a greater and greater perfection in the instrumentalities for pacific settlement of controversies between nations. In the creation and use of these instrumentalities we should support every sound method of conciliation, arbitration, and judicial settlement.... The way should, and I believe will, be found by which we may take our proper place in a movement so fundamental to the progress of peace....

I have lately returned from a journey among our sister Republics of the Western Hemisphere. I have received unbounded hospitality and courtesy as their expression of friendliness to our country. We are held by particular bonds of sympathy and common interest with them.... While we have had wars in the Western Hemisphere, yet on the whole the record is in encouraging contrast with that of other parts of the world. Fortunately the New World is largely free from the inheritances of fear and distrust which have so troubled the Old World. We should keep it so....

Peace can be contributed to by respect for our ability in defense. Peace can be promoted by the limitation of arms and by the creation of the instrumentalities for peaceful settlement of controversies. But it will become a reality only through self-restraint and active effort in friendliness and helpfulness. I covet for this administration a record of having further contributed to advance the cause of peace....

It appears to me that the more important further mandates from the recent election were the maintenance of the integrity of the Constitution; the vigorous enforcement of the laws; the continuance of economy in public expenditure; the continued regulation of business to prevent domination in the community; the denial of ownership or operation of business by the Government in competition with its citizens; the avoidance of policies which would involve us in the controversies of foreign nations; the more effective reorganization of the departments of the Federal Government; the expansion of public works; and the promotion of welfare activities affecting education and the home.

the additional burdens imposed on our judicial system by the eighteenth amendment	increased crime due to the nationwide prohibition of alcohol sales
the Great War	World War I
our sister Republics of the Western Hemisphere	the countries of Latin America and the Caribbean
race	not "race" in an ethnic sense, but rather in the sense of "the human race"
recent treaty for the renunciation of war	the Kellogg-Briand Pact, signed August 27, 1928

KELLOGG-BRIAND PACT PROCLAMATION (1929)

In April 1928, as a result of discussions between our Secretary of State of the United States and the Minister of Foreign Affairs of France, the President directed Secretary Kellogg to propose to the nations of the world that they should enter into a binding agreement as follows:

"Article 1—The high contracting parties solemnly declare in the names of their respective peoples that they condemn recourse to war for the solution of international controversies, and renounce it as an instrument of national policy in their relations with one another."

"Article 2—The high contracting parties agree that the settlement or solution of all disputes or conflicts of whatever nature or of whatever origin they may be, which may arise among them, shall never be sought except by pacific means."

That was a proposal to the conscience and idealism of civilized nations. It suggested a new step in international law, rich with meaning, pregnant with new ideas in the conduct of world relations. It represented a platform from which there is instant appeal to the public opinion of the world as to specific acts and deeds.

The magnificent response of the world to these proposals is well indicated by those now signatory to its provisions. Under the terms of the treaty there have been deposited in Washington the ratifications of the 15 signatory nations....Beyond this the Treaty has today become effective also with respect to 31 other countries, the Governments of which have deposited with the Government of the United States instruments evidencing their definitive adherence to the Treaty....

I congratulate this assembly, the states it represents, and indeed, the entire world upon the coming into force of this additional instrument of humane endeavor to do away with war as an instrument of national policy and to obtain by pacific means alone the settlement of international disputes.

I am glad of this opportunity to pay merited tribute to the two statesmen whose names the world has properly adopted in its designation of this Treaty. To Aristide Briand, Minister of Foreign Affairs of France, we owe the inception of the Treaty and to his zeal is due a very large share of the success which attended the subsequent negotiations. To Frank B. Kellogg, then Secretary of State of the United States, we owe its expansion to the proportions of a treaty open to the entire world and destined, as I most confidently hope, shortly to include among its parties every country of the world.

Mr. Stimson has sent forward today a message of felicitation to M. Briand and to the people of France for whom he speaks. I am happy, Mr. Kellogg, to extend to you, who represented the people of the United States with such untiring devotion and with such a high degree of diplomatic skill in the negotiations of this Treaty, their everlasting gratitude.

We are honored here by the presence of President Coolidge under whose administration this great step in world peace was initiated. Under his authority and with his courageous support you, Mr. Kellogg, succeeded in this great service. And I wish to mark also the high appreciation in which we hold Senators Borah and Swanson for their leadership during its confirmation in the Senate.

May I ask you who represent governments which have accepted this Treaty, now a part of their supreme law and their most sacred obligations, to convey to them the high appreciation of the Government of the United States that through their cordial collaboration an act so auspicious for the future happiness of mankind has now been consummated. I

Glossary

M.	abbreviation of *monsieur*, or "mister" in French
Mr. Stimson	Henry L. Stimson (1867–1950), Hoover's secretary of state
Senators Borah and Swanson	William Edgar Borah, a Republican from Idaho, and Claude A. Swanson, a Democrat from Virginia

dare predict that the influence of the Treaty for the Renunciation of War will be felt in a large proportion of all future international acts. The magnificent opportunity and the compelling duty now open to us should spur us on to the fulfillment of every opportunity that is calculated to implement this Treaty and to extend the policy which it so nobly sets forth.

ANNUAL MESSAGE TO CONGRESS (1931)

If we lift our vision beyond these immediate emergencies we find fundamental national gains even amid depression....For the first time in the history of our major economic depressions there has been a notable absence of public disorders and industrial conflict....Business depressions have been recurrent in the life of our country and are but transitory. The nation has emerged from each of them with increased strength and virility because of the enlightenment they have brought, the readjustments and the larger understanding of the realities and obligations of life and work which come from them....

The emergencies of unemployment have been met by action in many directions. The appropriations for the continued speeding up of the great Federal construction program have provided direct and indirect aid to unemployment upon a large scale.... Immigration has been curtailed by administrative action.... The expansion of Federal employment agencies under appropriations by the Congress has proved most effective. Through the President's organization for unemployment relief, public and private agencies were successfully mobilized last winter to provide employment and other measures against distress....The evidence of the Public Health Service shows an actual decrease of sickness and infant and general mortality below normal years. No greater proof could be adduced that our people have been protected from hunger and cold and that the sense of social responsibility in the nation has responded to the need of the unfortunate....

The fundamental difficulties which have brought about financial strains in foreign countries do not exist in the United States. No external drain on our resources can threaten our position, because the balance of international payments is in our favor; we owe less to foreign countries than they owe to us; our industries are efficiently organized; our currency and bank deposits are protected by the greatest gold reserve in history....

We must have insistent and determined reduction in government expenses. We must face a temporary increase in taxes. Such increase should not cover the whole of these deficits or it will retard recovery. We must partially finance the deficit by borrowing. It is my view that the amount of taxation should be fixed so as to balance the Budget for 1933 except for the statutory debt retirement. Such government receipts would assure the balance of the following year's budget including debt retirement....

A method should be devised to make available quickly to depositors some portion of their deposits in closed banks as the assets of such banks may warrant. Such provision would go far to relieve distress in a multitude of families, would stabilize values in many communities, and would liberate working capital to thousands of concerns.

I recommend the establishment of a system of home-loan discount banks as the necessary companion in our financial structure of the Federal Reserve Banks and our Federal Land Banks. Such action will relieve present distressing pressures against home and farm property owners....

In order that the public may be absolutely assured and that the government may be in position to meet any public necessity, I recommend that an emergency Reconstruction Corporation of the nature of the former War Finance Corporation should be established....The very existence of such a bulwark will strengthen confidence....

Our people have a right to a banking system in which their deposits shall be safeguarded and the flow of credit less subject to storms. The need of a sounder system is plainly shown by the extent of bank failures....

As an aid to unemployment the Federal Government is engaged in the greatest program of public building, harbor, flood control, highway, waterway, aviation, merchant and naval ship construction in all history....

We must avoid burdens upon the government which will create more unemployment in private industry than can be gained by further expansion of employment by the Federal Government. We can now stimulate employment and agriculture more effactually and speedily through the voluntary measures in progress, through the thawing out of credit, through the building up of stability abroad, through the home loan discount banks, through an emergency finance corporation and the rehabilitation of the railways and other such directions.

I am opposed to any direct or indirect government role. The breakdown and increased unemployment in Europe is due in part to such practices. Our people are providing against distress from unemployment in true American fashion by a magnificent response to public appeal and by action of the local governments....

I have referred in previous messages to the profound need of further reorganization and consolidation of Federal administrative functions to eliminate overlap and waste, and to enable coordination and definition of government policies now wholly impossible in scattered and conflicting agencies which deal with parts of the same major function....

I recommend that all building and construction activities of the government now carried on by many departments be consolidated into an independent establishment under the President to be known as the "Public Works Administration" directed by a Public Works Administrator....

I am opposed to any general congressional revision of the tariff. Such action would disturb industry, business, and agriculture. It would prolong the depression....

In reaching solutions we must not jeopardize those principles which we have found to be the basis of the growth of the nation.... If the individual surrenders his own initiative and responsibilities, he is surrendering his own freedom and his own liberty. It is the duty of the national government to insist that both the local governments and the individual shall assume and bear these responsibilities as a fundamental of preserving the very basis of our freedom.

Glossary

appropriations	funds set aside by government for a particular purpose
Federal Land Banks	a system of farm credit institutions created by Congress in 1916
Federal Reserve Banks	a system of central banks, overseen by the Treasury Department, created by the 1913 Federal Reserve Act
home loan discount banks	a system of financial institutions, authorized by Hoover in 1931, that provided low-interest loans to home buyers
Public Works Administration	a government agency designed to provide jobs while constructing bridges, roads, and other significant public works
statutory debt retirement	paying off of public debt that has been incurred by legislative means
tariff	tax on imports
War Finance Corporation	an agency created during World War I to support industries essential to the war

"THE CONSEQUENCES OF THE PROPOSED NEW DEAL" (1932)

This campaign is more than a contest between two men. It is more than a contest between two parties. It is a contest between two philosophies of government.

We are told by the opposition that we must have a change, that we must have a new deal. It is not the change that comes from normal development of national life to which I object, but the proposal to alter the whole foundations of our national life which have been builded through generations of testing and struggle, and of the principles upon which we have builded the nation. The expressions our opponents use must refer to important changes in our economic and social system and our system of government, otherwise they are nothing but vacuous words. And I realize that in this time of distress many of our people are asking whether our social and economic system is incapable of that great primary function of providing security and comfort of life to all of the firesides of our 25,000,000 homes in America, whether our social system provides for the fundamental development and progress of our people, whether our form of government is capable of originating and sustaining that security and progress....

Another proposal of our opponents, which would destroy the American system, is that of inflation of the currency. The bill, which passed the last session of the Democratic House, called upon the Treasury of the United States to issue $2,300,000,000 in paper currency that would be unconvertible into solid values. Call it what you will, greenbacks or fiat money. It was that nightmare which overhung our own country for years after the Civil War....

I have stated unceasingly that I am opposed to the Federal Government going into the power business. I have insisted upon rigid regulation. The Democratic candidate has declared that under the same conditions, which may make local action of this character desirable, he is prepared to put the Federal Government into the power business. He is being actively supported by a score of Senators in this campaign, many of whose expenses are being paid by the Democratic National Committee, who are pledged to Federal Government development and operation of electrical power.

If these measures, these promises, which I have discussed; or these failures to disavow these projects; this attitude of mind, mean anything, they mean the enormous expansion of the Federal Government; they mean the growth of bureaucracy such as we have never seen in our history. No man who has not occupied my position in Washington can fully realize the constant battle which must be carried on against incompetence, corruption, tyranny of government expanded into business activities. If we first examine the effect on our form of government of such a program, we come at once to the effect of the most gigantic increase in expenditure ever known in history. That alone would break down the savings, the wages, the equality of opportunity among our people. These measures would transfer vast responsibilities to the Federal Government from the States, the local governments, and the individuals. But that is not all; they would break down our form of government. Our legislative bodies cannot delegate their authority to

Glossary

fiat money	currency whose value is determined solely by the issuing government's fiat, or order, that it should be accepted at a particular value
greenbacks	government-issued currency, as opposed to Federal Reserve notes (the latter being the only variety now circulating in the United States)
inflation of the currency	in general, an economic situation of rising prices, but here tied to the idea of increased money supply, which was believed to lower the purchasing power of the dollar
unconvertible into solid values	not exchangeable for fixed units of value, such as precious metals (as opposed to paper currency, whose value depends on the strength of the government that issues it)

any dictator, but without such delegation every member of these bodies is impelled in representation of the interest of his constituents constantly to seek privilege and demand service in the use of such agencies. Every time the Federal Government extends its arm, 531 Senators and Congressmen become actual boards of directors of that business....

In the ebb and flow of economic life our people in times of prosperity and ease naturally tend to neglect the vigilance over their rights. Moreover, wrongdoing is obscured by apparent success in enterprise. Then insidious diseases and wrongdoings grow apace. But we have in the past seen in times of distress and difficulty that wrongdoing and weakness come to the surface, and our people, in their endeavors to correct these wrongs, are tempted to extremes which may destroy rather than build.

It is men who do wrong, not our institutions. It is men who violate the laws and public rights. It is men, not institutions, who must be punished.

J. Edgar Hoover (Library of Congress)

J. EDGAR HOOVER   1885–1972

First Director of the Federal Bureau of Investigation

Featured Documents
◆ Testimony before the House Un-American Activities Committee (1947)
◆ Letter to Harry Truman's Special Consultant, Sidney Souers (1950)
◆ Memo on the Leak of Vietnam War Information (1965)
◆ Memo on Martin Luther King (1965)
◆ Memo on Abbott Howard Hoffman (1970)

Overview

J. Edgar Hoover, who directed the Federal Bureau of Investigation (FBI) for eight different presidents over a forty-eight-year period, dominated federal law enforcement through much of the twentieth century. Hoover, however, was also a controversial figure. He maintained his power in Washington, D.C., in part by amassing enormous amounts of information on enemies both real and perceived. Many allege that Hoover regarded constitutional rights as an inconvenience and routinely engaged in illegal activities and "dirty tricks" in the investigation not only of criminals but also of those who held political beliefs he considered a threat to American security. His targets included such figures as the civil rights leader Martin Luther King, Jr., and Abbie Hoffman, leading member of the Youth International Party (Yippies) and one of the Chicago Seven, a group charged with conspiracy and inciting to riot for protests that took place in Chicago, Illinois, at the 1968 Democratic National Convention.

John Edgar Hoover was born on January 1, 1885, in Washington, D.C. Little is known about his early life. He attended George Washington University, taking a law degree in 1917. During World War I he worked at the U.S. Justice Department and rose to the head of the Enemy Aliens Registration Section at a time when the nation felt deep unease about immigration and subversive foreign influences. Then, in 1919, Hoover was appointed head of the Justice Department's Radical Division (later called the General Intelligence Division), which played a major role in the Palmer raids of 1919 and 1920. Some ten thousand suspected political radicals were arrested in the raids. Hoover was chosen to be deputy director of the Bureau of Investigation in 1921. In 1924 he was named acting head of the bureau. On May 10, 1924, President Calvin Coolidge appointed him director of the bureau, which became known as the Federal Bureau of Investigation in 1935. In this capacity he produced a large number of documents, many of them in the form of memos summarizing his activities or issuing directives to members of the FBI in connection with investigations.

In the 1930s, under Hoover's direction, "G-men," as FBI agents were known, focused their attention on organized crime and gangsterism. In the years leading up to World War II, Hoover's greatest concern was the threat of foreign subversives and saboteurs on American soil. This concern with subversion deepened during the cold war, when Hoover's focus was on Communism and then on antiwar and revolutionary groups, including members of the civil rights movement. His concern with subversion and revolutionary sentiments is reflected in various documents produced by Hoover during his tenure at the FBI. He also made his concern with Communists and subversion the subject of books, though it is likely that the books under his name were ghostwritten. Hoover died on May 2, 1972.

Explanation and Analysis of Documents

Throughout his career as director of the FBI, Hoover documented his concerns about Communism, subversion, and anti-American activities in the United States. These concerns are reflected in testimony he gave before the House Un-American Activities Committee as well as in reams of memoranda and letters he issued to the FBI's deputy director, agents in charge of FBI field offices, and others. An overriding theme is how the nation and the FBI should respond to these threats, whether real or imagined.

◆ Testimony before the House Un-American Activities Committee

On March 26, 1947, Hoover testified before the House Un-American Activities Committee. In his testimony he outlined his beliefs about the threat that Communism posed to the United States in the early cold war period. Hoover's concern about the spread of Communist ideology and revolution was part of a pattern that dated back some three decades during the early days of Hoover's career in public service. The Bolshevik Revolution in Russia in 1917 had struck fear into the hearts of Americans. This fear was stoked by an open "Letter to American Workers," written by Vladimir Lenin, the guiding hand of the Russian Revolution, and dated August 22, 1918. In this letter Lenin said that Communists were invincible "because the world proletarian revolution is invincible" (http://www.marxists.org/archive/lenin/works/1918/aug/20.htm).

Time Line

1885
- **January 1**
  John Edgar Hoover is born in Washington, D.C.

1917
- Hoover graduates from George Washington University with a law degree.

1919
- Hoover is appointed head of the Justice Department's Radical Division.

1919–1920
- The Palmer raids take place under the direction of the Radical Division.

1921
- Hoover is appointed deputy director of the Bureau of Investigation.

1924
- Hoover is appointed acting head of the Bureau of Investigation.
- **May 10**
  President Calvin Coolidge appoints Hoover director of the Bureau of Investigation.

1935
- The Bureau of Investigation becomes the Federal Bureau of Investigation.

1947
- **March 26**
  Hoover testifies before the House Un-American Activities Committee.

1950
- **July 7**
  Hoover outlines his plan for dealing with threats to the nation in a letter to Harry Truman's special consultant, Sidney Souers.

1965
- **June 29**
  Hoover issues a memo dealing with the source of a leak of information about escalation of the war in Vietnam.

In the years following World War I numerous factors conspired to spread the fear of Communism. One was immigration. In the 1910s and into the 1920s Americans were unsettled by the number of foreigners entering the country, particularly those from southern and eastern Europe. Between 1892 and 1914, seventeen million immigrants had passed through New York's Ellis Island. Most were not from northern European nations such as England, Germany, or the Scandinavian countries but from such places as Romania, Hungary, Greece, and Italy. Many Americans had begun to regard these so-called hordes of less desirable immigrants as the source of disease, crime, and anarchy. Many were Jewish and Slavic, but in the eyes of some Americans they were all "dirty Bolsheviks." The perception among many members of the public was that these immigrants were a subversive element.

Related to this concern was deep unease about the activities of organized labor. In the years following World War I, a wave of labor strikes rocked the country. Many turned violent. Panic began to spread when a bomb exploded at the home of U.S. Attorney General A. Mitchell Palmer on June 3, 1919. Similar bombs detonated in several other cities nationwide, and some sixteen additional bombs addressed to prominent persons were intercepted only because of an alert New York City postal worker. Hysteria grew as Americans concluded that the bombs were the work of Communists and other aliens, many of them members of the labor movement, who were thought to be plotting a revolution in the United States and the overthrow of American capitalism. It was in this climate that J. Edgar Hoover launched his professional career.

During the 1930s, as the specter of Fascism grew in Europe, many Americans became more tolerant of Communism, which they saw as a counterweight to the right-wing fanaticism of Adolf Hitler in Germany, Benito Mussolini in Italy, and their proxy Nationalist rebels during the Spanish Civil War (1936–1939). At this time the FBI was just as concerned with Fascism as it was with Communism. During the war Hoover and the bureau earned praise from President Harry Truman for their role in the so-called Quirin affair. In this incident the FBI successfully tracked down and rounded up Nazi saboteurs who had been landed by German U-boats off the shores of Long Island and Florida—though it has been noted that the FBI succeeded in large part because one of the saboteurs turned himself in to the FBI and confessed.

The Nazi-Soviet pact of 1939 put an end to this toleration, and once again Communism was on the defensive. Meanwhile, in the United States, the House Un-American Activities Committee (HUAC) was formed on May 26, 1938. In the climate of apprehension surrounding World War II and the early years of the cold war with the Soviet Union, HUAC acquired considerable power. In 1945 HUAC was made permanent, though it was abolished in 1975. In the late 1940s and early 1950s the committee adopted tactics that many people came to regard as overly threatening and severe. The committee conducted hearings in which accusations of Communist sympathies were leveled against people and their associates. The mere accusation often became a measure of guilt. Witnesses who refused to cooperate were suspected of disloyalty and treason, and they were often held in contempt. A particular target of HUAC was Hollywood, which the committee regarded as a hotbed of Communist sympathy. Seeming to fuel suspicions was the refusal of the Hollywood Ten, a group of screenwriters, to cooperate with the committee's investigations. Although HUAC failed to uncover a Communist network in Hollywood, film industry executives and later those in radio, television, and the theater refused to hire anyone suspected of Communist leanings. Many careers were destroyed as a result of HUAC investigations.

During World War II and in the early years of the cold war, Hoover was instrumental in ferreting out spies, and although many were critical of his tactics, it was difficult to argue with the results. One major undertaking Hoover directed was the so-called Venona Project (a name that has no particular significance). Before the outbreak of the war, the United States and Great Britain launched a project designed to locate and eavesdrop on Soviet spies in the two countries. Late in the war and beyond, thousands of encrypted Soviet dispatches to spies in the United States, England, and Australia were intercepted and decoded. Information from these documents was used to expose several high-profile Soviet agents, including Alger Hiss, Julius and Ethel Rosenberg, Kim Philby, and Guy Burgess. While many observers regarded Hoover as paranoid about Soviet spying, in fact these documents to a large extent confirm the suspicion the director outlined in his testimony to HUAC; some historians argue that they in part justify the anti-Communist hysteria whipped up by Senator Joseph McCarthy in the early 1950s. The project, however, remained a secret; revealing the source of the information would have alerted the Soviets that their codes had been broken. Hoover kept many Venona documents in a safe in his office, and it was not until 1995 that Venona Project materials were released to the public.

In the first two paragraphs of his remarks to HUAC, Hoover summarizes his view that Communists planned "bloody revolution" and the overthrow of American capitalism. He makes reference to *The History of the Communist Party of the Soviet Union*, a 1939 textbook of sorts written and published by the Soviet Communist Party's Central Committee. Hoover goes on to outline the aims of American Communists, arguing that their support for many of the aims of the New Deal (such as old-age pensions) is really a cover for more subversive goals. He notes the emergence of the Committee for the Constitutional Rights of Communists and its efforts to defend suspected Communists against legal action. Ironically, Hoover maintained a file on the U.S. Supreme Court based on his belief that the Court may have been sympathetic to Communists.

Hoover alludes to suspicions that Communists had infiltrated the labor unions and the entertainment industry. He goes on to raise a number of questions that might be asked about any organization or industry to determine whether it has Communist leanings. He uses the phrase

Time Line

1965

- **July 6**
  In a U.S. Department of Justice memorandum, Hoover discusses the issue of linkages between Martin Luther King, Jr., Communism, and the anti–Vietnam War movement.

1970

- **April 27**
  Hoover issues a memo directing the San Francisco FBI field office to investigate the identity of Grace Slick, an associate of the radical Abbie Hoffman.

1972

- **May 2**
  Hoover dies.

"fifth column" in reference to American Communists; the term continues to be used to refer to a subversive population residing within a country. (In 1936, during the Spanish Civil War, the general Emilio Mola coined the term when he stated that his four columns of troops marching on Madrid would be supported by a "fifth column" of citizens in the city.) Hoover concludes that only the vigilance of the American public and its resistance to Communist propaganda could neutralize the threat.

◆ Letter to Harry Truman's Special Consultant, Sidney Souers

A measure of Hoover's concern with internal subversion and sabotage is his letter of July 7, 1950, to Admiral Sidney Souers, former director of Central Intelligence working as a special consultant to President Harry Truman. This letter was written twelve days after the start of the Korean War. In this letter Hoover outlines a plan for dealing with four types of national emergency: an attack on the United States, a threatened invasion of the United States, an attack on U.S. troops in legally occupied territory, and rebellion. The proposal was far-reaching, and because of its dubious legality it was never enacted.

Under the heading "Action to Be Taken by the Department of Justice," Hoover outlines the essence of his proposed plan. Its chief feature was that in response to any of the four triggers he cites the president would have the authority to suspend the writ of habeas corpus. This is the constitutional guarantee that people cannot be detained without formal charges being leveled against them. Historically, suspension was a wartime measure used to deal with enemy aliens, terrorists, and saboteurs; during the Civil War, for example, President Abraham Lincoln suspended habeas corpus to deal with Confederate infiltrators in northern cities. Hoover's plan also calls for giving legal authority to this measure through a previously prepared joint resolution of Congress and an executive order issued by the president.

Hoover notes that under the plan's provisions, the FBI would be granted authority to round up and detain "individuals who are potentially dangerous to the internal security." Under the heading "Action to Be Taken by the FBI," Hoover notes that the bureau had a list of some twelve thousand of these people, 97 percent of whom were American citizens. These persons would be detained through the authority of a "master warrant" that would apply not to single individuals but to any person on the list.

In the final section of the letter, "Detention and Subsequent Procedures," Hoover specifies the procedures that would be followed after arrest. The detainees would be taken to military detention facilities, where the charges against them would be stated. Each accused person would have a hearing before a panel consisting of one judge and two American citizens. Such a hearing would not be bound by the rules of evidence that would normally apply in a criminal trial.

◆ Memo on the Leak of Vietnam War Information

This memo, dated June 29, 1965, provides a good example of the kind of routine memo Hoover would have produced in connection with the social and political upheavals of the 1960s, particularly those in connection with the war in Vietnam. Here he summarizes a conversation he had with President Lyndon Johnson about the leak of information concerning deepening U.S. involvement in Vietnam. This information had been leaked to the journalist Philip Geyelin, who, as a correspondent for the *Wall Street Journal*, had spent time in Vietnam and returned home extremely disillusioned by the war. He later continued his antiwar stance as deputy editor and then editor of the editorial pages of the *New York Times*.

Essentially, the memo outlines action the FBI had taken in response to the leak, including interviews with high-level officials at the Pentagon and State Department. On the basis of these interviews, Hoover concludes that a particular person was responsible for the leak. In the text of the memo, though, various names and other information have been blacked out; they are indicated by the bracketed word "redacted." This is a common practice when the FBI, the Central Intelligence Agency, and other federal agencies release documents that were originally confidential or secret. For various reasons, the agencies do not wish to make public details such as the names of individuals involved. Thus, although it is clear that Hoover has identified the person he believes is responsible for the leak, the name of that person is not revealed.

◆ Memo on Martin Luther King

Throughout the 1950s and early to mid-1960s, Hoover directed investigations of members and spokespersons of various social and political movements in the United States, including the New Left, the anti–Vietnam War movement, and student activist groups. Prominently, he investigated the possibility of ties between Communism and the civil rights movement. As arguably the most prominent civil rights leader, Martin Luther King, Jr., was a target of intense FBI investigation.

In a memo to Deputy Director Clyde Tolson and others (dated July 6, 1965), Hoover summarizes a discussion he had with the U.S. attorney general, Nicholas Katzenbach. The subject of the memo was possible linkages between King, Communism, and the antiwar movement. Hoover makes reference to Stanley Levison, a New York businessman who was prominent in leftist politics in the 1950s and 1960s. Levison, for example, had held a leadership position in the U.S. Communist Party during the 1950s and twice was called to testify before the U.S. Senate's Subcommittee on Internal Security; his testimony is still classified. Levison served as a speechwriter for King, and while Hoover never believed that King was actually a Communist, he feared that Communists such as Levison could manipulate King to foment civil unrest. On this basis, he authorized the bugging and wiretapping of King's offices and hotel rooms.

Hoover additionally references Clarence Jones, a member of King's inner circle of advisers. Hoover states that Jones, too, is a Communist and therefore represents further proof of a possible tie between the Communist and antiwar movements. Bayard Rustin, also named in the memo, was likewise a prominent civil rights activist and one of King's key advisers. Hoover asserts that Roy Wilkins, who at the time was the executive director of the National Association for the Advancement of Colored People, and James Farmer, cofounder of the Congress of Racial Equality, were opposed to some of the activities of King in reference to the Vietnam War.

◆ Memo on Abbott Howard Hoffman

Hoover's concern with subversion persisted through the 1950s and 1960s. Under his direction the FBI continued to investigate suspected Communists, but Hoover extended these investigations to an assortment of groups. These groups included Socialist organizations, sympathizers of the anti–Vietnam War movement, the vaguely defined New Left, radical student groups such as Students for a Democratic Society, white hate groups such as the Ku Klux Klan and the National States' Rights Party, and militant black organizations—or those he perceived to be militant, such as the Southern Christian Leadership Conference, the Congress of Racial Equality, the Nation of Islam, the Black Panthers, and the National Association for the Advancement of Colored People. By gathering extensive information about these organizations, along with their leaders and members, Hoover hoped to disrupt their activities and discredit them.

Abbott Howard Hoffman, better known as "Abbie" Hoffman, was one of the most well-known political and social activists of the 1960s, as much for his theatrics and flamboyant personality as for his viewpoints. He began his career in the civil rights movement and participated in the activities of the Student Nonviolent Coordinating Committee. He became active in the antiwar movement, at one time organizing a mass demonstration in which fifty thousand protesters attempted to use psychic energy to levitate the Pentagon, which, in their view, would bring the Vietnam War to an end. He became most widely known as a member of the Chicago Seven, a group of activists tried for conspiracy and inciting riot in connection with the turmoil surrounding the 1968 Democratic National Convention in Chicago. (The group was originally called the Chicago Eight but became the Chicago Seven when the trial of one of the accused was severed from that of the others.) Through these and other activities Hoffman became almost symbolic of the 1960s counterculture.

Again, Hoover's memo to the special agent in charge of the FBI's San Francisco office (dated April 27, 1970) is an example of the workaday communications of the bureau. Hoover calls attention to a "Mrs. Grace Slick." Hoover did not know it at the time ("Bufiles are negative on Mrs. Slick," meaning that the bureau did not have a file on her), but Slick, born Grace Barnett Wing, was a vocalist and songwriter for the rock band Jefferson Airplane. She and Tricia Nixon, the daughter of President Richard Nixon, were alumnae of Finch College. Because of this connection, Slick was invited to a party at the White House. She invited Abbie Hoffman to be her escort, and the two planned to spike the president's tea with the drug LSD. The two never entered, however, because security guards identified Hoffman. In this memo Hoover asks the San Francisco office to identify Slick and determine the nature of her connections with Hoffman.

Impact and Legacy

The legacy of J. Edgar Hoover is mixed. For nearly five decades he dominated federal law enforcement. Almost single-handedly, he forged the image of American G-men, who exhibited "Fidelity, Bravery, Integrity" (the FBI's motto) in fighting crime. From 1924 until his death in 1972 he turned the sometimes inept Bureau of Investigation, the FBI's predecessor organization, into a highly efficient professional organization. He kept firm control over the image of the FBI, in part by censoring movies and television shows that depicted the bureau, including films produced by the Walt Disney enterprise. He dedicated his life to public service at the sacrifice of personal concerns, and decades after his death his is still almost a household name. Indeed, Hoover and the FBI remain closely intertwined in the minds of most Americans.

Hoover's reputation was perhaps greatest during the 1930s. After the economic collapse that began with the stock market crash in 1929, many Americans began to identify the nation's financial institutions as adversaries. In particular, the high number of foreclosures on farms whose owners could not repay their debts gave banks throughout much of the nation, especially in the rural Midwest, a bad name. Accordingly, when a rash of daring bank robberies

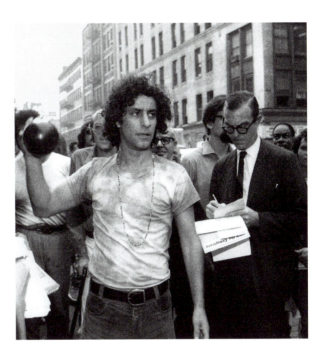

Yippie leader Abbie Hoffman holds a toy bomb in New York City on September 16, 1969, a week before his trial as part of the Chicago Seven. (AP/Wide World Photos)

broke out in the 1930s, some Americans were almost sympathetic to the colorful robbers and regarded them as romantic figures. Some of these outlaws became the stuff of legend: John Dillinger, Machine Gun Kelly, Ma Barker, and Clyde Champion Barrow and Bonnie Parker—the infamous bandits Bonnie and Clyde.

Local authorities were helpless to stop these robberies. Since many of the robbers made their getaways across state lines, however, the FBI had the authority to pursue them, so local authorities called in the bureau's help. Many of these pursuits, including the one that led to the gunning down of John Dillinger in Chicago, were highly publicized; much like the outlaws themselves, they captured the public's imagination. It was largely in response to these endeavors that the bureau's powers were expanded and its name changed. During the 1930s Hoover took advantage of the FBI's growing reputation and influence to expand recruitment efforts and to create the FBI Laboratory Services to examine forensic evidence and the Identification Division, which assembled the world's largest collection of fingerprints. It was Hoover, always concerned about the image and reputation of the bureau, who insisted that agents have college educations and that they dress in sober suits and ties. More important, he insisted that his agents remain loyal to him; young agents lived in fear that they would somehow offend the director and be fired or, at best, be shunted off to unattractive assignments. The iron fist with which Hoover presided over the FBI enabled him to engage in the kinds of activities depicted in these documents.

History has not been kind to Hoover's reputation. In 1976 the FBI's activities were investigated by the U.S. Sen-

> *"The best antidote to communism is vigorous, intelligent, old-fashioned Americanism, with eternal vigilance.... I...favor unrelenting prosecution wherever they are found to be violating our country's laws. As Americans, our most effective defense is a workable democracy that guarantees and preserves our cherished freedoms."*
>
> (Testimony before the House Un-American Activities Committee)

> *"What is important is the claim of the communists themselves that for every party member there are 10 others ready, willing and able to do the party's work. Herein lies the greatest menace of communism."*
>
> (Testimony before the House Un-American Activities Committee)

> *"For a long period of time the FBI has been accumulating the names, identities and activities of individuals found to be potentially dangerous to the internal security through investigation. These names have been compiled in an index...and will be attached to the master warrant referred to above. This master warrant will, therefore, serve as legal authority for the FBI to cause the apprehension and detention of the individuals maintained in this index."*
>
> (Letter to Harry Truman's Special Consultant, Sidney Souers)

ate's Select Committee to Study Governmental Operations with Respect to Intelligence Activities, usually referred to as the Church Committee after its chairman, Senator Frank Church of Idaho. The committee's investigation revealed that FBI investigations often relied on infiltration of suspected subversive groups; psychological warfare, including rumors, false reports, and other "dirty tricks"; harassment through the legal system; and illegal activities, such as wiretapping, break-ins, vandalism, and violence.

The Church Committee, in reference to a concerted series of FBI covert actions, concluded in their *Supplementary Detailed Staff Reports on Intelligence Activities and the Rights of Americans* that "many of the techniques [the FBI] used would be intolerable in a democratic society even if all of the targets had been involved in violent activity, but COINTELPRO [the FBI's covert action programs] went far beyond that." The committee accused the bureau of conducting a "sophisticated vigilante operation aimed squarely at preventing the exercise of First Amendment rights of speech and association, on the theory that preventing the

growth of dangerous groups and the propagation of dangerous ideas would protect the national security and deter violence" (http://www.icdc.com/~paulwolf/cointelpro/churchfinalreportIIIa.htm). In the eyes of many historians, these extralegal activities reflected the views and personality of the FBI's director. Presidents and attorneys general, his nominal bosses, feared that if they tried to replace him, he would reveal personal information they did not want made public.

By some measures, the concerns of the FBI under Hoover could be regarded as little short of absurd. The bureau kept a file, for example, on the issue of whether the lyrics to the Kingsmen's 1963 version of the classic rock song "Louie Louie" were obscene. Files were maintained on musicians such as the Beatles, Elvis Presley, and Frank Sinatra; artists such as Andy Warhol and Pablo Picasso; the baseball legend Mickey Mantle; actors such as Marilyn Monroe; and thousands of others, although it should be noted that many of these files had to do with investigation not of the individual but of threats against that individual. The FBI also kept extensive files on crime families, the Ku

Klux Klan, the murder of civil rights workers in Mississippi in 1964, and a host of other criminal activities and legitimate threats to the nation's security.

At his death, Hoover's body lay in state in the Rotunda of the U.S. Capitol, one of only twenty-eight public figures granted this honor (as of 2008). Yet in 2001 Senator Harry Reid sponsored legislation to have Hoover's name taken off the FBI headquarters, arguing that Hoover's illegal activities rendered his name a blemish on the building. Hoover, who never married, was an intensely personal man who devoted his life to the FBI, but after his death rumors began to emerge about his personal life, including allegations that he was a transvestite and perhaps a homosexual. Investigators have inquired into Hoover's ancestry as well. His birth certificate was not filed until 1938, and circumstantial evidence supports claims that family records were altered, perhaps to disguise African American roots in Mississippi. None of these claims has been conclusively proved. Such probing into the director's personal life and psyche is testimony to America' fascination with this complex man.

Key Sources

Hoover's own writings are contained in books that many students of the FBI believe were probably ghostwritten. One is *Masters of Deceit: The Story of Communism in America and How to Fight It* (1959). The other is *J. Edgar Hoover on Communism* (1969). James D. Bales compiled a volume titled *J. Edgar Hoover Speaks concerning Communism* (1970). Readers interested in various FBI investigations during the Hoover years should consult the Paperless Archives Web site at http://www.paperlessarchives.com/alphabetical.html and the FBI's own Freedom of Information Act Web site at http://foia.fbi.gov/. For example, information about the Venona Project can be found at http://foia.fbi.gov/venona/venona.pdf.

Further Reading

■ Books

Ackerman, Kenneth. *Young J. Edgar: Hoover, the Red Scare, and the Assault on Civil Liberties*. New York: Carroll and Graf, 2007.

Questions for Further Study

1. Discuss Hoover's testimony before the House Un-American Activities Committee in light of what is known today about actual Communist infiltration of the United States. Abuses of power by Joseph McCarthy, not to mention Hoover himself, helped bring about a reaction among intellectuals that has often been described as "anti-anti-Communist." This attitude, which became the conventional wisdom regarding Communism, held that Communists represented little danger compared with the witch-hunting excesses committed by anti-Communists. Is this really true? Were there, in fact, organizations that fit many of the characteristics of a front organization as outlined by Hoover? Were there certain basic principles of Communism that conflicted with loyalty to the United States?

2. In his letter to Sidney Souers, special consultant to President Harry Truman, Hoover outlines a stringent program of emergency measures for dealing with the threat of subversion in wartime. Examine the specifics of this plan and the reasons why the severity of the steps recommended would have made such practices unconstitutional. In particular, Hoover recommended suspension of habeas corpus rights. How does his plan compare with practices employed by President Abraham Lincoln some ninety years earlier, during the Civil War, or with those of President George W. Bush half a century later, in the war on terror?

3. Critique Hoover's memo on Martin Luther King, Jr. To what extent were his suspicions unjustified, and, conversely, was there anything about King's rhetoric, attitude, activities, and associates that might have justified fears of Communist influence? Compare King's views on Communism with those of two other African American leaders mentioned in the document, Roy Wilkins and Bayard Rustin.

4. For almost anyone who grew up in the rock 'n' roll era, Hoover's reference to "Mrs. Grace W. Slick, 2400 Fulton Street" in his memo on Abbott Howard ("Abbie") Hoffman is just a bit amusing. Apparently he had no idea that Slick was widely known as the vocalist for Jefferson Airplane on such hits as "Somebody to Love" and "White Rabbit." (An Airplane greatest-hits package released in 1987 was titled *2400 Fulton Street*.) As a solid member of "the Establishment," was Hoover simply incapable of understanding contemporary youth culture? How might he have avoided being so out of touch, and what effect would this have had on his actions and his success?

Charles, Douglas M. *J. Edgar Hoover and the Anti-Interventionists: FBI Political Surveillance and the Rise of the Domestic Security State, 1939– 1945.* Columbus: Ohio State University Press, 2007.

Garrow, David J. *The FBI and Martin Luther King, Jr., from "Solo" to Memphis.* Rev. ed. New Haven, Conn.: Yale University Press, 2001.

Gentry, Curt. *J. Edgar Hoover: The Man and the Secrets.* New York: W. W. Norton, 1991.

Lowenthal, Max. *The Federal Bureau of Investigation.* Westport, Conn.: Greenwood Press, 1971.

Powers, Richard Gid. *Secrecy and Power: The Life of J. Edgar Hoover.* New York: Free Press, 1987.

Schott, Joseph L. *No Left Turns: The FBI in Peace and War.* New York: Praeger, 1975.

Summer, Anthony. *Official and Confidential: The Secret Life of J. Edgar Hoover.* New York: G. P. Putnam's Sons, 1993.

Theoharis, Athan G., ed. *From the Secret Files of J. Edgar Hoover.* Chicago: Ivan R. Dee, 1993.

———, and John Stuart Cox. *The Boss: J. Edgar Hoover and the Great American Inquisition.* Philadelphia: Temple University Press, 1988.

■ Web Sites

Lenin, V. I. "Letter to American Workers," trans. Jim Riordan. V. I. Lenin Internet Archive Web site. http://www.marxists.org/archive/lenin/works/1918/aug/20.htm.

Select Committee to Study Governmental Operations. *Supplementary Detailed Staff Reports on Intelligence Activities and the Rights of Americans,* Book III: *Final Report of the Select Committee to Study Governmental Operations with Respect to Intelligence Activities, United States Senate, April 23, 1976.* AARC Public Library Web site. http://www.aarclibrary.org/publib/contents/church/contents_church_reports_book3.htm.

—Michael J. O'Neal

TESTIMONY BEFORE THE HOUSE UN-AMERICAN ACTIVITIES COMMITTEE (1947)

My feelings concerning the Communist Party of the United States are well known. I have not hesitated over the years to express my concern and apprehension. As a consequence its professional smear brigades have conducted a relentless assault against the FBI. You who have been members of this committee also know the fury with which the party, its sympathizers and fellow travelers can launch an assault. I do not mind such attacks. What has been disillusioning is the manner in which they have been able to enlist support often from apparently well-meaning but thoroughly duped persons....

The communist movement in the United States began to manifest itself in 1919. Since then it has changed its name and its party line whenever expedient and tactical. But always it comes back to fundamentals and bills itself as the party of Marxism-Leninism. As such, it stands for the destruction of our American form of government; it stands for the destruction of American democracy; it stands for the destruction of free enterprise; and it stands for the creation of a "Soviet of the United States" and ultimate world revolution....

The communist, once he is fully trained and indoctrinated, realizes that he can create his order in the United States only by "bloody revolution." Their chief textbook, "The History of the Communist Party of the Soviet Union," is used as a basis for planning their revolution. Their tactics require that to be successful they must have:

1. The will and sympathy of the people.

2. Military aid and assistance.

3. Plenty of guns and ammunition.

4. A program for extermination of the police as they are the most important enemy and are termed "trained fascists."

5. Seizure of all communications, buses, railroads, radio stations, and other forms of communications and transportation....

One thing is certain. The American progress which all good citizens seek, such as old-age security, houses for veterans, child assistance, and a host of others, is being adopted as window dressing by the communists to conceal their true aims and entrap gullible followers....

The mad march of Red fascism is a cause for concern in America. But the deceit, the trickery, and the lies of the American communists are catching up with them. Whenever the spotlight of truth is focused upon them they cry, "Red-baiting." Now that their aims and objectives are being exposed, they are creating a Committee for the Constitutional Rights of Communists, and are feverishly working to build up what they term a quarter-million-dollar defense fund to place ads in papers, to publish pamphlets, to buy radio time. They know that their backs will soon be to the wall....

What is important is the claim of the communists themselves that for every party member there are 10 others ready, willing and able to do the party's work. Herein lies the greatest menace of communism. For these are the people who infiltrate and corrupt various spheres of American life. So rather than the size of the Communist Party, the way to weigh its true importance is by testing its influence, its ability to infiltrate....

The communists have developed one of the greatest propaganda machines the world has ever known. They have been able to penetrate and infiltrate many respectable public opinion mediums. They capitalize upon ill-founded charges associating known honest progressive liberals with left-wing causes. I have always entertained the view that there are few appellations more degrading than "communist" and hence it should be reserved for those justly deserving the degradation.

The communist propaganda technique is designed to promote emotional response with the hope that the victim will be attracted by what he is told the communist way of life holds in store for him. The objective, of course, is to develop discontent and hasten the day when the communists can gather sufficient support and following to overthrow the American way of life....

Communists and their followers are prolific letter writers, and some of the more energetic ones follow the practice of directing numerous letters of protest to editors but signing a different name to each. Members of Congress are well aware of communists starting their pressure campaigns by an avalanche of mail which follows the party line....

The American communists launched a furtive attack on Hollywood in 1935 by the issuance of a directive calling for a concentration in Hollywood. The orders called for action on two fronts: One, an effort to infiltrate the labor unions; two, infiltrate the so-called intellectual and creative fields.

In movie circles, communists developed an effective defense a few years ago in meeting criticism. They would counter with the question "After all, what is the matter with communism?" It was effective because many persons did not possess adequate knowledge of the subject to give an intelligent answer....

I feel that this committee could render a great service to the nation through its power of exposure in quickly spotlighting existing front organizations and those which will be created in the future. There are easy tests to establish the real character of such organizations:

1. Does the group espouse the cause of Americanism or the cause of Soviet Russia?

2. Does the organization feature as speakers at its meeting known communists, sympathizers, or fellow travelers?

3. Does the organization shift when the party line shifts?

4. Does the organization sponsor causes, campaigns, literature, petitions, or other activities sponsored by the party or other front organizations?

5. Is the organization used as a sounding board by or is it endorsed by communist-controlled labor unions?

6. Does its literature follow the communist line or is it printed by the communist press?

7. Does the organization receive consistent favorable mention in the communist publications?

8. Does the organization present itself to be nonpartisan yet engage in political activities and consistently advocate causes favored by the communists?

9. Does the organization denounce American and British foreign policy while always lauding Soviet policy?

10. Does the organization utilize communist "double-talk" by referring to Soviet dominated countries as democracies, complaining that the United States is imperialistic and constantly denouncing monopoly-capital?

11. Have outstanding leaders in public life openly renounced affiliation with the organization?

12. Does the organization, if espousing liberal progressive causes, attract well-known honest patriotic liberals or does it denounce well-known liberals?

13. Does the organization have a consistent record of supporting the American viewpoint over the years?

14. Does the organization consider matters not directly related to its avowed purposes and objectives?

The Communist Party of the United States is a fifth column if there ever was one. It is far better organized than were the Nazis in occupied countries prior to their capitulation. They are seeking to weaken America just as they did in their era of obstruction when they were aligned with the Nazis. Their goal is the overthrow of our government. There is no doubt as to where a real communist's loyalty rests. Their allegiance is to Russia, not the United States....

What can we do? And what should be our course of action? The best antidote to communism is vigorous, intelligent, old-fashioned Americanism, with eternal vigilance. I do not favor any course of action which would give the communists cause to portray and pity themselves as martyrs. I do favor unrelenting prosecution wherever they are found to be violating our country's laws.

As Americans, our most effective defense is a workable democracy that guarantees and preserves our cherished freedoms.

I would have no fears if more Americans possessed the zeal, the fervor, the persistence and the industry to learn about this menace of Red fascism. I do fear for the liberal and progressive who has been hoodwinked and duped into joining hands with the communists. I confess to a real apprehension so long as communists are able to secure ministers of the gospel to promote their evil work and espouse a cause that is alien to the religion of Christ and Judaism. I do fear so long as school boards and parents tolerate conditions whereby communists and fellow travelers, under the guise of academic freedom, can teach our youth a way of life that eventually will destroy the sanctity of the home, that undermines faith in God, that causes them to scorn respect for constituted authority and sabotage our revered Constitution.

I do fear so long as American labor groups are infiltrated, dominated or saturated with the virus of communism. I do fear the palliation and weasel-worded gestures against communism indulged in by some of our labor leaders who should know better, but who have become pawns in the hands of sinister but astute manipulations for the communist cause.

I fear for ignorance on the part of all our people who may take the poisonous pills of communist propaganda.

Glossary

fascists	technically, a term for members of a specific radical right-wing political movement but often used by Communists for anyone who opposed them
fellow traveler	a person who does not belong to a Communist organization but nevertheless supports or sympathizes with the aims of Communists
fifth column	a term coined by Emilio Mola, a general in the Spanish Civil War (1936–1939), who said that his four marching columns of troops were supported by a fifth column of spies
front organizations	groups that pretend to represent the interests of peace, freedom, justice, and other ideals but are, in fact, paid for and supported by Communist governments
Marxism-Leninism	theory of Communism based on the writings of the German economist Karl Marx (1818–1883), with the practical means for seizing control of government deriving from the Russian revolutionary Vladimir Lenin (1870–1924)
Red	Communist
Red-baiting	denunciation of Communists or alleged Communists
Red fascism	terminology equating the extremism of left and right and implying that their actions are more important than their professed political beliefs
Soviet	in its original meaning, a workers' council—an idea developed independent of (and later taken over by) the Communists
when they were aligned with the Nazis	the period from the signing of the Nazi-Soviet Non-Aggression Pact on August 23, 1939, to Germany's invasion of Russia on June 22, 1941

LETTER TO HARRY TRUMAN'S SPECIAL CONSULTANT, SIDNEY SOUERS (1950)

Washington, July 7, 1950

My Dear Admiral:

For some months representatives of the FBI and of the Department of Justice have been formulating a plan of action for an emergency situation wherein it would be necessary to apprehend and detain persons who are potentially dangerous to the internal security of the country. I thought you would be interested in a brief outline of the plan.

Action to Be Taken by the Department of Justice

The plan envisions four types of emergency situations: (1) attack upon the United States; (2) threatened invasion; (3) attack upon United States troops in legally occupied territory; and (4) rebellion.

The plan contains a prepared document which should be referred to the President immediately upon the existence of one of the emergency situations for the President's signature. Briefly, this proclamation recites the existence of the emergency situation and that in order to immediately protect the country against treason, espionage and sabotage the Attorney General is instructed to apprehend all individuals potentially dangerous to the internal security.

In order to make effective these apprehensions, the proclamation suspends the Writ of Habeas Corpus for apprehensions made pursuant to it. The plan also contains a prepared joint resolution to be passed by Congress and an Executive Order for the President which too will validate the previous Presidential proclamation.

The next step in the plan is a prepared order from the Attorney General to the Director of the FBI to apprehend dangerous individuals, conduct necessary searches and seize contraband as defined in the plan. Together with the order to the Director of the FBI the Attorney General will forward a master warrant attached to a list of names of individuals which names have previously been furnished from time to time to the Attorney General by the FBI as being individuals who are potentially dangerous to the internal security.

It should be pointed out that the plan does not distinguish between aliens and citizens and both are included in its purview. If for some reason the full plan is not put into operation it has so been drawn that the section applicable only to alien enemies may be put into effect.

Action to Be Taken by the FBI

For a long period of time the FBI has been accumulating the names, identities and activities of individuals found to be potentially dangerous to the internal security through investigation. These names have been compiled in an index which index has been kept up to date. The names in this index are the ones that have been furnished to the Department of Justice and will be attached to the master warrant referred to above. This master warrant will, therefore, serve as legal authority for the FBI to cause the apprehension and detention of the individuals maintained in this index.

The index now contains approximately twelve thousand individuals, of which approximately ninety-seven per cent are citizens of the United States. Immediately upon receipt of instructions and the master warrant from the Attorney General the various FBI Field Divisions will be instructed by expeditious means to cause the apprehension of the indi-

Glossary

apprehensions made pursuant to it	arrests made under the authority of Hoover's proposed plan
Writ of Habeas Corpus	a petition for judicial relief from unlawful detention, as when a person is imprisoned without being formally charged

viduals within their various territories. Each FBI Field Division maintains an index of the individuals within its territory, which index is so arranged that it may be used for ready apprehension purposes. Upon apprehension the individuals will be delivered to the nearest jail for temporary detention and action by the Attorney General.

Detention and Subsequent Procedures

The permanent detention of these individuals will take place in regularly established Federal detention facilities. These facilities have been confidentially surveyed and the facilities have been found to be adequate in all areas except in the territory covered by the FBI's New York, Los Angeles and San Francisco Offices. In these three areas arrangements have been perfected with the National Military Establishment for the temporary and permanent detention in Military facilities of the individuals apprehended.

The plan calls for a statement of charges to be served on each detainee and a hearing be afforded the individual within a specified period. The Hearing Board will consist of three members to be appointed by the Attorney General composed of one Judge of the United States or State Court and two citizens. The hearing procedure will give the detainee an opportunity to know why he is being detained and permit him to introduce material in the nature of evidence in his own behalf. The hearing procedure will not be bound by the rules of evidence.

The Hearing Board may make one of three recommendations, that is; that the individual be detained, paroled or released. This action by the Board is subject to review by the Attorney General and the Attorney General's decision on the matter will be final except for appeal to the President.

The details of this plan as set forth in this communication have also been furnished on this date to Mr. James S. Lay, Jr., Executive Secretary, National Security Council.

With expressions of my highest esteem and best regards,

Sincerely yours,

J. Edgar Hoover

MEMO ON THE LEAK OF VIETNAM WAR INFORMATION (1965)

United States Department of Justice Memorandum 10:21 AM, June 29, 1965

Memorandum for: Mr. Tolson, Mr. De Loach, Mr. Sullivan, Mr. Wick

President Lyndon Johnson called and asked what I have learned in regard to the leak of information concerning the acceleration of war in Vietnam. I told the President we had interviewed about 75 persons and I was wrapping it up into a complete memorandum to send over this afternoon: that circumstantial evidence only is quite strongly pointing to [redacted] as being the one who may have told this writer (Philip Geyelin) the information. I told him that we have talked to various other persons such as Secretary of Defense Robert McNamara and others at a high level, but I think it would be unwise to go down to a lower level such as code clerks, et cetera, because I think it had to come, in view of the timing, from somebody at a high level. I stated we do not have proof on this [redacted] mixes around with what we call the Georgetown Set, in which this fellow moves.

I stated there is no indication that anyone in the Pentagon, and we have interviewed all of the Joint Chiefs of Staff and high level officials, knew the man. I stated they had not even heard of him and had no contact with him. I stated in the State Department practically all the high level people knew him, knew him socially and were friendly with him, but all denied they had given him any information. I stated we get down to a point where it is going to be one of these nebulous conclusions, but the finger of suspicion points more strongly to [redacted] than anyone else.

The President asked if there were any indication [redacted] talked to the writer any time after the decision was made. I stated there was not; that he claimed he did not have the opportunity to talk with Secretary Rusk. I stated in other words, McNamara talked to [redacted] was the first one notified in the State Department, [redacted] in turn notified various other persons who were probably entitled to know. I stated we interviewed all of them and, [redacted] denies he at any time gave any indication to this fellow of having information concerning this.

Glossary

the Georgetown Set	a reference not only to a university and the upscale neighborhood of Washington, D.C., surrounding it but also to upper-class leftists in general
redacted	edited

MEMO ON MARTIN LUTHER KING (1965)

United States Department of Justice Memorandum

5:53 PM, July 6, 1965

Memorandum for: Mr. Tolson, Mr. Belmont, Mr. Sullivan, Mr. De Loach

The Attorney General called. He stated he has been concerned about the Martin Luther King position on Vietnam and he wondered whether the Bureau could put together a memorandum on: 1. How King gets on to this extent; and 2. has there been any hard Communist Party line tieing [sic] together Vietnam and the civil rights movement. I stated we would get that together. The Attorney General stated he thought it would be helpful to have for the Secretary of State and the President something that would tie some of this together.

I stated there was no doubt in my mind from information we have had in the past few months that King, Levison and Jones in New York have been having these huddles together meeting at the Kennedy Airport motor inn. I stated, of course, Stanley Levison is a member of the Communist Party and Clarence Jones also. The Attorney General asked if we had any information independent of that that the Communist Party is trying to tie Vietnam and civil rights together. I stated I thought there was something along that line from informants in the Party that there is a definite tie in on that and we have had at various demonstrations over the last months, actual communists marching in the demonstrations. I referred briefly to the demonstrations on the Berkeley campus of the University of California.

The Attorney General stated there is a fair identity with civil rights groups of a lot of people who have taken the liberal line on civil rights and on Vietnam and there has always been that identity of view, but he is more interested in the hard part of it because he spoke with Roy Wilkins, who is somewhat upset and thinks it is wrong, as did James Farmer. The Attorney General stated they are concerned with what King is doing and he, the Attorney General, thought maybe Bayard Rustin was in it but he is inclined to think it is not Rustin. I stated I thought it was Levison and Jones.

Glossary

the hard part of it	the more radical, as opposed to liberal, members of civil rights groups
How King gets on to this extent	How King funds his political efforts (the implication being that he might have received Communist support)

Memo on Abbott Howard Hoffman (1970)

To: SAC, San Francisco
From: Director, FBI (100-449923)
ABBOTT HOWARD HOFFMAN
SM—ANA (KEY ACTIVIST)

On 4/24/70 information was received from Secret Service indicating a Mrs. Grace W. Slick, 2400 Fulton Street, San Francisco, California (born Evanston, Illinois), was to attend a tea at the White House on the afternoon of that date. Secret Service also received a rumor that Mrs. Slick might possibly try to smuggle Hoffman (one of the "Chicago 7") into the White House with her. Secret Service later reported that Mrs. Slick, accompanied by Hoffman, appeared at the White House gate and Mrs. Slick's invitation was withdrawn and neither Slick nor Hoffman was allowed to enter the White House grounds.

In view of the above, San Francisco is instructed to conduct appropriate investigation to fully identify Mrs. Slick and to determine, if possible, what her past connection have been with Hoffman.

Bufiles are negative on Mrs. Slick.

A bust of Charles Hamilton Houston at Howard University, where Houston was vice-dean of the Howard Marshall School of Law (AP/Wide World Photos)

CHARLES HAMILTON HOUSTON   1895–1950

Educator and Civil Rights Activist

Featured Documents
◆ "Educational Inequalities Must Go!" (1935)
◆ *Missouri ex rel Gaines v. Canada* (1938)
◆ *Hurd v. Hodge* (1948)

Overview

Charles Hamilton Houston, a leading African American civil rights lawyer and legal educator, was born on September 3, 1895. He graduated as a valedictorian from Amherst College in Massachusetts in 1915. After teaching at Howard University in Washington, D.C., for two years, he served as a U.S. Army officer in World War I. During the war he witnessed widespread discrimination against black soldiers, leading him to the conclusion that racial discrimination and segregation had to be attacked through the legal system. Accordingly, in 1919 he enrolled at Harvard University and, after completing a doctorate in law in 1923, entered private practice while returning to Howard University to teach part-time in the law school. In 1929 he was named vice-dean of the law school, though he was dean in all but title. In 1935 he moved to New York City to become litigation director for the National Association for the Advancement of Colored People (NAACP). That year, in an article in the *Crisis* titled "Educational Inequalities Must Go!," he announced the NAACP's strategy of attacking racial segregation by focusing on public education. In 1938 he returned to private practice in Washington, D.C., where he focused on civil rights litigation. Following his early death on April 22, 1950, he was eulogized by Supreme Court Justice Thurgood Marshall as the driving force behind the legal challenges that dismantled the Jim Crow system of racial segregation the U.S. Supreme Court had sanctioned in 1896 in *Plessy v. Ferguson*.

Houston argued numerous important cases in the U.S. Supreme Court that dealt with such issues as education, criminal procedure, and racial discrimination in housing. In *Hollins v. Oklahoma* (1935), the Supreme Court overturned the conviction of an African American accused of rape because African Americans had been systematically excluded from juries in that state. In *Missouri ex rel Gaines v. Canada* (1938), the Court opened the University of Missouri's law school to a black student, thus paving the way for subsequent challenges to racial segregation in schools, which culminated in the landmark 1954 *Brown v. Board of Education* decision. In *Hurd v. Hodge* (1948) (along with *Shelley v. Kraemer* that same year), the Court struck down the legal enforceability of private restrictive covenants that prevented racial minorities from occupying property they had purchased. Houston also argued numerous cases in the U.S. Court of Appeals.

Explanation and Analysis of Documents

Charles Hamilton Houston devoted his professional life to finding ways to use the legal system to attack racial inequality. He mounted that attack on two fronts. One was to improve the status of African Americans in the legal system by increasing the number of black lawyers—and in general by promoting educational opportunities for blacks. The other was to challenge racial inequality in the courts. An example of the first was his article "Educational Inequalities Must Go!" published in the NAACP's monthly journal *Crisis* in 1935. Examples of the second include his arguments in two Supreme Court case briefs: *Missouri ex rel Gaines v. Canada* (1938), his petition for the Court to hear a case to integrate the University of Missouri; and *Hurd v. Hodge* (1948), to prohibit the enforcement of covenants barring African Americans from living in property they had purchased in the District of Columbia.

◆ "Educational Inequalities Must Go!"

In the early 1930s Houston began publishing articles advocating equal treatment of African Americans by the legal system. The articles complemented his legal work in conjunction with the NAACP, which was pursuing a plan of political as well as legal mobilization against the Jim Crow system. (The term *Jim Crow* was based on a pre–Civil War minstrel show character and in time was popularly used to refer to a system of law and custom that perpetrated such outrages as lynchings, denial of voting rights, and biased criminal trials.) Houston wrote in numerous publications about his plans for forcing integration of schools. One such article was "Educational Inequalities Must Go!"

Nothing in Houston's essay is obscure or complicated. From the opening sentence he announces his intention, and that of the NAACP, with clarity and force: "The National Association for the Advancement of Colored People is launching an active campaign against race discrimination in public education." He points out that the campaign would extend to all levels of education, from elementary school to graduate school, and that the NAACP was already in the process of initiating legal action to have black students admitted to graduate schools in Maryland and Virginia. His goal was to end segregated schools, but failing that, he wanted to ensure at least that schools attended by blacks were equal to those attended by white students.

1895

- **September 3**
  Houston is born in Washington, D.C.

1915

- **June**
  Houston graduates from Amherst College

- **Fall**
  Houston begins teaching at Howard University.

1917

- Houston enters the U.S. Army, serving until 1919.

1923

- Houston obtains his law degree from Harvard.

1924

- Houston enters private practice and begins teaching at Howard Law School.

1929

- **June**
  Houston is appointed vice-dean at Howard Law School.

1935

- Houston moves to New York City to work as special counsel to the National Association for the Advancement of Colored People.

- **October**
  Houston publishes "Educational Inequalities Must Go!" in *Crisis*.

1938

- Houston returns to private practice in Washington, D.C.

- **November 8**
  Houston argues *Missouri ex rel Gaines* before U.S. Supreme Court.

1948

- **January 15–16**
  Houston argues *Hurd v. Hodge* before U.S. Supreme Court.

1950

- **April 22**
  Houston dies in Washington, D.C.

In the section titled "Linked to Other Objectives" Houston states that the NAACP's campaign was part of a broader effort to dismantle the Jim Crow system. As he forcefully puts it, "It ties in with the anti-lynching fight because there is no use educating boys and girls if their function in life is to be the playthings of murderous mobs." He goes on to note that improvements in education had to be part of a wider effort to improve all aspects of blacks' lives, and he laments the effects of the Great Depression of the 1930s on skilled black workers, who were often the first to lose their jobs.

In "Specific Objectives" Houston outlines the NAACP's plan of attack. The objectives he lists are self-explanatory, but he goes on to explain that the problems existed both where schools were segregated and where they were not. Even in integrated schools, black teachers met with professional obstacles, and black students were often excluded from, for example, extracurricular activities. He notes that at the graduate school level, the problem with segregation was largely confined to the South. He concludes the section by saying that the U.S. Supreme Court had sanctioned this system by holding that separate but equal schools did not violate the equal protection clause of the Fourteenth Amendment to the Constitution. Here he refers indirectly to the landmark 1896 case *Plessy v. Ferguson*, which played a major role in the emergence of the Jim Crow system that relegated African Americans to second-class status.

In "Inequalities Glaring," Houston gives examples, citing the work of other researchers. He notes, in particular, the "glaring" inequities in funding for white and black schools, where sometimes the disparity reached a factor of twenty. He notes that this condition had worsened during the first three decades of the century. The disparities were bad enough in 1900, but by 1930 they had grown much greater. He points out that in some 230 counties throughout the United States, no provision existed for educating African American high-school-age students.

In "No Graduate Training," Houston observes that in seventeen of the nineteen mainly southern states in which legal segregation existed there was no provision to admit black students to professional and graduate schools, though some offered scholarship funds, often inadequate, to send black students to other states, where they could gain admission. This problem, Houston writes, was simple to attack from a legal perspective. In states that maintained separate elementary and high schools for blacks and whites, complications arose from trying to compare the facilities in terms of their equality or inequality. But when a state provided funding for white graduate students but no funding for black students, the issue of inequality was unambiguous. For this reason, the NAACP's immediate focus was on cases involving graduate education.

In "Unwise Attempt," Houston discusses one such case, the effort by a young black woman to gain admission to graduate school at the University of Virginia. He quotes various Virginia newspapers that did not dispute the student's "abstract" right to attend the university but questioned the wisdom of her going where she was "not wanted." Houston responds by asserting, first, that the university was a public institution, so the question of whether the student was welcome was irrelevant. Further, in response to the notion that attending a school where they were not welcome was damaging to African American students' "self-respect," Houston notes that such students could maintain their self-respect by asserting their constitutional rights and that if they had to endure "snubs and insults," they had to do so in other contexts anyway. Houston concludes this section of the article by taking to task white southern "liberals" who paid "lip service" to the cause of equal rights but who, concerned that actions such as that taken by the NAACP would disturb "amicable race relations," ended up doing nothing to ensure that "amicable" relations were based on equal rights.

◆ Missouri ex rel Gaines v. Canada

In 1938 Houston challenged Missouri's segregation system in the U.S. Supreme Court in *Missouri ex rel Gaines v. Canada*. The document was Houston's petition for a writ of certiorari, a legal phrase that refers to a litigant's petition to a court to agree to hear the case; the court "grants cert" when it agrees to hear the case and places it on the court's docket. The Latin phrase *ex rel* is an abbreviation of *ex relatione*, meaning "upon being related." This term refers to any legal action undertaken by the government (for example, a state government) on behalf of a private person who needs that government to enforce his or her rights (in contrast to a case in which the litigant is suing for monetary damages). In this case, the litigant was Lloyd L. Gaines, who was denied admission to the University of Missouri law school because he was an African American. "Canada" was S. W. Canada, the university registrar who officially denied Gaines entrance (though Canada later said that he was forced to do so by administration officials).

At the time, Missouri excluded African American students from the University of Missouri's law school. In common with other states, Missouri provided instead a modest scholarship so that such students could attend school in another state. Houston used the precedent of a recent case in Maryland to get the U.S. Supreme Court to hear the case. Typically the Supreme Court hears only a fraction of the cases that are appealed to it. It usually accepts only cases that present significant constitutional issues, and it is more likely to grant certiorari if the petitioner can show conflicting decisions on the same matter in lower courts of appeal. In the case at hand the conflict was between the Maryland Court of Appeals and the Missouri Supreme Court.

In his petition, Houston points out the inequity of making some students attend school outside the state. He bases his argument primarily on the equal protection clause of the Fourteenth Amendment to the Constitution. The key portion of this amendment is Section 1:

All persons born or naturalized in the United States, and subject to the jurisdiction thereof, are citizens of

Lloyd Gaines, a young black American, who applied to University of Missouri's law school and was denied admission (AP/Wide World Photos)

the United States and of the State wherein they reside. No State shall make or enforce any law which shall abridge the privileges or immunities of citizens of the United States; nor shall any State deprive any person of life, liberty, or property, without due process of law; nor deny to any person within its jurisdiction the equal protection of the laws.

The kernel of Houston's argument is that in failing to provide black students with graduate education substantially equal to that provided to white students, the state was failing to extend "equal protection" to black students.

In tracing the history of the case before its arrival at the Supreme Court, Houston notes that the lower courts had "denied mandamus," a legal term that literally means "we command." By a writ of mandamus a court orders a public official to perform a duty. Houston also refers to the Lincoln University Act of 1921. Lincoln University was founded as a vocational school for freed slaves after the Civil War. It became a land-grant college under the Morrill Act of 1890, and in 1921 it was designated a university. As a historically black institution, it provided educational opportunities for African Americans in Missouri. In the legal wrangling associated with *Missouri ex rel Gaines v.*

Canada, officials argued that Gaines could obtain a legal education at Lincoln or through Lincoln in another state. Houston argues that this course of action would not provide Gaines with a "substantial equivalent" to the legal education he could receive at the University of Missouri law school. It should be noted that although Lincoln had no law school in 1938, the state hurriedly set up one that opened in 1939.

Houston's petition concludes with a simple, yet powerful statement of the magnitude of the problem: Nearly ten million African Americans lived in the sixteen states that excluded them from their state universities, and the nearly two million African American students in those states needed access to those universities. Therefore, Houston argues, "It is of the utmost public importance that a standard of equal protection of the laws under the Fourteenth Amendment to the Constitution of the United States be established for these students as they attempt to equip themselves to meet the highest standards of citizenship."

The Supreme Court ruled in Gaines's favor, but Gaines never attended the University of Missouri. On March 19, 1939, he disappeared from a rooming house in Chicago and was never heard from again. Some have speculated that he met with foul play, perhaps at the hands of the Ku Klux Klan; others suggested that he was tired of being in the public eye and wanted to disappear. In any event, in 2001 the University of Missouri renamed its Black Culture Center in his honor, and in 2006 Gaines was granted a posthumous honorary law degree and membership in the state bar association.

◆ Hurd v. Hodge

Houston's final appearance before the U.S. Supreme Court came with *Hurd v. Hodge*, a case in which he successfully challenged racially restrictive covenants. The covenants on the residential property in *Hurd* in Washington, D.C., prohibited African Americans from purchasing or renting the property. Covenants from other jurisdictions were challenged in a companion case the Court ruled on in the same decision, *Shelley v. Kraemer* (1948). A covenant is a provision a seller imposes on a property that restricts its use. As Houston points out, restrictive racial covenants were common, especially in the booming postwar suburbs of American cities. In the case at hand, James M. and Mary A. Hurd had purchased a house in Washington, D.C., that had attached to it a covenant "prohibiting the sale of the house to anyone of the Negro race." The house next door was occupied by the Hodges, who sued to have the covenant enforced. Ironically, two members of the Supreme Court had to recuse themselves from hearing the case because they lived in homes with similar covenants.

In this excerpt from his brief to the Court, Houston bases his argument on three issues, which he intertwines throughout the brief. The first is that restrictive racial covenants violated the due process clause of the Fifth Amendment to the Constitution. The key clause of the amendment reads that no person shall be "deprived of life,

liberty, or property, without due process of law." (Houston notes that in similar cases the due process clause of the Fourteenth Amendment had been cited. The Fourteenth Amendment, however, applies to the states, not the federal government; federal action is bound by the Fifth Amendment. In *Hurd* a complication arose because the District of Columbia was not a state; therefore, the Fifth Amendment applied.) Legally, the ownership of property consists of a bundle of rights associated with that property. Ownership implies the right, for example, to sell the property or, in the case of a home, to occupy it. Houston's argument was that the Hurds had been deprived of their property by being told that they could not live in it; in effect, preventing them from occupying the house stripped them of one of the rights of ownership, which amounted to stripping them of the property.

Houston's second argument was a corollary of the first. The legal question raised by this case was not whether such restrictive covenants were legal. Rather, the issue was whether the courts could enforce them. Ultimately, the Court in this case ruled that such covenants were legal but that, because they were "non-statutory" law, the court system had no power to enforce them. The court system could rule only on laws that had been passed by the legislature and that the courts therefore had the power to recognize and enforce. In essence, Houston argued successfully that the restrictive covenant was a private agreement, not governmental action. If a party to the agreement chose to violate it, the Court had no power to enforce it. The Court agreed.

In this regard, Houston points out that it would have been better for the legislature to have passed zoning requirements excluding African Americans and other "undesirable" groups. At least then, he observes, it would have been possible for the legislature to change the law or to provide areas where these groups of people would be allowed to live. Further, legislation is subject to "public scrutiny," and members of the community, to whom the legislature is responsible, can question and oppose the proposed laws. The evil of restrictive covenants was that they were not subject to public oversight and change. They were a function of "prejudice." Furthermore, they deprived other property owners of their rights. If a covenant was violated, it was usually only one or a handful of neighbors who objected and brought suit. In many cases most neighbors did not care, and for themselves liked to be able to dispose of their property in any way they saw fit, especially if the covenants in a neighborhood were routinely violated to the point where no one paid attention to them anymore. Thus, restrictive covenants had effects that rippled outward from the parties immediately affected to others who were not.

The first two arguments dealt with the legalities of the case, essentially establishing the Court's jurisdiction over the matter. The bulk of Houston's argument, however, was based on the social implications of racially restrictive covenants. They posed a threat to "national unity." They forced people to live in "virtual ghettoes." They led to "enormous overcrowding in slums" and "blighted areas." They exerted "a baneful influence upon the economic, social,

"It is not the purpose or the function of the national office of the N.A.A.C.P. to force a school fight upon any community. Its function is primarily to expose the rotten conditions of segregation, to point out the evil consequences of discrimination and injustice to both Negroes and whites, and to map out ways and means by which these evils may be corrected."

("Educational Inequalities Must Go!")

"Insults and snubs will not deter Negro students from insisting on their right to graduate and professional study."

("Educational Inequalities Must Go!")

"Sixteen states exclude Negroes from their State Universities solely because of race or color."

(*Missouri ex rel Gaines v. Canada*)

"Shall we in the United States have ghettoes for racial, religious and other minorities, or even exclude such minorities entirely from whole areas of our country, by a system of judicially enforced restrictions based on private prejudices and made effective through the use of government authority and power?"

(*Hurd v. Hodge*)

"A basic aim of the United States and the allied nations in World War II was the defeat of the same principle of racism which underlies the racial restrictive covenant in this case. To uphold this racial restrictive covenant would nullify the victories won by the United States and the allied nations at such great cost in that war."

(*Hurd v. Hodge*)

moral and physical well-being of all persons, white and black, young and old, rich and poor." The consequences of this violation of due process included "disease, death, crime, immorality, juvenile delinquency and racial tensions, increased strains on public facilities and services, and economic exploitation through artificially inflated rental and housing costs." They contributed to the "social disorganization of both the Negro people and the entire community."

Impact and Legacy

Charles Hamilton Houston was a leader of the movement to challenge segregation through the legal system. His constant advocacy, in conjunction with work by other leaders such as W. E. B. Du Bois and, later, Thurgood Marshall, demonstrated to the United States the multiple ways in which the legal system treated African Americans unfairly in such areas as education. Using a combination of legal and social arguments, NAACP lawyers, including Houston, led a transformation in the legal system.

In particular, Houston led a revolution in interpretations of the equal protection clause of the Fourteenth Amendment, passed in the wake of the Civil War to impose federal authority over state violations of constitutional rights. In a 1927 case, for example, Supreme Court justice Oliver Wendell Holmes, Jr., in upholding a Virginia statute providing for sterilization of developmentally disabled individuals, dismissed appeals to the Fourteenth Amendment. Less than thirty years later, however, the Supreme Court's decision in *Brown v. Board of Education* rested in large part upon a revolution in interpretations of that amendment's equal protection clause. In that landmark case the Court, echoing many changes in American culture, found that separation of the races in schools inherently failed to provide equal protection under the law. Laying the groundwork for *Brown* and the sweeping changes it launched was *Missouri ex rel Gaines v. Canada*. Although *Gaines* did not overturn *Plessy v. Ferguson*, it provided the legal framework that made the Court's ruling in *Brown* possible.

Houston is best remembered for his role in integrating education, but he fought against discrimination in employment as well. He successfully challenged discriminatory hiring and promotion by the government and its contractors during World War II. In *Tunstall v. Brotherhood of Locomotive Firemen and Enginemen* (1944), for example, he successfully used the Railway Labor Act to challenge a secret agreement between railroads and a union that, in essence, excluded African Americans from jobs as railroad firemen. The Court ruled that the act required unions to represent all its members without discrimination based on race.

Charles Houston is by no means a household name, but his accomplishments have been widely recognized in the legal community. In 1950 he was posthumously awarded the Spingarn Medal, and Howard University's main building was named Charles Hamilton Houston Hall in 1958. In 2005 Harvard Law School opened the Charles Hamilton Houston Institute for Race and Justice, and the law school maintains a professorship named in his honor.

Key Sources

Some of Houston's papers are available at Howard University's archives; others are available in the NAACP papers at the Library of Congress. Several of Houston's articles appeared in the NAACP's monthly magazine, *Crisis*, and other publications. Among them are "The George Crawford Case: An Experiment in Social Statesmanship," *Nation* (July 4, 1934); "The Need for Negro Lawyers," *Journal of Negro Education* (January 1935); "Cracking Closed University Doors," *Crisis* (December 1935); "Future Policies and Practices Which Should Govern the Relationship of the Federal Government to Negro Separate Schools," *Journal of Negro Education* (July 1938); and "Foul Employment Practice on the Rails," *Crisis* (October 1949). Unpublished works available on the Internet include Houston's report of February 1928, "Tentative Findings re Negro Lawyers" (http:// www.law.cornell.edu/houston/survey.htm) and his speech "An Approach to Better Race Relations," delivered on May 5, 1934, to the National Young Women's Christian Association Convention in Philadelphia (http://www.law.cornell.edu/houston/ywcatxt.htm).

Questions for Further Study

1. Houston's life spanned the era between two key Supreme Court decisions regarding civil rights: *Plessy v. Ferguson*, which was decided the year after he was born, and *Brown v. Board of Education*, a judgment passed four years after his death. Whereas *Plessy* upheld segregation in education and other public activities so long as separate facilities for blacks and whites were demonstrably equal in value, *Brown* struck down the "separate but equal" principle. Discuss Houston's approach, particularly in his 1935 piece on educational inequalities, to the notion of "separate but equal" facilities. In particular, analyze the figures spent for the education of black and white students and what those ratios demonstrate regarding the claim that the two groups received equal benefits.

2. Two civil rights cases of significance in Houston's work involved African American men named Gaines: *Donald Gaines Murray v. Raymond A. Pearson* (1935) and *Missouri ex rel Gaines v. Canada* (1938). Research and retell the narrative behind each case and the differing fate of each Gaines.

3. Discuss the distinctions between legislative and judicial power raised in *Hurd v. Hodge* as well as the principles of land use (covenants, zoning, and so on) involved in the case.

Further Reading

■ Articles

Kelleher, Daniel T. "The Case of Lloyd Lionel Gaines: The Demise of the Separate but Equal Doctrine." *Journal of Negro History* 56, no. 4 (October 1971):262–271.

Mack, Kenneth W. "Rethinking Civil Rights Lawyering and Politics in the Era before *Brown*." *Yale Law Journal* 115 (2005): 256.

———. "Law and Mass Politics in the Making of the Civil Rights Lawyer, 1931–1941." *Journal of American History* 93 (2006): 37–62.

■ Books

Greenberg, Jack. *Crusaders in the Courts: How a Dedicated Band of Lawyers Fought for the Civil Rights Revolution*. New York: Basic Books, 1994.

Kluger, Richard. *Simple Justice: The History of Brown v. Board of Education and Black America's Struggle for Equality*. 2 vols. New York: Knopf, 1975.

McNeil, Genna Rae. *Groundwork: Charles Hamilton Houston and the Struggle for Civil Rights*. Philadelphia: University of Pennsylvania Press, 1983.

Tushnet, Mark V. *The NAACP's Legal Strategy against Segregated Education, 1925–1950*. Chapel Hill: University of North Carolina Press, 1987.

■ Web Sites

Linder, Douglas O. "Before *Brown*: Charles H. Houston and the *Gaines* Case." Famous Trials Web site. http://www.law.umkc.edu/faculty/projects/ftrials/trialheroes/charleshoustonessayF.html.

—Michael J. O'Neal

"Educational Inequalities Must Go!" (1935)

The National Association for the Advancement of Colored People is launching an active campaign against race discrimination in public education. The campaign will reach all levels of public education from the nursery school through the university. The ultimate objective of the association is the abolition of all forms of segregation in public education, whether in the admission or activities of students, the appointment or advancement of teachers, or administrative control. The association will resist any attempt to extend segregated schools. Where possible it will attack segregation in schools. Where segregation is so firmly entrenched by law that a frontal attack cannot be made, the association will throw its immediate force toward bringing Negro schools to an absolute equality with white schools. If the white South insists upon its separate schools, it must not squeeze the Negro schools to pay for them.

It is not the purpose or the function of the national office of the N.A.A.C.P. to force a school fight upon any community. Its function is primarily to expose the rotten conditions of segregation, to point out the evil consequences of discrimination and injustice to both Negroes and whites, and to map out ways and means by which these evils may be corrected. The decision for action rests with the local community itself. If the local community decides to act and asks the N.A.A.C.P. for aid, the N.A.A.C.P. stands ready with advice and assistance.

The N.A.A.C.P. proposes to use every legitimate means at its disposal to accomplish actual equality of educational opportunity for Negroes. A legislative program is being formulated. Court action has already begun in Maryland to compel the University of Maryland to admit a qualified Negro boy to the law school of the university. Court action is imminent in Virginia to compel the University of Virginia to admit a qualified Negro girl in the graduate department of that university. Activity in politics will be fostered due to the political set-up of and control over public school systems. The press and the public forum will be enlisted to explain to the public the issues involved and to make both whites and Negroes realize the blight which inferior education throws over them, their children and their communities.

Linked to Other Objectives

This campaign for equality of educational opportunity is indissolubly linked with all the other major activities of the association. It ties in with the anti-lynching fight because there is no use educating boys and girls if their function in life is to be the playthings of murderous mobs. It connects up with the association's new economic program because Negro boys and girls must be provided with work opportunities commensurate with their education when they leave school. One of the greatest tragedies of the depression has been the humiliation and suffering which public authorities have inflicted upon trained Negroes, denying them employment at their trades on public works and forcing them to accept menial low-pay jobs as an alternative to starvation. Civil rights, including the right of suffrage, free speech, jury service, and equal facilities of transportation, are directly involved. The N.A.A.C.P. recognizes the fact that the discriminations which the Negro suffers in education are merely part of the general pattern of race prejudice in American life, and it knows that no attack on discrimination in education can have any far reaching effect unless it is bound to a general attack on discrimination and segregation in all phases of American life.

Specific Objectives

At the present time the N.A.A.C.P. educational program has six specific objectives for its immediate efforts:

(a) equality of school terms;

(b) equality of pay for Negro teachers having the same qualifications and doing the same work as white teachers;

(c) equality of transportation for Negro school children at public expense;

(d) equality of buildings and equipment;

(e) equality of per capita expenditure for education of Negroes;

(f) equality in graduate and professional training.

The first five objectives relate to segregated and separate school systems. Equality of educational opportunity in separate school systems is the greatest immediate educational problem of the Negro masses. But the problem of Negro education would not stand completely solved even if segregated schools were suddenly abolished. There would still be the question of the Negro's position in the unified system. At the present time Negro children and white children attend the same schools in the North, but Negroes suffer bitterly from prejudice in many northern schools. Negro students are frequently excluded from extra-curricular activities; they are kept out of class offices; cases are known where the white teacher has actively tried to discourage the Negro pupils from even attending the school. It is difficult for a Negro teacher to obtain placement in a nonsegregated school system; more difficult for a Negro teacher to rise to an administrative position in such a system; and apparently impossible for a Negro, regardless of merit, to become head of any public school system segregated or nonsegregated. The N.A.A.C.P. expects to fight race prejudice in nonsegregated school systems just as hard as it fights for equality in separate school systems.

The sixth objective: equality in graduate and professional training, is essentially a problem of the South. In the North Negroes are freely admitted to the state universities for graduate and professional training, except in some instances in medicine. The established policy of the South is segregated schools.

The United States supreme court has endorsed this policy to the extent of saying that segregated schools do not violate the guaranties of equal protection of the law under the Constitution of the United States provided equal facilities are offered to each race in the segregated system.

Inequalities Glaring

The South has never even made a serious effort to obey the mandate of the supreme court that the schools may be separate but they must be equal. The Commission on Interracial Cooperation in the fourth edition of its *Recent Trends in Race Relations* (revised May, 1935) states:

"In his excellent study, 'Financing Schools in the South in 1930,' Prof. Fred McCuistion shows that in the eleven Southern States in which separate records are kept, the public school outlay averaged $44.31

for the white and $12.57 for the colored child enrolled, or nearly four to one against the group most completely dependent upon public funds for its educational opportunity. In South Carolina the respective figures were $56.06 and $7.84; in Mississippi they were $45.34 and $5.45.

"But even these figures do not tell the worst. Within these averages there are unbelievable extremes. In Alabama, for example, where the averages for the State were $36.43 for the white child and $10.09 for the colored, there is one county in which the figures were found to be $75.50 for the white child and $1.82 for the Negro. In hundreds of counties in many of the states the proportion runs as high as ten to one, or twenty to one, in favor of the white child."

The Journal of Negro Education published by Howard University (4th Yearbook Number, July, 1935, P. 290) shows that

"in 1900 the discrimination in per capita expenditure for white and Negro children was 60 per cent in favor of the white; by 1930, this discrimination had increased to 253 per cent. Again, despite the fact that the training of Negro teachers, today, more nearly approximates that of the white teachers, the discrimination in salaries of white and Negro teachers increased from 52.8 per cent in 1900 to 113 per cent in 1930."

Ambrose Caliver, Senior Specialist in the Education of Negroes, the United States Office of Education, reports in the *National Survey of Secondary Education* that "in the 15 states comprising this investigation, 230 counties, with a Negro population of 12½ per cent or more of the total, are without high-school facilities for colored children. These counties contain 1,397,304 colored people, 158,939 of whom are 15 to 19 years of age. These young people represent 16.5 per cent of all Negroes between the ages of 15 and 19 in the 15 Southern States represented."

Yet every one of the 230 counties provided high school facilities for its white children.

No Graduate Training

Although the southern states provide a measure of undergraduate instruction for Negroes on the college level, not one of them provides any graduate or professional training for Negroes. The Journal of Negro Education above cited found that

"...there is not a single state-supported institution of higher learning in any one of 17 of the 19 states which require separation by law, to which a Negro may go to pursue graduate and professional education. On the other hand in 1930, some 11,037 white students were enrolled in publicly-supported higher institutions in 15 of these states, pursuing graduate and professional training."

West Virginia, Missouri, and this year Maryland provide certain scholarship money for their respective Negro students who desire graduate and professional training, toward their tuition fees in universities outside the state which will enroll them as students. But these scholarship grants do not include the differential in travel expense between the fare from the student's home to the state university which will not admit him, and his fare to the university outside the state which will. They do not include any differential in case of increased living expenses outside the state, and are frequently subject to conditions and restrictions not imposed upon white students taking the same work in the state university. In Maryland there was not even enough money to pay tuition fees for all the qualified Negro students who applied for scholarships.

For purely technical reasons the first problem the association attacked in court was the exclusion of qualified Negroes from graduate or professional training in state-supported universities, solely on account of race or color. The legal problem was simpler; and since much of its educational program will involve pioneer work the association began with the simpler problem first. As regards primary, secondary and collegiate education in the South, there is a system, albeit inadequate, of separate primary and secondary schools and colleges for Negroes supported from public funds. A challenge to the inadequacies of these primary [and] secondary schools and colleges would raise the question whether the facilities offered by them are equal to the facilities offered in similar schools to whites. This would involve complex problems of comparative budget analyses, faculty qualifications, and other facts. But in the case of the graduate or professional training there are no facilities whatsoever provided for Negroes by the state, and the question narrows down to a simple proposition of law: whether the state can appropriate public money for graduate and professional education for white students exclusively. The Baltimore City Court in the case of Donald Gaines Murray vs. Raymond A. Pearson, president of the University of Maryland, et al., has answered that this could not be done, and on June 25, 1935, issued its writ of mandamus commanding the officers of the university to admit Murray into the first year class of the law school. The university has appealed, and the case will be argued before the Court of Appeals of Maryland early this fall....

"Unwise Attempt"

The reactions of the white press of Virginia to this heretical attempt of a Negro girl to enter the graduate department of the University of Virginia are indicative of the opposition which the N.A.A.C.P. will face when its general educational program gets well under way. The editors admit the young woman has the legal right to attend the university, but urge her and the N.A.A.C.P. not to force the issue. Sample editorials state "it is inexpedient, ill-advised, and heavily charged with potential injury to the cause which the Association is designed to advance" (*Norfolk Ledger-Dispatch*). "The question here, it seems to us, is not what the Negro has an abstract right to do, but what it is wise to attempt" (*Richmond Times-Dispatch*). "Law bears on the question from one side; custom from another" (*Newport News Daily Press*). "The question instantly arises why any educated person should wish to impose his or her presence upon an institution where they are not wanted and where they could not possibly remain in justice to their own self-respect or to their hope of achievement" (*Northern Virginia Daily*).

White Virginians evidently cannot bring themselves to admit that the University of Virginia is a public institution, and not their own private property. It is a public institution, so the question put by the *Northern Virginia Daily* as to whether a Negro student "is wanted" at the university is beside the point. A Negro student can preserve her self-respect much more by standing up for her constitutional rights and facing the snubs and insults of the white students with calm and dignity than by supinely yielding up her constitutional rights. Unless the white students offer her actual physical violence, they cannot snub or insult her any worse than the white men students snubbed and insulted the first white woman student who dared enter the University of Virginia.

Insults and snubs will not deter Negro students from insisting on their right to graduate and professional study. Since the daily portion of Negroes in American life is snubs and insults, regardless how submissive they are, Negro students can afford to face a few more snubs and insults temporarily in defense of their constitutional rights to equal educational opportunities, until the white students and white authorities become reconciled to allowing them to pursue their education in peace. As a matter of fact, the young southern white students have not been heard from; but there are indications that there is a growing sentiment among them for recognition of the Negro as a real human being and citizen entitled to all the legal rights and public benefits as such.

Another point that the older white Virginians make is that any attempt to force the university issue will disturb "amicable race relations" in Virginia. It seems strange that white people always use "amicable race relations" as an excuse to discourage the Negro from insisting on his rights. The slaveholders told the abolitionists the same thing before the Civil War. If the "liberal" white Virginians would just manifest a little courage, and take a few chances with their own comfort and social position in a firm stand for real equality of opportunity between the races, there would be no occasion for "amicable race relations" to be disturbed. The difficulty is that white southern liberals give lip-service to equality before the law; but except in rare instances their qualms of conscience do not spur them into action.

Glossary

Ambrose Caliver	an African American educator who served in the Department of Education under the Herbert Hoover administration
Commission on Interracial Cooperation	a Christian-based civil rights group, founded in Atlanta in 1919
Donald Gaines Murray vs. Raymond A. Pearson	a 1935 Maryland civil rights case whereby Murray, an African American student, gained admission to the University of Maryland, whose president was Pearson
per capita expenditure	spending per person
portion	situation or misfortune
Prof. Fred McCuistion	an Arkansas scholar who focused on improving educational opportunities for African Americans
suffrage	the vote
supinely	passively
work	course of study
writ of mandamus	a court order requiring another court to perform a particular action

MISSOURI EX REL GAINES V. CANADA (1938)

Reasons Relied on for the Allowance of the Writ.

1. The State of Missouri denied petitioner the equal protection of the laws guaranteed him by the Fourteenth Amendment to the Constitution of the United States in that—

   a. The Curators of the University of Missouri refused him admission to the School of Law of the University of Missouri (the only public institution offering instruction in law in Missouri) solely because of race or color.

Petitioner challenged his exclusion as a denial of his Federal right to equal protection both in the Circuit Court and the Supreme Court of Missouri. The Circuit Court denied mandamus without opinion; the Supreme Court considered and denied the claim of Federal right.

   b. The Lincoln University Act of 1921 as applied to the facts of this case does not afford petitioner a substantial equivalent to the opportunity offered to white and other non-Negro students to study law in the School of Law of the University of Missouri.

Petitioner challenged the Lincoln University Act as a denial of his Federal right to equal protection both in the Circuit Court and the Supreme Court of Missouri. The Circuit Court denied mandamus without opinion; the Supreme Court considered and denied the claim of Federal right.

   c. The burden of proving that the State had otherwise afforded petitioner an opportunity to study law substantially equal to that accorded by the State to white and other non-Negro students in the School of Law of the University of Missouri was on the Registrar and Curators of the University of Missouri. They failed to sustain the burden.

Petitioner asserted both in the Circuit Court and the Supreme Court of Missouri that it was an incident to his Federal right to the equal protection of the laws that when he had established that the State had excluded him from the School of Law of the University of Missouri solely because of race or color, the burden was on the representatives of the State to establish that the State had otherwise accorded him an opportunity to study law substantially equal to that accorded white and other non-Negro students in the School of Law of the University of Missouri. Neither the Circuit Court nor the Supreme Court expressly ruled on this claim of Federal right.

2. There is a conflict of decision between the highest courts of the two states which have passed on the question as to what constitutes equal protection of the laws as guaranteed by the Fourteenth Amendment to the Constitution of the United States where the state has excluded a qualified Negro citizen of the state from the School of Law of the State University solely because of race or color.

The Court of Appeals of Maryland in *Pearson v. Murray*, 169 Md. 478, 182 A. 590, 103 A.L.R. 706 (1936), decided it was a denial of the Federal right to exclude the Negro student. The Supreme Court of Missouri in the instant case, 113 S.W. (2d) 783 (Mo. 1937), decided it was not a denial of Federal right to exclude the Negro student. There is no precedent in this court authoritatively settling the Federal question.

3. Sixteen states exclude Negroes from their State Universities solely because of race or color. Six of these sixteen states, and Maryland, have scholarship provisions for study outside the state. Ten make no provisions whatever for the graduate or professional training of Negroes.

Even if it be considered that under any circumstances a money grant could constitute the equal protection of the laws under the Fourteenth Amendment to the Constitution of the United States to a Negro citizen forced by the state to go outside the state solely because of race or color to study courses offered to all other students in the state university within the state border, nevertheless there is an irreconcilable conflict in the statutes of the scholarship laws as to size of grant, elements of compensation and other conditions which leaves the question in confusion and great uncertainty. There is no Federal precedent establishing whether a scholarship grant can constitute the equal protection of the laws; and if so, what the standard of equal protection should be.

4. According to the 1930 Census, 9,176,970 Negroes live in the sixteen states which exclude Negroes from the state university solely because of race or color. Negroes attending school in these states numbered 1,879,388. In 1933, these states had 17,893 Negroes enrolled in institutions of higher learning. It is of the utmost public importance that a standard of equal protection of the laws under the Fourteenth Amendment to the Constitution of the United States be established for these students as they attempt to equip themselves to meet the highest standards of citizenship.

A decision in this case will go far toward establishing a standard of conduct for the States under the equal protection clause of the Fourteenth Amendment.

Houston, Charles Hamilton

Glossary

Circuit Court	a federal court of appeals, so named because in frontier days, judges would "ride the circuit," or move from town to town, administering judgments
Curators	administrators
denied mandamus without opinion	refused, without explanation, to issue a court order requiring another court to perform a particular action
equal protection clause	a statement, in Section 1 of the Fourteenth Amendment, granting equal protection under the law to all citizens
ex rel	abbreviation for the Latin *ex relatione* ("on behalf of"), referring to a situation in which a governmental entity brings a lawsuit on behalf of a party deemed to be affected by the issue under question
Fourteenth Amendment	constitutional amendment, ratified in 1868, extending rights of citizenship and equal protection under the law to all Americans
incident to	part of
instant	present
Lincoln University Act of 1921	act of the Missouri legislature granting university status to a historically black college
Pearson v. Murray	a 1936 lawsuit whereby the University of Maryland appealed the ruling in *Murray v. Pearson* the preceding year
petitioner	the person bringing the case
precedent	a decision by a court that sets a standard for future judgments
Registrar	a college official responsible for admission, enrollment, and registration of students
Writ	court order

HURD V. HODGE (1948)

[7] These cases involve this fundamental issue: Shall we in the United States have ghettoes for racial, religious and other minorities, or even exclude such minorities entirely from whole areas of our country, by a system of judicially enforced restrictions based on private prejudices and made effective through the use of government authority and power?

The extensive area covered by these restrictions and the great number of persons and groups excluded from acquiring and occupying these lands for living space already constitute one of the greatest dangers to our national unity.

During the past two decades, racial restrictive covenants have been extensively imposed on most of the major cities of the nation on a large percentage of all newly constructed dwellings, new residential subdivisions, and existing residential properties contiguous to areas occupied by many of these excluded groups. Negroes have thus far been the major victims of this private, wholesale, and irresponsible "zoning" which, by placing such artificial yet impassable boundaries around the existing areas of Negro occupancy, has barred Negroes of all income groups from occupancy in most suburban areas where new construction has been concentrated, and has forced them into virtual ghettoes. Similar restrictions have been directed against persons of Mexican, Greek, Spanish, Armenian, Chinese, Korean, Filipino, Persian, Hindu, Ethiopian, Syrian, Japanese, Arabian and other ancestry, as well as "non-Caucasians," Latin-Americans, Jews, American Indians, Hawaiians, Puerto Ricans, and other groups, irrespective of their American citizenship or the use they would make of the land, and despite our pledge in the United Nations Charter "to practice tolerance and live together in peace with one another as good neighbors." Preamble, United Nations Charter, 59 Sta. 1035.

These restrictions have been a direct and major cause of enormous overcrowding into slums, with consequent substantial disorganization of family and community life. These effects have not been, and cannot be, in our fluid society, confined to the intended victims of the restrictions; they permeate the community and exert a baneful influence upon the economic, social, moral and physical well-being of all persons, white and black, young and old, rich and poor. They are incompatible with the foundations of our republic and their judicial approbation may well imperil our form of government and our unity and strength as a nation....

Judicial Enforcement of a restrict covenant which, solely on the basis of race, (1) forbids a person from acquiring, occupying and selling land and (2) forbids an owner of land from selling it to any member of the restricted group, is in violation of the due process clause of the Fifth Amendment. This Court has held that the legislative imposition of such restriction is unconstitutional under the due process clause of the Fourteenth Amendment. The guaranty of due process in the Fifth Amendment is similar to that of the Fourteenth Amendment and applies to the District of Columbia. The due process clause applies to judicial action and prohibits governmental action through judicial recognition and enforcement of non-statutory law which denies due process. Both the legislature and the judiciary are arms of the government. A result forbidden by the Constitution to the legislature cannot be achieved through the judiciary. Hence, the judicial enforcement of restrictive covenants, against willing sellers and willing buyers, who have never been parties to the covenants, violates the Constitution.

The enforcement of racial restrictive covenants has drastically curtailed the ability of "non-Aryans" to secure adequate housing and has hemmed them into slums, blighted areas, and ghettoes. Racial restrictive covenants have been a direct and major cause of enormous overcrowding in the few areas available to Negro residential occupancy, with consequent substantial increase in disease, death, crime, immorality, juvenile delinquency and racial tensions, increased strains on public facilities and services, and economic exploitation through artificially inflated rental and housing costs. They constitute a direct danger to the American principle of "equality before the law" and to our national unity. In the light of these effects and conditions, the judicial enforcement of restrictive covenants is clearly incompatible with the due process clause of the Constitution....

[28] Ironically, although it would be unconstitutional for a legislature to enact a statute imposing racial restrictions on land use, yet the wholesale and extensive imposition of these racial restrictive covenants has a more drastic effect than any legisla-

tive zoning statute. Through legislative control, even with all of its evils, it would at least have been possible to provide some sort of planned expansion of areas predominantly occupied by Negroes or other ethnic groups living in overcrowded or slum conditions. But the creation by individuals of racial restrictive covenants ordinarily takes no broader view than that dictated by racial prejudice. Furthermore, a statute may be, and frequently is, repealed or modified to accommodate changed conditions, or in response to changing concepts resulting from education. Most racial restrictive covenants, however, including the 1906 covenant here involved, purport to be *perpetual* restrictions, fossilizing eternally the prejudice pattern of a passing historical moment. In addition, legislative restrictions, subject to public scrutiny and opposition by the entire community, are imposed by public officials who are at least presumably responsible to the community. Racial restrictive covenants, however, are imposed by persons who are not responsible to the community and who neither represent those restricted nor desire to represent them. Moreover, under legislative zoning, the individuals who are opposed to a given restriction at least have the possibility of abolishing the restriction by trying to elect a majority of the legislature which would do so. In the case of racial restrictive covenants, however, suits are often instituted by only one or merely a few persons to dispossess others from their property and homes even through the majority of neighboring property owners in the area either oppose the initiation of such a suit or have affirmatively agreed to remove the restriction. The use of the government's power, through the courts, to enforce this private zoning and to deprive other individuals of their fundamental rights to dispose of their own property or to acquire and occupy that property as their home, is thus more arbitrary than judicial enforcement of racial zoning pursuant to the admittedly unconstitutional and vicious legislative zoning statutes....

[40] During the past two decades, racial restrictive covenants have been extensively and uniformly imposed in most of the major cities of the nation on a large percentage of all newly constructed dwellings, new residential subdivisions, and existing residential properties, contiguous to areas occupied by Negroes. This private, and wholesale, "zoning" has hemmed Negroes into virtual ghettoes by placing artificial yet impassable boundaries—iron rings in depth—around the existing areas of Negro occupancy, and barring Negroes of all income groups from occupancy in most suburban areas where new construction has been concentrated. The lack of suffi-

Glossary

Aryans	a term with deep and valid historical roots, referring to a group of Indo-European peoples who in prehistoric times settled in Iran, India, and Europe; in modern times, however, a term used by the Nazis and other racists to refer to a white "master race"
covenants	agreements whereby purchasers of real estate promise to abide by certain rules regarding their use of the property
due process clause of the Fifth Amendment	a guarantee of citizens' rights to due process under the law, meaning that an individual cannot be imprisoned without being charged for a crime and granted a speedy and fair trial
fossilizing eternally	settling in stone
ghettoes	a term often associated with poor areas; more broadly, any district or section occupied almost exclusively by members of a particular ethnic group—usually as a result of laws preventing them from living among the general population
positive correlation	a relationship whereby one factor serves as a function of another, increasing or decreasing as the other increases or decreases
statute	a law passed by a legislative body
zoning	the designation of particular city areas for specific uses, such as commercial or residential property

cient space for decent living and normal expansion which has resulted largely from these restrictions on the housing market and the increased urbanization of the Negro population have forced Negroes to "double-up" in excessively crowded dwellings and in congested neighborhoods; they have been grossly exploited by enormously inflated rents and selling prices; and the blighted slum areas into which they have been forced have, by virtue of such overcrowding, become further deteriorated.

This enforced living in slums has had universally known baneful effects upon the economic, social and moral life, not only of the Negroes, but also of the entire community....

[44] Restrictive covenants have been, in the cities, a prime factor contributing to the social disorganization of both the Negro people and the entire community. They have corrupted family life by promoting excessive density and congestion in ghetto-like communities of substandard houses. They have burdened Negroes with excessive housing and rental costs. Diseases, infant mortality, insanity, crime, juvenile delinquency, and family discord have been disproportionately stimulated by the effects of restrictive covenants. The covenants have been a direct cause of increased racial tensions and race riots. And they have provided the basic structure for other forms of segregation and discrimination in schools, health and welfare services, police protection, sanitation, and other municipal facilities, with consequent inefficiency and lowered standards for all. The "positive correlation between segregation [of Negroes] and tuberculosis mortality,...percentage of housing needing major repairs, infant mortality" etc., has been amply proven....

[131] A basic aim of the United States and the allied nations in World War II was the defeat of the same principle of racism which underlies the racial restrictive covenant in this case. To uphold this racial restrictive covenant would nullify the victories won by the United States and the allied nations at such great cost in that war, and deliberately ignore the tensions and misery which the exaltation of racism has imposed on the entire world.

Sam Houston (Library of Congress)

SAM HOUSTON

1793–1863

President of the Texas Republic, U.S. Senator, and Governor

Featured Documents
♦ **Inaugural Address as President of the Republic of Texas (1836)**
♦ **Speech Supporting the Compromise of 1850 (1850)**
♦ **Speech Opposing the Kansas-Nebraska Act (1854)**
♦ **Speech on Refusal to Take the Oath of Loyalty to the Confederacy (1861)**

Overview

Samuel Houston—military hero, governor of two states, president of the Texas Republic, and U.S. senator—was born on March 2, 1793. He lived his early life in Tennessee, where he spent most of his time with the Cherokee and was even adopted into the Cherokee Nation. He later enlisted in the army during the War of 1812, worked as an Indian subagent, and pursued a law career in Tennessee. By 1819 Houston's political career was starting to evolve; he served as adjunct general of the state militia and attorney general for the district of Nashville. With the support of Andrew Jackson, Houston was elected to the U.S. House of Representatives, where he served from 1823 to 1827. Then, in 1827, he ran for and won the governorship of Tennessee, though he resigned on April 16, 1829, heading west into Indian Territory and eventually to Texas.

Once in Texas, Houston became enmeshed in the events unfolding there. He was one of the Texas representatives at the Convention of 1833, through which Texas sought a peaceful independence from Mexico. Hopes for peace were dashed when war broke out in October 1835. As commander in chief of the Texas army, Houston led Texas to victory over Mexican forces in 1836. In September that year, Houston was elected as the first president of the Republic of Texas, serving until December 1838. He was elected again in December 1841, to serve until December 1844. After Texas became a state in 1845, Houston was elected as one of the state's first senators, a post he held for thirteen years.

Without doubt, Houston's most eloquent documents were speeches. In his early days in Tennessee he was known as a gifted orator. While his oratory might be considered flowery in the twenty-first century, in that respect his was little different from that of other great orators of the day. In addition, his speeches, such as his 1836 inaugural address, were infused with common sense and gentle humor, and when he spoke, he could attract crowds and move people to action. It was as a senator that Houston delivered two of his most powerful speeches, on the Compromise of 1850 and on the 1854 Kansas-Nebraska Act. In late 1859 Houston became Texas's seventh governor, but he resigned less than two years later over the controversy surrounding his refusal to take the Confederate loyalty oath. Houston retired into private life and died at home on July 26, 1863.

Explanation and Analysis of Documents

Houston was involved in some of the most dramatic events in American history. Aside from his successful military career, he proved to be a passionate and dedicated politician. Unlike many of his southern counterparts, he was sympathetic to Native Americans and firmly believed that secession was a mistake. A charismatic orator and eloquent writer, Houston's writings and speeches often stirred people to action. Four documents that demonstrate his commitment to peace, his zeal, and his love of Texas and the Union are his inaugural address as the first president of the Republic of Texas, his speech on the Compromise of 1850, his speech on the Kansas-Nebraska Act, and his letter to the people of Texas refusing to take an oath of loyalty to the Confederacy.

♦ Inaugural Address as President of the Republic of Texas

Many Americans "Remember the Alamo"—a battle cry in memory of the soldiers who fought there—but the events that led to the annexation of Texas as part of the United States, in which the defense of the Alamo in San Antonio played a central part, are less widely known. Prior to 1836, Texas was under the rule of Mexico. In 1832 Houston traveled from Tennessee to Texas partly to engage in land speculation, partly to help local authorities negotiate with Native Americans. Some historians believe that there was also a third motivation: They argue that President Andrew Jackson dispatched him to foment insurrection against Mexico. Whether that claim is true or not, Houston was quickly caught up in the events that led to Texan independence. Tensions between settlers and Mexico led to hostilities, and Houston was appointed provisional head of the Texas army. Then, on March 2, 1836, Texas declared itself independent from Mexico. Hostilities continued; when the Alamo fell on March 6 after a twelve-day siege, Houston and his small army, accompanied by panicked civilians, began a retreat that ended with the Battle of San Jacinto on April 21, which resulted in the destruction of the Mexican army and the capture of the Mexican president Antonio López de Santa Anna.

The election of Houston as the first president of the Republic of Texas happened quickly, with Houston commanding 79 percent of the 6,449 votes. He had only a few hours' notice before being sworn in as president of the

1793

■ **March 2**
Samuel Houston is born on Timber Ridge, near Lexington, Virginia.

1813

■ **March 24**
Houston enlists in the U.S. Army.

1814

■ **March**
Houston serves in the campaign against the Creek Nation under Andrew Jackson.

1818

■ **March**
Houston resigns his commission after being falsely accused of involvement in the slave trade and returns to Tennessee, to study law and pass the bar later that year.

1821

■ Houston is made a major general in the Tennessee militia.

1827

■ **October 1**
Houston takes office as the elected governor of Tennessee.

1836

■ **March 4**
Houston is appointed major general of the army of the Republic of Texas.

■ **April 21**
Houston wins the Battle of San Jacinto, defeating Antonio López de Santa Anna.

■ **October 22**
Houston is sworn in as president of the Republic of Texas and delivers his inaugural address.

1845

■ **December 29**
Texas becomes a state.

1846

■ **February 21**
Houston takes office as a U.S. senator from Texas, to serve for thirteen years.

Republic of Texas, and while his inaugural speech was extemporaneous, it was nonetheless eloquent. He begins the speech with a modest tone, expressing his awe and sense of responsibility at being elected president. He then turns his attention to the region's Native Americans. With Texas bordered by Indian lands, Houston promoted the desire for peace as "the most rational grounds" for seeking the Indians' friendship. Unlike his mentor and friend Andrew Jackson, Houston was sympathetic to Native Americans, having lived with them from time to time over the course of years. He urged his fellow Texans to avoid aggression and establish fair commerce with neighboring tribes. For the remaining bulk of the speech, Houston praises the volunteers who came to the aid of Texas and reminds everyone that Mexico still posed a real danger to the people of Texas.

At the end of the speech, Houston drew his sword, which he had worn at San Jacinto, and stated that it was a symbol of his past office but that he would bear it again in the defense of Texas. From this point on, he would be a man of peace, fighting only to defend Texas. Houston went on to serve nonconsecutive terms as president of the new Republic of Texas, the first spanning 1836–1838 and the second 1841–1844. Throughout those years the issue of American statehood was central in Texas politics. In 1837 the United States actually rejected the annexation of Texas as a state, and Houston as governor carried on negotiations with both France and England about aligning Texas with one or the other. Not until 1845 and the administration of John Tyler was Texas annexed as a state.

◆ Speech Supporting the Compromise of 1850

As early as 1820 the nation was entangled in bitter debates surrounding new territories and the entrance of states into the Union as either free or slave states. The issue was important because neither side of the debate wanted the other to gain a majority in Congress. In the 1820s one crisis was averted by the Kentucky senator Henry Clay's Missouri Compromise, which prohibited slavery in the Louisiana Territory north of latitude 36°30' while allowing the new state of Missouri to enter the Union as a slave state, thus maintaining the balance of power in Congress.

Similar issues arose again in 1850. The Compromise of 1850, likewise authored by Clay, was in large part a consequence of the Mexican-American War of 1846–1848. Despite the outcome of the Texas insurrection of 1836, which led to Texan independence, Mexico still claimed ownership of Texas. That nation regarded the U.S. annexation of Texas in 1845 as a hostile act and moved to reclaim at least some of its lost territory in the American Southwest. The war that erupted quickly divided Americans. Members of the Whig Party, particularly in the North, bitterly opposed the war as an act of unjust aggression and an effort to expand slave territories; it was in response to the war that Henry David Thoreau wrote his famous essay "Civil Disobedience." Democrats, particularly those in the southern states, eagerly embraced the war, seeing it as an opportunity to expand southern reaches of the nation that the South hoped would become slave states. The war ended in 1848 with the Treaty of Guadalupe Hidalgo, which established the Rio Grande as the border between Texas and Mexico and allowed the United States to acquire territories in the American Southwest. In many respects, the Mexican-American War served as a training ground for young officers such as Jefferson Davis, Ulysses S. Grant, George McClellan, Ambrose Burnside, James Longstreet, Thomas "Stonewall" Jackson, Robert E. Lee, and others who would gain fame during the Civil War.

The outcome of the war left the nation divided over four key questions: Should the territory recently acquired from the war with Mexico be free or allow slavery? Should California's petition to enter the Union as a free state be allowed? How should a dispute over territory claimed by Texas be resolved? And should Washington, D.C., continue to be home to one of the nation's largest slave markets?

Clay's suggested compromise on the issues was debated for eight months. Southern Democrats opposed the compromise because admitting California as a free state, as per the conditions, would upset the balance of power in the Senate. They further claimed that the proposed abolition of the slave trade in Washington, D.C., would be unconstitutional. Northern Whigs, meanwhile, opposed the terms of the compromise's reinforced Fugitive Slave Act, which would significantly strengthen the Fugitive Slave Act of 1793 by mandating that all citizens assist in the return of runaway slaves to their owners as well as by establishing penalties to deal with law officials and others who aided runaway slaves. A number of people, however, including Houston, felt that whatever needed to be done to preserve the Union should be done. On February 8, 1850, Houston, though he was a slave owner who opposed abolition, delivered a passionate speech supporting the Compromise of 1850.

Houston begins his speech by humbly thanking the Senate for allowing him to speak. He informs the gathering that he feels it to be his duty to speak frankly and candidly and that his hope is that the discord between factions will end. (At this point Houston was asked to pause so that the Senate could suspend its rules to allow a number of women to enter the chamber to hear the speech.) Houston then spends a good portion of the speech explaining that Congress has no authority over the states or territories to permit or prohibit slavery and asking the North to refrain from insisting on stepping on the rights of the states and territories.

The heart of the document is Houston's passionate plea to preserve the Union at all cost, which he holds as more important than the potential gains of any one region or individual. He calls on the "friends of the Union" to come "forward like men" for the good of the country as a whole and even asks the Senate to consider what message the dissolution of the Union would send to foreign countries. Further, he recites a poem from a Virginia newspaper that reminds his audience that the North and South served together to establish the Union. Dramatically, Houston warns that if the North were to continue to violate the rights of the southern states, then the consequences would

Time Line

1850	■ **February 8** Houston delivers a speech in support of the Compromise of 1850.
1854	■ **February 14–15** Houston delivers his speech opposing the Kansas-Nebraska bill.
1859	■ **December 21** Houston takes office as the elected governor of Texas.
1861	■ **February 1** Texas secedes from the United States, to join the Confederacy on March 2. ■ **March 16** Houston refuses to take the Confederate loyalty oath and is removed as governor by the Texas Secession Convention.
1863	■ **July 26** Houston dies in Huntsville, Texas.

"lie at their own door" and the ensuing war would be a "war of brothers." Houston ends his speech asking for everyone to pray for the Union because a "nation divided against itself cannot stand."

In the end, a series of five acts constituted the Compromise of 1850: California entered the Union as a free state; both the Utah Territory and the New Mexico Territory would decide the free-or-slave question by popular sovereignty; Texas relinquished its claim to the disputed territory in exchange for $10 million; the slave trade was abolished in Washington, D.C.; and the Fugitive Slave Act of 1850 strengthened the existing law. Neither side was entirely content with the compromise, and the issue would reenter the spotlight in 1854.

◆ Speech Opposing the Kansas-Nebraska Act

Authored by Senator Stephen Douglas, the Kansas-Nebraska Act was designed to move the issue of slavery from the federal arena to the individual territories, to thereby ease tensions between the North and South because the South would be able to expand slavery while states in the North could still abolish the institution. The act originated with Douglas's desire to see a transcontinental railroad built through his home state of Illinois. But the proposed railroad could follow such a route, and thereby benefit the people of

A pro-Democrat cartoon forecasting the collapse of Whig opposition to the annexation of Texas (Library of Congress)

Illinois, only if it could continue westward into what would become Nebraska Territory. This territory, however, would lie north of the dividing line between free and slave states established by the Missouri Compromise. Accordingly, senators from the southern states opposed its inception. Douglas's bill was intended to be a new compromise; it would divide the territory into two potential states, Nebraska and Kansas, while at the same time repealing the Missouri Compromise line. It was expected that Nebraska, the more northerly territory, would be free territory and that Kansas, the more southerly, would elect to be a slave territory.

In February 1854, Houston delivered a passionate and dramatic speech to the U.S. Senate opposing the Kansas-Nebraska bill that took almost two complete days. He focused on two main issues that he had with the legislation. The first issue centered on the Native Americans living in the territories in question. Houston begins by acknowledging that as a supporter of the Indians and their rights, he is alone but remains duty bound to advocate for them. At this point he begins referring to and quoting from a series of agreements between the government and various Indian nations starting as far back as 1785. Houston skillfully points out each broken promise made by the U.S. government. He then encourages the Senate to civilize and Christianize the Indians, stating, "They seem not be regarded in the light of human beings, and are driven like wild beasts; and when their habitation is made in one place, they are considered as temporary residents." He adds that by civilizing the Indians, the federal government could abandon its forts along the Rio Grande and in Texas and New Mexico, saving money and men for other purposes.

At the point in the speech marking the beginning of the second day, Houston resumes his plea for the Native Americans within the Kansas-Nebraska territory by outlining the advantages he sees gained "when they [the Indians] are justly treated." As an example, he points to the Cherokee in Tennessee. As a boy, he lived with the Cherokee before they had adopted modes of white American civilization; in time, they learned to work as farmers and mechanics and gained education. Houston does not advocate for the preservation of native cultures, but he believes that the country and the Indian nations would be better off working together. He believes that by honoring its treaties, the government could establish meaningful and permanent relationships with native nations.

With his plea on behalf of Native Americans finished, Houston turns his attention to his second issue with the bill, the repeal of the Missouri Compromise. By declaring that the people of the new territories would decide whether to allow slavery by popular sovereignty, the Kansas-Nebraska bill was in direct violation of the 1820 Missouri Compromise, which outlawed slavery north of latitude 36°30'; indeed, the bill included a clause that would repeal the Missouri Compromise. Calling the compromise their "wall of fire," Houston argues that it remained a binding agreement between North and South that had kept peace for more than thirty years and was "essential to the preservation of this Union." He emphasizes that the repeal of that compromise would certainly bring about disunion.

Only one other southerner, John Bell of Tennessee, stood with Houston in opposition to the Kansas-Nebraska bill. On March 4, just over two weeks after Houston's two-day speech and despite his passionate effort in opposition, the Senate voted thirty-seven to fourteen in favor of the bill. On May 22, 1854, the bill passed the House narrowly, by a vote of 113 to 100. Houston's predictions proved accurate. In undoing the Missouri Compromise, the passage of the Kansas-Nebraska Act further divided the nation and split political parties, giving rise to the Republican Party. Meanwhile, Houston's strong Unionism and opposition to the expansion of slavery into the territories drove a wedge between him and both the Texas legislature and the southern states. For Houston, the events would reach a painful climax in March 1861, when he refused to take an oath of loyalty to the Confederacy.

◆ Speech on Refusal to Take the Oath of Loyalty to the Confederacy

Throughout the tumultuous 1850s, Houston advocated for a peaceful solution to the growing discord over whether new states and territories should be admitted to the United States allowing slavery or as free. Houston waited as long as possible to call a special session of his state's legislature to debate secession. The Texas legislature met on January 21, 1861, at which time South Carolina, Mississippi, Georgia, Florida, and Alabama had already seceded. In addressing the legislature, Houston tried to sway the group by pointing out how Texas was different from other southern states. For instance, no other southern state bordered a foreign country or was susceptible to Indian attacks, and Texas relied on the support of the federal government to defend itself.

Ultimately, Houston argued that the people of Texas should decide the issue. The Texas Secession Convention assembled a week later, promptly voted 171 to six in favor of secession, and named a committee to draft an ordinance on which the people of Texas would vote. In a bill titled "An Ordinance: To Dissolve the Union between the State of Texas and the Other States, United under the Compact Styled 'The Constitution of the United States of America,'" the convention outlined its motives for withdrawing from the Union:

> Whereas, the Federal Government has failed to accomplish the purposes of the compact of union between these States, in giving protection either to the persons of our people upon an exposed frontier, or to the property of our citizens; and, whereas, the action of the Northern States of the Union is violative of the compact between the States and the guarantees of the Constitution; and whereas the recent developments in Federal affairs, make it evident that the power of the Federal Government is sought to be made a weapon with which to strike down the inter-

ests and prosperity of the people of Texas and her Sister slaveholding States, instead of permitting it to be, as was intended, our shield against outrage and aggression." (http://www.tsl.state.tx.us/ref/abouttx/secession/1feb1861.html)

In the only case where the people directly voted on the issue of secession, the people of Texas voted to secede. Even though Texas delegates had already traveled to Montgomery, Alabama, to take their seats in the First Confederate Congress, Houston insisted that Texas had merely reclaimed its independence and had not yet agreed to become a part of another government. The members of the Texas Secession Convention were outraged and sent a messenger to Houston's home instructing him to appear the next day to take the Confederate oath of allegiance. During the night, Houston wrote a letter addressed to the people of Texas, which he read to the convention the next day.

In his address to the Texas Secession Convention, Houston begins by explaining that he would not take the oath of allegiance because the convention had not obtained its authority from the Texas legislature or people. As he put it, "That convention, besides being revolutionary in its character, did not receive the sanction of a majority of the people." He further notes that the convention had held its meetings in secret and appointed military personnel to operate under its authority. He then states that he refuses to recognize the authority of the convention and declares its actions null and void. At the end he declares, "I solemnly protest against the act of its members who are bound by no other than themselves, in declaring my office vacant, and I refuse to appear before it and take the oath prescribed." As a result of his refusal to take the Confederate oath, Houston was replaced as governor by the lieutenant governor, Edward Clark.

Impact and Legacy

Sam Houston is a complex historical figure. He was sympathetic to Native Americans, even living with them on two occasions and taking a Cherokee wife, in an era when most Americans considered them savages. He was known to say that he preferred living among the "red man" to living among "bloodthirsty" whites. He was also an ardent Unionist who opposed extending slavery into new states and territories, even though he owned slaves and opposed outright abolition. Although he was known for being impulsive, drinking too much, and having a temper, Houston in his writings shows himself to be a thoughtful and passionate man dedicated to Texas and to the Union. His ability to stir people's emotion with his oratory and writing ability made him an effective leader both on the battlefield and in the political arena.

Perhaps Houston's most lasting legacy was his impact on Texas. From his defeat of Santa Anna at the Battle of San Jacinto through his service to the Republic of Texas and the state of Texas to his resignation as governor of

"We are only in the outset of the campaign of liberty. Futurity has locked up the destiny which awaits our people."

(Inaugural Address as President of the Republic of Texas)

"A subject of no small importance is the situation of an extensive frontier, bordered by Indians, and open to their depredations. Treaties of peace and amity, and the maintenance of good faith with the Indians, present themselves to my mind as the most rational grounds on which to obtain their friendship."

(Inaugural Address as President of the Republic of Texas)

"But I call upon the friends of the Union from every quarter, to come forward like men, and to sacrifice their differences upon the common altar of their country's good."

(Speech Supporting the Compromise of 1850)

"For a nation divided against itself cannot stand."

(Speech Supporting the Compromise of 1850)

"I never knew an Indian nation violate a treaty which was made in good faith, and observed by the white man."

(Speech Opposing the Kansas-Nebraska Act)

"I assert the principle that Congress has no right to legislate upon the subject of slavery in any of our territories of this Union."

(Speech Opposing the Kansas-Nebraska Act)

"I do not wish to be sectional. I do not wish to be regarded as for the South alone. I need not say that I am for the whole country.... But, sir, my all is in the South."

(Speech Opposing the Kansas-Nebraska Act)

"I went back into the Union with the people of Texas. I go out from the Union with them; and though I see only gloom before me, I shall follow the 'Lone Star' with the same devotion as of yore."

(Speech on Refusal to Take the Oath of Loyalty to the Confederacy)

Texas over secession, Houston served according to his conscience and with passion. Remaining true to his inaugural address as the first president of the Republic of Texas and despite the fact that he was a military hero, Houston spent his political career advocating for peace. His legacy lives on in the names of the city of Houston, incorporated in 1837, and of such institutions as Sam Houston State University.

Key Sources

The Sam Houston Papers, spanning the period 1814–1957, are housed at the Center for American History at the University of Texas at Austin and are available online (http://www.lib.utexas.edu/taro/utcah/00005/cah-00005.html). The collection includes documents from his personal life, his military service, and his service as Tennessee congressman and governor, Republic of Texas president, and Texas senator and governor. His collected writings were published as *The Writings of Sam Houston, 1813–1863*, 8 vols. (1938–1943), edited by Amelia W. Williams and Eugene C. Barker. Houston's personal correspondence has been compiled and edited by Madge Roberts into a four-volume series entitled *The Personal Correspondence of Sam Houston* (1996–2001). Houston also wrote memoirs of his life, which were edited by Donald Day and Harry H. Ullom and published as *The Autobiography of Sam Houston* (1954).

Further Reading

■ Books

Braider, Donald. *Solitary Star: A Biography of Sam Houston*. New York: Putnam, 1974.

De Bruhl, Marshall. *Sword of San Jacinto: A Life of Sam Houston*. New York: Random House, 1993.

Haley, James L. *Sam Houston*. Norman: University of Oklahoma Press, 2002.

James, Marquis. *The Raven: A Biography of Sam Houston*. Indianapolis, Ind.: Bobbs-Merrill, 1929.

Williams, John Hoyt. *Sam Houston: A Biography of the Father of Texas*. New York: Simon & Schuster, 1993.

■ Web Sites

"An Ordinance: To Dissolve the Union between the State of Texas and the Other States, United under the Compact Styled 'The Constitution of the United States of America.'" Texas State Library and Archives Commission Web site. http://www.tsl.state.tx.us/ref/about tx/secession/1feb1861.html.

—Michael J. O'Neal and Lisa Ennis

Questions for Further Study

1. In the twenty-first century Americans in general regard Texas as simply another state in the Union. However, Texas as an organized territory has not always been a U.S. state. Summarize the sequence of events that led to eventual statehood. What role did Sam Houston play in these events?

2. During the early decades of the nineteenth century, the United States underwent rapid expansion westward. In this light, why was the acquisition of Texas, California, and the Southwest a source of controversy? How was the controversy resolved? What role did Houston play in these controversies?

3. The two major U.S. political parties in Sam Houston's day were the Whigs and the Democrats. On what basis did the two parties differ? Was Sam Houston more sympathetic with the views of the Whigs or the Democrats (or neither)? Explain.

4. On what basis did Texas secede from the Union in 1861? How did the state's motives for secession differ from those of other southern states? What was Sam Houston's position on the secession issue?

5. Compare and contrast Houston's views regarding slavery and North-South relations with those of Henry Clay as expressed in his remarks on the Compromise of 1850 resolutions.

6. Houston did not live to see the end of the Civil War or the developments that took place in its aftermath. How would Houston have reacted to Salmon Chase's opinion in the case of *Texas v. White*?

Inaugural Address as President of the Republic of Texas (1836)

Deeply impressed with a sense of responsibility devolving on me, I can not, in justice to myself, repress the emotion of my heart, or restrain the feelings which my sense of obligation to my fellow-citizens has inspired....

We are only in the outset of the campaign of liberty. Futurity has locked up the destiny which awaits our people....

If, then, in the discharge of my duty, my competency should fail in the attainment of the great objects in view, it would become your sacred duty to correct my errors and sustain me by your superior wisdom. This much I anticipate—this much I demand. I am perfectly aware of the difficulties that surround me, and the convulsive throes through which our country must pass.... A country situated like ours is environed with difficulties, its administration is frought with perplexities.... Nothing but zeal, stimulated by the holy spirit of patriotism, and guided by philosophy and wisdom, can give that impetus to our energies necessary to surmount the difficulties with which our political path is obstructed.

By the aid of your intelligence, I trust all impediments in our advancement will be removed; that all wounds in the body politic will be healed, and the Constitution of the Republic will derive strength and vigor equal to all opposing energies....

A subject of no small importance is the situation of an extensive frontier, bordered by Indians, and open to their depredations. Treaties of peace and amity, and the maintenance of good faith with the Indians, present themselves to my mind as the most rational grounds on which to obtain their friendship. Let us abstain on our part from aggressions, establish commerce with the different tribes, supply their useful and necessary wants, maintain even-handed justice with them, and natural reason will teach them the utility of our friendship....

Admonished by the past, we can not, in justice, disregard our national enemies; vigilance will apprise us of their approach, a disciplined and valiant army will insure their discomfiture.... We must keep all our energies alive, our army organized, desciplined, and increased agreeably to our present necessities. With these preparations we can meet and vanquish despotic thousands. This is the attitude we at present must regard as our own....

The course our enemies have pursued has been opposed to every principle of civilized warfare—bad faith, inhumanity, and devastation marked their path of invasion. We were a little band, contending for liberty; they were thousands, well appointed, munitioned, and provisioned, seeking to rivet chains upon us, or extirpate us from the earth. Their cruelties have incurred the universal denunciation of Christendom. They will not pass from their nation during the present generation....

At this moment I discern numbers around me who battled in the field of San Jacinto, and whose chivalry and valor have identified them with the glory of the country, its name, its soil, and its liberty.... It now, Sir, becomes my duty to make a presentation of this sword—this emblem of my past office!...

I have worn it with some humble pretensions in defence of my country; and should the danger of my country again call for my services, I expect to resume it, and respond to that call, if needful, with my blood and life.

Glossary

depredations	attacks
discomfiture	frustration, disappointment, defeat
extirpate	eliminate
San Jacinto	the site in Texas of a major battle between Texas and Mexico in 1836

SPEECH SUPPORTING THE COMPROMISE OF 1850 (1850)

Mr. President: However incompetent I may be to repay the Senate for their courtesy in permitting me to address them at this time, and upon this subject, I feel that it is my duty to offer my views in a respectful, frank, and candid manner, as the representative of that State whose interests are involved in the resolutions offered for our consideration by the distinguished Senator from Kentucky [Mr. Clay]....

These considerations awaken my solicitude for the adoption of the resolution which I had the honor a few days since to submit to the Senate....

Mr. President, my object in the introduction of this resolution was to present a ground which I believed was equitable and just, between the conflicting interests and prejudices in this country. I believe, in the first place, that the Congress of the United States does not possess the power to legislate upon the subject of slavery, either within the Territories or in any other section of the Union.... The North contend that they have a right to interfere with the subject of slavery; hence the Wilmot proviso. The South contend that the North has no such right—no right to interfere with the subject of slavery anywhere; and hence the principle is contended for that Congress does not possess this power as applicable to the Territories—no power arising from the terms of the union between the North and the South—none growing out of the Constitution by which they are bound together. Nor do I believe that Congress has, under the Constitution, any authority to impose upon States asking for admission into the Union any condition whatever, other than that of having a republican form of government....

I maintain that when the Territories are erected into States by their own action, that, in the formation of their constitutions, under which they ask admission, the people of the Territories have the right to give their own form to their own institutions, and in their own way.

Let these grounds be assumed—and they are grounds, which it seems to me, the North and South can take without the sacrifice of any principle—then no collision can occur, and all complaint will cease. It will be a reconciliation, an adjustment of all the causes of difference which now agitate the Union. And I trust that these views may prevail. We do not ask the North to concede anything. We merely ask them to abstain from aggression. The South only asks that her rights be respected in relation to the Constitution of the United States, by which all the States are bound.

If the compromise line of 36° 30' is continued, inhibiting slavery north of that line, and the States which may be formed south of it be authorized to claim admission into the United States with such municipal regulations as they may choose to form, according to the nature of their social and domestic institutions, the whole matter is at an end. How trifling the sacrifice would be?...

Congress has the power to make needful rules and regulations for the Territories and other property of the United States; and these rules are temporary....

I believe that the exercise of a power not clearly given is nowhere so dangerous as in the Congress of the nation—more so than in any of the coördinate branches of the Government....

Unfortunately, Mr. President, when these dissensions first commenced between the North and the South, they were comparatively unimportant in their extent, but time added fuel to the flame, and has now brought it to a conflagration difficult to extinguish....

But I call upon the friends of the Union from every quarter, to come forward like men, and to sacrifice their differences upon the common altar of their country's good, and to form a bulwark around the Constitution that cannot be shaken. It will require manly efforts, sir; and they must expect to meet with prejudices growing up around them that will assail them from every quarter. They must stand firm to the Union, regardless of all personal consequences....

Sir, the Union is not dissolved; and I apprehend there will be less danger of it when the people are awakened to the slightest apprehension of real danger....

Do you think that if there be real danger of a disunion, they will not be awakened from their lethargy? Do you think that they will not feel themselves called upon to act by the apprehension of such danger? Then, sir, you will have a sincere expression, when you carry it to the hearths of the farmer, the mechanic, who has every comfort of life around him, acquired by industry, or inherited from patriotic ancestry, under the broad aegis of this Union, and tell him you have now to encounter the hazard of civil broils—of a war of disolution—the worst of all wars; a war, not of race—a war, not of language, or of tongue, or of religion, but a war of brothers—the most sanguinary of mortal strife....

But, Mr. President, it is not alone the North and the South—not alone these two sections of this vast Union, who are interested. Where are the Middle States?... Sir, if the North does not refrain, if they persist in their threatened aggressions upon the South, and invasions upon their rights established under the Constitution, the sin must lie at their own door, and their own threshold will be defiled with the consequences of injustice to their brethren....

The passage of the proviso would be an indignity, and, if the North choose to take this firebrand and thrust it into the bosom of southern society, then they may reproach themselves, and not the South, for the conflagration which they have kindled....

Permit me—and I say it because it is history not embelished, it is truth—when I gave the first evidence of manhood it was in earnest devotion to the South.... There I offered the richest libation of my youth, the blood of my early manhood, to consecrate the soil to freedom and the Union. This was in the centre of the South. Now, war is no more heard on our borders, the mountains speak peace, and joy is in all our valleys. The warrior is careless, his arms lie idle; he can now point to them and speak to his sons of his valient deeds. In what I have done, if I have contributed my mite to human freedom, I will let history tell, and say to what extent I have done it; or, if I have failed in the offices of humanity, let it be visited upon me. With my gallant associates I have struck manacles from the limbs of a captive chieftain and restored him, with his vanquished comrades, to their nation and their homes, without ransom. I ask no recompense. Was not all this done for the South, and am I to be questioned of having a southern heart, when that heart is large enough, I trust, to embrace the whole Union, if not the whole world?... But I beseech those whose piety will permit them reverently to petition, that they will pray for this Union, and ask that He who buildeth up and pulleth down nations will, in mercy, preserve and unite us. For a nation divided against itself cannot stand. I wish, if this Union must be dissolved, that its ruins may be the monument of my grave, and the graves of my family. I wish no epitaph to be written to tell that I survive the ruin of this glorious Union.

Glossary

aegis	protection, support, guardianship
conflagration	fire; more generally, a conflict or war
sanguinary	bloody
solicitude	a state of uneasiness or concern
Territories	organized areas west of the early United States that were later admitted to the Union as states
Wilmot proviso	a rider, attached to an 1846 congressional appropriations bill and named after its sponsor, Congressman David Wilmot, intended to prevent the introduction of slavery into any territory acquired from Mexico but that did not pass in Congress

SPEECH OPPOSING THE KANSAS-NEBRASKA ACT (1854)

I am aware, Mr. President, that in presenting myself as the advocate of the Indians and their rights, I shall claim but little sympathy from the community at large, and that I shall stand very much alone, pursuing the course which I feel it my imperative duty to adhere to. It is not novel for me to seek to advocate the rights of the Indians upon this floor and elsewhere. A familiar knowledge of them, their manners, their habits, and their intercourse with this Government for the last half century, from my early boyhood through life, have placed within my possession facts, and, I trust, implanted in me a principle enduring as life itself. That principle is to protect the Indian against wrong and oppression, and to vindicate him in the enjoyment of rights which have been solemnly guaranteed to him by this Government; and *that* is the principle, Mr. President, which I shall insist grows out of the course of policy avowed by this Government as far back as 1785. The Hopewell treaty was then negotiated with the Cherokee Indians of Tennessee....

Successive promises were made from 1785 to 1802, during the administration of General Washington; and the pledges of amity and regard that were made to the Indians by him, inured to Mr. Jefferson, for he, in 1809, made solemn promises to them, provided they would migrate west of the Mississippi.... They continued there up to 1814, 1816 and 1817, under the promises of the Government, battling against the hostile, wild Indians, and relying upon the pledges of the different Presidents of the United States, their great father, that they should not be molested in their settlement there....After that, the policy of the Government became more stringent upon them; and a disposition arising, owing to pressure from surrounding States, to remove them to Arkansas, it was proposed that the whole nation of Cherokees east of the Mississippi should migrate, and exchange their lands on the east for lands lying to the far west....

These were the suggestions, and the most solemn pledges were made by this Government—that if they would remove to the west of the Mississippi they should never again be surrounded by white men, and that they should have a boundless and interminable outlet, as far as the jurisdiction of the United States extended....I need not rehearse to gentlemen who are familiar with the past, the tragedies that followed, the

sanguinary murders and massacres, the mid-night conflagrations—these attest the inharmonious action which arose from this faithless conduct on the part of the Government or its agents. I know this may appear a very harsh assertion to make here, that our Government acts in bad faith with the Indians....Look at the Creeks, at the Choctaws, the Chickasaws; look at every tribe that has ever been within our jurisdiction, and in every instance our intercourse has resulted in their detriment or destruction....

It seems to be a foregone conclusion that the Indians must yield to the progress of the white man—that they must surrender their country—that they must go from place to place, and that there is to be no rest for them. Is not the earth wide enough for all the creatures the Almighty has placed upon it? But they seem not to be regarded in the light of human beings, and are driven like wild beasts; and when their habitation is made in one place, they are only considered as temporary residents, to be transferred at will to some more distant station....

I have a proposition to make, and I will submit it to the intelligence of Senators, though the destruction of the Indians seems to be a foregone conclusion.

Military posts are distributed throughout New Mexico and Texas, along the borders of the Rio Grande, to a great extent. It takes an immense amount of money to supply the various garrisons and to carry on the transportation for the provisioning of the troops.... If you appropriate that money to the Indians, you can civilize every Indian east of the Rocky Mountains. Place capable men among them—men who feel higher impulses than a disposition to rob the defenseless—and you will be enabled to collect these people together, and to teach them the arts of agriculture and mechanics. You will civilize them preparatory to their christianization; you can do all this, and yet have a large surplus left out of the money which you are now expending for the support of these garrisons....

I will speak in reference to the Indians, and the advantage which arises when they are justly treated.

Within my recollection, the first missionary, or schoolmaster, went to the Cherokee nation on the Tennessee river; for that was the northern boundary of the nation; and I found myself in boyhood located within six miles of that boundary, and every scene upon the banks of the river and its adjacent tributaries are as familiar to me as my right hand. I had every opportunity of becoming acquainted with them.... I was familiar with them then. They were in a savage state; they had no refinement....What are they now? They are a civilized people....

Sir, aid them in their progress.... They are not inferior in intellect, sagacity, or moral excellence to any people who are born upon the earth; and though the charge of perfidy has been made against them for ages back, I have lived for many years in connection with them, and, as a strict observer, can bear testimony that I never knew an Indian nation violate a treaty which was made in good faith, and observed by the white man....

Here, Mr. President, I shall terminate my remarks on the subject of the Indians.... As my position in relation to the repeal of the Missouri compromise, if unexplained, might not exactly be comprehended, I must speak of it.... Although I stood alone in the South, with the exception of a southwestern Senator [Mr. Benton, of Missouri]. I expressed my opinion, and voted my principle upon it. I supported the Missouri compromise, Mr. President, in its application to Oregon.... Although I had determined to vote against the bill, and the Indian provisions furnished insuperable objections to it, I have not denounced its general features....

I adopt no new course, but have heretofore maintained my present position; and the reasons which I gave on that occasion I will take care, sir, to reassert on this, and will show that it is no new ground to me; that it is one which I have maintained since Texas was annexed to the United States, and since she formed one star of our constellation.

If I voted, Mr. President, on a former occasion, in 1848, for the Missouri Compromise, I voted for it in accordance with the sanction of Texas.... Among the conditions expressed in that enactment, to which the consent of the Republic of Texas was peremptorily exacted, as a prerequisite to her admission into the Union, will be found the following. It provides that all new States formed north of 36° 30', within the limits of Texas, as she then rightfully claimed, slavery should be prohibited; that in all south of that, they could come into the Union with or without slavery, as they might think proper. This was accepted by Texas, with all the sanctity and solemnity that could attach to any compact whatever. She adopted the Missouri compromise....

The Missouri compromise has been repeatedly recognized and acted upon by Congress as a *solemn* compact between the States; and as such, it has received the sanction of each individual member of the Confederacy. I consider that the vital interests of all the States, and *especially of the South*, are dependent, in a great degree, upon the preservation and sacred observance of that compact....*I assert the principle that Congress has no right to legislate upon the subject of slavery in any of our territories of this Union....*

I would oppose to the last by all means of rational resistance the repeal of the Missouri compromise, because I deem it essential to the preservation of this Union, and to the very existence of the South. It has heretofore operated as a wall of fire to us....

I do not wish to be sectional. I do not wish to be regarded as for the South alone. I need not say that I am for the whole country. If I am, it is sufficient without rehearsing it here. But, sir, my all is in the South. My identity is there. My life has been spent there....I claim the Missouri compromise, as it now stands, in behalf of the South. I ask Senators to let its benefits inure to us. I do not want it taken away....

I am now called upon to vote for the repeal of the Missouri compromise, which I esteem everything to the South—under which it has prospered, and in which we have always acquiesced since its adoption—which the South united in applying to Texas when it was admitted into the Union; and even Texas has prospered under the infliction....

Mr. President, in the far distant future I think I perceive those who come after us, who are to be affected by the action of this body upon this bill. Our

Glossary

Hopewell treaty	three treaties, named for the South Carolina estate where they were signed, between the United States and the Cherokee (November 28, 1785), the Choctaw (January 3, 1786), and the Chicasaw (January 10, 1786)
perfidy	treachery, disloyalty
sagacity	wisdom

children have two alternatives here presented. They are either to live in after times in the enjoyment of peace, of harmony, and prosperity, or the alternative remains for them of anarchy, discord, and civil broil. We can avert the last. I trust we shall. At any rate, so far as my efforts can avail, I will resist every attempt to infringe or repeal the Missouri Compromise.

SPEECH ON REFUSAL TO TAKE THE OATH OF LOYALTY TO THE CONFEDERACY (1861)

When on account of the election of Mr. Lincoln to the Presidency of the United States, I was urged to call the Legislature, I refused to do so until such time as I believed the public interests required it....

In the meantime, the Convention had been called....That convention, besides being revolutionary in its character, did not receive the sanction of a majority of the people. As the representative of a minority, however large, it could not claim the right to speak for the people. It was without the pale of the Constitution, and was unknown to the laws which I had sworn to support. While sworn to support the Constitution, it was my duty to stand aloof from all revolutionary schemes calculated to subvert the Constitution. The people who were free from such solemn obligations, might revolutionize and absolve me from mine, my oath only having reference to my acts in the capacity of their Chief Executive; but as a sworn officer, my duty was too plain to be misunderstood....

Fellow Citizens, I have refused to recognize this Convention....

I have declared my determination to stand by Texas in whatever the position she assumes. Her people have declared in favor of a separation from the Union. I have followed her banners before, when an exile from the land of my fathers. I went back into the Union with the people of Texas. I go out from the Union with them; and though I see only gloom before me, I shall follow the "Lone Star" with the same devotion as of yore.

You have withdrawn Texas from her connection with the United States. Your act changes the character of the obligation I assumed at the time of my inauguration. As Your Chief Executive, I am no longer bound to support the Constitution of the United States.

I love Texas too well to bring civil strife and bloodshed upon her. To avert this calamity, I shall make no endeavor to maintain my authority as Chief Executive of this State, except by the peaceful exercise of my functions. When I can no longer do this, I shall calmly withdraw from the scene, leaving the Government in the hands of those who have usurped its authority; but still claiming that I am its Chief Executive.

I protest in the name of the people of Texas against all the acts and doings of this convention, AND I DECLARE THEM NULL AND VOID! I solemnly protest against the act of its members who are bound by no other than themselves, in declaring my office vacant, and I refuse to appear before it and take the oath prescribed.

Glossary

Lone Star	a reference to the Texas state flag, which features a single star
without the pale of the Constitution	outside the bounds of the Constitution, referring to the pickets, or "pales," of a fence

Andrew Jackson (Library of Congress)

ANDREW JACKSON   1767–1845

Seventh President of the United States

Featured Documents
◆ **Proclamation Regarding the Opening of U.S. Ports to British Vessels (1830)**
◆ **Second Annual Message to Congress (1830)**
◆ **Veto of the Bill to Limit the Power of the Bank of the United States (1832)**
◆ **Proclamation to the People of South Carolina Regarding Nullification (1832)**

Overview

Andrew Jackson, the seventh president of the United States, was born on March 15, 1767, just south of the border between North and South Carolina. His birth marked the beginning of an extraordinarily eventful life. As a teenager, he was taken prisoner during the Revolutionary War, an experience that left him with a lifelong animosity toward the British. He studied law, and during the 1780s and 1790s he held various judicial and legislative posts, including congressman, senator (a post he held again in the 1820s), and justice of the Tennessee Supreme Court. In the early decades of the nineteenth century he embarked on a military career, gaining a reputation for heroism during the War of 1812, particularly at the Battle of New Orleans. He also served as military governor of Florida after leading a controversial expedition against the Seminole Indians. Meanwhile, he was the owner of a plantation worked by slaves. The injuries he received in battle and in at least thirteen duels rendered him one of the nation's sickliest presidents. Nevertheless, his frontier toughness earned him the nickname "Old Hickory."

Jackson entered presidential politics in 1824 when he was nominated for president by the Democratic-Republican Party. Although he received a plurality of the popular vote in a four-candidate race, he failed to win a majority in the Electoral College, throwing the election to the House of Representatives, which chose John Quincy Adams. In 1828, however, Jackson was elected to the first of his two terms as president under a revived Republican Party, which had changed its name to the Democratic Party.

Jackson was a forceful and active president and outlined his positions on several issues in the accompanying state documents, which represent just a fraction of the numerous papers, addresses, and proclamations he issued as president. Despite the resentment he bore toward the British— a resentment deepened by the War of 1812—he opened U.S. ports to British merchants in 1830. He was a firm believer in the doctrine of Manifest Destiny—the belief that European settlers were destined by divine providence to spread their civilization across the entire breadth of North America—so he was the motive force behind the removal of Indians from their lands in eastern states to western reservations. He opposed the existence of a national bank, which he believed concentrated financial power in

the hands of the few at the expense of the common people, yet at the same time he was a proponent of a strong federal government. Although he was a slave owner, he never supported the grumblings of secession in the southern states that would eventually spark the Civil War, and as president he spoke out forcefully during the nullification crisis in South Carolina in 1832. In 1837 Jackson retired to Nashville, Tennessee. He died at his nearby plantation, the Hermitage, on June 8, 1845.

Explanation and Analysis of Documents

During his eight years as president, Jackson took forceful positions on numerous issues. Four of the issues that defined his administration were his opening of U.S. ports to British merchants, his role in the removal of American Indians to reservations in the West, his veto of a bill to recharter the Second Bank of the United States, and his opposition to efforts by South Carolina to nullify acts of Congress. He outlines his positions on these matters in the state documents excerpted here.

◆ Proclamation Regarding the Opening of U.S. Ports to British Vessels

In discussions of Andrew Jackson, the term *Jacksonian democracy* is sometimes used, but historians debate the true meaning of this term, with some arguing that the term is so ambiguous as to have no meaning at all. On the one hand, "Old Hickory" was a champion of the common people; his opposition to the chartering of a national bank was based on his belief that it concentrated too much power in the hands of too few. On the other hand, he was a proponent of a strong federal government, as he would later indicate in his response to the South Carolina nullification crisis. His efforts to engage in trade negotiations with Great Britain and to open American ports to British merchant vessels was significant because it represented a federal as opposed to a state effort. In effect, the proclamation asserted the power of the federal government to arrange the nation's business affairs.

In 1830 relations with Great Britain were still tense. Jackson himself, along with virtually his entire family, had suffered greatly during the Revolutionary War. Moreover, the War of 1812 with Britain, in which the British had

1767

- **March 15**
  Andrew Jackson is born at Waxhaw settlement, South Carolina.

1780–1781

- Jackson serves in the American Revolution and is taken as a prisoner of war.

1788

- Jackson is appointed public prosecutor for the Western District of North Carolina and migrates west.

1796

- Jackson participates in the Tennessee Constitutional Convention.

- Jackson is elected to the U.S. House of Representatives.

1797

- Jackson is elected to the U.S. Senate.

1798

- Jackson is elected judge of the Tennessee Superior Court.

1802

- Jackson is appointed major general of the Tennessee militia.

1812–1815

- Jackson leads troops in the War of 1812.

1821

- Jackson is appointed governor of Florida Territory.

1822

- Jackson is nominated for president by the Tennessee legislature.

1823

- Jackson is elected a U.S. senator.

1828

- Jackson is elected the seventh president of the United States and serves two terms, ending in 1837.

---

burned much of Washington, D.C., was fresh in the nation's memory. By the 1820s Great Britain and its colonies, particularly in the West Indies and South America, maintained lucrative trade arrangements, but U.S. merchants and farmers were excluded as a consequence of acts of Congress passed in 1818, 1820, and 1823. Jackson, in an effort to boost the prosperity of American workers and farmers, wanted the nation to participate in that trade.

Soon after he took office, Jackson dispatched negotiators to Great Britain, chiefly with the purpose of reassuring the British that American sentiments no longer opposed trade with Great Britain. After considerable negotiation, the British indicated that they were amenable to opening trade with the United States. On May 29, 1830, an act of Congress authorized the president to open American ports to British vessels and to import British goods with tariffs not to exceed those charged by any of Britain's colonies in the West Indies and South America ("duties of tonnage or impost or charges of any other description")—but only if the president had firm evidence that Great Britain would open its ports in its colonies to American vessels under the same terms. Jackson received this evidence from his trade negotiators on August 17 of that year. Accordingly, he issued his proclamation on October 5. Note that tariffs are a kind of tax levied on imported goods; they have a tendency to dampen trade, for they make imported goods more expensive. By removing or lowering tariffs, imported goods on both sides become less expensive, expanding the market for those goods.

At first glance the issue of opening ports would not seem to be a particularly dramatic one, but one more along the lines of conducting the routine affairs of state as they pertain to foreign trade. However, the matter must be looked at in a larger context, given the tension that has existed between the states and the federal government, a tension that even in the twenty-first century has not been fully resolved. In the 1830s numerous issues had a strong bearing on federal-state relations. One of these issues, for example, was transportation, often discussed at the time under the more general heading of "internal improvements." In the Northeast, along the mid-Atlantic coast, and in the West, business interests favored the construction of national roads and canals as a way of stimulating economic development and linking the far-flung sectors of a growing nation. The southern states, in contrast, opposed national roads, preferring to rely on rivers for transportation. But the larger issue for some citizens and lawmakers was whether the federal government was overstepping its authority in backing the construction of roads and canals by, for example, requiring new states to dedicate a percentage of funds raised from the sale of public lands to road and canal building. Sectional rivalries and tensions such as this would eventually rend the nation with the outbreak of civil war, and some of these tensions can be traced directly back to the policies of the Jackson administration.

Although U.S. negotiators made some concessions in their talks with Great Britain, in general, the opening of trade relations with Great Britain worked in favor of American interests. Jackson was a firm believer in a balanced budget, especially since his administration had inherited a significant deficit. By 1837 the administration had reduced that deficit to a mere $11 million (although the Panic of 1837 would wipe out much of the progress on reducing the national debt). Thus, throughout the bulk of Jackson's term in office, U.S. business flourished, and federal revenues increased. The power of the federal government to act in the interests of the nation as a whole seemed to have been vindicated.

◆ Second Annual Message to Congress

Each year, usually in January, the U.S. president delivers a State of the Union address to a joint session of Congress. The title "State of the Union," though, was not used until 1935, during the administration of Franklin D. Roosevelt. Until then, it was referred to as the president's annual message to Congress and, since Thomas Jefferson's presidency, had been delivered in writing; Woodrow Wilson was the first president to revive the tradition of giving the message as a speech. Thus Jackson's second annual message to Congress in December 1830 was delivered in written, not oral form.

Jackson's message was a lengthy recital of the nation's accomplishments during the preceding year and touched on a wide range of issues, including trade relations with Britain, internal improvements, the federal budget, and the like. But one further significant issue he addressed was relations with Indian tribes and his justification for removing Indians from their lands in the East and resettling them on lands in the expanding West. The section of the annual message reproduced here is that bearing on the question of Indian removal.

In the twenty-first century the attitude that Jackson expresses toward the Indian tribes with such words as "rude" and "savage" would be considered condescending and racist. Further, his policies were predicated on the assumption that the land inhabited by Indians was in effect wasted when it could instead be filled by prosperous farmers supported by cities and towns, civilization, and Christianity. From the perspective of the twenty-first century it is difficult to justify government policies that stripped Indians of their ancestral lands to make way for white settlers and removed Indians to unfamiliar lands farther to the west. Looked at from the perspective of the 1830s, however, it was perhaps inevitable that Indians would be forced off their lands by the sheer growth of the white population, along with the development of commerce, trade, manufacture, and transportation networks. In 1800, for example, the U.S. population stood at just over five million; by 1830 the population had burgeoned to nearly thirteen million. Had Jackson not proposed specific policies for Indian removal, the process would most likely have still taken place, but with what consequences will never be known.

From the beginning of the nineteenth century, U.S. policy had been to allow Indians east of the Mississippi River to remain on their lands. However, Indians who chose to do so were required to become "civilized" by speaking English,

Time Line

1830

■ **October 5**
Jackson issues a proclamation reopening American ports to British West Indian trade.

■ **December 6**
Having signed the Indian Removal Act earlier in the year, Jackson explains his position on Indian affairs in his Second Annual Message to Congress.

1832

■ **July 10**
Jackson outlines his objections to a national bank in vetoing the recharter of the Second Bank of the United States.

■ **December 10**
Jackson issues a proclamation to the people of South Carolina on nullification.

1845

■ **June 8**
Jackson dies at the Hermitage near Nashville, Tennessee.

practicing Christianity, and engaging in settled farming. This system proceeded in a piecemeal way, often under the authority of individual states. In the Northeast, where tribes tended to be smaller and less consolidated, the effect was to drive these tribes virtually out of existence. In the South some tribes succumbed to the pressure and assimilated themselves to white society. In particular, the so-called Five Civilized Tribes—the Chickasaw, Choctaw, Creek, Seminole, and Cherokee—had adopted many characteristics of the white society in which they lived. Numerous Cherokee, for example, grew cotton and other cash crops, often using the labor of black slaves. The tribe had a formal system of government modeled on the federal system, with an elected chief, a bicameral council, and a court system. The tribe also published a newspaper and books written in both English and Cherokee after the Cherokee leader Sequoyah developed a syllabary for recording the Cherokee language using the letters of the alphabet.

During the early years of the nineteenth century a policy proposed by Thomas Jefferson began to take hold. This policy was to discontinue buying land from the Indians and instead to exchange lands with them in the East by giving them comparable lands in the West. The first such exchange had taken place in 1817, when the Cherokee traded land in the East for a tract in Arkansas. Meanwhile, individual states were demanding that Indian lands within

Four Cherokee Indians from North Carolina end their retracing of the tribe's historic 1838 "Trail of Tears" in Westville, Oklahoma, on May 16, 1951. (AP/Wide World Photos)

their jurisdictions be placed under their control. One example is Georgia, which passed a law forbidding whites to live on Indian lands—a law motivated by a desire to exclude from those lands white Christian missionaries who were encouraging Indians to resist removal.

Jackson, in an effort to assert federal authority over Indian affairs, made Indian removal one of the chief planks of his 1828 campaign for the presidency. Accordingly, on May 28, 1830, he signed into law the Indian Removal Act, in part to help resolve the jurisdictional dispute Georgia was having with the Cherokee. Under the new law, the federal government reserved the power to negotiate land exchange treaties with the Indian nations. The first of these treaties was the Treaty of Dancing Rabbit Creek, concluded with the Choctaw in September of that year. The most infamous such treaty was the Treaty of New Echota in 1835, which led to what is now called the Trail of Tears, when fifteen thousand Cherokee were forced to march from Georgia to Indian Territory (present-day Oklahoma). Severe winter weather, combined with poor planning and a lack of provisions by government authorities, led to the death of four thousand people. Although the movement of the Indian peoples was supposed to be voluntary, in fact, great pressure was exerted on tribal leaders to move. Many did, but some stayed, the most notable example being part of the Cherokee tribe that remained in the East to form the Eastern Band Cherokee. Additionally, the Seminole in Florida refused to abandon their homeland, leading to the Second Seminole War, which did not end until 1842.

In this portion of his annual message to Congress, Jackson justifies his policies on Indian removal. In the first paragraph he refers to the federal government's "benevolent policy" with regard to Indians and announces that with

the passage of the Indian Removal Act the matter has reached a "happy consummation." In the second paragraph, he enumerates the advantages of Indian removal. It will open large tracts of land to white settlers, with resulting "pecuniary advantages" to the nation. It will strengthen the states in the Southwest, enabling them to repel invasion. For the Indians, it will remove them from white settlements and the authority of state governments, allowing them to pursue their own way of life in peace. Most important, in Jackson's view, it will allow them to survive rather than have their numbers dwindle.

In the third paragraph Jackson becomes slightly obscure. He professes a "friendly feeling" toward the Indian tribes and argues that the federal government has tried to impress on the Indians the advantages of placing themselves under the protection of the federal government. He then alludes to the efforts of states to control Indian affairs ("the laws passed by the States within the scope of their reserved powers") and acknowledges that the states are not "responsible to" the federal government. And while he notes that individuals might oppose the policies of states (that is, "entertain and express our opinion of their acts"), the federal government, without the Indian Removal Act, had no authority to intervene in state affairs (the federal government "has little right to control" the states"). This was yet another example of the tension between the authority of the states and that of the federal government that threatened to dissolve the Union in the nineteenth century.

In the fourth paragraph Jackson notes that already treaties have been forged with the Cherokee and Choctaw. He points out that by removing themselves from the authority of the states, they can pursue their own way of life in the West and eliminate the "vexations" of having to live in Alabama and Mississippi. In the fifth paragraph Jackson acknowledges that Indian removal causes hardship. The policy displaces people from their ancestral lands and puts them in new surroundings. Jackson justifies this course of action by noting that white settlers, too, left their ancestral lands for a new life. He also comments that throughout the far western reaches of the country, evidence shows that other civilizations had risen and then disappeared. In the sixth paragraph Jackson argues that removal is a course to be preferred over the annihilation that many eastern tribes suffered. Jackson concludes by finessing the issue of the relations between Indians, state governments, and the federal government, noting that the states can retain jurisdiction over those Indians who choose to remain.

In the twenty-first century the very concept of Indian removal is abhorrent. Jackson, in particular, has been criticized for the role he played in this policy. However, a more balanced assessment would note that, given the time at which he lived, Jackson saw only two alternatives. One was for the federal government to assert authority over Indian affairs and use its power to grant lands to the Indians in the West, principally Oklahoma. The other was to allow states to regulate Indian affairs, often with the effect of virtually wiping out the tribes by depriving them of their land but giving them no place else to go. Faced with these alternatives, Jackson chose the course that he believed most likely to ensure the continued existence of the eastern and southern tribes. The program was an ambitious one. During Jackson's administration, in excess of forty-five thousand Indians were relocated to the West, and the administration bought up some one hundred million acres of Indian land at a total price of $68 million.

◆ Veto of the Bill to Limit the Power of the Bank of the United States

The story of the Second Bank of the United States, which Jackson opposed with his bank veto, begins with the First Bank of the United States, proposed by Alexander Hamilton and chartered by Congress in 1791 for twenty years. The purpose of the bank, which was based in Philadelphia and had eight branches, was to put the financial affairs of the new nation on a sounder footing, given that at the time at least fifty different forms of currency were in circulation and it was impossible for anyone to know the real value of these currencies relative to one another. Congress chartered the bank over the objections of Thomas Jefferson and his supporters, who argued that the bank would represent mercantile interests at the expense of agriculture. The bank's charter expired in 1811 and was not renewed because of opposition from state banks and business owners, who complained that the bank's cautiousness was hampering economic development.

In the years after the War of 1812 the country was in deep debt. As a result of this debt, private banks were issuing their own bank notes, which in turned boosted the inflation rate. In response to this crisis, President James Madison urged Congress to charter the Second Bank of the United States. Congress complied, issuing the bank a twenty-year charter in 1816. Like the First Bank, the Second Bank, located in Philadelphia, was the repository of U.S. Treasury funds.

The Second Bank was mired in controversy from the outset. Despite the country's economic woes, a significant boom was under way, in large part thanks to the Napoleonic Wars in Europe that had devastated European agriculture. Food exports led to an agricultural expansion, but the unfortunate side effect of this expansion was land speculation. Banks issued loans to speculators, who bought fifty-five million acres of land in 1819 alone, forcing the price of land up and creating an economic bubble. In this fevered speculative climate, fraudulent transactions became commonplace, and many critics regarded the Second Bank as corrupt. As the managers of the bank began to recognize the precarious situation they had created, they began calling in loans, which slowed land sales and the U.S. production boom, a slowdown worsened by the recovery of Europe after the Napoleonic Wars. The result was the Panic of 1819. Meanwhile, individual states were trying to compete with the national bank by imposing a tax on banks not chartered within their state. Maryland, for example, levied a 2 percent tax on outside banks. This tax led to a landmark U.S. Supreme Court case, *McCulloch v. Maryland* (1819), in which the Court ruled that any state law that ran contrary to federal law—in this case, the tax—was null and void.

Normally, the Second Bank's charter would have expired in 1836. The issue of extending the charter was injected into Jackson's 1832 reelection campaign when his opponent, Representative Henry Clay, urged the bank's president, Nicholas Biddle, to apply for extension of the charter in 1832, which was four years early. Clay ushered the bill to recharter the bank through Congress, but when the bill arrived on Jackson's desk for his signature, he returned it to Congress with his veto message. In his veto message, Jackson outlines five reasons for his opposition to the bank. The first was that it concentrated the nation's financial affairs in a single institution, creating a "monopoly." Second, he believed that the bank had the injurious effect of making the rich richer. He points out, for example, that the value of the bank's stock was already far above the stock's "par value"—that is, the value of the stock when it was issued. Rechartering the bank would lead to a further significant increase in the stock's value, perhaps as much as 20 or 30 percent. The result was a "gratuity," or gift, to already "opulent" stockholders.

A chief objection to the national bank, one that Jackson shared with many business owners and western farmers, was that too much of the stock was owned by foreigners. Jackson suggests that if the increase in the bank's stock value accrued to the benefit of Americans, his objection on this score might not be as strong, but given that some "eight millions"—a third of the stock—were in the hands of foreigners, it was the foreigners who would be the recipients of the "bounty of our Government." But this money would not materialize out of nowhere. Rather, it would come "directly or indirectly out of the earnings of the American people." Put differently, Jackson was a firm believer that the nation's future could best be ensured by encouraging the development of an agricultural republic rather than an elite circle of industrialists and commercial entrepreneurs. The national bank, in Jackson's view, served the ends of the latter rather than those of laborers and farmers—giving rise to Jackson's fourth objection, that the bank favored the interests of the northeastern states at the expense of the states of the South and West.

Jackson was troubled by a fifth consideration. With so much of the stock, and therefore so much of the nation's wealth, in foreign hands and in the hands of a few wealthy American stockholders, the bank was able to exercise too much control over Congress. While Jackson was a proponent of a strong federal government, he distrusted monied interests that could control that government at the expense of common people, not to mention the states, whose own banks existed only through the "forbearance" of the national bank. Jackson concludes by noting a practical danger of placing so much American wealth in the hands of foreign investors. In the event of a war, American resources could be in the hands of the very nation that is America's enemy. This control over American wealth could be more of a danger to American interests than hostile armies and navies.

Jackson's veto and the actions that followed it have been referred to as the "Bank War." Jackson anticipated that the bank would again seek to have its charter renewed in 1836.

To preempt this move, in 1833, over the objections of congressional committees and members of his cabinet, Jackson ordered that all U.S. funds be withdrawn from the Second Bank and that no further Treasury funds be deposited in it. U.S. Treasury funds were instead deposited in twenty-three state banks, referred to disparagingly as "pet banks." As a consequence, numerous state and local banks took over the Second Bank's lending functions, leading to issuance of bank notes that were not backed by gold or silver. The result was inflation and crushing state indebtedness. After Jackson ordered in 1836 that all purchases of government land had to be in "specie"—that is, precious metal coins—there was a run on specie that the state and local banks could not meet. Many of these banks went under, leading to the Panic of 1837, a collapse with aftereffects that were felt for years. Meanwhile, the Senate censured Jackson for removing U.S. funds from the Second Bank, though that censure was later expunged after his supporters regained a majority in the Senate.

◆ Proclamation to the People of South Carolina Regarding Nullification

In 1832 Andrew Jackson faced down South Carolina in what came to be called the "nullification crisis." In this context, the word *nullification* refers to a declaration that a federal law is "null," or without effect, in this case in the state of South Carolina. The issue that led to the nullification crisis was tariffs, but the far larger issue was the relationship between the federal and state governments. In attempting to nullify the nation's tariff laws, South Carolina was reserving to itself the right to declare a federal law unconstitutional and unenforceable. Jackson responded by asserting the authority of the federal government to pass laws that were applicable in all the states.

The crisis had been brewing for a number of years. It started with the Tariff of 1816, which required American merchants to pay tariffs of up to 25 percent of the value of imported goods such as iron and wool. The public largely supported this tariff, but resistance to high tariffs began to grow with the Tariff of 1824, which increased tariff rates to 35 percent and was passed to raise funds for "internal improvements"—chiefly the building of roads and canals. Then Congress passed the Tariff of 1828, which quickly became known in the South as the "Tariff of Abominations." Southern states such as South Carolina were bitterly opposed to these tariffs because, in their view, they favored the interests of northern industrialists at the expense of the agricultural South. Additionally, the southern states in general opposed the nation's plans for internal improvements, believing again that the system of roads and canals funded by the tariffs favored northern manufacturing interests. Portions of New England were also opposed to the tariffs.

Opponents of the tariffs believed that the new president, Andrew Jackson, would move to lower them. While he did lower tariffs, he did so only slightly, and South Carolina, with its major port cities, was not satisfied—though it must be noted that even South Carolina was divided

between the "Nullifiers" and those who wished to remain loyal to the Union. Meanwhile, South Carolina had been hurt badly by the Panic of 1819 and the country's general economic malaise in the 1820s. Prior to that, the state had enjoyed a booming economy, primarily through such crops as rice, indigo, and cotton. The state blamed the tariffs for its declining economic fortunes, though other factors, such as soil erosion (cotton, in particular, depletes the soil) and competition from newer states in the West and Southwest, contributed. After the Tariff of 1828 was passed, South Carolina attempted to mount a concerted southern response to it. When that effort failed, radicals in the state began to argue that the state should act on its own. Jackson and his vice president, John C. Calhoun, openly split when Calhoun agreed to write a document called "Exposition and Protest" in 1828 in which he argued that states had the right to nullify laws they regarded as unconstitutional.

In the years that followed, the issue of tariffs remained very much on the front burner, and passions in the state ran high as the Nullifiers gained momentum and support. Finally—as Jackson points out in the opening paragraphs of his proclamation—the state's lawmakers held a Nullification Convention in November 1832. At this convention, the lawmakers declared the Tariff of 1828, as well as a new tariff bill passed in 1832, to be unconstitutional and unenforceable in the state; asserted that the issue was not one that could be resolved by the federal courts; and threatened withdrawal from the Union if the federal government attempted to enforce the tariffs in South Carolina. Jackson makes clear his opposition to South Carolina's position and warns "of the consequences that must inevitably result from an observance of the dictates of the Convention."

The remainder of the document is a passionate plea for the supremacy of the Union and the Constitution. Jackson argues that South Carolina's actions seem to be based on the "strange position" that a state can be a member of the Union and a signatory to its Constitution yet at the same time decide on its own that it will not adhere to a particular law that it regards as unconstitutional. Jackson goes on to argue that two mechanisms check the federal government if it passes or attempts to pass an unconstitutional law: the court system and the people of the country who elect their lawmakers. After Jackson states his unequivocal belief that nullification is inconsistent with the Union and the Constitution, he devotes the remainder of the proclamation to defending his position: that the United States are one people; that members of Congress are paid by the United States and are required to act for the "general good"; that the United States is not a league but rather a single government; and that as president, he will exercise his duty to enforce the laws that he is sworn to uphold. Finally, Jackson appeals directly to the people of South Carolina, urging them not to be deluded by a small majority who want to enjoy the advantages of the Union but bear none of its burdens. He further argues that the Nullifiers "are not champions of liberty emulating the fame of our Revolutionary fathers, nor are you an oppressed people,

"The ports of the United States are from the date of this proclamation open to British vessels coming from the said British possessions, and their cargoes, upon the terms set forth in the said act."

(Proclamation Regarding the Opening of U.S. Ports to British Vessels)

"Toward the aborigines of the country no one can indulge a more friendly feeling than myself, or would go further in attempting to reclaim them from their wandering habits and make them a happy, prosperous people."

(Second Annual Message to Congress)

"To follow to the tomb the last of his race and to tread on the graves of extinct nations excite melancholy reflections. But true philanthropy reconciles the mind to these vicissitudes as it does to the extinction of one generation to make room for another."

(Second Annual Message to Congress)

"It is easy to conceive that great evils to our country and its institutions might flow from such a concentration of power in the hands of a few men irresponsible to the people."

(Veto of the Bill to Limit the Power of the Bank of the United States)

"I consider, then, the power to annul a law of the United States, assumed by one State, incompatible with the existence of the Union, contradicted expressly by the letter of the Constitution, unauthorized by its spirit, inconsistent with every principle on which It was founded, and destructive of the great object for which it was formed."

(Proclamation to the People of South Carolina Regarding Nullification)

"The Constitution of the United States, then, forms a government, not a league, and whether it be formed by compact between the States, or in any other manner, its character is the same. It is a government in which all the people are represented, which operates directly on the people individually, not upon the States."

(Proclamation to the People of South Carolina Regarding Nullification) contending … against worse than colonial vassalage. You are free members of a flourishing and happy Union."

Impact and Legacy

Despite the controversy surrounding him, Andrew Jackson is counted among the nation's most influential presidents. At least nine states, including South Carolina, have a city or town named Jackson, and three others have a Jacksonville. At least twenty-one states have a Jackson County. Numerous streets and schools, town squares, state parks, military bases, and memorials are named after him. His image appears on the $20 bill. Jackson's appeal was in his ability to tap into the disaffection that was widespread during the 1820s and

1830s. He created a national party—the Democratic Party—that at the time democratized American politics. He denounced monied interests and the nation's aristocracy and promoted the virtues, industry, and sound common sense of farmers and laborers—those who had not benefited from the expansion of the free market economy. He repeatedly called for a constitutional amendment to eliminate the Electoral College, believing that in a true democracy, the president and vice president should be elected directly by the people they serve, not by the states. Put differently, he promoted egalitarianism, though his position as a slave owner and the stance he took with regard to Indian removal argues against that egalitarianism. His legacy, therefore, remains mixed, and the political realignment he forged was shattered by growing tensions over slavery and, finally, the Civil War.

Questions for Further Study

1. In his proclamation regarding the opening of U.S. ports, Jackson had to face a number of politically sensitive issues, including the relationship between the United States and Britain (with which it had fought a war, in which Jackson had served with distinction as general), the relative power of the federal and state governments, and the matter of tariffs on imports. Discuss these and other problems dealt with in the proclamation and the means by which Jackson—both in words and actions—addressed them.

2. To a modern person, aware of the tragedies that resulted from the policy of Indian removal initiated by Jackson, his second annual message to Congress makes for melancholy reading. Yet it is likely that he believed his claims that removal would actually benefit the native peoples. Examine his speech and his principal points of justification. How effectively did he defend his position? Were his arguments valid? If so, how? Note his reference to vanished peoples in the Southwest—a group now termed by archaeologists *Anasazi*. How much, if anything, was known about these people in his time? Would greater knowledge about them, or indeed about Native Americans as a whole, have changed his perspective?

3. Evaluate Jackson's arguments against the Bank of the United States. What are his best and least effective points in making this case? How might history have been different if the bank had been allowed to continue in existence? Finally, how might Jackson regard the present-day Federal Reserve System?

4. Compare and contrast Jackson's position regarding states' rights and the South, as expressed in his 1832 proclamation to the people of South Carolina, with those of his vice president (and fellow native South Carolinian) John C. Calhoun. What were the major points of contention between the two men, and in what ways might they have found common ground? How did disagreement between them influence their effectiveness as leaders?

5. It is interesting to read Jackson's South Carolina proclamation in view of the fact that he was both a southerner (born, as he observes in the document, in that state, though he is more commonly associated with his adopted home of Tennessee) and a Democrat. Had he lived another decade, these facts might have created for him divided loyalties as southern Democrats began to speak openly, and increasingly, of secession. How would Jackson, as a loyal defender of the Union, have dealt with the crisis that led to the Civil War? Would he have remained true to his vision of a federal government, which he clearly cherished, or would sectional and political loyalties have swayed him to take the side of the Confederacy?

Key Sources

Various of the papers of Andrew Jackson can be found at the Avalon Project at Yale Law School at http://www.yale.edu/lawweb/avalon/presiden/jackpap.htm. The University of Tennessee in Knoxville since 1971 has been in the process of gathering, editing, and publishing a seventeen-volume edition of Jackson's papers that will represent his entire output; as of 2008, seven volumes, covering the period through 1829, have been published. Numbers of Jackson's papers are housed at the Library of Congress and reproduced on microfilm (http://www.loc.gov/rr/mss/text/jacksona.html). Additional resources for study can be found at the Web site of the Hermitage at http://www.thehermitage.com.

Further Reading

■ Articles

Cave, Alfred A. "Abuse of Power: Andrew Jackson and the Indian Removal Act of 1830." *Historian* 65 (Winter 2003): 1330–1353.

Sellers, Charles Grier, Jr. "Andrew Jackson versus the Historians." *Mississippi Valley Historical Review* 44, no. 4 (March 1958): 615–634.

■ Books

Brands, H. W. *Andrew Jackson: His Life and Times*. New York: Doubleday, 2005.

Bugg, James L. *Jacksonian Democracy: Myth or Reality?* New York: Holt, Rinehart, and Winston, 1965.

Burstein, Andrew. *The Passions of Andrew Jackson*. New York: Knopf, 2003.

Hammond, Bray. "Andrew Jackson's Battle with the 'Money Power.'" In *Banks and Politics in America: From the Revolution to the Civil War*. Princeton, N.J.: Princeton University Press, 1957.

James, Marquis. *The Life of Andrew Jackson*. Indianapolis, Ind.: Bobbs-Merrill, 1938.

Latner, Richard B. *The Presidency of Andrew Jackson: White House Politics, 1829–1837*. Athens: University of Georgia Press, 1979.

Remini, Robert Vincent. *Andrew Jackson and the Course of American Freedom, 1822–1832*. New York: Harper and Row, 1981.

———. *Andrew Jackson and the Course of American Democracy, 1833–1845*. New York: Harper and Row, 1984.

———. *The Legacy of Andrew Jackson: Essays on Democracy, Indian Removal, and Slavery*. Baton Rouge: Louisiana State University Press, 1988.

Satz, Ronald N. *American Indian Policy in the Jacksonian Era*. Norman: University of Oklahoma Press, 2002.

Schlesinger, Arthur M. *The Age of Jackson*. Boston: Little, Brown, 1945.

Syrett, Harold Coffin. *Andrew Jackson: His Contribution to the American Tradition*. Indianapolis, Ind.: Bobbs-Merrill, 1953.

Taylor, George Rogers. *Jackson versus Biddle: The Struggle over the Second Bank of the United States*. Boston: D.C. Heath, 1949.

Wallace, Anthony F. C., and Eric Foner. *The Long, Bitter Trail: Andrew Jackson and the Indians*. New York: Hill and Wang, 1993.

Wilentz, Sean. *Andrew Jackson*. New York: Times Books, 2005.

—Michael J. O'Neal

PROCLAMATION REGARDING THE OPENING OF U.S. PORTS TO BRITISH VESSELS (1830)

Whereas by an act of the Congress of the United States passed on the 29th day of May, 1830, it is provided that whenever the President of the United States shall receive satisfactory evidence that the Government of Great Britain will open the ports in its colonial possessions in the West Indies, on the continent of South America, the Bahama Islands, the Caicos, and the Bermuda or Somer Islands to the vessels of the United States for an indefinite or for a limited term; that the vessels of the United States, and their cargoes, on entering the colonial ports aforesaid, shall not be subject to other or higher duties of tonnage or impost or charges of any other description than would be imposed on British vessels or their cargoes arriving in the said colonial possessions from the United States; that the vessels of the United States may import into the said colonial possessions from the United States any article or articles which could be imported in a British vessel into the said possessions from the United States; and that the vessels of the United States may export from the British colonies aforementioned, to any country whatever other than the dominions or possessions of Great Britain, any article or articles that can be exported therefrom in a British vessel to any country other than the British dominions or possessions as aforesaid, leaving the commercial intercourse of the United States with all other parts of the British dominions or possessions on a footing not less favorable to the United States than it now is—that then, and in such case, the President of the United States shall be authorized, at any time

before the next session of Congress, to issue his proclamation declaring that he has received such evidence, and that thereupon, and from the date of such proclamation, the ports of the United States shall be opened indefinitely or for a term fixed, as the case may be, to British vessels coming from the said British colonial possessions, and their cargoes, subject to no other or higher duty of tonnage or impost or charge of any description whatever than would be levied on the vessels of the United States or their cargoes arriving from the said British possessions; and that it shall be lawful for the said British vessels to import into the United States and to export therefrom any article or articles which may be imported or exported in vessels of the United States; and that the act entitled "An act concerning navigation," passed on the 18th day of April, 1818, an act supplementary thereto, passed the 15th day of May, 1820, and an act entitled "An act to regulate the commercial intercourse between the United States and certain British ports," passed on the 1st day of March, 1823, shall in such case be suspended or absolutely repealed, as the case may require....

Now, therefore, I, Andrew Jackson, President of the United States of America, do hereby declare and proclaim that such evidence has been received by me, and that by the operation of the act of Congress passed on the 29th day of May, 1830, the ports of the United States are from the date of this proclamation open to British vessels coming from the said British possessions, and their cargoes, upon the terms set forth in the said act.

Glossary

Caicos	the Turks and Caicos Islands, British possessions in the West Indies
dominions	former British colonies, such as those in Canada and Australia, that were granted limited but increasing degrees of independence
duties of tonnage	taxes on ships according to the tonnage or weight of goods they carry
impost	a tax
Somer Islands	small islands (usually spelled "Sommer") near Bermuda

SECOND ANNUAL MESSAGE TO CONGRESS (1830)

It gives me pleasure to announce to Congress that the benevolent policy of the Government, steadily pursued for nearly 30 years, in relation to the removal of the Indians beyond the white settlements is approaching to a happy consummation. Two important tribes have accepted the provision made for their removal at the last session of Congress, and it is believed that their example will induce the remaining tribes also to seek the same obvious advantages.

The consequences of a speedy removal will be important to the United States, to individual States, and to the Indians themselves. The pecuniary advantages which it promises to the Government are the least of its recommendations. It puts an end to all possible danger of collision between the authorities of the General and State Governments on account of the Indians. It will place a dense and civilized population in large tracts of country now occupied by a few savage hunters. By opening the whole territory between Tennessee on the north and Louisiana on the south to the settlement of the whites it will incalculably strengthen the SW frontier and render the adjacent States strong enough to repel future invasions without remote aid. It will relieve the whole State of Mississippi and the western part of Alabama of Indian occupancy, and enable those States to advance rapidly in population, wealth, and power. It will separate the Indians from immediate contact with settlements of whites; free them from the power of the States; enable them to pursue happiness in their own way and under their own rude institutions; will retard the progress of decay, which is lessening their numbers, and perhaps cause them gradually, under the protection of the Government and through the influence of good counsels, to cast off their savage habits and become an interesting, civilized, and Christian community. These consequences, some of them so certain and the rest so probable, make the complete execution of the plan sanctioned by Congress at their last session an object of much solicitude.

Toward the aborigines of the country no one can indulge a more friendly feeling than myself, or would go further in attempting to reclaim them from their wandering habits and make them a happy, prosperous people. I have endeavored to impress upon them my own solemn convictions of the duties and powers of the General Government in relation to the State authorities. For the justice of the laws passed by the States within the scope of their reserved powers they are not responsible to this Government. As individuals we may entertain and express our opinions of their acts, but as a Government we have as little right to control them as we have to prescribe laws for other nations.

With a full understanding of the subject, the Choctaw and the Chickasaw tribes have with great unanimity determined to avail themselves of the liberal offers presented by the act of Congress, and have agreed to remove beyond the Mississippi River. Treaties have been made with them, which in due season will be submitted for consideration. In negotiating these treaties they were made to understand their true condition, and they have preferred maintaining their independence in the Western forests to submitting to the laws of the States in which they now reside. These treaties, being probably the last which will ever be made with them, are characterized by great liberality on the part of the Government. They give the Indians a liberal sum in consideration of their removal, and comfortable subsistence on their arrival at their new homes. If it be their real interest to maintain a separate existence, they will there be at liberty to do so without the inconveniences and vexations to which they would unavoidably have been subject in Alabama and Mississippi.

Humanity has often wept over the fate of the aborigines of this country, and Philanthropy has been long busily employed in devising means to avert it, but its progress has never for a moment been arrested, and one by one have many powerful tribes disappeared from the earth. To follow to the tomb the last of his race and to tread on the graves of extinct nations excite melancholy reflections. But true philanthropy reconciles the mind to these vicissitudes as it does to the extinction of one generation to make room for another. In the monuments and fortifications of an unknown people, spread over the extensive regions of the West, we behold the memorials of a once powerful race, which was exterminated or has disappeared to make room for the existing savage tribes. Nor is there any thing in this which, upon a comprehensive view of the general interests of the human race, is to be regretted. Philanthropy could not wish to see this continent restored to the condition in which it was found by our forefathers. What good man would prefer a country covered with forests and ranged by a few thousand savages to our extensive Republic, studded with cities, towns, and prosperous farms, embellished with all the improvements which art can devise or industry execute, occupied by more than 12,000,000 happy people, and filled with all the blessings of liberty, civilization, and religion?

The present policy of the Government is but a continuation of the same progressive change by a milder process. The tribes which occupied the countries now constituting the Eastern States were annihilated or have melted away to make room for the whites. The waves of population and civilization are rolling to the westward, and we now propose to acquire the countries occupied by the red men of the South and West by a fair exchange, and, at the expense of the United States, to send them to a land where their existence may be prolonged and perhaps made perpetual....

It is, therefore, a duty which this Government owes to the new States to extinguish as soon as possible the Indian title to all lands which Congress themselves have included within their limits. When this is done the duties of the General Government in relation to the States and the Indians within their limits are at an end. The Indians may leave the State or not, as they choose. The purchase of their lands does not alter in the least their personal relations with the State government. No act of the General Government has ever been deemed necessary to give the States jurisdiction over the persons of the Indians. That they possess by virtue of their sovereign power within their own limits in as full a manner before as after the purchase of the Indian lands; nor can this Government add to or diminish it.

Glossary

aborigines	native peoples
the Choctaw and Chickasaw tribes	two of the "Five Civilized Tribes" who originated in the southeastern United States, generally cooperated with the U.S. government, and were forced to move to Oklahoma and other western regions
the General Government	the federal government
remote aid	help from afar
an unknown people...a once powerful race	a reference to the vast structures left behind in the American Southwest by peoples, often lumped under the term *Anasazi* (Navajo for "ancient ones"), whose history became an object of archaeological research a century after Jackson's speech

Veto of the Bill to Limit the Power of the Bank of the United States (1832)

The bill "to modify and continue" the act entitled "An act to incorporate the subscribers to the Bank of the United States" was presented to me on the 4th July instant. Having considered it with that solemn regard to the principles of the Constitution which the day was calculated to inspire, and come to the conclusion that it ought not to become a law, I herewith return it to the Senate, in which it originated, with my objections.

A bank of the United States is in many respects convenient for the Government and useful to the people. Entertaining this opinion, and deeply impressed with the belief that some of the powers and privileges possessed by the existing bank are unauthorized by the Constitution, subversive of the rights of the States, and dangerous to the liberties of the people, I felt it my duty at an early period of my Administration to call the attention of Congress to the practicability of organizing an institution combining all its advantages and obviating these objections. I sincerely regret that in the act before me I can perceive none of those modifications of the bank charter which are necessary, in my opinion, to make it compatible with justice, with sound policy, or with the Constitution of our country.

The present corporate body, denominated the president, directors, and company of the Bank of the United States, will have existed at the time this act is intended to take effect twenty years. It enjoys an exclusive privilege of banking under the authority of the General Government, a monopoly of its favor and support, and, as a necessary consequence, almost a monopoly of the foreign and domestic exchange. The powers, privileges, and favors bestowed upon it in the original charter, by increasing the value of the stock far above its par value, operated as a gratuity of many millions to the stockholders.

An apology may be found for the failure to guard against this result in the consideration that the effect of the original act of incorporation could not be certainly foreseen at the time of its passage. The act before me proposes another gratuity to the holders of the same stock, and in many cases to the same men, of at least seven millions more. This donation finds no apology in any uncertainty as to the effect of the act. On all hands it is conceded that its passage will increase at least 20 or 30 per cent more the market price of the stock, subject to the payment of the annuity of $200,000 per year secured by the act, thus adding in a moment one-fourth to its par value. It is not our own citizens only who are to receive the bounty of our Government. More than eight millions of the stock of this bank are held by foreigners. By this act the American Republic proposes virtually to make them a present of some millions of dollars. For these gratuities to foreigners and to some of our own opulent citizens the act secures no equivalent whatever. They are the certain gains of the present stockholders under the operation of this act, after making full allowance for the payment of the bonus.

Every monopoly and all exclusive privileges are granted at the expense of the public, which ought to receive a fair equivalent. The many millions which this act proposes to bestow on the stockholders of the existing bank must come directly or indirectly out of the earnings of the American people. It is due to them, therefore, if their Government sell monopolies and exclusive privileges, that they should at least exact for them as much as they are worth in open market. The value of the monopoly in this case may be correctly ascertained. The twenty-eight millions of stock would probably be at an advance of 50 per cent, and command in market at least $42,000,000, subject to the payment of the present bonus. The present value of the monopoly, therefore, is $17,000,000, and this the act proposes to sell for three millions, payable in fifteen annual installments of $200,000 each.

It is not conceivable how the present stockholders can have any claim to the special favor of the Government. The present corporation has enjoyed its monopoly during the period stipulated in the original contract. If we must have such a corporation, why should not the Government sell out the whole stock and thus secure to the people the full market value of the privileges granted? Why should not Congress create and sell twenty-eight millions of stock, incorporating the purchasers with all the powers and privileges secured in this act and putting the premium upon the sales into the Treasury?

But this act does not permit competition in the purchase of this monopoly. It seems to be predicated on the erroneous idea that the present stockholders have a prescriptive right not only to the favor but to the bounty of Government. It appears that more than a fourth part of the stock is held by foreigners and the residue is held by a few hundred of our own citizens, chiefly of the richest class. For their benefit does this act exclude the whole American people from competition in the purchase of this monopoly and dispose of it for many millions less than it is worth. This seems the less excusable because some of our citizens not now stockholders petitioned that the door of competition might be opened, and offered to take a charter on terms much more favorable to the Government and country.

But this proposition, although made by men whose aggregate wealth is believed to be equal to all the private stock in the existing bank, has been set aside, and the bounty of our Government is proposed to be again bestowed on the few who have been fortunate enough to secure the stock and at this moment wield the power of the existing institution. I can not perceive the justice or policy of this course. If our Government must sell monopolies, it would seem to be its duty to take nothing less than their full value, and if gratuities must be made once in fifteen or twenty years let them not be bestowed on the subjects of a foreign government nor upon a designated and favored class of men in our own country. It is but justice and good policy, as far as the nature of the case will admit, to confine our favors to our own fellow citizens, and let each in his turn enjoy an opportunity to profit by our bounty. In the bearings of the act before me upon these points I find ample reasons why it should not become a law....

The modifications of the existing charter proposed by this act are not such, in my view, as make it consistent with the rights of the States or the liberties of the people. The qualification of the right of the bank to hold real estate, the limitation of its power to establish branches, and the power reserved to Congress to forbid the circulation of small notes are restrictions comparatively of little value or importance. All the objectionable principles of the existing corporation, and most of its odious features, are retained without alleviation....

In another of its bearings this provision is fraught with danger. Of the twenty-five directors of this bank five are chosen by the Government and twenty by the citizen stockholders. From all voice in these elections the foreign stockholders are excluded by the charter. In proportion, therefore, as the stock is transferred to foreign holders the extent of suffrage in the choice of directors is curtailed. Already is almost a third of the stock in foreign hands and not represented in elections. It is constantly passing out of the country, and this act will accelerate its departure. The entire control of the institution would necessarily fall into the hands of a few citizen stockholders, and the ease with which the object would be accomplished would be a temptation to designing men to secure that control in their own hands by monopolizing the remaining stock. There is danger that a president and directors would then be able to elect themselves from year to year, and without responsibility or control manage the whole concerns of the bank during the existence of its charter. It is easy to conceive that great evils to our country and its institutions might flow from such a concentration of power in the hands of a few men irresponsible to the people.

Is there no danger to our liberty and independence in a bank that in its nature has so little to bind it to our country? The president of the bank has told us that most of the State banks exist by its forbearance. Should its influence become concentrated, as it may under the operation of such an act as this, in the hands of a self-elected directory whose interests are identified with those of the foreign stockholders, will there not be cause to tremble for the purity of our elections in peace and for the independence of our country in war? Their power would be great whenever they might choose to exert it; but if this monopoly were regularly renewed every fifteen or twenty years on terms proposed by themselves, they

From all voice	from all right to participate or determine the outcome of
instant	of this year
par value	the stated or face value of currency
prescriptive	established through time-honored practice
small notes	unit of paper currency representing relatively small units of value

might seldom in peace put forth their strength to influence elections or control the affairs of the nation. But if any private citizen or public functionary should interpose to curtail its powers or prevent a renewal of its privileges, it can not be doubted that he would be made to feel its influence.

Should the stock of the bank principally pass into the hands of the subjects of a foreign country, and we should unfortunately become involved in a war with that country, what would be our condition? Of the course which would be pursued by a bank almost wholly owned by the subjects of a foreign power, and managed by those whose interests, if not affections, would run in the same direction there can be no doubt. All its operations within would be in aid of the hostile fleets and armies without. Controlling our currency, receiving our public moneys, and holding thousands of our citizens in dependence, it would be more formidable and dangerous than the naval and military power of the enemy.

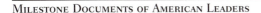

PROCLAMATION TO THE PEOPLE OF SOUTH CAROLINA REGARDING NULLIFICATION (1832)

Whereas a convention, assembled in the State of South Carolina, have passed an ordinance, by which they declare that the several acts and parts of acts of the Congress of the United States, purporting to be laws for the imposing of duties and imposts on the importation of foreign commodities, and now having actual operation and effect within the United States, and more especially "two acts for the same purposes, passed on the 29th of May, 1828, and on the 14th of July, 1832, are unauthorized by the Constitution of the United States, and violate the true meaning and intent thereof, and are null and void, and no law," nor binding on the citizens of that State or its officers, and by the said ordinance it is further declared to be unlawful for any of the constituted authorities of the State, or of the United States, to enforce the payment of the duties imposed by the said acts within the same State, and that it is the duty of the legislature to pass such laws as may be necessary to give full effect to the said ordinances:

And whereas, by the said ordinance it is further ordained, that, in no case of law or equity, decided in the courts of said State, wherein shall be drawn in question the validity of the said ordinance, or of the acts of the legislature that may be passed to give it effect, or of the said laws of the United States, no appeal shall be allowed to the Supreme Court of the United States, nor shall any copy of the record be permitted or allowed for that purpose; and that any person attempting to take such appeal, shall be punished as for a contempt of court:

And, finally, the said ordinance declares that the people of South Carolina will maintain the said ordinance at every hazard, and that they will consider the passage of any act by Congress abolishing or closing the ports of the said State, or otherwise obstructing the free ingress or egress of vessels to and from the said ports, or any other act of the Federal Government to coerce the State, shut up her ports, destroy or harass her commerce, or to enforce the said acts otherwise than through the civil tribunals of the country, as inconsistent with the longer continuance of South Carolina in the Union; and that the people of the said State will thenceforth hold themselves absolved from all further obligation to maintain or preserve their political connection with the people of the other States, and will forthwith proceed to orga-

nize a separate government, and do all other acts and things which sovereign and independent States may of right do.

And whereas the said ordinance prescribes to the people of South Carolina a course of conduct in direct violation of their duty as citizens of the United States, contrary to the laws of their country, subversive of its Constitution, and having for its object the instruction of the Union—that Union, which, coeval with our political existence, led our fathers, without any other ties to unite them than those of patriotism and common cause, through the sanguinary struggle to a glorious independence—that sacred Union, hitherto inviolate, which, perfected by our happy Constitution, has brought us, by the favor of Heaven, to a state of prosperity at home, and high consideration abroad, rarely, if ever, equaled in the history of nations; to preserve this bond of our political existence from destruction, to maintain inviolate this state of national honor and prosperity, and to justify the confidence my fellow-citizens have reposed in me, I, Andrew Jackson, President of the United States, have thought proper to issue this my PROCLAMATION, stating my views of the Constitution and laws applicable to the measures adopted by the Convention of South Carolina, and to the reasons they have put forth to sustain them, declaring the course which duty will require me to pursue, and, appealing to the understanding and patriotism of the people, warn them of the consequences that must inevitably result from an observance of the dictates of the Convention....

The ordinance is founded, not on the indefeasible right of resisting acts which are plainly unconstitutional, and too oppressive to be endured, but on the strange position that any one State may not only declare an act of Congress void, but prohibit its execution—that they may do this consistently with the Constitution—that the true construction of that instrument permits a State to retain its place in the Union, and yet be bound by no other of its laws than those it may choose to consider as constitutional. It is true they add, that to justify this abrogation of a law, it must be palpably contrary to the Constitution, but it is evident, that to give the right of resisting laws of that description, coupled with the uncontrolled right to decide what laws deserve that character, is to give the power of resisting all laws. For, as by the theory, there is no appeal, the reasons alleged by the State, good or bad, must prevail. If it should be said that public opinion is a sufficient check against the abuse of this power, it may be asked why it is not deemed a sufficient guard against the passage of an unconstitutional act by Congress. There is, however, a restraint in this last case, which makes the assumed power of a State more indefensible, and which does not exist in the other. There are two appeals from an unconstitutional act passed by Congress—one to the judiciary, the other to the people and the States. There is no appeal from the State decision in theory; and the practical illustration shows that the courts are closed against an application to review it, both judges and jurors being sworn to decide in its favor. But reasoning on this subject is superfluous, when our social compact in express terms declares, that the laws of the United States, its Constitution, and treaties made under it, are the supreme law of the land; and for greater caution adds, "that the judges in every State shall be bound thereby, anything in the Constitution or laws of any State to the contrary notwithstanding." And it may be asserted, without fear of refutation, that no federative government could exist without a similar provision. Look, for a moment, to the consequence. If South Carolina considers the revenue laws unconstitutional, and has a right to prevent their execution in the port of Charleston, there would be a clear constitutional objection to their collection in every other port, and no revenue could be collected anywhere; for all imposts must be equal. It is no answer to repeat that an unconstitutional law is no law, so long as the question of its legality is to be decided by the State itself, for every law operating injuriously upon any local interest will be perhaps thought, and certainly represented, as unconstitutional, and, as has been shown, there is no appeal....

I consider, then, the power to annul a law of the United States, assumed by one State, *incompatible with the existence of the Union, contradicted expressly by the letter of the Constitution, unauthorized by its spirit, inconsistent with every principle on which It was founded, and destructive of the great object for which it was formed....*

The people of the United States formed the Constitution, acting through the State legislatures, in making the compact, to meet and discuss its provisions, and acting in separate conventions when they ratified those provisions; but the terms used in its construction show it to be a government in which the people of all the States collectively are represented. We are ONE PEOPLE in the choice of the President and Vice President. Here the States have no other agency than to direct the mode in which the vote shall be given. The candidates having the majority of all the votes are chosen. The electors of a majority of States may have given their votes for one candidate, and yet another may be chosen. The people, then, and not the States, are represented in the executive branch.

In the House of Representatives there is this difference, that the people of one State do not, as in the case of President and Vice President, all vote for all the members, each State electing only its own representatives. But this creates no material distinction. When chosen, they are all representatives of the United States, not representatives of the particular State from which they come. They are paid by the United States, not by the State; nor are they accountable to it for any act done in performance of their legislative functions; and however they may in practice, as it is their duty to do, consult and prefer the interests of their particular constituents when they come in conflict with any other partial or local interest, yet it is their first and highest duty, as representatives of the United States, to promote the general good.

The Constitution of the United States, then, forms a government, not a league, and whether it be formed by compact between the States, or in any other manner, its character is the same. It is a government in which all the people are represented, which operates directly on the people individually, not upon the States; they retained all the power they did not grant. But each State having expressly parted with so many powers as to constitute jointly with the other States a single nation, cannot from that period possess any right to secede, because such secession does not break a league, but destroys the unity of a nation, and any injury to that unity is not only a breach which would result from the contravention of a compact, but it is an offense against the whole Union....

This, then, is the position in which we stand. A small majority of the citizens of one State in the Union have elected delegates to a State convention; that convention has ordained that all the revenue laws of the United States must be repealed, or that they are no longer a member of the Union. The governor of that State has recommended to the legislature the raising of an army to carry the secession into effect, and that he may be empowered to give clearances to vessels in the name of the State. No act of violent opposition to the laws has yet been committed, but such a state of things is hourly apprehended, and it is the intent of this instrument to PRO-

CLAIM, not only that the duty imposed on me by the Constitution, "to take care that the laws be faithfully executed," shall be performed to the extent of the powers already vested in me by law or of such others as the wisdom of Congress shall devise and Entrust to me for that purpose; but to warn the citizens of South Carolina, who have been deluded into an opposition to the laws, of the danger they will incur by obedience to the illegal and disorganizing ordinance of the convention—to exhort those who have refused to support it to persevere in their determination to uphold the Constitution and laws of their country, and to point out to all the perilous situation into which the good people of that State have been led, and that the course they are urged to pursue is one of ruin and disgrace to the very State whose rights they affect to support.

Fellow-citizens of my native State! let me not only admonish you, as the first magistrate of our common country, not to incur the penalty of its laws, but use the influence that a father would over his children whom he saw rushing to a certain ruin. In that paternal language, with that paternal feeling, let me tell you, my countrymen, that you are deluded by men who are either deceived themselves or wish to deceive you. Mark under what pretenses you have been led on to the brink of insurrection and treason on which you stand! First a diminution of the value of our staple commodity, lowered by over-production in other quarters and the consequent diminution in

Glossary

case of law or equity	reference to the fact that under common law, modeled on the English system, regular lawsuits had to conform to very specific guidelines, whereas suits in equity allowed more freedom
coeval with	taking place at the same time as
duties and imposts	taxes
electors	elected representatives from each state whose vote, in the Electoral College, decides presidential elections
federative	referring to a federal system of government, in which states exercise a degree of independence on some issues yet submit to the rule of a central authority on matters of national importance
for greater caution	for good measure
a government, not a league	reference to the fact that states are ultimately under the authority of the federal government, as opposed to constituting a "league," or a confederation of independent political entities such as nations
indefeasible	incapable of being rendered null and void
ingress or egress	entrance or exit
instrument	law
mark	consider
sanguinary	bloody
settled design	concerted effort
sovereign	self-governing
they retained all the power they did not grant	a reference to the fact that the Constitution, in addressing the relationship between federal and state governments, explicitly grants only certain powers to the federal government while reserving all other powers for the states
vassalage	the stage of being subject to someone possessing greater power

the value of your lands, were the sole effect of the tariff laws. The effect of those laws was confessedly injurious, but the evil was greatly exaggerated by the unfounded theory you were taught to believe, that its burdens were in proportion to your exports, not to your consumption of imported articles. Your pride was aroused by the assertions that a submission to these laws was a state of vassalage, and that resistance to them was equal, in patriotic merit, to the opposition our fathers offered to the oppressive laws of Great Britain. You were told that this opposition might be peaceably—might be constitutionally made—that you might enjoy all the advantages of the Union and bear none of its burdens. Eloquent appeals to your passions, to your State pride, to your native courage, to your sense of real injury, were used to prepare you for the period when the mask which concealed the hideous features of DISUNION should be taken off. It fell, and you were made to look with complacency on objects which not long since you would have regarded with horror. Look back to the arts which have brought you to this state—look forward to the consequences to which it must inevitably lead! Look back to what was first told you as an inducement to enter into this dangerous course. The great political truth was repeated to you that you had the revolutionary right of resisting all laws that were palpably unconstitutional and intolerably oppressive—it was added that the right to nullify a law rested on the same principle, but that it was a peaceable remedy! This character which was given to it, made you receive with too much confidence the assertions that were made of the unconstitutionality of the law and its oppressive effects. Mark, my fellow-citizens, that by the admission of your leaders the unconstitutionality must be *palpable*, or it will not justify either resistance or nullification! What is the meaning of the word *palpable* in the sense in which it is here used? that which is apparent to

everyone, that which no man of ordinary intellect will fail to perceive. Is the unconstitutionality of these laws of that description? Let those among your leaders who once approved and advocated the principles of protective duties, answer the question; and let them choose whether they will be considered as incapable, then, of perceiving that which must have been apparent to every man of common understanding, or as imposing upon your confidence and endeavoring to mislead you now. In either case, they are unsafe guides in the perilous path they urge you to tread. Ponder well on this circumstance, and you will know how to appreciate the exaggerated language they address to you. They are not champions of liberty emulating the fame of our Revolutionary fathers, nor are you an oppressed people, contending, as they repeat to you, against worse than colonial vassalage. You are free members of a flourishing and happy Union. There is no settled design to oppress you. You have, indeed, felt the unequal operation of laws which may have been unwisely, not unconstitutionally passed; but that inequality must necessarily be removed. At the very moment when you were madly urged on to the unfortunate course you have begun, a change in public opinion has commenced. The nearly approaching payment of the public debt, and the consequent necessity of a diminution of duties, had already caused a considerable reduction, and that, too, on some articles of general consumption in your State. The importance of this change was underrated, and you were authoritatively told that no further alleviation of your burdens was to be expected, at the very time when the condition of the country imperiously demanded such a modification of the duties as should reduce them to a just and equitable scale. But as apprehensive of the effect of this change in allaying your discontents, you were precipitated into the fearful state in which you now find yourselves.

Jesse Jackson (AP/Wide World Photos)

JESSE JACKSON

1941–

Civil Rights Activist and Presidential Candidate

Featured Documents
- "The Struggle Continues" (1988)
- "The Fight for Civil Rights Continues" (2005)

Overview

The Reverend Jesse L. Jackson, one of the nation's most prominent civil rights leaders and spokespersons for African Americans, was born to a teenage single mother in Greenville, South Carolina, on October 8, 1941. After attending the University of Illinois and graduating from the North Carolina Agricultural and Technical State University, he devoted his energies to the civil rights movement by organizing sit-ins, marches, and other events with the goal of ending segregation. In 1965 he joined with Martin Luther King, Jr., and the Southern Christian Leadership Conference (SCLC). Throughout the 1960s he was especially active in Chicago, particularly in leading the SCLC's Operation Breadbasket, which pressured businesses to hire more minority employees. In 1971, frustrated with the conservatism of the SCLC and its leader, Ralph Abernathy, he resigned to form People United to Save Humanity (PUSH). Meanwhile, in 1968, he was ordained as a Baptist minister.

Jackson entered the political arena with a run for the presidency in 1984, only the second African American (after Shirley Chisholm) to mount a nationwide campaign for the presidency. He surprised observers by winning 3.3 million votes in the Democratic Party's primaries, finishing third behind Gary Hart and the eventual nominee, Walter Mondale. That year, too, he formed an organization called the Rainbow Coalition in an effort to unite a "rainbow" of minorities, the poor and working class, gays, and other oppressed groups in a political movement; the Rainbow Coalition and PUSH would merge in 1996. He carried his message of affirmative action, voting rights, social programs, and the war on drugs into the 1988 presidential campaign. If the success of his 1984 campaign was surprising, his run in 1988 stunned many observers by more than doubling his previous results. In his 1988 speech "The Struggle Continues," he outlines many of his social preoccupations.

Throughout the 1990s Jackson continued to speak out on social concerns while serving a six-year term as a "shadow senator" in Washington, D.C. This was a post created by the district to push for statehood. After his term expired in 1996, Jackson turned his attention to American corporations, working to persuade them to include more minorities in higher level positions. Whenever newsworthy events occurred that had a bearing on race relations or the rights and condition of the African American community, Jackson spoke out. He remained in the public eye as a television and radio-show host and with speeches and magazine articles, such as his 2005 article in *Ebony* magazine, "The Fight for Civil Rights Continues."

Explanation and Analysis of Documents

The theme that has dominated Jesse Jackson's public life is racial and social equality. This theme runs through his speeches and published writings, including his speech at the 1988 Democratic National Convention and an article he wrote for *Ebony* magazine in 2005. Throughout his career, Jackson kept the pressure on in his speeches and writing. He challenged white America to recognize the civil and economic rights of the African American community. He also challenged African Americans to assert their rights and to look to their own development. In this way he became one of the most prominent—if not *the* most prominent—civil rights advocates of his generation.

◆ "The Struggle Continues"

In the 1984 presidential election, Jesse Jackson launched a campaign that many political observers thought of as quixotic. However, he won more votes in the primaries than anyone expected, emboldening him to run again in 1988. In March of that year, after a series of primary wins and strong second-place finishes, he was regarded as the front-runner for the Democratic Party's nomination. Eventually Massachusetts governor Michael Dukakis was the party's nominee, but Jackson had shown his ability to register new voters—not just African Americans but also progressive whites who shared his vision—and to win votes in a crowded Democratic field. By the end of the primary season Jackson had garnered some 6.9 million primary votes. He won seven primaries (Alabama, District of Columbia, Georgia, Louisiana, Mississippi, Puerto Rico, and Virginia), five state caucuses (Alaska, Delaware, Michigan, South Carolina, and Vermont), and the state party conventions in Texas (although he did not win the Texas primary). He particularly astounded skeptics by winning 55 percent of the vote in Michigan. He arrived at the Democratic National Convention in second place, with more than twelve hundred pledged delegates. Jackson's supporters believed that because of his strong showing, Dukakis would select him as his running mate. Instead, Dukakis picked Senator Lloyd Bentsen of Texas. The breadth of Jackson's support, however, left him in the position of a power broker who could deliver votes. The Dukakis camp made

Time Line

1941

- **October 8**
  Jesse Jackson is born in Greenville, South Carolina.

1965

- Jackson joins Martin Luther King, Jr., and the Southern Christian Leadership Conference.

1966

- Jackson begins work on the Southern Christian Leadership Conference's economic program, Operation Breadbasket.

1971

- Jackson resigns from the Southern Christian Leadership Conference and forms his own organization, People United to Save Humanity.

1984

- Jackson campaigns for the Democratic Party's presidential nomination and also forms the Rainbow Coalition.

1988

- Jackson again campaigns for the Democratic Party's presidential nomination.

- **July 19**
  Jackson delivers an address at the Democratic National Convention, "The Struggle Continues."

1991–1996

- Jackson serves as "shadow senator" for the District of Columbia.

1996

- Jackson leads the merger of People United to Save Humanity and the Rainbow Coalition to form a single nonprofit organization called Rainbow/PUSH.

2005

- **November**
  Jackson writes "The Fight for Civil Rights Continues" for *Ebony* magazine.

---

numerous concessions to Jackson, including at least nine changes in the party's platform proposed by Jackson.

In this excerpt from his speech to his delegates on July 22, at the close of the 1988 convention, Jackson inspires them to sustain the struggle for influence and impact in the Democratic Party. In the first paragraph, he attacks the administration of the current president, Ronald Reagan, for its foreign policies and notes that Reagan never met with the Congressional Black Caucus. He makes reference to Reagan's state campaign headquarters in Philadelphia, Mississippi, noteworthy for an infamous event in 1964 when three young civil rights workers, Michael Schwerner, Andrew Goodman, and James Chaney, were murdered by authorities. Their bodies were later found near the town of Philadelphia. Jackson also expresses his concern with South Africa and its apartheid policies, which, he argues, Reagan was doing nothing to oppose. In this regard, Jackson was inaccurate. Reagan repeatedly said that he found apartheid repugnant, but he believed that the United States could not force South Africa to change its policies; rather, his administration worked to put quiet, steady pressure on the South African regime to do so.

Jackson goes on to point out the extraordinarily narrow margin by which John Kennedy had won the 1960 presidential election, a win that expressed for African Americans the "margin of our hope." In contrast, the Republican Richard Nixon's more comfortable victory over Hubert Humphrey in 1968 reflected the "margin of our despair." Jackson then argues that, in contrast to 1968, in 1988 African Americans and Jackson supporters in general have more "strength" and ability to "knock down doors in the DNC." He indicates that his supporters are "still knocking on doors," producing change in the attitudes of the party leadership, including the party chairman Paul Kirk.

Jackson uses the image of "street heat" in referring to civil rights successes. He notes, for example, that while John Kennedy supported civil rights in the South (a conclusion that some historians have cast some doubt on, for Kennedy did not want to alienate the Democratic South), it was "children in Birmingham" who "wrote" civil rights with their deaths. Jackson here is referring to yet another infamous incident, when the Ku Klux Klan bombed the 16th Street Church in Birmingham, Alabama, killing four young girls. He also argues that while President Lyndon Johnson signed the 1964 Civil Rights Act, it was the people of Selma, Alabama, who got the legislation passed. Jackson is talking about the Selma-to-Montgomery (Alabama) civil rights marches in 1965 and particularly to "Bloody Sunday," or March 7, when state and local authorities attacked the marchers with clubs and tear gas. Jackson urges his followers to keep up the "street heat," in part by registering new voters. He makes reference to the "contra vote," congressional investigations into the complicated Iran-Contra "arms for hostages" scandal that plagued the last months of the Reagan administration, and to efforts to gain statehood for the District of Columbia led by Mayor Marion Barry and Walter Fauntroy, a civil rights activist who served as a nonvoting representative for the district in Congress.

Jesse Jackson raises a clenched fist from a police van after he and eleven others from Operation Breadbasket were arrested during a sit-in at the Atlantic and Pacific Tea Co. offices in New York City on February 2, 1971. (AP/Wide World Photos)

Jackson indicates his excitement about movements in the Democratic Party that affect African Americans. He refers to the "Dellums Bill," introduced in Congress by Ron Dellums to impose sanctions on South Africa. He also refers to the "Conyers Bill," introduced by Representative John Conyers to secure federal voting rights. More important than these pieces of legislation, though, is a new unity based on newfound support from those who did not support Jackson in his 1984 presidential bid. He urges, then, more grassroots politics, exhorting his supporters to keep an eye on what their congressional representatives are doing and to vie for leadership positions in their state party organizations. Jackson asserts that "we were humiliated on Wednesday night because we won the popular vote but the superdelegates imposed their will on us." (Superdelegates are party leaders who have votes at the convention but are not elected in the primary process.) In response to Jackson's influence, Dukakis and other party leaders pledged to revise the process of selecting superdelegates in a way that would work in Jackson's favor should he choose to run again in the future. Although Jackson states that "we won the popular vote," it is unclear what he means. Although he won nearly seven million primary votes, Dukakis garnered nearly ten million.

◆ "The Fight for Civil Rights Continues"

Jackson's purposes in this 2005 article from *Ebony* magazine are twofold. One is to summarize the progress of the civil rights movement. The other is to suggest the future direction it should take. His overall themes are that every generation is a "Civil Rights generation" and that genuine freedom can be achieved only if progress is made on the economic front.

In the opening paragraph Jackson begins by noting that concepts of the civil rights movement should not be restricted to the 1960s. Rather, the struggle for civil rights, he states, has been going on since before the nation's founding. He goes on to say that it extends back at least 346 years, which would place the year at 1659. Until the 1650s slavery did not exist in what would become the United States. Some blacks were indentured servants, meaning that they were obligated by contract to function as servants or laborers for a fixed span of time. Upon the expiration of that time period, however, they were released from their indenture, and their children were not born into a condition of servitude. Blacks until the end of the 1650s enjoyed access to the court system, owned land, and in general were not regarded as property. But as a shortage of white indentured workers began to develop on the colonies' growing tobacco plantations and as consciousness of race-based differences began to grow, statutes were passed that in effect created the institution of slavery in such colonies as Virginia.

Jackson also points out that as early as the 1830s "Colored" men began to form organizations whose goal was the end of slavery and the achievement of civil rights. Jackson is most likely alluding to the efforts of such activists as Austin Steward. Steward was a former slave who settled in Rochester, New York, and who actively supported runaway slaves and contributed to the establishment of a black settlement in Wilberforce, Ontario. His book *Twenty-Two Years a Slave and Forty Years a Freeman* became an important document in the struggle for abolition. Steward served as vice president of the First Annual Convention of People of Color, held in Philadelphia in 1831, the first of several such conventions to call for the end of slavery.

In the fourth paragraph Jackson alludes to the hundredth anniversary of the Niagara Movement, which led to the creation of the National Association for the Advancement of Colored People in 1909. The Niagara Movement was the result of efforts by W. E. B. Du Bois and other black leaders, who had to meet on the Canadian side of Niagara Falls because they were barred from registering in any hotel in New York State on the American side. The goal of the meeting was to draft a list of demands to end discrimination and segregation and to foster economic opportunities for African Americans. The Niagara Movement had little immediate impact, but it laid the groundwork for civil rights struggles later in the century.

In the same paragraph, Jackson speaks about the efforts of southern whites to block implementation of the Thirteenth, Fourteenth, and Fifteenth Amendments to the Constitution. These three amendments, often referred to as the Civil Rights Amendments or the Reconstruction Amendments, were passed during Reconstruction in the wake of the Civil War. The Thirteenth Amendment abolished slavery. The Fourteenth Amendment, written to secure the rights of former slaves, calls for "due process" and "equal protection of the laws" in each state. The Fifteenth Amendment was written to secure the right to vote regardless of a person's "race, color, or previous condition of servitude." While these three amendments created hopes that the nation could put its history of slavery behind, many states found ways to thwart the intentions of the amendments. So-called Jim Crow laws, particularly in the South, led to a deeply segregated society. ("Jim Crow" was the name of a pre–Civil War minstrel show character, and the term came to be applied to both laws and customs that kept African Americans in a subservient position.) Fear was spread in the African American community by lynchings (nearly five thousand recorded from 1882 to 1968, though the true number was undoubtedly much higher) and the terrorism of the Ku Klux Klan. Blacks were routinely denied their right to vote through such measures as poll taxes and literacy tests, and black participation in governmental affairs was negligible.

Jackson then notes that changes began to take place in the second half of the twentieth century. One factor that promoted these changes was "Black migration to the North." Such migrations had already begun in the 1910s and the 1920s. Chicago's black population, for example, grew from forty-four thousand to 110,000 between 1910 and 1920. In New York City the black population grew from approximately fifty thousand in 1914 to 165,000 in 1930. Similar patterns developed in such cities as Detroit and Cleveland. This movement of people, coupled with the demands for troops and manufacturing workers during World War II and the cold war (the rivalry between the United States and the Soviet bloc) that followed, created conditions that would lead to the civil rights movement in the 1950s.

Jackson enumerates some of the successes of the movement in the paragraphs that follow. Among them were the U.S. Supreme Court's decision in the landmark case *Brown v. Board of Education*, which outlawed school segregation and overturned the doctrine of "separate but equal" enshrined by the Supreme Court in *Plessy v. Ferguson* (1896); the national attention given to race relations by events in Little Rock, Arkansas, and the infamous case of Emmett Till, a fourteen-year-old Chicago boy who, in 1955, was kidnapped and murdered in Mississippi after supposedly speaking disrespectfully to a white woman; and Rosa Parks's historic refusal in 1955 to relinquish her seat on a bus to a white man in Montgomery, Alabama. Parks's arrest for violating the laws pertaining to segregation in public transit led to a major civil rights success. From December 1, 1955, to December 20, 1956, African Americans in the city boycotted the transit system. The Montgomery bus boycott was successful (black taxicab drivers, for example, charged black passengers an amount equal to bus fares, 10 cents), leading to the U.S. Supreme Court's upholding a federal district court ruling that the city's segregation laws for public transit were unconstitutional.

Jackson then recounts additional successes such as the "freedom rides." These were organized by the Congress of Racial Equality to test the U.S. Supreme Court's decision in *Boynton v. Virginia*, which outlawed racial segregation in public areas—restrooms, restaurants, waiting rooms, terminals—that served interstate travelers. Similar nonviolent tactics were used to desegregate public accommodations in other parts of the country. The "power of this movement… hit its zenith with the March on Washington" that Martin Luther King led in 1963. The purpose of the march was to urge passage of the Civil Rights Act, which had stalled in Congress. Organizers expected that perhaps one hundred thousand people would attend. In fact, two hundred thousand attended, and it is likely that few ever forgot Dr. King's soaring "I have a dream" speech, delivered on August 28. As Jackson notes, the march had its desired effect on President John Kennedy and his successor, Lyndon Johnson, leading to the passage of the Civil Rights Act of 1964, the Voting Rights Act of 1965, and the Fair Housing Act of 1968.

Jackson asserts that these civil rights successes helped create a growing black middle class. Blacks could be found in increasing numbers in education, and, thanks to court decisions that upheld affirmative action in the awarding of federal contracts to minorities, blacks were increasingly visible in government programs as well as in major corporations and government itself. He notes that in 2005 the U.S. secretary of state (Condoleezza Rice), third in line to the presidency, was black. The number of blacks living in poverty had declined, and income among blacks was up. Jackson states, however, that while progress has been made, much remained to be done. He points out that the poverty rate among blacks was still twice that of whites. Whites continued to hold a disproportionate percentage of managerial jobs, and gaps in such areas as income and home ownership remained stable—to the disadvantage of blacks. He theorizes that the chief obstacle to black progress is the lack of capital for economic development. This lack of capital made it impossible for blacks to own businesses, and this impossibility had become a form of "structural discrimination"—that is, not deliberate discrimination on the part of individuals or companies but a form of discrimination emanating from the structure of the American economy itself. A further obstacle to black progress, according to Jackson, is that some of the earlier gains were being "rolled back." The Office of Federal Contract Compliance, which monitored contracting with government agencies, was understaffed and underfunded, and provisions of the Voting Rights Act were under assault. Indeed, Jackson was a highly vocal critic of voting procedures in Ohio, which George W. Bush narrowly won in the 2004 presidential election, giving him the crucial electoral votes that resulted in his victory.

In the final paragraphs of the article Jackson urges black leaders to remain vigilant. While acknowledging that much progress had been made, he notes that there remained plenty of "unfinished business" and asks leaders to "shine the light" on practices such as "redlining" by banks. (The term refers to a bank's refusal to grant loans to buy property or businesses in certain areas of a city, usually black areas, delineated on a map by a red line.) He also recommends that leaders ensure that banks and other lending institutions adhere to the provisions of the 1977 Community Reinvestment Act, which required these lending institutions to offer credit throughout their entire market area and not just to target wealthier borrowers and neighborhoods (and which prohibits the practice of redlining). It is likely that Jackson in 2005 was responding to changes made in the law that year. Previously, smaller banks and similar institutions had argued that the accounting and documentation requirements of the law were too onerous. In response to this concern, the law was changed to apply only to institutions with $1 billion in assets, rather than the $250 million of the original law. Many civil rights leaders and others were highly critical of these changes, for they created the opportunity for medium-sized lending institutions to ignore the spirit of the law. In 2008 the Community Reinvestment Act and similar legislation came under heavy fire when banks and other financial institutions failed because of so-called subprime loans, or loans made to those who could not afford them. Jackson concludes by saying that every generation, not just the 1960s generation, is a civil rights generation, for freedom can be achieved only when blacks achieve economic equality.

Impact and Legacy

Jesse Jackson has oftentimes been a highly controversial figure. His critics, for example, maintain that he is overly self-aggrandizing, sometimes given to showboating. His claim that he cradled the head of the dying Martin Luther King has been disputed by others who were present the day King was assassinated (April 4, 1968), and they were highly critical of his later appearances in a shirt supposedly stained with King's blood. He irritated the head of the Southern Christian Leadership Conference, Ralph D. Abernathy (who assumed control of the organization after King's assassination), who found him too freewheeling and given to grandstanding in order to gain the leadership of the SCLC. Critics have questioned the operations of PUSH and the Rainbow Coalition, pointing to irregularities both in the management of personnel and the expenditure of funds, and some have questioned the tax-exempt status of Rainbow/PUSH. Some critics have argued that his economic efforts in the late 1990s amounted in effect to extortion and that he threatened to organize boycotts of businesses that did not accommodate his demands. Still others have criticized him for meddling in foreign affairs. Over the years he has traveled to such trouble spots as South Africa, the Middle East, the former Yugoslavia, Cuba, Syria, Kenya, Venezuela, and Sierra Leone to try to broker peace agreements or to secure the release of hostages. While he enjoyed some successes, he sometimes angered government officials by negotiating with the Palestinian Liberation Organization and Cuba's Communist dictator, Fidel Castro.

Jackson has also attracted criticism for his tendency to speak without thinking. He once publicly referred to New York City as "Hymietown," a disparaging reference to Jews, and his close association with the Black Muslim leader Louis Farrakhan, an outspoken anti-Semite, has long offended Jews. More recently, in 2008, Jackson once again provoked controversy when he made a vulgar remark about presidential candidate Barack Obama in the vicinity of a microphone that he did not know was open. To some observers, the remark, which itself had racist overtones, suggested resentment on the part of the veteran that newcomer Obama had found the success that had eluded Jackson in running for president.

Despite these gaffes and the criticism he has drawn, for four decades Jesse Jackson has been one of the nation's most energetic forces for African Americans, minorities in general, and the poor, leading to his receipt of the Presidential Medal of Freedom in 2000. At one point or another, he has spoken out about a wide range of social issues, including voting rights, discrimination, segregation, poverty, affirmative action, health care, education, job placement for youths, drug use, and crime. He has been able to attract a wide following among both blacks and whites with his

"*And so here we are today, still knocking on doors. We're still winning every day and winning in every way.*"

("The Struggle Continues")

"*My friends, if we put on two to three million new voters between now and October 8, there will be enough heat to cook our meat.*"

("The Struggle Continues")

"*In truth, every generation for the past 346 years has been and is still today engaged in the struggle for full citizenship and equality.*"

("The Fight for Civil Rights Continues")

"*The reason civil rights activists have been important to Black advancement is that they are not anointed to become cheerleaders for the progress that has been achieved. Rather, they have a responsibility to acknowledge progress and continue to exploit opportunities to shine the light on the unfinished business of equality in every generation.*"

("The Fight for Civil Rights Continues")

vitality and the force of his soaring oratory. Listeners might disagree with him, but they cannot help but be moved by his words and his unique ability to give expression to the hopes and dreams of African Americans. His efforts have led to greater African American participation in the political process, and many observers would argue that the pace of minority representation in politics and corporate life increased as a direct result of the steady pressure he placed on the nation to correct the racial ills of the past.

Key Sources

There is no collection of Jesse Jackson's papers and speeches, so readers interested in his words must locate articles, interviews, and speeches in a variety of sources. Jackson is the author of numerous articles and has taken part in many interviews that can be found in publications such as *Ebony* and *Jet*. Some of his speeches can be found in *Keep Hope Alive: Jesse Jackson's 1988 Presidential Campaign*, edited by Frank Clemente and Frank Watkins (1989). His 1984 address to the Democratic National Convention and other material is in Lucius J. Barker's *Our*

Time Has Come: A Delegate's Diary of Jesse Jackson's 1984 Presidential Campaign (1988). Jackson was the author of *Straight from the Heart* (1987) and coauthored two books with his son, Jesse Jackson, Jr.: *Legal Lynchings: Racism, Injustice, and the Death Penalty* (1996) and *It's about the Money!* (1999).

Further Reading

■ **Articles**

Monroe, Sylvester. "Personalities: Does the Rev. Jesse Jackson Still Matter?" *Ebony* 62, no. 1 (2006): 170.

■ **Books**

Abernathy, Ralph David. *And the Walls Came Tumbling Down.* New York: Harper & Row, 1989.

Bruns, Roger. *Jesse Jackson: A Biography.* Westport, Conn.: Greenwood Press, 2005.

Colton, Elizabeth O. *The Jackson Phenomenon: The Man, the Power, the Message.* New York: Doubleday, 1989.

Frady, Marshall. *Jesse: The Life and Pilgrimage of Jesse Jackson*. New York: Simon and Schuster, 2006.

Henry, Charles P. *Jesse Jackson: The Search for Common Ground*. Oakland, Calif.: BlackScholar Press, 1991.

House, Ernest R. *Jesse Jackson and the Politics of Charisma*. Boulder, Colo.: Westview Press, 1988.

Reed, Adolph L. *The Jesse Jackson Phenomenon: The Crisis of Purpose in Afro-American Politics*. New Haven, Conn.: Yale University Press, 1986.

Reynolds, Barbara A. *Jesse Jackson: America's David*. Washington, D.C.: JFJ Associates, 1985.

Stanford, Karin L. *Beyond the Boundaries: Reverend Jesse Jackson in International Affairs*. Albany: State University of New York Press, 1997.

—Michael J. O'Neal

Questions for Further Study

1. In "The Struggle Continues," Jesse Jackson focuses much of his attention on black progress within the Democratic Party. What were some of the gains, and how did they affect African American involvement in the political process?

2. In his presidential bids, Jackson attracted support not only from African Americans but from others as well, including many whites. What do you believe was the source of his appeal to a range of voters? Cite specifics from the two documents.

3. Jackson places considerable emphasis on the economic condition of the black community. He cites gains by African Americans and the growth of a black middle class. What contributed to the improved economic condition of many African Americans?

4. Jackson argues that the "civil rights movement" was a phenomenon not limited to the 1960s, when blacks in modern life made significant gains. What were some other significant events and developments in the struggle for civil rights?

5. Compare and contrast Jesse Jackson's rhetoric with that of earlier African American activists and civil rights leaders, including William Lloyd Garrison, Frederick Douglass, Ida B. Wells, Ella Baker, Malcolm X, and W. E. B. Du Bois. How do these various writers and speakers appeal to their audiences?

"The Struggle Continues" (1988)

These last seven years have been especially painful. While our sons and daughters have died in Grenada and Lebanon and Europe, this President has not met with the Congressional Black Caucus one time. Denial of access. In these last seven years, this man suggested that those in South Africa who were shot in the back had provoked the shootings. In these last seven years, our complicity with South Africa, in Angola, in Namibia and inside South Africa, continues. In these last seven years, Reagan opened up his presidential campaign in Philadelphia, Mississippi, sending a signal that was missed by too many people. There's not even a railroad in Philadelphia, Mississippi, not even a small airport. The only thing it is known for is that it is where the civil rights activists Schwerner, Goodman and Chaney were found murdered. On that day of Reagan's announcement, even the Klan were there in their paraphernalia. I tell you from Philadelphia, Mississippi, to Bitburg, Germany, to Johannesburg, South Africa, it's been an unbroken line by Reagan, unchallenged by Bush.

My friends, I'm going to keep on arguing a preferable case to you about our live options. We might think now that in 1960 John Kennedy won unanimously. But he won by 112,000 votes—less than one vote per precinct. Kennedy won against Nixon with less than one vote per precinct difference in the American mind.

In 1960, we won by the margin of our hope, because Kennedy took the risks to relate to us publicly and to reach out to Dr. King.

In 1968, the psychology shifted. Dr. King was killed on April 4. Robert Kennedy was killed on June 5. There were riots at the Chicago Democratic Convention. With all of that death, all of that despair, all of those broken hearts, all of that lost blood, Nixon beat Humphrey by 550,000 votes.

The difference between Nixon and Humphrey was tremendous. But we could not make a distinction between the Great Society and the lost society. We lost by the margin of our despair what we had won eight years before by the margin of our hope.

Now we come forth in 1988, with much more strength and much greater capability. We've had to knock down doors in the DNC. It's not unusual. We give thanks that we have the ability to knock them down, and open them up. We can do that. We've always had the paradoxical burden of fighting to save the nation just to save ourselves.

If you're in the back seat of a truck, and you don't like the driver and the car's going over the cliff, don't take solace in the fact that he's going over the cliff, because he isn't going to push a button and eject you. You'll have to save the driver just to save yourself. And so here we are today, still knocking on doors. We're still winning every day and winning in every way.

Many things have changed this week in Atlanta—among other things, relationships. There have been serious meetings this week with Paul Kirk and the DNC leadership, and there will be serious changes in the DNC as of this morning because of you—not because those doors voluntarily opened up and certainly not because you stopped knocking. Some combination of your knocking and determination to get in has changed things.

He had the will but not the capacity because there are checks and balances in this government. He told Dr. King, "I'm for it, but we can't get it because the Congress is too conservative. I just can't get it passed." But "street heat" in Selma gave him a new alternative. He then could say, "I'm for some change, now we shall overcome."

I'll tell you one reason I want to be close enough to serve and far enough away to challenge—because change requires a combination of new leadership and "street heat." John Kennedy and Robert Kennedy could not go to Birmingham and say, I feel ashamed, therefore I will enact a Public Accommodations bill. It took a combination of their leadership and our "street heat."

We've got to keep up the "street heat." My friends, if we put on two to three million new voters between now and October 8, there will be enough heat to cook our meat, and enough heat for George Bush to get out of the kitchen.

You do understand that the contra vote that comes up again next week—they can't get that vote now. You do understand that when Mayor Marion Barry and Rep. Walter Fauntroy try to get the D.C. statehood bill passed, that the wing of the party that's been holding it back—they have to deliver now. That's the art and science of politics. It takes different temperatures to cook different kinds of meat. That's "street heat."

I'm excited. There's going to be a change. Why are Republicans already talking about "They're running a three-man ticket—Dukakis, Bentsen and Jackson"? Well, they're trying to create some mess. That's a trick to drive us away, but we're not leaving.

There isn't a three-man ticket. Psychologically, I don't require it. A political ticket doesn't need it. We're more grown than that. We got this commitment on the Dellums Bill, and Mandela can rejoice, and on the Conyers Bill, and unregistered voters can rejoice, and on two senators and a governor in D.C., which could completely change the balance in the U.S. Senate, and we can all rejoice.

Let's look at a few more things here. I suppose the first victory for us is that we're together. People who didn't support us in 1984 supported us in 1988. There are those who didn't support us in 1988 who

are going to support us from now on because it's clear what time of day it is.

We're also in major league politics now. This isn't softball. The next step is to go back to your states—to every state we won, every district we won—and see how your congressperson voted, see how your senator voted, and see how your DNC member voted. That's the basis for new politics right where you live.

That's the first thing you've got to do. In Mississippi they got themselves lawyers, organized over the long haul and now they are the leaders of the state Democratic Party. Our Mississippi delegation ran a ticket and won the leadership positions in the state party. We must do this in every state we won—from Maine to Delaware to Virginia to South Carolina to Georgia to Alabama to Louisiana—in every one of those states where we the people were humiliated on

Glossary

Angola	a nation in south-central Africa embroiled in civil war from 1975 to 2002, a conflict that in its early years was a proxy war in the cold war between the United States and its allies and the Communist Soviet Union and its allies
Bitburg, Germany	the site of a cemetery where World War II German troops are buried and where President Ronald Reagan provoked controversy by agreeing to lay a wreath at the site on May 5, 1985, in commemoration of the end of the war in Europe
Bush	George H. W. Bush (b. 1924), Republican U.S. president
Great Society	name given to President Lyndon Johnson's social and civil rights programs in the 1960s
Grenada	a Caribbean island nation invaded by a U.S.-led force on October 25, 1983, to depose a Communist dictator
Humphrey	Hubert Humphrey (1911–1978), prominent Democratic U.S. senator and presidential candidate in 1968 and U.S. vice president under Lyndon B. Johnson
Lebanon	a country on the eastern shore of the Mediterranean Sea, which was embroiled in civil war from 1975 to 1990; its capital, Beirut, was the site of a terrorist bombing on October 23, 1983, in which more than two hundred U.S. Marines and other military personnel were killed
Mandela	Nelson Mandela (b. 1918), South African civil rights activist who later served as first president of South Africa after the dismantling of apartheid in that country
Namibia	a nation in southern Africa annexed by South Africa and its apartheid regime after World War II
Nixon	Richard Nixon (1913–1994), Republican U.S. president
Robert Kennedy	U.S. attorney general, U.S. senator, and leading contender for the Democratic Party presidential nomination at the time of his assassination (1925–1968)
superdelegates	prominent party members who vote at the major party nominating conventions but are not elected as delegates in the primary process

Wednesday night because we won the popular vote but the superdelegates imposed their will on us.

Some people say what did we get? Well, we got new rules and the party can't run over us again in 1992.

"THE FIGHT FOR CIVIL RIGHTS CONTINUES" (2005)

Defining the proper role and place of the movement for Civil Rights in America has been difficult because of the shorthand that has characterized the 1960s uniquely as that era. In truth, every generation for the past 346 years has been and is still today engaged in the struggle for full citizenship and equality. In fact, in 1830 the first series of national meetings of Colored men began with a civil rights agenda that stood for an end to slavery, the provision of the vote and education and a stake in the new America as full citizens.

Fighting slavery and its progeny was necessary because it had built the foundation for our social space at the bottom of society. It also distorted the project of American democracy and led almost logically to a civil war, and it would also follow that the Constitution should be amended to create a new framework of racial relations based on equality.

Thus the goals in these amendments defined the task of Black leadership and their allies to make them meaningful for subsequent generations.

This year, we observe the 100th anniversary of the Niagara Movement that, in 1905, led to the birth of the NAACP and the civil rights movement of that era. The success of Southern Whites in solidifying control of the states in that region largely eliminated the implementation of the 13th, 14th and 15th amendments. Instead, they launched an attack on Blacks, marked by lynchings, rigid segregation, cultural inferiorization, exclusion from politics and other negative outcomes.

This framework of social life for Blacks remained remarkably stable for the first 50 years of the 20th century, but was eventually altered by such factors as Black migration to the North, World War II, the humanitarian principles of the United Nations, Cold War competition and, of course, the superb legal leadership of the NAACP.

The 1954 victory of the NAACP in the case of *Brown v. Board of Education* initiated a new phase in the civil rights struggle, creating the optimistic possibility that segregation could successfully be confronted in other areas.

The following year, 1955, featured other dramatic events such as President Dwight Eisenhower using federalized troops to protect Black youth attempting to integrate Central High School in Little Rock, Ark., and the death of the young Emmett Till, killed in Mississippi on August 28, 1955, for "ogling" a White woman that stirred emotions nationally.

Just months later, on December 5, 1955, Rosa Parks sat down and refused to go to the back of the bus.

Doubtless, these emotions of both deep victory and deep defeat, contributed to the Montgomery Bus Boycott, which inaugurated another kind of era.

The defense against the discrimination of Blacks in public transportation in Montgomery, Ala., was a flash point for the mobilization of large numbers of ordinary citizens in the South. Led by Dr. Martin Luther King Jr., whose genius was articulating the methods and goals of the mobilization, their marching feet became a powerful movement that not only broke open the segregated bus system in Montgomery, it also started "freedom rides" across state lines and sparked the imagination of millions of young people who used similar tactics of nonviolent protest to open lunch counters, swimming pools and other places of public accommodations all over the country.

The power of this movement at every phase in the 1960s, whether in Birmingham, Selma, Nashville, Greenville or even St. Louis, Chicago and Detroit, shook the structure of discrimination in the social realm that had held Blacks in deep poverty, in rigid ghettoes, in subordinate employment, in inferior schools and away from the voting booth. This movement hit its zenith with the March on Washington, led by Dr. King on August 28, 1963.

The Civil Rights Movement challenged the political system, and political parties in particular, and caused their leaders to respond. Thus, Presidents John F. Kennedy and Lyndon B. Johnson were pushed by the winds of this Movement toward the proposition that America could not move forward, either domestically or internationally, without enacting significant policies of social change.

The Civil Rights Movement—an independent "third rail" for social change—caused both Democrats and Republicans to join in the passage of legislation such as the 1964 Civil Rights Act, Title VII (which prohibited discrimination in employment), the 1965 Voting Rights Act, the 1968 Fair Housing Act and, in 1971, led the courts to approve affirmative action in the awarding of federal contracts.

The success of this stage of the Movement built the foundation for the emergence of the Black middle class, which took advantage of the greater openness of society in higher education, in employment, in the awarding of contracts by cities, counties and the federal government. Education was central, and although confined to historically Black colleges and universities in the '50s and '60s, Blacks now attend a wide variety of higher education institutions and hold professorships and chairs at some of the nation's most prestigious institutions.

As a result, in the past 60 years, some marvelous things have happened. Whereas in 1960 at the beginning of the Civil Rights Movement, only 10 percent of Blacks made the average income, 30 percent have such income today. And whereas over half of the Black population was in officially declared poverty in 1960, about one-third exists in that situation today.

Many Blacks have also broken out of the ghetto to reside in housing in many desirable areas, in both cities and metropolitan neighborhoods. In addition, a number of Blacks today also hold positions as managers in some Fortune 500 companies and have risen to high positions in government, including Secretary of State, who is third in succession to the President of the United States.

The goal of Black progress, however, was never just freedom, but full equality and citizenship, and therefore, while we point to the progress which had been made, we must also continue to keep the emerging challenges in view. For example, in 2004, the poverty rate for all citizens was 12 percent, but double that for Blacks at 24 percent, and only 8 percent for Whites. Unemployment in the Black community has also continued to be double that of Whites since the Civil Rights Movement, a structural condition that has led to deep social crises such as poor health, criminal involvement, low educational performance, and other situations which have not been ameliorated. On the other hand, a similar proportion (20 percent) of Black men and White men are now employed in technical, sales and administrative support jobs, but within that category, Whites have 33 percent of the managerial jobs and Blacks only 18 percent. The income gap between Blacks and Whites has remained remarkably stable, with Blacks at about 58 percent (about $20,000) of Whites since 1980; but Blacks spend, on average, 76 percent of what Whites spend. The home ownership gap is also substantial, with nearly half of Blacks owning their homes, compared to 75 percent of Whites.

Perhaps the most serious of the current challenges faced by the Black community—and, therefore, by those who would accept the leadership to foster more achievement—is economic development. Freedom was never the goal; freedom was part of the process of getting to the goal of equality. The Freedom bills of 1964–65 did not delve into the infrastructure of denial of access to capital and economic empowerment for people of color.

The focus on business ownership by Blacks has resulted in some successes. For example, there are more than 350 McDonald franchises owned by Blacks. But in other industries, the lack of inclusion is glaring. Coke, for instance, has been in business for 117 years, yet there is only one Black bottler.

In fact, the exclusion of Blacks from many business opportunities resides in the fact that at the time when franchises were given out in such multi-city, multi-national enterprises, those in line with the resources to obtain them were almost exclusively White. This holds true for radio and TV stations in 1948, and more recently for many of the franchises in automotive and other retail establishments.

This structural discrimination and denial of access to capital has become embedded in the American economic culture, which sees Blacks as essentially consumers, and it grows stronger with the emergence of a conservative culture that's counter to general Black social advancement. We have disturbed the epidermal level, but the deep structure has not yet been touched. And now, gains of the Civil Rights Movement—relating to economic empowerment, minority procurement and access to capital—are being rolled back. For example, a recent report of the U. S. Civil Rights Commission indicates that the least increase in budget and staff in the past few years has gone to the Office of Federal Contract Compliance, the office that monitors affirmative action contracting with government agencies.

More critically, key anti-discrimination provisions of the landmark Voting Rights Act are now threatened. Forty years after its enactment, this administration and Department of Justice have not aggressively enforced the Act, and have yet to commit to reauthorization of critical enforcement provisions (Sections 203 and Section 5) that give the Act its teeth. That's why Rainbow/PUSH initiated the march and rally in Atlanta on August 6, the 40th anniversary of the signing of the Voting Rights Act, and along with civil and human rights leadership, took this case back to the streets. Civil rights leadership fought for, and won, the Voting Rights Act in 1965; it must enforce, protect and extend it in 2005.

The reason civil rights activists have been important to Black advancement is that they are not anointed to become cheerleaders for the progress that has been achieved. Rather, they have a responsibility to acknowledge progress and continue to exploit opportunities to shine the light on the unfinished business of equality in every generation. As such, they should not settle for an easy version of freedom, but to make freedom, equality, equity and parity meaningful in terms of achieving full access to the opportunities and resources available to all Americans.

This goal cannot be achieved by leaders alone, but fundamentally by a community that remains disciplined and sensitive to the challenges and does not settle for an easy definition of freedom located in violence, spiritual materialism or the liberation of self. Most important, it will require the willingness to support all relevant strategies, including civil methods of lobbying, demonstrations and other methods of nonviolent social change, to affect public atten-

tion to our agenda, an agenda that has generally empowered most of the American people.

So, whether it's fighting for the right of workers to organize for higher wages and secure benefits, or preventing neighborhood redlining by banks, or pressuring them to abide by the guidelines of the Community Reinvestment Act, or installing more minority pension fund managers and using those funds for community development, or demanding fair corporate investment in communities for their market influence, or promoting more women and minority CEOs in large firms, or opposing trade deals that send jobs abroad, or obtaining more and better franchises and contracts, this is an agenda for economic equity and parity.

In this sense, this generation is a "Civil Rights generation," and every generation will be one, until real freedom has come.

Glossary

Black bottler	reference to the fact that the Coca-Cola Company is the parent of some three hundred companies that bottle and distribute the company's beverages
Fortune 500	the five hundred largest U.S. companies, as determined by *Fortune* magazine
infrastructure	a figure of speech referring to roads, bridges, utilities, and other public facilities; the underlying structure or system of organization
Little Rock, Arkansas	reference to civil unrest that surrounded the integration of Little Rock High School in September 1957
Reagan	Ronald Reagan (1911–2004), Republican U.S. president
third rail	a figure of speech that refers to the rail that carries electrical power to trains; an issue so "charged" and dangerous that politicians do not like to deal with it

Robert H. Jackson (Library of Congress)

ROBERT H. JACKSON   1892–1954

Supreme Court Justice

Featured Documents
- ◆ "The Federal Prosecutor" (1940)
- ◆ *West Virginia State Board of Education v. Barnette* (1943)
- ◆ Opening Statement before the International Military Tribunal, Nuremberg, Germany (1945)
- ◆ Closing Statement before the International Military Tribunal, Nuremberg, Germany (1946)

Overview

Robert Houghwout Jackson was born in Spring Creek, Pennsylvania, in 1892. The son of William Eldred and Angelina Houghwout Jackson, he grew up in Frewsburg, New York. The last person to serve as associate justice on the Supreme Court without obtaining a law degree, Jackson passed his bar exam after two years apprenticing for a law firm in nearby Jamestown, New York, and taking a year of course work at Albany Law School in Albany, New York. Following a successful career in private practice, Jackson in 1931 accepted a nomination from then governor Franklin D. Roosevelt to serve on the New York State Commission to Investigate the Administration of Justice. This was to prove formative for his career, much of which focused on the problems inherent in the criminal justice system, such as equality before the law and the pursuit of justice and truth rather than simply pursuit of convictions.

Jackson carried this approach with him into federal service, where he served in the Department of Internal Revenue and as assistant attorney general in the Tax Division and the Antitrust Division, before being named solicitor general in 1938 and then U.S attorney general in 1940. His reputation for fairly pursuing truth and justice as objectively as possible earned him high renown among his peers, and he brought that same resolve to the Supreme Court, to which he was appointed in 1941. Although Jackson was a staunch defender of individual liberties, he nevertheless strove in his opinions to delineate both individual rights and liberties and the constitutional powers of the state and federal governments, leaving behind a nuanced intellectual legacy.

Jackson's chief legacy, however, rests on the Nuremberg war crimes tribunals, which he was instrumental in creating and seeing through. In the closing days of World War II, one of President Harry Truman's first actions in office was to ask Jackson to represent the United States in the creation of a postwar criminal tribunal to bring the deposed heads of the Nazi state to justice. The Allies had agreed in principle to such proceedings earlier in the war, and Jackson worked throughout the summer of 1945 to turn that agreement into a working tribunal. His efforts paid off, and on August 8, 1945, the Allies signed the London Charter, outlining the aims and methods of the war crimes tribunal, which began in the fall of 1945. Jackson, selected to serve as U.S. chief

of counsel during the proceedings, delivered the opening and closing statements for the first trial, speeches that rank among the most eloquent and important of his career. With the trials in Germany over, Jackson returned to the bench in 1946. On October 9, 1954, Jackson suffered a fatal heart attack and was buried in Frewsburg, New York.

Explanation and Analysis of Documents

Jackson is widely remembered for his fluency in language and his ability to concisely convey complicated arguments understandably. He possessed a clear-sighted view of the limitations of the law, both in terms of preventing problems and as having itself the potential to cause problems. He also held a strong belief that the law, properly cared for and implemented by those responsible for doing so, could be a powerful, active force in protecting rights and liberties and redressing wrongs. The four documents included here—Jackson's speech addressing the responsibilities of the federal prosecutors, his opinion in a First Amendment dispute, and his opening and closing statements at the Nuremberg Nazi war crimes tribunal—all speak to these problems with and hopes for the law. Each demonstrates Jackson's commitment to creating working legal systems that treated all people equally, including heads of state, and each speaks to his belief that the law can protect individual liberties without weakening government itself.

◆ "The Federal Prosecutor"
On April 1, 1940, Jackson, who had been appointed attorney general only three months earlier, gave one of the most important speeches of his career. Entitled "The Federal Prosecutor" and delivered to a gathering of U.S. attorneys serving in each of the nation's federal judicial districts, the speech laid out Jackson's understanding of the duties and role of U.S. attorneys—the federal prosecutors. The speech outlined Jackson's aspirations in reorganizing and cleaning up the Department of Justice, which was badly disorganized and demoralized at the time that Jackson was appointed attorney general.

The theme of the speech is that with great power comes grave responsibility. Delineating the powers of the prosecutor, Jackson reveals how few factors limit that power. As Jackson notes, the primary limitations on prosecutorial

Time Line

1910
- Jackson undertakes a one-year apprenticeship with two lawyers in Jamestown, New York.

1911
- Jackson begins a year of courses at Albany Law School in New York.

1912
- Jackson continues apprenticing with lawyers in Jamestown, New York, for a year.

1913
- Jackson is admitted to the New York Bar.

1931
- Governor Franklin D. Roosevelt appoints Jackson to the New York Commission to Investigate the Administration of Justice.

1934
- President Franklin D. Roosevelt appoints Jackson general counsel of the Internal Revenue Service.

1936
- Jackson is named assistant attorney general for the Tax Division.

1937
- Jackson is named assistant attorney general for the Antitrust Division.

1938–1940
- Jackson serves as U.S. solicitor general.

1940–1941
- Jackson serves as U.S. attorney general.

1940
- **April 1**
  Jackson delivers a speech, "The Federal Prosecutor," outlining his understanding of the role of the prosecutor in the federal criminal justice system.

---

power are logistical: There simply are not enough people in the prosecutor's office to investigate every potential crime, and there is a distinction between the jurisdictions of federal and local law enforcement. These limitations, in turn, create the greatest of the prosecutors' powers—the ability to pursue cases at their discretion. It is the decision of a prosecutor whether citizens will be indicted, investigated, charged, or made the subject of public or private whisper campaigns—that is, the coordinated circulation of rumors, in public or in private circles, designed to defame or injure an individual's reputation.

Jackson approaches the question of power and responsibility from a slightly different angle in order to make his greater point. The prosecutor does not choose simply which cases to pursue but also which defendants to prosecute. This is the crux of the prosecutor's responsibility, to choose cases on the merits of the alleged crimes rather than on the basis of who the defendant is or what he or she represents. This was a particularly pertinent point in the months shortly before the United States entered World War II, and Jackson voices a strong warning about the negative impact that an overzealous prosecutor might have on civil liberties and what he refers to as traditional American concepts of liberty and freedom. He emphatically advises prosecutors against targeting "subversive" elements, reminding them that most constitutional freedoms Americans enjoy were once punishable, subversive offenses. Moreover, Jackson says, it is best to keep in mind that at one time both "Republican" and "Democrat" were not descriptors of political affiliation, but epithets denoting radicalism and subversiveness. The prosecutor's duty is to protect the spirit as well as the letter of American civil liberties, Jackson notes, and thus the prosecutor is constrained to act fairly and apolitically at all times.

Jackson directed the Department of Justice along the lines he laid out in this speech. His articulation of the responsibilities incumbent on the federal prosecutor and his precise formulation of the dilemma faced by the prosecutor—to seek to punish and eliminate crime but to do so while respecting the American tradition of civil liberties—foreshadowed his approach to problems of civil liberties as an associate justice on the Supreme Court. "The Federal Prosecutor" retains such relevance that numerous subsequent attorneys general have directly quoted from it to summarize their own views of the duties and responsibilities of federal prosecutors.

◆ West Virginia State Board of Education v. Barnette

In 1940 the Supreme Court decided *Minersville School District v. Gobitis*, which held that school districts could compel students to salute the flag despite any religious objections they might have. The Jehovah's Witnesses had brought the case before the court, arguing that saluting the flag amounted to idolatry according to their beliefs and thus that they had a First Amendment right not to be forced to violate their religious conscience. The Court disagreed, ruling against them. Shortly, however, public opinion turned against the *Gobitis* decision, provoked by reports of physical violence committed against Jehovah's Witnesses who refused to salute the flag and by several prominent patriotic organizations calling for legislation to make flag observance voluntary.

Given the change in public opinion, Walter Barnette and several other Jehovah's Witnesses brought suit against the West Virginia State Board of Education, again arguing that they had a right not to be compelled to violate their religious beliefs by participating in actions that they believed were contrary to those beliefs. This time the Witnesses were successful, and the Supreme Court struck down West Virginia's law, voiding the idea that students could be compelled to salute the flag.

The *Gobitis* opinion rested on four foundations, each of which Jackson dismantles in his opinion in *Barnette*. First, *Gobitis* claimed that when faced with the dilemma of choosing between a weak government and one strong enough to threaten the liberties of the people, the latter should be preferred. In *Barnette*, Jackson dismisses this argument as incorrect and beside the point. Carried to its conclusion, he notes, there would be no foundation for individual liberties. Further, that government which does not threaten the people's liberties is not necessarily weak; indeed, Jackson cites preservation of individual freedom as the mark of a strong government.

Second, *Gobitis* held that striking down school board requirements would entangle the Supreme Court too deeply in local affairs, making the Court, in effect, a national school board. Again, Jackson says that this claim is false, noting that the Fourteenth Amendment protects the citizen from the states and their offices, including local school boards. Third, *Gobitis* held that the Court was ill equipped to interfere in matters such as local school board policy. Because the Court was not competent to rewrite the rules, *Gobitis* states, the legislatures are the proper venue for dictating policy changes. Not so, counters Jackson. The Court is certainly competent to adjudge whether freedoms protected by the Bill of Rights are being infringed upon, and in cases where fundamental rights are in question, such as the right to conscience or free speech, then the Court can and must intervene.

Last, *Gobitis* found that because national unity forms the basis for national security, measures promoting this unity should not be hindered. Jackson does not take exception to this idea itself, but rather the means by which it is to be achieved. As always, he defers to persuasion and force of argument, rather than validating compulsion. Where persuasion fails, he notes, conflict follows, leading inevitably to persecution. This being the case, Jackson's opinion concludes that coercing unity of expression by enforcing the flag salute is an unconstitutional abridgment of free speech, and thus he overturns *Gobitis*.

The *Barnette* decision is remarkable in three ways. First, it is unusual for a case to be overturned so swiftly after being decided, as *Gobitis* was. Second, in the midst of World War II, the decision protected the rights of a religious minority in the face of laws designed to enforce national unity. Last, the *Barnette* decision was a major vic-

Time Line	
1941	■ **July 7** Jackson is confirmed associate justice of the U.S. Supreme Court.
1943	■ **June 14** Jackson delivers the Court's opinion in *West Virginia State Board of Education v. Barnette*.
1945	■ **May 2** President Harry S. Truman names Jackson U.S. chief of counsel for the Nazi war criminal trials. ■ **July 7** Jackson visits Nuremberg, Germany, and recommends the city as the site for the trials. ■ **November 21** Jackson delivers his opening statement in the trial of *The United States of America, the French Republic, the United Kingdom of Great Britain and Northern Ireland, and the Union of Soviet Socialist Republics v. Hermann Wilhelm Goering, et al.*, the first of the Nazi war crimes trials.
1946	■ **July 26** Jackson delivers his closing argument in the first of the Nuremberg war crimes trials.
1954	■ **October 9** Jackson dies in Washington, D.C.

tory for religious minorities and their right to practice their faith, but the fact that it was decided on freedom of speech grounds also marked a major turning point in constitutional jurisprudence. For the remainder of the century, religious freedom cases came more and more to be argued and won on free speech grounds and not on the basis of freedom of religion.

◆ **Opening Statement before the International Military Tribunal, Nuremberg, Germany**

On October 30, 1943, the United States, United Kingdom, Soviet Union, and China signed the Moscow Decla-

Former Nazi defendants (among them, Hermann Goering standing) in the dock at the Nuremberg war crimes tribunal (AP/Wide World Photos)

ration, which declared that Nazi war criminals would be arrested and submitted to judicial proceedings. On May 2, 1945, President Harry S. Truman named Jackson the U.S. chief of counsel for the future trials. On August 8 the United States, the Soviet Union, the United Kingdom, and France signed the London Agreement, which mandated trying the Nazi war criminals in an international military tribunal. On October 6 the four powers published their joint statement of indictment against the defendants; on November 21, Jackson gave one of the most famous speeches of his life, the opening statement in the trial of *The United States of America, the French Republic, the United Kingdom of Great Britain and Northern Ireland, and the Union of Soviet Socialist Republics v. Hermann Wilhelm Goering, et al.*

Jackson's statement is an expression of the necessity of the conjoined development of civilization and international law. It is, he says, civilization itself that is the plaintiff in the case against Nazi aggression and horrors and civilization itself that would be existentially threatened by a resurgence of the same hatreds and nationalisms that gave rise to the Nazi movement. Can civilization, he wonders, long be protected unless the law develops the mechanisms by which to deal with crimes of this magnitude? The victorious Allied nations have paid their due to reason, Jackson says, by staying the hand of vengeance and dealing with the defeated fairly, rationally, and in courts of law, rather than by ignoring the crimes against peace and humanity committed by the Nazis and reacting in hot blood. It is the responsibility of the tribunal, Jackson says, to put into place mechanisms whereby the powerful can be held to account for their actions, thereby initiating a process that will work against future wars of aggression and future tyrannies.

Jackson's statement is a remarkably humble declaration of the justice and wisdom of the trials and lays out the array of charges against the defendants, broken down into sections. Describing the Nazi's "Lawless Road to Power," Jackson summarizes the rise of the Third Reich, while he describes "The Consolidation of Nazi Power" by focusing on three elements in particular: "The Battle against the Working Class," "The Battle against the Churches," and "The Battle against the Jews," the last of which details the progressive legal changes and pogroms that culminated in the Holocaust. Continuing by describing Nazi "Terrorism and Preparation for War," "Experiments in Aggression," the "War of Aggression," and the "Conspiracy with Japan," Jackson finishes laying out the framework of the case against the defendants and moves into "The Law of the Case." In the latter section he details the legal structures defining the prosecution and the grounds for the tribunal. Jackson concludes his statement by describing "The Crime against Peace," in which he gives a definition of war of aggression; "The Law of Individual Responsibility," or the degree to which individuals in a totalitarian state are responsible for war crimes; "The Political, Police, and Military Organizations," describing the roles of these groups in the commission of the crimes under trial; and, finally, his view of "The Responsibility of this Tribunal."

Jackson's answer to the question of responsibility of the tribunal ranks among his most eloquent and profound speeches. The goal of the tribunal, Jackson says, is to try to put in place mechanisms whereby future wars might be prevented. This is no idealistic venture, along the line of World War I's failure to end all wars, but rather a legal and judicial desire. By punishing the vanquished after the fact and by taking steps to ensure that this prosecution applies in all cases, war may gradually be seen less and less as a viable policy action.

The recognition of and call to broadly applicable standards of international law and justice are the strengths of Jackson's statement. Jackson believes it important to demonstrate that the powerful can and will sit in judgment before the law and that the leaders of nations will be held accountable for their crimes. He also highlights the racial hatreds that supported the Nazi's systematic terrorism and violence, to expose the foundations while judging the crimes that resulted. Jackson notes that all of the evidence to be presented against the defendants would be from German sources.

Instead of utilizing American, French, British, or Soviet sources, Jackson says that there is enough evidence created and retained by the defendants themselves to prove the prosecution's case. More important, it is critical for two main reasons to demonstrate the fairness of the proceedings: First, although Jackson acknowledges that the victor will determine history, he nevertheless wants the proceedings to be as fair and judicious as possible, to the extent of excluding evidence against the defendants compiled by their wartime enemies. Second, recognizing the importance of the occasion and the desire that it become an international precedent in the event of future wars, Jackson reminds the court that they need to get it right the first time. The tribunal, if it is perceived to be unfair, will cast doubt not only upon the sentences rendered but also on the viability of an international tribunal to adjudicate future war crimes. In order to preserve the form and function of the tribunal, Jackson says, it must be conducted as much in line with fairness as possible. He revisited these themes eight months later in his closing statement.

◆ Closing Address before the International Military Tribunal

Over the eight months of testimony held between November 1945 and July 1946, the Allied nations presented evidence in rotating phases, with evidence of the atrocities committed at Auschwitz presented during the French phase and evidence of German atrocities in Eastern Europe presented during the Soviet phase. On July 26, 1946, Jackson delivered his closing statement as the prosecution began its summation toward the end of the first set of trials.

In his closing statement, Jackson revisits several themes he had developed in his opening statement. He again refers to the notion that civilization itself is on trial as much as are the Nazi war criminals. If civilization cannot adequately and justly respond to the crimes that have been perpetrated, then the events and beliefs that led to those crimes might be repeated, again resulting in catastrophic war and culminating, in Jackson's words, in "the doom of civilization." Jackson also defends the proceedings to which the Nazi defendants were submitted. Consulting the trial record, he says, will dispel any questions regarding the fundamental justice of the trials. If this is the first case in history in which the defeated were tried in such a way, it is also the first time that they were able to defend themselves against the charges facing them. The defendants in this trial, Jackson says, will have had their chance to be heard in the kind of trial that they never provided those accused of crimes against the Nazi regime. All the same, he warns against seeing fairness as weakness, contending that fairness and justice are always strengths and reminding the court that the proceedings have relied on German sources of evidence and documentation. Rather than letting the victorious Allies formulate the case against the German defendants, the prosecution instead allowed the defendants' own words, records, and documents to build the case against them.

Jackson constructs his statement with the logic that provided the framework for the tribunal, treating the Nazi government as a criminal plot and prosecuting the Nazi wars of aggression as inherently criminal. In so doing, he systematically dismantles the arguments put forward by the defendants, that they were insignificant "role players" or that they had no knowledge of events happening beyond their departments or even within their departments. All of those truly guilty, the defendants claimed, were already dead. What sort of situation do we then confront, Jackson wonders sardonically, when the guilty are already dead and those left living are themselves innocent of the crimes of which they are accused? The evidence, he says, leads clearly to the opposite conclusion. At no time were those in power not aware of their actions and of the consequences of those actions. At no time were they not planning the next steps that their regime would take to increase its power, territorial holdings, and ability to utilize "undesirable" peoples, such as Eastern Europeans and Jews, as slave labor en route to eventual extermination.

In pursuing the prosecution as a criminal conspiracy, Jackson also seeks to discredit the notion that "following orders" was sufficient defense against the charges brought by the tribunal. At best, he argues, this line of defense can extend only to mitigation, not to exculpation. This is a critical moment in the statement, in which Jackson takes on the idea that there can be no charge of conspiracy within a dictatorial government, because the dictator, in this case Adolf Hitler, held everyone under him within his grasp. If the men on trial became slaves to Hitler, Jackson says, it was their own doing, for without their active support on his behalf, he could never have consolidated his own power over them or over Germany. Likening this argument to that of the boy who killed his parents and begged for mercy because he was an orphan, Jackson reiterates one of the principal aims of the tribunal in dismissing this claim, that those who created the power to which they were subject remained culpable for their actions, that the force of law must not fall solely upon the petty criminals on the streets but also upon those who create and utilize the machinery of the state to commit crimes against their own people, against world peace, and against civilization and humanity itself.

Impact and Legacy

In many ways, it would be difficult to overstate the legacy that Jackson left behind. Although he served on a bitterly divided Supreme Court and among justices who voted reflexively along principles sometimes in defiance of the facts of the cases before the bench, Jackson stayed above the infighting and always considered the facts of the case at hand in rendering his verdict. This is not to suggest that Jackson was unprincipled. It is quite the opposite: Jackson believed that it was vitally important to deal with each case in terms of the facts, and he was interested in creating a workable interpretive framework. Such a framework would best preserve both individual liberties and the constitutionally defined powers of the state and federal governments. This framework, he believed, would best permit individuals to remain free while not denuding government of the power to enforce the law.

Jackson's opinions are remarkably clear-sighted and articulate statements of the problems of the cases and the problems of applying the law. As he had throughout his career, he wrote and ruled in favor of what he saw as the best interests of justice. Most of his career on the Supreme Court was occupied by World War II and the cold war, two periods in American history notorious for attempts to squelch dissent. Jackson steadfastly resisted such measures, however, arguing repeatedly that freedom and liberty depended on the right of an individual to believe and speak as he or she saw fit. A final element of Jackson's judicial legacy is the shift in cases brought to the Supreme Court by religious litigants. Before *Barnette*, religious cases tended to focus on either the establishment or free exercise clause. After *Barnette*, religious litigants raised free speech claims more often, and with greater success, than claims based on either the establishment clause of the First Amendment (which states that Congress will not make laws concerning the establishment of religion) or the free exercise clause of the same amendment (which states that Congress will not prohibit the free exercise of religion).

Nuremberg, however, stands as Jackson's greatest achievement and legacy. The tribunal gave Jackson a platform from which to repeat his views on issues he held to be of vital importance in a free society, if only by contrast. In contrast to the Nazi regime, he points out, we do and must allow dissent. In contrast to the Nazi regime, he points out, we provide for a fair and just defense of even those who have committed the most horrific of crimes. Justice, individual liberty, and the equality of strong and weak alike before the law were common themes in Jackson's activities in his various professions, and it is as a defender of these ideals and for his profound impact on the development of international law that he is known today.

Key Sources

The Robert H. Jackson Papers at the Library of Congress is the single largest collection of Jackson's writings and material, with extensive holdings covering every period of his professional life. The Oyez Project, an online Supreme Court archive, has links to several of Jackson's opinions (http://www.oyez.org/justices/robert_h_jackson/opinions/). A prolific author, Jackson left an extensive body of writings. Prominent among them are *The Struggle for Judicial Supremacy: A Study of a Crisis in American Power Politics* (1941), *The Case against the Nazi War Criminals* (1946), *The Nüernberg Case* (1947), *The Supreme Court in the American System of Government* (1955), and *That Man: An Insider's Portrait of Franklin D. Roosevelt* (2003), the last two of which were published posthumously.

Further Reading

■ Articles

Barrett, John Q. "*Recollections of* West Virginia State Board of Education v. Barnette: *Closing Reflections on Jackson and* Barnette." *St. John's Law Review* 81, no. 3 (Fall 2007): 755, 793–796.

———. "The Nuremberg Roles of Justice Robert H. Jackson." *Washington University Global Studies Law Review* 6 (September 2007): 511–525.

Jaffe, Louis. "Mr. Justice Jackson." *Harvard Law Review* 68 (April 1955): 940–998.

"*If the prosecutor is obliged to choose his cases, it follows that he can choose his defendants. Therein is the most dangerous power of the prosecutor: that he will pick people that he thinks he should get, rather than pick cases that need to be prosecuted.*"

("The Federal Prosecutor")

"*One's right to life, liberty, and property, to free speech, a free press, freedom of worship and assembly, and other fundamental rights may not be submitted to vote; they depend on the outcome of no elections.*"

(*West Virginia State Board of Education v. Barnette*)

"*If there is any fixed star in our constitutional constellation, it is that no official, high or petty, can prescribe what shall be orthodox in politics, nationalism, religion, or other matters of opinion, or force citizens to confess by word or act their faith therein.*"

(*West Virginia State Board of Education v. Barnette*)

"*That four great nations, flushed with victory and stung with injury stay the hand of vengeance and voluntarily submit their captive enemies to the judgment of the law is one of the most significant tributes that Power has ever paid to Reason.*"

(Opening Statement before the International Military Tribunal)

"*The common sense of mankind demands that law shall not stop with the punishment of petty crimes by little people. It must also reach men who possess themselves of great power and make deliberate and concerted use of it to set in motion evils which leave no home in the world untouched.*"

(Opening Statement before the International Military Tribunal)

"*Only those who have failed to learn the bitter lessons of the last decade can doubt that men who have always played on the unsuspecting credulity of generous opponents would not hesitate to do the same, now.*"

(Closing Statement before the International Military Tribunal)

■ **Books**

Gerhart, Eugene C. *America's Advocate: Robert H. Jackson*. Indianapolis, Ind.: Bobbs-Merrill, 1958.

Schubert, Glendon. *Dispassionate Justice: A Synthesis of the Judicial Opinions of Robert H. Jackson*. Indianapolis, Ind.: Bobbs-Merrill, 1969.

Stone, Geoffrey R. *Perilous Times: Free Speech in Wartime from the Sedition Act of 1798 to the War on Terrorism*. New York: W. W. Norton, 2004.

■ **Web Sites**

"Robert H. Jackson." The Robert H. Jackson Center Web site. http://www.roberthjackson.org/index.html.

"The International Military Tribunal for Germany: Contents of the Nuremberg Trials Collection." The Avalon Project at Yale Law School Web site. http://avalon.law.yale.edu/subject_menus/imt.asp.

—Anthony Santoro

Questions for Further Study

1. Robert Jackson took office as the nation's attorney general (1940) at about the same time that J. Edgar Hoover was reaching the height of his influence as the director of the Federal Bureau of Investigation. At this time Hoover was growing increasingly concerned about foreign subversives. How might he have responded to Jackson's speech "The Federal Prosecutor"—or, conversely, how might Jackson have responded to the concerns Hoover raised in his?

2. Do you believe that Jackson's opinion in *West Virginia State Board of Education v. Barnette* is consistent with the opinions of Justice Oliver Wendell Holmes, Jr., particularly in *Abrams v. United States* and *Schenck v. United States*? Explain.

3. Explain Jackson's views with regard to the importance of international law. How are these views consistent with those of James Monroe and John Jay as expressed in their documents?

4. Throughout his documents Jackson repeatedly makes reference to "mankind" and "civilization." Explain how these concepts played a role in Jackson's jurisprudence.

"THE FEDERAL PROSECUTOR" (1940)

Jackson, Robert H.

The prosecutor has more control over life, liberty, and reputation than any other person in America. His discretion is tremendous. He can have citizens investigated and, if he is that kind of person, he can have this done to the tune of public statements and veiled or unveiled intimations. Or the prosecutor may choose a more subtle course and simply have a citizen's friends interviewed. The prosecutor can order arrests, present cases to the grand jury in secret session, and on the basis of his one-sided presentation of the facts, can cause the citizen to be indicted and held for trial. He may dismiss the case before trial, in which case the defense never has a chance to be heard. Or he may go on with a public trial. If he obtains a conviction, the prosecutor can still make recommendations as to sentence, as to whether the prisoner should get probation or a suspended sentence, and after he is put away, as to whether he is a fit subject for parole. While the prosecutor at his best is one of the most beneficent forces in our society, when he acts from malice or other base motives, he is one of the worst....

Nothing better can come out of this meeting of law enforcement officers than a rededication to the spirit of fair play and decency that should animate the federal prosecutor. Your positions are of such independence and importance that while you are being diligent, strict, and vigorous in law enforcement you can also afford to be just. Although the government technically loses its case, it has really won if justice has been done. The lawyer in public office is justified in seeking to leave behind him a good record. But he must remember that his most alert and severe, but just, judges will be the members of his own profession, and that lawyers rest their good opinion of each other not merely on results accomplished but on the quality of the performance. Reputation has been called "the shadow cast by one's daily life." Any prosecutor who risks his day-to-day professional name for fair dealing to

build up statistics of success has a perverted sense of practical values, as well as defects of character. Whether one seeks promotion to a judgeship, as many prosecutors rightly do, or whether he returns to private practice, he can have no better asset than to have his profession recognize that his attitude toward those who feel his power has been dispassionate, reasonable and just....

If the prosecutor is obliged to choose his cases, it follows that he can choose his defendants. Therein is the most dangerous power of the prosecutor: that he will pick people that he thinks he should get, rather than pick cases that need to be prosecuted.... It is here that law enforcement becomes personal, and the real crime becomes that of being unpopular with the predominant or governing group, being attached to the wrong political views, or being personally obnoxious to or in the way of the prosecutor himself.

In times of fear or hysteria political, racial, religious, social, and economic groups, often from the best of motives, cry for the scalps of individuals or groups because they do not like their views. Particularly do we need to be dispassionate and courageous in those cases which deal with so-called "subversive activities." They are dangerous to civil liberty because the prosecutor has no definite standards to determine what constitutes a "subversive activity," such as we have for murder or larceny. Activities which seem benevolent and helpful to wage earners, persons on relief, or those who are disadvantaged in the struggle for existence may be regarded as "subversive" by those whose property interests might be burdened or affected thereby. Those who are in office are apt to regard as "subversive" the activities of any of those who would bring about a change of administration. Some of our soundest constitutional doctrines were once punished as subversive. We must not forget that it was not so long ago that both the term "Republican" and the term "Democrat" were epithets with sinister meaning to denote per-

Glossary

grand jury	a body of people who determine whether there is sufficient evidence to charge a person with a crime

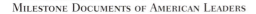

sons of radical tendencies that were "subversive" of the order of things then dominant.

In the enforcement of laws which protect our national integrity and existence, we should prosecute any and every act of violation, but only overt acts, not the expression of opinion, or activities such as the holding of meetings, petitioning of Congress, or dissemination of news or opinions. Only by extreme care can we protect the spirit as well as the letter of our civil liberties, and to do so is a responsibility of the federal prosecutor.

WEST VIRGINIA STATE BOARD OF EDUCATION V. BARNETTE (1943)

To sustain the compulsory flag salute, we are required to say that a Bill of Rights which guards the individual's right to speak his own mind left it open to public authorities to compel him to utter what is not in his mind.

Whether the First Amendment to the Constitution will permit officials to order observance of ritual of this nature does not depend upon whether as a voluntary exercise we would think it to be good, bad or merely innocuous. Any credo of nationalism is likely to include what some disapprove or to omit what others think essential, and to give off different overtones as it takes on different accents or interpretations. If official power exists to coerce acceptance of any patriotic creed, what it shall contain cannot be decided by courts, but must be largely discretionary with the ordaining authority, whose power to prescribe would no doubt include power to amend. Hence, validity of the asserted power to force an American citizen publicly to profess any statement of belief, or to engage in any ceremony of assent to one, presents questions of power that must be considered independently of any idea we may have as to the utility of the ceremony in question.

Nor does the issue, as we see it, turn on one's possession of particular religious views or the sincerity with which they are held.... It is not necessary to inquire whether nonconformist beliefs will exempt from the duty to salute unless we first find power to make the salute a legal duty....

Government of limited power need not be anemic government. Assurance that rights are secure tends to diminish fear and jealousy of strong government, and, by making us feel safe to live under it, makes for its better support. Without promise of a limiting Bill of Rights, it is doubtful if our Constitution could have mustered enough strength to enable its ratification. To enforce those rights today is not to choose weak government over strong government. It is only to adhere as a means of strength to individual freedom of mind in preference to officially disciplined uniformity for which history indicates a disappointing and disastrous end....

It was also considered in the *Gobitis* case that functions of educational officers in States, counties and school districts were such that to interfere with their authority "would in effect make us the school board for the country."

The Fourteenth Amendment, as now applied to the States, protects the citizen against the State itself and all of its creatures—Boards of Education not excepted. These have, of course, important, delicate, and highly discretionary functions, but none that they may not perform within the limits of the Bill of Rights. That they are educating the young for citizenship is reason for scrupulous protection of Constitutional freedoms of the individual, if we are not to strangle the free mind at its source and teach youth to discount important principles of our government as mere platitudes....

The *Gobitis* opinion reasoned that this is a field "where courts possess no marked, and certainly no controlling, competence," that it is committed to the legislatures, as well as the courts, to guard cherished liberties, and that it is constitutionally appropriate to "fight out the wise use of legislative authority in the forum of public opinion and before legislative assemblies, rather than to transfer such a contest to the judicial arena," since all the "effective means of inducing political changes are left free."

The very purpose of a Bill of Rights was to withdraw certain subjects from the vicissitudes of political controversy, to place them beyond the reach of majorities and officials, and to establish them as legal principles to be applied by the courts. One's right to life, liberty, and property, to free speech, a free press, freedom of worship and assembly, and other fundamental rights may not be submitted to vote; they depend on the outcome of no elections....

Nor does our duty to apply the Bill of Rights to assertions of official authority depend upon our possession of marked competence in the field where the invasion of rights occurs.... We act in these matters not by authority of our competence, but by force of our commissions. We cannot, because of modest estimates of our competence in such specialties as public education, withhold the judgment that history authenticates as the function of this Court when liberty is infringed.

Lastly, and this is the very heart of the *Gobitis* opinion, it reasons that "National unity is the basis of national security," that the authorities have "the right to select appropriate means for its attainment," and hence reaches the conclusion that such compulsory measures toward "national unity" are constitutional.

Upon the verity of this assumption depends our answer in this case.

National unity, as an end which officials may foster by persuasion and example, is not in question. The problem is whether, under our Constitution, compulsion as here employed is a permissible means for its achievement....

As governmental pressure toward unity becomes greater, so strife becomes more bitter as to whose unity it shall be. Probably no deeper division of our people could proceed from any provocation than from finding it necessary to choose what doctrine and whose program public educational officials shall compel youth to unite in embracing. Ultimate futility of such attempts to compel coherence is the lesson of every such effort from the Roman drive to stamp out Christianity as a disturber of its pagan unity, the Inquisition, as a means to religious and dynastic unity, the Siberian exiles as a means to Russian unity, down to the fast failing efforts of our present totalitarian enemies. Those who begin coercive elimination of dissent soon find themselves exterminating dissenters. Compulsory unification of opinion achieves only the unanimity of the graveyard.

It seems trite but necessary to say that the First Amendment to our Constitution was designed to avoid these ends by avoiding these beginnings....

The case is made difficult not because the principles of its decision are obscure, but because the flag involved is our own. Nevertheless, we apply the limitations of the Constitution with no fear that freedom to be intellectually and spiritually diverse or even contrary will disintegrate the social organization. To believe that patriotism will not flourish if patriotic ceremonies are voluntary and spontaneous, instead of a compulsory routine, is to make an unflattering estimate of the appeal of our institutions to free minds.... But freedom to differ is not limited to things that do not matter much. That would be a mere shadow of freedom. The test of its substance is the right to differ as to things that touch the heart of the existing order.

If there is any fixed star in our constitutional constellation, it is that no official, high or petty, can prescribe what shall be orthodox in politics, nationalism, religion, or other matters of opinion, or force citizens to confess by word or act their faith therein. If there are any circumstances which permit an exception, they do not now occur to us.

Glossary

anemic	weak, lacking energy
Gobitis **case**	a 1940 case, *Minersville School District v. Gobitis,* about a student who was expelled from school for refusing to salute the American flag
innocuous	harmless
Inquisition	beginning in the twelfth century, tribunals and commissions established by the Roman Catholic Church to stamp out heresy
vicissitudes	changes

Opening Statement before the International Military Tribunal, Nuremberg, Germany (1945)

The privilege of opening the first trial in history for crimes against the peace of the world imposes a grave responsibility. The wrongs which we seek to condemn and punish have been so calculated, so malignant, and so devastating, that civilization cannot tolerate their being ignored, because it cannot survive their being repeated. That four great nations, flushed with victory and stung with injury stay the hand of vengeance and voluntarily submit their captive enemies to the judgment of the law is one of the most significant tributes that Power has ever paid to Reason.

This Tribunal, while it is novel and experimental, is not the product of abstract speculations nor is it created to vindicate legalistic theories. This inquest represents the practical effort of four of the most mighty of nations, with the support of 17 more, to utilize international law to meet the greatest menace of our times—aggressive war. The common sense of mankind demands that law shall not stop with the punishment of petty crimes by little people. It must also reach men who possess themselves of great power and make deliberate and concerted use of it to set in motion evils which leave no home in the world untouched. It is a cause of that magnitude that the United Nations will lay before Your Honors.

In the prisoners' dock sit twenty-odd broken men. Reproached by the humiliation of those they have led almost as bitterly as by the desolation of those they have attacked, their personal capacity for evil is forever past. It is hard now to perceive in these men as captives the power by which as Nazi leaders they once dominated much of the world and terrified most of it. Merely as individuals their fate is of little consequence to the world.

What makes this inquest significant is that these prisoners represent sinister influences that will lurk in the world long after their bodies have returned to dust. We will show them to be living symbols of racial hatreds, of terrorism and violence, and of the arrogance and cruelty of power. They are symbols of fierce nationalisms and of militarism, of intrigue and war-making which have embroiled Europe generation after generation, crushing its manhood, destroying its homes, and impoverishing its life. They have so identified themselves with the philosophies they conceived and with the forces they directed that any tenderness to them is a victory and an encourage-

ment to all the evils which are attached to their names. Civilization can afford no compromise with the social forces which would gain renewed strength if we deal ambiguously or indecisively with the men in whom those forces now precariously survive....

If these men are the first war leaders of a defeated nation to be prosecuted in the name of the law, they are also the first to be given a chance to plead for their lives in the name of the law....

We will not ask you to convict these men on the testimony of their foes. There is no count in the Indictment that cannot be proved by books and records. The Germans were always meticulous record keepers, and these defendants had their share of the Teutonic passion for thoroughness in putting things on paper. Nor were they without vanity. They arranged frequently to be photographed in action. We will show you their own films. You will see their own conduct and hear their own voices as these defendants re-enact for you, from the screen, some of the events in the course of the conspiracy....

It is my purpose to open the case, particularly under Count One of the Indictment, and to deal with the Common Plan or Conspiracy to achieve ends possible only by resort to Crimes against Peace, War Crimes, and Crimes against Humanity....

The end of the war and capture of these prisoners presented the victorious Allies with the question whether there is any legal responsibility on high-ranking men for acts which I have described. Must such wrongs either be ignored or redressed in hot blood? Is there no standard in the law for a deliberate and reasoned judgment on such conduct?

The Charter of this Tribunal evidences a faith that the law is not only to govern the conduct of little men, but that even rulers are, as Lord Chief Justice Coke put it to King James, "under God and the law." The United States believed that the law long has afforded standards by which a juridical hearing could be conducted to make sure that we punish only the right men and for the right reasons....

I am too well aware of the weaknesses of juridical action alone to contend that in itself your decision... can prevent future wars. Judicial action always comes after the event. Wars are started only on the theory and in the confidence that they can be won. Personal punishment, to be suffered only in the event the war is lost, will probably not be a sufficient deterrent to prevent a war where the warmakers feel the chances of defeat to be negligible.

But the ultimate step in avoiding periodic wars, which are inevitable in a system of international lawlessness, is to make statesmen responsible to law. And let me make clear that while this law is first applied against German aggressors, the law includes, and if it is to serve a useful purpose it must condemn aggression by any other nations, including those which sit here now in judgment. We are able to do away with domestic tyranny and violence and aggression by those in power against the rights of their own people only when we make all men answerable to the law. This trial represents mankind's desperate effort to apply the discipline of the law to statesmen who have used their powers of state to attack the foundations of the world's peace and to commit aggressions against the rights of their neighbors....

The real complaining party at your bar is Civilization. In all our countries it is still a struggling and imperfect thing. It does not plead that the United States, or any other country, has been blameless of the conditions which made the German people easy victims to the blandishments and intimidations of the Nazi conspirators....

Civilization asks whether law is so laggard as to be utterly helpless to deal with crimes of this magnitude by criminals of this order of importance. It does not expect that you can make war impossible. It does expect that your juridical action will put the forces of international law, its precepts, its prohibitions and, most of all, its sanctions, on the side of peace, so that men and women of good will, in all countries, may have "leave to live by no man's leave, underneath the law."

Lord Chief Justice Coke	Sir Edward Coke (1552–1634), a prominent jurist whose writings on common law in England were influential long after his death
Teutonic	referring to the Teutons, an early Germanic tribe

Closing Statement before the International Military Tribunal, Nuremberg, Germany (1946)

It is common to think of our own time as standing at the apex of civilization, from which the deficiencies of preceding ages may patronizingly be viewed in the light of what is assumed to be "progress." The reality is that in the long perspective of history the present century will not hold an admirable position, unless its second half is to redeem its first.... No half-century ever witnessed slaughter on such a scale, such cruelties and inhumanities, such wholesale deportations of peoples into slavery, such annihilations of minorities. The terror of Torquemada pales before the Nazi Inquisition. These deeds are the overshadowing historical facts by which generations to come will remember this decade. If we cannot eliminate the causes and prevent the repetition of these barbaric events, it is not an irresponsible prophecy to say that this twentieth century may yet succeed in bringing the doom of civilization....

Of one thing we may be sure. The future will never have to ask, with misgiving, what could the Nazis have said in their favor. History will know that whatever could be said, they were allowed to say. They have been given the kind of a Trial which they, in the days of their pomp and power, never gave to any man.

But fairness is not weakness. The extraordinary fairness of these hearings is an attribute of our strength. The Prosecution's case, at its close, seemed inherently unassailable because it rested so heavily on German documents of unquestioned authenticity. But it was the weeks upon weeks of pecking at this case, by one after another of the defendants, that has demonstrated its true strength. The fact is that the testimony of the defendants has removed any doubt of guilt which, because of the extraordinary nature and magnitude of these crimes, may have existed before they spoke. They have helped write their own judgment of condemnation....

The central crime in this pattern of crimes, the kingpin which holds them all together, is the plot for aggressive wars. The chief reason for international cognizance of these crimes lies in this fact. Have we established the Plan or Conspiracy to make aggressive war?...

While a credulous world slumbered, snugly blanketed with perfidious assurances of peaceful intentions, the Nazis prepared not as before for a war but now for the war. The Defendants Goering, Keitel, Raeder, Frick, and Funk, with others, met as the Reich Defense Council in June of 1939. The minutes, authenticated by Goering, are revealing evidences of the way in which each step of Nazi planning dovetailed with every other. These five key defendants, 3 months before the first Panzer unit had knifed into Poland, were laying plans for "employment of the population in wartime," and had gone so far as to classify industry for priority in labor supply after "5 million servicemen had been called up." They decided upon measures to avoid "confusion when mobilization takes place," and declared a purpose "to gain and maintain the lead in the decisive initial weeks of a war." They then planned to use in production prisoners of war, criminal prisoners, and concentration camp inmates. They then decided on "compulsory work for women in wartime." They had already passed on applications from 1,172,000 specialist workmen for classification as indispensable, and had approved 727,000 of them. They boasted that orders to workers to report for duty "are ready and tied up in bundles at the labor offices." And they resolved to increase the industrial manpower supply by bringing into Germany "hundreds of thousands of workers" from the Protectorate to be "housed together in hutments."...

Thus, the war crimes against Allied forces and the crimes against humanity committed in occupied territories are incontestably part of the program for making the war because, in the German calculations, they were indispensable to its hope of success.

Similarly, the whole group of prewar crimes, including the persecutions within Germany, fall into place around the plan for aggressive war like stones in a finely wrought mosaic....

The activities of all these defendants, despite their varied backgrounds and talents, were joined with the efforts of other conspirators not now in the dock, who played still other essential roles. They blend together into one consistent and militant pattern animated by a common objective to reshape the map of Europe by force of arms....

The dominant fact which stands out from all the thousands of pages of the record of this Trial is that the central crime of the whole group of Nazi crimes—the attack on the peace of the world—was clearly and deliberately planned....

Nor were the war crimes and the crimes against humanity unplanned, isolated, or spontaneous offenses. Aside from our undeniable evidence of their plotting, it is sufficient to ask whether 6 million people could be separated from the population of several nations on the basis of their blood and birth, could be destroyed and their bodies disposed of, except that the operation fitted into the general scheme of government. Could the enslavement of 5 millions of laborers, their impressment into service, their transportation to Germany, their allocation to work where they would be most useful, their maintenance, if slow starvation can be called maintenance, and their guarding have been accomplished if it did not fit into the common plan? Could hundreds of concentration camps located throughout Germany, built to accommodate hundreds of thousands of victims, and each requiring labor and materials for construction, manpower to operate and supervise, and close gearing into the economy—could such efforts have been expended under German autocracy if they had not suited the plan? Has the Teutonic passion for organization suddenly become famous for its toleration of nonconforming activity? Each part of the plan fitted into every other. The slave-labor program meshed with the needs of industry and agriculture, and these in turn synchronized with the military machine. The elaborate propaganda apparatus geared with the program to dominate the people and incite them to a war their sons would have to fight. The armament industries were fed by the concentration camps. The concentration camps were fed by the Gestapo. The Gestapo was fed by the spy system of the Nazi Party. Nothing was permitted under the Nazi iron rule that was not in accordance with the program. Everything of consequence that took place in this regimented society was but a manifestation of a premeditated and unfolding purpose to secure the Nazi State a place in the sun by casting all others into darkness....

One of the chief reasons the defendants say there was no conspiracy is the argument that conspiracy was impossible with a dictator. The argument runs that they all had to obey Hitler's orders, which had the force of law in the German State, and hence obedience could not be made the basis of an original charge. In this way it is explained that while there have been wholesale killings, there have been no murderers.

This argument is an effort to evade Article 8 of the Charter, which provides that the order of the Government or of a superior shall not free a defendant from responsibility but can only be considered in mitigation....

These men destroyed free government in Germany and now plead to be excused from responsibility because they became slaves. They are in the position of the fictional boy who murdered his father and mother and then pleaded for leniency because he was an orphan.

What these men have overlooked is that Adolf Hitler's acts are their acts. It was these men among millions of others, and it was these men leading millions of others, who built up Adolf Hitler and vested in his psychopathic personality not only innumerable lesser decisions but the supreme issue of war or

Glossary

apex	height, highest point
Gestapo	the secret police of Nazi Germany
Goering, Keitel, Raeder, Frick, and Funk	Hermann Goering, Nazi leader and commander of the German air force; Wilhelm Keitel, commander of the German military; Erich Raeder, commander of the German navy; Wilhelm Frick, German minister of the interior; Walther Funk, German minister for economic affairs
Panzer	a German tank; more generally, German armored military forces
perfidious	treacherous, deceptive
Praetorian Guard	the specially selected guards of the ancient Roman emperors
6 million people	reference to Europe's Jews who were killed in the Nazi Holocaust
Torquemada	Tomás de Torquemada (1420–1498), a notorious leader of the Catholic Church's Inquisition

peace. They intoxicated him with power and adulation. They fed his hates and aroused his fears. They put a loaded gun in his eager hands. It was left to Hitler to pull the trigger, and when he did they all at that time approved. His guilt stands admitted, by some defendants reluctantly, by some vindictively. But his guilt is the guilt of the whole dock, and of every man in it.

In conspiracy we do not punish one man for another man's crime. We seek to punish each for his own crime of joining a common criminal plan in which others also participated. The measure of the criminality of the plan and therefore of the guilt of each participant is, of course, the sum total of crimes committed by all in executing the plan....

These men in this dock, on the face of this record, were not strangers to this program of crime, nor was their connection with it remote or obscure. We find them in the very heart of it. The positions they held show that we have chosen defendants of self-evident responsibility. They are the very top surviving authorities in their respective fields and in the Nazi State....

These men had access to Hitler and often could control the information that reached him and on which he must base his policy and his orders. They were the Praetorian Guard, and while they were under Caesar's orders, Caesar was always in their hands....

Credibility is one of the main issues of this Trial. Only those who have failed to learn the bitter lessons of the last decade can doubt that men who have always played on the unsuspecting credulity of generous opponents would not hesitate to do the same, now....

If you were to say of these men that they are not guilty, it would be as true to say that there has been no war, there are no slain, there has been no crime.

John Jay (Library of Congress)

JOHN JAY   1745–1829

First Chief Justice of the United States

Featured Documents
♦ Letter to George Washington (1779)
♦ "Circular-Letter from Congress to Their Constituents" (1779)
♦ Federalist 2–5 and 64 (1787–1788)
♦ "Charge to the Grand Juries" (1790)
♦ Draft of the Proclamation of Neutrality (1793)

Overview

John Jay was born in the colony of New York on December 12, 1745. Jay's paternal great-grandfather, Pierre Jay, was a Huguenot who left France for England to avoid persecution. Jay's paternal grandfather, Augustus, grew up in England but moved to the American colonies and became a successful import-export businessman. By the time John was born, John's father, Peter, was rich, retired, and married to Mary Van Cortlandt, a member of a large and powerful Dutch banking and trade family. The Jays' multinational origins and their focus on trade and comity for their livelihoods would be themes of John Jay's long career.

In 1764 Jay graduated from what was then called King's College but became Columbia University. He was admitted to the bar and began his law practice in 1768. By 1774 he had begun his political career by serving on the Committee of Fifty to select New York's delegates to the Constitutional Convention. He also married Sarah Livingston, the daughter of the New Jersey governor William Livingston. In 1776 Jay began his service as a delegate to the New York State constitutional convention, and in 1778 he began a two-year term as president of the First Continental Congress. He was also the chief justice of New York State during this period. Beginning in 1779, Jay spent three years seeking diplomatic recognition for the newly independent country of the United States of America. He focused his negotiations on the recognition of the new country, on trade and commerce, and on the establishment of alliances based on mutual commercial interests. His efforts abroad led to the execution of the Treaty of Paris in 1783, which brought formal peace between England and the United States. Although the treaty was controversial at home, where many people were still angry at England, formal peace with England was necessary for the new country to make the transition from the Revolutionary War mode to one of economic growth grounded in peaceful international relations. Upon his return home in July 1784, Jay was installed as secretary for foreign affairs. His tenure as secretary was consumed by constant negotiations over trade violations and other breaches of the Treaty of Paris by both countries. The challenges Jay dealt with as secretary led him to embrace the concept of a more powerful central government than had been established by the Articles of Confederation. Although he did not attend the Philadelphia convention, he would prove instrumental in the adoption of the new Constitution.

As one of the authors of the Federalist Papers, along with James Madison and Alexander Hamilton, Jay was instrumental in persuading the citizens of the country to adopt the new Constitution. He was also one of the primary shepherds of the document through the ratification debates in New York and is credited with swaying those delegates who were leery of a strong central government as well as those who were concerned with the power of small states under the new constitutional design. When the Constitution was approved and George Washington had become president, one of Washington's earliest acts was to nominate Jay to be chief justice of the United States. Jay's time as chief justice has perhaps been eclipsed by the length and impact of John Marshall's tenure, but Jay served during a critical time in the nation's development. He helped establish the United States as a credible trade partner and a legitimate member of the community of nations. While serving as chief justice, Jay was dispatched by President Washington in 1794 to negotiate a broad peace and trade agreement with England. While it was controversial at the time, driven by residual hostility from the war with Britain, the Jay Treaty led to an economic relationship that proved beneficial over the near and long terms. When Jay was negotiating the treaty, his allies in New York nominated him and the voters elected him governor of the state. He accepted the position in 1795 and resigned his post at the Supreme Court. Throughout Jay's long career of public service, he helped guide the United States into the international economy and helped solidify its position as a member of the community of nations.

Explanation and Analysis of Documents

John Jay was president of the Continental Congress and active in New York politics when the country was making the transition from the Articles of Confederation to the new Constitution. His in-depth understanding and appreciation of the role of trade and international commerce proved critical in establishing the new country as a legitimate member of the family of nations. He viewed credible

1745

■ **December 12**
John Jay is born in New York City.

1764

■ Jay graduates from King's College (now Columbia University) and becomes a law clerk.

1768

■ Jay is admitted to the New York bar and starts his law practice.

1774

■ Jay is appointed to the Committee of Fifty to select the New York delegates to the Continental Congress.

1776– 1777

■ Jay serves as a delegate to New York's constitutional convention and helps draft the state constitution

1777– 1778

■ Jay serves as chief justice of New York State.

1778– 1779

■ Jay serves as president of the Continental Congress while also serving as New York's chief justice.

1779

■ Jay begins a three-year effort as a commissioner to Spain to obtain a treaty of alliance and commerce as well as diplomatic recognition.

■ **April 26**
Jay corresponds with George Washington about the need to bolster the economy and the threat belligerent privateers are posing to trade relations.

■ **September 13**
Jay drafts and delivers the "Circular-Letter from Congress to Their Constituents," which explains the host of economic problems faced by the country and organizational problems in the Continental Congress.

trade and stable, viable economic relationships with the other nations of the world as the only path the American Revolutionists could take to attain the status of a respected nation. Jay carried this commitment to economic viability in the international arena onto the bench when he became the first chief justice of the United States. Jay perceived the world through the lens of what might now be called globalization. He saw the emerging country as a part of a larger world system. From his perspective, if the United States could not pay its debts and therefore be trusted by other nations in matters of trade, it would eventually be conquered and divided. Four documents, along with his contributions to the Federalist Papers, demonstrate his ability to make lucid and persuasive economic arguments: his letter to George Washington (April 26, 1779), the "Circular-Letter from Congress to Their Constituents" (September 8, 1779), the Federalist Papers 2–5 and 64 (1787–1788), his charge to the grand jury of the circuit court for the District of New York (April 12, 1790), and his draft of the Proclamation of Neutrality (April 1793).

◆ **Letter to George Washington**

In April 1779, President George Washington wrote to Jay gravely concerned about the privateers—or pirates— who were harbored throughout the islands of Bermuda. Washington was concerned first that the privateers were trading salt for flour and were taking these basic commodities out of the American economy at a time when those goods were needed most. Washington was also concerned that trade with the privateers enabled them to raid the ships of the trading partners of the new country and harm international trade relations generally and the economy of the United States specifically. Jay responded to Washington and expressed his own concern that the committee system in the Continental Congress would perpetually inhibit the growth of maritime trade. Jay argued that as long as "maritime affairs" were controlled and directed by a committee in the Continental Congress, the policies would fail to be systematic or comprehensive, would be given little attention, and would be determined by people with scant knowledge of the issues. Although the marine committee had a delegate from each state, attendance of the delegates was unpredictable and erratic. The committee might have two consecutive meetings with no member present at both. Continuity of agenda and expertise on the committee were not likely. Very few of the members had any interest in the topic or any time to attend the meetings.

Jay thought the committee on commerce was equally useless for the same reasons. Jay argued that the self-interest of the individual members of the Continental Congress defeated common interests because the collective was not able to move easily or efficiently. His observation that the Continental Congress had the intrigue of the Vatican but the secrecy of a boarding school expressed his frustration that the members of Congress were more concerned about their own narrow self-interest than about firmly establishing the viability of the new country. This letter to Washington sets forth the problems with collective action that both

Washington and Jay perceived to be impediments to a consolidation of the new country and the new economy. It demonstrates Jay's sharp understanding of the importance of institutional design. The letter also underscores Jay's commitment to establishing the new country as a trusted trading partner in the international arena. It also gives insight into the relationship between Washington and Jay. It shows that Jay was a trusted and close confidant of Washington and also that their visions of the role of international trade and commerce in the development of the country were parallel.

◆ "Circular-Letter from Congress to Their Constituents"

As president of the Continental Congress and at the request of the men in Congress, Jay wrote the "Circular-Letter from Congress to Their Constituents" on September 13, 1779. The letter accompanied a series of resolutions passed to address the growing economic crisis that was driven in large part by default on the part of states and domestic merchants on contracts with and loans from foreign interests. The cost of credit for both states and merchants was soaring because of the high rate of default across the new country. Jay was convinced that the survival of the new country depended on its establishing itself as a reliable trading partner with the other nations of the world. Jay was gravely concerned about the possibility of American defaults—whether by states, by merchants, or by citizens—on foreign contracts and loans. He was convinced that if independence was followed by insolvency, the new country would be destroyed by its creditors and by nations defending the interests of those creditors. His fear was that the new country's resources would be a powerful incentive encouraging foreign invasion under the guise of defending aggrieved foreign citizens and that these resources would be parsed out to its economic rivals after defeat. The purpose of this letter was to put the general legislative efforts toward economic accountability and stability into a broader and unified context. The Revolutionaries had been rightly wary of government power, and the Continental Congress was an inefficient, unwieldy, and weak institution. Jay undercut arguments about concerns of a power grab or an unwanted expansion of government with his persuasive line of reasoning.

Jay's arguments in the "Circular-Letter" reflected his career-long interest in trade, international economics, and the relations of nations as demonstrated through commerce. The letter also set forth some of the major arguments that would become the rationales for replacing the Articles of Confederation with the Constitution. The letter argued for the economic coordination and harmonization that the new Constitution would ultimately adopt. Jay's vision of sound national and international economics as a prerequisite to a strong state proved persuasive to many and predictive of the nation's development at the outset of its history. The involvement of Congress in stabilizing the economy after the adoption of the Constitution was foreshadowed in both form and substance by the "Circular-Letter."

Time Line

1783
- **September**
  Jay helps negotiate the Treaty of Paris with Britain to end the Revolutionary War.

1784
- **July**
  Jay becomes secretary of foreign affairs for the Confederation.

1787–1788
- Jay collaborates with James Madison and Alexander Hamilton on *The Federalist* and shepherds the new Constitution through ratification by the state of New York.

1789
- **September**
  Washington nominates, and the Senate confirms Jay as the first chief justice of the United States.

1790
- **April–May**
  Jay delivers the grand jury charge, which explains the role and importance of the judiciary in the new governmental system.

1793
- **April 11**
  Jay delivers the first draft of the Proclamation of Neutrality to George Washington.

1794
- Jay completes negotiations for the Jay Treaty, which resolved a series of ongoing disputes with Great Britain.

1795
- Jay steps down from the Supreme Court and becomes governor of New York.

1799
- **July 4**
  Jay signs into law a legislative act declaring all children born of slaves from that date forward to be born free.

1801
- Jay completes his second term as governor, declines to run for president of the United States, and retires.

1829
- **May 17**
  Jay dies at the age of eighty-three at his home in Bedford, New York.

◆ Federalist 2–5 and 64

Throughout 1787 and 1788, Jay, James Madison, and Alexander Hamilton published a series of articles designed to persuade the public to support the new Constitution. The articles, published as *The Federalist*, each addressed some specific benefit to or rationale of the new institutional framework of the Constitution. Jay had expressed his concern over the institutional design of the Articles of Confederation in a variety of ways, and his apprehension about the ongoing viability of the country without adoption of the Constitution was clear. His careful and persuasive arguments in Federalist Papers 2, 3, 4, 5, and 64 became part of the national discourse and without doubt were instrumental in ratification of the Constitution not only by New York but also generally across the former colonies. Much of the public was wary of a strong central government or any replication of a royal rule like England's. The notion that a strong central government might be necessary to protect the rights of the people as well as preserve the Union was central to the arguments made in the Federalist Papers.

Jay argues in Federalist 2 that the peace and prosperity of the country depend upon its being united and warns against the perils of many sovereign and rival nations arising out of the rubble of the Articles of Confederation. His central theme is that the individual states could not persevere in the international arena and only through uniting could the people of the country hope to preserve the freedom won through the Revolution. In Federalist 3, Jay warns that only a strong central government can properly defend the people from foreign aggression, even in the face of just war, and keep the country engaged in international commerce. He points out that if foreign powers were able to set state against state, there would be no hope of the states collectively or individually avoiding re-colonization at the hands of the established countries of the world. In Federalist 4, Jay makes a complementary argument that a strong central government is less likely to provoke war with foreign powers. He urges that a slow and deliberative central government would be less likely to provoke aggression while pushing parochial interests. In Federalist 5, he argues that a strong central government would also diminish the possibility of hostility among the states. Essentially, Jay posits the federal government as the peacekeeper and arbiter among the states. In Federalist 64, Jay discusses the power of making treaties and argues that the president must be able to negotiate treaties while ratification by the Senate would ensure broad support for the substance of any agreement reached. That is, he insists that the country must speak with one voice—the president's—when addressing the world but that some popular control—Senate ratification—would ensure general acceptance of the decisions of the executive.

◆ "Charge to the Grand Juries"

Jay's first public elaboration as chief justice of his view of the role of the Supreme Court and the law was in his charge to the grand juries. Jay presented his vision of the Court and the role of the judiciary in the larger societal and global context to several grand juries in New York, Connecticut, Massachusetts, and New Hampshire during April and May 1790. This first foray into the administration of justice by the federal judiciary laid the groundwork for the future development of the Supreme Court as well as the lower courts. It also set forth Jay's wish that the United States abide by the international rules of conduct that other nations followed. The judiciary was framed as an instrument of international relations and a guardian of international peace. Jay instructed the grand jury panels that even the best-designed constitution or government faced peril and extinction unless it was well administered and its laws were obeyed. He also went to great lengths to explain to the juries that the law of nations was part of the law of the land and it was critical for the new nation to be seen as a good international citizen. These instructions proved to be reflective of Jay's tenure on the Court. Overwhelmingly, the docket of the Court dealt with trade and international issues throughout Jay's stewardship. His depth of understanding of the international economy and the importance of good credit to the ongoing viability of the new nation helped shape the first era of the Court. Jay saw the Court as an administrative avenue for aggrieved nations to assert their claims. By providing the international community with a means of redress, the Court made the commitments of the new country more credible because they could be enforced. This early establishment of credible commitments helped stabilize the new economy and helped the new country claim a seat at the table of nations.

◆ Draft of the Proclamation of Neutrality

Few documents so clearly demonstrate Jay's concern with trade and foreign relations as does his draft of the Proclamation of Neutrality. It also shows the close relationship between Jay and George Washington and the degree to which the president sought his counsel and advice. The proclamation issued by Washington on April 22, 1793, while consistent in tone and spirit with the Jay draft, was less specific and briefer than Jay's. Jay points out in his draft that although the leaders in government in the United States regret the sad fate of the deposed and deceased king of France, the new government of France is a fact, and it should be recognized by other nations as the legitimate government. Jay sets forth an argument that not only is it in the best interests of the United States to abide by the law of nations but also that the United States has a duty to do so.

In this context, Jay suggests that the law of nations dictates an acceptance of the revolutionary government of France. Jay cautions against the problems that the United States would face if it were to act in any fashion other than neutrally toward all nations regardless of the relationship among the other nations. From Jay's perspective, no good could come from the United States becoming enmeshed in the conflict between France and Austria or Prussia—or indeed any conflict between any two other nations unless the interests of the United States were clearly at risk. Jay argues that only a strictly neutral position as to any belligerence could cultivate peace and prosperity through international relations. Both the Jay's draft and the actual proclamation delivered by Washington warned the citizens of the United States to take no action that could imperil the position of neutrality and to avoid provoking, through private acts, any of the belligerent powers. This warning that the government would not tolerate or support any private action that could provoke an attack on or the entanglement of the United States in belligerence established an important monopoly of power for the federal government over foreign affairs. In essence, the Proclamation of Neutrality made clear that only the central government had power in the international relations arena; private citizens were not free to engage other nations in conflict.

Impact and Legacy

John Jay has been underestimated in his impact on, his vision of, and his role in the founding of the country. His lifelong interest in trade and international relations carried through to his understanding of the institutional role and systemic purpose of the Supreme Court. His time as chief justice was so effective in establishing his vision that a general assumption that things have always been so has taken hold. The disregard in which many hold the first chief justice and the early Court is quite likely attributable both to the extended time period of John Marshall's career on the bench and the importance of Marshall's major decisions. The Court under Jay was so accomplished at managing the early international relations of the United States that the credibility of commitments made by the new country was soundly established before John Marshall donned the judicial robes. The first era of the Court was successful in establishing the United States as a member of the community of nations in part because of Jay's approach to the law of nations and to the judiciary. Even in the twenty-first century, other sovereign nations; the international commercial, academic, and legal communities; and the public in general all expect international trade to be conducted under enforceable contracts and the country and the states to pay their debts. The international trade reputation of the country has become what Jay worked to establish.

John Jay's legacy and the legacy of the first era of the Supreme Court are economic and systemic credibility. Thanks to Jay's vision and guidance, within a decade of a revolution deemed to be a violation of international law by most of the nations of the world, the rogue nation run by the anarchic mob of Revolutionists became a respected and viable creditor and trading partner. Under Chief Justice Jay, the U.S. Supreme Court developed the specific institutional role of providing an administrative remedy to nations with grievances and therefore deprived those potentially hostile nations of any trade-based or economic excuse for aggression. The original jurisdiction of the Supreme Court as outlined in the Constitution was geared toward the provision of a remedy for trade disputes, and that was the primary field of concern addressed by Jay as chief justice. The existence of a judiciary that was independent of control by the executive or legislative branches helped create more credible trade agreements and reduced the likelihood that a nation could validly turn to self-help or belligerence to resolve trade conflicts.

By providing an independent and disinterested Court through which aggrieved nations could seek an administrative remedy for conflict and by reducing the economic uncertainty associated with trading with the Revolutionaries, Jay helped claim a legitimate seat for the new country at the international table of nations. By enhancing the credibility of the new government among the world's great nations, as well as by reassuring its trading partners, Jay and the Framers of the Constitution allowed time for the economic growth of the new country. This was a prerequisite to consolidation of the economy and thus to consolidation of the government itself. Jay's vision and legacy inform larger questions of nation building and democratic consolidation. The lesson to be taken from the early era of the Supreme Court as directed by Jay is that credibility of commitments made to foreign interests is integral to stability and development.

Key Sources

The collected papers of John Jay are available at the library of Columbia University in New York City. Columbia has also created an online database of many of the documents, which can be accessed at http://www.columbia.edu/cu/lweb/digital/jay/biography.html. Many of Jay's most important papers and works are contained in the two volumes of *The Life of John Jay: With Selections from His Correspondence and Miscellaneous Papers* (1833), edited by his son William Jay. Additionally, Maeva Marcus's *Documentary History of the Supreme Court of the United States 1789–1800* (1998) contains the original documents from Jay's time as chief justice of the United States. The Web site of the Museum of History provides a comprehensive set of resources about John Jay and contains photographs of many of his actual documents (http://www.johnjay.net/). Previously unpublished documents are collected in Richard B. Morris, ed., *John Jay, the Making of a Revolutionary, 1745–1780: Unpublished Papers* (1975).

"There is as much intrigue in this State-house as in the Vatican, but as little secrecy as in a boarding-school."

(Letter to George Washington)

"Let it never be said, that America had no sooner become independent than she became insolvent, or that her infant glories and growing fame were obscured and tarnished by broken contracts and violated faith in the very hour when all the nations of the earth were admiring and almost adoring the splendour of her rising."

("Circular-Letter from Congress to Their Constituents")

"They who promote the idea of substituting a number of distinct confederacies in... the plan of the convention, seem clearly to foresee that the rejection of it would put the continuance of the Union in the utmost jeopardy.... I sincerely wish that it may be as clearly foreseen by every good citizen, that whenever the dissolution of the Union arrives, America will have reason to exclaim, in the words of the poet: 'FAREWELL! A LONG FAREWELL TO ALL MY GREATNESS.'"

(Federalist 2)

"Let candid men judge, then, whether the division of America into any given number of independent sovereignties would tend to secure us against the hostilities and improper interference of foreign nations."

(Federalist 5)

"The most perfect constitutions, the best governments, and the wisest laws are vain, unless well administered and well obeyed.... We are now a nation and it equally becomes us to perform our duties as to assert our rights."

("Charge to the Grand Juries")

"It is no less the duty than the interest of the United States strictly to observe that conduct towards all nations which the law of nations prescribes."

(Draft of the Proclamation of Neutrality)

Further Reading

■ Articles

Smith, Charles Anthony. "Credible Commitments and the Early American Supreme Court." *Law and Society Review* 42, no. 1 (March 2008): 75–110.

■ Books

Monaghan, Frank. *John Jay: Defender of Liberty*. New York: Bobbs-Merrill, 1935.

Pellew, George. *John Jay*. 1890. Reprint. New York: Chelsea House, 1980.

—Tony Smith

Questions for Further Study

1. John Jay makes a clear distinction between a "union" and a "confederacy" in reference to the United States. What is the distinction between the two, and why did Jay argue that union was to be preferred over a confederacy or group of confederacies?

2. While other Founders of the United States focused on such issues as the rights of citizens, Jay's focus was more on economic affairs. Based on the documents, summarize the major economic issues Jay believed the young United States faced and how he proposed to deal with these issues.

3. In the twenty-first century it seems inconceivable that hostility and perhaps even armed aggression could erupt between states in the United States—and even less conceivable that a single U.S. state could enter into conflict with a foreign nation. Would John Jay have accepted this generalization? Cite at least two reasons Jay gave for arguing that giving individual states too much power could lead to conflict.

4. Among the nation's Founders, Jay arguably had the most international outlook. In what specific ways did Jay work throughout his career to make the United States an equal in the community of nations?

5. Jay was one of the authors of the Federalist Papers, along with James Madison and Alexander Hamilton. Compare and contrast Jay's essays with those of Madison and Hamilton. What concerns did they share? On what separate issues did the three writers focus?

LETTER TO GEORGE WASHINGTON (1779)

Philadelphia, 26th April, 1779

Dear Sir:

The questions contained in your favour of the—April instant are as important as the manner of introducing them is delicate.

While the maritime affairs of the continent continue under the direction of a committee, they will be exposed to all the consequences of want of system, attention, and knowledge. The marine committee consists of a delegate from each State; it fluctuates; new members constantly coming in, and old ones going out; three or four, indeed, have remained in it from the beginning; and few members understand even the state of our naval affairs, or have time or inclination to attend to them. But why is not this system changed? It is, in my opinion, convenient to the family compact. The commercial committee was equally useless. A proposition was made to appoint a commercial agent for the States under certain regulations. Opposition was made. The ostensible objections were various. The true reason was its interfering with a certain commercial agent in Europe and his connections.

You will, if I am not greatly mistaken, find Mr. Gerard disposed to be open and communicative. He has acquired an extensive knowledge of our affairs; I have no reason to believe he will use it to our prejudice. There is as much intrigue in this State-house as in the Vatican, but as little secrecy as in a boarding-school. It mortifies me on this occasion to reflect that the rules of Congress on the subject of secrecy, which are far too general, and perhaps for that reason more frequently violated, restrains me from saying twenty things to you which have ceased to be private.

The state of our currency is really serious. When or by what means the progress of the depreciation will be prevented, is uncertain. The subject is delicate, but the conduct of some men really indicates at least great indifference about it. It will not be many days before measures having a great though not immediate influence on this subject, will be either adopted or rejected. I shall then have an opportunity of being more particular.

I am, my dear sir,

With perfect esteem and regard,

Your obedient servant,

John Jay.

Glossary

Gerard	probably Conrad Alexander Gerard, a French diplomat
instant	of the present month
Vatican	the seat of the Roman Catholic Church, an independent state surrounded by Rome, Italy

"Circular-Letter from Congress to Their Constituents" (1779)

Friends and Fellow-Citizens:

In government raised on the generous principles of equal liberty, where the rulers of the state are the servants of the people, and masters of those from whom they derive authority, it is their duty to inform their fellow citizens of the state of their affairs.…The ungrateful despotism and inordinate lust of domination which marked the unnatural designs of the British king and his venal parliament to enslave the people of America, reduced you to either asserting your rights by arms or ingloriously passing under the yoke. You nobly preferred war. Armies were to be raised, paid, and supplied; money became necessary for these purposes. Of your own there was but little; and of no nation in the world could you then borrow.… You had no other resource but the natural value and wealth of your fertile country. Bills were issued on the credit of this bank, and your faith was pledged for their redemption.… Thus a national debt was unavoidably created.… The United States must depend on two things: first, the success of the present revolution; and secondly, on the sufficiency of the natural wealth, value, and resources of the country. That the time has been when honest men might, without being chargeable with timidity, have doubted the success of the present revolution, we admit, but that period is passed. The independence of America is now fixed as fate, and the petulant efforts of Britain to break it down are as vain and fruitless as the raging of the waves which beat against her cliffs.… A bankrupt, faithless republic would be a novelty in the political world, and appear among reputable nations like a common prostitute among chaste and respectable matrons. The pride of America revolts from the idea.… If, then, neither our ability nor our inclination to discharge the public debt is justly questionable, let our conduct correspond with this confidence, and let us rescue our credit from its present imputations.…Let it never be said, that America had no sooner become independent than she became insolvent, or that her infant glories and growing fame were obscured and tarnished by broken contracts and violated faith in the very hour when all the nations of the earth were admiring and almost adoring the splendour of her rising.

Glossary

British king	King George III (1738–1820)

FEDERALIST 2–5 AND 64 (1787–1788)

Federalist 2

To the People of the State of New York:

When the people of America reflect that they are now called upon to decide a question, which, in its consequences, must prove one of the most important that ever engaged their attention, the propriety of their taking a very comprehensive, as well as a very serious, view of it, will be evident.

Nothing is more certain than the indispensable necessity of government, and it is equally undeniable, that whenever and however it is instituted, the people must cede to it some of their natural rights in order to vest it with requisite powers. It is well worthy of consideration therefore, whether it would conduce more to the interest of the people of America that they should, to all general purposes, be one nation, under one federal government, or that they should divide themselves into separate confederacies, and give to the head of each the same kind of powers which they are advised to place in one national government.... It has often given me pleasure to observe that independent America was not composed of detached and distant territories, but that one connected, fertile, wide-spreading country was the portion of our western sons of liberty.... It is worthy of remark that not only the first, but every succeeding Congress, as well as the late convention, have invariably joined with the people in thinking that the prosperity of America depended on its Union. To preserve and perpetuate it was the great object of the people in forming that convention, and it is also the great object of the plan which the convention has advised them to adopt.... They who promote the idea of substituting a number of distinct confederacies in the room of the plan of the convention, seem clearly to foresee that the rejection of it would put the continuance of the Union in the utmost jeopardy. That certainly would be the case, and I sincerely wish that it may be as clearly foreseen by every good citizen, that whenever the dissolution of the Union arrives, America will have reason to exclaim, in the words of the poet: "FAREWELL! A LONG FAREWELL TO ALL MY GREATNESS."
PUBLIUS.

Federalist 3

To the People of the State of New York:

It is not a new observation that the people of any country (if, like the Americans, intelligent and well informed) seldom adopt and steadily persevere for many years in an erroneous opinion respecting their interests. That consideration naturally tends to create great respect for the high opinion which the people of America have so long and uniformly entertained of the importance of their continuing firmly united under one federal government, vested with sufficient powers for all general and national purposes....

Among the many objects to which a wise and free people find it necessary to direct their attention, that of providing for their SAFETY seems to be the first.... At present I mean only to consider it as it respects security for the preservation of peace and tranquillity, as well as against dangers from FOREIGN ARMS AND INFLUENCE, as from dangers of the LIKE KIND arising from domestic causes.... Let us therefore proceed to examine whether the people are not right in their opinion that a cordial Union, under an efficient national government, affords them the best security that can be devised against HOSTILITIES from abroad.

The number of wars which have happened or will happen in the world will always be found to be in proportion to the number and weight of the causes, whether REAL or PRETENDED, which PROVOKE or INVITE them. If this remark be just, it becomes useful to inquire whether so many JUST causes of war are likely to be given by UNITED AMERICA as by DISUNITED America; for if it should turn out that United America will probably give the fewest, then it will follow that in this respect the Union tends most to preserve the people in a state of peace with other nations....

It is of high importance to the peace of America that she observe the laws of nations towards all these powers, and to me it appears evident that this will be more perfectly and punctually done by one national government than it could be either by thirteen separate States or by three or four distinct confederacies....

Because, under the national government, treaties and articles of treaties, as well as the laws of nations, will always be expounded in one sense and executed in the same manner,—whereas, adjudications on the same points and questions, in thirteen States, or in three or four confederacies, will not always accord or be consistent; and that, as well from the variety of independent courts and judges appointed by different and independent governments, as from the different local laws and interests which may affect and influence them. The wisdom of the convention, in committing such questions to the jurisdiction and judgment of courts appointed by and responsible only to one national government, cannot be too much commended....

But not only fewer just causes of war will be given by the national government, but it will also be more in their power to accommodate and settle them amicably.

    PUBLIUS.

Federalist 4

To the People of the State of New York:

My last paper assigned several reasons why the safety of the people would be best secured by union against the danger it may be exposed to by JUST causes of war given to other nations; and those reasons show that such causes would not only be more rarely given, but would also be more easily accommodated, by a national government than either by the State governments or the proposed little confederacies.

But the safety of the people of America against dangers from FOREIGN force depends not only on their forbearing to give JUST causes of war to other nations, but also on their placing and continuing themselves in such a situation as not to INVITE hostility or insult; for it need not be observed that there are PRETENDED as well as just causes of war....

The people of America are aware that inducements to war may arise out of these circumstances, as well as from others not so obvious at present, and that whenever such inducements may find fit time and opportunity for operation, pretenses to color and justify them will not be wanting. Wisely, therefore, do they consider union and a good national government as necessary to put and keep them in SUCH A SITUATION as, instead of INVITING war, will tend to repress and discourage it. That situation consists in the best possible state of defense, and necessarily depends on the government, the arms, and the resources of the country.

As the safety of the whole is the interest of the whole, and cannot be provided for without government, either one or more or many, let us inquire whether one good government is not, relative to the object in question, more competent than any other given number whatever.

One government can collect and avail itself of the talents and experience of the ablest men, in whatever part of the Union they may be found. It can move on uniform principles of policy. It can harmonize, assimilate, and protect the several parts and members, and extend the benefit of its foresight and precautions to each. In the formation of treaties, it will regard the interest of the whole, and the particular interests of the parts as connected with that of the whole. It can apply the resources and power of the whole to the defense of any particular part, and that more easily and expeditiously than State governments or separate confederacies can possibly do, for want of concert and unity of system. It can place the militia under one plan of discipline, and, by putting their officers in a proper line of subordination to the Chief Magistrate, will, as it were, consolidate them into one corps, and thereby render them more efficient than if divided into thirteen or into three or four distinct independent companies....

But whatever may be our situation, whether firmly united under one national government, or split into a number of confederacies, certain it is, that foreign nations will know and view it exactly as it is; and they will act toward us accordingly.... If they see that our national government is efficient and well administered, our trade prudently regulated, our militia properly organized and disciplined, our resources and finances discreetly managed, our credit re-established, our people free, contented, and united, they will be much more disposed to cultivate our friendship than provoke our resentment. If, on the other hand, they find us either destitute of an effectual government (each State doing right or wrong, as to its rulers may seem convenient), or split into three or four independent and probably discordant republics or confederacies, one inclining to Britain, another to France, and a third to Spain, and perhaps played off against each other by the three, what a poor, pitiful figure will America make in their eyes! How liable would she become not only to their contempt but to their outrage, and how soon would dear-bought experience proclaim that when a people or family so divide, it never fails to be against themselves.

    PUBLIUS.

Federalist 5

To the People of the State of New York:

Queen Anne, in her letter of the 1st July, 1706, to the Scotch Parliament, makes some observations on the importance of the UNION then forming between England and Scotland, which merit our attention. I shall present the public with one or two extracts from it: "An entire and perfect union will be the solid foundation of lasting peace: It will secure your religion, liberty, and property; remove the animosities amongst yourselves, and the jealousies and differences betwixt our two kingdoms. It must increase your strength, riches, and trade; and by this union the whole island, being joined in affection and free from all apprehensions of different interest, will be ENABLED TO RESIST ALL ITS ENEMIES." "We most earnestly recommend to you calmness and unanimity in this great and weighty affair, that the union may be brought to a happy conclusion, being the only EFFECTUAL way to secure our present and future happiness, and disappoint the designs of our and your enemies, who will doubtless, on this occasion, USE THEIR UTMOST ENDEAVORS TO PREVENT OR DELAY THIS UNION."

It was remarked in the preceding paper, that weakness and divisions at home would invite dangers from abroad; and that nothing would tend more to secure us from them than union, strength, and good government within ourselves. This subject is copious and cannot easily be exhausted....

Should the people of America divide themselves into three or four nations, would not the same thing happen? Would not similar jealousies arise, and be in like manner cherished? Instead of their being "joined in affection" and free from all apprehension of different "interests," envy and jealousy would soon extinguish confidence and affection, and the partial interests of each confederacy, instead of the general interests of all America, would be the only objects of their policy and pursuits. Hence, like most other BORDERING nations, they would always be either involved in disputes and war, or live in the constant apprehension of them....

Let candid men judge, then, whether the division of America into any given number of independent sovereignties would tend to secure us against the hostilities and improper interference of foreign nations.
　　PUBLIUS.

Federalist 64

To the People of the State of New York:

...The power of making treaties is an important one, especially as it relates to war, peace, and commerce; and it should not be delegated but in such a mode, and with such precautions, as will afford the highest security that it will be exercised by men the best qualified for the purpose, and in the manner most conducive to the public good. The convention appears to have been attentive to both these points: they have directed the President to be chosen by select bodies of electors, to be deputed by the people for that express purpose; and they have committed the appointment of senators to the State legislatures. This mode has, in such cases, vastly the advantage of elections by the people in their collective capacity, where the activity of party zeal, taking the advantage of the supineness, the ignorance, and the hopes and fears of the unwary and interested, often places men in office by the votes of a small proportion of the electors.... There are a few who will not admit that the affairs of trade and navigation should be regulated by a system cautiously formed and steadily pursued; and that both our treaties and our laws should correspond with and be made to promote it. It is of much consequence that this correspondence and conformity be carefully maintained; and they who assent to the truth of this position will see and confess that it is well provided for by making concurrence of the Senate necessary both to treaties and to laws....

However useful jealousy may be in republics, yet when like bile in the natural, it abounds too much in the body politic, the eyes of both become very liable to be deceived by the delusive appearances which that malady casts on surrounding objects. From this cause, probably, proceed the fears and apprehensions of some, that the President and Senate may make treaties without an equal eye to the interests of all the States. Others suspect that two thirds will oppress the remaining third, and ask whether those gentlemen are made sufficiently responsible for their conduct; whether, if they act corruptly, they can be punished; and if they make disadvantageous treaties, how are we to get rid of those treaties?

As all the States are equally represented in the Senate, and by men the most able and the most willing to promote the interests of their constituents, they will all have an equal degree of influence in that body, especially while they continue to be careful in appointing proper persons, and to insist on their punctual attendance. In proportion as the United States assume a national form and a national character, so will the good of the whole be more and more an object of attention, and the government must be a weak one indeed, if it should forget that the good of the whole can only be promoted by advancing the good of each of the parts or members which compose the whole. It will not be in the power of the President and Senate to make any treaties by which they and their families and estates will not be equally bound and affected with the rest of the community; and, having no private interests distinct from that of the nation, they will be under no temptations to neglect the latter....

With respect to their responsibility, it is difficult to conceive how it could be increased. Every consideration that can influence the human mind, such as honor, oaths, reputations, conscience, the love of country, and family affections and attachments, afford security for their fidelity. In short, as the Constitution has taken the utmost care that they shall be men of talents and integrity, we have reason to be persuaded that the treaties they make will be as advantageous as, all circumstances considered, could be made; and so far as the fear of punishment and disgrace can operate, that motive to good behavior is amply afforded by the article on the subject of impeachments.

PUBLIUS.

Glossary

adjudications	judgments
Chief Magistrate	the head of the executive branch; the president
confederacy	a compact or agreement for providing mutual support or engaging in mutual action
late convention	the Constitutional Convention
Publius	a pseudonym in honor of the ancient Roman consul Publius Valerius Publicola, Publicola being a nickname that means "friend of the people"
Queen Anne	queen of England during whose reign the 1707 Act of Union linked England and Scotland (1665–1714)
supineness	the state of lying on one's back

"CHARGE TO THE GRAND JURIES" (1790)

Whether any people can long govern themselves in an equal, uniform, and orderly manner, is a question which the advocates for free government justly consider as being exceedingly important to the cause of liberty. This question, like others whose solution depends on facts, can only be determined by experience. It is a question on which many think some room for doubt still remains. Men have had very few fair opportunities of making the experiment; and this is one reason why less progress has been made in the science of government than in almost any other. The far greater number of the constitutions and governments of which we are informed have originated in force or in fraud, having been either imposed by improper exertions of power, or introduced by the arts of designing individuals, whose apparent zeal for liberty and the public good enabled them to take advantage of the credulity and misplaced confidence of their fellow citizens.... Wise and virtuous men have thought and reasoned very differently respecting government, but in this they have at length very unanimously agreed, viz., that its powers should be divided into three distinct, independent departments—the executive, legislative and judicial. But how to constitute and balance them in such a manner as best to guard against abuse and fluctuation, and preserve the Constitution from encroachments, are points on which there continues to be a great diversity of opinions, and on which we have all as yet much to learn. The Constitution of the United States has accordingly instituted these three departments, and much pains have been taken so to form and define them as that they may operate as checks one upon the other, and keep each within its proper limits; it being universally agreed to be of the last importance to a free people, that they who are vested with

executive, legislative, and judicial powers should rest satisfied with their respective portions of power, and neither encroach on the provinces of each other, nor suffer themselves to intermeddle with the rights reserved by the Constitution to the people. If, then, so much depends on our rightly improving the before-mentioned opportunities, if the most discerning and enlightened minds may be mistaken relative to theories unconfirmed by practice, if on such difficult questions men may differ in opinion and yet be patriots, and if the merits of our opinions can only be ascertained by experience, let us patiently abide the trial, and unite our endeavors to render it a fair and an impartial one....We had become a nation. As such we were responsible to others for the observance of the Laws of Nations.... The most perfect constitutions, the best governments, and the wisest laws are vain, unless well administered and well obeyed....

It cannot be too strongly impressed on the minds of us all how greatly our individual prosperity depends on our national prosperity, and how greatly our national prosperity depends on a well organized, vigorous government.... Let it be remembered that civil liberty consists not in a right to every man to do just what he pleases, but it consists in an equal right to all the citizens to have, enjoy, and to do, in peace, security, and without molestation, whatever the equal and constitutional laws of the country admit to be consistent with the public good. It is the duty and the interest, therefore, of all good citizens, in their several stations, to support the laws and the government which thus protect their rights and liberties.

I am persuaded, gentlemen, that you will cheerfully and faithfully perform the task now assigned you, and I forbear, by additional remarks, to detain you longer from it.

Glossary

credulity	excessive trustfulness
encroachments	gradual intrusions
viz.	abbreviation for Latin word *videlicet*, meaning "namely" or "that is to say"

DRAFT OF THE PROCLAMATION OF NEUTRALITY (1793)

Whereas every nation has a right to change and modify their constitution and government in such a manner as they may think most conducive to their welfare and happiness, and whereas a new form of government has taken place and actually exists in France, that event is to be regarded as the act of the nation until that presumption shall be destroyed by fact; and although certain circumstances have attended that revolution, which are greatly to be regretted, yet the United States as a nation have no right to decide on measures which regard only the internal and domestic affairs of others. They who actually administer the government of any nation are by foreign nations to be regarded as its lawful rulers so long as they continue to be recognized and obeyed by the great body of their people.

And whereas royalty has been in fact abolished in France, and a new government does there at present exist and is in actual operation, it is proper that the intercourse between this nation and that should be conducted through the medium of the government in fact, and although the misfortunes, to whatever cause they may be imputed, which the late King of France and others have suffered in the course of that revolution, or which that nation may yet experience, are to be regretted by the friends of humanity, and particularly by the people of America to whom both that king and that nation have done essential services, yet it is no less the duty than the interest of the United States strictly to observe that conduct towards all nations which the laws of nations prescribe.

And whereas war actually exists between France on the one side and Austria, Prussia, Great Britain, and the United Netherlands on the other; and whereas on the one hand we have abundant reason to give thanks unto Almighty God that the United States are not involved in that calamity, so on the other hand it is our duty by a conduct strictly neutral and inoffensive to cultivate and preserve peace, with a firm determination, nevertheless, always to prefer war to injustice and disgrace.

I do therefore most earnestly advise and require the citizens of the United States to be circumspect in their conduct towards all nations and particularly those now at war, to demean themselves in every respect in the manner becoming a nation at peace with all the world, and to unite in rendering thanks to a beneficial Providence for the peace and prosperity we enjoy, and devoutly to entreat the continuance of these invaluable blessings. I do expressly require that the citizens of the United States abstain from acting hostilely against any of the belligerent powers under commissions from either. Such conduct would tend to provoke hostilities against their country, and would in every respect be highly reprehensible; for while the people of all other states abstain from doing injury to any of our people, it would be unjust and wicked in any of our people to do injuries to them.

I do also enjoin all magistrates and others in authority to be watchful and diligent in preventing any aggressions from being committed against foreign nations and their people; and to cause all

Glossary

animadversions	censure, harsh criticisms
demean themselves	to behave themselves
exemplary manner	in a way that makes an example of someone
King of France	Louis XVI (1754–1793), deposed in 1792 and put to death by French Revolutionaries
Prussia	formerly an independent kingdom, now part of Germany
war actually exists between France on the one side…	reference to the Napoleonic Wars (1799–1815) between France, led by Napoléon Bonaparte (1769–1821), and various European countries

offenders to be prosecuted and punished in an exemplary manner. I do also recommend it to my fellow-citizens in general to omit such public discussions as may tend not only to cause divisions and parties among ourselves, and thereby impair that union on which our strength depends, but also give unnecessary cause of offence and irritation to foreign powers.

And I cannot forbear expressing a wish that our printers may study to be impartial in the representation of facts, and observe much prudence relative to such strictures and animadversions as may render the disposition of foreign governments and rulers unfriendly to the people of the United States.

April 11th, 1793